Lecture Notes in Computer Science 8513

Commenced Publication in 1973
Founding and Former Series Editors:
Gerhard Goos, Juris Hartmanis, and Jan van Leeuwen

T0212619

Constantine Stephanidis   Margherita Antona (Eds.)

Universal Access in Human-Computer Interaction

Design and Development Methods for Universal Access

8th International Conference, UAHCI 2014
Held as Part of HCI International 2014
Heraklion, Crete, Greece, June 22-27, 2014
Proceedings, Part I

 Springer

Volume Editors

Constantine Stephanidis
Foundation for Research and Technology - Hellas (FORTH)
Institute of Computer Science
N. Plastira 100, Vassilika Vouton, 70013 Heraklion, Crete, Greece
and University of Crete, Department of Computer Science
Heraklion, Crete, Greece
E-mail: cs@ics.forth.gr

Margherita Antona
Foundation for Research and Technology - Hellas (FORTH)
Institute of Computer Science
N. Plastira 100, Vassilika Vouton, 70013 Heraklion, Crete, Greece
E-mail: antona@ics.forth.gr

ISSN 0302-9743   e-ISSN 1611-3349
ISBN 978-3-319-07436-8   e-ISBN 978-3-319-07437-5
DOI 10.1007/978-3-319-07437-5
Springer Cham Heidelberg New York Dordrecht London

Library of Congress Control Number: 2014939292

LNCS Sublibrary: SL 3 – Information Systems and Application, incl. Internet/Web and HCI

Typesetting: Camera-ready by author, data conversion by Scientific Publishing Services, Chennai, India

Printed on acid-free paper

Springer is part of Springer Science+Business Media (www.springer.com)

Foreword

The 16th International Conference on Human–Computer Interaction, HCI International 2014, was held in Heraklion, Crete, Greece, during June 22–27, 2014, incorporating 14 conferences/thematic areas:

Thematic areas:

- Human–Computer Interaction
- Human Interface and the Management of Information

Affiliated conferences:

- 11th International Conference on Engineering Psychology and Cognitive Ergonomics
- 8th International Conference on Universal Access in Human–Computer Interaction
- 6th International Conference on Virtual, Augmented and Mixed Reality
- 6th International Conference on Cross-Cultural Design
- 6th International Conference on Social Computing and Social Media
- 8th International Conference on Augmented Cognition
- 5th International Conference on Digital Human Modeling and Applications in Health, Safety, Ergonomics and Risk Management
- Third International Conference on Design, User Experience and Usability
- Second International Conference on Distributed, Ambient and Pervasive Interactions
- Second International Conference on Human Aspects of Information Security, Privacy and Trust
- First International Conference on HCI in Business
- First International Conference on Learning and Collaboration Technologies

A total of 4,766 individuals from academia, research institutes, industry, and governmental agencies from 78 countries submitted contributions, and 1,476 papers and 225 posters were included in the proceedings. These papers address the latest research and development efforts and highlight the human aspects of design and use of computing systems. The papers thoroughly cover the entire field of human–computer interaction, addressing major advances in knowledge and effective use of computers in a variety of application areas.

This volume, edited by Constantine Stephanidis and Margherita Anton, contains papers focusing on the thematic area of Universal Access in Human-Computer Interaction, addressing the following major topics:

- Design for all methods, techniques, and tools
- Development methods and tools for Universal Access

- User models, adaptation and personalization
- Natural, multimodal, and multisensory interaction
- Brain-computer interfaces

The remaining volumes of the HCI International 2014 proceedings are:

- Volume 17, LNCS 8526, Virtual, Augmented and Mixed Reality: Applications of Virtual and Augmented Reality (Part II), edited by Randall Shumaker and Stephanie Lackey
- Volume 18, LNCS 8527, HCI in Business, edited by Fiona Fui-Hoon Nah
- Volume 19, LNCS 8528, Cross-Cultural Design, edited by P.L. Patrick Rau
- Volume 20, LNCS 8529, Digital Human Modeling and Applications in Health, Safety, Ergonomics and Risk Management, edited by Vincent G. Duffy
- Volume 21, LNCS 8530, Distributed, Ambient, and Pervasive Interactions, edited by Norbert Streitz and Panos Markopoulos
- Volume 22, LNCS 8531, Social Computing and Social Media, edited by Gabriele Meiselwitz
- Volume 23, LNAI 8532, Engineering Psychology and Cognitive Ergonomics, edited by Don Harris
- Volume 24, LNCS 8533, Human Aspects of Information Security, Privacy and Trust, edited by Theo Tryfonas and Ioannis Askoxylakis
- Volume 25, LNAI 8534, Foundations of Augmented Cognition, edited by Dylan D. Schmorrow and Cali M. Fidopiastis
- Volume 26, CCIS 434, HCI International 2014 Posters Proceedings (Part I), edited by Constantine Stephanidis
- Volume 27, CCIS 435, HCI International 2014 Posters Proceedings (Part II), edited by Constantine Stephanidis

I would like to thank the Program Chairs and the members of the Program Boards of all affiliated conferences and thematic areas, listed below, for their contribution to the highest scientific quality and the overall success of the HCI International 2014 Conference.

This conference could not have been possible without the continuous support and advice of the founding chair and conference scientific advisor, Prof. Gavriel Salvendy, as well as the dedicated work and outstanding efforts of the communications chair and editor of *HCI International News*, Dr. Abbas Moallem.

I would also like to thank for their contribution towards the smooth organization of the HCI International 2014 Conference the members of the Human–Computer Interaction Laboratory of ICS-FORTH, and in particular George Paparoulis, Maria Pitsoulaki, Maria Bouhli, and George Kapnas.

April 2014

Constantine Stephanidis
General Chair, HCI International 2014

Organization

Human–Computer Interaction

Program Chair: Masaaki Kurosu, Japan

Jose Abdelnour-Nocera, UK
Sebastiano Bagnara, Italy
Simone Barbosa, Brazil
Adriana Betiol, Brazil
Simone Borsci, UK
Henry Duh, Australia
Xiaowen Fang, USA
Vicki Hanson, UK
Wonil Hwang, Korea
Minna Isomursu, Finland
Yong Gu Ji, Korea
Anirudha Joshi, India
Esther Jun, USA
Kyungdoh Kim, Korea

Heidi Krömker, Germany
Chen Ling, USA
Chang S. Nam, USA
Naoko Okuizumi, Japan
Philippe Palanque, France
Ling Rothrock, USA
Naoki Sakakibara, Japan
Dominique Scapin, France
Guangfeng Song, USA
Sanjay Tripathi, India
Chui Yin Wong, Malaysia
Toshiki Yamaoka, Japan
Kazuhiko Yamazaki, Japan
Ryoji Yoshitake, Japan

Human Interface and the Management of Information

Program Chair: Sakae Yamamoto, Japan

Alan Chan, Hong Kong
Denis A. Coelho, Portugal
Linda Elliott, USA
Shin'ichi Fukuzumi, Japan
Michitaka Hirose, Japan
Makoto Itoh, Japan
Yen-Yu Kang, Taiwan
Koji Kimita, Japan
Daiji Kobayashi, Japan

Hiroyuki Miki, Japan
Shogo Nishida, Japan
Robert Proctor, USA
Youngho Rhee, Korea
Ryosuke Saga, Japan
Katsunori Shimohara, Japan
Kim-Phuong Vu, USA
Tomio Watanabe, Japan

Engineering Psychology and Cognitive Ergonomics

Program Chair: Don Harris, UK

Guy Andre Boy, USA
Shan Fu, P.R. China
Hung-Sying Jing, Taiwan
Wen-Chin Li, Taiwan
Mark Neerincx, The Netherlands
Jan Noyes, UK
Paul Salmon, Australia

Axel Schulte, Germany
Siraj Shaikh, UK
Sarah Sharples, UK
Anthony Smoker, UK
Neville Stanton, UK
Alex Stedmon, UK
Andrew Thatcher, South Africa

Universal Access in Human–Computer Interaction

**Program Chairs: Constantine Stephanidis, Greece,
and Margherita Antona, Greece**

Julio Abascal, Spain
Gisela Susanne Bahr, USA
João Barroso, Portugal
Margrit Betke, USA
Anthony Brooks, Denmark
Christian Bühler, Germany
Stefan Carmien, Spain
Hua Dong, P.R. China
Carlos Duarte, Portugal
Pier Luigi Emiliani, Italy
Qin Gao, P.R. China
Andrina Granić, Croatia
Andreas Holzinger, Austria
Josette Jones, USA
Simeon Keates, UK

Georgios Kouroupetroglou, Greece
Patrick Langdon, UK
Barbara Leporini, Italy
Eugene Loos, The Netherlands
Ana Isabel Paraguay, Brazil
Helen Petrie, UK
Michael Pieper, Germany
Enrico Pontelli, USA
Jaime Sanchez, Chile
Alberto Sanna, Italy
Anthony Savidis, Greece
Christian Stary, Austria
Hirotada Ueda, Japan
Gerhard Weber, Germany
Harald Weber, Germany

Virtual, Augmented and Mixed Reality

**Program Chairs: Randall Shumaker, USA,
and Stephanie Lackey, USA**

Roland Blach, Germany
Sheryl Brahnam, USA
Juan Cendan, USA
Jessie Chen, USA
Panagiotis D. Kaklis, UK

Hirokazu Kato, Japan
Denis Laurendeau, Canada
Fotis Liarokapis, UK
Michael Macedonia, USA
Gordon Mair, UK

Jose San Martin, Spain
Tabitha Peck, USA
Christian Sandor, Australia

Christopher Stapleton, USA
Gregory Welch, USA

Cross-Cultural Design

Program Chair: P.L. Patrick Rau, P.R. China

Yee-Yin Choong, USA
Paul Fu, USA
Zhiyong Fu, P.R. China
Pin-Chao Liao, P.R. China
Dyi-Yih Michael Lin, Taiwan
Rungtai Lin, Taiwan
Ta-Ping (Robert) Lu, Taiwan
Liang Ma, P.R. China
Alexander Mädche, Germany

Sheau-Farn Max Liang, Taiwan
Katsuhiko Ogawa, Japan
Tom Plocher, USA
Huatong Sun, USA
Emil Tso, P.R. China
Hsiu-Ping Yueh, Taiwan
Liang (Leon) Zeng, USA
Jia Zhou, P.R. China

Online Communities and Social Media

Program Chair: Gabriele Meiselwitz, USA

Leonelo Almeida, Brazil
Chee Siang Ang, UK
Aneesha Bakharia, Australia
Ania Bobrowicz, UK
James Braman, USA
Farzin Deravi, UK
Carsten Kleiner, Germany
Niki Lambropoulos, Greece
Soo Ling Lim, UK

Anthony Norcio, USA
Portia Pusey, USA
Panote Siriaraya, UK
Stefan Stieglitz, Germany
Giovanni Vincenti, USA
Yuanqiong (Kathy) Wang, USA
June Wei, USA
Brian Wentz, USA

Augmented Cognition

**Program Chairs: Dylan D. Schmorrow, USA,
and Cali M. Fidopiastis, USA**

Ahmed Abdelkhalek, USA
Robert Atkinson, USA
Monique Beaudoin, USA
John Blitch, USA
Alenka Brown, USA

Rosario Cannavò, Italy
Joseph Cohn, USA
Andrew J. Cowell, USA
Martha Crosby, USA
Wai-Tat Fu, USA

Rodolphe Gentili, USA
Frederick Gregory, USA
Michael W. Hail, USA
Monte Hancock, USA
Fei Hu, USA
Ion Juvina, USA
Joe Keebler, USA
Philip Mangos, USA
Rao Mannepalli, USA
David Martinez, USA
Yvonne R. Masakowski, USA
Santosh Mathan, USA
Ranjeev Mittu, USA

Keith Niall, USA
Tatana Olson, USA
Debra Patton, USA
June Pilcher, USA
Robinson Pino, USA
Tiffany Poeppelman, USA
Victoria Romero, USA
Amela Sadagic, USA
Anna Skinner, USA
Ann Speed, USA
Robert Sottilare, USA
Peter Walker, USA

Digital Human Modeling and Applications in Health, Safety, Ergonomics and Risk Management

Program Chair: Vincent G. Duffy, USA

Giuseppe Andreoni, Italy
Daniel Carruth, USA
Elsbeth De Korte, The Netherlands
Afzal A. Godil, USA
Ravindra Goonetilleke, Hong Kong
Noriaki Kuwahara, Japan
Kang Li, USA
Zhizhong Li, P.R. China

Tim Marler, USA
Jianwei Niu, P.R. China
Michelle Robertson, USA
Matthias Rötting, Germany
Mao-Jiun Wang, Taiwan
Xuguang Wang, France
James Yang, USA

Design, User Experience, and Usability

Program Chair: Aaron Marcus, USA

Sisira Adikari, Australia
Claire Ancient, USA
Arne Berger, Germany
Jamie Blustein, Canada
Ana Boa-Ventura, USA
Jan Brejcha, Czech Republic
Lorenzo Cantoni, Switzerland
Marc Fabri, UK
Luciane Maria Fadel, Brazil
Tricia Flanagan, Hong Kong
Jorge Frascara, Mexico

Federico Gobbo, Italy
Emilie Gould, USA
Rüdiger Heimgärtner, Germany
Brigitte Herrmann, Germany
Steffen Hess, Germany
Nouf Khashman, Canada
Fabiola Guillermina Noël, Mexico
Francisco Rebelo, Portugal
Kerem Rızvanoğlu, Turkey
Marcelo Soares, Brazil
Carla Spinillo, Brazil

Distributed, Ambient and Pervasive Interactions

**Program Chairs: Norbert Streitz, Germany,
and Panos Markopoulos, The Netherlands**

Juan Carlos Augusto, UK
Jose Bravo, Spain
Adrian Cheok, UK
Boris de Ruyter, The Netherlands
Anind Dey, USA
Dimitris Grammenos, Greece
Nuno Guimaraes, Portugal
Achilles Kameas, Greece
Javed Vassilis Khan, The Netherlands
Shin'ichi Konomi, Japan
Carsten Magerkurth, Switzerland

Ingrid Mulder, The Netherlands
Anton Nijholt, The Netherlands
Fabio Paternó, Italy
Carsten Röcker, Germany
Teresa Romao, Portugal
Albert Ali Salah, Turkey
Manfred Tscheligi, Austria
Reiner Wichert, Germany
Woontack Woo, Korea
Xenophon Zabulis, Greece

Human Aspects of Information Security, Privacy and Trust

**Program Chairs: Theo Tryfonas, UK,
and Ioannis Askoxylakis, Greece**

Claudio Agostino Ardagna, Italy
Zinaida Benenson, Germany
Daniele Catteddu, Italy
Raoul Chiesa, Italy
Bryan Cline, USA
Sadie Creese, UK
Jorge Cuellar, Germany
Marc Dacier, USA
Dieter Gollmann, Germany
Kirstie Hawkey, Canada
Jaap-Henk Hoepman, The Netherlands
Cagatay Karabat, Turkey
Angelos Keromytis, USA
Ayako Komatsu, Japan
Ronald Leenes, The Netherlands
Javier Lopez, Spain
Steve Marsh, Canada

Gregorio Martinez, Spain
Emilio Mordini, Italy
Yuko Murayama, Japan
Masakatsu Nishigaki, Japan
Aljosa Pasic, Spain
Milan Petković, The Netherlands
Joachim Posegga, Germany
Jean-Jacques Quisquater, Belgium
Damien Sauveron, France
George Spanoudakis, UK
Kerry-Lynn Thomson, South Africa
Julien Touzeau, France
Theo Tryfonas, UK
João Vilela, Portugal
Claire Vishik, UK
Melanie Volkamer, Germany

HCI in Business

Program Chair: Fiona Fui-Hoon Nah, USA

Andreas Auinger, Austria
Michel Avital, Denmark
Traci Carte, USA
Hock Chuan Chan, Singapore
Constantinos Coursaris, USA
Soussan Djamasbi, USA
Brenda Eschenbrenner, USA
Nobuyuki Fukawa, USA
Khaled Hassanein, Canada
Milena Head, Canada
Susanna (Shuk Ying) Ho, Australia
Jack Zhenhui Jiang, Singapore
Jinwoo Kim, Korea
Zoonky Lee, Korea
Honglei Li, UK
Nicholas Lockwood, USA
Eleanor T. Loiacono, USA
Mei Lu, USA

Scott McCoy, USA
Brian Mennecke, USA
Robin Poston, USA
Lingyun Qiu, P.R. China
Rene Riedl, Austria
Matti Rossi, Finland
April Savoy, USA
Shu Schiller, USA
Hong Sheng, USA
Choon Ling Sia, Hong Kong
Chee-Wee Tan, Denmark
Chuan Hoo Tan, Hong Kong
Noam Tractinsky, Israel
Horst Treiblmaier, Austria
Virpi Tuunainen, Finland
Dezhi Wu, USA
I-Chin Wu, Taiwan

Learning and Collaboration Technologies

Program Chairs: Panayiotis Zaphiris, Cyprus, and Andri Ioannou, Cyprus

Ruthi Aladjem, Israel
Abdulaziz Aldaej, UK
John M. Carroll, USA
Maka Eradze, Estonia
Mikhail Fominykh, Norway
Denis Gillet, Switzerland
Mustafa Murat Inceoglu, Turkey
Pernilla Josefsson, Sweden
Marie Joubert, UK
Sauli Kiviranta, Finland
Tomaž Klobučar, Slovenia
Elena Kyza, Cyprus
Maarten de Laat, The Netherlands
David Lamas, Estonia

Edmund Laugasson, Estonia
Ana Loureiro, Portugal
Katherine Maillet, France
Nadia Pantidi, UK
Antigoni Parmaxi, Cyprus
Borzoo Pourabdollahian, Italy
Janet C. Read, UK
Christophe Reffay, France
Nicos Souleles, Cyprus
Ana Luísa Torres, Portugal
Stefan Trausan-Matu, Romania
Aimilia Tzanavari, Cyprus
Johnny Yuen, Hong Kong
Carmen Zahn, Switzerland

External Reviewers

Ilia Adami, Greece
Iosif Klironomos, Greece
Maria Korozi, Greece
Vassilis Kouroumalis, Greece

Asterios Leonidis, Greece
George Margetis, Greece
Stavroula Ntoa, Greece
Nikolaos Partarakis, Greece

HCI International 2015

The 15th International Conference on Human–Computer Interaction, HCI International 2015, will be held jointly with the affiliated conferences in Los Angeles, CA, USA, in the Westin Bonaventure Hotel, August 2–7, 2015. It will cover a broad spectrum of themes related to HCI, including theoretical issues, methods, tools, processes, and case studies in HCI design, as well as novel interaction techniques, interfaces, and applications. The proceedings will be published by Springer. More information will be available on the conference website: http://www.hcii2015.org/

General Chair
Professor Constantine Stephanidis
University of Crete and ICS-FORTH
Heraklion, Crete, Greece
E-mail: cs@ics.forth.gr

Table of Contents – Part I

Design for All Methods, Techniques, and Tools

Development Methods and Tools for Universal Access

User Models, Adaptation and Personalisation

Natural, Multimodal and Multisensory Interaction

Brain-Computer Interfaces

Table of Contents – Part II

Access to Mobile Interaction

Access to Text, Documents and Media

Access to Education and Learning

Access to Games and Ludic Engagement

Access to Culture

Table of Contents – Part III

Design for Aging

Health and Rehabilitation Applications

Accessible Smart and Assistive Environments

Assistive Robots

Mobility, Navigation and Safety

Table of Contents – Part IV

Web Accessibility

Design for all in the Built Environment

Global Access Infrastructures

User Experience in Universal Access

Design for All Methods, Techniques, and Tools

Empathic and Ethical Design of Technology

Rachel Batchelor[1] and Ania Bobrowicz[2]

[1] Kent Law School/School of Engineering and Digital Arts, University of Kent,
Canterbury, CT2 7NT, UK
[2] School of Engineering and Digital Arts, University of Kent,
Canterbury, CT2 7NT, UK
{Rb392,A.Bobrowicz}@kent.ac.uk

Abstract. A generation which relies on constant communication and digital information has a different view point and language use to older generation for whom modes of communication are less constant. How do we convey intangible qualities such as empathy, creativity and ethics to a young technologically literate generation who are comfortable with its use, but who may lack understanding of life experiences of other users? We examine themes emerging from the findings of a study into the ways older people (60+) use technology. The questions guiding our enquiry are as follows: How could learning about social history of technology help bridge the gap between generations and lead to a more empathic design? Can the teaching of empathy and ethical understandings assist this process?

Keywords: Empathy, design, ethics, technology.

1 Introduction

The need for designers to be able to examine viewpoints of the users of digital technology is paramount for successful design to succeed. The word "designer" can carry several meanings depending on the academic discipline and training routes. In this context we use the term 'designer' to represent those who are involved in finding creative solutions to problems in the fields of engineering and technology. For HCI educators this presents particular pedagogical challenges of how to convey intangible qualities such as empathy, creativity and ethics to a young generation of designers who are technologically literate and very comfortable with its everyday use, but who may lack understanding of the diverse life experiences of others, for example, older users, and especially of digitally dis-engaged non-users.

Findings from an EPSRC (Engineering and Physical Sciences Research Council) project indicate that older users (60+) are much more comfortable with domestic technologies, while finding digital technology generally obscure, confusing and baffling. We have learnt that older people did not recognize digital technologies as tools for everyday use within a domestic context, and considered that they had no need for most of them. This paper aims to contribute to the debate among the pedagogical design community about how to teach empathic and ethical design. We specifically

C. Stephanidis and M. Antona (Eds.): UAHCI/HCII 2014, Part I, LNCS 8513, pp. 3–10, 2014.

aim to consider what can be learnt from older people's use of domestic technology, and how might an understanding of this inform the teaching of HCI design practice.

2   Empathy and Ethical Design

Empathy and ethical design are, we argue, core features of good human-computer interaction (HCI) design, i.e. design which is ultimately successful for a diverse, inclusive range of user groups. 'Know your user' is a key design principle in HCI, and empathic approaches to design have been explored by a number of commentators from a variety of perspectives [1, 2, 3, 4]. Similarly, ethical issues in relation to the "Internet of things" are an emerging area. Given the inter-connected use of various devices and data sharing that arises, there is arguably a need to teach ethical frameworks which consider the needs and competencies of those older users who are not familiar with emergent technologies. This is particularly clear in the context of use of mobile devices and the cross over with medical and social care devices with consumer technologies [5].

Though concepts which may promote empathic design [6] through reflexive consideration of one's own perspectives and that of others, such as theories relating to 'beholder's share' [7], the 'period eye' [8] and 'ways of seeing' [9] are familiar to those with design training through art and design schools, they are not necessarily included in the engineering and technology curriculum. These and similar theories help to analyse social constructs and intellectual frameworks which inform art and design history and critical studies modules. The reflective self-analytical aspects of these broad theories encourage students to question the familiar and to consider their own and others responses to material and visual cultures, and in doing so, promote reflective practice. Intuitive and emotional responses are part of the process of qualitative research as well as reflective practice as advocated by Donald Schön. Schön's notions of reflection-in-action and reflection-on-action encourages engagement with lived experiences, feelings and emotions [10]. It is also supportive of ethical frameworks in which to consider wider impact of design on users.

To return to the use of domestic technologies, the intuitive use of tools and technologies cannot be assumed. A simple domestic tool such as a wooden spoon has a basic design, which can be easily understood across many cultures. The use to which it is put may however be less clear – as a device for stirring, scooping, measuring, dipping. It might be used at different stages in a process, for cooking with, serving with or eating with. The same domestic tool can be a tool for preparing non-food stuffs, and has a symbolic, iconic value, especially in the context of food preparation, café signs, recipe books, and similar.

The shape of this simple tool allows for other uses (see affordances). In contrast, the functions of a mobile phone may be multiple, but they are not always obvious, especially to a new user. The functionality of a mobile phone may not be seen at first glance; though visually simple, the use is complex as is the hidden technology which enables it to function. It is this gap between intended use, the user and the functionality of the device which, we think, needs empathic consideration. Rather than teaching a reluctant user to struggle with a product which is not suitable, it may be more useful to design inclusively and empathically. Work carried out by the Royal College of Arts at the Helen Hamlyn centre as well as Cambridge Engineering Design Centre demonstrates diversity in process and problem solving, and may serve as a useful reference point here [11].

3   UK Education System, and Educational Experiences of Engineering and Technology Students

Ken Robinson, an international advisor on education, has noted that mass systems of public education were developed primarily to meet the needs of the Industrial Revolution, and, in many ways, they mirror the principles of industrial production. They emphasise linearity, conformity and standardization. One of the reasons they are not working now is that 'real life is organic, adaptable and diverse' [12]. Engineering and technology training traditionally has a greater reliance on linear quantitative methodologies and commercial approaches, which are not necessarily embedded in empathic modes of research [13]. In addition, the intellectual challenges and resources required to support good design education are not necessarily recognized by the leaders of engineering and technology institutions [14]. However,

> "For something to be designed well, it needs to have been designed in consideration of more than mathematical integrity, cognitive models of 'users,' or usability; it needs to have been designed in consideration of contexts, environments, inter-relations, markets, emotions, aesthetics, visual forms, semiotic references and a whole host of considerations that are part of the assumed nature of successful designs. It needs to be construed as part of a dialogue between product, anti-product (i.e. reclaiming old things as new), and lifestyle and notions of ecology and futures." [15]

Russian philosopher and scholar Mikhail Bakhtin considered dialogue and 'aesthetic seeing' to be an essential part of our human existence [16]. Part of our way of being in the world is recognizing each other as unique individuals, each with own values and ways of seeing the world.

Our own experiences as students, educators and inter-disciplinary researchers within the UK education system has led us to question the premise of the system which severely constraints learning and pursuit of interdisciplinary knowledge. Although sciences, arts and humanities subjects are taught in all schools, there is encouragement to specialize early in the student's education (often at 14 and certainly by the age of 16). This means students entering university have an early specialist, not generalist education background. This early specialisation commonly falls between the sciences/mathematics, and arts/humanities strands. The early emphasis on subject selection at school level, which promotes rapid specialism rather than broad conceptual basis often works against a student taking STEM (science/technology/engineering/mathematics) subjects as well as ethics/philosophy/reflective subjects (or humanities subjects plus mathematics). We will argue from experience, that this early split results in early barriers to inter-disciplinary understanding which can in turn hinder good inter-disciplinary working and research. In terms of pedagogical construct it has an impact on the teaching of skills needed for complex design solutions. Teaching the creative, flexible process described by Ken Robinson can be challenging when those same processes have been excluded from earlier study. Indeed, the authors' own experience of working on this paper demonstrated different 'ways of seeing', from a task-oriented and solution-based approach of the sciences to the posing of probing, exploratory questions practiced in the arts and humanities. How do we pedagogically value the qualitative and nuanced data of the "lived experience" in order to enable young designers to engage in respectful dialogues and empathic conversations as part of the creative processes which promote reflexive practice? One issue that arises is how to recognize and value that within creative exploration of a problem that "failed" ideas are an important part of the process while still meeting the requirements of a field which relies on quantitative (linear, conformed, standardized) rather than qualitative (organic, adaptable, diverse) data.

4   SEEDS: An Approach to Participatory Design

In order to inform our view, we are considering the data from the SEEDS project funded by the Engineering and Physical Sciences Research Council, UK. A collaborative venture between the School of Engineering and Digital Arts at the University of Kent, School of Computing at the University of Dundee, and School of Mechanical Engineering at Leeds University. Project SEEDS was an 18-month long feasibility study, which collected data from older people relating to their use of technology. The central theme of the project, 'what would you like to be able to do which you currently cannot, and will technology help?' effectively resulted in the collection of contextually rich social stories. Altogether 29 interviews with older people (60+) from diverse socio-demographic groups (professionals, military, public and private sector) were recorded. The interviews were taken in different geographical locations (Scotland, Kent, the Midlands). We video recorded response sessions to social stories from undergraduate and postgraduate students in engineering, HCI, and technology and design. Our archive is an exciting repository of socially rich material, initial findings of which were discussed in Valentine et al [17]. Our aim through the SEEDS project was to find out whether or not access to such social stories would enhance the understanding of older people's needs among young designers and result in better design solutions. In other words, will understanding of the context of use help inform better, more user-friendly design solutions?

The interviews we collected are revealing in terms of how differences in life experiences between generations impact upon the engagement and understanding of different technologies. The importance of contextual and social understanding of interview data was particularly evident in viewing student responses to it. The contextual information included socio economic, geographical and regional differences, work experiences and previous use of differing technologies by the interviewees. Those interviewees who had experienced workplace technologies reported a greater degree of acceptance of e-mail and word-processing in a domestic context, but were still unlikely to see the need for digital technologies at home, seeing it as intrusive. This presents an interesting comparison with the Technology Acceptance Model (TAM) which supports the use of computerized technologies in the workplace. TAM provides a useful framework for understanding user interaction with technology, and in many cases explains users' reluctance to engage with it. However, it is somewhat lacking in consideration of the empathic and ethical dimensions. The focus is on the workplace management science and workplace information systems rather than on the human-centred design process. Given that the first TAM paper was published in 1989 [18], the SEEDS data indicated that there is a continuing reluctance to engage with new technologies among older people.

5   What Can Young Designers Learn About Older People from Our Study?

As a result of undertaking the study, we learnt that differences in life experiences between young designers and older users bear upon the uptake, use and understanding of digital technology. Each group and the individuals within them bring with them their own 'beholder's share' to their view both of technology and the visual culture in which they are submerged. For example, when an older person was asked where she would go for information, she responded that she would ask friends/family, or use the library, she did not 'Google it'. Interviewees were more familiar with domestic and non-digital technology. They frequently referred to domestic technology, which they find less problematic in usage. For instance, garden equipment and domestic appliances have a clear function, and though can sometimes be used for other purposes; there is a general principle that the function is singular and limited. The use of such technology is often mechanical and physical in user engagement rather than electronic, and largely passive.

Respondents from the SEEDS data collection were not on the whole, technophobes. Two of the video interviewees had previously held technologically sophisticated jobs (dentist and RAF air traffic). These respondents were more assured in talking about technology than other interviewees. Though there was a clear understanding of the potential use of digital technology (e-mail and research), neither seemed to have a particularly enthusiastic response to the domestic use of digital technology; the concerns of the broader group about use and necessity seem to be shared.

In our study older participants talk about hand written letters, tactile reminders of the person as well as written communication in preference to e-mail. Several respondents indicated letters as particularly valuable. For a generation of young designers used to constant uploads this is an illustrative point. Rapidity of communication is not the key issue, reliability (post boxes and post offices don't lose signal or battery) is more important, as is the quality of information and the concomitant sense of personal contact. E-mail was recognised by one interviewee (Kent male) as being quicker and useful for formal communication. This again may reflect a 'beholder's share' which indicates that technological aspects of communication are essentially business and formal in use.

For some elderly people landline telephones used to occupy the same niche, the use limited to those who needed them for work or who were wealthy. The use was limited and delineated by need, and not constant drive for communication and 'being connected'. Landline telephones are available – again a single use device and seem preferred to mobile phones which have multiple applications. The key advantage of a mobile phone is that it is not restricted to place, however interviewees often used phrases relating to 'intrusion' in relation to mobiles. This seems to reflect concerns about usage rather than the technology itself, again possibly pointing to functionality and perceived usefulness. Compare this to our favourite domestic technology – the wooden spoon, a device which has clear functionality and purpose. Young designers may benefit from some engineering/design history based on products available (domestically and in the workplace) and the restrictions on telecommunication devices that the older people have experienced.

To return to the perceived intrusive nature of mobile phones, it may be useful for young designers seeking to improve design or encourage usage, to consider some of the social background that the older people grew up with - long waits for letters and parcels, rationing and queuing during the 1940's and 1950's, for example. Colloquial phrases relating to children from the early twentieth century in the UK include 'being seen and not heard', 'speaking when spoken to', 'careless talk costs lives' and being treated 'firm but fair'. These phrases do not promote the need to continually be in communication with others. It also raises differences in language relating to the technology of communication and leisure. What would the comparable phrases be now? Shall I join you on Wii? Shall I nuke some lunch? Check online? Look up Wikipedia?

For a generation of online social network users 'posting' has a clear meaning (digital), distinctly different to that of older generations (paper based). Slang abbreviations and slang use such as "lol" (laugh out loud),"fb" (Facebook), "omg" (Oh my God), are frequently used by young people in texting. These abbreviations are increasingly finding their way into more formal contexts. University tutors are reporting such phrases being used in formal assignments. Although considered 'standard' and 'normal' to teens, and initially framed by technological use, they can be baffling to older generations. The responses in interviews to the digital communication in particular may reflect these attitudes. There may then be a need to promote clarity and respectful communication between students and those they wish to design for.

Digital technology often has multiple applications and this seems to cause some barriers to use – interviewees see that there are alternatives for different aspects of digital technology. This caused respondents concern over confused functions and remembering how to access different options (Kent female, Dundee male). This seems to be compounded with the need for guidance to demonstrate how to access and 'set up' the equipment, both in the first instance and in updating and problem solving. Clear, none screen based, printed instructions would be a key feature here.

Although interviewees were asked a series of questions relating to the use of digital technologies, they were not asked what they considered 'the purpose of the technology' to be. There are references in responses to 'the computer' but often little clarity over what it is that 'the computer' is for, which contrasts with responses referring to other tools and technology. Unlike the example of the wooden spoon whose purpose can easily be determined. We find this a particularly important perspective on the possible barriers to use.

In seeking to address our themes, 'how could learning about social history of technology help bridge the gap between generations and lead to a more empathic design? Can the teaching of empathy and ethical understandings assist this process, and if so, how? We suggest that different, more empathic, approaches to collecting initial data may be of value. The use of cultural probes [19], user diaries [20], technology biographies [21], or narrative vignettes [22] may prove fruitful in gathering information, building empathy and a dialogue of mutual understanding and respect between generations.

6   Conclusions

A generation which relies on constant communication and digital information has a different view point and language use to older generations for whom modes of communication are less constant. Additionally, a picture emerges that generations involved in the study have differing ideas on what constitutes the related concepts of communication, friendship, and privacy. A generation which is familiar with Facebook, is in constant contact with 500 'friends', and is comfortable with the open disclosure which is part of that forum, will necessarily have a very different perspective to a generation in which an occasional handwritten letter from a friend of 50 years standing is highly valued.

In order to further design students' understanding of differing user groups we would like to develop their appreciation of broader design history as well as history of social constructs. Though there have been useful developments in recent years in the study of history of science, ethical and inclusive design, it is harder to find the history of, or social critiques of, engineering and technology design. We would like to call for a discussion on the use of inter-disciplinary critical thinking and reflection on the social context of design in undergraduate and graduate training.

Acknowledgements. This research was carried out under the auspices of the SEEDS project (An organic approach to virtual participatory design), EPSRC Grant No. EP/H006834/1.

References

1. Wright, P., McCarthy, J.: Empathy and Experience in HCI. In: CHI 2008 Proceedings of the SIGCHI Conference on Human Factors in Computing Systems, pp. 637–646 (2008)
2. Koskinen, I., Battarbee, K.: Introduction to user experience and empathic design. In: Koskinen, I., Battarbee, K., Mattelmäki, T. (eds.) Empathic Design: User Experience in Product Design, pp. 37–50. Edita IT Press, Helsinki (2003)
3. Dandavate, U., Sanders, E.B.N., Stuart, S.: Emotions matter: User empathy in the product development process. In: Proceedings of the 40th Annual Meeting of the Human Factors and Ergonomics Society, pp. 415–418. HFES, Santa Monica (1996)

4. Black, A.: Empathic design: User focused strategies for innovation. In: Proceedings of the Conference on New Product Development, pp. 1–8. IBC, London (1998)
5. Batchelor, R., Bobrowicz, A., Mackenzie, R., Milne, A.: Challenges of ethical and legal responsibilities when technologies' uses and users change: social networking sites, decision-making capacity and dementia. Ethics & Information Technology 14, 99–108 (2012)
6. Leonard, D., Rayport, J.F.: Spark innovation through empathic design. Harvard Business Review 75, 102–113 (1997)
7. Gombrich, E.H.: Art and Illusion: A study in the psychology of pictorial representation. Princeton University Press, Princeton (2000)
8. Baxandall, M.: Painting and Experience in Fifteenth-Century Italy: A Primer in the social history of pictorial style. Oxford University Press, Oxford (1988)
9. Berger, J.: Ways of Seeing. British Broadcasting Corporation and Penguin Books, London (1972)
10. Schön, D.: The Reflective Practitioner: How Professionals Think in Action. Temple Smith, London (1983)
11. Coleman, R., Clarkson, J., Dong, H., Cassim, J.: Design for Inclusivity: A Practical Guide to Accessible, Innovative and User-Centred Design. Gower Publishing, Aldershot (2007)
12. Robinson, K.: Out of Our Minds: Learning to be Creative. Capstone, Chichester (2001)
13. Hosking, I., Waller, S., Clarkson, P.J.: It is normal to be different: Applying inclusive design in industry. Interacting with Computers 22, 496–501 (2010)
14. Dym, C.L., Agogino, A.M., Eris, O., Frey, D.D., Leifer, L.J.: Engineering Design Thinking, Teaching, and Learning. Journal of Engineering Education, 103–120 (2005)
15. Blevis, E., Lim, Y.K., Stolterman, E.: Regarding Software as a Material of Design. In: Wonderground Design Research Society Conference. Design Research Society (2006)
16. Bakhtin, M.: Speech Genres and Other Late Essays. University of Texas Press, Austin (1986)
17. Valentine, E., Bobrowicz, A., Coleman, G., Gibson, L., Hanson, V., Kundu, S., McKay, A., Holt, R.: Narrating Past to Present: Conveying the Needs and Values of Older People to Young Digital Technology Designers. In: Stephanidis, C. (ed.) Universal Access in HCI, Part II, HCII 2011. LNCS, vol. 6766, pp. 243–249. Springer, Heidelberg (2011)
18. Davis, F.D.: Perceived Usefulness, Perceived Ease of Use, and User Acceptance of Information Technology. MIS Quarterly, 319–340 (1989)
19. Gaver, B., Dunne, T., Pacenti, E.: Design: Cultural Probes. ACM Interactions 6(1), 21–29 (1999)
20. Colbert, M.: A diary study of rendezvousing: implications for position-aware computing and communications for the general public. In: Proc. of the 2001 Int ACM SIGGROUP Conference on Supporting Group Work, pp. 15–23 (2001)
21. Blythe, M., Monk, A., Park, J.: Technology Biographies: Field Study Techniques for Home Use Product Development. In: Proc. CHI 2002 (Extended Abstracts), pp. 658–659. ACM Press (2002)
22. Orr, J.: Talking about Machines: An Ethnography of a Modern Job. Cornell University Press, New York (1999)

Structured Knowledge: A Basic Aspect for Efficient User Applications

Laura Burzagli and Pier Luigi Emiliani

Institute of Apply Physics "Nello Carrara" National Research Council of Italy
{l.burzagli,p.l.emiliani}@ifac.cnr.it

Abstract. Designing a user ICT application in the Ambient Intelligence (AmI) Information Society requires an accurate study of the knowledge relevant to all the domains of interest for the application, in order to favour a holistic approach to the well-being of all users in their living environment instead of accessibility to the available interfaces. In the framework of a new approach for the design of user applications in the Information Society, a number of examples are provided, which highlight basic elements of the knowledge relevant and its structure.

Keywords: knowledge, ontology, expert system.

1   Introduction

The design of an ICT user application frequently starts from the selection and implementation of a technological infrastructure (for example a platform as Android and other hardware and software building blocks) and the identification of the general layout of its human-system interface. The contents of the application are often considered in a subsequent phase, when the system providing the service is supplied with information that, after appropriate processing, is presented to the user as a response to his/her request. In this paper, a methodology for setting up efficient applications, with special reference to the field of eInclusion, is described, showing that it requires a previous analysis of the information content of the application and of its structure. To make the explanation more effective, a specific application field was selected in order to present and to discuss relevant examples. Food, with its many related activities that affect the user, was considered an appropriate reference.

This paper starts with the introduction of new living environments as they emerge in the Information Society. It then introduces a new approach for the design and implementation of user applications relevant for eInclusion, in comparison with the traditional one. Next, for the specific kitchen environment (a food-related environment), it presents the relevance of a correct structuring and use of knowledge as a starting point of implementation of any application. Finally, several examples are introduced, and certain unusual characteristic are pointed out.

C. Stephanidis and M. Antona (Eds.): UAHCI/HCII 2014, Part I, LNCS 8513, pp. 11–18, 2014.
© Springer International Publishing Switzerland 2014

2   Application Environments

The field of application of Information and Communication Technologies (ICT) has rapidly expanded from single devices, such as smart phones, to the entire environment in which people spend all their time. So far, the vast majority of analyses and implementations of ICT have been concerned with a few specific environments. First, the office, because activities carried out in this environment are often related to the management, delivery and reception of information in electronic format. Another environment where ICT plays an important role is the classroom, due to the possibilities offered by these technologies in the learning and educational processes. A third environment, which is no less important than the previous ones, is the hospital, both due to the importance of health in human life and to the possibility of a structured organization of information offered by ICT.

However, the house is recently receiving a particular attention. At home, each person carries out a number of activities, which assume a fundamental role for the quality of his/her life. A primary function can be related to each room, such as sleeping to the bedroom, even if additional activities are also related to it. Special importance is attributed to the kitchen, with special reference to all activities related to food and eating. The list of activities contains several aspects, from planning meals to their cooking, up to the social level, in which people, who are perhaps seated around a table and eating good food, can improve their social relationships. ICT shows its importance in the kitchen, in simplifying several tasks and thus improving people's quality of life. This positive impact is increased if the different elements of the kitchen are networked and connected to Internet, in order to have access to external services and applications.

An intelligent kitchen is under development in the context of the FOOD project [1] part of the Ambient Assisted Living Joint Programme (AAL).The project is setting up a set of services and applications to improve the quality of life of elderly people. Some of these applications are specifically related to feeding, addressing, for example, menu definitions based on nutritional needs or health conditions. Others also address more general aspects such as safety or communication related socializing activities, connected to feeding.

3   A Structured and Knowledge-Based Approach to the Design of User Applications

According to this vision of interconnected and intelligent environments, the concept of applications is changing as well. Until now, the analysis of the behaviour of a person in the environment, especially in e-Inclusion, started from an analysis of barriers or limitations of activities that users might experience. A specific answer to such limitations was pursued in order to attain a complete inclusion of people in the environment, namely one that is also supported by technology. For example, in the office the main questions were related to the access of people to computers and the use of applications for interpersonal communications, such as social networks. Safety, security and the control of the health status are other domains of main concern. The related applications normally start with the acquisition of data by sensors. These data have different sources: a few data are about environmental status, such as temperature or gas presence, but they can also be about user conditions, such as health-care parameters (blood pressure, or insulin value). This information can be processed at local level or can be sent to a control centre for continuous monitoring.

Even if this approach has demonstrated its validity over the past twenty years, recently the objective of ICT applications has been moving form accessibility, inclusion and, consequently, independent living, towards a more general concept, i.e. well-being. This implies that a service or application is no longer limited to address a solution for a specific user activity, but is aimed at helping people to reach a higher level of quality of life. For example, for a user affected by diabetes, an application is supposed not be limited to measuring and recording glycaemia values and giving alarms, but also to suggest the most appropriate food in each moment of the day, according to the patient's diet, even when s/he is shopping. A new concept of application is introduced, which is not limited to a specific activity, but follows the dovetailed daily activities of the user.

In order to design an application according to the previous approach, the knowledge to be used in the implementation and the general structure of the resulting application are essential. The structure describes all the hardware and software building blocks, at a level abstraction allowing the selection of available commercial products. The knowledge includes data relevant for the application (e.g. data about food) and the user's data including his/her physical, sensory and cognitive changes in real time. In addition, a clear description and measurement of the above knowledge as related to the context is necessary.

If activities that are important for the user's quality of life must be pointed out in order to design applications aimed to favour their performance, their survey cannot be limited to results of tests with a small number of users. Since the main goal is to consider the variety of users, it is important to utilize international classifications that are produced and approved by a wide range of stakeholders. The document that best fits these requirements is the International Classification of Functioning and Disabilities, produced by the World Health Organization (WHO) in 2001[2]. In its main sections, it presents a classification of Body Functions, Body Structures, Activities and Participation, and Environmental Factors. These classifications can also be expanded, and a few modifications have already been approved by the WHO[3]. With reference to a specific example such as diabetes, not only the health aspects are considered, but also the more general aspects related to well-being [4][5]. Fourteen categories of the "Activity and Participation" components are considered influential from the patient's perspective. Among many, Acquisition of goods and services (d620), Preparing meals (d630), Doing housework (d640), Caring for household objects (d650), Complex interpersonal interactions (d720), and Informal social relationships (d750) can be cited. These few examples are sufficient to show how health conditions and activities in various environments are closely connected. These are the relationships to be taken into consideration in setting up a user application.

In any case, in order to obtain a collection and formalization of the knowledge required, the adoption of an ontology is appropriate. This is because it describes both the structure and the relationship between all the elements relevant for the problem. A comparison of the different knowledge available allows an analysis of the approaches adopted by other researchers.

As a preliminary summary, it is clear that in a complex environment as the kitchen, where many networked appliances are present and complex activities are carried out, it is not possible to use the approach used so far in eInclusion, where single difficulties are addressed and specific solutions for them are looked for. It is necessary to look for holistic approaches, where a set of tasks, for example connected to feeding as in the FOOD project, are addressed concurrently and coherently. Moreover, when application is designed it is not convenient to start from scratch. A lot of knowledge is available and most of it is structured and formalized in ontologies. Finally, some of these applications, as the one aimed to suggest diets for people with diabetes are so complex, that it is necessary to be able to reason about the individual situations (experts systems have been already used).

From the above considerations, it is clear that the concern about interaction, i.e. about accessibility, so far predominant in eInclusion, becomes only one of the aspects to be considered. Moreover, it is clear that, as far as possible, the interaction, and therefore the human-system interface, must be suggested by the type and quantity of information to be transferred and adapted to the functionalities that the service or application is able to offer to the users.

4   Examples of Structured Knowledge

As already mentioned before, in many cases applications are designed without taking into account that in many application environments a lot of information is available and formalized (for example in the form of an ontology) to be easily incorporated in reasoning systems (as expert systems). This is the case with food in general and with diets for different medical information (for example diabetes),

In the following, a summary of the knowledge available to be used in the implementation of applications in the feeding sector is made available. Only when this information is integrated in the structure of the application, the identification of suitable interaction becomes again the main concern, with the main constraint that interaction should be designed to be suitable for the different users and not resulting from the adaptation of an interface designed for the average user.

Example 1: An example of food ontology for diabetes control is presented in [6] within the domain of nutritional and health care. This ontology has been produced in the context of the PIPS (Personalized Information Platform for Health and Life Services) international project[7], to manage heterogeneous knowledge coming from different sources. In an application, which collects information from different sources, brings together different stakeholders and includes structured, semi-structured and unstructured data, an ontological solution has been identified as the best approach *for achieving a common understanding of the domains in which the system works.*

Fig. 1. PIPS project logo

The starting point is the identification of existing classifications, by selecting a food coding system and integrating it with a database developed by a consortium partner for data management in healthcare applications. A process in seven steps is adopted, which leads to 177 classes, 53 properties and 632 instances. A specific step for considering the reuse of existing ontologies is included, among the seven steps of the complete process (from the identification of the domain and the scope of the ontology to the creation of instances).

Example 2: A second example of ontological knowledge is presented in [8]. This ontology makes no direct reference to diabetes or to health problems, but it refers to food in general. It covers four main areas: food, kitchen utensils, actions and recipes. The context is now related to a dialogue system, where an electronic agent answers to voice input allowing the control of home devices using only voice. It presents a first example of how it is possible to integrate structured information within a more complex system: in this case, a dialogue system. Among the many aspects, at least two add elements of interest to the present discussion: the separation between knowledge and the processing system, and the possibility of easily adding new domains to the system. This is important when the designed applications do not address a specific and defined problem, but a much more general condition of the user well-being. Also in this example, the starting point is represented by an acknowledgment as to what is available and what is not. In addition, among the modules of this ontology three auxiliary modules can also be found, related to units, measurements and equivalences. In a general system for diet advice, this aspect is important, because, according to most health guidelines, the daily or weekly food intake is indeed relevant. The calories contained in a meal or a dish are often not meaningful if they are not evaluated over the space of a day.

Example 3: In this example [9], a still more complete system related to food, based on three main modules, is shown. It is based on an ontology for knowledge about food, an expert system for reasoning about diets, and a user interface for presentation, in order to set up a counselling system for food or menu planning in different contexts, such as a restaurant, a hospital, or at home. The presentation layer is also included, with different renderings within different contexts. This example show how more and more complex ontologies assume a growing importance in systems, especially when the system will be used in different contexts and with different interfaces. An additional element of interest is the review of existing Databases examined in order to set up the system: USDA (the USDA National Nutrient Database for Standard Reference, is a database published by the United Stated Department of Agriculture[10]); AGROVOC [11](a multi-lingual thesaurus compiled by the Food and Agriculture Organization of the United Nations (FAO) that contains nearly 20,000 concepts and 3 types of relations: preferred term, related term and broader term).

Example 4: In this example [12], a specific system for food recommendations for people with diabetes is presented. It is a complete intelligent system and can provide a plan in accordance with a person's preferences and health conditions.

In this example, the user profile influences the results coming from the system, so that the general level and the personal level are interconnected to give the user an even more accurate result.

Example 5: The importance of this example is based on the context in which the work was carried out. It comes from the European project OASIS (Open architecture for Accessible Services Integration and Standardisation)[13]. A precise reference to the aforementioned PIPS project is made within the framework of a service platform for health and life, which includes domains such as nutrition or physical activity. A dimension of well-being is presented in the project. Concepts such as diet, menus or food are essential to the activities of the project. It uses an ontology based on standards in nutrition such as Eurocode 2[14]; however, an even more interesting element in this discussion is that the ontology related to food is integrated with the others coming from different fields. A structured knowledge of people activities and their integration for each context is presented and the user and her/his characteristics are shown within a unified perspective.

Fig. 2. OASIS logo

Example 6 [15] shows the importance of a well-defined structure of the information also with the introduction of new devices. In this example, another element enriches the discussion. So far, in all the presented examples, the starting points were identified by previous ontologies or codes. Here, the large numbers of existing applications on mobile phones is considered. It is a new way to consider work, ideas and activities carried out in this field of interest. Even if international codes or standards maintains their importance, the results coming from new communication ways are taken into account. This means that, together with standards, international codes and scientific outcomes, knowledge can come also from a sort of distributed intelligence, such as (in this case) applications on tablets and mobile phones that are normally referred to as apps. The methodology presented by this example is a survey of existing apps to lists of the most common terms referring to diabetes. The application is intended for the health context, but, as said before, contexts are no longer kept very separate.

Example 7: Before concluding, as a final example, LanguaL™ [16] is reported. LanguaL is an automated method for describing, capturing and retrieving data regarding food. It provides a standard language for describing food, and serves specifically for classifying food products with the purpose of information retrieval. LanguaL™ is based on the concept that any food (or food product) can be systematically described by using a combination of characteristics. These characteristics can be classified into viewpoints and coded for computer processing. The resulting viewpoint/characteristic codes can be used to retrieve data relative to food from external databases.

5   Collection of Elements

In order to set up applications in the context of e-Inclusion, the previous examples contain several useful aspects of the knowledge, which is involved in such applications. The first example shows how the starting point for the process can be an ontology for the specific problem. An ontology allows designers to adopt a conceptual structure rather than a data oriented approach, which result much more useful for an application, able to evolve with the changes of users requirements. The second reference introduces an example of a structured information in complex processing system, such as a dialogue system. In this case, the split between knowledge and processing becomes a design criterion. The split also suggests that for an open system addition of different domains becomes easier. This is a basic aspect in implementing well-being applications, in comparison with service devoted only to a specific problem. Another aspect to be taken into account for effective services is the introduction of the concept of measure, as a basic component. Warning messages are not sufficient to guarantee an efficient application, which must also be able to provide specific values for each user. Since the first two building blocks of the system have been identified as a knowledge component (e.g. an ontology) and an expert system, the third element to be considered is the interface. This means that applications for the new environments not only require data from different domains, for example health and leisure, but they must also address different final users, who interact with the system at different levels and with different interaction needs and abilities. For example, in a health application, the final user is not only the patient, but also the caregivers, the nutritionists and the shopkeepers have to be considered. The importance of the user profile is particularly stressed in the following example, together with the need of connection with the other information for applications that adapt themselves to modification of user needs and preferences. This aspect assumes a particular importance for elderly people, because they often experience change in their conditions, which require modifications in the application, in real time too.

If the previous mentioned aspects are the basis of a well-being application, at least two additional characteristics have been identified. The first, coming from the sixth example, is related with the importance of already existing data collections, which represent a common reference for different community to make easier their interconnections and the second to the importance of standard languages for the description of the elements in a domain.

6   Conclusions

In the Information Technology Society, the approach to applications capable of giving effective help in improving the quality of life must be discussed. An approach, which takes the role of knowledge in the entire process into much more consideration in comparison to other aspects, as for example the interface, must be considered. The importance of the availability and an efficient structure of information is discussed in the paper by means of several different examples related to food and to a heath condition such as diabetes. The examples show how an ontological approach has been recognized and adopted by several communities, even if with some differences. The ontology can represents a building block, which together with an appropriate expert system to reason about user problems and a user interface provide users with the appropriate application, even when the context changes and new domains, new requirements from the user or from the contexts of use intervene.

References

1. AAL FOOD project, http://www.aal-europe.eu/
2. WHO: ICF International Classification of Functioning, Disability and Health. World Health Organization, Geneva (2001)
3. List of Official ICF Updates, http://www.who.int/classifications/icfupdates/en/
4. Ruof, J., Cieza, A., Wolff, B., Angst, F., Ergeletzis, D., Omar, Z., Kostanjsek, N., Stucki, G.: ICF CORE SETS FOR DIABETES MELLITUS. J Rehabil. Med.; Suppl. 44, 100–106 (2004)
5. Kirchberger, I., Coenen, M., Hierl, F.X., Dieterle, C., Seissler, J., Stucki, G., Cieza, A.: Validation of the International Classification of Functioning, Disability and Health (ICF) core set for diabetes mellitus from the patient perspective using focus groups. Diabetic Medicine 26, 700–707 (2009)
6. Cantais, J., Dominguez, D., Gigante, V., Laera, L., Tamma, V.: An example of food ontology for diabetes control. In: Proceedings of the International Semantic Web Conference 2005 Workshop on Ontology Patterns for the Semantic Web, Galway (2005)
7. PIPS project, http://www.hon.ch/Global/pdf/pips_sanna.pdf
8. Ribeiro, R., Batista, F., Pardal, J.P., Mamede, N.J., Pinto, H.S.: Cooking an Ontology. In: Euzenat, J., Domingue, J. (eds.) AIMSA 2006. LNCS (LNAI), vol. 4183, pp. 213–221. Springer, Heidelberg (2006)
9. Snae, C., Brückner, M.: FOODS: A Food-Oriented Ontology-Driven System. In: Second IEEE International Conference on Digital Ecosystems and Technologies (IEEE DEST 2008) Proceedings, pp. 168–176 (2008)
10. USDA National Nutrient Database for Standard Reference, http://ndb.nal.usda.gov/
11. AGROVOC Agricultural Information Management Standards, http://aims.fao.org/standards/agrovoc/about
12. Lee, C., Wang, M., Li, H., Chen, W.: Intelligent Ontological Agent for Diabetic Food Recommendation. In: IEEE International Conference on Fuzzy Systems (FUZZ 2008) Proceedings, pp. 1803–1810 (2008)
13. Kehagias, D., Kontotasiou, D., Mouratidis, G., Nikolaou, T., Papadimitriou, I.: Ontologies, typologies, models and management tools, OASIS Deliverable D1.1.1 (2008)
14. Eurocode2 Food Coding System, http://www.ianunwin.demon.co.uk/eurocode7
15. Sutton, D., Aldea, A., Martin, C.: An Ontology of Diabetes Self Management. In: Proceedings of the First International Workshop on Managing Interoperability and Complexity in Health Systems, pp. 83–86. ACM, New York (2011)
16. LanguaL™ - The International Framework for Food Description, http://www.langual.org/Default.asp (2012)

Designer Requirements for Visual Capability Loss Simulator Tools: Differences between Design Disciplines

Katie Cornish, Joy Goodman-Deane, and P. John Clarkson

University of Cambridge, Department of Engineering, Cambridge, UK
{klc49,jag76,pjc10}@cam.ac.uk

Abstract. There is a low uptake of inclusive design tools in industry, partly due to a poor fit between design tools and the thought and work processes of designers. Simulating visual capability losses is a technique with great potential in helping designers improve inclusivity and accessibility. However, we need to understand the needs of designers from different disciplines to improve the fit of these tools and their uptake in industry.

This study aims to determine designers' needs for vision loss simulators, and how this varies between disciplines. Interviews were carried out with 15 designers from five disciplines. The results suggest that one tool is not suitable for all. The graphic and web designers interviewed required a tool to aid communication with clients, hoever, the industrial and engineering designers required two tools, depending on the stage of the design process. To increase their uptake, simulator tools should be used in education.

Keywords: Design Tools, Inclusive Design, Simulation, Vision Impairment, Design Discipline.

1   Introduction

Inclusive design is an "approach to designing in which the designers ensure that their products and services address the needs of the widest possible audience, irrespective of age or ability" [1]. The ageing population is making inclusive design more important than ever. The Disability Discrimination Act [2] and the Americans with Disabilities Act [3] also add legal drivers. Its successful implementation can provide businesses with access to a wider market, and increased customer satisfaction [4]. Despite this, products that are inclusively designed are still rare [5].

One explanation for a lack of inclusively designed products is the low uptake of inclusive design in industry [6, 7]. This is, in part, because the tools, methods and materials required for inclusive design are not being fully utilized [8]. The utilization of these tools could be encouraged by improving the fit between them, and the way in which designers think and work [6, 7].

The simulation of the loss of visual capabilities is an effective technique that is liked by designers [9]. Losses in visual capability are particularly important to consider as the likelihood of developing a visual impairment increases with age [10]. Vision simulation can take the form of a software tool where a design is uploaded and the

C. Stephanidis and M. Antona (Eds.): UAHCI/HCII 2014, Part I, LNCS 8513, pp. 19–30, 2014.

effect of a visual impairment is applied to it on screen. It can also take the form of a wearable tool such as a set of glasses which the designer wears to replicate the effects of a visual impairment. By generating empathy, vision simulation increases designers' understanding of their users [11]. This assists in the creation of more accessible products, services and built environments. The technique is particularly important as designers are often young and healthy [12] making it difficult for them to understand those with reduced capabilities [13].

As previously mentioned, the utilization of these tools could be encouraged by improving the fit between them, and the way in which designers think and work [6, 7]. Designers from different disciplines work in different ways and so it is important to identify how their requirements for a simulator tool differ. By adopting a user-centered process we can increase our understanding of designers' needs [14].

This paper details a study involving interviews with practicing designers from different disciplines, with the aim of improving the fit between vision loss simulators and designers' thought and work processes.

2   Previous Work

2.1   Existing Visual Capability Loss Simulator Tools

Vision simulation for designers has been used in industry by Ford, IDEO, Interval Research Corporation, and Siemens and Bosch Home Appliances [15 - 18].

Formal simulation tools include software tools such as the Inclusive Design Toolkit's Simulation Software [4] and the VisionSim App [19]. They also include wearable tools such as the Cambridge Simulation Glasses [4] and the Fork in the Road SimSpecs [20]. Informal techniques include smearing Vaseline on glasses to blur the wearer's vision [21].

Research that evaluates existing vision loss simulators with regard to the needs of designers is limited. Dong et al. [14] evaluated a range of tools including the Cambridge Simulation Glasses and the Inclusive Design Simulation Software. She identified a number of designer requirements not currently met by the tools. Cardoso [22] also identified designer requirements for a simulator tools. However, he concluded that the simulator tools he evaluated "required further revision in order to be effectively and efficiently utilized". This highlights the need for more work in this area.

2.2   Design Disciplines

Design practice encompasses a spectrum of disciplines, but vision loss simulators are created for 'designers' in general. Lawson [23] recognizes this spectrum of design as ranging from art to science. He suggests that an engineer works in a "precise, systematic and mechanical" way whereas a fashion designer is more "imaginative, unpredictable and spontaneous". Although this may be an overly simplistic view of the complex differences between design disciplines, it highlights that different disciplines may have different requirements from a tool.

In addition to this it is widely reported that we need to increase our understanding of design practice and create design tools in a user-centered way [6], [14], [23, 24]. Therefore we should investigate the needs of designers from different disciplines in a user-centered way, to create tools that have a better fit with their individual thought and work processes.

2.3   Barriers and Drivers for Inclusive Design

There is limited research on what makes a successful vision loss simulator. However, some lessons can be learnt from research focusing more generally on the barriers and drivers for inclusive design. These include the designer's individual preferences, the company, client, design process, and design discipline [6]. Barriers include concerns that tools may limit a designer's creativity and impact on the aesthetics of the finished product, as well as client barriers [26]. Recommendations for successful tools include making them quick and easy to use, flexible, stimulating, concise, inspiring, usable and useful [14], [27]. However, we may need to be cautious in applying these general findings to vision loss simulators.

3   Method

3.1   Aim

The aim of this study is to understand whether one visual capability loss simulator tool is suitable for all designers, and how tool requirements vary between design disciplines on the art-to-science spectrum.

3.2   Sample

The participants consisted of 15 practicing designers, three from each of the following disciplines: graphic design, web design, industrial design, architecture and engineering design. These design disciplines were selected based on the most common disciplines listed in designer directories and design school courses throughout the world. They represent a range of disciplines on the art-to-science spectrum, and create products, buildings or services that need to be visually accessible. This will allow us to investigate the differences between designers from different disciplines.

3.3   Data Collection and Analysis

Designers were contacted by e-mail using design directories [28 - 30] and personal contacts. They confirmed which discipline they felt they belonged to prior to their interview, and the aim of the study was explained to them. All designers were located in Cambridge or London, except one who was based in the US. They were offered no incentives to take part.

Each designer took part in a semi-structured interview lasting between 30 minutes and an hour. These were carried out in the participant's chosen location (except for the designer in the US where Skype was used). The interviews covered the following topics: background questions on the designer's current job and education relevant to it; their current consideration of visual accessibility; and their use of tools for both visual accessibility and in other areas of design. The designers were then given an explanation of the Cambridge Simulation Glasses and how they work with the opportunity to try them out. They were asked about their opinion of the tool, their likelihood of using it and an explanation for this. They were also asked how the tool might be improved to suit them, and whether they would use other tools, such as a software-based vision loss simulator.

All designers were asked to complete a consent form before taking part. The interviews were recorded on a digital audio recorder and with hand-written notes, and transcribed and analyzed using QSR NVivo 8 software [31]. This was in accordance with a general inductive approach for qualitative data analysis [32] where data are reduced to identify the main themes. One interview was double coded by an independent researcher, which facilitated an in-depth discussion about the themes and their definitions. This led to the refinement, re-organization and clarification of the themes, and the inclusion of previously missing themes. The full data set was re-coded where necessary in accordance with the new themes. This helped to ensure the reliability of the coding.

4   Results

The results of the 15 interviews are presented in the following section, grouped according to the five design disciplines: graphic design, web design, industrial design, architecture and engineering design. A participant number has been included where direct quotes have been used. For example G1, G2 and G3 have been used for the three graphic designers, and W1, W2 and W3 for the three web designers.

4.1   Graphic Design

The graphic designers considered visual accessibility to be important in their discipline. However, they felt that some graphic designers do not currently carry out tests to ensure their designs are visually accessible. One participant added that "*a designer that is not doing some legibility tests, to me, is not a good designer*" (G1) suggesting that there is a 'best practice' but there might be a divide within the discipline.

The participants added that visual accessibility is particularly important in graphic design because "*everything is visual*" (G1). They suggested that testing visual accessibility should be a requirement of all projects and that if they had access to the Cambridge Simulation Glasses they would use them. This suggests that considering visual accessibility could be less project-dependant in graphic design than in other disciplines, and therefore a vision loss simulator would be most useful to them.

Graphic designers currently use informal methods to test their designs. These include removing their glasses, asking the opinions of colleagues, using Photoshop to blur designs, and printing small versions of their designs. However, they agreed that a formal tool such as a vision loss simulator would be useful.

The graphic designers emphasized the importance of the client when considering visual accessibility. For example the client may have a really developed brief. Alternatively, they may have *"a tiny understanding about what they want"* (G1). This requires the designer to spend a lot of time trying to understand the client's needs, but it does allow for a discussion about visual accessibility. They added that a vision loss simulator would be beneficial in aiding this discussion, but emphasized the importance of being able to calculate population exclusion. For example, if they could tell their client that *"20% of the potential customers can't read that sort of series two font, then they'd take notice"* (G2).

The graphic designers felt that both a wearable tool and a software tool would be useful in their industry. However, there were concerns that when using the tool a designer would use it *"for the first couple of months, and then put it away and like forget about it"* (G3). Therefore the tool would have to be easily accessible and embedded in the design process.

Finally, the graphic designers were in agreement that including vision loss simulators in education would improve their uptake in industry. One graphic designer stated that *"to be able to see a simulator tool in university would make you think about it all the time, and understand how it actually works"* (G3) making her more likely to consider using it in the future.

4.2   Web Design

There was a higher level of recognition of the importance of visual accessibility amongst the web designers, in comparison with the graphic designers. It was suggested that this was due to the existence of guidelines and standards in the industry such as the W3C Web Content Accessibility Guidelines [33]. One designer added that using them has *"become so natural and common sense"* (W1).

There is still a variety in the level of understanding amongst clients, with one web designer reporting that "normally in the brief that you get from a public facing organization, such as a university or a charity, they will stipulate what level of accessibility they want their website to be at" (W3) which demonstrates the high level of awareness of some clients. However, another web designer regularly has to convince his clients of the importance of visual accessibility, and often the client doesn't agree. This results in the designer adapting his design to meet the client's requirements by "biting their tongues and making the changes" (W2), often making it less accessible. He added that the client sometimes returns at a later date, asking for it to be more visually accessible, and the designer reverts to his original ideas. They suggested that a vision loss simulator could help them convince clients of the importance of visual accessibility.

Web designers were also slightly more in favor of a wearable tool. One graphic designer stated that the Cambridge Simulation Glasses would be really useful as *"you*

*could actually show them to a client in a meeting... getting people involved and shar-
ing that experience so everyone understands is much better than an isolated plug in
for me... it's the group awareness and the group knowledge especially from the
client's perspective because as designers we're aware of this anyway"* (W3). This
demonstrates their preference for a wearable tool over a software tool as it allows
better communication with the client. Another web designer was worried about the
complexities of a software-based tool, with the third web designer being happy to use
either type.

Again, there was a clear acknowledgement of the importance of education in promoting designer's awareness of inclusive design and the tools and methods available.
One web designer stated that *"when people in education are actually using these sorts
of tools, it will invariably filter down into industry"* (W3).

4.3   Industrial Design

The industrial designers gave a mixture of responses with regard to whether visual
accessibility is considered. This may be due to the larger diversity of products created.
For example, the designer working in medical device design, suggested that designers
in the area have to consider visual accessibility as it is required by the legislation. He
added that *"in development (of a medical device) you'd have to prove that you tested
it"* (I2) for visual accessibility. However, he suggested that this may be less important
in areas that are not subject to such strict legislation.

Their likelihood of using a tool also varied depending on the structure and focus of
the company. For example one designer worked in a company with a dedicated human factors team, and felt it was the job of this team to ensure visual accessibility,
rather than his. However, he added that the Cambridge Simulation Glasses would be
useful within the company.

Again, it was noted that there are different types of client. Those clients wanting a
medical device seem to accept the need for visual accessibility tests, as this is a factor
covered by the legislation. However, those who want a consumer product are less
likely to recognize the importance of visual accessibility. One designer added that
*"probably one of the key benefits, of the Cambridge Simulation Glasses, is at the start
of a lot of projects you have a workshop with the client, and that's basically where
you explore the problem space... with the client. So you get them to think about all the
stuff that they're not doing at the moment. So a nice little exercise could be if everyone
wore these glasses, and they realized how the extreme user isn't experiencing it like
they thought they would"* (I2). This process would be really useful in communicating
with clients who didn't already recognize the need for visual accessibility.

One industrial designer took this further, suggesting the need for two tools with
different aims depending on the stage of the design process. The first tool would be
for use early in the design process to generate empathy and encourage the understanding of clients and other stakeholders. *"We do workshops with clients where we get
them, with their stakeholders, involved... empathy tools in those scenarios are quite
good"* (I1). The designer added that a tool for use with a client needs to appear reliable and robust so as not to undermine the designer's competence.

The second tool would be used to calculate population exclusion (and validate a product against industry legislation where needed) later in the design process. This tool would also need to *"cover several different conditions... color blindness, some sort of occlusion, cataracts... I would absolutely 100% use this"* (I3). This would be much more complex and data driven, based on large amounts of population data, but would only be used by designers. Participants felt that this would be more useful than an empathy tool later in the design process and when validating highly regulated and safety critical products.

Again, the importance of education in promoting the use of vision loss simulators was highlighted. One industrial designer recounted: *"my first experience with empathy tools came in my third year of university with simulator goggles... it was the first real empathy tool I ever used, and it sort of stuck with me. If I ever did a project where I had to design to be inclusive I'd definitely use it"* (I2). He suggested that in addition using them in education they could be promoted through industry social media, magazines and conferences.

4.4   Architecture

The architects reported that a simulator tool would be of very little use to their industry due to the design process that they typically use. They felt that a wearable vision loss simulator could potentially be used at the end of the process to test designs. However, the designs are often one-offs without large-scale prototypes so cannot be tested early on. Furthermore, if a flaw was found with a building after it had been completed they are unlikely to go back and change it. The architects did state that *"elements within a building such as pre-manufactured pod bathrooms"* (A1) could be tested using the glasses before multiple copies were made.

A software-based simulator tool could potentially be beneficial, but only on larger projects such as the design of an airport terminal. Smaller architectural firms are less likely to create a 3D computer design of the building before it is built and so a software tool would be of no use to them. *"We are not creating a 3D space as such... I suspect some firms are moving on towards actually creating the 3D model of the building... but because we haven't got that 3D model there's nothing really at this point that a plug in would give to us"* (A3).

Furthermore, budgeting for a *"final stage check"* with the glasses would be difficult as budgets often get used up on other unforeseen areas, leaving little or no money at the end. One architect explained that often during the design process *"there have been a lot of... unexpected things that come up, and put pressure on the budget... it would be tough to hold money back until that point for those kind of activities and not have it get used up by other unforeseen things"* (A2).

4.5   Engineering Design

The engineering designers were similar to the industrial designers in a number of ways. They also gave mixed responses with regard to whether visual accessibility is considered. Again, this could be due to the large diversity of products created.

Furthermore, they also suggested that a number of different tools may be needed depending on the stage of the design process. One engineer stated that "I think it depends on what stage in the process you're actually working at, I think if you're very early concept a quick look see is brilliant, you don't need it to be calibrated"(E1). He added that a later stage test would have to be much more rigorous as "with any test approach you have to validate your test protocol to be confident that your results are any good". This would need to take into account factors such as different visual impairments and lighting levels and work with industry standards and legislation.

Similarly to the industrial designers, the company structure in engineering design also impacts on the designer's likelihood of using a visual loss simulator. One engineer working in a company with a particular focus on usability felt that it was important that all members of the company (including engineers, human factors specialists, graphic designers, marketing, clients and managers) had as much knowledge about the user as possible. He felt that although this gave them a competitive advantage. However, he felt that this company's ethos was in the minority, albeit in the context of a growing trend.

Another engineer outsources all human factors work stating that "we are a small company with 10 people… we have got a huge range of expertise in house but we can't do everything" (E2). Although he added that a simple visual loss simulator would be interesting to use and have around the office. These examples highlight the need for different types of tool depending on the stage of the design process.

5   Discussion

The aim of this study was to understand whether one visual capability loss simulator tool is suitable for all designers, and how tool requirements vary between design disciplines on the art-to-science spectrum. A comparison across the disciplines demonstrates that one tool is not suitable for all designers as they have different requirements depending on their discipline.

5.1   Comparison Across Disciplines

A comparison of the results across the disciplines highlighted the main themes with regard to requirements for vision loss simulators.

Firstly, most designers questioned recognised the importance of visual accessibility in their discipline (whether they currently tested for it or not). The majority of designers suggested that a vision loss simulator would be useful in their discipline, and that if they had access to a set of the Cambridge Simulation Glasses they would probably use them. The exception to this rule was the architects who didn't feel that a vision loss simulator would be useful to them.

Secondly, the architects would not use the tool because of the design process that they follow. They suggested that it is difficult for them to budget for final stage checks and so a wearable tool would not be useful. Furthermore they often do not create a full 3D model of each project, so they wouldn't be able to use a software tool.

Thirdly, it was clear across all disciplines (again with the exception of architecture) that the client has a large impact on whether visual accessibility is considered. There appears to be a variety in the level of understanding of the importance of visual accessibility amongst clients.

Therefore, a simulator tool to help designers discuss the importance of visual accessibility with their clients would be useful. This would be particularly useful in graphic and web design as these disciplines rely so heavily on vision. The vision loss simulator would need to be formal and generate empathy as well as allowing the calculation of population exclusion data. There was also a slight preference for a wearable tool as it can be used in workshops with clients.

However, industrial and engineering designers would be more likely to require two tools depending on the stage of the design process. Similarly to the graphic and web designers, they would like an empathy tool for use early on in the design process. This would be particularly useful in less regulated areas or where the client doesn't already acknowledge the need for visual accessibility. However, they were also interested in a more complex tool for use solely by designers that validated products against industry standards and legislation. This would need to be more rigorous and reliable and for use later in the design process.

Finally, most designers suggested that including a vision loss simulator in education would improve its uptake in industry. Some added that they should also be featured in industry blogs, magazines, conferences and journals.

5.2   Limitations of the Study

It is important to note that as only three designers were interviewed from each discipline the generalizability of the findings to the rest of the discipline is limited. Furthermore, only five disciplines were studied and therefore these results are specific to them. It is also important to recognize that sub-specialisms within each discipline may affect tool requirements. However, this is the first part in a larger project focusing on the improvement of vision loss simulators and provides a solid foundation for future work.

6   Conclusion

The main conclusion of this study is that one visual capability loss simulator tool is not suitable for all designers as designers' requirements vary depending on their discipline. The main requirements for a vision loss simulator (with the exception of the architects) are as follows;

1. The tool must be easily accessible. The designers generally agreed that they would find a vision loss simulator useful and would use it if they had access to one.
2. For graphic and web designers the tool must work well in discussions with clients. The graphic and web designers in particular felt that a vision loss simulator would help the client understand the need for visual accessibility. The tool should be formal, generate empathy and allow the calculation of population exclusion data. It should also be wearable so it can be used in workshops with clients.

3. For industrial and engineering designers there must be two tools depending on the stage of the design process. The first tool is similar to the one required by the graphic and web designers: for use early in the process in discussion with clients. The second tool is for use later in the process to validate products against industry standards.
4. The tool must feature in design education. This will lead to its adoption in industry and can be helped by promoting the tool in industry blogs, magazines, conferences and journals.

7   The Impact of the Results and Future Work

This paper highlighted not only that designers from different disciplines require a subtly different vision loss simulator, but the importance of acknowledging the differences between design disciplines. This has a wider impact in the field and should be acknowledged, particularly when improving the fit between inclusive design tools and the way in which designers think and work.

Future work could investigate the development of two tools. One tool could be used at an early stage when communicating with clients. The second tool could be used to validate products later in the design process. Exactly how this is achieved requires further research which should continue to be conducted in a user-centered way.

This paper is part of a larger study that also investigated the requirements that each designer felt would make a vision loss simulator useful to them. The results of this work have not yet been published but highlight factors such as the need for a tool to be quick and easy to use, available and easily accessible, and to allow the calculation of population exclusion data.

Acknowledgement. We would like to thank the EPSRC for funding this work, and Wolfson College Cambridge for their support.

References

1. The Design Council,
   http://www.designcouncil.info/inclusivedesignresource/
2. The Disability Discrimination Act lation, http://www.legisgov.uk/ukpga/1995/50/contents
3. The Americans with Disabilities Act, http://www.ada.gov/
4. Waller, S., Bradley, M., Hosking, I., Clarkson, P.J.: Making the case for inclusive design. Applied Ergonomics, 1–7 (2013)
5. Bontoft, M., Pullin, G.: What is an inclusive design process? In: Clarkson, P.J., Coleman, R., Keates, S., Lebbon, C. (eds.) Inclusive Design: Design for the Whole Population, p. 250. Springer, London (2003)
6. Goodman-Deane, J., Langdon, P., Clarkson, P.J.: Key influences on the user-centred design process. Journal of Engineering Design 21, 345–373 (2010)

7. Mieczakowski, A., Langdon, P., Clarkson, P.J.: Investigating designers' and users' cognitive representations of products to assist inclusive interaction design. Universal Access in the Information Society, 1–18 (2012)
8. Cardoso, C., Keates, S., Clarkson, P.J.: Supplementing User Information During the Inclusive Design Process. In: International Conference of Inclusive Design and Communications (2005)
9. Keates, S., Clarkson, P.J.: Countering Design Exclusion: an introduction to inclusive design. Springer, London (2003)
10. Harvey, P.T.: Common Eye Diseases of Elderly People: Identifying and Treating Causes of Vision Loss. Gerontology 49, 1–11 (2003)
11. Goodman-Deane, J., Langdon, P., Clarkson, P.J., Caldwell, N., Sarhan, A.: Equipping designers by simulating the effects of visual and hearing impairments. In: Proceedings of the 9th international ACM SIGACCESS Conference on Computers and Accessibility, pp. 241–242 (2007)
12. Zitkus, E., Langdon, P., Clarkson, P.J.: Accessibility Evaluation: Assistive Tools for Design Activity in Product Development. In: Proceedings of the 1st International Conference on Sustainable Intelligent Manufacturing (2011)
13. Goodman-Deane, J., Waller, S., Sarhan, A., Caldwell, N., Clarkson, P.J.: Simulation Software: Providing Insight into the Effects of Vision and Hearing Impairments. INCLUDE (2011)
14. Dong, H., McGinley, C., Nickpour, F., Cifter, A.S.: Designing for designers: Insights into the Knowledge Users of Inclusive Design. Applied Ergonomics, 1–8 (2013)
15. Hitchcock, D., Taylor, A.: Simulation for Inclusion-true User-Centred Design. In: Proceedings of International Conference on Inclusive Design (2003)
16. IDEO's Human-Centred Design Toolkit, http://www.ideo.com/work/human-centered-design-toolkit/
17. Leonard, D., Rayport, J.F.: Spark Innovation Through Empathic Design. Harvard Business Review 75, 102–115 (1997)
18. Siemens: Cooking Up a Better Life, http://www.siemens.com/innovation/apps/pof_microsite/_pof-fall-2010/_html_en/cooking-up-a-better-life.html
19. Apple Inc. VisionSim by Braille Institute, https://itunes.apple.com/gb/app/visionsim-by-braille-institute/id525114829?mt=8
20. Fork in the Road Vision Rehabilitation Services, http://www.lowvisionsimulators.com/sitecontent/product/full-set
21. Nicolle, C., Maguire, M.: Empathic Modelling in Teaching Design for All. In: Proceedings of International Conference on Human-Computer Interaction (2003)
22. Cardoso, C.: Design for Inclusivity: Assessing the Accesibility of Everyday Products. PhD Thesis: University of Cambridge (2005)
23. Lawson, B.: How Designers Think: The Design Process Demystified, 4th edn. Architectural Press, Oxford (2005)
24. Blessing, L., Chakrabarti, A.: DRM, a Design Research Methodology. Springer, London (2009)
25. Nickpour, F., Dong, H.: Developing User Data Tools: Challenges and Opportunities. Designing Inclusive Interactions, 79–88 (2010)
26. Dong, H., Keates, S., Clarkson, P.J.: Inclusive Design in Industry: Barriers, Drivers and the Business Case. User-Centred Interation Paradigms for Universal Access in the Information Society, 305–319 (2004)

27. Goodman, J., Langdon, P., Clarkson, P.J.: Formats for User Data in Inclusive Design. In: Stephanidis, C. (ed.) HCI 2007. LNCS, vol. 4554, pp. 117–126. Springer, Heidelberg (2007)
28. The Directory of Design Consultants ndirectory, http://www.desig.co.uk/
29. The Dexigner Directory, http://www.dexigner.com/directory/
30. Designer Listings, http://www.designerlistings.org/
31. QSR   International: NVivo   8,   http://www.qsrinternational.com/products_previous-products_nvivo8.aspx
32. Thomas, D.R.: A General Inductive Approach for Analyzing Qualitative Evaluation Data. American Journal of Evaluation 27, 237–246 (2006)
33. The Web Content Accessibility Guidelines 1.0, http://www.w3.org/TR/WCAG10/

Inclusive Design and Anthropological Methods to Create Technological Support for Societal Inclusion

Anita H.M. Cremers[1], Yvonne J.F.M. Jansen[2], Mark A. Neerincx[1,3],
Dylan Schouten[1,3], and Alex Kayal[3]

[1] TNO, P.O. Box 23, 3769 ZG Soesterberg, The Netherlands
{anita.cremers,mark.neerincx}@tno.nl
[2] TNO, P.O. Box 718, 2130 AS Hoofddorp, The Netherlands
yvonne.jansen@tno.nl
[3] Delft University of Technology, P.O. Box 5, 2600 AA Delft, The Netherlands
{d.g.m.schouten,a.kayal}@tudelft.nl

Abstract. Large groups in society lack the necessary skills to be sufficiently self-reliant and are in need of personal assistance. They include ageing people, people with low literacy skills, non-natives, but also children. They could all be supported by information and communication technology (ICT), but only if this technology is designed to fit their (cognitive) abilities. Inclusive design theory and methods have already been developed to support participatory design, but they should benefit more from insights of qualitative research and analysis methods developed in the field of anthropology. This allows identifying and interpreting theory-based patterns in generic user needs and human values. We present two case studies of how these methods have been applied to develop ICT for self-reliance of various target groups. By incorporating pattern descriptions in the 'situated Cognitive Engineering' framework, this knowledge becomes available for future ICT design and development processes, for other target groups and application areas.

Keywords: ICT, self-reliance, grounded theory, focus group, interview, observation, cultural probe, situated Cognitive Engineering.

1 Introduction

Information and communication technology (ICT) has a large impact on personal and social lives of people. More and more, in order to access, request or provide information (e.g. to make personal choices in health care), and to participate actively in society (e.g. to use social media to maintain contacts with peers), people take ad-vantage of the benefits of this technology. Governments applaud this development, since they expect citizens to become more self-reliant in many areas of society, but in particular in social security, health care and well-being, and societal participation.

Large groups in society, however, lack the necessary skills to be sufficiently self-reliant and to use ICT independently. An important cause is their lack of self-efficacy, which is the ability and belief to act adequately and efficiently in a given situation [1].

C. Stephanidis and M. Antona (Eds.): UAHCI/HCII 2014, Part I, LNCS 8513, pp. 31–42, 2014.
© Springer International Publishing Switzerland 2014

These groups include people with physical and cognitive limitations, ageing people, people with a low education or a low socioeconomic status, people with low literacy skills, non-natives, but also children. In order to become more self-reliant, they could still be supported by ICT, but only if this technology is designed to take their personal human values into account, to fit their personal needs and abilities, to be integrated in their personal and social context (situated) and to enhance self-efficacy.

An important question is how to design ICT applications which offer smart support for self-reliance of these special target groups, and stimulate their self-efficacy. The solutions should not be developed in an ad hoc fashion, but they should be evidence-based, more or less generic, re-usable but situated. This can be achieved by developing and applying validated theory and methods and to lay down the results in a structured format. The situated Cognitive Engineering (sCE) methodology has been developed to offer a coherent specification framework for the user requirements and interaction design, and their theoretical and empirical grounding [32]. Part of the theory is knowledge of the target groups; about their characteristics, abilities, needs, experience, physical and social context and technology use.

Traditionally, to gather this knowledge, inclusive design methods are being used. Inclusive design is defined as the design of mainstream products and/or services that are accessible to, and usable by, as many people as reasonably possible, without the need for special adaptation or specialized design [4], [30]. However, a theoretical base is lacking to describe data collected from various (both qualitative and quantitative) methods into generic concepts. This inhibits re-usability of findings for other personal human values, needs and abilities, and personal and social contexts. We propose to enrich inclusive design methods with qualitative method approaches from the social sciences as they are used within the field of anthropology. These methods are used in anthropology to discover, interpret and explain patterns in human values. These insights should be more systematically addressed in inclusive design practices, as they allow for better tailoring of   ICT applications [6].

This paper first describes the sCE method (section 2). Then an overview of current inclusive design methods, standards and guidelines is presented, and some shortcomings are identified (section 3). Following is an overview of qualitative research methods from anthropology, their added value for personalized design of ICT applications for self-reliance, their selection and analysis (section 4). Two illustrative case studies are presented for children and their parents and people of low literacy, showing the befits of a systematic qualitative approach (section 5). Finally, some conclusions are drawn from the current work (section 6).

2   Situated Cognitive Engineering

Human-centered development of interactive information and communication systems should be built on theory and empirical research in such a way that the results feed into an explicit definition of the design rationale [5]. Whereas software engineering methods provide formal and traceable specifications that development teams can share and refine, User Centered Design methods provide relatively ambiguous design descriptions that support the creative process but less the justification and completion. The sCE method (see Fig. 1) was developed to bridge this gap with a coherent specification framework for the user requirements and interaction design, and their theoretical and empirical grounding [32]. Recently, Value Sensitive Design (VSD) approaches were incorporated in this method to establish a sound and traceable transfer of stakeholders' values and policies into the design specification [10]. VSD is a theoretically grounded approach to the design of technology that accounts for human values in a principled and comprehensive manner throughout the design process [15].

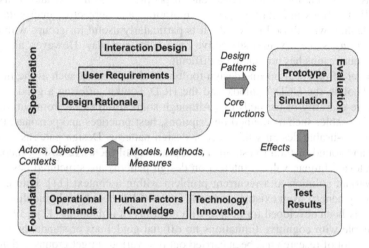

Fig. 1. Situated Cognitive Engineering (sCE) method

In sum, the current sCE method establishes a 'self-explaining' requirements baseline consisting of three components: (1) the domain, human factors and technological foundation; (2) the design specification of the requirements and the corresponding use cases, claims and interaction design patterns; (3) the evaluations that validate these claims. However, the methodology should provide two extensions. First, to address the policies, values and characteristics for groups citizens that might experience accessibility problems, core elements of the inclusive design knowledge base should be included (see section 3). Second, to acquire a good understanding of the needs of these citizens and establish a sound foundation for the design, it should provide core elements of anthropological methods (see section 4).

3   Inclusive Design Methods, Standards and Guidelines

The term 'inclusive design' stands in the tradition of the terms 'design for all', 'universal design' and '(universal) accessibility'. A large collection of (inclusive) design methods is currently available, quantitative as well as qualitative, for both specification and evaluation, and applicable in various phases of the design process. However, current methods are not always suitable for systematically deriving and securing the knowledge of the target groups, in order to include these in the iterative designing and testing of ICT applications and re-use them in future design processes. In particular qualitative methods (observation, interview, focus group, cultural probe) are not always carried out in a systematic and thus re-usable manner. Also, data analysis is problematic given the nature of the data, which is often multimodal, (speech, text, drawings and non-verbal expressions).

For example, cultural probes is a design-led approach to understanding users that stresses empathy and engagement. Probes are collections of evocative tasks meant to elicit inspirational responses from people. The approach is valuable in inspiring design ideas for technologies that could enrich people's lives in new and pleasurable ways [17]. It values uncertainty, play, exploration, and subjective interpretation as ways of dealing with those limits [18]. It is particularly useful for groups with cognitive limitations, since it values subjective experience and play. However, analysis of cultural probe results has proven to be difficult.

A number of practical on-line design toolboxes already exist, such as the Inclusive De-sign Toolkit, the UCD Toolbox and the HCD Toolkit, offering a good basis for prac-tical re-usability of methods [8]. Although some information from current toolboxes is re-usable, such as method descriptions, best practices and personas, they do not contain re-usable design guidelines or design patterns. Design patterns provide a practical and sound method to establish best practices of inclusive design, incorporating the relevant human values. Interaction design patterns are structured descriptions of an invariant solution to a recurrent problem within a context [11]. Future design patterns may benefit from existing sets of 'Universal Accessibility' guidelines which have already been developed for people with a variety of limitations [12], [39].

For people with cognitive limitations no official guidelines or standards exist yet. However, a lot of research has been carried out into various target groups and applications, which has often resulted in lists of design recommendations or guidelines. There are design principles for elderly people [14], for children [22], design considerations for persons with a cognitive disability [33], [38], and for people of low literacy [7]. These guidelines may form a valuable starting point for construction of design patterns for these target groups.

4   Anthropological Research

4.1   Role of Theory

Anthropology is the discipline that studies races, cultures, identity, language, and the very meaning of human differences [28]. Whereas in the early days anthropology was more concerned with the study of non-Western cultures to discover the primitive origins of Western customs, anthropology evolved as a field within the social sciences that studies and tries to explain the diversity of institutionalized cultural beliefs and practices within societies and organizations, by means of studying different communities and subcultures [2], [3]. The study of culture and social aspects and how they are socially constructed is the core of the anthropological field. Within anthropology, culture is often defined as the complex whole which includes knowledge, belief, art, morals, law, custom, and any other capabilities and habits acquired by man as a member of society [28].

The field of anthropology has come to know different theoretical perspectives [28]. However, all perspectives acknowledge the role of theory to be essential to discover and explain patterns in cultural and human values. Central to these perspectives is the notion that cultural aspects should be studied holistically, neither in isolation of their historically formed contexts, nor from one single viewpoint. Theory in itself is also a construction about 'reality', accumulated and constructed through discourse, debate, consensus and dissensus, by scholars using a specific theoretical perspective [26], [27], [29]. For example, a large body of knowledge exists on individualism and social cohesion, on the inclusion and exclusion mechanisms in group formations, identity formation and the social construction of identity. These theoretical concepts can be informative when studying the situatedness of a particular phenomenon within communities or societies, such as the phenomenon of self-reliance, to contribute to successful personalization of design [19], [24].

4.2   Research Methods

In order to be able to understand and explain differences in cultural aspects, one needs to interpret and understand these aspects from an insider's point of view, the emic perspective [16]. One is only able to understand and explain cultural aspects if one systematically, over a longer period of time, gathers empirical data by immersing oneself completely in the culture and everyday lives of the people who are the subject of one's study [35]. Below, the research methods (participant) observation, interview and focus group are described from an anthropological perspective.

Observation. The method of (participant) observation is one of the key methods within anthropological research. It is used to explore a phenomenon in depth in its natural setting over a sustained period of time [9], [16], [35], by thoroughly describing the daily routines of target group members from an emic perspective. Through (participant) observations it is possible to observe the 'real' actions of all actors, both human and non-human (e.g. symbols, cultural artifacts, technical apparatus), without any a priori implicit or explicit interpretations of those actions [16]. The (participant) observations are reflected in observational notes and transcripts that are made preferably on site and during the period of observation.

Interview. Interviews are a good manner for gathering information on how individual members of target groups interpret and explain their actions, experiences, perspectives, their cultural and social values. Informal interviews provide insights in how potential users interpret their actions in real life, their use of technology and their perspectives on self-reliance [13], [35]. Topics and questions in informal interviews are not predefined and open in nature. In contrast, formal semi-structured interviews are guided by an ordered list of topics to be discussed during the interview, of which the order can be adapted according to the dynamics of the conversation that develops. Also, it allows interviewees to elaborate and to go into depth about specific topics [3], [9]. In order to conduct formal interviews, thorough preparation an pilot testing are essential. Interviews are preferably held at locations that are familiar to the interviewees. This enables them to relate more to their emic perspectives on the phenomenon that is studied, and it creates openness [13].

Focus Group. Focus groups are often used to describe the consensus that may exist among the members of the target group about the phenomenon that is studied. Focus groups are considered a suitable method for research among members with a shared cultural or social background. Because of the discussion and group dynamics, they provide more in-depth information on cultural and social values that exist within a certain target group. Similar to interviews, focus groups require extensive preparation. Topic lists to guide the group discussions have to be developed, pilot tested and adjusted where needed. Focus groups are preferably held at locations that are important and familiar within the community or the target group, such as community centers. Also, they are preferably guided by interviewers who are known to the target groups and speak their language, such as bi-lingual and/or bi-cultural interviewers in case of ethnic minorities.

4.3   Application and Analysis of Methods

A careful selection should be made of which method to use for which target group, application domain and circumstances, including the choice for quantitative or qualitative, for specification or evaluation, and for which phase in the design process. Other existing qualitative methods from the (inclusive) design domain which have already proven their value, such as cultural probes, should be added to this collection and a similar body of knowledge should be accumulated from application of these methods to contribute to existing theory-based patterns.

   The information in the different materials (observational notes, transcripts, relevant documents etc.) should be analyzed by confronting the different perspectives, interpretations of potential users and observations of real daily life actions with each other. When doing so, patterns within the material can be discovered, which than has to be interpreted and described using relevant theoretical perspectives and bodies of knowledge. For example, transcriptions of interviews and focus groups, preferably verbatim, allow re-reading and re-using the expressions used by the participants. For analysis purposes, results from qualitative methods should be related to and, if possible, supported by results from quantitative methods.

5   Technological Support for Societal Inclusion: Two Case Studies

Two qualitative studies, one with people of low literacy and one with children and their parents, have been carried out in The Netherlands. Both case studies address similar high level goals: to support citizens in societal participation. Also, they have used similar methods (focus group and cultural probe) to elicit needs and wishes of target group members. Although some of the resulting user requirements are specific, also more general results were found.

5.1 People of Low Literacy

Target Group, Goal and Methods. In the Netherlands, five levels of literacy have been defined: level 1 indicates that a person is low-literate [36]. There are currently 1.1 million level 1 people between the ages of 15 and 65, whose ability to read and write is too low to function well in Dutch society [21], of whom 69% are native citizens. Level 3 ('functional literacy') is required to participate in society, have economic independence and increased participation in life-long learning [31].

The goal of the workshops was to gain qualitative insight into the daily lives of people of low literacy, and the issues related to societal participation and reading and writing they experience. As input, an earlier model to describe societal participation was used [34] (see Fig. 2). In this model, social situations are described on two axes: context and skill. The context axis describes the kind of social situation the participatory behavior takes place in, and ranges from formal to informal. The skill axis describes the type of social skill required to be proficient and successful at the participatory behavior, and ranges from information to communication.

The methods used in the preference elicitation process were two focus groups and one cultural probe. The focus group studies were held one month apart; the cultural probe was deployed in the first week after the first focus group. The goal of the first focus group study was to learn about the issues related to societal participation and reading and writing that the low-literate participants encountered in their daily lives. An initial overview of possible issues, inspired by the model of societal participation (Fig. 2), was used as input. Participants (nine) were shown four selected examples of possibly problematic issues, and were encouraged to talk about their similar experiences and to share any stories related to the topic. The cultural probe was designed to gain insight into the participants' daily lives. Participants were provided with a disposable analog camera, a digital audio recorder, and a selection of cardboard cards, each corresponding to a certain day of the week. The participants were asked to provide examples of situations related to reading and writing in their daily lives that they were either proud of or hindered by, using any of the materials provided. The second focus group had two goals. First, the results of the cultural probes (eight) were discussed. Second, the participants (six) were asked to rate a selection of technology devices and technology services on two axes displayed on a poster: 'difficult to use' vs. 'easy to use' and 'I use this' vs. 'I don't use this'.

Analysis and Results. Results were analyzed in three ways. The physical artifacts produced by the two focus groups and the cultural probes were analyzed by the researchers in a qualitative 'expert analysis'. The audio recordings were transcribed, and the transcriptions were coded and analyzed using Grounded Theory methodology [12]. The observation notes were used to craft Grounded Theory methodology memos. The outcomes of the focus groups and the cultural probes validated the accuracy of the earlier model used to describe societal participation (Fig. 2). Important lessons

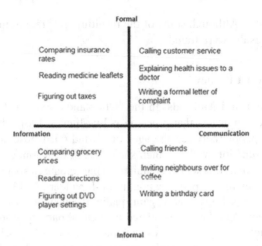

Fig. 2. Matrix with axes: context (formal-informal) vs. skill(information-communication). The cells contain example situations that cause problems for the illiterate target group.

about engaging in studies with people of low literacy were learned. Because of low technological self-efficacy, many participants expressed doubt and uncertainty about their ability to use the audio recorder. While the recorder used had specifically been selected for its low complexity (as perceived by the researchers), several participants still encountered serious issues while trying to use it during the cultural probe. More hands-on practice during the explanatory part might have been beneficial.

5.2   Children and Their Parents

Target Group, Goal and Methods. The group of elementary school children in The Netherlands contains children who are between 6 and 12 years of age. Our target group for this study was this group of children and their parents, where six parents and six of their children (between 6-8) were recruited. The goal was to gain an overall understanding about children and their family and school life, to gain ideas that will guide the design of a mobile social and navigational support platform for these children. The methods used were three focus groups and one cultural probe study.

The goal of the first focus group (parents only) was to introduce our research to the participants, explain other methodologies we want to use, familiarize the participants with our research issues, and obtain a few possible early insights from our participants as well as the green light to proceed with further sessions. To stimulate discussion, we displayed a few pre-made usage scenarios and design claims about a few positive and negative effects of the software's features within our scenarios. Then we asked the participants (individually) to rate to what extent they agree with our claims. At the end of focus group 1, we gave the cultural probing kits to the participants, containing a map of the neighborhood, an instant camera, post it notes, post cards, pens, and some glue. The main question was to provide an idea of their activities in the neighborhood as well as thoughts and experiences related to these.

The goal of the second focus group was to understand "what it is like to live their lives". This session was held three weeks later. It included the same group that participated in the first session. The parents brought back the material they (along with their children) had collected during that period, and then proceeded to describe the data (e.g., pictures, drawings, scrabbling, map highlights, etc.) they collected. Several of the parents' and their childrens' life issues, values, and concerns were discussed.

In the third focus group (children only) we tried to understand how children within that age group interact with technology, their interaction with their families, teachers, and peers within various contexts such as their school, home and other social activities. It was led by an experienced elementary school teacher, and consisted of a discussion where the teacher asked the children a number of open ended questions about their knowledge and usage of current technology, what activities they are allowed to do, how they connect with other children at school, sport clubs, and other places.

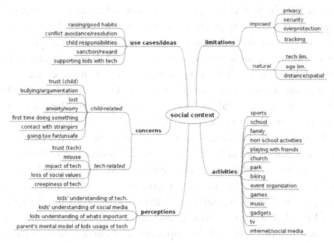

Fig. 3. Result tree for children and their parents based on grounded theory analysis

Analysis and results. We transcribed the audio recordings from all three focus group sessions and imported these transcriptions into QSR NVivo. We used Grounded Theory [9] as a main method for analysis, whereby codes are formed into a tree-structure that represents common themes and the links among them (see Fig. 3). The themes and concepts in the tree were later used to build a model that represents the relationship between the social context of the target demographic and the requirements for a normative, regulatory structure for the platform to be designed [25].

Lessons learned from these user studies can be summarized as follows. First, having a session moderator (an experienced elementary school teacher) who is relevant to the target group can generally lead to more favorable outcome in terms of collected data. Second, open-ended questions will generate more discussion, but may lead sometimes to unfavorable states such as divergence from the topic or side conversations. Third, while cultural probing is a data collection method by itself, its results served more as stimuli feeding into another method (focus groups). So data collected from a previous session can always be used to stimulate discussion in later sessions.

6   Discussion, Conclusions and Future Work

This article has addressed the important question of how to design ICT applications which offer smart support for user groups who lack the necessary skills to be sufficiently self-reliant and to use ICT independently, in order to stimulate their self-efficacy. We showed that a large collection of (inclusive) design methods is currently available, quantitative as well as qualitative, for both specification and evaluation, and applicable in various phases of the design process. However, we also identified the fact that application of current methods not always allows systematically deriving and securing the personal goals of users, the relevant human factors aspects and the appropriate technology. In particular qualitative methods, such as observation, interview, focus group and cultural probes, are not always carried out in a systematic manner. Data analysis for these methods is also problematic given the nature of the data, which is essentially multimodal. Finally, we found that a theoretical base is lacking, to describe data collected from various methods in generic concepts that can be translated to user requirements and design patterns. This inhibits re-usability of findings for other personal human values, personal needs and abilities, and personal and social contexts, in future design processes for enhancing self-efficacy.

We have shown that inclusive design methods enriched with qualitative methods from anthropology, not only enable deriving specific design requirements that allow for personalized systems, but also generic requirements which can be used for other target groups and application areas. The reason is that anthropological methods are systematically prepared and executed, and existing theoretical concepts stemming from bodies of knowledge are used to systematically analyze the empirical materials.

Two case studies have illustrated the application of two qualitative methods, focus group and cultural probes, for people of low literacy and children and their parents. The case studies show that through the combination of appropriate inclusive design and anthropological research methods we have been able to find not only specific design requirements, but also generic requirements. For people of low literacy, the context and situation where the participatory behavior takes place (critical practice situations) could be described in generic concepts of information acquisition and communication skills in formal and informal contexts. For children and their parents, it turned out to be possible to define support for self-reliance as a normative system, which contains all values of stakeholders in the neighborhood.

Both knowledge from inclusive design and anthropology provide input to the foundation of the sCE method. They contribute to the policies, values and characteristics for groups of citizens that might experience accessibility problems, and provide a good understanding of the needs of these citizens and establish a sound foundation for the design. Applying theoretical patterns from this foundation contributes to both effective and efficient research and development activities and concise and coherent design specifications. Through situated application of the methods, new theoretical patterns are derived, that can be added to the foundation for future use. In addition, other qualitative and quantitative methods could be applied, to add concepts derived from other perspectives and integrating them with existing ones, thereby contributing to the existing body of knowledge.

Acknowledgements. The current work was carried out as part of COMMIT, a Dutch national public-private research program on information and communication technology, project P02: Interaction for universal access (http://www.commit-nl.nl).

References

1. Bandura, A.: Self-efficacy: the exercise of control. Freeman, New York (1997)
2. Bernard, R.H.: Handbook of Methods in Cultural Anthropology. AltaMira Press (1998)
3. Bowling, A.: Research methods in health: investigating health and health services. Open University Press, Buckingham (2002)
4. British Standards Institute, British Standard 7000-6:2005. Design management sys-tems - Managing inclusive design – Guide (2005)
5. Carroll, J.M., Rosson, M.B.: Design rationale as theory. In: Carroll, J.M. (ed.) HCI Models, Theories, and Frameworks (Chapter 15), Morgan Kaufmann, San Francisco (2003)
6. Cheng, A.-S., Fleischmann, K.R.: Developing a meta-inventory of human val-ues. Proc. Am. Soc. Info. Sci. Tech. 47, 1–10 (2010)
7. Cremers, A.H.M., Kranenborg, K., Kessens, J.M.: Guidelines for user interfaces for illiterates. Draft TNO Report (2012)
8. Cremers, A.H.M., Neerincx, M.A., De Jong, J.G.M.: Inclusive design: bridging theory and practice. In: Harris, D. (ed.) Engineering Psychology and Cognitive Ergonomics, HCII 2013, Las Vegas, USA (July 2013)
9. Creswell, J.W.: Research design: qualitative, quantitative and mixed methods approaches. Sage, London (2003)
10. De Greef, T., Mohabir, A., Van der Poel, I., Neerincx, M.A.: sCEthics: embedding ethical values in cognitive engineering. In: Proceedings of the 31st European Conference on Cognitive Ergonomics, August 26-28, pp. 26–28 (2013)
11. Dearden, A., Finlay, J.: Pattern languages in HCI: a critical review. Human–Computer Interaction 21(1), 49–102 (2006)
12. ETSI, Human Factors (HF); Guidelines for ICT products and services; "Design for All". Sophia Antipolis Cedex, ETSI Guide ETSI EG 202 116 V 1.2.2 ETSI (2009-3) (2009)
13. Evers, J.: Kwalitatief interviewen: kunst én kunde. Uitgeverij Lemma, Den Haag (2007)
14. Fisk, A.D., Rogers, W.A., Charness, N., Czaja, S.J., Sharit, J.: Designing for older adults: principles and creative human factors approaches, 2nd edn. Human Factors & Aging Series. CRC Press Taylor & Francis Group, Boca Raton (2009)
15. Friedman, B., Kahn, P.H., Borning, A.: Value Sensitive Design and Information Systems. Technology 3, 6, 1–27 (2003)
16. Garfinkel, H.: Studies in Ethnomethodology. Polity Press in association with Blackwell Publishing Ltd., Cambridge (2003)
17. Gaver, B., Dunne, T., Pacenti, E.: Design: cultural probes. Interactions 6(1), 21–29 (1999)
18. Gaver, B., Boucher, A., Pennington, S., Walker, B.: Cultural probes and the value of uncertainty. Interactions 11(5), 53–56 (2004)

19. Hackett, E.J., Amsterdamska, O., Lynch, M., Wajcman, J.: The handbook of science and technology Studies. The MIT Press, Cambridge (2008)
20. HCD Toolkit: http://www.hcdconnect.org/methods
21. Houtkoop, W., Allen, J., Buisman, M., Fouarge, D., Van der Velden, R.: Kernvaardigheden in Nederland. Expertisecentrum Beroepsonderwijs (2012)
22. Hourcade, J.P.: Interaction Design and Children. Foundations and Trends in Human–Computer Interaction 1(4), 277–392 (2008)
23. Inclusive Design Toolkit, http://www.inclusivedesigntoolkit.com/
24. Jasanoff, S.: Designs of nature: science and democracy in Europe and the United States. Princeton University Press (2005)
25. Kayal, A., Van Riemsdijk, M.B., Brinkman, W.-P., Gouman, R., Neerincx, M.: Norms for electronic partners in socio-geographical support. In: Proceedings of the 15th Workshop on Coordination, Organization, Institutions, and Norms, COIN@AAMAS 2013 (2013)
26. Knorr Cetina, K.: Laboratory studies: The cultural approach to the study of science. In: Jasanoff, S., Markle, G.E., Petersen, J.C., Pinch, T. (eds.) Handbook of Science and Technology Studies, pp. 140–166. Sage Publications, Thousand Oaks (1995)
27. Knorr Cetina, K.: Epistemic cultures: how the sciences make knowledge. Harvard University Press, Cambridge (2003)
28. Kottak, C.P.: Cultural anthropology: appreciating cultural diversity. McGraw-Hill (2011)
29. Kuhn, T.: The structure of scientific revolutions. University of Chicago Press (2012)
30. Langdon, P., Thimbleby, H.: Editorial: Inclusion and interaction: designing interaction for inclusive populations. Interacting with Computers 22, 439–448 (2010)
31. Murray, T.S., Kirsch, I.S., Jenkins, L.: Adult Literacy in OECD Countries: Technical Report on the International Adult Literacy Survey. US Dept. of Education (1997)
32. Neerincx, M.A.: Situated Cognitive Engineering for Crew Support in Space. Personal and Ubiquitous Computing 15(5), 445–456 (2011)
33. van der Pijl, D.J., Cremers, A.H.M., Soede, M.: Personalized PDA accessibility for intellectually disabled persons: concept guidelines based on the development of an electronic travel companion, July 22-27. HCI International, Las Vegas (2005)
34. Schouten, D., Smets, N., Driessen, M., Hanekamp, M., Cremers, A.H.M., Neerincx, M.A.: User requirement analysis of social conventions learning applications for non-natives and low-literates. In: Harris, D. (ed.) EPCE 2013, Part I. LNCS, vol. 8019, pp. 354–363. Springer, Heidelberg (2013)
35. Spratley, J.P.: Participant observation. Harcourt Brace College Publ., Fort Worth (1980)
36. Steehouder, P., Tijssen, M.: Opbrengsten in beeld; Rapportage Aanvalsplan Laaggeletterdheid 2006-2011. CINOP, Den Bosch. (2011)
37. UCD Toolbox, http://www.ucdtoolbox.com
38. WebAIM. Cognitive disabilities Part 1 (We Still Know Too Little, and We Do Even Less) and Part 2 (Conceptualizing Design Considerations). Web Accessibilit In Mind, http://webaim.org/articles/cognitive
39. World Wide Web Consortium. Web Content Accessibility Guidelines 1.0; User Agent Accessibility Guidelines 1.0, http://www.w3.org

A Simple Procedure for Using Vision Impairment Simulators to Assess the Visual Clarity of Product Features

Joy Goodman-Deane, Sam Waller, Katie Cornish, and P. John Clarkson

Engineering Design Centre, University of Cambridge, Cambridge, UK
{jag76,sdw32,klc49,pjc10}@cam.ac.uk

Abstract. Capability loss simulators give designers a brief experience of some of the functional effects of capability loss, thus helping them to understand capability loss better. Wearable simulators, such as vision simulator glasses, can also be worn while using products and prototypes to help identify usability problems. However, this process can be confusing. This paper presents a simple procedure for using vision impairment simulators to assess the visual clarity of product features. The procedure provides clear results that are linked to the numbers of people in the population affected by the issues identified. It was tested with eight accessibility specialists and product developers. Results indicate that they can use this method effectively, and find it useful.

Keywords: Vision loss, Simulation, Inclusive design, Product assessment.

1 Introduction

In order to design inclusively, designers need to understand the challenges faced by people with capability loss. Capability loss simulators are one way to do this. They give designers a brief experience of some of the functional effects of capability loss for themselves [1, 2]. This can be done by wearing equipment that restricts one's motor or sensory capability, such as body suits [3] or pairs of glasses [4]. Software can also be used to show how things might appear to someone with a sensory impairment, e.g. [5].

Capability loss simulators can help designers and other stakeholders to understand capability loss, and to develop empathy with people with impairment. Wearable simulators can also be worn while using products and prototypes to provide insight into the effect of capability loss on product use and to identify usability problems. As such, they are not intended as a replacement for involving users, because they are limited and cannot convey the full experience of someone with an impairment. However, they provide a useful complement to user involvement, providing initial usability feedback before designs are taken to users and helping designers to internalise information gained through other methods.

However, identifying usability problems using simulators can be confusing. Simulators often do not specify what level of impairment is simulated (e.g. [3]), or how

C. Stephanidis and M. Antona (Eds.): UAHCI/HCII 2014, Part I, LNCS 8513, pp. 43–53, 2014.

many people have that level of impairment. This can make it difficult to determine whether a usability problem will affect many of the target user group or just a few.

This issue has been addressed through work on the Cambridge Simulation Glasses [6]. These vision impairment simulators can be layered to simulate greater levels of impairment. Recent work has calculated the level of visual ability loss simulated by different numbers of glasses. This can be used to estimate how many people would be excluded from using a product based on the number of glasses it is useable with [4]. However, experience with designers indicates that the figures on vision capability and exclusion levels can be confusing to understand, calculate and apply.

This paper presents a simpler procedure for assessing a product using simulator glasses. The procedure gives clear advice on whether the product needs further work or not, depending on whether it passes or fails a standard benchmark. It is described in Section 2, with examples in Section 3. The statistics and calculations behind the procedure are described in Section 4. Results from evaluating the method with accessibility specialists and product developers are given in Section 5.

2   Assessment Method

2.1   Testing the Assessor's Vision

The first part of the assessment method is a very simple test of the assessor's vision. In this paper, "assessor" refers to the person doing the product assessment. The vision test is important because a person's starting vision affects their level of visual ability when wearing the simulator glasses. With the same number of simulator glasses, someone with average starting vision experiences worse visual ability than someone with excellent starting vision [4]. Furthermore, there is some variation in starting vision, even within a group of young designers with "normal" vision. Knowing the assessors' starting vision abilities means that they can each wear the right number of glasses so that they all experience roughly the same level of visual ability.

The test chart used is shown in Figure 1 on the following page. It is attached to a wall at eye level at a distance of 150cm. Assessors wear their normal corrective glasses or contact lenses, but no simulation glasses. They read down the chart to identify the smallest row on which they can read at least 7 letters correctly. The instructions next to this row indicate which sheet to use in the rest of the procedure. An assistant may be needed, to confirm whether assessors have read the letters correctly or not.

The assessment method is not suitable for use by people with poorer levels of vision (worse than 20/281), i.e. people who cannot read the second line on the test chart. This is because the primary aim of the method is to help designers with good levels of vision to understand the needs of people with vision impairments. By focusing on just

---

[1]   In this paper, visual ability is described using Snellen notation (20/X). 20/20 is often described as "normal" visual ability, although many people have better vision than this. Smaller values of X (e.g. 20/16) indicate better visual ability, and larger values indicate worse.

this target group of designers, the assessment procedure can be greatly simplified to use only two very similar flowcharts (see Section 2.2). The simulators themselves can be used by designers with all levels of starting vision [4] but the assessment procedure is more complicated.

The test chart is based on the letter charts used in the Towards Better Design survey [7, 8]. This means that the levels of simulated visual ability can be compared with results from the survey to indicate the numbers of people with those levels of vision, as described in Section 4. The particular levels of vision assessed in the chart were chosen so that the vision levels while wearing the simulator glasses correspond to particular percentages of people in the population (see Section 4.3).

Fig. 1. Vision chart used in testing the assessor's vision (For illustrative purposes only: note that this is not printed at the appropriate size for use in testing vision)

2.2   Assessing the Visual Clarity of a Product Feature

First of all, assessors specify the product they are going to assess. Rather than assessing the whole product at once, they specify a particular user goal with that product, and then assess the clarity of the product features required to achieve that goal. For example, using a mobile phone can involve many different goals, such as charging the phone, making a phone call, and reading a text message. These involve different product features and thus have different levels of accessibility. By examining a single goal at a time, the assessment is more focused and effective. Assessors also specify a use scenario, as levels of accessibility vary depending on aspects such as lighting and the user's prior knowledge.

In the assessment itself, assessors use assessment sheet A or B, depending on their starting vision. The sheets each contain a flowchart, summarizing the procedure to follow, as shown in Figures 2 and 3 on the following page. The flowcharts (and thus the procedure) are identical except for the number of glasses to wear at each stage. Assessors with excellent vision wear more simulator glasses than those with good/average vision to achieve the same levels of simulated vision ability.

Assessors start by wearing the number of simulator glasses listed in the first diamond. The glasses used are the Cambridge Simulation Glasses (Figure 4). These restrict the ability to see fine detail and perceive contrast differences, and can be layered to simulate greater levels of impairment [6].

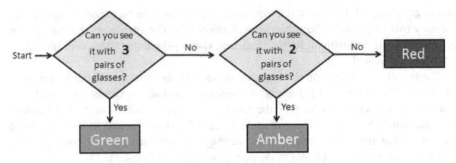

Fig. 2. The assessment procedure flowchart for assessors with good/average vision (visual ability between 20/16 and 20/28)

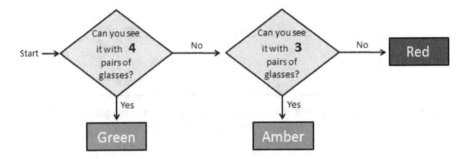

Fig. 3. The assessment procedure flowchart for assessors with excellent vision (visual ability better than 20/16)

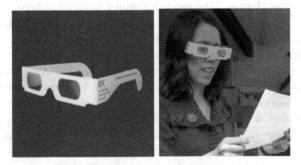

Fig. 4. Cambridge Simulation Glasses

The assessors examine the product features while wearing the specified number of glasses. This may involve trying to read text on the product, discern icons, perceive salient details in images or distinguish parts of a product from each other visually. It is important that assessors keep the product at a normal working distance while doing this, to avoid skewing the results.

If the assessor can see the product feature successfully, it is rated "Green" as indicated by the leftmost box in the flowchart. This indicates that less than 1% of the population is excluded from using that product feature on visual grounds (see Section 4 for calculations). The product has passed this basic visual accessibility check, although this does not, of course, guarantee that there are no accessibility problems overall. Ideally, this procedure should be used together with user involvement as part of an overall inclusive design process [9].

If the assessors cannot distinguish the product feature successfully, they remove one set of glasses. Thus people with good vision wear two pairs of glasses, and those with excellent vision wear three, as shown in the second diamond in the flow charts. They then examine the product feature again. If they can distinguish it successfully this time, it is rated "Amber". This indicates that between 1 and 6% of the population is excluded from using that product feature on visual grounds. The design of the feature should be improved if possible, but it may not be the highest priority.

If the assessors cannot distinguish the product feature successfully while wearing the second set of glasses, then it is rated "Red". This means that more than 6% of the population is excluded from using it on visual grounds. It really needs to be improved to reduce user frustration, avoid losing customers, and include the senior market.

3   Example Assessments

Before examining any products, the assessor's vision was tested using the test chart in Fig 1. She could read all the letters on the bottom line of this chart, and thus used the flowchart in Fig 3 for the assessments below.

3.1   Assessment 1: Box of Biscuits

The assessor examined the visual clarity of the ingredients list on a box of biscuits, shown in Fig 5. The product goal was to determine whether the biscuits contained milk. The scenario involved the biscuits being selected by someone unfamiliar with the biscuits or their ingredients, in an indoor setting with good daytime lighting.

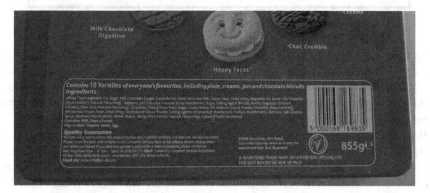

Fig. 5. Portion of the biscuit box used in the assessment, showing the ingredients list

Following the procedure in Fig 3, the assessor started with four pairs of simulator glasses. With these, she could not read the ingredients sufficiently clearly to tell if they contained milk. Therefore, she tried again with three pairs of glasses, as indicated in the second diamond in Fig 3. This time, she could read the ingredients successfully. Thus, this product feature was rated Amber. This means that between 1% and 6% of the population would be excluded from reading the ingredients list. The list should be improved if possible. An obvious way to do this is by increasing the font size. However, there are other ways of doing so without taking up more space on the packaging, such as using a bolder font, or darkening the background to increase the contrast of the letters.

3.2   Assessment 2: Digital Camera

The second assessment examined the visual clarity of the PC/AV port on a digital camera (see Fig 6). The product use task was to insert the cable into the port, in good lighting, without knowing the location of the port on the camera.

Fig. 6. Digital camera used in the assessment, with close-up of the PC/AV slot

As before, the assessor started with four pairs of glasses. While wearing these, she was able to find a slot of approximately the right size and shape. By trying to insert the cable in this slot, she determined that it was indeed the right slot, and succeeded at the task. Thus the slot was rated Green, as shown in Fig 3. Less than 1% of the population would be excluded from using it on visual grounds alone.

However, users with lower levels of prior knowledge or confidence may not be willing to insert a cable into an unknown slot. Furthermore, many could not rely on touch feedback to determine if the cable fits properly. It is, therefore, also important to examine the visual clarity of the text label next to the slot, which reads "PC/AV". The assessor was unable to read this while wearing four pairs of glasses, or even with three pairs of glasses. The text label is therefore rated Red, meaning that more than 6% of the population would not be able to read it. It fails our benchmark, and needs to be improved. This could be done by increasing the contrast of the text. To avoid the cost of having to print an additional label, the text could be printed on an existing nearby label (such as that containing the serial number), which could be repositioned appropriately.

4   Underlying Calculations

4.1   Exclusion Calculations

Product features are rated as Green, Amber or Red, depending on the proportion of the population that would be unable to see them, and thus be excluded from their use. The exclusion calculations are best explained using an example, summarized in Table 1. Consider the assessor from Section 3. She could read the bottom line on the vision chart and thus has visual ability better than 20/16. The best human visual ability is around 20/9 [12]. However, this is rare, and the distribution of visual ability in the population means that most assessors in this range actually have vision between 20/16 and 20/11.

Table 1. Exclusion calculations for an example (Amber) assessment

	Example assessor with "excellent" vision (i.e. who can read the bottom line on the test chart)	
	Worst vision in this range	Good vision in this range (most assessors in this range have vision worse than this)
Starting visual ability (VA) (Snellen visual acuity)	20/16	20/11
VA with 3 pairs of simulator glasses	20/49	20/34
Estimated exclusion for a product that is just viewable with 3 pairs of glasses (weighted percentage of survey sample with VA worse than that simulated by 3 pairs)	1.0%	4.9%

We measured twenty participants to determine the effect of different numbers of simulator glasses on people's vision (unpublished study, c.f. [4]). There is some variation between individuals, but it is small enough that the mean values can be used to estimate the assessor's visual ability while wearing three (or four) pairs of glasses (see Table 1).

The assessor could read the ingredients list on the box of biscuits with three pairs of glasses, but not with four (Section 3.2). It is reasonable to assume that people with visual ability (VA) equivalent to (or worse than) four pairs of glasses would not be able to read the ingredients list. They would thus be excluded from it. Similarly, we assume that people with VA equivalent to (or better than) three pairs would be able to read the ingredients and thus not be excluded.

The precise level of VA required to read the ingredients is unknown but lies somewhere between these two values. In the worst-case (most exclusive) scenario, it lies just below the VA with three pairs of glasses. People who have VA equivalent to three glasses can just manage to read the ingredients, and so are included. Everyone with worse VA is excluded. This forms a *conservative* estimate of exclusion. Using this estimate ensures that anyone who is actually excluded is counted in the estimate, at the risk of counting some people who may not actually be excluded (but may still find the product difficult to use). Using a conservative estimate encourages designers to think inclusively.

Thus exclusion is estimated by adding up all the people in the dataset with vision worse than that simulated by three pairs of glasses (see Table 1 for results). More details of how this is done can be found in [4]. The dataset used comes from the Towards Better Design survey [7, 8]. This survey tested a range of user capabilities related to product design. It was chosen because it covers a wide range of vision and other capability measures, meaning that exclusion for other impairments and combinations of impairments can also be calculated [10, 11]. However, in this paper, we focus only on the vision results.

Although the survey was relatively small (362 people), it was postcode sampled across England and Wales and weighted for age and gender. Thus, it can give a good indication of exclusion on a wider scale.

In the example, it is likely that between 1.0% and 4.9% of the population would be excluded (see Table 1). The ingredients list is thus rated Amber (1-6% exclusion). Similar calculations were done for assessors with different starting vision, and different numbers of simulator glasses.

4.2   Choice of Assessment Bands

The assessment procedure gives banded results (Green, Amber and Red) rather than exact exclusion values. This was chosen for two main reasons. Firstly, it is of little interest to a designer whether the exclusion is exactly 2.6%. It is more practically useful to know whether it falls within a band that requires further action (e.g. between 1% and 6%). Secondly, the exact level of exclusion depends on the exact visual ability of the assessor. However, in practice, it is difficult to measure visual ability exactly. For practical reasons, the assessment uses a simplified vision test to estimate the assessor's visual ability within a range (e.g. between 20/16 and 20/28).

The Green, Amber and Red bands correspond to: less than 1%; 1% to 6%; and greater than 6% exclusion. These were chosen because they roughly correspond to levels of exclusion that designers can relate to. Ergonomics books commonly refer to

95th and 99th percentiles, corresponding to 5% and 1% exclusion (e.g. [13], p28). Thus, designers are unlikely to be interested in levels of exclusion below 1%, while values above 5% are high enough for them to realise that something really is remiss.

However, if wearing three pairs of simulator glasses corresponds to about 1% exclusion, then removing one pair increases the exclusion value to about 6%, not 5%. Thus the boundary for the Red band was set at 6% instead of 5%. Ideally, simulator glasses would be chosen that alter exclusion by about 5%. However, the filters for such glasses are not commercially available. The Cambridge Simulator Glasses use the smallest gradation in filters that are easily obtainable commercially.

4.3   Test of Starting Vision

Assessors start the assessment procedure by taking a simple vision test (see Section 2.1). To make this test as simple as possible, different levels of starting vision were combined into ranges, e.g. 20/16 and 20/12 were placed in the same range. The ranges were set so that the exclusion results for people in the same range corresponded to the same band: under 1% (Green), 1-6% (Amber) or over 6% (Red) exclusion. Two people within the same starting vision range should get the same banded result (Green, Amber or Red) with the same number of simulator glasses.

For people with fairly "normal" vision (better than 20/28), only two vision ranges were needed (good/average vision; and excellent vision). Thus only two rows were really needed on the test chart in Figure 1. An extra row was added at the top, to help avoid confusion for people whose vision is worse than 20/28. It also helps people get accustomed to the test chart procedure.

5   Testing the Method

5.1   Workshop

The method was tested in a workshop with eight accessibility specialists and product developers. Level of professional experience varied from 10 months to 15 years. The workshop started with an introduction to the simulators. After this, the starting vision of each person was measured, and they were given the appropriate assessment sheet, as described in Section 2. The assessment method was then explained to them with an example.

The group was then split into pairs. Each pair worked together to assess a variety of items in the meeting room. Choices included TV remote controls, mobile phones, a fire extinguisher, an air conditioning control unit, a packet of adhesive tack, and a microwave. The members of each pair took it in turns to carry out the assessment, while the other person recorded the results. After completing the assessments, the workshop attendees completed a short questionnaire about their experiences of and opinions of the method.

5.2   Results

The results from this initial workshop indicate that participants were able to understand and use the assessment method effectively. However, some clarifications may be helpful to further improve the method. In particular, it would be helpful to provide more worked examples, covering the full range of Green, Amber and Red outcomes, and clarifying how borderline cases should be assessed (where text is difficult but not impossible to see).

All attendees said that they would like to use the simulators again. Seven of the eight said that they would use them to assess visual clarity, with several describing it as a useful technique. For example, one person described it as a *"very useful and consistent check"*.

6   Conclusions and Future Work

This paper has presented a simple procedure for using vision impairment simulators to assess the visual clarity of product features. The procedure gives clear advice on whether the product needs further work or not, depending on whether it passes or fails a standard benchmark. Assessors wear two different sets of simulator glasses while trying to use the product feature. Depending on whether they are successful or not in using the feature, it is rated Green, Amber or Red. These bands reflect the numbers of people who would be excluded from that product feature, and thus the importance of action in improving it.

Participants in a workshop could understand and use the method effectively. Further work is required to test the effectiveness of alternative approaches to resolving the issue of borderline assessment cases, and presenting results in terms of difficulty and/or exclusion. Further testing is also needed with a wider range of industry professions.

Acknowledgements. This work was funded by EPSRC through the KT-EQUAL programme. We would also like to thank the RNIB for helping to organise the workshop where the method was tested. Thanks are also due to the members of the 'Design and Usability Community' group who took part in the workshop.

References

1. Nicolle, C.A., Maguire, M.: Empathic Modelling in Teaching Design for All. In: Stephanidis, C. (ed.) International Conference on Human-Computer Interaction; Universal Access in HCI: Inclusive Design in the Information Society, vol. 4, pp. 143–147 (2003)
2. Cardoso, C., Clarkson, P.J.: Impairing Designers: Using Calibrated Physical Restrainers to Empathise with Users. In: Kose, S. (ed.) 2nd International Conference for Universal Design. International Association for Universal Design, Kyoto (2006)

3. Hitchcock, D.R., Lockyer, S., Cook, S., Quigley, C.: Third Age Usability and Safety - An Ergonomics Contribution to Design. International Journal of Human-Computer Studies 55(4), 635–643 (2001)
4. Goodman-Deane, J., Waller, S., Collins, A.-C., Clarkson, J.: Simulating Vision Loss: What Levels of Impairment are Actually Represented? In: Anderson, M. (ed.) Contemporary Ergonomics and Human Factors 2013, Institute of Ergonomics & Human Factors (2013)
5. Goodman-Deane, J., Waller, S., Clarkson, J.: Simulating Impairment. In: Bryan-Kinns, N., Lloyd, T., Sheridan, J.G. (eds.) (re)Actor3/HCI 2008 (2008)
6. Engineering Design Centre: Inclusive Design Tools. In: Inclusive Design Toolkit, http://www.inclusivedesigntoolkit.com/betterdesign2/inclusiv etools/inclusivedesigntools.html
7. Clarkson, P.J., Huppert, F.A., Tenneti, R., Waller, S., Goodman-Deane, J., Langdon, P., Myerson, J., Nicolle, C.: Towards Better Design, 2010 [computer file]. Colchester, Essex: UK Data Archive [distributor]. SN: 6997 (2012), http://dx.doi.org/10.5255/UKDA-SN-6997-1
8. Tenneti, R., Langdon, P., Waller, S., Goodman-Deane, J., Ruggeri, K., Clarkson, P.J., Huppert, F.A.: Design and Delivery of a National Pilot Survey of Capabilities. Applied Ergonomics (2014)
9. Engineering Design Centre: Inclusive Design Toolkit, http://www.inclusivedesigntoolkit.com/
10. Keates, S., Clarkson, J.: Countering Design Exclusion: An Introduction to Inclusive Design. Springer, London (2003)
11. Goodman-Deane, J., Waller, S., Williams, E., Langdon, P., Clarkson, P.J.: Estimating Exclusion: A Tool to Help Designers. In: Proceedings of Include 2011. Royal College of Art, London (2011)
12. Kirschen, D.G., Laby, D.M.: Sports Vision Testing: An Innovative Approach To Increase Revenues. Optometric Management (May 2006), http://www.optometricmanagement.com/articleviewer.aspx?articleid=71635
13. Pheasant, S.: Bodyspace, 2nd edn. Taylor & Francis (1999)

The Role of Simulation in Designing for Universal Access

Simeon Keates[1] and Peter Olaf Looms[2]

[1] School of Engineering, University of Greenwich, Medway, Kent, UK
s.keates@gre.ac.uk
[2] Technicsl University of Denmark, Lyngby, Denmark
polooms@gmail.com

Abstract. It is known that the adoption of user-centred design processes can lead to more universally accessible products and services. However, the most frequently cited approach to user-centred design, i.e. participatory design, can be both problematic and expensive to implement., particularly over the difficulty of finding and recruiting suitable participants. Simulation aids offer a potentially cost-effective replacement or complement to participatory design. This paper examines a number of the issues associated with the use of simulation aids when designing for Universal Access. It concludes that simulation aids can play an effective role, but need to be used with due consideration over what insights they provide.

Keywords: User-centred design, universal access, simulation, impairments.

1 Introduction

What makes a successful product? This is a question that designers and design commissioners ponder regularly. In many cases, the question can be answered by reference to a property or attribute of the design, such as, for example, the fastest, the cheapest or the most reliable. Such attributes can be measured and quantified by direct empirical analysis.

However, when designing for use by people, the attributes commonly cited suddenly become decidedly more woolly and imprecise. Words and phrases such as "user friendliness," "intuitiveness" and "user experience" are used. While these phrases make some sense at a surface level, once you start to examine them more closely, they become increasingly unsatisfactory as design requirements. For example, there is no universally accepted definition of what constitutes a user-friendly or intuitive design. Similarly, and as a direct consequence of the difficulty in defining them, there is no clear approach to how to measure them.

A review of the literature shows many different approaches and no single, uniform, "best practice" approach to designing for people. The closest to a conformity of opinion in this area is that a user-centred design approach is the most reliable option for generating a usable, user-friendly, intuitive, etc., design.

In an attempt to minimise the variability in the design requirements and specifications, designers will typically try to reduce the users to a simple homogeneous

C. Stephanidis and M. Antona (Eds.): UAHCI/HCII 2014, Part I, LNCS 8513, pp. 54–63, 2014.

representative. As Cooper warns [7], unless they are presented with a very specific view of who the users are, the designers will often substitute themselves as the target users. This is a seductive assumption to make. After all, designers are people and the users are people, so who is to say that the designers are not suitably representative of the target users?

Of course, taking a quick step back to view the problem and the problem with that assumption becomes clear. For example, not all users, and indeed very few users, will have the insights into the operation of the product or system that the designer will have. Consequently, the designers will be power users, whereas most target users will not. A single designer is also, by definition, homogenous. By designing for him or herself, the designer is making the assumption that all users will share his or her knowledge and also his or her physical attributes and functional capabilities. This raises the question of how valid is that assumption? The answer is often that it is not valid. Furthermore, if the assumption is not valid, how can the designers be assisted in designing products or services that better meet the needs of the wider population?

Those who endorse user-centred design typically focus on the direct participation of users in the scoping, development or subsequent optimisation of their products. Others make use of proxies for target users in the design process by using personas. In this paper, however, we will examine the role that simulation can play in assisting designers design for the widest possible range of users.

2   Designing for Universal Access

For many people, a disabled person is typified by either a young man in a wheelchair or an older blind man walking with either a white cane or a guide dog. However, these are both anachronistic stereotypes that do not reflect the true variety or prevalence of functional impairments across the whole population. For designers, it is functional impairment – i.e. a limitation in someone's capabilities – that is important. Disability is a consequence of a person's functional impairments preventing them from interacting with a product or service successfully within a given context [11]. If the product or service is designed to be sufficiently robust to support or accommodate a wide enough range of functional impairments or limitations, then no disability or handicap should be experienced by that person.

The most common approach to designing for Universal Access is to adopt a participatory design approach, i.e. recruiting users into the design. This is the basis taken for the Design Business Association (DBA) Inclusive Design Challenges, organised in conjunction with the Helen Hamlyn Centre [4]. DBA member consultancies from all design disciplines are set a design challenge to create a mainstream product or service that can be enjoyed equally by users of all abilities. The teams work with the Helen Hamlyn Centre, disabled users and other experts to ensure that all aspects of inclusivity are considered throughout the Challenge. Prizes are awarded at the end of each Challenge.

While participatory design approaches do, in general, lead to more inclusive designs when appropriate users have been selected, it can be difficult to find and recruit the users. Even when users have been found and recruited successfully, the costs of organizing consultation sessions can be significant. Furthermore, there are questions over the representative nature of such a design approach. How, for example, does the design team choose which participants to select and include? Fundamentally, how can the design team ensure that the outcome of the participatory design process is a product or service that is accessible by many potential users and not simply those who are sufficiently similar to the members of the participatory design team? Many accessibility audit panels typically consist of a very small number of users. How does the design team ensure that the capabilities of those users reflect the wider population? We can go further, can such panels ever truly represent the wider population?

These are difficult questions to answer. To begin to do so, it is necessary to understand the prevalence of functional impairments.

3   Prevalence of Functional Impairments

Functional impairments are surprisingly prevalent across the population. For example, in 1996/7 it was estimated that 17.8% of the population of Great Britain (i.e., England, Wales and Scotland) had at least one functional impairment [9]. These impairments could be further broken down into:

- 14.7% having a motor impairment, such as locomotion, dexterity, reach and stretch, strength)
- 5.7% having a cognitive impairment, such as difficulty with memory, recall, recognition, understanding and communication
- 8.7% having a sensory impairment, such as vision or hearing

It can be seen that 14.7% + 5.7% + 8.7% > 17.8%. This inequality arises because approximately 8.8% of the population has more than one class of functional impairment, e.g., a motor and a cognitive impairment. 2.5% of the population has all three classes of impairment, i.e., motor, cognitive and sensory.

This overall prevalence pattern is believed to be typical of the developed world. The US Census Bureau's 1999-2004 American Community Survey [1] asked respondents if they had any kind of disability, defined here as "a long-lasting sensory, physical, mental or emotional condition," a definition that fits well with that in Article 1 of the UN Convention on the Rights of Persons with Disabilities [18]. The data collected were as follows:

- 16.0% reported any type of disability (cf. 17.8% from the British survey)
- 4.7% reported a sensory disability (cf. 8.7% for a sensory impairment)
- 10.6% reported a physical disability (cf. 14.7% for a motor impairment)
- 5.2% reported a mental disability (cf. 5.7% for a cognitive impairment)
- 3.1% reported a self-care disability (no direct comparison available)
- 4.9% reported a go-outside-home disability (no direct comparison available)
- 5.6% reported an employment disability (no direct comparison available)

Again, it can be seen that multiple impairments/disabilities are common. From the same survey:

- 6.7% reported one type of disability (cf. 5.9%)
- 7.6% reported two or more types of disability (cf. 8.8%)

Some of the differences in prevalence will arise from the different definitions used for each survey. A second issue is that of self-reporting: some individuals may well have an impairment of which they are not aware or that they do not consider to be serious. A study from 2012 of the intelligibility of television audio from the public service broadcaster DR in Denmark, discussed in [16], suggests that the prevalence of hearing impairments may be markedly higher than was shown in the studies by Grundy and American Community. However, if we restrict ourselves to the methodologies used in these two studies, the overall pattern is sufficiently similar for it to be assumed that no less than 1 in 6 adults in a developed country will have a functional impairment and approximately 1 in 12 will have two or more classes of impairment types.

It is also worth noting that prevalence of disability typically increases with age [5]. Although older adults are increasingly healthy compared with their predecessors, the ageing process is still accompanied by an overall decrease in functional capabilities. Typically several capabilities will degrade over time and this leads to the widespread prevalence of multiple impairment classes. Someone who is older could easily have arthritis, cataracts and be a little hard of hearing, for example.

One very useful source of information is quantified data about the extent of exclusion caused by each item on the list of issues to be fixed. Effectively, each source of exclusion can be ranked by how many people are excluded by that particular problem, e.g. how many people cannot see that label and how many people cannot hear that beeper. Exclusion calculators, based on the data collected for the UK 1996/7 Disability Follow-Up Survey are available at:

- http://www.inclusivedesigntoolkit.com/
- http://www.eng.cam.ac.uk/inclusivedesign/

These calculators allow designers to specify the capability demands placed on the users by each stage of the interaction with the product. The calculators then display how many adults within the population of Great Britain cannot meet those demands, and thus would be excluded from using the product. Worked examples of how to use the calculators have been provided by Keates and Clarkson [6, 10].

These data can be used to inform user-centred design processes when designing for Universal Access.

4   Implementing User-Centred Design

The principal methods most commonly associated with user-centred design are participatory design, co-operative design and contextual design. Participatory design and co-operative design are largely very similar, with the principal difference being that participatory design is more widely used in Europe and co-operative design in the US.

However, they both focus on the role of users as equal members within the design team. Contextual design arose from ethnographic methods, building up a better understanding of who the users are and the wider context of use of the product to be designed [2].

Where a wholly new design for a product or service is required, any of these user-centred approaches are valid and, if implemented correctly with an appropriate choice of users, should yield an accessible and inclusive design. However, these methods are expensive and time-consuming to adopt and so organisations are typically looking for cheaper and faster options for achieving similar outcomes. Such options can include:

- **Empathy.** Empathising with the users is a very cheap method for implementing user-centred design. Put simply, the designers try to picture themselves as the users and cognitively walk through the process of using a product or service from that users perspective. Indeed, contextual design could be considered a highly developed variant of this. The effectiveness of this approach can be enhanced through videos, photographs, multimedia stories, etc. of the users. There are numerous websites available that offer invaluable information to support this approach, such as the Inclusive Design Toolkit. The principal disadvantage to this approach is how it is calibrated. In other words, how do the designers ensure that what they think is the case, really is the case? That calibration needs to happen via supplementary or complementary methods, such as user evaluation / observation sessions.

- **User evaluation or user observation sessions.** Rather than recruiting users for the entirety of the design process, organisations may opt to recruit them for intensive sessions where the users interact with the product or service. The observations are then used in the re-designing of features that were problematic for the users. However, further iterations of user sessions are then required to ensure that the re-designed product is genuinely an improvement. One common approach is a frequent cycle of user evaluations at defined gateways in the design and development process. However, there is also a balance to be reached regarding the frequency of such sessions. Too frequent and the process becomes expensive and time-consuming. Too infrequent and the design being evaluated may have acquired more inaccessible features as the design will have progressed substantially in the intervening time period. The user sessions are required to keep the design "on track."

- **Simulation aids.** The physical aspects of particular impairments or capability limitations can be simulated through the use of aids, such as thick gloves (loss of feeling), ear defenders (hearing impairment), fuzzy screen shots (minor visual impairments) and a blindfold (blindness). Such aids can help identify many basic accessibility issues quite quickly. However, it is possible to read too much into simulation and both designers and researchers have been known to regard simulation as reproducing the entire experience of what it is to have a particular impairment instead of recognising that only one aspect of the impairment is actually being simulated.

The remainder of this paper will focus on the potential role of simulation and simulation aids in designing for Universal Access.

5   Approaches to Simulation

There are two principal approaches to the role of simulation and simulation aids:

- **Formative simulation.** It is possible to use simulation as a formative component during the creative stages of design, where concepts, prototypes and solutions are being developed. Formative simulation may involve the prototype product or the underlying system that gives rise to the prototype (for example a TV programme with subtitles/closed captions or the end-to-end system for the production and distribution of a programme with subtitles/closed captions). If a simulation aid affords a sufficiently high fidelity insight into the difficulties faced by potential users, designers can benefit from this to proactively design solutions that accommodate the needs of those users. Effectively, the simulation aids help shape, or form, the designers' understanding as they generate new solutions.
- **Summative simulation.** The other approach to using simulation aids is when reviewing designs to evaluate the accessibility of a design once it has been created. Designers can use the simulation aids to retrospectively amend and optimise a design as part of an iterative design process. It could be argued that this is a reactive, rather than proactive, use of simulation aids. EIII, a major research project looking into 'crowd-sourcing' to get users of Internet resources to assess the accessibility of (public) websites uses this approach [8].

Many simulation aids can be used as part of either of the above approaches.

While it is generally appreciated that proactive design approaches are more effective and cost-effective than reactive ones, especially in the area of Universal Access, there is a fundamental question about how much of an insight into a user's true condition can be gained through a simulation aid. For example, does closing your eyes really help in understanding what it is like to be blind? It could be argued, on a surface level, that indeed it does. Certainly, closing your eyes does bring home the immediacy of dangers, such as nearby hazards. However, it can equally be argued that this level of understanding is largely symptomatic, not causal. In other words, you can simulate the consequence of being blind, but not really the full experience of it as a long-term condition.

This distinction is important. Anyone who has spent time working with or observing people with severe impairments will usually notice that such people often develop unexpected techniques for interacting with everyday products and technologies. These are the so-called "coping strategies." Users develop these strategies to take advantage of their comparatively non-impaired capabilities. For example, there are cases of people who cannot use their hands developing the skill of holding a cup with their feet. It is questionable whether a temporary simulation of one aspect of someone's functional impairment would necessarily lead to a designer attempting this particular feat.

Consequently, it could be argued that simulation aids serve a much better purpose as reactive design tools, where simply closing your eyes will help evaluate whether the functionality of a product can be accessed by someone who is blind. However, even this approach is not without its limitations. The principal drawback is that this approach is based on the notion that the designers will only really learn whether a product is basically accessible, i.e. that a user can gain basic access to its functions. It does not guarantee that the product will be usable or accessible in an acceptable amount of time. It also, almost certainly, does not allow for whether a user's coping strategies may help overcome some of the difficulties encountered by adopting a different approach, based on potentially years of experience, that a user may take that a designer may not predict.

However, to truly evaluate the usefulness and role of simulation, it is worth examining a few examples of it in use.

6   Simulation in Practice

There are many different types of simulation aid ranging from very simple simulation of one type of functional impairment, such as closing your eyes or covering your ears, to highly sophisticated simulators of multiple impairment types.

6.1   Simulating Colour Blindness

About 8% of the western male population is colour blind. Vischeck [19] is a freely available online tool that can simulate the effects of Deuteranopia (red/green colour deficit), Protanopia (red/green colour deficit) and Tritanopia (blue/yellow colour deficit) by applying different colour filters to screenshots or web sites. The tool is straightforward to use and the results are believed to be realistic.

However, when used by postgraduate students in a Masters course at the IT University of Copenhagen, it was found that the output was sometimes difficult for the students to interpret correctly. A small number of groups tried to adjust the colour schemes of their sites to still look visually appealing to themselves, while not appreciating that their colour preferences (with unimpaired colour vision) were not the same as for someone with a colour vision impairment. Most students, though, used Vischeck to look for insufficient colour contrast for each of the three colour vision impairment types, which was usually more successful and is the generally accepted correct use of the tool.

6.2   Simulating Computer Access Difficulties

There are several possible methods for simulating the potential difficulties experienced when access computer and IT systems. For example, simulating the effects of vision impairment can be achieved at some level by switching off the monitor or computer display and relying upon a screen reader, such as JAWS, to provide information about the display. This is a common accessibility evaluation technique and provides good insight into potential problems, especially when combined with the use of the W3C HTML validation tools.

Similarly, simulating the effects of hearing impairment is straightforward. All that needs to be done is to mute the sound output from the computer system.

Simulating motor impairment is more difficult. While work has been done on understanding, quantifying and modelling the movements of users with motor impairments (e.g. [13, 14]), there is a question over the most appropriate method of using such quantified and calibrated models. For example, consider modelling the effects of spasms on user cursor control. A spasm can occur at any point in an interaction, but is most commonly experienced close to a target. A probabilistic model for the onset of a spasm can be developed based on sufficient empirical data. Similarly, it is straightforward to perform a frequency analysis of essential tremor to develop a mathematical model of the resultant cursor movements.

However, there is then the issue of what to do with such models. It is also straightforward to apply them to the cursor movement of an able-bodied user and thus introduce artificial noise into the cursor behaviour. The problem, though, is that such noise would only be experienced visually by the user and the kinaesthetic feedback loop between the user's eyes and arm/hand movements would be broken, i.e. the user would see the noise, but not feel it. It is debatable how useful such simulation would be in terms of establishing how easy an on-screen target would be to hit using such an approach. One solution is the use of haptic force feedback, so the user can feel the noise being generated, thus re-establishing the kinaesthetic feedback paths [15].

In the absence of haptic feedback, the most appropriate solution here would be to run the model as a full probabilistic simulation of the interaction, i.e. one where the computer controls the cursor and the noise and simply reports back the expected time to complete the task [3].

6.3   Simulating Ageing – The "Third Age Suit"

Ford cars have traditionally been at or near the top of car sales in the UK for many years. As the venerable Ford Escort approached the end of its manufacturing lifespan, Ford began to develop a replacement model, the Ford Focus.

Unlike any car built by previously by Ford, the designers of the Focus were encouraged to design for the needs of older. Ford even went so far as to develop a novel method of simulating the effects of old age using what became known as the 'Third Age Suit' in conjunction with Loughborough University [10].

The suit was designed to simulate the equivalent of another 30 years of ageing to the wearer. This ageing effect was achieved by joint stiffeners in the neck, back, stomach and knees to simulate the reduced flexion from conditions such as arthritis. The suit added both weight and bulk around the torso to replicate both the change in body shape and the difficulty in getting into and out of cars often associated with ageing. Visual impairments, such as cataracts, are also simulated through the use of spectacles with different lenses where each lens type was marked with different patterns or colours.

Designers were encouraged to wear the suit to increase their empathy with older users by letting them experience some of the difficulties faced by older drivers. As a result of their use of the suit, the Focus offers many innovative features. For example,it has the most headroom of any cars in its class. The front door is wider and higher than in the Escort and the seats are higher. This combination of door size and seat height makes it significantly easier to get in and out of the Focus. The dashboard controls are larger than those of its predecessor and were designed to be easier to locate, grab and operate.

All of the features developed to make the car easier to operate and drive for older adults have not adversely affected the enjoyment of the Focus for younger drivers. Indeed, many of the features introduced are of benefit to all drivers. For example, the easier access to the car is good for parents with small children. Larger, easy to use controls are good for everyone.

6.4   Simulating Cognitive Impairments

One area of simulation that is known to be problematic is that of simulating cognitive impairments. While those with visual and hearing impairments have vocal and persuasive advocates, those with cognitive impairments rarely have the same organisational support. Public awareness of the issues is lower as a result.

One category of cognitive impairments includes aphasias. Olesen and Slynge [17] report on their work in the development of rehabilitation software for people with aphasias and the need to recognise the multiplicity of manifestations this impairment may have.

Other cognitive impairments can be simulated temporarily through chemical intervention, e.g. alcohol. While possible, this is ethically dubious, to say the least. Forms of distraction or deliberate cognitive overloading of an able-bodied user may produce similar effects to lack of concentration or some memory impairments. Again, though, this is ethically questionable since it usually involves stressing the user to induce such symptoms. Arguably the safest option for designing for cognitive impairments is to follow recommended design guidelines, such as in [12].

7   Conclusion

Simulation aids clearly have a valuable role to play when designing for Universal Access. However, their strengths and weaknesses need to be understood by designers attempting to use them to inform the design process, whether as proactive or reactive design tools. Designers, or designer evaluators, need to understand what the simulation aid is intended to simulate. They also need to be aware that it is highly unlikely that such aids will provide a full, high-fidelity understanding of what it is to be functionally impaired as a long-term condition. As such, simulation aids need to be handled with caution. However, when they are used correctly they are capable of assisting designers in creating more universally accessible products, as clearly demonstrated in the examples given in this paper.

References

1. ACSO, American Community Survey, subject definitions. American Community Survey Office, US Census Bureau (2007)
2. Beyer, H., Holtzblatt, K.: Contextual Design: Defining customer-centered systems. Morgan Kaufmann, San Francisco (1998)

3. Biswas, P., Robinson, P.: Automatic evaluation of assistive interfaces. In: Proceedings of the 13th ACM International Conference on Intelligent User Interfaces, pp. 247–256 (2008)
4. Cassim, J.: Cross-market product and service innovation – the DBA Challenge example. In: Designing a More Inclusive World, pp. 11–19. Springer, London (2004)
5. Christensen, K., Doblhammer, G., Rau, R., Vaupel, J.W.: Ageing populations: The challenges ahead. Lancet. 374(9696), 1196–1208 (2009)
6. Clarkson, P.J., Keates, S.: Quantifying design exclusion. In: Keates, Clarkson, Langdon, Robinson (eds.) Universal Access and Assistive Technology, pp. 23–32. Springer, London (2002)
7. Cooper, A.: The inmates are running the asylum. SAMS Publishing, Indianapolis (1999)
8. EIII, European Internet Inclusion Initiative (2014), http://eiii.eu/ (accessed February 2, 2014)
9. Grundy, E., Ahlburg, D., Ali, M., Breeze, E., Sloggett, A.: Disability in Great Britain: results from the 1996/7 disability follow-up to the Family Resources Survey. Charlesworth Group, Huddersfield (1999)
10. Keates, S., Clarkson, P.J.: Countering design exclusion: An introduction to inclusive design. Springer, London (2003)
11. Keates, S.: Designing for accessibility: A business guide to countering design exclusion. Lawrence Erlbaum Associates / CRC Press, Mahwah, NJ (2007)
12. Keates, S., Adams, R., Bodine, C., Czaja, S., Gordon, W., Gregor, P., Hacker, E., Hanson, V., Kemp, J., Laff, M., Lewis, C., Pieper, M., Richards, J., Rose, D., Savidis, A., Schultz, G., Snayd, P., Trewin, S., Varker, P.: Cognitive and learning difficulties and how they affect access to IT systems. Int. J. on Universal Access in the Information Society 5(4), 329–339 (2007)
13. Keates, S., Langdon, P., Clarkson, P.J., Robinson, P.: User models and user physical capability. User Modeling and User-Adapted Interaction (UMUAI), Wolters Kluwer Publishers 12(2-3), 139–169 (2002)
14. Keates, S., Hwang, F., Langdon, P., Clarkson, P.J., Robinson, P.: The use of cursor measures for motion-impaired computer users. Int. J. on Universal Universal Access in the Information Society (UAIS) 2(1), 18–29 (2002)
15. Langdon, P., Hwang, F., Keates, S., Clarkson, P.J., Robinson, P.: Investigating haptic assistive interfaces for motion-impaired users: Force-channels and competitive attractive-basins. In: Proceedings of Eurohaptics 2002 Int'l Conference, Edinburgh, pp. 122–127 (2002)
16. Looms, P.: Making TV Accessible in the 21st Century. In: Liu, Y.-l., Picard, R.G. (eds.) Chapter 3: Policy and Marketing Strategies for Digital Media, Routledge, Abingdon, UK (in Press, 2014)
17. Olesen, R., Slynge, C.: Sharp - Rehabilitation Software for Aphasics. Aalborg University, Department of Media Technology, Aalborg, Denmark (2012), http://projekter.aau.dk/projekter/files/63417640/SHARPreport_full.pdf
18. UN (2006), UN Convention on the Rights of Persons with Disabilities, http://www.un.org/disabilities/convention/conventionfull.shtml (accessed February 2, 2014)
19. Vischeck (2008), Vischeck, http://www.vischeck.com/ (accessed February 2, 2014)

'In My Shoes' Interaction Sandbox for a Quest of Accessible Design: Teaching Sighted Students Accessible Design for Blind People

Cosima Rughiniş[1] and Răzvan Rughiniş[2]

[1] University of Bucharest, Department of Sociology, Bucharest, Romania
cosima.rughinis@sas.unibuc.ro
[2] University Politehnica of Bucharest, Department of Computer Science, Splaiul Independenţei 313, Bucharest, Romania
razvan.rughinis@cs.pub.ro

Abstract. This paper examines current practices in motivating students to design accessible technologies, and proposes an additional method to promote a long-term, steadfast commitment to accessibility. We examine recent reports of teaching accessibility for blind users to sighted students, and we find three types of motivational devices: 1) a 'web of arguments' as to morality, legality, and usefulness, 2) empathy, and 3) framing accessibility through mainstreaming. We observe that the challenge of interactional malaise between sighted and blind people is often neglected, and we propose an 'Interaction Sandbox' to overcome it. We also put forward an additional way of framing accessible design, in order to position it as a work of autonomy, mastery, and purpose: the 'Quest' metaphor. Accessible design is thus introduced as the pursuit of a daring goal against widespread adversity, through mastery, in the company of powerful characters. The Quest is set in motion by bringing students to appreciate the technical wizardry of accessible design, its aesthetics, and the heroism of blind people as skilled navigators of a dangerous world.

Keywords: Accessibility, blindness, student motivation, interactional malaise, Quest.

1 Introduction

This paper reports our ongoing work of designing a course to introduce accessibility to Computer Science students in a European university. Specifically, we focus on introducing accessible design for blind users to sighted students.

The starting point of our work was an increased awareness that many IT companies place multiple, stringent priorities that compete with accessibility requirements. Professionals must balance the ideal of accessible technology with a plethora of economic, aesthetic, and technical counterclaims. Even when they believe that accessibility should be introduced, they have to face objections from team members and leaders (Putnam et al., 2012). This raises the following question: How can we teach

C. Stephanidis and M. Antona (Eds.): UAHCI/HCII 2014, Part I, LNCS 8513, pp. 64–74, 2014.
© Springer International Publishing Switzerland 2014

accessible design so that students will feel inspired to pursue it, against considerable adversity and persistent indifference in their workplace, years after graduation? In brief: how can we turn accessibility into an energizing and unwavering professional orientation?

The paper is structured as follows: in the next section we review several articles on teaching accessibility to Computer Science students and we analyze their motivational approaches. We then propose two ways to strengthen students' commitments to accessible design:

1. We propose that a stumbling block in inspiring long term, persistent motivation for accessible design consists in the experienced and imagined **interactional malaise** when encountering or just thinking about impaired people – in this case, blind people. Starting from this analysis, we introduce the **'In My Shoes' Interaction Sandbox,** a gateway to online resources designed to support sighted students and teachers in imagining and making sense of interactions with blind people, thus transforming latent discomfort into a sense of clear thinking and mastery.
2. In order to frame accessibility-oriented work, we introduce a **'Quest of Accessible Design'** highlighting technical mastery, aesthetics, and empathy with heroic characters.

We finally discuss the risk of romanticizing blindness, and we conclude the paper.

2   Why Bother?

There is a significant thread of research dedicated to teaching accessible design to Computer Science students. Most authors, who report on their own teaching and curricular design, do not take accessibility to be a self-evident matter, and they offer reasons for engaging in accessible design. Articles frequently include a dedicated section for discussing pros and occasional cons (R. F. Cohen, Fairley, Gerry, & Lima, 2005; Harrison, 2005; Ludi, 2002; Rosmaita, 2006), thereby assembling a *web of arguments*. Authors also introduce two other motivational resources for teachers: *empathy* with blind users, and framing accessibility as normal, through *mainstreaming* it in the curriculum.

2.1   The Web of Arguments

The reviewed articles discuss many reasons for considering accessibility in design. To begin with, it is ethically correct (Wang, 2012) and socially responsible (Rosmaita, 2006). In many countries it is demanded by law (R. F. Cohen et al., 2005; Rosmaita, 2006; Wang, 2012); in these cases skills for accessible design are also valued by employers, becoming directly useful for graduates (R. F. Cohen et al., 2005; Ludi, 2002). Besides employability, appeals to interest (rather than ethics) also include the observation that blind (and otherwise impaired) users represent a significant proportion of customers and citizens. Moreover, they represent a segment of society that will likely include many of us, through our own or significant others' aging and other life meanders (Ludi, 2002; Rosmaita, 2006). Last but not least, there are technical reasons: accessible design promotes interoperability and compliance with standards (Wang, 2012), and it helps unimpaired users use technology in what we could term 'impaired situations': "automobile drivers—who otherwise have normal vision—are blind with respect to the web while they are driving. Likewise, a person surfing the web on a small mobile handheld device is, for all intents and purposes, a low-vision person accessing the web" (Rosmaita, 2006).

In the flip side of these pros, one can read the implicit cons: that accessible design benefits only a minority, is costly, and hinders aesthetic design, stifling creativity (Waller, Hanson, & Sloan, 2009). Some authors do engage them explicitly; for example, accessibility can be 'lightweight' to introduce (R. F. Cohen et al., 2005), and definitely easier to plan from the beginning than to retrofit (R. F. Cohen et al., 2005; Rosmaita, 2006). The aesthetic issue is discussed in the literature on accessible design - see for example (Mbipom & Harper, 2011; Regan, 2004) but less so in the reviewed articles on teaching.

2.2   Empathy

The paramount method of cultivating sighted students' empathy with blind persons consists in face-to-face interaction (Harrison, 2005; Kurniawan, Arteaga, & Manduchi, 2010; Rosmaita, 2006; Waller et al., 2009). Some teachers invite blind persons in the classrooms, to talk about and demonstrate their practices of working with technology; courses that are dedicated to accessible design may also involve students in project-based collaboration with blind people. These experiences are coupled with students' own experiments with assistive technologies, for example by navigating the internet with the monitor turned off, through a screen reader (Freire, de Mattos Fortes, Barroso Paiva, & Santos Turine, 2007; Harrison, 2005; Rosmaita, 2006). Less frequently, teachers also introduce students to accounts of blindness from the scientific or autobiographical literature (Kurniawan et al., 2010; Rosmaita, 2006).

2.3   Interactional Malaise

We find that the literature on teaching accessibility pays virtually no attention to the interactional troubles between sighted and blind people and the negative emotions that such encounters can stir, such as disorientation, discomfort, frustration, anxiety, self-blaming, and fear (Coates, 2003; Hebl, Tickle, & Heatherton, 2000; Higgins, 1980; Titchkosky, 2008). By analyzing a set of online blind personas, we find a similar absence. A potentially stifling burden on engineers' thinking about blind people remains unaddressed.

We rely on psychological research reporting that positive imagined interactions with outgroup members decrease anxiety and improve one's emotional makeup for other contact occasions (Crisp & Turner, 2010; Giacobbe, Stukas, & Farhall, 2013; West, Holmes, & Hewstone, 2011). We propose a learning resource, the 'In My Shoes'

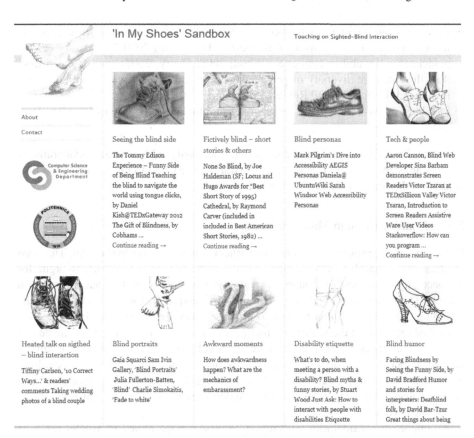

Fig. 1. 'In My Shoes' Interaction Sandbox – Gateway Architecture

Interactional Sandbox, which assists teachers and students not only in experiencing real and imagined positive interactions with blind people, but also in understanding the mechanics of discomfort and conceptualizing their ways out.

We design a gateway that invites sighted students to meet blind characters, real and fictive, and enables them to reflect on such encounters. There are two types of resources: some construct a conceptual framework, while others facilitate online encounters, mediated by text, image, or video.

The main entry points include (see Figure 1):

— Meeting blind people through short filmed accounts, chosen to illustrate interesting achievements or performances, with a focus on IT - such as (Edison, 2013; Kish, 2012);
— Meeting fictional blind people – either through short stories (Haldeman, 1995) (Carver, n.d.), experiments with simulated blindness (Ball, 2013), or specialized, design-oriented personas (Pilgrim, 2002; AEGIS, 2012);
— Observing artists' portraits of blind people, thus becoming de-familiarized and then re-familiarized with looking at faces that display signs of blindness (Fullerton-Batten, n.d.; Ivin, n.d.; Simokaitis, n.d.);

— Reading about interactions between sighted and blind people: analytical accounts from social research - 'Awkward moments' (Hebl et al., 2000; Titchkosky, 2008), guidelines - 'Disability etiquette' (Wood, 2008; Henry, 2007) and 'Heated talk' that illustrates the diversity of perspectives on what constitutes a meaningful interaction (Carlson, 2013; DP Review Contributors, 2012);
— Last but not least, humoristic perspectives on blindness as a way of life (Bradford, 2013).

Future developments will enable students to easily add content collaboratively through an academic wiki (Deaconescu & Matei, 2013), and to rank information thus modifying the order of elements on each entry point page.

2.4   Framing through Mainstreaming

We can organize resources for motivating students in a three-layered model. The *'web of arguments'* appeals to reason, and provides a much needed repertoire to argue for the necessity of accessible design, in dialogues with others or, for that matter, with oneself. The web of arguments is essentially a discursive, rhetorical resource for self- and other- persuasion. *Empathy* transforms this assemblage of reasons into a deeper, embodied experience: the reality of blind people's interests becomes vivid, the details of their experiences become memorable. Accessibility becomes a matter of human interest, rather than a matter of rhetoric. Also at this layer, the 'Interaction Sandbox' encourages students to overcome malaise in interacting with blind persons. A third layer involves *framing* the way in which students learn to make sense of the work of accessible design.

An important consideration of framing discussed in the reviewed articles refers to *mainstreaming* accessibility: that is, including topics of accessible design throughout a given course (Harrison, 2005; Ludi, 2002; Wang, 2012) and, preferably, throughout the curriculum (Waller et al., 2009), rather than marking it as a special, isolated topic. From a skill-based perspective, the advantage of mainstreaming accessibility is that it becomes a requirement in multiple hands-on assignments, and students learn to do it by practice. From a motivational perspective, its benefit consists in a 'routinization of concern': students learn to just do it, without too much examination and argumentation. This is how accessibility gets under the radar of competing priorities and considerations – avoiding a competition in which it often stands to lose.

2.5   Framing through a Quest of Accessible Design

We propose an additional way of framing accessible design – a way that, we argue, would support future professionals' unwavering motivation for promoting universal access, against considerable noise and adversity. This supplementary frame relies on the metaphor of a Quest of accessible design, and it involves getting students to recognize the value of *heroism* in their own work and in the lives of those who inspire it – in this case, blind persons. Such framing, relying on the gamification vocabulary (Rughiniş, 2013a, 2013b), would reposition the pursuit of accessibility from a domain of mainly extrinsic motivation (legality, interest, social responsibility) to a domain of passion – or, following Pink's inspiring trichotomy, to life driven by autonomy, mastery and purpose (Pink, 2009). The metaphor of the Quest is well suited to capture this frame, not least because it is longingly familiar to many computer engineers, from digital gaming. A *Quest* involves *a pursuit of a daring goal, against widespread adversity, through mastery, in company of powerful characters.* Readers can probably already see that this description is a highly plausible representation of accessible design. In the next sections we sketch it in more detail and we illustrate some helpful online resources for this modus operandi.

Technical Mastery: Dare to Change the World

As we have seen in the 'web of arguments', there is a strong case to be made that accessible design is essentially a feat of technical excellence. An orientation towards accessibility is in effect an orientation towards usability in non-traditional environments and restricted situations, proving creativity and the ability to see beyond the status quo.

A stronger use of this formulation consists in the appraisal of accessible design as endeavoring to change the world – *our* world, nothing less. Engineers are well accustomed to appreciate the power of technology to create new realities out of old ones: distance, time, communication, thinking, feeling, perceiving – so many fundamental aspects of human existence have been thoroughly transformed through technology. The point to be made is that accessible design transforms *our* world – not a limited version of the world, the 'world of the blind'. It is important to convey the understanding that impaired and unimpaired people live in a shared environment and in a web of reciprocal interactions; it is this environment and social fabric that enable or, conversely, disable persons. The social model of disability is a powerful conceptual device to highlight our shared universe: "disability is the active and purposive social exclusion and disadvantaging of people with impairment (...); disability becomes a product and oppressive quality of the social relationships that exist between people who are socially marked as having impairment and those who are marked as physically, sensorially, and cognitively normal" (Thomas & Corker, 2002). Autonomy, for impaired and unimpaired people as well, is highly dependent on technology and the built environment, and on supportive social relations; after all, how would sighted students be *students,* were it not for the impressive infrastructure that supports their lives, professors' lives, and so on? This infrastructure remains invisible unless it fails, as it is often the case for impaired persons. Engineers are called upon to repair and expand the world, to inspect and restructure its hidden machinery.

The Beauty of Accessible Design

As Regan points out (Regan, 2004) there is a feeling, among IT professionals, that accessibility inhibits aesthetics, and that accessible technologies are rather dull. This implies that few designers work with accessibility in mind, because there are few works that they could take as inspiration. This is a serious obstacle in stirring a passion for accessible design: professionals aspire to create aesthetically beautiful or interesting objects. Back to the metaphor, a Quest advances at its best through beautiful equipment, in stunning landscapes.

There are several ways to point out the beauty of accessible design. At a conceptual level, it is useful to cultivate an appreciation of *minimalist design*: simple, clear, well organized interfaces can be uplifting (Thorlacius, 2007) – and they impose, on average, fewer hurdles by way of accessibility (Mbipom & Harper, 2011). At an emotional level, the beauty of accessible technologies can be directly experienced in contrast with inaccessible versions, by navigating them with assistive technologies. Students can thus directly perceive the vexing repetition of redundant navigation links, the cumbersome reading of URL's for images lacking an ALT caption, or the chaos of improperly organized content. By tagging such un-navigable systems as sloppy and amateurish, and by inviting students to display their own Halls of Fame and of Shame (Kurniawan et al., 2010), teachers can present a moral and aesthetic contrast that would hopefully function as a persisting benchmark for future professionals when evaluating their own and others' work.

In Company of Powerful Characters: Portraits of the Blind

What is the point of accessible design? What can justify standing up for it, when it is pushed down in the priority stack? We have highlighted the challenge of proving engineering mastery, and the beauty of accessible designs; still, the most forceful drive must reside in the appreciation of the company of blind persons. Accessible design is a means to enable us to readily go into relationships with blind people, and for them to join social spaces handily.

The most important challenge for framing accessible design as a Quest consists in highlighting blind people as able navigators of a troublesome, dangerous world – rather than as vulnerable and dependent characters. It is about understanding them as bearers of interests and skills, rather than as bearers of needs. This requires an empathic understanding of life in a world where vision is not an option, or at least not a pervasive, taken for granted property.

It is also important to observe that blindness is by no means the equivalent of a lack of vision. On the one hand, blind people often have some forms of vision, which they put to use to successfully navigate the 'sighted world'(R. L. Michalko, 1977); on the other hand, blindness is better understood as a way of being in the social and material world, rather than as a 'missing thing' (Titchkosky, 2002).

There is no shortage of portraits of blind people that present sighted readers with wisdom, enhanced abilities, arduous training and perseverance, sacrifice, and friendship. Sighted students can read memoirs and other accounts of blind people's lives – in online journals of general interest (A. Cohen, 2009; Robertson, 2004), on Quora's Q&A pages (Hartmann, 2013; Strange, 2013), in printed books (R. Michalko, 1998), documentaries (Stoble & Cole, 2004) and TED presentations of IT blind professionals (Tsaran, 2009), to name but a few. Reading about blind people also offers students the chance to see the humor of blindness as it is lived by the blind themselves, to relate through self-irony, as well as to recognize themselves in so many sketches of sighted-blind interaction.

The interaction between sighted and blind people is often painfully impeded by sighted people's discomfort and misdirected attention when seeing a blind face. Some visual familiarity, an equivalent of a sandbox for interaction, can be cultivated through looking at portraits of blind people, such as Gaia Squarci's exhibition (Gonzalez, 2013), Sam Ivin's photography (Ivin, n.d.), Julia Fullerton-Batten's 'Blind' series (Fullerton-Batten, n.d.), or Charlie Simokaitis' 'Fade to white' (Simokaitis, n.d.).

3   Romanticizing Blindness?

The risk of framing accessible design through the Quest metaphor is to romanticize blindness, and thus to ignore the *normality* of blind people's lives, as well as the many occasions of frustration and despair, and the experiences of loss for people who become blind. We propose the Quest frame as a tool for acquainting students with accessibility, in the hope that their understanding of blindness will be refined through repeated human interaction, trial and error, and reflection: that is, through engagement and learning. Therefore, the peril of romanticizing the blind is, we argue, a risk of a *productive misunderstanding*, to the extent that it upholds a stronger commitment to accessible design.

4   Conclusion

In this paper we propose two supplementary resources for teaching accessibility for blind users to sighted students. We aim for adamant, stubborn motivation to support accessible design in the years after graduation, when engineers confront concurrent priorities and massive indifference. At a practical level, we propose to address the interactional malaise between sighted and blind persons through an online 'Interaction Sandbox', in which students can gain familiarity with blind people without the hurdles of face-to-face encounters.

As regards the 'big picture' of accessibility work, we propose to frame accessible design with the metaphor of the Quest - the adventurous pursuit of a noble goal, defying enmity and hard times through mastery, in the company of forceful characters. By focusing on accessibility as a feat of engineering savvy, on the beauty of accessible technologies, and the heroism of blind characters encountered in various narrative and visual portrayals, students can recognize accessible design for what it is: an invitation to boost the invisible infrastructure of the sighted world.

Acknowledgments. This article has been supported by the research project "Sociological imagination and disciplinary orientation in applied social research", with financial support of ANCS / UEFISCDI with grant no. PN-II-RU-TE-2011-3-0143, contract no. 14/28.10.2011.

References

1. AEGIS (2012), Open Accessibility Everywhere - Personas, http://www.aegis-project.eu/index.php?option=com_content&view=article&id=63&Itemid=53 (retrieved from September 01, 2013)
2. Ball, D.: Things I learned by pretending to be blind for a week (2013), http://blog.silktide.com/2013/01/things-learned-pretending-to-be-blind-for-a-week/ (retrieved from September 01, 2013)
3. Bradford, D.: Facing blindness by seeing the funny side. The Guardian (2013), http://www.theguardian.com/lifeandstyle/2013/may/17/facing-blindness-cope-sight-loss (retrieved from September 01, 2013)
4. Carlson, T.: 10 Correct Ways to Interact with People with Disabilities. The Mobility Resource (2013),http://www.themobilityresource.com/10-correct-ways-to-interact-with-people-with-disabilities/ (retrieved from September 01, 2013)
5. Carver, R. (n.d.): Cathedral, http://nbu.bg/webs/amb/american/6/carver/cathedral.htm (retrieved from September 01, 2013)
6. Coates, D.C.: Social order and the construction of meaning in social interaction: Troubled communication between sighted and partially sighted/blind people. Wayne State University (2003), http://search.proquest.com/docview/305279654
7. Cohen, A.: Going Deaf and Blind in a City of Noise and Lights. New York Magazine (2009), http://nymag.com/news/features/53787/ (retrieved from September 01, 2013)
8. Cohen, R.F., Fairley, A.V., Gerry, D., Lima, G.R.: Accessibility in Introductory Computer Science. In: Proceedings of the 36th SIGCSE Technical Symposium on Computer Science Education - SIGCSE 2005, vol. 37, pp. 17–21. ACM Press, New York (2005)
9. Crisp, R.J., Turner, R.N.: Can imagined interactions produce positive perceptions? Reducing prejudice through simulated social contact. The American Psychologist 64(4), 231–240 (2010)
10. Deaconescu, R., Matei, S.: The Negotiation of Knowledge and Knowing: The Challenge of Using Wiki Technology in Computer Supported Collaborative Learning. In: 2013 19th International Conference on Control Systems and Computer Science, pp. 575–581. IEEE (2013), doi:10.1109/CSCS.2013.68
11. Review Contributors, D.P.: Taking photos of blind people. In: Digital Photography Review - DP Review (2012), http://www.dpreview.com/forums/post/42366882 (retrieved from September 01, 2013)
12. Edison, T.: The Tommy Edison Experience (2013), http://www.youtube.com/user/TommyEdisonXP?feature=watch (retrieved from September 01, 2013)
13. Freire, A.P., de Mattos Fortes, R.P., Barroso Paiva, D.M., Santos Turine, M.A.: Using screen readers to reinforce web accessibility education. ACM SIGCSE Bulletin 39(3), 82–86 (2007)
14. Fullerton-Batten, J. (n.d.): Blind. Julia Fullerton-Batten Web Site - Fine art collection (2013), http://www.juliafullerton-batten.com/small.html (retrieved from September 01, 2013)
15. Giacobbe, M.R., Stukas, A.A., Farhall, J.: The Effects of Imagined Versus Actual Contact With a Person With a Diagnosis of Schizophrenia. Basic and Applied Social Psychology 35(3), 265–271 (2013), http://dx.doi.org/10.1080/01973533.2013.785403

16. Gonzalez, D.: Guided by Blindness. New York Times Blogs (2013),
    http://lens.blogs.nytimes.com/2013/03/22/
    guided-by-blindness/ (retrieved from September 1, 2013)
17. Haldeman, J.: None So Blind (1995),http://www.sff.net,
    http://www.sff.net/people/joe.haldeman/story1.html (retrieved from
    September 1, 2013)
18. Harrison, S.M.: Opening the eyes of those who can see to the world of those who can't.
    ACM SIGCSE Bulletin 37(1), 22–26 (2005)
19. Hartmann, C.: Cristina Hartmann, can you speak up a bit? I can't hear you. Quora (2013),
    https://www.quora.com/Disability-and-Disabilities/How-does-
    romance-change-if-you-lose-your-sight-Your-hearing-Both   (re-
    trieved from September 1, 2013)
20. Hebl, M.R., Tickle, J., Heatherton, T.F.: Awkward Moments in Interactions between Non-
    stigmatized and Stigmatized Individuals. In: Heatherton, T.F. (ed.) The Social Psychology
    of Stigma, pp. 275–306. The Guildford Press, New York (2000),
    http://www.dartmouth.edu/~thlab/pubs/00_Hebl_etal_Stigma.pdf
    (retrieved)
21. Henry, S.L.: Just Ask: Integrating Accessibility Throughout Design. Lulu.com (2007),
    http://www.uiaccess.com/accessucd/print.html (retrieved)
22. Higgins, P.C.: Societal Reaction And The Physically Disabled: Bringing The Impariment
    Back In. Symbolic Interaction 3(1), 139–156 (1980)
23. Ivin,   S.   (n.d.):   Blind   Portraits.   Sam   Ivin   Photography.,   http://
    www.samivin.co.uk/gallery_476907.html (retrieved September 1, 2013)
24. Kish, D.: Teaching the blind to navigate the world using tongue clicks. TEDxGateway
    (2012), http://www.youtube.com/watch?v=ob-P2a6Mrjs (retrieved from
    September 1, 2013)
25. Kurniawan, S.H., Arteaga, S., Manduchi, R.: A general education course on universal
    access, disability, technology and society. In: Proceedings of the 12th International ACM
    SIGACCESS Conference on Computers and Accessibility, ASSETS 2010, pp. 11–18.
    ACM Press, New York (2010)
26. Ludi, S.: Access for everyone: introducing accessibility issues to students in Internet pro-
    gramming courses. In: Frontiers in Education FIE 2002, vol. 3, pp. S1C-7–S1C-9. IEEE
    (2002)
27. Mbipom, G., Harper, S.: The interplay between web aesthetics and accessibility. In: The
    proceedings of the 13th International ACM SIGACCESS Conference on Computers and
    Accessibility, ASSETS 2011, pp. 147–154. ACM Press, New York (2011)
28. Michalko, R.: The Two-in-One. Walking with Smokie, Walking with Blindness. Temple
    University Press, Philadelphia (1998)
29. Michalko, R.L.: Accomplishing the Sighted World. The University of British Columbia
    (1977), https://circle.ubc.ca/bitstream/handle/2429/20966/UBC_
    1977_A8M52.pdf (retrieved)
30. Pilgrim, M.: Dive Into Accessibility (2002),
    http://diveintoaccessibility.info/ (retrieved September 1, 2013)
31. Pink, D.: The Puzzle of Motivation. TED Talks (2009), http://www.ted.com/
    talks/dan_pink_on_motivation.html (retrieved from February 2, 2010)
32. Putnam, C., Wozniak, K., Zefeldt, M.J., Cheng, J., Caputo, M., Duffield, C.: How do pro-
    fessionals who create computing technologies consider accessibility? In: Proceedings of
    the 14th International ACM SIGACCESS Conference on Computers and Accessibility,
    ASSETS 2012, pp. 87–94. ACM Press, New York (2012)

33. Regan, B.: Accessibility and Design: A Failure of the Imagination. In: Proceedings of the International Cross-Disciplinary Workshop on Web Accessibility-W4A, pp. 29–37. ACM Press, New York (2004)
34. Robertson, C.: Vision Loss in Later Life: My Personal Story. Canadian Blind Monitor (2004), http://www.blindcanadians.ca/publications/cbm/17/vision-loss-later-life-my-personal-story (retrieved)
35. Rosmaita, B.J.: Accessibility first! A New Approach to Web Design. In: Proceedings of the 37th SIGCSE Technical Symposium on Computer Science Education, SIGCSE 2006, vol. 38, pp. 270–274. ACM Press, New York (2006)
36. Rughini, R.: Gamification for Productive Interaction. Reading and Working with the Gamification Debate in Education. In: The 8th Iberian Conference on Information Systems and Technologies, CISTI 2013, pp. 1–5. IEEE, Lisbon (2013a)
37. Rughini, R.: Scaffolding a Technical Community of Students Through Social Gaming: Lessons from a Serious Game Evaluation. In: 10th International Conference on Computer Supported Collaborative Learning, CSCL 2013, pp. 141–144. ISLS, Madison (2013b)
38. Simokaitis, C. (n.d.): Fade to White. Charlie's Simokaitis Photography, http://www.charliesimokaitisphotography.com/#mi=2&pt=1&pi=10000&s=19&p=1&a=0&at=0 (retrieved from September 1, 2013)
39. Stoble, J., Cole, J.: Freedom Machines. PBS (2004), http://www.pbs.org/pov/freedommachines/ (retrieved from September 1, 2013)
40. Strange, J.: Quora Profile. Quora (2013), https://www.quora.com/Janice-Strange (retrieved from September 1, 2013)
41. Thomas, C., Corker, M.: A Journey around the Social Model. In: Corker, M., Shakespeare, T. (eds.) Disability/Postmodernity: Embodying Disability Theory, pp. 18–31. Continuum, London (2002)
42. Thorlacius, L.: The Role of Aesthetics in Web Design. Nordicom Review 28(1), 63–76 (2007)
43. Titchkosky, T.: Cultural Maps: Which Way to Disability? In M. Corker & T. Shakespeare (Eds.). In: Disability/Postmodernity: Embodying Disability Theory, London, pp. 101–111 (2002)
44. Titchkosky, T.: Looking Blind. A Revelation of Culture's Eye. In: Sandahl, C., Auslander, P. (eds.) Bodies in Commotion: Disability and Performance, pp. 219–229. The University of Michigan Press, Ann Arbor (2008)
45. Tsaran, V.: Victor Tsaran at TEDxSilicon Valley (2009), http://www.youtube.com/watch?v=BsJB73c38yw (retrieved)
46. Waller, A., Hanson, V.L., Sloan, D.: Including accessibility within and beyond undergraduate computing courses. In: Proceeding of the Eleventh International ACM SIGACCESS Conference on Computers and Accessibility, ASSETS 2009, pp. 155–162. ACM Press, New York (2009)
47. Wang, Y.D.: A holistic and pragmatic approach to teaching web accessibility in an undergraduate web design course. In: Proceedings of the 13th Annual Conference on Information Technology Education, SIGITE 2012, pp. 55–60. ACM Press, New York (2012)
48. West, K., Holmes, E., Hewstone, M.: Enhancing imagined contact to reduce prejudice against people with schizophrenia. Group Processes & Intergroup Relations 14(3), 407–428 (2011), http://gpi.sagepub.com/content/14/3/407.short (retrieved)
49. Wood, S.: Blind Myths & Funny Stories, September 01, 2013 (2008), http://waywood.wordpress.com/2008/01/20/blind-myths-legends-and-funny-stories-part-1-dispelling-the-myths/ (retrieved September 1, 2013)

Supporting the Design of AAL through a SW Integration Framework: The D4All Project

Marco Sacco[1], Enrico G. Caldarola[2], Gianfranco Modoni[2], and Walter Terkaj[1]

[1] Institute of Industrial Technologies and Automation, National Research Council, Milan, Italy
{marco.sacco,walter.terkaj}@itia.cnr.it
[2] Institute of Industrial Technologies and Automation, National Research Council, Bari, Italy
{enrico.caldarola,gianfranco.modoni}@itia.cnr.it

Abstract. Contemporary design is characterized by the paradigm shift from a one-size-fits-all, oriented to the standard man, to an holistic and inclusive one-size-fits-one, that takes into account the full range of human diversity. Following the new paradigm, the "Design for All" Italian research project aims at realizing an effective demonstrator of a framework that promotes a design of an AAL oriented to the real individual, considering everybody in his peculiarities. On the one hand, the framework handles the knowledge about the home environment, also through innovative approaches aimed at modeling specific scenarios representing the relevant states of the individuals (situation and context awareness). On the other hand, it allows various software tools supporting the entire home's life cycle to exchange the knowledge in a smart manner. Mainly focused on interoperability aspects, the paper describes the motivations behind the "Design for All" project concepts, together with the goals and the first findings. Finally, it presents a demonstration scenario that aims at testing and validating the framework.

Keywords: Design For All, Ambient Assisted Living, Interoperability, Semantic Data Model.

1 Introduction

Traditional design is focused on the standard man, which is an abstraction of the real man. However, this approach neglects the real object of study: users with their variety of skills, knowledge, wishes and ambitions. To overcome this limitation it is emerging a new inclusive and holistic paradigm, the Universal Design [1], also known as Design for All, which takes into account a broad spectrum of human diversity. It proposes an adaptable design that offers basic universal features which can be easily adjusted to the needs of a specific user. The new approach has been deepened in different areas of research also through the involvement of modern information technologies. For example, in the context of the Design for All for eInclusion European Coordination Action, a detailed study has been conducted under the responsibility of the IFAC-CNR [2].

C. Stephanidis and M. Antona (Eds.): UAHCI/HCII 2014, Part I, LNCS 8513, pp. 75–84, 2014.
© Springer International Publishing Switzerland 2014

The principles of Universal Design can also be applied in the field of the design of Ambient Assisted Living (AAL); in this case, it is necessary to face the crucial challenge of handling the continuously growing complexity resulting from the applied paradigm shift. The development and the administration of a home automation environment based on the new approach requires, indeed, the use of various heterogeneous tools supporting the entire home's life cycle (e.g. design, utilization, control and monitoring), in this way extending their applicability traditionally limited to the design process. Moreover, it is necessary to represent the articulated scenario in which the real user acts and to have a strong awareness of specific user activities (e.g. doors that open as people walk towards them). This leads to deal with several ubiquitous devices [3], such as sensors, actuators and controllers. The latter are often managed by different software which generate large amount of data (also in the form of Big Data) in a proprietary format, thus difficult to integrate.

In such a complex scenario, one of the AAL research topics that needs to be addressed is the enhancement of the semantic interoperability of the involved heterogeneous SW systems. Thus it's necessary to improve their capability to join distributed data sources, represented in various formats, into a view that facilitates the exchange of information and the use of the information to exchange [4]. Since the number of devices related and software applications increases, as well as the number of technology suppliers, it is fundamental to make software tools interoperable in order to fully exploit their functionalities. For this reason, in the last decade, many vendors have started to propose suites, in order to supply integrated alternatives to the customer. Despite this, the semantic interoperability problem has become relevant since no company is able to produce a full optional service, capable to satisfy all the customers' needs.

This paper introduces a new interoperability framework for an inclusive and sustainable home automation design, which integrates and harmonizes the knowledge related to the domestic environments, thus satisfying the holistic requirements for the next generation of AAL. The research represents the first finding of an Italian research project founded by the Ministry of University and Research called: "Design for All - SW integration and advanced Human Machine Interfaces in design for Ambient Assisted Living". The main project goal is the development of the previous mentioned software architecture that will support mainly the design phase (but not just this) of the future home automation environment addressing any type of users (Design for All … "users") and making application able to adapt to the context and to react. Moreover the platform will represent a unique integration point (Design for All …"applications").

Several recent studies have demonstrated that a valid solution to achieve interoperability is the approach based on the Semantic Web technology; e.g. in the context of Virtual Factory Framework (VFF) project [5], a semantic technologies-based framework for the interoperability was already designed, implemented and validated within the manufacturing domain for supporting the whole factory's life cycle. Thus, it can be considered a valid starting point for the Design for All project, but applying it to a new domain: the home automation.

The paper is structured as follows. Section 2 presents the outcomes of main studies carried out by others in the area of home automation systems interoperability. Section 3 introduces the architecture of the proposed interoperability framework. Section 4 defines the demonstration scenario that aims at testing and validating the framework. Finally Section 5 draws the conclusions summarizing the major findings.

2   Related Works

In order to enable an enhanced interoperability among the different software tools supporting the home automation system's life cycle, it is necessary to bridge the "knowledge gap" existing among them. A simple way to get interoperable two devices is to create a one-to-one bridge, but this solution cannot always be practically applicable because the number of the required bridges grows up too fast with the number of devices to be connected and the functionalities provided. Moreover, the framework deals with the information and knowledge produced by the software application themselves (from design to control, monitoring and automation). Thus, it is necessary to overcome this limit and search for a sufficiently scalable solution able to integrate data but also to capture the knowledge. The Korean Electronics and Telecommunications Research Institute proposes an Universal Home Network Middleware (UHNM) [6] to guarantee a seamless interoperability of appliances and services characterized by heterogeneous communication protocols. However this solution is far from an ideal interoperability based on open-standard technologies such as Web Services [7] or XML-based formats [8] and Internet protocols. In this regard an interesting approach has been provided by the Open Building Information Exchange group (oBIX) [9] that is working to create a standard XML and Web Services guideline to facilitate the exchange of information in the building automation field. Another important solution comes from Device Profile for Web Services [10]: a Service Oriented Architecture (SOA) [11] that allows devices to automatically discover each other and abstract the interface that they expose from the implementation, thus enabling an enhancement of the interoperability [12].

A mostly used approach to face the interoperability challenge is the adoption of the XML Schema Definition (XSD) technology [13]. This allows applications to share a common language to communicate each other. In this regard Sacco et al. [14] conceived the VFF data model as a set of XSD files defining the structure of the XML files that implement the schema. This solution offers relevant advantages in terms of syntactic validation of the XML files according to the defined XSD schemas; also, it provides a rich expressiveness, since several default data types can be further extended and complex constraints and properties can be modelled. However, XSD technology alone is not suitable for knowledge representation since it lacks an explicit characterization of the data at a semantic level. Moreover, since interoperable software applications can consume and publish data in a distributed way, different data repositories can be accessed by various software at the same time. For this reason consistency of the data plays a key role in making an effective collaboration among tools in such a scenario. Although XSD technology supports the references within the document, inter-document references, e.g. cross-references, are modeled so poorly to put at risk the consistency of the model.

The presented considerations led to evaluate and finally adopt a semantic model-based solution, represented via an ontology. This is a specification of a conceptualization [15], that is a formal description of the concepts and their semantic links within a knowledge domain. A valid approach to describe an ontology is based on Semantic Web first-order logic-based languages such as RDF [17] and OWL [18]. Thanks to their expressiveness, it is possible to represent a formal semantics for the knowledge in the domestic environment in a much more significant manner compared with the above mentioned XSD schemas.

The ontology model provides a systematic approach to classify and integrate the knowledge of the home automation environment; it represents an holistic view of the home as a whole, both considering its physical dimensions, its actors with their needs and its evolution over time. Furthermore, standardized models, based on a consistent description language, allow many existing tools to automatically infer and reason over the data model, bringing out new derived knowledge about the concepts and their relationships, in addition to those initially asserted. Finally, the ontology model is expected to support a new and more flexible design methodology, based on virtual reality technologies, aimed at a smarter evaluation of human-environment interactions scenarios. For this reason the application of semantic technologies can be considered the critical success factor of "Design for all" project.

3   The Virtual Home Framework – VHF

This section presents the Virtual Home Framework (VHF), an integrated platform whose main objectives are to handle the knowledge about the home environment and, on the other hand, to allow various software tools to exchange the knowledge in a smart manner, supporting the entire home automation system's life cycle.

VHF is based on four key Pillars (Fig. 1): (I) Semantic Shared Data-Model, (II) Virtual Home (VH) Manager, (III) Decoupled modules and (IV) the "Real Home". All the functionalities required by the Real Home are provided by different decoupled modules (Pillar III) that work on a consistent reference model (Pillar I) for the domestic environment domain. This can be realized thanks to the VH Manager (Pillar II) that plays an integrating role by interfacing all the modules. An interoperability framework can be effective only if all the applications coupled to it share a common language. This is achieved through the "Data Model" (DM) which represents the first pillar of the framework.

3.1   Pillar I – Semantic Shared Data Model

The Semantic Shared Data Model provides a common, standard and consistent representation of the knowledge related to the domestic environment. Moreover it has to be extensible and guarantee the proper granularity, providing at the same time the enablers for data consistency, data safety and proprietary data management. Taking advantage of its flexibility and expressiveness, it is possible to formally describe some concepts related to the home environment and their semantic links, such as resources, appliances, facilities, building components and also users who have an active role in the home environment. The Data Model can be conceived as a common meta-language that provides all applications a shared knowledge definition within the framework.

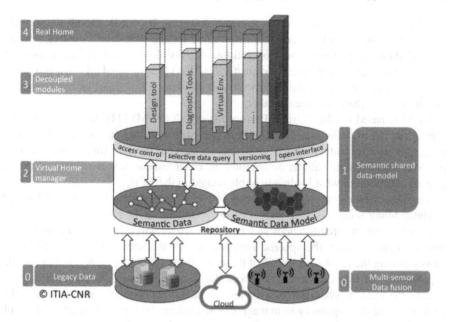

Fig. 1. Virtual Home Interoperability - VHF

While implementing a data model, an essential practice to follow is to refer to the state-of-the-art technical standards or other reference works available in different domains. One important reference comes from buildingSMART international organization [19] which has developed the ICF (Industry Foundation Classes) standard. This is a common data schema concerning the Building Information Modeling (BIM) aimed at representing physical and functional characteristics of buildings or facilities in order to exchange relevant data among different design software applications. Specifically regarding the domestic environment modeling, Konnex alliance [20] has proposed a model including objects grouped in four classes: measurement tools, house-hold appliances and systems, multimedia appliances and telecommunication tools. Another interesting work is DomoML [21], a markup language aimed at the definition of interoperability standard for domestic resources. It describes operational and functional aspects together with some preliminary architectural and positioning information. Furthermore in the context of ubiquitous computing, the SOUPA ontology [22] provides a modular modeling structure that includes vocabularies for representing intelligent agents, time, space, events, etc.

The home ontology is expected to facilitate the use of generic tools which can infer and reason about the ontology, thus giving a support that is not limited to the a priori asserted knowledge. In this regard, rule-based mechanisms and case-based reasoning techniques will be investigated.

3.2   Pillar II – Virtual Home Manager (VHM)

The "Manager" is the "core" of the entire framework. It coordinates all the modules connected to the framework and it is responsible for the data access control, versioning and data query management operations. A possible communication architecture could be based on "High Level Architecture" (HLA) [23], a standard that provides a common Application Program Interface (API) allowing all modules to invoke specific primitives to exchange data each other.

VHM is based on the "Virtual Factory Manager" (VFM) [24] that acts as a server supporting the I/O communications within the framework for the modules needing to access its data repository. Since VHM has to manage the real time communication between software applications in the domestic environment, it is necessary to investigate an extension to what is already implemented in the VFF.

The Data Repository is the backbone of the VHM and can be accessed by each module. Many solutions of repositories are available in literature, everyone works best under certain circumstances and may be more suitable in a case rather than in another, depending on the specific requirements of the scenario. For this reason, a survey among the most widespread of these solutions should be carried out to find the appropriate one that can host and expose the data related to domestic environment. Due to the specific characteristics of this scenario, main criteria used to apply this evaluation are the capability to manage live streaming data, to keep track of the multiple versions and to host large amount of data; also the scalability and performance of these systems under workloads with various characteristics will be taken into account.

3.3   Pillar III – Decoupled Modules

The Virtual Home modules are the decoupled functional tools used to support the whole home automation system's life cycle, following an approach based on the Design for All principles. They include both commercial or non-commercial applications; diagnostic and monitoring tools, design tools, human-machine interfaces and also virtual environment applications are some examples. All tools have their specific features and are addressed to a specific purpose, but, if they can share the same data model of the domestic environment, they result more coupled each other, and so more useful and powerful in the design phase as well for the user. For example, the output of a one tool can be easily given as input to another tool without the need for an ad hoc adaptation. They are able to understand each other. If the module cannot directly access the VH Manager in order to query the data repository, it is necessary to develop a module adapter to enable the communication between them. The module with the adapter is referred to as coupled module.

3.4   Pillar IV – The Real Home

The last pillar of the VHF is the "Real Home". It is an abstraction representing an effective and efficient solution for an AAL that takes into account the above mentioned Design for All approach. Real Home can be meant as an holistic concept used to described the full range of services that the "Home for All" is expected to satisfy. It must be able to respond to the different situations in which real individuals are involved also considering variables coming from different contexts. For example, wake up scenario can require some alarm clock adjustment depending on weather or traffic and can trigger some operations such as the ignition of the heater in the bath or the start to prepare coffee in the kitchen.

The Real Home is also an adaptive system able to modify its characteristics in accordance with the user actions and the environment, also anticipating the user's behavior.

D4All project is part of the Italian cluster "technology for the living environment" in which a second project called "SHELL" ("Shared interoperable Home Ecosystems for a green, comfortable and safe Living") is specifically dealing with the real house and it will provide input for the presented framework.

4   Validation

The main purpose of the VHF is to support the various software tools used in the entire home's life cycle. New methodologies and technologies for design, validation and market analysis of the domestic environment has been taken into consideration (e.g. 3D visualization, haptic interfaces, Virtual and Augmented Reality, etc.). These technologies allow designers to evaluate, in a flexible manner, the human-machine interactions in the home automation environment, also by adopting virtual prototyping in order to carry out a real home simulation and analysis.

In order to test and validate the introduced framework, a demonstration scenario has been identified. This scenario is thought to represent activities and habits that occur on a regular basis in a domestic environment, whose main operating context is represented by the home, the residential aggregates and the AAL, connected to the outside in different ways, depending on the specific needs. For example, one scenario focuses on the man while he sleeps (Fig. 2); in this situation, the idea is to check information related to physiological parameters of the user (e.g. heart rate, blood pressure, sweating, etc.) and subsequently identify the user's status (e.g. health status, posture, etc.).

Moreover, it is required to monitor specific user behavior, based on specific identified behavioral patterns (e.g. recognize when the user has not taken the prescribed drug before sleeping; recognize when, during the night, the user has woken up and has wandered, since there may be a greater chance of a fall, due to poor light conditions).

This can be realized implementing a new user-environment interaction system performing various tasks:

- collect and gather data and information related to the user's physiologic parameters coming from wireless technology based smart objects, also exploiting the potential of the emerging multi-sensor data fusion technology;
- derive the user health shape, the posture, emotional being and so forth;
- call different available services using data coming from several sensors within the environment related to the context of interaction between the user and the environment (e.g. activating an alarm, fading lights, activate a phone call);
- adoption of new user interfaces to interact with the domestic environment, exploiting also the most innovative and latest technologies of Virtual Reality.

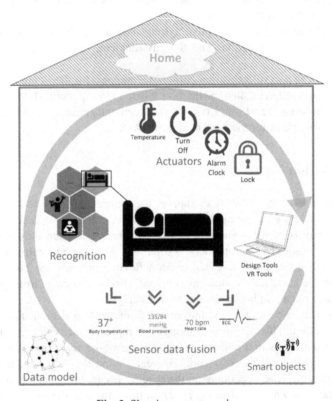

Fig. 2. Sleeping man scenario

Moreover, since the final goal of the Design For All project is to improve the effectiveness of an AAL based on the Universal Design principles, it is necessary to verify the impact of the new proposed approach. This need asks for the cooperation of industrial partners to provide their structures and labs for ambient assisted living. Thus, the validation of the obtained results and the developed prototypes will be performed by mean of experimental campaigns brought within the AUXOLOGICO structures in collaboration with industrial partners such as ABMEDICA, CALEARO, TEOREMA, EUROTECH, LAB IDEA and LOGICAL SYSTEM, and external interested companies like BTICINO, WHIRPOOL, ELECTROLUX, some already part of the

Cluster. Also, the industrial partners will evaluate possible collaborations and future developments for industrialization and commercialization of the proposed platform.

5   Conclusion

Low interoperability is the most important barrier slowing a wide spread of AAL systems based on a design oriented to the Universal Design principles.

To overcome such a limit, this paper, starting from the study of the state of the art, illustrated the structure of the Virtual Home Framework, its goals and how to reach them in order to realize the idea of the home as a holistic and inclusive environment, thus satisfying the requirements for the next generation of AAL.

Finally, as the impact of the new approach on the real home has to be evaluated, a demonstration scenario has been defined to allow the test and validation of the proposed framework.

Acknowledgments. This work has been co-funded by the Ministry of University and Research of Italy within the cluster "Tecnologie per gli ambienti di vita – Technologies for Ambient Assisted Living" initiatives, with the overall objective of increasing quality of life in the domestic environment through the use of the modern technologies.

References

1. Mace, R.L., Hardie, G.J., Place, J.P.: Accessible Environments: Toward Universal Design (1991)
2. Emiliani, P.L., Burzagli, L., Billi, M., Gabbanini, F., Palchetti, E.: Report on the impact of technological developments on eAccessibility, DfA@eInclusion Project deliverables (2008), http://www.dfaei.org
3. Poslad, S.: Ubiquitous Computing. Smart Devices, Environments and Interactions (2009)
4. IEEE Standard Computer Dictionary: A Compilation of IEEE Standard Computer Glossaries, 610, IEEE (1990)
5. Sacco, M., Pedrazzoli, P., Terkaj, W.: VFF: Virtual Factory Framework. In: Proceedings of 16th International Conference on Concurrent Enterprising, Lugano, Switzerland (2010)
6. Lee, C.E., Moon, K.D.: Design of a Universal Middleware Bridge for Device Interoperability in Heterogeneous Home Network Middleware. In: CCNC Conference (2005)
7. Richardson, L., Ruby, S.: RESTful Web Services. Web services for the real world. O'Reilly Media (2007)
8. Extensible Markup Language (XML) 1.0 (2008), http://www.w3.org/XML/
9. oBIX (Open Building Information Xchange), http://obix.org/
10. A Technical Introduction to the Devices Profile for Web Services, http://msdn.microsoft.com/en-us/library/ms996400.aspx
11. Understanding Service-Oriented Architecture, Microsoft Developer Network (2004), http://msdn.microsoft.com/en-us/library/aa480021.aspx
12. Jammes, F., Smit, H., Martinez Lastra, J.L., Delamer, I.M.: Service-Oriented Paradigms in Industrial Automation. IEEE Transactions on Industrial Informatics 1(1), 62–70 (2005)

13. W3C. XML Schema Part 1: Structures Second Edition (2004),
    http://www.w3.org/TR/xmlschema-1/
14. Terkaj, W., Pedrielli, G., Sacco, M.: Virtual Factory Data Model. In: Proceedings of 2nd OSEMA (Ontology and Semantic Web for Manufacturing) Workshop (2012)
15. Gruber, T.R.: What is an Ontology? Summary statement of Gruber's defintion of ontology as a specification of a conceptualization (1995),
    http://www-ksl.stanford.edu/kst/what-isan-ontology.html
16. Fisseha, F.: The Basics of Ontologies. Nordic Agricultural Ontology Service (AOS) Workshop Royal Veterinary and Agricultural University Copenhagen, Denmark (2003)
17. W3c   RDF   Primer,   http://www.w3.org/TR/2004/REC-rdf-primer-20040210/
18. W3C.OWL 2 Web Ontology Language - Document Overview (2009),
    http://www.w3.org/TR/owl2-overview/
19. Industry Foundation Classes (IFC) data model,
    http://www.buildingsmart.org/standards/ifc
20. KNX international site, http://www.knx.org/
21. Miori, V., Tarrini, L., Manca, M.: An Open Standard Solution for Domotic Interoperability
22. Chen, H., Finin, T., Joshi, A.: The SOUPA Ontology for Pervasive Computing. In: Ontologies for Agents: Theory and Experiences, pp. 233–258. Birkhäuser, Basel (2005)
23. IEEE Standard for modeling and simulation high level architecture (HLA) - framework and rules. IEEE Std. 1516-2000, pp. i–22 (2000)
24. Ghielmini, G., Pedrazzoli, P., Rovere, D., Terkaj, W., Dal Maso, G., Milella, F., Sacco, M., Boer, C.R.: Virtual Factory Manager of Semantic Data. In: Proceedings of DET 2011 (2011)

Empathy Building through Co-design

Shu Yuan[1] and Hua Dong[2]

[1] College of Architecture and Urban Planning, Tongji University, Shanghai, China
yuanshu66@gmail.com
[2] College of Design and Innovation, Tongji University, Shanghai, China
donghua@tongji.edu.cn

Abstract. As a user-designer face-to-face design approach, co-design needs the two sides standing at each other's perspectives for problem solving. In co-design, the key point is building empathy between designers and users. This paper went through the literature about "design empathy". A practical co-design workshop was organized which proved the effectiveness of design probes for empathy building. Other findings include the three modes of designers' participation in co-design.

Keywords: Design empathy, co-design, participatory design.

1 Introduction

Co-design, a user-involved approach for design innovation, integrates designers and design researchers with non-designers to create better experience [1]. In co-design, it is hoped that, designers' professional skills and users' specific knowledge would inspire each other and lead to an equal and effective dialogue, thus helping develop appropriate solutions to meet the user needs. However, it is often a challenge for designers and non-designers (normally with little design knowledge) to have a harmonious dialogue.

Empathy in co-design includes two aspects: creating a respectful dialogue and supporting empathic understanding with users [2]. In empathic design, designers and researchers continually develop and check their creative understanding of users' experiences in dialogues with users over time [3]. Empathic design is a relatively low-cost, low-risk way to identify potentially critical customer needs [4].

The term 'design empathy' has been in use since the late 1990s to describe the role of the designer/researcher [4-6]. Design empathy makes use not only of the emotions of the users, but also those of the designers [7]. One of the most frequently cited definitions of empathy comes from Fulton Suri [8] who defines empathy as "our intuitive ability to identify with other people's thoughts and feelings – their motivations, emotional and mental models, value, priorities, preferences, and inner conflicts". There are also other definitions or descriptions of design empathy, for example:

C. Stephanidis and M. Antona (Eds.): UAHCI/HCII 2014, Part I, LNCS 8513, pp. 85–91, 2014.

"Empathy in design is the ability to step into another person's shoes, imagine how that person feels, would think and act, in order to use that understanding in designing." [9].

"Empathy has been used as a defining characteristic of designer-user relationships when design is concerned with user experience." [10]

"Empathy is the critical component that deepens the designer's understanding of users who may be very different from the designer". [11]

Postma et al. [3] quoted Wright and McCarthy [12]'s definition of creative understanding - the combination of a rich, cognitive and affective understanding, and the ability to translate this understanding into user-centered products and services - to explain that empathic design is a design research approach that is directed towards building creative understanding of users and their everyday lives for new product development (NPD).

Sleeswijk Visser [13] synthesized literature about empathy and explained it from three aspects. (1) Empathy is a kind of ability, which could be affected by designers' willingness and the specific situation. (2) In the psychological literature, empathy has two components, i.e., affective and cognitive. For designers, "having an emotional response (affective) to another's emotional state and being able to reflect on that by perspective-taking (cognitive) is a core mechanism of empathy." (3) Empathizing is a process, including stepping in, walking around and stepping out phases.

In this paper, the authors implanted empathy into a co-design workshop. The purpose of introducing empathy was to emphasize the mutual understanding between the designer and the user.

2   Methods

In October 2013, a co-design workshop was conducted in Tongji University, Shanghai. It was the second one of a series of co-design workshops. Before the workshop, four users were recruited to collect data (through probes) for building empathic understanding when co-designing with designers. Two of them (U1 and U2) took part in the first co-design workshop in 2012, while the other two were new members (U3 and U4). User 1 is a retired chef with poliomyelitis. User 2 is a 74-year-old lady who used to be a university lecturer. Users 3 and 4 are two active ladies (aged between 25-30) with hearing loss. They communicate with the help of hearing aids. The two ladies are very good friends and are both interested in hip-hop dancing. Six professional designers participated in the co-design workshop. Three of them took part in the first workshop while the other three were new. All the designers and users were divided into three groups; each group with one or two users and two designers.

Several researchers make suggestion on the techniques and methods of empathic design. Leonard and Rayport [4] suggested watching consumers use products or services (i.e., observation) in their own environment as a basic technique for empathic design. Some visual techniques for communication are described, for instance, photo diaries [2], context-mapping [14], and generative tools [15]. McDonagh and Thomas [16] conducted a series of empathic modeling activities (for instance, designers without physical disabilities using wheelchairs and/or restricting their mobility or handgrip dexterity) to enhance empathy with design students.

Fulton Suri [3] distinguished the empathic methods into three categories: "looking at what people really do [looking], asking people to participate [participating], trying things ourselves [trying]." Kouprie and Sleeswijk Visser [17] classified all the tools and techniques into three types: "techniques for direct contact between designers and users (research), techniques for communicating findings of user studies to design teams (communication) and techniques for evoking the designer's own experiences in a domain relevant to the user (ideation)."

"We learn about what other people think and feel through empathic interpretation of what they say and do." [3] This study used design probes (a kind of static saying) and video ethnography (doing) to capture the users' "behavior" and "thinking". Visual data such as video clips, persona cards and photos were shot and classified by the users and researchers, together with textual data (e.g. quotes).

Barros & Duarte [18] surveyed many publications [19-21] and concluded that participatory design is one of the best ways when developing products to be used by people with disabilities. Finally, all the collected data from design probes and video ethnography were shared with the designers and users in the co-design workshop. The co-design topic of each group was determined according to the user's personal life focus and personal interests. Concerning the "trying" [3] level of empathic design, a designer-user co-cooking session was added to the U1 group, whose co-design topic was around cooking and kitchen. The topic of U2 (a retired teacher) group was in relation to taking care of patients in hospital, as U2's husband got cancer a year ago and her daily life now was taking care of her husband in hospital. U3 and U4 wished to design something that could express their positive living attitude towards hearing impairments.

At the co-design venue, besides the participants (designers and users), there was one facilitator and one recorder in each group. The facilitator controlled every group's procedure while the recorder objectively recorded the detailed reactions in the dialogue. The whole process was video recorded. Stationary and basic model making materials (such as strings and small pieces of blocks) were prepared for brainstorming and prototyping.

3   Results and Discussion

The data collected via probes proved effective when co-designing. Users narrated their own stories to designers under the assistance of visual materials. Most designers were curious about the users' experiences and then conversations began. When evoked, the users expressed more and designers got a deeper empathic understanding. Unlike the first co-design workshop in 2012 [22], this time, designers had more curiosities about the users' narrations and the users had greater motivation to explain their problems and express their ideas. The visual materials helped ideas to converge between the designers and the users. From the questionnaire, all the participants thought the designers were fully or almost fully standing at the users' perspectives when considering the situation. Designers listened patiently and sometimes were "surprised by various aspects that influence the user's experience [13]." This proved that designers empathized with the users. On the other side, from the follow-up discussion, the users learned useful design concepts and understood designers' ways of working. All the users thought that the designers had made great contribution to the final solution. This process has shown the three aspects of empathetic design [13]: i.e. (1) Empathy is a kind of ability. (2) Empathy has affective and cognitive components. (3) Empathizing includes stepping in, walking around and stepping out phases.

3.1   User Participation Modes

Concerning user participation in the co-design process, Yuan and Dong [23] summarized four user participation modes, i.e., active, semi-active, indirect and passive modes. In the active mode, users are able to propose problems and solutions or related ideas, which has much contribution to design outcomes. In the semi-active mode, users are aware of their intentions or problems, but can hardly propose any design solutions. In the indirect mode, users do not know what they need very clearly, but they are willing to talk, which may inspire designers. In the passive mode, users have little contribution to the design outcomes. They only give feedback when they see the design solution or concept.

In this co-design workshop, all the four users behaved naturally and were willing to express their ideas and thinking. No users were in a passive mode, which may not lead to successful design outcomes or collaborative design experience. U1 was in a semi-active mode, which meant he proposed his problems and was willing to answer the designers' questions, but with no initial design solutions. U2 was in an active mode. She not only collected all the problems she had when taking care of her husband, but also had professional knowledge to think the problems out. In the co-design workshop, it was a good chance for her to share her ideas with the designers and then form the final solutions together. U3 and U4 belong to the indirect mode, in which designers' strong mind determined the design directions. U3 and U4 actively participated in the discussion and offered key information on certain topics that inspired the designers. It proved that in active modes, users' contribution to design final outcomes could be greater. It was true in this co-design workshop. "The final design solution was proposed by the Granny [U2]. We just encouraged her to recall her memory!" explained one designer in Group U2. "I really appreciate the designers in our group. They gave me many good suggestions about how to arrange my kitchen to enlarge the working space," said U1.

3.2   Designers' Roles

Based on the observation of the three groups, the designers' roles can be classified into three: i.e., listening, controlling, and inspiring. In the "listening" mode, designers often keep quiet most of the time and listened to the users attentively, letting them express their experiences and ideas. Normally, designers take notes down and express his/her own thinking after users' talking. This mode of designers matches the "active" mode of users very well. In the "controlling" mode, designers strongly lead the design direction and procedure. In this mode, users are easy to be inspired, and, sometimes, ignored as well. In the third mode "inspiring", designers also listen to users, but with appropriate intervention, e.g. inquiry, which gives opportunities for users to propose creative solutions by themselves. This mode of designers best suits open-minded and thoughtful users.

3.3   Interactions between Users and Designers

Based on the co-design workshop, U2 (in the "active" mode) and the designers in her group (one in the "inspiring" mode while the other in the "listening" mode) collaborated best: all had good experiences and the design outcomes were generated by the user under the designers' encouragement. Figure 1 shows the discussion scenario of the group. The "inspiring" designer carefully listened to the Granny's ideas and then explored deeply according to her experiences. The left male designer was in the "listening" mode while the person at the right corner was the facilitator.

The U1 group was the combination of a "semi-active" user and "listening" designers. Sometimes, they got stuck when no one was talking. This kind of design process

Fig. 1. The "active" user with "inspiring" and "listening" designers

was not smooth. The designers expected the users to talk much more than them. They wished to have more than one user.

The U3 & U4 group was a combination of "indirect" users and a "listening" designer and a "controlling" designer. They worked very well together. It was observed that the "listening" and "controlling" or "listening" and "inspiring" combinations tend to get more harmonious results.

3.4   Suggestions for Improvements

The designers proposed suggestions for improving the co-design workshop. As the user data were collected and roughly classified by the users and researchers before the co-design workshop, the designers had little time to digest the data. It was at the workshop venue that the designers firstly get all the data. "It's better to let us know about our users before we came here and then we can prepare some material at home," said one designer. In addition, there was also a gap about the understanding of the user data between the researchers and the facilitators. When the user data were shared with all the participants, it is important to classify the data in advance, and present them with a logical sequence.

4   Conclusions

Under the direction of literature, this study mainly applied the technique - design probes - for empathy building in co-design. The key findings of this study are:

- The design probe proves a good approach for empathic design. All the designers and users had a positive response to this kind of methods and both sides learned from each other.
- The visual data collected from design probes, which included the real user environment, indeed helped build an equal dialogue and encourages the designers' empathic understanding with users.
- While there are four user participation modes (active, semi-active, indirect and passive) in co-design, three designer participation modes were also identified, i.e. listening, controlling and inspiring.
- The combinations of different modes of designers and users may lead to different co-design results and affect participant's experiences. In this workshop, it was observed that when there was a 'listening' designer with a 'controlling' or 'inspiring' designer, the co-design process was smoother. This will need to be tested in further research.

Acknowledgments. We thank all the participants and the research assistants who helped collect data and organize the workshop.

References

1. Sander, E.B.-N., Stappers, P.J.: Co-creation and the New Landscapes of Design. CoDesign: International Journal of CoCreation in Design and the Arts 4(1), 5–18 (2008)

2. Mattelmäki, T.: Design Probes. Doctoral Thesis. University of Art and Design, Helsinki, Finland (2006)
3. Postma, C.E., Zwartkruis-Pelgrim, E., Du, J.: Challenges of Doing Empathic Design: Experiences from Industry. International Journal of Design 6(1), 59–70 (2012)
4. Leonard, D., Rayport, J.F.: Spark Innovation through empathetic Eesign. Harvard Business Review 75(6), 102–113 (1997)
5. Segal, L.D., Fulton Suri, J.: The Empathic Practitioner. Measurement and Interpretation of User Experience. In: Proceedings of the 41st Annual Meeting of the Human Factors and Ergonomics Society, pp. 451–457 (1997)
6. Koskinen, I., Battarbee, K., Mattelmäki, T.: Empathic Design. User Experience for Product Design. IT Press, Helsinki (2003)
7. Battarbee, K., Koskinen, I.: Co-experience: user experience as interaction. CoDesign 1(1), 5–18 (2005)
8. Fulton Suri, J.: Empathic design: Informed and inspired by other people's experience. In: Koskinen, I., Battarbee, K., Mattelmäki, T. (eds.) Empathic Design. IT Press, Finland (2003)
9. Mattelmäki, T.: Handouts of presentation at "user inspired design course", Helsinki (2006)
10. Wright, P., McCarthy, J.: Empathy and Experience in HCI. In: CHI 2008 Proceedings Dignity in Design (2008)
11. McDonagh, D., Thomas, J.: Disability+relevant desigh: empathic design strategies supporting more effective new product design outcomes. The Design Journal 13(2), 180–198 (2010)
12. Wright, P., McCarthy, J.: The value of the novel in designing for experience. In: Pirhonen, A., Roast, C., Saariluoma, P., Isom, H. (eds.) Future Interaction Design, pp. 9–30. Springer, London (2005)
13. Sleeswijk Visser, F.: Bringing the Everyday life of People into Design. Doctoral Thesis. Technical University of Delft, Delft, Netherland (2009)
14. Sleeswijk Visser, F., Stappers, P.J., Van der Lugt, R., Sanders, E.B.-N.: Contextmapping: Experiences from Practice. CoDesign: International Journal of Co Creation in Design and the Arts 1(2), 1–30 (2005)
15. Stappers, P.J.: Generative Tools for Codesigning. In: Scrivener, S.A.R., Ball, et al. (eds.) Collaborative Design. Springer, UK (2000)
16. McDonagh, D., Thomas, J.: Rethinking design thinking: empathy supporting innovation. Australasian Medical Journal 3(8), 458–464 (2010)
17. Kouprie, M., Visser, F.S.: A framework for empathy in design: stepping into and out of the user's life. Journal of Engineering Design 20(5), 437–448 (2009)
18. Barros, A.C., Duarte, C.: Dear users.. empathy building methods for assistive product design. In: Proceedings of 8th International Design and Emotion Conference, London (2012)
19. Demirbilek, O., Demirkan, H.: Universal product design involving elderly users: a participatory design model. Applied Ergonomics 35, 361–370 (2004)
20. Dong, H., Clarkson, P.J., et al.: Critical user forums-an effective user research method for inclusive design. The Design Journal 8(2), 49–59 (2005)
21. Storni, C.: Multiple forms of appropriation in self-monitoring technology: reflections of the role of evaluation in future self-care. International Journal of Human-Computer Interaction 26(5), 537–561 (2010)
22. Dong, H., Yuan, S.: Learning from Co-designing. In: Proceedings of 2nd International Conference for Design Education Researchers (2013)
23. Yuan, S., Dong, H.: Co-design in China: Implications for Users, Designers and Researchers. Under Press (2014)

Development Methods and Tools
for Universal Access

Ergonomic Aspects of Software Engineering

Andrzej Borucki

IME , Poznan University of Technology, Poznan, Poland
andrzej.borucki@put.poznan.pl

Abstract. The practice of applying rigid software development rules has killed creativity as processes and tools take precedence over technical solutions and client satisfaction. A key role in developing software is played by the intellectual resources of project teams, i.e. their knowledge. The knowledge used to produce software may be either open or hidden. In order to manage software development effectively, advantage needs to be taken of the knowledge held by each design team member. Two distinctive knowledge management strategies are available for managing software development. These are the knowledge codification strategy and the knowledge personalization strategy. The knowledge codification strategy requires the use of expensive technology to apply CASE tools. Based on two decades of experience in managing IT projects, we have grown somewhat critical of the use of CASE tools. Our experience in managing IT projects shows that a strategy of knowledge personalization in software development helps improve designer knowledge in a given business field and boosts their productivity.

Keywords: Project Management, Software Engineering, Reguirement Engineering.

1 Introduction

The prime purpose of software development ergonomics is to ensure the best possible working conditions for programmers while minimizing work onerousness and maximizing worker productivity. A study of the effectiveness displayed by our team1 on software development projects performed between 2000 and 2013 shows that, in project management practice, excessive emphasis is commonly placed on the technical aspects of project management while neglecting the innovation side. We have observed that the use of standard software development procedures does not make a project more cost efficient nor speed up the design process. What it often does, however, is keep project team members from devoting their time to forging friendly relationships with one another. Practice has shown that mutual relations among designers are pivotal for creating an environment which will unlock the intellectual potential of individual project team members and inspire the team's innovative spirit.

---

[1] Since 1990, during his employment in PPH Softmar, the author has led numerous deployments of management information systems. Between 1990 and 2001, he and his team developed and unrolled dozens of proprietary applications in logistics and finance.

C. Stephanidis and M. Antona (Eds.): UAHCI/HCII 2014, Part I, LNCS 8513, pp. 95–103, 2014.
© Springer International Publishing Switzerland 2014

Every innovation process requires positive interaction between the authors of ideas and their protectors responsible for approving a new solution and incorporating it into the project. The innovations achieved by project teams should help shift project focus from effectiveness and efficiency to innovation. Therefore, software design managers need to recognize the influence of non-environmental factors on designer productivity and select management methods and techniques which will minimize the arduousness of intellectual work and bring out the innovation potential of the design team.

The non-environmental factors which in our view are the most critical for ensuring ergonomically-sound software development and which remain within the discretion of project managers include project-specific knowledge management strategies, software development models applied in the design process and project and team management methods. By and large, the classic software development ergonomics is a study of the impact of environmental factors on the onerousness of intellectual work (including the influence of lighting, noise, screen radiation and the ergonomics of CASE tool interfaces) which downplays or fully ignores the non-environmental impacts that relate to the human factor and tie closely to the quality and innovative value of given software.

2   Ergonomics of Software Development vs. Productivity

Today's software engineering should provide efficient software design tools and define the boundary conditions to govern their use. To that end, developers need to ascertain:

— Whether a unified approach to software development does not kill designer individuality and consequently reduce designer productivity and innovation;
— Whether the things of importance for increasing the overall efficiency of project team management do not reduce the effectiveness of individual designers;
— The extent to which the stress experienced by designers during software development affects their efficiency and innovation;
— The reasons why project managers seeking to meet client expectations neglect the personal intellectual potential of individual designers.

Experience with a great number of IT projects which varied in the degree of their innovation and complexity points to the following key factors which undermine the productivity of designer teams (Borucki,2012),(Cushman,Rosenberg,1991):

1. The stress experienced by designers in developing and implementing IT projects results from:

— Their post-go-live accountability for software defects;
— Their inability to process a flood of input data supplied during software development or having to complete their assignments based on incomplete information;
— Having to cope with gaps in knowledge, especially technological, needed to complete their project,
— Changes to software requirements made in mid-project, especially by the prospective user.

2. Mismanagement of the intellectual potential of individual project team members;
3. Excessive reliance on CASE tools to aid design at the expense of pure project innovation;
4. Adopting the regime of a specific IT project management method;
5. The pressure of having to meet project deadlines and budgets after the labor intensity of a project has been underestimated;
6. Having adopted a knowledge management strategy which fails to fit project profile.

Developers frequently forget the simple fact that, as individuals, employees differ in their personalities and intellectual potential. Little is done to harness their talent for project purposes to allow staff members to derive personal satisfaction from their work (Marco ,Lisner,2002). In seeking to achieve project goals and meet deadlines (especially where clients allow too little time for document preparation), it is often believed that good and efficient management is all about pushing employees to work harder with little regard for their off time. Where the entire focus is placed squarely on the technical aspects of project management, very little time remains for finding the best way to complete a given project task, especially where standard operating procedures are followed. Having watched a number of designers at work over the last two decades, I have seen them dedicate their time overwhelmingly to performing specific project tasks while giving little attention to identifying the best possible solution. Most designers had to be "forced" by company management to read designer books or attend conferences and training. Our observations show also that, regrettably, the present design practice is geared towards getting designers to become as "efficient" as possible and to making entire projects highly effective. This makes design work extremely strenuous and often described as "the dark side of intellectual work". The reason for this lies in underestimating the importance in the design process of the human factor and, in particular, people's intellectual and psychological dimensions. Figure 1 shows three key non-environmental factors which affect the ergonomics of software development and which can be influenced by team manager.

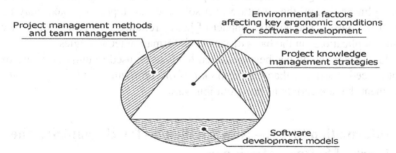

Fig. 1. Factors affecting key ergonomic conditions for software development

In searching for ways to make project teams more productive, the majority of project managers choose to use various CASE support techniques in design work and project management. Such tools are viewed as facilitators for the efficient development of complex IT systems which are more functional, reliable and efficient and allow for easier maintenance and system transferability.

The key advantages of using CASE tools to improve software design efficiency are:

— The option of modeling systems at various levels of abstraction,
— The capability to produce project documentation in a uniform format at each stage of design,
— Easier communication between project developers and the future software user,
— Facilitated two-way (vertical and horizontal) communication between designers,
— Access to knowledge from other projects for the purposes of the new undertaking,
— Reliance on standard system development methods,
— The capability to use uniform methods to evaluate project quality,
— A knowledge repository created to support future projects – the repository is a database of specifications to be used to assess the labor-intensity of projects, developers, design items, diagrams, algorithms, etc.,
— Standard formats for input and output data,
— An ability to rapidly produce a user interface and automatically generate software source codes based on diagram designs created in e.g. the UML language.

The majority of CASE functionalities are designed to help gather knowledge on the project at hand, create a knowledge-base for future reference, build a project management model and develop a knowledge and team management strategy. Our 20-years' experience in managing IT projects suggests there is a pressing need for revising the way CASE tools are being used. Despite their widespread application, such tools do little to keep developers from exceeding deadlines or overspending budgets. The key reason for that lies in poorly formulated knowledge management strategies and excessive reliance on CASE tools in software design. Such problems are particularly pronounced in innovative projects where designing is non-linear and involves a sequence of fixed steps performed up to a certain point in the process after which the developers go into feedback loops not envisioned in the initial project model. In non-linear design, the structure of a software development project may be unknown at the outset. The adverse impact of heavy reliance on CASE tools is seen in designing applications on the basis of various information technologies.

The knowledge which has been acquired tends to be used to unify software development procedures rather than create the kinds of ergonomic conditions for software development that are certain to bring out innovation.

3   Information Stress – New Challenges for Humanizing the Work of Software Designers

Contemporary software engineers employ a range of CASE tools designed primarily to create knowledge repositories for gathering and storing the information needed in software design. In designing IT systems, use is made of basically 10 areas of knowledge which are software configuration management, logic software model structure management, software design management, software engineering infrastructure, software engineering management, testing, requirements analysis, software quality analysis, software evolution & maintenance and software engineering. Once obtained, information about current project and any relevant past projects may "come in handy" in current design work. Such information comprises powerful databanks which should be accessible to designers on an equal basis. Figure 2 illustrates a sample complex knowledge repository used in software design. Repositories of non-confidential knowledge hold information of high as well as low relevance for software design.

Many designers become overloaded with various types of data. Without proper selectiveness, developers may end up being overloaded with data and subjected to what literature refers to as "information stress". Commonly, information stress results from the inability of employees to process excessive input data supplied to them in the course of software development or from not having enough information to complete their work. At the start of the design process, it is difficult to tell which information will be of use and value. Information stress results from the discord between the volume of information provided during software development and the individual processing capabilities of the designers. Such stress can be seen to affect developers with varying intensity at all stages of software design and deployment – it affects all persons involved in creating software as well as its would-be users (who are also involved in the design process). Recent literature provides articles on intellectual work ergonomics and specifically on the impact of information overflow on the efficiency of intellectual work (Ledzińska, 2011),(Hankała, 2009). The severity of the impact of information overload depends on a personality trait which the literature refers to as "the cognitive drive" (Ledzińska, 2011). A number of factors determine an individual's sensitivity to information stress. Such factors include inquisitiveness manifesting itself as hunger for knowledge, temperament, personality and rational intelligence. Information stress may be experienced at various stages of information processing. One of the primarily responsibilities of software design management is to process information at the stages at which information is identified, analyzed and used. Excessive or insufficient information at various design stages may affect the severity of the stress experienced by designers.

Stress may also harm the working efficiency of developers who are bombarded daily with aggressive information. The resulting information glut may impair their ability to process and select information causing them to make misguided judgments. Information stress may distort cognition and result in delivering products based on false or incomplete assumptions. In extreme cases, it may contribute to project failures.

Our observations of dozens of software development projects suggests that designers experience the most severe information stress while identifying and examining functional software requirements. At this stage, conflicts abound due to excessive functional demands made by various groups of would-be users as well as functions left out by designers and the system functionalities unnoticed by future software users. Such circumstances are illustrated in Figure 3.

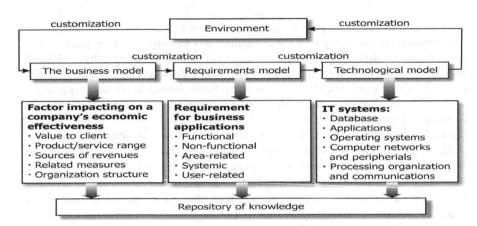

Fig. 2. Elements of knowledge gathered in software project repository

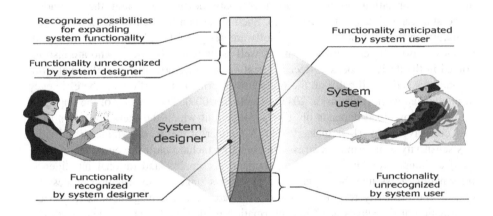

Fig. 3. Areas of knowledge about the functionalities of software in development

The simultaneous occurrence of information gluts and information deficiencies, as faced by software designers while defining software requirements, is caused additionally by the fact that prospective software users define their software functionality demands very generally or express functional requirements in their industry jargon (the so called "tribal language"). This makes it difficult to identify the precise requirements and assign priorities to the individual demands in the design process. A great number of the requirements submitted by various individuals are mutually exclusive. In designing large systems in projects which go on for months on end, requirements concerning specific functionalities may change considerably over time. This may be due to the persons responsible for selecting software functionalities changing their minds, changes in the effectiveness factors applied on the business parts of IT architecture for which a given software package is being developed and changes in the legal environment of a given enterprise.

One way to arrange knowledge into an orderly structure is to divide it into the categories of basic, advanced and innovative (Ashok, 2004). Another is to define a hierarchy of importance of the knowledge to be used in project implementation. Depending on project size and complexity and the degree of innovation involved, a layer may be set aside in the knowledge repository for exclusive knowledge with the most critical information, particularly that related to the innovative technologies to be employed in the design process. Other layers would contain knowledge generally accessible to all designers as well as knowledge on the CASE methods and programs applied in the project (Borucki,2012). Needless to say, a design firm derives most of its competitive edge from the exclusive knowledge concerning innovation. A crucial consideration in creating a knowledge repository is also how the knowledge is stored and accessed by individual project developers. My experience with various projects shows that much designer stress comes from not having the knowledge needed to solve a specific problem and being aware of gaps in one's knowledge, especially where the knowledge that is missing is essential for completing a project task.

4   Project Management Methods Mitigating Adverse Stress Impact

An overview of software development management methods shows that many traditional solutions ignore the significance of designer productivity, or the so called human factor, in its intellectual, psychological and sociological aspects. The fact of the matter, however, is that it is actually essential for project managers to recognize not only technical and economic considerations but also the soft factors. Such managers should therefore (Martin,2008),(Highsmith,2007):

1. Secure individual and collective capabilities to develop software;
2. Minimize the impact of non-environmental factors which undermine the capacity to develop software: such factors include employee stress, lack of motivation and heavy reliance on "rigid" software development methodologies;
3. Retain key personnel with critical skills on project teams;
4. Optimally select the environmental factors which enhance software development capabilities;
5. Ensure software is developed with agility, i.e. keep the designers and software users working at a swift pace;
6. Communicate osmotically to allow free circulation of information within project teams with equal access to project information ensured for all team members;
7. Ensure all staff members feel secure and free to express their opinions on project-related matters;
8. Select the right project team members with experience in the field in question to staff short- and long-term projects;
9. Flexibly apply technical support and CASE tools in software production so as not to constrain designers' individuality.

In order to satisfy the need for recognizing the human factor, new "agile" project management methods have been developed. The methods satisfy the criteria of being ergonomically sound as they rest on the assumption that project success comes from successfully utilizing the human factor and creatively engaging with clients at each stage of project implementation. The software projects which rely on agile methodologies are easier to accept for future users which in itself reduces the risk of project failure. In any enterprise, IT infrastructure is only optimal in real life when its applications can be adjusted rapidly to new business challenges and fit well into the enterprise management concept. This is made considerably easier with the arrival of agile methodologies in IT system design, especially where it is essential that the system is customized to a company's business model with as little harm as possible and without interrupting the continuity of IT processes.

5   Knowledge Personalization Strategy as a Key to Humanizing Project Work

A key role in software development is played by the knowledge resources that, if used competently, have the potential of boosting project innovativeness. Both covert and overt knowledge should be used optimally at each stage of system design. An overview of successful IT projects in recent years, particularly those relying on internet technologies, shows that a key to their success is to employ a proper knowledge management strategy which helps bring out and effectively utilize the intellectual potential of individual design team members. Interestingly, in the majority of the reviewed cases, the use of knowledge management strategies followed the collapse of markets for previously produced products.

Knowledge management cycle as applied in software development

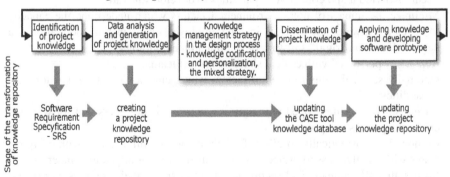

Fig. 4. Knowledge management cycle as applied in software development.

Many companies which faced such tribulations have been forced to redefine themselves on the market and adopt new competitiveness strategies to unlock their potential for product innovation. Figure 4 presents the knowledge management cycle as applied in software development.

6   Conclusions

Design firms churn out ever more sophisticated software systems which they are expected to deliver within ever shorter lead times by relying on continuous progress in software engineering. Unfortunately, the practice, at least that seen on innovative projects, is plagued by randomness and uncertainty of schedules and costs. Design firms look for effective ways to increase the productivity of their designers and entire design teams. In doing so, they usually consider the two options of either increasing process efficiency, which involves a strategy of knowledge codification, or developing innovative project solutions, possibly by means of a knowledge personalization strategy.

Our observations from numerous projects confirm that the choice of a path for knowledge personalization to support design innovation requires the use of ergonomic software development methods and properly managing the overall software design process.

References

1. Ashok, J.: Knowledge Management: An Integrated Approach. Peearson Education Limited (2004)
2. Borucki, A.: Factors Adversely Affected the Productivity of Software Designers Applying CASE Tools. In: Vink, P. (ed.) Advances Social and Organizational Factors, pp. 317–329. CRC Press Taylor & Francis Group (2012)
3. Cushman, W.H., Rosenberg, D.J.: Human Factors in Product Design. Elsevier, Amsterdam (1991)
4. Hankała, A.: Aktywność umysłu w procesach wydobywania informacji pamięciowych. Wydawnictwo Uniwersytetu Warszawskiego, Warsaw (2009)
5. Heeg, F.J., Shrader, M., Scgrader, S.: Analyse und Neugestaltung betrieblicher DV-Systeme unter besonderen Beucksichtingung Software-ergonomicher Kriterien. In: Schonplug, W. (ed.) w Software-Ergonomie 1987: Nutzen Informatiuunssytems dem Benutzer, Tanbuer, Berlin, pp. 440–453 (1987)
6. Highsmith, J.: APM: Agile Project Management, PWN (2007)
7. ISO/IEC-15939-Software engineerng-Software measurement process, Reference number
8. ISO 9241-100 Ergonomies of human system interraction - Introduction to Software ergonomics
9. ISO 9241-129 Ergonomics of human system interraction-Guidance on invidualization
10. ISO 9241-20 Ergonomic of Human system interaction-Accessibility quideline for Information communication equipment and service-General quidelines (2008)
11. Marco, T., Lister, T.: Czynnik ludzki, skuteczne przedsięwzięcie i wydajne zaspoły. WNT, Warszawa (2002)
12. Martin, R.C., Martin, M.: Agile. Programowanie zwinne. Zasady, wzorce, praktyki zwinnego wytwarzania oprogramowania w C#, Wydawnictwo Helion (2008)
13. Ledzińska, M.: Człowiek współczesny w obliczu stresu informacyjnego. Wydawnictwo Psychologii PAN, Warsaw (2008)
14. Ledzińska, M.: Nowe czasy-nowe źródła stresu w pracy. In: Juliszewski, T. (ed.) Obciążenie psychiczną pracą-nowe wyzwania dla ergonomii. Komitet Ergonomii PAN, Kraków (2011)

Tests with Blind Programmers Using AWMo: An Accessible Web Modeling Tool

Filipe Del Nero Grillo and Renata Pontin de Mattos Fortes

Computer Science Department, Institute of Mathematics and Computer Sciences at University of São Paulo, São Carlos, Brazil. Av. Trabalhador São-carlense 400 - Centro, P.O.Box 668. 13560-970 - São Carlos/SP, Brazil
{grillo,renata}@icmc.usp.br
http://www.icmc.usp.br

Abstract. With the increase of public utility services being offered by many organizations, such as companies and government institutions, over the Internet and on other electronic medium, the concern related to the access blind and visually impaired citizens is raised. But still, some types of data remain intrinsically unaccessible such as software models, that are generally represented by visually rich diagrams which are inaccessible to screen readers. The goal of this paper is to categorize and evaluate the navigation strategies of blind users using a web application that allows access to UML class diagrams by using a specialized textual language. The investigation was done by analyzing videos with screen capture that were collected as part of a case study conducted with two blind programmers to evaluate the AWMo efficacy in enabling access to visual diagrams for blind and visually impaired software developers. We identified three navigation strategies adopted by the users during the study and the results of the analysis suggest that the navigation in long texts may become a burden on users memories, despite their strategies to improve their speed, non sequential text navigation methods must be further investigated.

Keywords: Web Accessibility, Case Study, Navigation, Modeling, UML.

1 Introduction

With the increase of public utility services being offered by many organizations, such as companies and government institutions, over the Internet and on other electronic medium, the concern related to the access of the blind and visually impaired is raised. In fact, a variety of laws all around the world has been established to support the rights of all people, including the disabled people such as the Section 508 [1] in United States and e-MAG (Electronic Government Accessibility Model) in Brazil [2].

Although the legislation helps to enforce accessibility to everyone that produce content and provide services on the web, some types of data remain intrinsically dependent on specific senses, such as vision. The software models, for instance,

C. Stephanidis and M. Antona (Eds.): UAHCI/HCII 2014, Part I, LNCS 8513, pp. 104–113, 2014.

are generally represented as visual diagrams, usually composed of geometric forms and connectors associating the geometric forms.

The models have semantics so the people involved with the software process could communicate rationale in a concise way. Most of the times there is also textual content inside these diagrams, but the meaning of the visual notations is so relevant that the understanding of the content is almost impossible when only listening to the textual content of the model. In this context, the AWMo (Accessible Web Modeler) was developed.

AWMo is a prototype Web tool designed to allow users to model software artifacts using a subset of UML class diagrams in two distinct ways. The first one is a graphical view, in which sighted software developers can draw diagrams in the traditional way by dragging elements and connecting them visually. The second view is a textual view, in which software developers with or without visual impairment can create the exact same elements of the diagrams using a textual language developed specially for AWMo.

Based on AWMo, we have conducted user tests with two blind people to evaluate the proposed approach, the tests are briefly described in Section 4. This paper uses the data collected during the mentioned user tests to analyze the navigation strategies of blind users during their interaction with a web application that allows access to UML class diagrams by using a specialized textual language. The recordings captured both the screen where the user were interacting with AWMo and the webcam where it was able to capture the facial expressions of the user while they worked on a set of five pre established tasks.

The analysis concentrated on the textual language content navigation inside the text editor, but was also extended to the rest of the web application in an attempt to compare the strategies used in hyper documents and simple text. Although there were several other aspects evaluated to reach objectives of the case study itself, this paper focuses solely on the identification and analysis of the navigation strategies adopted by the two blind programmers while interacting for the first time with the textual editor inside a web application they were not previously familiar with.

The remainder of this paper is organized as follows: Section 2 presents work found in the Literature that relates to the work presented in this paper. Section 3 presents the developed prototype tool. Section 4 briefly describes the case study that was conducted to evaluate the AWMo, from where the data used in this paper was collected. Section 5 evaluates the navigation strategies used by the two blind software developers that participated in the case study both in the application interface and inside the tool's textual editor. Finally, Section 6 presents a discussion over the obtained results and concludes the paper with some final remarks.

2   Related Work

There are several studies in the Literature that relates to this work from several different aspects.

As a Web modeling tool, in [3] the authors have developed GEMSJax, a Web version of the Eclipse GEMS software. It was designed to allow remote access via REST API. Similarly there is SLIM [4] which is also a Web modeling tool, but aims at enabling synchronous collaboration on modeling activities. Both these studies present good quality modeling tools but lack accessibility, in other words, for blind and visually impaired users, it would be just as difficult to use the mentioned tools as it would be to use a desktop modeling tool. This is precisely the point that make AWMo different from its peers, AWMo was set out to be accessible from its inception.

AWMo first prototype version was developed to work with UML class diagrams, in this field the work of King et al. (2004) [5] addressed the access of UML software engineering diagrams by blind people. They have developed a tool called TeDUB that allows read access to four of the twelve UML diagrams and their approach was well-received by the participants who have tested it. However, one of the requirements raised by the users was the possibility of editing the diagrams in addition to read it. Without the ability to modify and create new diagrams the access of blind people is only partial, they are able to access and understand the information they seek to convey but are unable to participate in its construction or collaborate in software modeling activities by using TeDUB. With this in mind, AWMo had its scope narrowed to only one of the UML diagrams, the class diagram, but sought out to allow the user to read, modify and create diagrams.

In [6], the authors compare browsing behavior of blind and sighted users. They made use of a proxy and AJAX technology to collect information about the pages that the subjects were browsing. This study had the participation of 10 blind and 10 sighted people and the results indicated that blind users employ coping strategies when facing accessibility problems and find their way to overcome these problems.

The authors of [7] have conducted studies to analyze the interaction of blind and visually impaired users on the Web. They categorized the main problems that the users faced and identified 17 tactics employed to overcome them that were explained in light of coping theory [8]. More than that, they related the tactics employed by the user with technical problems. Similarly, [9] proposed an automatic analysis method of webpage navigability and confuted a survey with 30 real users to evaluate their behavior on online shopping sites. The results indicated that blind users strongly depend on scanning navigation and a landmark-oriented navigation model was proposed based on their findings.

In [10], a set of nine guidelines was developed to assist the development of text interfaces as alternatives to graphical user interfaces (GUI). During the study they conducted an experiment with 39 blind subjects and discovered that the text interface is more usable for the blind. Therefore, the first approach that was explored with AWMo prototype was to allow access to visual models to blind software engineers using a textual language inside a Web application.

Finally, [11] reports a case study similar to the one conducted by the authors, they used a semi structured interview to know the participants and an observation phase to collect data about blind users navigation.

3   The AWMo

The AWMo is a prototype tool developed by the authors in the search of a proposal that would enable blind and visually impaired software developers to work with graphical software models and diagrams. The prototype is restricted to UML class diagrams in order to evaluate the approach.

The key concept behind AWMo approach is to provide two distinct views where the users can work with UML class diagrams: the graphical view, where sighted software developers can draw diagrams in the traditional way (by dragging elements and connecting them visually) and the textual view, where software developers with or without visual impairment can create the exact same diagrams using a textual language developed especially for AWMo.

The main goal of providing two views for the edition of the same model is that both views allow users to accomplish the same tasks and get the same results. By making all the changes made in one view available to the other, AWMo also foster the use of the models as a communication tool for teams of software developers composed of both blind and sighted people, while it does not represent an overhead to sighted users, since they will not necessarily need to learn the textual language in order to use the tool.

AWMo is a Web application developed in JavaServer Faces (JSF) 2.1. The textual language was developed using Eclipse's Xtext project. The Xtext provides a set of tools to allow the definition of grammars using the Extended Backus-Naur Form (EBNF) and generates the resources for textual languages such as the parser of the language, validators and code generators. Also, by making available the Ecore metamodel and the EMF classes for the designed language, it allows programatic access to both models and metamodels. The technology behind AWMo is better described in [12].

Figure 1 shows the interface of the AWMo's textual editor. We can observe that there is a context box on the top showing to the user which diagram is open and allows the user to close it. On the right of the context box is the accessibility toolbar, it allows the user to enable high contrast, control the font size of the application as a whole and also select the language in which the application is presented. On the left side of the main content area there is a menu that is also affected by the context of the application: if there are no open diagrams it will display only the options "Home" and "Help" while if there is an open diagram it will also display the "Textual view" and "Graphical view" options where the user can quickly switch between both textual and graphical editors for the same open diagram.

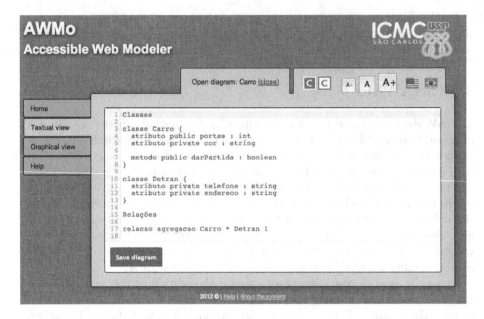

Fig. 1. Screen capture of AWMo interface displaying a diagram open with the textual view

For its interface design, AWMo was developed based on a reference architecture [13], including the visual style, menus and accessibility features such as high contrast, font size control and also the ability to be translated to multiple languages. The fact that both architecture and interface were inherited from the reference architecture and had good accessibility and usability features gave the AWMo tool development a great start up speed. Moreover, it allowed the development be focused on the inner workings and business logic of the proposed modeling environment.

AWMo has earned the second place in Brazilian Web Accessibility Recognition Program - All@Web[1], organized by W3C Brazil, at the Apps and Assistive Technologies category.

4   Case Study and Data Set

In order to evaluate the AWMo approach, a case study was conducted with one subject [14] and later on with a second subject that allowed us to gather more data and enrich the work with comparative analysis of the executions.

This study was composed of three phases: an initial interview to know the subjects, an observation phase where the subject performed a series of pre established tasks with AWMo on an instrumented computer and finally a final

---

[1] http://premio.w3c.br/english/

interview to collect the user thoughts and more subjective data regarding the tool and the performed tasks.

Audio of the interviews were recorded and transcribed. The computer screens and webcam were also captured and recorded with the use o Morae Recorder[2] and this data were used to carry out an initial analysis of AWMo approach.

One of the data gathered during the use of Morae was that time each participant took to complete each of the tasks defined for the case study. Figure 2 shows the time spent by each participant plotted as lines. We can see that although there were certainly differences in the times spent in each task, the general pattern of the curves is similar. We can see the amount of time increasing in task 3, reducing around task 4 and spiking again in task 5. This pattern was expected and relates directly to the level of difficulty of the tasks. The differences in the curves can be related to personal differences from the subjects, one had harder time working with the existing diagrams and the other had a harder time when creating a new diagram from the scratch.

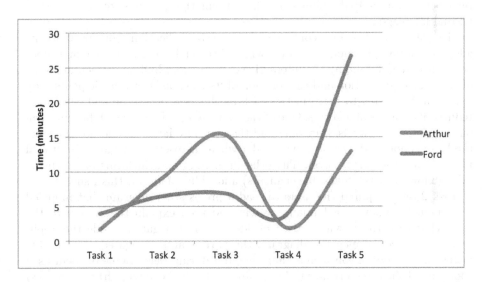

Fig. 2. Chart displaying the time used by the subjects to complete each task proposed by the case study

The results of the case study indicated that the AWMo approach is viable for leveraging collaboration and communication between sighted and visually impaired users on software modeling activities. However, we believe that richness of the gathered data can be further explored and that it can be analyzed from different perspectives. In this study we have analyzed the data evaluating the navigation strategies used by the participants both on the application as a whole and inside textual editor.

---

[2] http://www.techsmith.com/morae.html

5 Navigation Strategies

This work uses the data gathered during the case study mentioned above under a different perspective. By analyzing the footage collected during the case study containing both the computer screen and the users faces we identified navigation strategies the subjects used to navigate inside AWMo and how these strategies evolved during the course of the experiment.

Both participants were completely blind and they made use of the NVDA[3] screen reader, the same screen reader they use on their daily use computers.

The task 1 of the case study consisted in the subject using the AWMo accessibility features on the top right toolbar, however since both participants were completely blind and used screen reader to access the web, the features presented were of little help and they both used their time to learn how the interface was structured and the location of the menus, toolbars and other interactive elements. This was the first contact they were having with the tool, all they have read before was a PDF manual teaching them the grammar of the AWMo's textual language.

Since this was their first contact with the web application, both participants adopted scanning techniques, they navigated through the entire page in a moderate pace, understanding the interactive elements and building a mental model of the page organization and the location of its controls. Both participants took less than 2 minutes to perform this task as this is a prototype and, therefore, reduced in number of features. One of the users detected an accessibility problem on the font size controls, they only had the attribute label set and not the title, the label is not read by the screen reader when the user is navigating in virtual mode (using the arrow keys). The other user navigated in forms mode (using tab to move over the focusable elements) and didn't detected this issue.

Task 2 only required the users to read a pre-existing diagram that modeled a simplified version of a banking system and then explain the system to the researcher with their own words. Considering the navigation inside the application interface to open the diagram, the participants navigated considerably faster on the application menus than they did during task 1. One of them used shortcuts of the screen reader to jump directly to the headers (<h1> html tags) of the page and consequently getting much faster to the table with the existing diagrams. Considering only the navigation inside the text editor, following the same principle that on Task 1, the participants have scanned the whole text, line by line in a moderate speed because they were having the first contact with the model in question.

For task 3, the participants needed to modify the banking system diagram to specialize the person class into natural person and legal person classes using inheritance between them. In text navigation one of the participants started using a different strategy to access the person class, he jumped to the end of the text and moved upwards to find the desired class. The person class was located much closer to the bottom of the text so it allowed him to get there faster.

---

[3] http://www.nvaccess.org/

The same participant also employed the same strategy when navigating the application. After saving the diagram AWMo displays a message informing the user whether the operation was successful or any errors were found in the diagram. For navigating to the message, he navigated backwards, from the bottom of the page until the feedback message. Again the path from below was quicker than the regular top-down approach.

In task 4 participants were expected to remove the savings account class and any of its references from the diagram. Both participants navigated line by line but in a much faster way. One of them only let the NVDA red the first word of the line to identify if it was the line it was looking for and then jumped to the next line. We called it directed scanning, as the user quickly ignored the lines with definition of methods and attributes, since he was looking for a class definition, he listened more carefully the lines with class definitions. The other participant did basically the same with a slight difference: he seemed to have acquired a good notion of the size of each class (in terms of number of lines) and after its declaration (when wasn't the class he was looking for) he jumped line by line so fast that the NVDA wasn't able to not even start reading the sentence. After this short burst, he reduced the speed and listened to the beginning of the next class

Task 5 required the users to create a new diagram using simple specifications provided by the task description. Since the diagram was small and they created it from the beginning, not much navigation strategies were employed inside the text. Except when users were correcting errors pointed by AWMo when they saved the diagram, where line by line navigation sufficed.

6   Discussion and Concluding Remarks

Even in situations where there were no common accessibility problems detected, it was possible to observe that the blind users were constantly trying to improve their navigation around the application environment. Three were the strategies adopted by them to speed up their text navigation:

- **Bottom-up (web page)**: sometimes, knowing that the target was closer to the end of the page, the user jumped to the bottom of page and navigated backwards (using shift + tab) to get the point he wanted.
- **Bottom-up (text editor)**: same strategy used on the application, page down key to travel instantly to the bottom of the text area and then move up line by line. If the understanding of the user is correct about the position he is trying to go, this strategy result in less lines read by screen reader and, consequently, less time to reach the objective.
- **scanning with landmarks**: Fast navigation line by line stoping at landmarks like class definitions. This builds on the knowledge about the estimated number of lines that the class have to speed up the cursor over its lines and get the to desired location even faster.

One interesting fact to observe, is that both participants of the case study rarely used the link to skip to the content of the page. Even though it was there and was read by the screen reader, they ignored it and navigated through the menus jumping fast until they reached the page content. According to [9] its is common that most users prefer to scan the whole page and menu to make sure they haven't missed anything.

The possibility of non sequential navigation must be further investigated. We believe that textual navigation will pose as the greatest drawback of the AWMo approach to modeling for blind users. Despite its innovation in allowing edition models by blind and visually impaired users, as systems get complex their models get bigger and bigger and, consequently, strategies for reducing the memory burden on the users might be required.

As a future work, the authors intend to prototype and evaluate different navigation strategies for the textual language of AWMo, allowing the users to navigate throughout the textual content in a non sequential way.

Acknowledgements. We thank all the participants who voluntarily performed the experiments, ICMC-USP for providing the infrastructure that allowed this project to be developed and CNPq and CAPES for the financial support.

References

1. US Government: Section 508 of the rehabilitation act (29 u.s.c. 794d), as amended by the workforce investment act of 1998, pp. 105–220 (1998)
2. Executive power: Ordinance N° 3, from 7 of may of 2007. Institutionalizes the Accessibility Model in Electronic Government - e-MAG in scope of the "Sistema de Administração dos Recursos de Informação e Informática" - SISP. Official Gazette of the Union [from] Federarive Republic of Brazil 103 (87), Section 1 (May 2007) ISSN 1677-7042
3. Farwick, M., Agreiter, B., White, J., Forster, S., Lanzanasto, N., Breu, R.: A web-based collaborative metamodeling environment with secure remote model access. In: Benatallah, B., Casati, F., Kappel, G., Rossi, G. (eds.) ICWE 2010. LNCS, vol. 6189, pp. 278–291. Springer, Heidelberg (2010)
4. Thum, C., Schwind, M., Schader, M.: SLIM—A Lightweight Environment for Synchronous Collaborative Modeling. In: Schürr, A., Selic, B. (eds.) MODELS 2009. LNCS, vol. 5795, pp. 137–151. Springer, Heidelberg (2009)
5. King, A., Blenkhorn, P., Crombie, D., Dijkstra, S.J., Evans, G., Wood, J.: Presenting UML Software Engineering Diagrams to Blind People. In: Miesenberger, K., Klaus, J., Zagler, W.L., Burger, D. (eds.) ICCHP 2004. LNCS, vol. 3118, pp. 522–529. Springer, Heidelberg (2004)
6. Bigham, J.P., Cavender, A.C., Brudvik, J.T., Wobbrock, J.O., Lander, R.E.: Webinsitu: A comparative analysis of blind and sighted browsing behavior. In: Proceedings of the 9th International ACM SIGACCESS Conference on Computers and Accessibility, Assets 2007, pp. 51–58. ACM, New York (2007)
7. Vigo, M., Harper, S.: Coping tactics employed by visually disabled users on the web. Int. J. Hum. -Comput. Stud. 71(11), 1013–1025 (2013)
8. Lazarus, R.S., Folkman, S.: Stress, appraisal, and coping. Springer Pub. Co., New York (1984)

9. Takagi, H., Saito, S., Fukuda, K., Asakawa, C.: Analysis of navigability of web applications for improving blind usability. ACM Trans. Comput. -Hum. Interact. 14(3) (September 2007)
10. Leuthold, S., Bargas-Avila, J.A., Opwis, K.: Beyond web content accessibility guidelines: Design of enhanced text user interfaces for blind internet users. Int. J. Hum. -Comput. Stud. 66(4), 257–270 (2008)
11. Hillen, H., Evers, V.: Website navigation for blind users. John Wiley & Sons, Ltd. (2007) ISBN-13: 978-0-470-01866-8
12. Grillo, F.D.N., Fortes, R.P.M.: Awmo: Accessible web modeler. In: WebMedia 2013 - 19th Brazilian Symposium on Multimedia and the Web - XVII Workshop on Tools and Applications (2013)
13. Fortes, R.P.M., Dias, A.L., Grillo, F.D.N., Masiero, P.C.: Creating a project towards universal access: is it possible? In: INTERACT 2013 Workshop on Rethinking Universal Accessibility: A Broader Approach Considering the Digital Gap, Cape Town, South Africa (2013)
14. Grillo, F.D.N., Fortes, R.P.M.: Accessible modeling on the web: a case study. In: Procedia Computer Science, Proceedings of the 5th International Conference on Software Development for Enhancing Accessibility and Fighting Info-exclusion, DSAI 2013 (2013)

Choice-Based Authentication:
A Usable-Security Approach

Yasser M. Hausawi, William H. Allen, and Gisela Susanne Bahr

Department of Computer Sciences
Florida Institute of Technology
Melbourne, FL 32901, USA
{yhausawi@my., wallen@, gbahr@}fit.edu

Abstract. Authentication is an important security component of almost any software application. It serves as the application's security front door by controlling access with the goal of protecting the confidentiality and integrity of the system. However, with the large variety of software applications that an end user interacts with daily, authentication is becoming a usability issue that has the potential to weaken a system's overall security. The increasing complexity of dealing with a variety of authentication mechanisms often causes end users to develop negative security behaviours, such as writing down passwords. Moreover, some of the currently available authentication mechanisms, such as alphanumeric passwords, raise universal access issues due to both the issue of remembering a complex sequence of characters and the difficulty some individuals may have in entering that exact sequence on a keyboard or mobile device. This article proposes an authentication approach that seeks to address these usability, universal access, and security issues.

1 Introduction

Computing systems have become some of the most important tools for easily exploring and investigating the intricate nature of art, sciences, and engineering. Humans interact with systems on a daily basis to get their jobs done efficiently and effectively. However, with the revolution of information technology, humans tend to use these systems with both good and bad intentions. Consequently, security and usability have become two important quality attributes that need to be adjusted, integrated, and properly balanced. Usability assumes that humans interact with systems for the purposes for which they were built in order to perform an appropriate task, while security considers that humans may interact with systems with malevolent intent. Those two contradicting goals lead to a conflict of interest between the two attributes that is evident in irrational interaction design [2].

Human-Computer Interaction (HCI) specialists and security experts addressed this problem by forming a new solution field called usable-security [3]. Whitten and Tygar [26] define usable-security as a security system where users are aware of security tasks that need to be performed, able to figure out how those tasks are

C. Stephanidis and M. Antona (Eds.): UAHCI/HCII 2014, Part I, LNCS 8513, pp. 114–124, 2014.

properly performed, do not make harmful errors, and are comfortable with the interface. Usable-security has become a new hybrid software quality attribute with the goal of making security and usability synergistic rather than dissonant [9,11,22,25]. To this end, HCI and security experts have provided various approaches and design techniques to merge, align, and integrate usable-security, such as: user-centered interface design [5], early involvement of both security and usability [8], designation design [27], user decision-based security information [24], filtering users and transmitted data [15], using biometrics [14], using principles and patterns [9], and incorporating post-hoc security layers [10].

Authentication is one area that illustrates the security-usability conflict of interest [19]. Kumar [14] concluded that alphanumeric-password-based authentication cannot be both usable and secure at the same time and suggested graphical passwords and biometrics as alternatives to alphanumeric passwords. In contrast, Sasse et al. [23] concluded that alphanumeric passwords are not usable because usability is not considered as a fundamental security requirement.

This article proposes an authentication system that addresses usability, universal access, and security issues based on two concepts. The first concept is to allow end users to select their authentication method based on their preferences in order to provide better usability and universal access, and the second concept is to increase the difficulty for adversaries by displaying all of the possible authentication methods at one time, increasing the complexity of guessing the user's chosen authentication approach.

The next section presents background information about security, usability, usable-security, and Universal Access. Section 3 introduces our Choice-Based Authentication Approach (CBAA) along with a demonstration to the approach. Section 4 describes an informal heuristic analysis. Section 5 discusses the results of the heuristic evaluation, and Section 6 concludes this article.

2   Background

The CBAA involves two main areas in general, namely: usability and security. In addition, universal access and authentication are particularly involved. In the following, some background information is provided about the involved areas.

2.1   Security

Security is a set of related methods and techniques used together as one mechanism to protect computer systems from being negatively impacted by both legitimate users and adversaries. Any computer system has weaknesses that can be exploited to harm the system itself, its users, or its owners. As of today, there is no computer system that can be perfectly secured nor a security mechanism that can make other systems fully secure [9]. Pfleeger and Pfleeger define computer security as "preventing the weaknesses from being exploited and understanding preventive measures that make the most sense" [20]. By making the weaknesses more difficult to exploit, an acceptable degree of security may be achieved and a system's behavior can be controlled. Security researchers attempt to provide mechanisms that are reliable and cause secured systems to behave as expected. As stated by Garfinkel and Spafford: "a computer is secure if you can depend on it and its software to behave as you expect it to" [9]. To meet the above definitions, there are three primary security properties: confidentiality, integrity, and availability. Confidentiality involves restricting a system and its information so that it is only accessible to legitimate users. Integrity ensures that the alteration of system's behavior and its information is only done in an appropriate way. Availability assures that the system, its information and other resources are accessible whenever needed.

Among the above three properties, confidentiality has been the subject of considerable security research, thus many security methods and techniques have been developed to ensure confidentiality, such as authentication and access control [4,20]. Authentication is a security process that verifies an individual's identity upon access request. Access control is another security process that manages what an user can access based on policies or on a user's roles [4]. The scope of this work is limited to the authentication process. Therefore, some background information about authentication is provided here.

There are three common authentication approaches: *what an individual knows*, such as passwords, *what an individual has*, such as ID cards, and *who an individual is*, such as biometrics. The first two approaches are more traditional, while the third approach has emerged more recently. All three approaches have advantages and disadvantages (see Table 1). On one hand, the traditional authentication approaches are prone to memorability, theft and loss problems. The more modern biometric authentication is prone to privacy problems because it uses individuals' private traits that cannot be returned or changed by the individuals after they are taken. Moreover, the newer approach has not yet proven to be as reliable as the others. On the other hand, all three approaches have advantages. The traditional approaches can verify authentication methods with a high degree of accuracy, however, they cannot identify the authentication method's user. The modern approach (biometrics) can identify individuals, but cannot provide 100% accuracy.

2.2   Usability

The International Standard Organization (*ISO*) defines usability as the individuals' ability to perform a particular task effectively, efficiently, and with an accepted degree of satisfaction [12]. The ISO definition summaries a complete usability engineering process. The definition has three primary usability properties that need to be met, namely: effectiveness, efficiency, and satisfaction. Effectiveness is a product's ability to help individuals to perform a particular task successfully with a lowest number of errors. Efficiency is a product's ability to help individuals to perform a particular task effectively and within an acceptable amount of time. Satisfaction is a products ability to help individuals to perform a particular task effectively and efficiently along with an acceptable degrees of easiness, happiness, and confidence. Moreover, there are secondary properties that

Table 1. Advantages and Disadvantages of Primary Authentication Approaches

Category	Traditional		Modern
Approach	*What individuals know*	*What individuals have*	*Who individuals are*
Methods	Passwords, PINs	IDs, Tokens	Biometrics
Memory Problems	Major	Minor	Minor
Theft Problems	Major	Major	Minor
Loss Problems	Major	Major	Minor
Privacy Concerns	Moderate	Moderate	High
Matching Accuracy	High	High	Medium
Verification	Yes	Yes	Yes
Identification	No	No	Yes
Cost	Low	Medium	High
User Acceptance	Moderate	Moderate	Moderate
Universal Access	Moderate	Moderate	Moderate

have both direct and indirect impact on the three primary properties. These properties are: memorability, learnability, accuracy, and users' knowledge.

2.3 Usable-Security and Universal Access

Whitten and Tygar [26] define usable-security as a security system where users are aware of security tasks that need to be performed, are able to figure out how those tasks are properly performed, do not make harmful errors, and are comfortable with the interface. Universal Access is defined as set of techniques and methods that "seek to provide the utility of modern information technology to as broad a range of individuals as possible" [16]. Consequently, usable-security and Universal Access can be jointly defined as: a security system that can be utilized by as broad a range of individuals as possible where those individuals are aware of security tasks that need to be performed, able to figure out how those tasks are properly performed, do not make harmful errors, and are comfortable with the interface. It becomes obvious that usability is essential to Universal Access to provide universal usability for software products [16]. Moreover, usability has direct impact on a security mechanism's success through providing usable-security. From the above observations we can conclude that in order to develop a system that provides both security and Universal Access, usability must be highly considered [16].

3   Choice-Based Authentication Approach

Typical authentication systems provide one method for verifying users (passwords, ID cards, tokens, or biometrics) [13]. In some advanced authentication systems, two-factor authentication is used to verify users. Two-factor authentication is a methodology that uses two different factors, such as combining passwords, tokens or biometrics together to authenticate individuals [13]. However, the user still does not have the option to select the most suitable method of interaction with the system. It appears that two-factor authentication increases the complexity of security systems enough to make penetration more difficult [3]. This observation prompts two questions: **Is increased computational complexity necessary to make authentication systems difficult to penetrate?** and **Is there a simpler way to make security systems simultaneously usable and difficult to penetrate rather than simply adding complexity?** [10] To address the above concerns, we propose a Choice-Based Authentication Approach (CBAA) as a way to make security and usability synergistic to achieve an acceptable level of usable-security without increasing users' cognitive load.

The approach is based on two concepts. The first concept is allowing end users to select their authentication method for better usability in order to decrease users' cognitive load and increase their desire to cooperate with the system. In addition, this concept supports increasing universal access because it allows users to select from a group of authentication approaches that are most suitable for a broad range of users [16]. The second concept is increasing the difficulty for adversaries by displaying all of the possible authentication methods during the login process. The goal of this work is not to produce a novel authentication method, but rather to demonstrate that it is possible to employ currently available authentication technologies in a way that is both more secure and more usable.

3.1   CBAA Demonstration

Figures 1 and 2 show an authentication system that is based on the CBAA approach. The system uses three different authentication methods, namely: alphanumeric password based on the NIST SP 800 Series [6], graphical password based on the recall-based method [7,21], and fingerprint biometrics [1,13,16,25]. The purpose of the CBAA demonstration is to investigate whether usable-security can be achieved by giving end-users the freedom to select the authentication method they prefer. Each of the three authentication methods will be described in details as follows.

Alphanumeric Password. For the purposes of this demonstration, we derived a simplified password creation policy that was adapted from the password strength guidelines provided by the National Institute of Standards and Technology (NIST SP 800 Series) [6]. The justification for lowering the standard for this paper is to reduce the cognitive load for password creation so that it was more in line with the other techniques. However, for a real system, both the password and graphical authentication methods should have stronger requirements. The guidelines used for this paper consist of the following policy points:

1. The length of the password must be at least eight characters.
2. Must contain at least one digit (number).

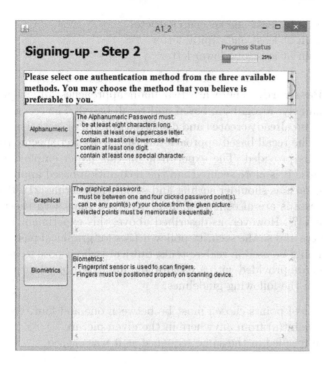

Fig. 1. A snapshot of the CBAA signing-up window that works towards usability

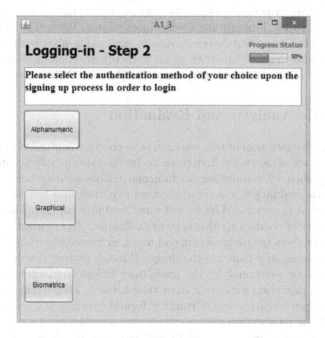

Fig. 2. A snapshot of the CBAA logging-in window that works towards security

3. Must contain at least one special character.
4. Must contain at least one capital letter.
5. Must contain at least one lower letter.

Graphical Password. There are two main approaches for graphical passwords [7,21] namely: recognition based and recall based. The recognition based approach relies on already created and displayed grids or objects that users select as passwords. The recall based approach has the user select specific points from a picture that is provided. The experiment in this paper employs the second approach because it is more secure than the recognition based approach against many attacks, such as shoulder surfing and social engineering [21]. Recall based graphical passwords are also more difficult to guess than with the recognition based approach [7]. However, as described above, this experiment is concerned with user choices and so the security policy it uses for graphical passwords is less secure than should be used in real systems. Subjects who choose to use graphical authentication are provided with a picture and are asked to select points on the image, based on the following guidelines:

1. The number of points chosen must be between one and four.
2. It can use point(s) from anywhere in the given picture.
3. It must be recalled in the same sequence as it was chosen.

Biometrics. There are many biometric traits available for authentication, such as face, fingerprint, voice, iris, signature, gait, hand geometry, palm-print, and soft biometrics [13,16]. Fingerprints are the most popular biometric trait that can easily be extracted in a controlled environment such as for lab experiments [1,25]. The subjects who choose biometrics as an authentication method are provided with a commercially-available fingerprint sensor to scan their fingerprints.

4   Heuristic Analysis and Evaluation

Although the ultimate goal of this research is to conduct controlled experiments with a wide range of users, we first chose to investigate the effectiveness of our proposed approach by conducting an informal usable-security heuristic evaluation. Heuristic evaluation is a critique-based expertise and heuristic feedback investigation that is performed by security and usability experts. There are four main advantages of conducting this type of evaluation [18]: 1) identifying minor issues to resolve them before involving end users, so formal experiments focus on major design issues, 2) enhancing the design through getting new improvement ideas that may be presented by the evaluators before conducting the official experiment, 3) providing indicative data that helps in identifying the possible directions and potential success of running formal experiments, and 4) helping to smooth off the rough edges.

Our informal usable-security heuristic evaluation for the demonstration of the proposed CBAA depends on checking the CBAA-based demonstration system's compliance with the heuristic usability principles of Jakob Nielsen [17]. Moreover, the usable-security principles of Simson Garfinkle [9] were added to the list of the principles. The informal evaluation was done with several individuals. Each expert walked through the demonstration twice and went over all of the tasks during each run. Seven persons participated in the heuristic evaluation, five males and two females. Their security and usability experience is between one and over 20 years. The following list represents the heuristics used for evaluating the demonstration:

- H_1 : **Visibility of System Status:** The system provides feedback on the status of performed.
- H_2 : **Match between System & World:** The system speaks the users' language (meaningful vocabulary, phrases, and concepts).
- H_3 : **User Control & Freedom:** The system provides the choice of "exit" at any time.
- H_4 : **Design Consistency & Security Standards:** The system provides enough consistency on flow control and objects placement, and follow standard Policies.
- H_5 : **Error Prevention:** The system itself encourages error avoidance by controlling the process flow.
- H_6 : **Recognition Support:** The system supports recognition though minimizing recall (minimizing cognitive load).
- H_7 : **Flexibility & Efficiency of Use:** The system allows skipping unnecessary or known steps (shortcut) to save time.
- H_8 : **Aesthetic & Minimalist Design:** The system provides only relevant information for each dialog.
- H_9 : **Help Users Recognize, Diagnose, and Recover from Errors:** The system provides error messages that indicate the problems and suggest proper solutions.
- H_{10} : **Help & Documentation:** The system provides instant and informative help.
- H_{11} : **Least Surprise & Astonishment:** The system avoids surprising and astonishing users with unexpected information or actions.
- H_{12} : **Good Security Now:** The system adopts up-to-date security techniques.
- H_{13} : **No External Burden:** The system avoid affecting other systems and applications negatively.

5 Results and Discussion

Results of the heuristic evaluation are displayed in Figure 3. The heuristic evaluation levels are ranged between 6.7 and 9.3 with an overall average evaluation level of 8.1.

Both H_2 and H_{12} received the highest evaluation level (9.3). This indicates that the CBAA system uses meaningful vocabulary, phrases, and concepts that

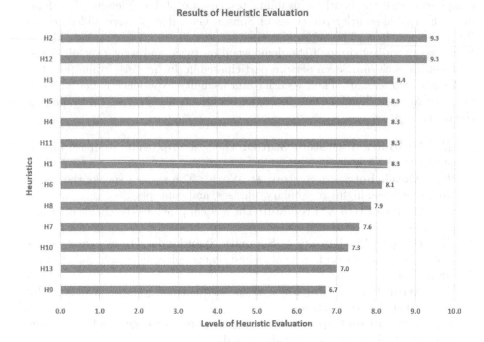

Fig. 3. The Results of Heuristic evaluation

speak end users' language. Moreover, the system adapts up-to-date security techniques through using graphical passwords and biometrics (fingerprints). H_1, H_3, H_4, H_5, and H_{11} were evaluated at levels between 8.4 and 8.1, which indicates that the system provides feedback on the status of user's progress. Moreover, it allows users to exit at any time, provides consistent flow control and object placement of the design along with following the standard authentication policies, encourages error avoidance by controlling the process flow, avoids unexpected information and/or actions. However, these points could be enhanced more. The rest of the heuristic points (i.e. H_6, H_7, H_8, H_9, H_{10}, and H_{13}) were evaluated at levels below 8, which indicates that more work is needed to enhance the usable-security of the proposed system through improving these heuristics. We concluded that the system should be enhanced in the following ways:

- Helping end users to recognize the authentication processes without having to recall much information or need experience to interact with the proposed authentication approach.
- Allowing end users to skip unnecessary steps through providing shortcuts, so users can move to the other authentication methods at any time.
- Focusing on only providing relevant information for each dialog.
- Supporting end users with helpful error messages that clearly explain the error and suggest solutions.
- Providing adequate help and documentation.

After analyzing the results of the heuristic evaluation, we revised the demonstration version of the CBAA to address the usability and security points that were shown to need further enhancement. The latest version of the interface will be used for future usable-security research that compares usable-security level between the proposed CBAA and the currently available standard-based authentication systems, to determine whether the CBAA that we proposed provides better usable-security than the authentication systems that are currently available. A full-scale survey of a wide range of users is planned and the results will be submitted for publication in the future.

6   Conclusion

We proposed a Choice-Based Authentication Approach (CBAA) that is based on two concepts: end-users' preference of authentication method to address usability and universal access concerns, and improved security by raising the bar for adversaries. Future work will focus on investigating whether this approach provides better usable-security than the standard single-authentication approach, as more work is needed to determine how responsive this approach is to end-users with differing levels of security experience.

References

1. AL-Harby, F., Qahwaji, R., Kamala, M.: Users' acceptance of secure biometrics authentication system: Reliability and validate of an extended UTAUT model. In: Zavoral, F., Yaghob, J., Pichappan, P., El-Qawasmeh, E. (eds.) NDT 2010. CCIS, vol. 87, pp. 254–258. Springer, Heidelberg (2010)
2. Bahr, G.S., Allen, W.H.: Rational interfaces for effective security software: Polite interaction guidelines for secondary tasks. In: Stephanidis, C., Antona, M. (eds.) UAHCI 2013, Part I. LNCS, vol. 8009, pp. 165–174. Springer, Heidelberg (2013)
3. Balfanz, D., Durfee, G., Smetters, D.K., Grinter, R.E.: In search of usable security: Five lessons from the field. IEEE Security & Privacy 2(5), 19–24 (2004)
4. Bertino, E., Martino, L., Paci, F., Squicciarini, A.: Security for Web Services and Service-Oriented Architectures. Springer Publishing Company (2009) (Incorporated)
5. Braz, C., Robert, J.-M.: Security and usability: The case of the user authentication methods. In: Proceedings of the 18th International Conferenceof the Association Francophone d'Interaction Homme-Machine, pp. 199–203. ACM (2006)
6. Burr, W.E., Dodson, D.F., Newton, E.M., Perlner, R.A., Polk, W.T., Gupta, S., Nabbus, E.A.: Sp 800-63-1. electronic authentication guideline (2011)
7. Dirik, A.E., Memon, N., Birget, J.C.: Modeling user choice in the passpoints graphical password scheme. In: Proceedings of the 3rd Symposium on Usable Privacy and Security, pp. 20–28. ACM (2007)
8. Flechais, I., Mascolo, C., Sasse, M.A.: Integrating security and usability into the requirements and design process. International Journal of Electronic Security and Digital Forensics 1(1), 12–26 (2007)
9. Garfinkel, S.: Design Principles and Patterns for Computer Systems that are Simultaneously Secure and Usable. Ph.D. thesis, Massachusetts Institute of Technology (2005)

10. Gutmann, P., Grigg, I.: Security usability. IEEE Security & Privacy 3(4), 56–58 (2005)
11. Hausawi, Y.M., Mayron, L.M.: Towards usable and secure natural language processing systems. In: HCI International 2013 Extended Abstracts, pp. 109–113. Springer (2013)
12. ISO, W.: 9241-11. ergonomic requirements for office work with visual display terminals (VDTs). The international organization for standardization (1998)
13. Jain, A.K., Ross, A.A.A., Nandakumar, K.: Introduction to biometrics. Springer (2011)
14. Kumar, N.: Password in practice: An usability survey. Journal of Global Research in Computer Science 2(5), 107–112 (2011)
15. Lampson, B.: Privacy and security usable security: How to get it. Communications of the ACM 52(11), 25–27 (2009)
16. Mayron, L.M., Hausawi, Y., Bahr, G.S.: Secure, usable biometric authentication systems. In: Stephanidis, C., Antona, M. (eds.) UAHCI 2013, Part I. LNCS, vol. 8009, pp. 195–204. Springer, Heidelberg (2013)
17. Nielsen, J.: Heuristic evaluation. Usability inspection methods 17, 25–62 (1994)
18. Nielsen, J.: How to conduct a heuristic evaluation (2001) (retrieved November 10)
19. Payne, B.D., Edwards, W.K.: A brief introduction to usable security. IEEE Internet Computing 12(3), 13–21 (2008)
20. Pfleeger, C.P., Pfleeger, S.L.: Security in Computing. Prentice Hall PTR (2006)
21. Sarohi, H.K., Khan, F.U.: Graphical password authentication schemes: Current status and key issues (2013)
22. Sasse, M.A.: Computer security: Anatomy of a usability disaster, and a plan for recovery. In: Proceedings of CHI 2003 Workshop on HCI and Security Systems, Citeseer (2003)
23. Sasse, M.A., Brostoff, S., Weirich, D.: Transforming the weakest link a human/computer interaction approach to usable and effective security. BT Technology Journal 19(3), 122–131 (2001)
24. Stoll, J., Tashman, C.S., Edwards, W.K., Spafford, K.: Sesame: Informing user security decisions with system visualization. In: Proceedings of the Twenty-Sixth Annual SIGCHI Conference on Human Factors in Computing Systems, pp. 1045–1054. ACM (2008)
25. Toledano, D.T., Pozo, R.F., Trapote, Á.H., Gómez, L.H.: Usability evaluation of multi-modal biometric verification systems. Interacting with Computers 18(5), 1101–1122 (2006)
26. Whitten, A., Tygar, J.D.: Why johnny cant encrypt: A usability evaluation of pgp 5.0. In: Proceedings of the 8th USENIX Security Symposium, vol. 99, McGraw-Hill (1999)
27. Yee, K.-P.: Aligning security and usability. IEEE Security & Privacy 2(5), 48–55 (2004)

3D Facial Biometric Database – Search and Reconstruction of Objects Based on PCA Modes

Michal Rychlik, Witold Stankiewicz, and Marek Morzynski

Poznan University of Technology, Department of Virtual Engineering,
Piotrowo 3, 60965 Poznan, Poland
{Michal.Rychlik,Witold.Stankiewicz,
Marek.Morzynski}@put.poznan.pl

Abstract. This article presents application of modal analysis for the computation of biometric data base (3D faces) and extraction of three dimensional geometrical features. Traditional anthropometric database contains information only about some characteristic points recorded as linear or angular dimensions. The current face recognition systems are also based on the two-dimensional information. To increase level of security the methods need to operate on three-dimensional data. In the article authors present of 3D modal analysis, for decomposition, extraction features and individual coding of analyzed objects sets. Authors apply empirical modal analysis PCA (Principal Component Analysis) for 3D data of human faces. Additionally for face recognition, the comparison of reconstruction with different number of modes are presented and discussed.

Keywords: 3D geometry reconstruction, data registration, low-dimensional model, modal analysis, Principal Component Analysis (PCA).

1 Introduction

Human face is the one of the elements of our being, which is using for recognition of the people. This is the most natural and one of the oldest (next to voice recognition) known biometric systems that are in daily use for thousands of years.

From the first days of life man develops the ability to memorize and recognize facial features. Skill of the face recognition with voice recognition ability gives us the possibility almost 100% effective in identifying persons. However, this high efficiency is reserved only for the people we know. In case that we do not know the person (thereby her facial features and voice), we are not able to capture the subtle differences but only the general features and significant differences.

Biometrics identifies people by measuring some individual aspects of anatomy, physiology or other behavioral characteristic [1]. Nowadays can biometric systems can used many different elements e.g.: face, fingerprints, hand geometry, signature or voice. Type features used to identify persons determines use of the different input data, such as the shape of the face [3, 17], hand [8, 18] and even the whole human body [2].

C. Stephanidis and M. Antona (Eds.): UAHCI/HCII 2014, Part I, LNCS 8513, pp. 125–136, 2014.
© Springer International Publishing Switzerland 2014

Facial identification reads the peaks and valleys of facial features, known as nodal points. In a human face there exist 80 points, but usually only 15-20 of them, known as „Golden triangle", are used for identification.

The problem with face recognition is not only acquisition of the clear data, but also many other aspects like illumination, clothing parts (hat, sunglasses, jewelry), hairiness (beard, long hair), makeup. Some of these elements can be used in everyday life to face beautify, but also somebody can specifically used to falsify the true facial features [5]. Another aspect of face geometry except facial expression is lip movements and facial muscles during speaking.

Insufficient reliability of the currently used 2D recognition techniques (photos contain less information then the 3D surface) stimulates interest in 3D or even 4D techniques [11].

In future research works, more aspects of using 3D/4D biometrical systems should be considered include also the ergonomics. Ergonomic quality, is not as earlier dependent on one or several factors that a user can affect, but results from a whole range of elements of the macro environment [4].

Rapid increase of the amount of data to be analyzed leads to the need for modal analysis methods. These methods are used to simplify and minimize the number of parameters which describe objects. The kind of used modal method: mathematical, physical or empirical (PCA/POD), has a fundamental influence on the results [12, 13].

This paper will present advances in use of 3D face biometric database based on Principal Component Analysis. In further sections will be presents and discuss procedure of collecting 3D data, PCA decomposition and 3D face geometry reconstruction of the real data.

2   Acquisition of 3D Face – Input Data

There are several methods which can be used to collect data of the 3D face geometry. In 2D biometric systems usually the single camera is used. In this approach, the most important is adequate lighting of the face and ensure visibility of the most important points in the area of the so-called. "golden triangle".

It is possible to create the 3D object from single two-dimensional image [9], but obtained model is not always high accuracy. From this reason it can be not enough for more complex 3D systems. For better results the stereo acquisitions systems or 3D scanners can be used. Stereo acquisition systems based on images, collected in the same time from two or more cameras [15]. Depending on used algorithms the different results are obtained. The newest systems are fast enough to acquire and processing 3D data in real time, creating 4D systems in which the fourth dimension is time [11]. The more accurate 3D models (higher resolution data) offer 3D scanners. Usually for biometrics the touch less (optical) methods are used. There are two most often techniques used: structural light scanners and laser scanners. Disadvantage of such solution is necessary to use, in addition to camera, an extra medium (as a structured light pattern or laser beam) and longer time off data acquisition (laser scanners). Furthermore the laser scanners are slower than stereo acquisition systems and structural light scanners.

In presented work the professional 3D structural light scanner was used. For this scanner the measuring volume is 400x300x210mm with resolution 0.05mm.

In order to provide equal conditions of scanning for all objects (human faces) during measuring process, the special face positioner was used (Fig. 1. a). The purpose of positioner is providing a similar setting for each scanned face: optimal measuring distance (about 90cm from the scanner detector), increase stability (elimination of involuntary head movement during data recording) and repeatability position regardless of the individual features of the scanned person. The positioner has a special pitch angle with lock, allowing head set in the range of angles of +/− 75^0 (Fig. 1. b).

a)   b)

Fig. 1. The special face positioner: a) general view, b) pitch angle with the locking position

Each person subjected the scan takes place on a chair and puts his face to the abutment elements of the positioner. The face of a person is measured from three different directions in the three consecutive measurements (Figure 2 a, b, c). The first measurement is set "an face" corresponding to an angle of 0^0 to the positioner, the second measurement refers to the right facial profile and is made with 45^0 set on the positioner, third measurement shows left profile face (-30^0 angle positioner). The asymmetry of the angular set positioner result of the construction of a scanner having only one detector. Each measurement is performed with a facial expression similar to recommended in the performance of two-dimensional images of biometric documents.

a)   b)   c)

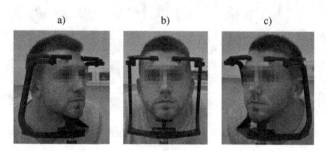

Fig. 2. The face scanning procedure: a) right profile of the face (positioner angle $+45^0$, b) an face direction, c) left profile of the face (positioner angle -30^0).

The result of the scanning process is a set of three point clouds (Fig. 3. a) containing a total of about 750k measuring points describing the geometry of the face from three different directions.

Each obtained point cloud were subjected to processing of: removing the errors of points (called noise), smoothing and removing the discontinuity areas that contain other components such as ears, fragments of the neck, the hairs (Fig. 3 b).

The next steps have been to overlapping (the registration process) and connect the individual point clouds into one homogenous (Fig. 3 c).

a)   b)   b)

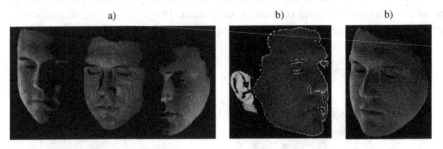

Fig. 3. The point clouds processing: a) set of scanned data from three directions, b) removing of the errors (bright color), c) final homogenous point cloud of the face

In the last stage the point cloud were subjected to triangulation process – "coupling" triangle mesh at each points of the cloud. The resulting surface model still requires further treatment related with the removal of triangulation errors and fill gaps in the data source. The final result of processing is three-dimensional surface mesh consisting of about 500k triangles, describing the face of the person being scanned.

In this work more than 100 faces of different persons (male and female, age: 22-24 years old) with neutral expression was acquired.

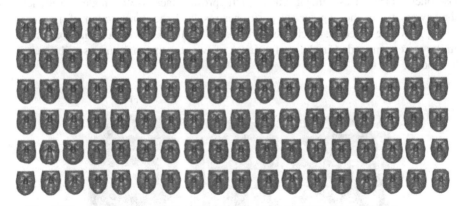

Fig. 4. Visualization of the 3D face database – more than 100 faces of different persons.

3   3D Data Registration

To enable fast work with the large number of data – 3D face database – the modal decomposition can be used. There are several types of modal methods but one of the well known are methods based Proper Orthogonal Decomposition (POD) or Principal Component Analysis (PCA). These methods have some variants like: Snapshot method, Kernel PCA [6], Multilinear PCA [10] or Generalized POD.

PCA provides a "relevant" set of basis functions, which allows construction of a low-dimensional subspace. PCA modes are optimal from viewpoint of information included inside of the each modes. The shape of each object is represented in the data base as the set of 3D polygonal surface and stored as a vector. PCA consists in centering of objects (by subtracting the average geometry) and the calculation of the covariance matrix [7]. Eigenvectors of this matrix (PCA modes) represent the geometrical features (shape) of the object

The Principal Component Analysis requires the same position, orientation and topology of the data input (the same number of nodes, matrix connection, etc.) for all objects. To achieve this, each new object added to database must be registered.

The registration process used in this work is performed by special developed algorithm and numerical tool (based on kd-tree searching algorithm) which is consists of three stages [14].

First stage (preliminary registration) – involves series of affine transformations (shift, rotation and scaling) to set scanned face on position in a coordinate system.

The second stage (elastic registration) consists of five steps:

1. Detection of edge elements lying on the boundary of the face;
2. Automatic detection of 16 specific points on the surface of the registrant face defining regional features: eyes, nose, mouth, beard / chin;
3. The displacement of boundary curve points of reference grid onto new position on registrant grid;
4. Displacement of characteristic points of the reference grid in the corresponding position on the registrant grid;
5. Interpolation of the position of other nodes on reference grid basing on the known boundary conditions.

The third stage (finishing registration) – is the transfer of all the nodes in the reference grid to the position defined by the points lying on the registered grid.

The result of the applied registration procedure is description of all faces in data base by the same (in topological meaning) surface mesh. The value of standard deviation between source and registered faces was 0.054mm and average distance 0.008mm.

4   Modal Decomposition of 3D Faces Database

PCA decomposition gives orthogonal directions of principal variation of input data. Variation is described by eigenvalue related to the first principal component. The further principal components, describe the next in order, orthogonal directions in the space with the largest variation of data.

Generally only few first principal components are describing majority variations of the data. Data projected onto other principal components often has small amplitude, lower than value of measurement noise (scanner error). Therefore they can be deleted, without decreasing the accuracy. The used algorithm is based on statistical representation of the random variables [16].

Because few first modes carry most information, therefore each original object S_i is reconstructed by using some K principal components (1):

$$S_i = \overline{S} + \sum_{k=1}^{K} a_{ki} \Psi_k, \; i = 1, 2, \ldots, M, \tag{1}$$

where Ψ_k is an eigenvector representing the orthogonal mode (the feature computed from data base), a_{ki} is coefficient of eigenvector.

For prepared database of human faces the PCA analysis was performed. The result of this operation is the mean face, modes and a set of coefficients values (Fig. 5). To reconstruct 90% of information about decomposed geometry, it is enough to used the first 19 modes (Table 1).

Table 1. Participation of the first 20 modes in PCA decomposition of 3D faces

Number of the mode	Participation of the mode [%]	Total participation of the modes [%]
1	24,6826618	24,6826618
2	13,8607809	38,5434427
3	9,2869719	47,8304146
4	8,0263284	55,8567429
5	6,6289872	62,4857302
6	5,4689992	67,9547294
7	4,2335093	72,1882386
8	3,4046341	75,5928727
9	3,0812213	78,6740939
10	2,0491344	80,7232284
11	1,9885962	82,7118246
12	1,4060026	84,1178272
13	1,2429369	85,3607641
14	1,0910051	86,4517692
15	0,9615076	87,4132768
16	0,8416507	88,2549274
17	0,7555748	89,0105023
18	0,7096819	89,7201841
19	0,6701088	90,3902929
20	0,6467980	91,0370909

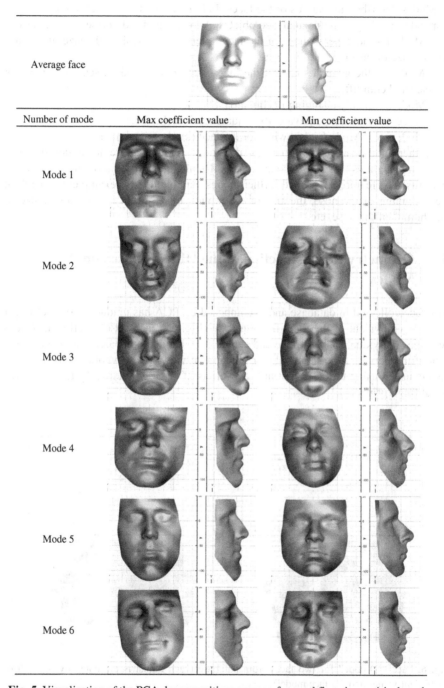

Fig. 5. Visualization of the PCA decomposition: average face and first six empirical modes

Modes describe the features of the faces. Individual modes geometric changes correspond to the largest in the analyzed objects. Another modes describes accordingly:

- Mode 1 - the general shape of the face - slenderness, scaling the size of the face and the size of the chin;
- Mode 2 - the general shape of the face - trapezoidal ovality, scaling the size of the face and chin lift;
- Mode 3 - mainly changing in chin area;
- Mode 4 - ovality or equivalently "squareness" of the face;
- Mode 5 and Mode 6 - "skewing" of the face (kind of asymmetry).

Further modes with lower energy determine another more local deformations (biometric features), in consequence more difficult for interpretation and description in words. The features described further modes may include for example: the depth of the beginning of the nose, the size of the mouth, the position of the mouth, size of the "hump" of the nose, etc.

5   Geometry Reconstruction of the Objects Based on PCA Modes

Any face collected in database and decomposed by PCA has unique set of coefficient values – equivalent of the identification code (Fig. 6). Each set of coefficient values describes individual shape of face and can be decoded and compared with the original data of the person. Also identical (for human eye view) monozygotic twins might be distinguished using these "faceprints" as well as 2D face biometrics systems or traditional fingerprints [5].

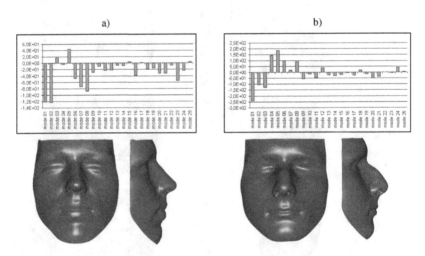

Fig. 6. Face "ID code" for two faces from database (each object is presented by – graph of coefficient values and 3D face model)

For randomly selected face from the database the reconstruction of the geometry was done. Presented reconstruction was performed with a different number of modes: 1, 4, 12 and 25 modes (Fig. 7 - row 1). For each reconstruction step - starting from the average face - a comparative analysis was made of the surface mesh of the model obtained in reconstruction (Fig. 7 – row 2) to the reference face model (original source 3D face model used for the analysis of PCA).

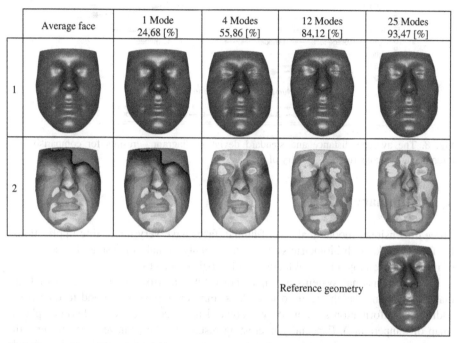

Fig. 7. Visualization of the reconstruction with using a different number of modes: 1) the surface mesh shape, 2) maps of the average deviation between a reference and reconstructed grid (bright color – max "+" deviation, dark color min "–"negative deviation).

The numerical values of the average distance and standard deviation of the compared surfaces (reference and reconstructed faces) are shown in Table 2 and illustrated on the graph (Figure 8).

Table 2. Results of the surfaces comparison of reference and reconstructed face

Number of the modes used for reconstruction	Average distance [mm]	Standard deviation [mm]
Average face	-1,630373	2,544203
1	-1,760347	2,515758
4	-0,918404	2,202656
12	-0,144863	0,825188
25	0,027492	0,577073

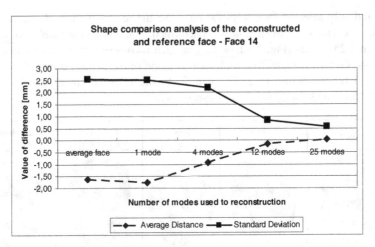

Fig. 8. The average distance and standard deviation diagram – results for comparison of reference and reconstructed geometry of the faces.

6   Summary

Three dimensional modal analyses of human faces have very interesting implications for future works with biometric systems. Such analysis makes possible the extraction of mean shape and geometrical features of biological object set.

Three dimensional systems are more powerful and stronger on any kind of fake than 2D systems which are used nowadays. Further is possible to add to data base additional information's (not only geometrical data) like e.g. thermal photo (map of temperature). Especially interesting results can be achieved with using 4-th dimension – time. Such "real time" systems can be applied for extraction individual movements of some regions of the face.

Presented method as the source of data-input, apply full 3D face information – instead of "control" points set (few nodal points in "golden triangle" area). The 3D geometry of the face (3D faceprint) is more complicated than "flat" image and by this way more proof onto fake than 2D face recognition systems.

The quality of the registration process has a fundamental importance onto results obtained in modal analysis. For 3D faces three-step registration process allows obtaining very precise final model. In presented article accuracy of registration process was better than accuracy of 3D scanning (0.05mm) used for data acquisition.

For testing of sensitivity level of proposed faceprints method the twin's faces can be used. Numerical experiments confirm that even the similarity faces of monozygotic twin's can be analyzed and coded with using PCA analysis.

Presented in article results of face reconstruction (with using different numbers of modes), showing that it is possible to obtain high quality 3d models with using low number of data. This is very important if such system will be work with data collected from all citizens of the country.

Additional mean shape and geometrical features of the faces (knowledge about shape and trends of deformations) can be used to create new three dimensional data base for forensics and police departments. Such 3D database can be important in anthropology, gives information about the changes that appear in the human skeletal structure in different populations or ages.

References

1. Anderson, R.J.: Security Engineering: A Guide to Building Dependable Distributed Systems. Wiley Publishing Inc., Indiana (2008)
2. Brett, A., Curless, B., Popović, Z.: The space of human body shapes: reconstruction and parameterization from range scans. ACM Transactions on Graphics (TOG) 22(3) (2003)
3. Bruce, D.A., et al.: Recognizing faces with PCA and ICA. Computer Vision and Image Understanding 91(1), 115–137 (2003)
4. Butlewski, M., Tytyk, E.: The assessment criteria of the ergonomic quality of anthropotechnical mega-systems. In: Vink, P. (ed.) Advances in Social and Organizational Factors, pp. 298–306. CRC Press, Taylor and Francis Group, Boca Raton, London (2012)
5. Gökberk, B., Salah, A.A., Akarun, L., Etheve, R., Riccio, D., Dugelay, J.L.: 3D face recognition. In: Guide to Biometric Reference Systems and Performance Evaluation, pp. 263–295. Springer, London (2009)
6. Hoffmann, H.: Kernel PCA for Novelty Detection. Pattern Recognition 40, 863–874 (2007)
7. Holmes, P., Lumley, J.: Turbulence, Coherent Structures, Dynamical Systems and Symmetry. Cambridge University Press, Cambridge (1998)
8. Jain, A.K., Ross, A., Pankanti, S.: A prototype hand geometry based verification system. In: Proceeding 2nd Int. Conf. Audio- and Video-Based Biometric Person Authentication, pp. 166–171 (1999)
9. Kuo, C.J., Huang, R.-S., Lin, T.-G.: 3-D facial model estimation from single front-view facial image. IEEE Transactions on Circuits and Systems for Video Technology 12(3), 183–192 (2002)
10. Lu, H., Plataniotis, K.N., Venetsanopoulos, A.N.: MPCA: Multilinear principal component analysis of tensor objects. IEEE Trans. Neural Netw. 19(1), 18–39 (2008)
11. Papatheodorou, T., Rueckert, D.: Evaluation of automatic 4D face recognition using surface and texture registration. In: Proceedings of the Sixth IEEE International Conference on IEEE Automatic Face and Gesture Recognition, pp. 321–326 (2004)
12. Rychlik, M., Stankiewicz, W.: Extraction of 3D Geometrical Features of Biological Objects with 3D PCA Analysis and Applications of Results. In: Naik, G.R. (ed.) Applied Biological Engineering – Principles and Practice, pp. 85–112. InTech (2012)
13. Rychlik, M., Stankiewicz, W., Morzyński, M.: Application of modal analysis for extraction of geometrical features of biological objects set. In: BIODEVICES 2008: Proc. 1st Int. Conf. Biomed. Electronics and Devices, vol. 2, pp. 227–232 (2008)
14. Rychlik, M., Stankiewicz, W., Morzynski, M.: Biological Objects Data Registration Algorithm for Modal (Low Dimensional) Analysis. In: HCI International 2013 - Posters' Extended Abstracts, Communications in Computer and Information Science, vol. 373, pp. 655–659. Springer, Heidelberg (2013)

15. Seitz, S.M., Curless, B., Diebel, J., Scharstein, D., Szeliski, R.: A comparison and evaluation of multi-view stereo reconstruction algorithms. In: 2006 IEEE Computer Society Conference on Computer Vision and Pattern Recognition, vol. 1, pp. 519–528 (2006)
16. Stankiewicz, W., Roszak, R., Morzynski, M., Noack, B.R., Tadmor, G.: Continuous Mode Interpolation between Multiple Operating and Boundary Conditions for Reduced Order Modelling of the Flow. AIP Conference Proceedings 1389(1), 94–97 (2011)
17. Xuerong, C., Jing, Z., Xiao, G.: Nonlinear fusion for face recognition using fuzzy integral. Comm. Nonlin. Science and Num. Sim. 12(5), 823–831 (2007)
18. Yörük, E., Dutağaci, H., Sankur, B.: Hand biometrics. Image and Vision Computing 24(5), 483–497 (2006)

Improved Model-Driven Engineering of User-Interfaces with Generative Macros

Anthony Savidis[1,2], Yannis Valsamakis[1], and Yannis Lilis[1]

[1] Institute of Computer Science, FORTH
[2] Department of Computer Science, University of Crete, Greece
{as,jvalsam,lilis}@ics.forth.gr

Abstract. Model-driven engineering entails various modeling, abstraction and specialization levels for user-interface development. We focus on model-driven tools generating user-interface code, either entire or partial, providing a tangible basis for programmers to introduce custom refinements and extensions. The latter introduces two maintenance issues: (i) once the generated code is modified the source-to-model extraction path, if supported, is broken; and (ii) if the model is updated, code regeneration overwrites custom changes. To address these issues we proposed an alternative path: (i) instead of directly generating code, the model driven tool generates source fragments in the form of abstract syntax trees (ASTs) as XML files; (ii) the application deploys compile-time metaprogramming to manipulate, generate and insert code on-demand from such ASTs, using calls similar to macro invocations. The latter leads to improved separation of concerns: (a) the application programmer controls when and where interface source is generated and integrated in the application source; and (b) interface regeneration overwrites no source code as it only produces ASTs that are manipulated (input) via generator macros.

Keywords: Model-Driven Development, Model-Based User-Interfaces, Code Generation, Compile-Time Metaprogramming.

1 Introduction

In general, model-driven engineering (MDE) of user interfaces [3] involves tools, models, processes, methods and algorithms addressing the demanding problem of automated user-interface engineering. An important authoring requirement for MDE tools is to involve notions and concerns inherent in the design domain, typically including tasks, user profiles, context characteristics, interaction controls, abstract behaviors, and input events. Then, a target implementation is incrementally derived, usually with an intermediate transition from the modeling domain to an instantiation domain that is in most cases platform independent. This discipline is outlined under Fig. 1, showing the typical specialization from abstract to platform that most MDE tools adopt, and the shift from abstract to concrete implying a sort of transformation.

C. Stephanidis and M. Antona (Eds.): UAHCI/HCII 2014, Part I, LNCS 8513, pp. 137–148, 2014.
© Springer International Publishing Switzerland 2014

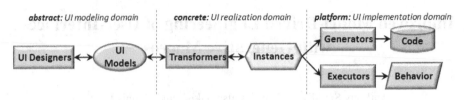

Fig. 1. High-level overview of the model-driven user-interface development process showing tool roles with respective inputs and outputs

Currently, many MDE tools emphasize the delivery of user-interface source code (like wxFormBuilder and Microsoft Visual Studio), thus encompassing user-interface code generators, sometimes capable to cater for varying programming languages and target platforms. Alternatively, MDE tools may provide executors, usually falling in the domain of interaction interpreters, which directly offer the required end-user dialogue (such as the XCode Interface Builder). The latter actually interpret the various produced concrete instances and their accompanying internal interface representations, as resulting from the transformations on the abstract modeling domain. In our work we generally focus on MDE tools that eventually generate user-interface source code, such tools ranging from common interface builders to entire model-driven application framework generators.

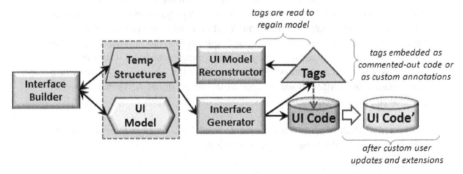

Fig. 2. General architecture of interface builders involving: (1) interactive editing with the builder; (2) code generation from an explicit interface model or temporary structures; and (3) only when temporary structures are used, tags are inserted in the source code.

In the context of our case study we considered interface builders – their general process diagram is outlined under Fig. 2. Interface builders usually support an explicit interface model, usually in a custom user-interface description language (UIDL). Alternatively, they may rely on special tags carrying model information, such tags explicitly embedded in the generated source as commented-out code. Through tags, no interface model is explicitly stored, except temporary structures which are available only during authoring time.

We continue with the identification of the maintenance problem inherent in user-interface code generation, and then brief the key contributions of our work to address this issue.

1.1   Identification of the Problem

MDE tools, whether finally offering user-interface source code generation or an execution system at the platform level, can hardly address all required aspects of an interactive user-interface. As a result, custom user-interface source code amendments and modifications are always anticipated. Even there are evolved tools in Model-Driven of user-interfaces area; none of them can completely construct the user-interface of applications. In our context we focus only on MDE tools generating user-interface source code because we consider they are more flexible by supporting evolution and customization of the user-interface directly at the source level.

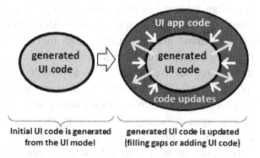

Fig. 3. Typical growth of user-interface application code around generated user-interface code with custom extensions and updates, eventually leading to bidirectional dependencies.

With such MDE tools, the typical lifecycle of the generated user-interface code is outlined under Fig. 3. In particular, typical updates relate to user-interface application functionality importing and invocation, event handling extensions, custom user-interface management logic, and linkage to third-party libraries that are not known to the MDE tool. This situation very quickly results into many bidirectional dependencies as indicated at the right part of **Fig. 3**.

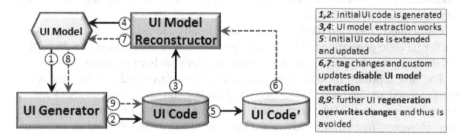

Fig. 4. The primary maintenance issue inherent in user-interface source generation under model-driven development

The problem with this scenario is that it introduces serious maintenance issues (see Fig. 4). Initially, once the user-interface code is not changed, user-interface regeneration and user-interface model reconstruction is well-defined (steps 1 to 4). In other words, the MDE tool works perfectly for both steps of the processing loop. However, once the generated UI code is updated (step 5), two problems directly appear. Firstly, tag editing and misplacing may break model reconstruction (steps 6 and 7), while the manually inserted UI logic outside the MDE tool causes a model-implementation conflict. Secondly, source regeneration overwrites all manually introduced updates (steps 8 and 9). For real life applications of a considerable scale the latter may lead to adoption of the MDE tool only for the first version, or worse avoiding using an MDE tool at all.

1.2   Primary Contributions

Our main contribution is an inversed responsibility model for generator MDE tools where: (a) UI generation takes place only in the form of ASTs; and (b) the actual code generation is applied on-demand and in-place through metaprograms (macros) that are included in the implementation of the interactive system and are evaluated at compile-time (i.e. during the build process). This approach, not only resolves the maintenance issues of traditional UI generators, but also sets user-interface code manipulation as a first-class concept in user-interface management and reveals the value of metaprogramming languages in the engineering of interactive systems.

Overall, we propose an improved process where the MDE tool outcome is read-only, decoupled from UI code generation, letting interactive applications directly deploy and manipulate code fragments, instead of being built around them. In this context, we discuss the most common composition practices on user-interface code fragments through ASTs as consolidated from our case study.

2   Related Work

Several UI source code generators exist in the arena of MDE tools and most of them are incorporated into UI Builders. Some of them are GrafiXML [10], GuiBuilder [11], GtkBuilder [12], wxFormBuilder [9] etc none of which has addressed the maintenance issues we have discussed.

Furthermore, there are relevant works that partially address the maintenance issues not for UI code generation but for general purpose source code generation. In particular, there are two different ways in which the problem has been approached.

The first approach includes special tags or annotations which are inserted within the generated source code. Developers may further edit such annotations to specify whether certain parts of the source code should be maintained or not upon regeneration. However, free editing may cause tag misplacement and thus result in manual updates being discarded upon regeneration. In the one hand, tags address the problem; on the other hand there is extra responsibility for developers. Tools which adopt this approach are EMF [13], Acceleo [14], Actifsource [15] etc.

The second approach is based on the full MDE development cycle allowing both model-to-source and source-to-model transformations. For the latter, they parse source files locating specific code structures (e.g. Classes, Attributes, Operations etc.) in order to regenerate the model, while treating any additional code they include as metadata. This is an important step towards resolving the maintenance issues; however, it cannot be applied in case of MDE tools for UI code generation, because it is practically impossible to recognize the widget elements by parsing manually written source code. Tools which adopt this approach are Papyrus [16] and Modelio [17].

3   Staged Metaprograms

Generally, metaprogramming relates to functions which generate code, i.e. programs producing other programs, while metaprogramming languages take the task of code generation and support it as a first-class language feature. This is a sort of reification of the language code generator enabling programmers write code which generates extra source code. When available as a macro system before compilation, the method is known as compile-time metaprogramming. Alternatively, if offered during runtime, usually built on top of the language reflection mechanism, it is called runtime metaprogramming. We focus on compile-time metaprogramming being more powerful to its runtime case. In this context, code generating macros are functions manipulating code in the form of ASTs, and are evaluated by a separate stage preceding normal compilation. Then, they are substituted in the source text by the code they actually produce. Due to the introduction of an extra stage, and because macros may generate further macros, thus requiring extra staging, such languages are also called multistage languages [2, 4]. In our work we use Delta [1], a recent publicly available dynamic object-oriented language, its wx widgets library, and its compile-time metaprogramming extension [5, 6]. Popular meta-languages include Lisp, Scheme, Macro ML [7], Meta OCaml [8], Meta Lua and Converge.

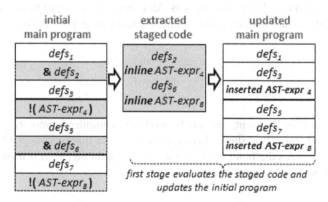

Fig. 5. Metaprogram evaluation as a compilation stage

In the Delta language, meta-code involves meta definitions and inline directives (i.e., code generation), prefixed with the **&** and **!** symbols respectively. In particular, inline directives accept an expression returning an AST and are the only way to insert extra code into the main program.

As shown under Fig. 5, in the first stage the compiler: (i) collects all scattered meta-code into a single metaprogram; (ii) evaluates the program while internally recording the output the inline calls; and (iii) removes all meta-code from the initial program and replaces inline directives by the code they actually produced. For example, consider the following Delta code.

```
1: using wx;
2: &ast = ui::load_ast ("<some ast path>");
3: !(ast);   ← code generation (inline) directive
```

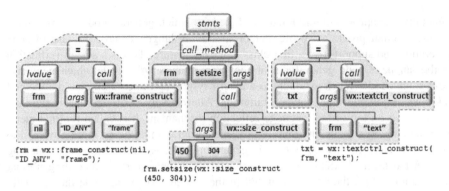

Fig. 6. Example of an abstract syntax tree for three statements using the wx widgets library: (i) *left*: creating a frame widget; (ii) *middle*: setting its size; and (iii) *right*: creating a text widget

The first line is normal code, a typical directive to import the wx widgets library. But the next two lines are meta-code, distinguished by **&** and **!** prefixes. The second line loads an AST from a file, assume the loaded AST to be the one of Fig. 6. The third line inserts the code implied by this AST into the main program. As a result, after the first stage, and before normal compilation, the main program is:

```
using wx;
frm = wx::frame_construct(nil, "ID_ANY", "calculator");
frm.setsize(wx::size_construct(450, 300);
txt = wx::textctrl_construct(frm, "text");
```

Such code is only transient, and exists inside the compiler temporarily during the first compilation stage. It is shown here for clarity. After this first stage, the resulting source text constitutes the input to the normal compilation phase, as if it was originally written this way by the programmer.

4   Improved Model-Driven Process

The primary motivation for our work has been the serious user-interface source code maintenance issue inherent in model-driven UI code generators. Although we needed to avoid this problem, in the mean time we wished to retain the powerful generational character of MDE tools. Thus we started thinking of an alternative path, in which: (i)

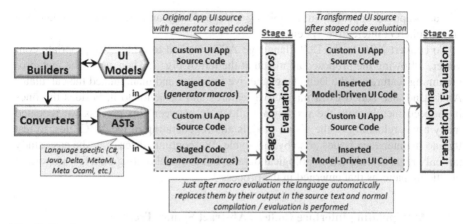

Fig. 7. The improved model-driven process with inverted responsibility: user-interface programmers deploy generator macros to produce resulting code on-demand and in-place without affecting the originally produced ASTs by the MDE tools

the MDE tool output would somehow remain invariant; and (ii) the source code of the interactive application could still grow in an unconstrained manner around it. This led us to the idea of bringing metaprogramming into the pipeline by enabling interface engineers algorithmically manipulate the generated interface code including: loading, processing and transforming using macros that are evaluated during build time. Such a process is detailed under Fig. 7.

As shown, we suggest that the MDE tools should generate the concrete produced user-interfaces in a user-interface description language (UIDL), such definitions naturally involving all the necessary structural, algorithmic and event management details, but in a language neutral form. This is only proposed to allow language independent MDE tools, but is not strict, meaning MDE tool developers may choose to directly produce ASTs for a specific target programming language. The general approach for code manipulation and insertion using ASTs is the one earlier described and relates to compile-time metaprogramming languages, involving two stages that are also depicted under Fig. 7: meta-code evaluation (stage 1), and normal compilation (stage 2).

5   Development Case Study

To test our approach and assess its expressive power and engineering validity, we have carried out a case study. We have adopted wx Form Builder [9], a popular publicly available interface builder for the wx widgets cross-platform library. This tool offers a typical rapid-application development cycle with interactive user-interface construction, and outputs interface descriptions into its custom language-neutral format called XRC (XML Interface Resources). Then, using wxFormBuilder we constructed a full-scale scientific calculator application. The latter was actually practiced in alternative ways, such as with single authoring project or alternatively with multiple independent projects. This way we could also assert the compositional flexibility of our proposed approach in combining independently authored interfaces under a single coherent interactive system.

To convert XRC to the Delta language ASTs we had to build an appropriate converter, following the proposed approach at the left of Fig. 7. Then, using the metaprogramming features of the Delta language, we imported and manipulated the calculator ASTs, and also added extra interactive features and behavior to it, besides the ones introduced merely with the wx Form Builder. In-between this process we repeated many times reloading of the visual models and regenerating of the XRC files, to test that no maintenance issues arise by this cycle. We continue discussing the case study not only regarding the methodological details, but also elaborating on a few important practicing patterns that emerged in the process.

5.1   Manipulating Interface Code as Abstract Syntax Trees

The goal of our case study was dual: (a) to show that the maintenance is effectively eliminated; and (ii) to demonstrate the huge expressive power of metaprogramming for flexible interface code composition. In this context, as part of the case study, we have identified and deployed a number of operations on ASTs to assist in code composition when implementing user-interface metaprograms. In Fig. 8, two of the composition scenarios which have been implemented are outlined.

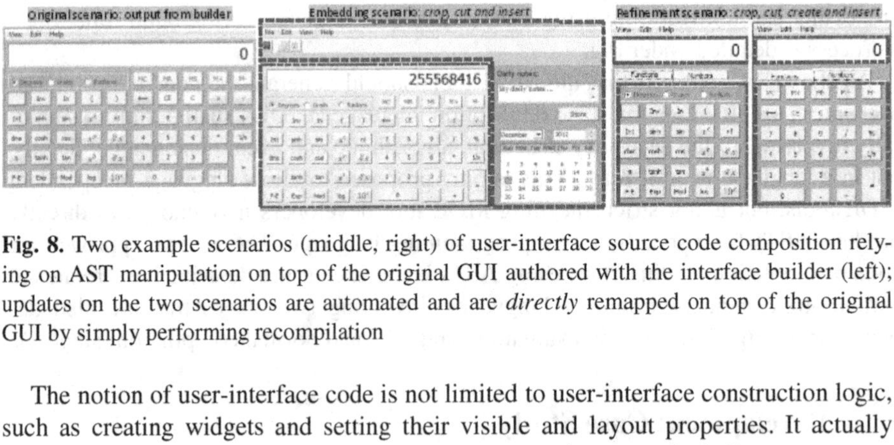

Fig. 8. Two example scenarios (middle, right) of user-interface source code composition relying on AST manipulation on top of the original GUI authored with the interface builder (left); updates on the two scenarios are automated and are *directly* remapped on top of the original GUI by simply performing recompilation

The notion of user-interface code is not limited to user-interface construction logic, such as creating widgets and setting their visible and layout properties. It actually concerns the full range of dialogue management requirements, including event management and all types of dynamic interface updates. For instance, composition may well concern scenarios where event management code is injected within a user-interface construction code snippet.

In the following table, we enumerate and briefly describe the manipulation operators. A few automations for easier user-interface code composition were provided on insertion, such as renaming of local variables in case of conflicts at the new context, and automatic relinking of widgets to the container produced by the previous code fragment.

Table 1. Manipulation Operators for User-Interface

Operator	Description
Cut	Addresses the need to extrapolate the code snippet of an entire user-interface component, and is expected to be followed by appropriate merge or insert operations. It was needed to extract the code creating the numeric and function pads of the calculator case study. When directly followed by an insert operation it implements re-parenting.
Clone	Concerns cases where a copy of the source code for a user-interface component is required. Typically, alone this operation is rarely needed, thus it is anticipated to be followed by radical changes of the user-interface code with operations such as merge, insert and modify.
Crop	It is required when the source code creating some outer parts (i.e. containers) of user-interface components is not needed. In our case we deployed the operator to drop the containing frame window that is by default inserted by the wx Form Builder on all projects.
Create	This is not an operator on the input source code fragments per se. It reflects the necessity to introduce extra custom user-interface source code in the form of AST, to be actually combined with the parts produced by the MDE tool. In our case study the latter concerned the tab-box with the Functions and Numbers entry (see Figure 8, right part).
Merge	It is a combined composition action on ASTs and is introduced to enable mixing of independent interface code snippets under a common parent. Usually, such components are either authored independently in the modeling process, or they may constitute the outcome of earlier cut operations.
Insert	It allows (re)linking of an existing user-interface code fragment inside another one. Practically, this action is the dynamic form of all manual editing actions that UI programmers would have to apply in order to insert custom code inside the generated code. It is anticipated as the most frequent editing operation on ASTs.
Modify	It reflects the need to algorithmically apply localized changes on the AST, such as: renaming variables and functions, changing argument ordering, changing invocation styles, etc. Although expected to introduce small scale changes, it can be very useful to keep the generated code synced with newer versions of widget libraries when the MDE tool is not yet up-to-date.

5.2   Composing Interface Code In-Place and On-Demand

We elaborate on the way composition on user-interface code through ASTs has been applied in the context of our case study. It should be noted that, although at some points it may look like the effect can be also accomplished by typical runtime composition at the level of widgets, in general it is not. In particular, not all widget libraries offer runtime name-based registries for widgets, neither all of them facilitate the runtime registration of event handlers in the form of typical method invocations.

In other words, if linkage is required between interaction objects that are constructed by the generated interface code to custom event handlers provided by the application, then it may the case that the only option is making such code fragments coexist at the same source context. In our case study, the initial source code corresponding to the outcome of the wxFormBuilder has the following structure (pseudo code, many details removed), and creates the calculator instance shown at the left part of Fig. 8:

```
1: new main frame m_frame0       : null
2: new panel m_panel0            : m_frame0
3: new num panel m_panel1        : m_panel0
4: new num buttons m_button<i>   : m_panel1
5: new func panel m_panel2       : m_panel0
6: new func buttons m_button<j>  : m_panel2
```

The colon is used to indicate the GUI parent object typically required, while line numbering is used only to help in our explanations. Now, we need to perform the following changes: (1) drop the code producing the outer frame (line 1); (2) insert code for event handling implementing calculations on the numeric and function buttons (after lines 4 and 6); (3) crop the numeric and functions panel (lines 3 and 5); and (4) introduce a tab-box were to insert the cropped code fragments for the calculator numeric and the functions pad. In all these cases we also rely on the automatic relinking of the parent objects offered by the insertion operator, as mentioned earlier.

```
& calc = nil;           ← a global meta-code variable, carrying the entire AST of the user-interface code
& {                     ← an entire block of meta-code begins here
calc = Converter::xrc2ast("calc.xrc");        ← load XRC definitions and convert to respective AST
Tree::Crop(calc, "calcFrame");                ← drop the outer Frame inserted by wx Form Builder    ①
Tree::Insert(                                 ← insert an application event handler for = button
  calc, "buttEqual", "EVT_COMMAND_BUTTON_CLICKED",
  "CalcApp::OnEqual"                          ← handler function provided by the application
);                                                                                                   ②
Tree::Insert(                                 ← insert an application event handler for + button
  calc, "buttAdd", "EVT_COMMAND_BUTTON_CLICKED",
  "CalcApp::OnAdd"                            ← handler function provided by the application
);
...rest of event handlers are inserted here for the rest of the calculator buttons...
local numbers = Tree::Cut(calc, "panelNums");  ← cut the code constructing the numeric panel    ③
local funcs   = Tree::Cut(calc, "panelFuncs"); ← cut the code constructing the functions panel
local panel   = Tree::Get(calc, "panelMain");  ← get the code creating the main calculator panel
local tabBox  = << code here to create the tab box >>;  ← code placed around <<>> is automatically converted to AST
Tree::Insert(panel, tabBox);                   ← insert the code for the tab-box after the code of the calculator panel   ④
local numsTab = << code here to create the numbers tab entry >>;
local funcsTab = << code here to create the functions tab entry >>;
Tree::Insert(numsTab, numbers);                ← insert the code for the numeric panel after the code of its tab entry
Tree::Insert(funcsTab, funcs);                 ← insert the code for the functions panel after the code of its tab entry
}
...any other meta or normal code may be freely placed here...
!(calc);                                       ← inline the entire AST carried by calc at this source location
```

Fig. 9. Meta-code to load, manipulate (four labeled steps) and inline the source code for the modified calculator.

The meta-code implementing these four composition steps is outlined under Fig. 9, with many details removed for clarity. Also, the actual conversion from XRC to ASTs is cached and is applied only when an internally produced and stored AST file is older than the supplied XRC file. There is code in Fig. 9 appearing with a form << some code >>. This is not a conceptual symbolism, but is syntax relating to meta-language construct known as quasi-quoting. Essentially, it is a compile-time operator that converts the surrounded raw source-text to its respective AST representation. For instance <<1+2>> is equivalent to the AST of the expression 1+2, not merely the character string '1+2'. This is useful when one needs to combine in-place an explicitly written source code snippet with other code fragments that are available directly as AST values. In our example, we quasi-quote the source text producing the numeric and function tab entries (middle of step 4 in **Fig. 9**) and compose them via `Tree::Insert` with the ASTs earlier extracted from the calculator code.

6   Summary and Conclusions

Currently, MDE of User-Interfaces represents a domain of very powerful development tools for rapid development of interactive systems. Their evolution in the last decade consolidated the disciplined view of model-based user-interface generation as a transformation process from abstract to concrete models, eventually down to the physical platform level. Generational MDE tools support the production of concrete user-interface implementations directly at the source code level. Such a facility is overall very helpful, powerful and flexible for user-interface programmers. However, it also causes maintenance issues once extensions and updates are manually introduced over the generated user-interface.

To cope with such maintenance issues we propose the exploitation of the metaprogramming language facilities and suggest an improved model-driven code of practice relying on the manipulation of user-interface code fragments by clients directly as data. In this approach, the generator components of MDE tools need output Abstract Syntax Trees (ASTs), not source code, while clients should import and compose ASTs as needed, before eventually performing on-demand and in-place code generation.

We have also carried out a case study to experiment and validate the engineering proposition using a publicly available compile-time metaprogramming language and an interface builder. Overall we were truly impressed by the compositional flexibility which allowed us to safely and easily manipulate and extend the produced interface without suffering from maintenance issues. We believe our work reveals the chances by combining metaprogramming and generational MDE user-interface engineering tools, and anticipate more efforts to further exploit this field.

References

1. Savidis, A.: Delta Programming Language (2012), http://www.ics.forth.gr/hci/files/plang/Delta/Delta.html (accessed february 2014)

2. Taha, W.: A gentle introduction to multi-stage programming. In: Lengauer, C., Batory, D., Blum, A., Odersky, M. (eds.) Domain-Specific Program Generation. LNCS, vol. 3016, pp. 30–50. Springer, Heidelberg (2004)
3. Schramm, A., Preußner, A., Heinrich, M., Vogel, L.: Rapid UI Development for Enterprise Applications: Combining Manual and Model-Driven Techniques. In: Petriu, D.C., Rouquette, N., Haugen, Ø. (eds.) MODELS 2010, Part I. LNCS, vol. 6394, pp. 271–285. Springer, Heidelberg (2010)
4. Sheard, T., Benaissa, Z., Martel, M.: Introduction to multi-stage programming using MetaML. Technical report, Pacific Software Research Center, Oregon Graduate Institute (2000)
5. Lilis, Y., Savidis, A.: Implementing Reusable Exception Handling Patterns with Compile-Time Metaprogramming. In: Avgeriou, P. (ed.) SERENE 2012. LNCS, vol. 7527, pp. 1–15. Springer, Heidelberg (2012)
6. Lilis, Y., Savidis, A.: Implementing Reusable Exception Handling Patterns with Compile-Time Metaprogramming. In: Avgeriou, P. (ed.) SERENE 2012. LNCS, vol. 7527, pp. 1–15. Springer, Heidelberg (2012)
7. Foley, J., Kim, W.C., Kovacevic, S., Murray, K.: Defining Interfaces at a High Level of Abstraction. IEEE Software 6(1), 25–32 (1989)
8. MetaOCaml, A compiled, type-safe multi-stage programming language (2003), http://www.metaocaml.org/
9. wx Form Builder (2006), A RAD tool for wx GUIs, http://sourceforge.net/projects/wxformbuilder/ (accessed online January 2014)
10. Michotte, B., Vanderdonckt, J.: GrafiXML, a Multi-target User Interface Builder Based on UsiXML. In: Proceedings of ICAS 2008 4th International Conference on Autonomic and Autonomous Systems, Gosier, Guadeloupe, March 16-21, pp. 15–22. IEEE (2008)
11. Sauer, S., Engels, G.: Easy model-driven development of multimedia user interfaces with guiBuilder. In: Stephanidis, C. (ed.) HCI 2007. LNCS, vol. 4554, pp. 537–546. Springer, Heidelberg (2007)
12. GtkBuilder – Build an interface from an XML UI definition, https://developer.gnome.org/gtk3/stable/GtkBuilder.html (accessed online January 2014)
13. The Eclipse Foundation. Eclipse Modeling Framework, EMF (2008), http://www.eclipse.org/modeling/emf/ (accessed online January 2014)
14. Obeo (2006), Acceleo: MDA generator, http://www.acceleo.org/pages/home/en (accessed online January 2014)
15. Actifsource GmbH (2010), Actifsource Code Generator for Eclipse, http://www.actifsource.com/_downloads/actifsource_code_generator_for_Eclipse_en.pdf (accessed online January 2014)
16. Lanusse, A., Tanguy, Y., Espinoza, H., Mraidha, C., Gerard, S., Tessier, P., Schnekenburger, R., Dubois, H., Terrier, F.: Papyrus UML: an open source toolset for MDA. In: Proceedings of the Tools and Consultancy Track of the Fifth European Conference on Model-Driven Architecture Foundations and Applications (ECMDA-FA 2009), University of Twente. Enschede, The Netherlands, June 23-26 (2009)
17. Desfray, P.: Modelio: Globalizing MDA. In: Proceedings of the Tools and Consultancy Track of the Fifth European Conference on Model-Driven Architecture Foundations and Applications (ECMDA-FA 2009), University of Twente. Enschede, The Netherlands, June 23-26 (2009)

Nested Compositing Window Managers

Anthony Savidis[1,2] and Andreas Maragudakis[1]

[1] Institute of Computer Science, Foundation for Research and Technology – Hellas (FORTH)
[2] Department of Computer Science, University of Crete, Greece
{as,maragud}@ics.forth.gr

Abstract. Compositing is currently the prevalent rendering paradigm for window managers. It applies off-screen drawing of managed windows with final image composition by the window manager itself. In this context, a compositing system is presented, enabling the concurrent presence of multiple window managers, being arbitrarily nested while facilitating switch managers on-the-fly. Two distinct managers are implemented, 2d desktop and custom 3d book, that can be freely combined into nested hierarchies. To allow such nesting two extensions are introduced. Firstly, the compositing process is turned to a rendering pipeline with window managers directly in-the-loop, with an imaging model combining diverse geometries. Secondly, to facilitate focus control in such geometric spaces, a cascaded pointing translation process is implemented, enabling geometric mapping of pointing events across nested window managers. The entire compositing system is implemented in a custom widget toolkit named sprint (in C++ with OpengGL and shaders) that is publicly available.

Keywords: Development methods, Interaction techniques, platforms and metaphors, Window managers, Toolkits.

1 Introduction

Currently, the imaging model of most window managers is compositing. The latter relies on the drawing of managed (top-level) windows into off-screen buffers (normal rendering phase), with the window manager responsible to eventually compose the final picture from such buffers (compositing rendering phase), shown in Fig. 1. Also, compositing does not radically affect individual window rendering, since it is still performed as before, however, with output redirected in off-screen-buffers.

Effectively, it brought two changes: (i) the final rendering stage; and (ii) initial pointing filtering from window manager space to local (planar) window space. While the amendments are overall simple, they are powerful in terms of the visual scenarios they support, and radical regarding the underlying implementation rework they require (i.e., GPU rendering).

We discuss two novel extensions along the standard compositing features. Firstly, we extend the imaging model to support nested window managers, thus enabling arbitrarily nested interactive spaces. In this context, nesting is possible on different window managers, while enabling users switch managers on-the-fly. Secondly, we extend

C. Stephanidis and M. Antona (Eds.): UAHCI/HCII 2014, Part I, LNCS 8513, pp. 149–160, 2014.

the initial pointing filtering process towards a cascaded translation process in order to support focus control across nested window managers and their custom geometries.

We continue with the novel features of the compositing system. Then, we discuss the primary implementation aspects and patterns to accommodate them. Finally, we compare with related work, draw key conclusions and outline future steps.

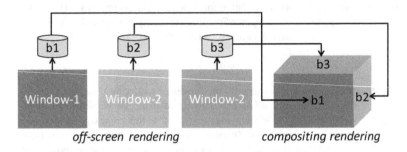

Fig. 1. Compositing rendering process combining buffers from off-screen rendering

2   Related Work

Window managers (Myers, 1988) with compositing implementations appeared originally under X windows more than a decade ago, following early pioneering work with first 3d window managers such as the Task Gallery (Robertson et al., 2000). Event today compositing managers like Compiz (Canonical, 2013), KWin (KDE, 2013) and Quartz (Apple, 2013) do not have interoperating variations and always work in a standalone fashion. Currently, for users to alternate across different spaces the notion of virtual desktops is offered (Ringel, 2011), but always with a similar window management style.

Additionally, they still operate outside the toolkit loop: after the toolkit in terms of display composition, and before the toolkit in terms of the initial input translation. While not related to compositing, the work on facades (Stürzlinger et al., 2006) revealed the need for compositional user-interfaces, something that inspired us towards dynamic window manager switching.

Display improvements for various scenarios have been proposed, like optimal space exploitation (Bell & Feiner, 2000), improved desktop rendering for importance-driven compositing (Waldner et al., 2011), optimal display usage for different monitor sizes (Hutchings et al., 2004; Hutchings & Stasko, 2004). In general, display improvements could be modeled in window managers as modular layout add-ons implementing different policies; however, we did not focus on this particular problem in the reported work. A constraint-based approach to model such policies is proposed in (Badros, 2001).

Various research efforts on compositing systems have been carried out, but little progress is made in extending the compositing pipeline with radical refinements such multiple and nested window managers. Metisse is a flexible compositing system (Chapuis et al., 2005) relying on FvwmCompositor which allows 3d transformations on window rendering, thus offering a framework for rendering windows beyond typical desktop topologies. However, it still cannot combine different window managers, while pick translation is typical single-stage preprocessing involving the window 3d transformation matrix.

3   Features

We implemented a compositing toolkit with two distinct window managers: (i) desktop window manager with a 2d geometric space and rectangular planar geometry; and (ii) custom book window manager with a 3d geometric space with a typical perspective view frustum. A snapshot with nested desktop and book managers, showing texturing and triangulation involved in compositing is provided in Fig. 2, while cross nesting with book and desktop managers is provided under Fig. 3.

Typical live taskbars with window miniatures are implemented, as in most compositing window managers, relying on the off-screen-buffers for the contents of managed windows. In our implementation they are currently included in desktops, while we are working on a geometric model suited to the book window manager.

Fig. 2. Mixed window managers with windows as textured (two triangles) rectangles

Switching from one window manager to another is facilitated on-the-fly, and, as we discuss later, in an automated implementation manner. Since switching is also an operation on window managers it is also included in their special local toolbar (see Fig. 3, top-left window areas, right to eye icons, showing a desktop or book icons).

Because of nesting, window maximization can have a dual meaning. The common meaning, as observed in (standalone) desktop managers, is making windows occupy the full-screen space. However, in managers with non-desktop rendering plugins, like the cubic renderers of Compiz and KWin, the behavior is different with maximization adjusted to the rendering space were windows geometrically 'live' - in the previous cases the actual cube sides. Since the two interpretations are different, we decided to separate them as follows.

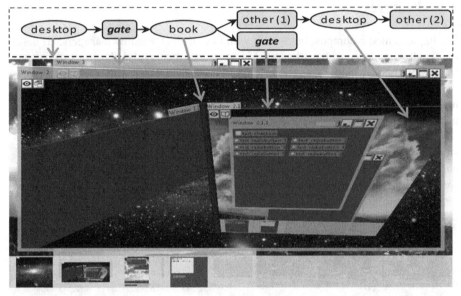

Fig. 3. Desktop encompassing a book encompassing a desktop

Manager maximization / restoration, offered to window managers only, not to windows, allowing them exploit full screen space. It enables give the impression that a window manager is standalone, (see Fig. 4, right part). In our implementation this mode is interactively offered by a local toolbar at the top-left of the window-manager rendering area, and concerns to the 'eye' icon (see Fig. 3 and Fig. 4, toolbars at top-left window areas). Additionally, successive manager maximize requests are allowed on nested managers, with the restore operation always returning to the full-screen state of the hierarchically-closest parent manager.

Window maximization / restoration, an operation on managed windows, is optionally offered by individual window managers depending on their individual rendering models. In our case it is only supplied by desktops and is included in the standard window frame toolbar. Through this operation windows take the full space in area of their parent window manager (see Fig. 4, 'window maximize'). In our context, if a desktop is the root manager or is maximized, this operation maximize behaves exactly as in existing desktops and makes the window occupy full-screen space.

When supporting nested window managers the resulting interactive spaces not only become visually rich, but also sometimes visually complex. In particular, the desktop with its overlapped windows may cause nested window managers to be obscured. To allow users quickly inspect what is behind we introduced an extra item in the desktop toolbar for interactive transparency control (see Fig. 4). Our implementation concerns appearance and does not allow obscured content to be interactive without the focus, as in (Robertson et al., 2000) were interaction with hidden content is enabled.

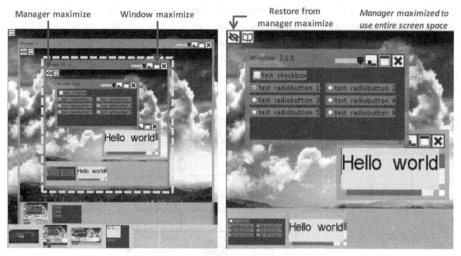

Fig. 4. Dual maximization operation applying on window managers (eye icon) and on managed windows (standard icon)

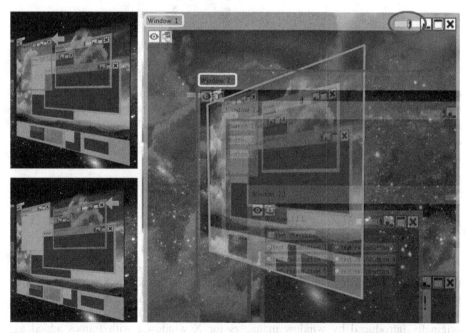

Fig. 5. Transparency control; Left: on windows of a desktop nested in a book; Right: book nested in 'Window 1' of desktop ('Window 2' is transparent and in-front of 'Window 1')

4   Implementation

In compositing toolkits, the classes regarding managed windows have always a local off-screen-buffer. Under OpenGL implementations the latter is typically a frame buffer object with a texture rendering target. In this context, to support dynamically nested window managers we introduced a managed window subclass named *gate* (see Fig. 6), with a dynamically associated window manager instance (optional, can be null). The root of the entire window hierarchy is always a gate, while gates may be freely nested within any container window. However, only instances of managed windows can have a gate instance as a parent.

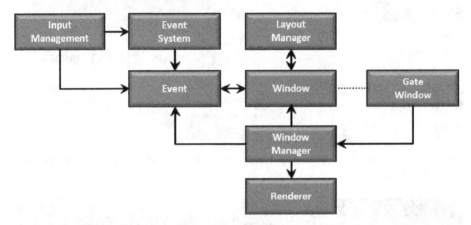

Fig. 6. General architecture of our toolkit, with *Gate* window class playing a key role

The class design to accommodate our requirements is outlined under Fig. 7 (many details omitted for clarity). Overall, window managers rely on decorators, one decorator added per managed window. The latter concerns the WindowManager (WM) abstract class, its Decorate abstract method, and the WindowDecorator (WD) abstract class. This way, managed windows are added / removed to / from window managers as follows:

*static **WM::Add** (ManagedWindow win)*
        *{ decorators[win] = **Decorate**(win); }*
*static **WM::Remove** (ManagedWindow win)*
        { decorators[win].Destroy( ); decorators.erase(win); }

As also shown under Fig. 7, subclasses of window manager and decorator are defined in pairs, something reflected in the desktop and book window managers we implemented. One role of the decorator is to optionally introduce extra widgets necessary for interactive window control. The latter is a standard approach on desktops, originally introduced by window managers for X windows, with frames added as extra windows. We continue with the implementation details of the rendering pipeline, dynamic switching and cascaded input translation.

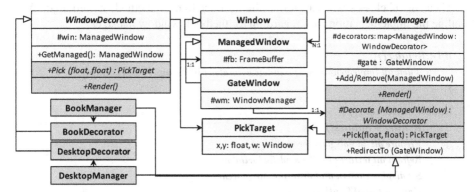

Fig. 7. Class schema to support dynamic and hybrid nesting of compositing window managers - key methods and members are only shown for clarity

The rendering process is recursive as in all toolkits. When a gate window is asked to render itself it simply delegates the rendering work to its window manager instance:

GateWindow::Render() {
    Set rendering target to **this.***GetFrameBuffer( )*
    Draw any background image
    ***GetWindowManager().Render*()**
}

We continue with the *Render*() methods at the level of super-classes. There are also three non-abstract methods, two for rendering managed windows and decorators, and one to render the local toolbar (this is discussed later).

WM::RenderWindows() {   ←*non-abstract method*
    foreach *x* **in** *decorators* **do**
        x.GetKey().Render()
}
WM::RenderDecorators() {   ←*non-abstract methods*
    foreach *x* **in** *decorators* **do**
        x.GetValue().Render()
}
WM::Render() {
    RenderWindows( )
    RenderDecorators( )
    RenderLocalToolbar()
}

Then, in subclasses we may refine the abstract Render methods as required. We outline the implementation case regarding for the book window manager:

WD::Render(){
    // default implementation of window decorator (WD) super-class is empty
}

BookWM::Render() {
    RenderWindows()
    Prepare all 3d polygons for book
    Refresh all textures for the modified windows
    Set display camera and draw the entire scene
    RenderLocalToolbar()
}

As observed, in the book implementation the decorator subclass has no particular role in rendering. This is no general rule, but reflects our choice to gather all triangles for managed windows into one rendering batch (it is much faster than having separate batches per window). As mentioned, the entry points for dynamically attaching window managers are gate window instances. Interactively, the dynamic switching options are included in the local toolbar of window managers. In our implementation, the construction of this toolbar is automatic and can accommodate any future window manager subclasses that may be possibly implemented.

In other words, if an extra window manager is implemented, it will directly appear with a reserved entry in this toolbar. For this to work, a specific design pattern needs to be adopted, as outlined under Fig. 8. In particular, a factory has to be implemented and a factory instance should be initially (at startup) registered to a factory directory with a suitable unique class identifier.

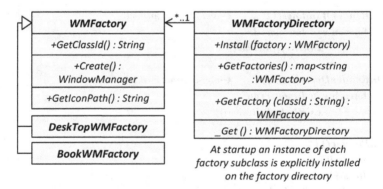

Fig. 8. Abstract superclass for window manager factories and the singleton registry with all factories indexed using their unique class ids

The local window-manager toolbar is placed on top of the rendering output that is drawn in the gate frame buffer, while it is interactively a standard toolbar with clickable behavior. It is prepared on-demand during rendering (i.e., when changed, it is internally cached) as follows:

WM::RenderLocalToolbar() {
>   *Get a copy of all factories from the factory directory*
>   *Remove the entry for the wm class id of the caller (this)*
>   *Draw manager maximization entry and set its click handler*
>   **foreach** *x in factories* **do** {
>>   *Draw the texture corresponding to* *x.GetIconPath()*
>>   *Set the click handler of the toolbar entry to invoke* *WM::Switch()*
>
>   }
}

Once a toolbar item is selected, the associated window manager is instantiated and set as the current in its respective gate instance, destroying the previous manager. This approach enables any number of window managers to be interactively activated and combined. The previous behavior is possible through the Switch method below:

static *WM::Switch* *(GateWindow gate, string wmClassId)* {
>   *gate.GetWindowManager().Destroy()*
>   *gate.SetWindowManager(Create(wmClassId))*

}
static *WM WM::Create* *(string wmClassId)* {
>   *factory = get factory entry from directory for wmClassId*
>   *return factory.Create()*

}

```
uniform    mat4       projectionMatrix;
in         vec3       inVertex;
void main()
           { gl_Position = projectionMatrix * vec4(inVertex, 1.0); }
```

```
uniform    vec4       color;
void main()
           { gl_FragColor = color; }
```

```
uniform    sampler2D  tex;
uniform    float      transparency;
uniform    bool       useTransparency;
in         vec2       textureCoordinates;
void main() {
           gl_FragColor = texture(tex, textureCoordinates);
           if (useTransparency)
                   gl_FragColor.a = transparency;
}
```

Fig. 9. The simple shaders for applying compositing rendering; the vertex shaders should use orthographic matrices

For the rendering of the windows we used custom GLSL vertex and fragment shaders. Specifically, we had to use different very simple shaders for the rendering of the desktop window manager and the contents of the top-level windows and other shaders for the 3d shapes of the book window manager. Also, the shaders are divided to the shaders with and without texturing (see Fig. 9). The shaders that are not using textures, such as clearing backgrounds, apply a color to the triangle surface that is provided as a uniform variable.

In Fig.9, we see the GLSL shaders that were used for the rendering of the 2d orthographic scenes. In the first program the vertex shader applies the orthographic projection to the input vertices. Usually, the input vertices are the window rectangles, which are converted to two triangles. The second program is the fragment shader that applies the uniform color to every fragment of the window rectangle. Finally, in the last program, we see how the texturing is performed in the fragment shader that renders the rectangles with background images, such as the gate window, the icons and the text. The texture coordinates are provided from the vertex shader, which simply passes through the input variable. The texture function, provided by the GLSL language, is used to get the color from the texture. In some cases, such as when the transparency slider is moved, we want to force a transparency value to the output window. In that case, we assign the transparency value to a uniform.

5   Cascaded Pick Translation

Picking through pointing is of key importance in toolkits and windows managers since it is used others for focus control. In our context, pointing is translated from the top window manager to the nested ones via a cascaded translation process (Fig. 10).

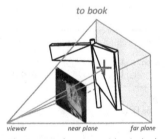

The *desktop* propagates hierarchically pick to *managed* windows which apply point-in-rectangle tests by default, except *gates* delegating window managers to pick

The *gate window* passes pick to its *book* which performs typical 3d ray-object intersection to find the *managed* window that will further process the pick

Fig. 10. Cascaded pick processing enabling to support precise pointing interaction and focus window shifting across the diverse geometries of nested window managers

More specifically, every window manager is able to translate from a planar position, whose coordinates are given relative to its gate, to a pair carrying the actual picked managed window and a relative position inside it. Then, the managed window invokes pick recursively to child windows. As with rendering, gates always delegate pick requests directly to their window manager:

> *PickTarget GateWindow::Pick (float x, float y)* {
>   **return** *GetWindowManager( ).Pick(x,y)*
> }

The initial pick request is always in screen coordinates and is supplied to the root gate instance. The implementation of the default pick logic at the level of the window manager superclass is to iteratively test managed windows. The latter is directly sufficient for the desktop manager subclass.

PickTarget WM::Pick (float x, float y) {
        foreach *x* in *decorators* **do** {
            PickTarget target = x.GetKey( ).Pick( )
            if *target.GetWindow( ) ≠ null* **then**
                return *target*
        }
        return *null*   ←*fallback means no pick target was found*
}

However, when it comes to the book manager subclass, the pick logic is more comprehensive and is provided below. Initially, the planar pick event is translated to the geometry of the book by producing a ray on the perspective view frustum using the current camera. Then, translation proceeds by recursively invoking the Pick method on the managed window corresponding to hit book page. The latter is done after translating the ray intersection point to the local planar space of the window.

PickTarget BookWM::Pick (float x, float y) {
        Translate the pick coordinates x,y to an 3d ray
        Using this ray *determine the closest intersecting book page and its hit point*
        if *a book page element is intersected* **then** {
            Let win *be the managed window for this book page*
            Translate hit point to page plane coordinates x',y'
            return *win.Pick(x',y')*   ←*this call will recursively pick to nested managers*
        }
}

6   Conclusions and Future Work

We have implemented a low-fidelity experimental toolkit named sprint, supporting compositing rendering and hosting of arbitrarily nested window managers. We enabled users switch window managers on-the-fly to any registered alternative window manager. To experiment with different geometries we implemented a desktop and book window managers and tested various dynamic nesting configurations between them. In this context, we mainly focused on the technical amendments and implementation for nested compositing window managers, rather than on the human factors and interaction quality inherent in hybrid and nested workspaces. In summary, we propose the involvement of window managers into the loop with a cascaded rendering and pick-translation pipeline.

Our implementation also indicated that a few extensions on the toolkit side are required, the most prominent being the need for a special window class, called gate in our work, to offer hosting of embedded window managers. The tests also showed that switching is extremely fast, since it only involves the initial creation of the window manager custom geometry. The contained windows and window managers are by default cached due to compositing rendering.

References

1. Myers, B.: A taxonomy of window manager user interfaces. IEEE Computer Graphics and Applications 8(5), 65–84 (1988)
2. Robertson, G., Van Dantzich, M., Robbins, D., Czerwinski, M., Hinckley, K., Risden, K., Thiel, D., Gorokhovsky, V.: The Task Gallery: a 3D window manager. In: Proc. CHI 2000, pp. 494–501. ACM (2000)
3. Bell, B.A., Feiner, S.K.: Dynamic space management for user interfaces. In: Proc. UIST 2000, pp. 239–248. ACM (2000)
4. Badros, G.J., Nichols, J., Borning, A.: Scwm: An Extensible Constraint-Enabled Window Manager. In: USENIX Annual Technical Conference, FREENIX Track 2001, pp. 225–234 (2001)
5. Ishak, E.W., Feiner, S.K.: Interacting with hidden content using content-aware free-space transparency. In: Proc. UIST 2004, pp. 189–192. ACM (2004)
6. Waldner, M., Steinberger, M., Grasset, R., Schmalstieg, D.: Importance-driven compositing window management. In: Proc. CHI 2011, pp. 959–968. ACM (2011)
7. Stürzlinger, W., Chapuis, O., Phillips, D., Roussel, N.: User interface façades: towards fully adaptable user interfaces. In: Proc. UIST 2006, pp. 309–318. ACM (2006)
8. Chapuis, O., Roussel, N.: Metisse is not a 3D desktop! In: Proc. UIST 2005, pp. 13–22. ACM (2005)
9. Hutchings, D.R., Smith, G., Meyers, B., Czerwinski, M., Robertson, G.: Display space usage and window management operation comparisons between single monitor and multiple monitor users. In: Proc. AVI 2004, pp. 32–39. ACM (2004)
10. Hutchings, D.R., Stasko, J.: Shrinking window operations for expanding display space. In: Proc. AVI 2004, pp. 350–353. ACM (2004)
11. Ringel, M.: When one isn't enough: an analysis of virtual desktop usage strategies and their implications for design. In: CHI Extended Abstracts, pp. 762–763. ACM (2003)
12. Apple. Quartz Compositor, http://apple.wikia.com/wiki/Quartz_Compositor (accessed April 2013)
13. Canonical LTD. Compiz, https://launchpad.net/compiz (accessed April 2013)
14. KDE. KWin, http://techbase.kde.org/Projects/KWin (accessed April 2013)

Automatic Detection of Features (Markers) on a Three-Dimensional Model of a Human Face

Witold Stankiewicz and Michał Rychlik

Poznan University of Technology, Division of Virtual Engineering, Poland
witold.stankiewicz@put.poznan.pl
http://virtual.edu.pl

Abstract. The post-processing and correlation analysis (like Proper Orthogonal Decomposition) requires the same topology for all objects in the database. Thus, in the case of 3D scanned data, registration is required. One of possible choices is elastic registration based on the known positions of certain markers (features) on the surface of each scanned object.

The present paper targets the method of automatic detection of such markers on the scanned human faces and the elastic deformation resulting in the same topology of the triangular meshes after the registration. Resulting data might be analyzed using methods like POD.

Keywords: data registration, 3D scanning, POD, PCA.

1 Introduction

The increasing globalization, growth of tourism and labor migration affect the increase in passenger traffic as well as increasing frequency of terrorist threat alerts. The challenges of the modern world cause increased demand for the systems of auto-matic recognition and identification of individuals.

Such a recognition might be based on the individual anatomical / physiological features or on the basis of persons behavior. Commonly used biometric methods are based among others on the retinal, fingerprint, hand, dental or facial identification, as well as voice or signature analysis.

Face recognition, based so far on flat photographs and analysis of eigenfaces, in-creasingly relies on the spatial data coming from three-dimensional scanning.

Point cloud and resulting from the following processing computational mesh may consist of the large number of degrees of freedom. The database containing several thousand objects might require processing the data of the order of 10^9, which obviously causes great difficulties in the storage and processing. Therefore, it is important to use methods reducing the size (dimensionality) of the data while maintaining high accuracy of the mapping of full spatial information about the object. The methods used to reduce and simplify the database and thus making an analysis of geometrical features possible are modal analysis.

The paper targets the method of automatic detection of the most important markers on the human face, basing on the curvature of the facial surface. Such markers, used together with the definition of the facial surface's boundary and

C. Stephanidis and M. Antona (Eds.): UAHCI/HCII 2014, Part I, LNCS 8513, pp. 161–170, 2014.
© Springer International Publishing Switzerland 2014

mesh deformation algorithms, constitute elastic registration technique, resulting in the mesh defining the geometry of new object and remaining the topology (number of nodes, element connectivity) of base mesh.

The paper is organized as follows. In the next, second section the data acquisition based on 3D scanning is described. Next, The Proper Orthogonal Decomposition and it's requirements on the input data are briefly introduced. The algorithm of automatic detection of the markers is described in fourth section and the elastic registration method is summarized in section 5. Finally, the whole approach is summarized.

2   3D Scanning

The input data for numerical experiment and biometric PCA/POD analysis has been obtained using 3D optical, structural light scanner (fig. 1). In this work the geometry for more than 100 human faces of different persons with neutral expression has been acquired.

Fig. 1. Left: 3D structural light scanner. Middle: face setting with positioner. Right: scanning using the measurement stripes

The following procedure of 3D scanning and post-processing has been used: each input object has been scanned from three directions: front and both (left and right) profiles (fig. 2,left-middle). Left and right profiles were measured from the angles $-30°$ and $45°$ to the sagittal plane, respectively.

After the scanning process the three separate point clouds have been merged into one, single point cloud. In the next steps the 3D surface model has been computed basing on the point cloud and an individual polygonal surface mesh (containing 50k triangles, instead of few markers from "golden triangle" area) has been created (fig. 2, right).

3   Data Registration for Modal Decomposition

One of the most popular methods of modal analysis is Proper Orthogonal Decomposition (POD), also known as Principal Component Analysis (PCA) [1,2],

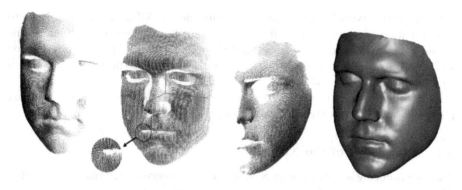

Fig. 2. Scanning of human face: set of three basic point clouds of the face (right, front and left profile, total ca. 500k mln points) and resulting surface model of the face (ca. 50k triangles). White spots represent the areas not illuminated while scanning at a given angle

as well as its variations like Snapshot method, Kernel PCA [3], Multilinear PCA [4] and Generalized POD. In this family of methods, the modal information is obtained from the solution of an eigenproblem for auto-correlation matrix based on input snapshots.

PCA is based on the assumption, that the snapshots v_i containing data (here: geometry) for successive obects are correlated.

The first step is the computation of time-averaged solution $\bar{u}$ and the centering of the snapshots by the subtraction $\acute{v}_i = v_i - \bar{u}$.

Resulting vectors $\acute{v}_i$ describe the differences between the snapshots and the mean geometry. This data is required to compute the autocorrelation matrix C:

$$C = \frac{1}{M} S S^T, \qquad \text{where} \quad S = [\acute{v}_1, \acute{v}_2, ...\acute{v}_M]. \tag{1}$$

Eigenvectors u of standard eigenproblem $Cu = \lambda I u$, related to eigenvalues λ of largest magnitude, are the most dominant PCA/POD modes.

A necessary prerequisite to carry out the modal decomposition is to preserve the same topology for all input data. In particular, the same number of nodes and mesh connectivity is required. The processing of raw input data to obtain the same topology for all input objects is called data registration. Unfortunately, the human face is characterized by a quite complex geometry, that makes 3D registration difficult.

4   Curvature-Based Feature Detection

In order to solve the problem of registration of data from 3D scanning, the program automatically detecting the characteristic points (markers) on the surface of the face has been developed. The algorithm of the program is as follows: triangular mesh (stored in Wavefront OBJ format) is cut by the designated plane (parallel to the axis of the coordinate system, such as XZ or YZ), which leads to the formation of a new curve. After an initial sorting of the vertices lying on the curve, it is possible to rotate it around the axis normal to the aforementioned surface. After the (optional) rotation , the extremes of the (parametric) function defining the curve are calculated.

Particular features (markers) on the face are searched using various cutting planes, rotations and extremes, in the following order.

4.1   Apex (Tip) of the Nose

The face is cut by a YZ-plane at coordinate $X = 0$ (symmetry plane, fig.3, left). The intersection of the facial surface and the cutting-plane is a curve, on which maximal Z value is searched. This point is used as the location where second cutting-plane, parallell to XZ-plane, is placed (fig.3, right).

Again, maximum value of Z coordinate is searched on the intersecting curve. This approach, possible to be repeated iteratively, allows the correction of the first marker's position and is especially important in the case of distortion of the nose.

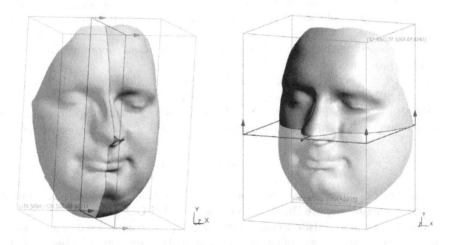

Fig. 3. Marker detection - apex of the nose. For the visualisation of meshes, markers and cutting planes, gmsh tool [8] is used

4.2   Nasal Bridge (Root, Nasion) and the "End" of the Nose

Second marker is defined as a mid-point of the nasal bridge - a point on the forehead between the eyes (fig.4, left). It is detected using the first intersection curve (YZ-plane at coordinate $X = 0$). Approximate position of this point is defined as the point lying above the Y-coordinate of nose tip, where the Z-coordinate is minimal. Again, iterative correction of the coordinates using various cutting-planes is possible.

Third marker defines the point between the philtrum and columella, where the nasolabial angle is measured. Again, it's approximate position is detected on the same curve as the second marker. This time, the first local minimum of the Z-coordinate below the apex of the nose is searched (fig.4, left).

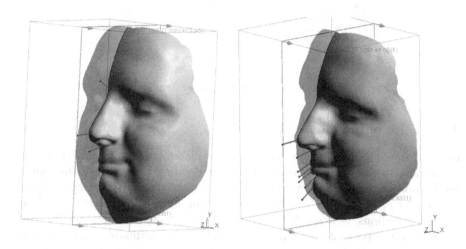

Fig. 4. Marker detection - bridge and "end" of the nose

4.3   Lips and Chin

The curve lying on the intersection of the surface and YZ-plane is used in the detection of a few another points (fig.4, right).

Fourth marker, defining the "center of the mouth", is located in the second minimum of the Z-coordinate, considering the points below the apex of the nose.

Fifth and sixth markers, lying on the top and bottom lines of the lips, are defined as two local maxima of Z-coordinate lying in the vicinity of the fourth marker.

Another two points lying on the aforementioned curve approximate the coordinates of markers 7 and 8, lying on the chin. These are, respectively, the points of the biggest depression and maximal protuberance.

4.4   Correction of the Third Marker's Position

After determining the coordinates of the markers 4-6 defining the lips, the position of the marker defining "end" of the nose is corrected. Previously used curve is rotated by 45 degrees (fig. 5), then the lowest point between the first and fifth marker is searched.

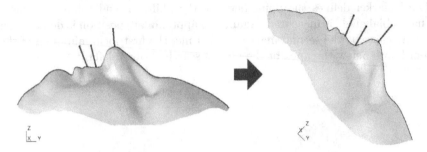

Fig. 5. Correction of the position of the "end" of the nose

4.5   Width of the Mouth

For the rest of the markers, horizontal cutting-planes are used for initial position estimation. In the case of markers 9 and 10, defining the width of the mouth, the Y-coordinate of XZ-plane is set on the value of the fourth marker, defining the "center of the mouth" (fig.6). The resulting intersection curve is analysed in both directions, starting from the marker 4 ("center of the mouth"). New markers' initial positions are the local minima of Z-coordinate. These positions are adjusted in the iterative search of smallest Z-coordinate in the vicinity of the initial location.

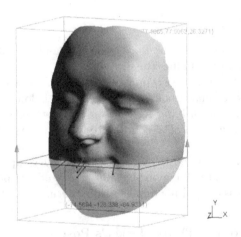

Fig. 6. Search for the markers defining the width of the mouth

4.6   Width of the Nose

Markers 11 and 12, defining the width of the nose, are initially found on the curve resulting from the intersection of facial surface and XZ-plane on marker 1 (apex of the nose), as shown on the left of the fig.7. These approximate positions are corrected by the search - in the close vicinity of initial location - of the maximum or minimum of X-coordinate, respectively (fig.7, right). If this approach fails, the curve is rotated about Y-axis and iterative procedure is repeated.

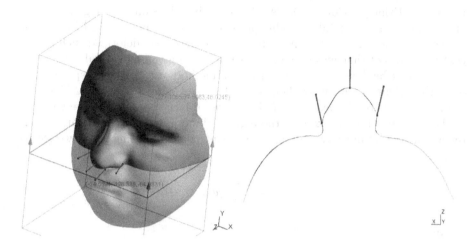

Fig. 7. Detection of the markers defining width of the nose

4.7 Eyes

The last four markers are placed in the corners of the eyes, as depicted in fig.8. They are approximately defined by the local minima of Z-coordinate on the intersection of facial surface and XZ-plane at $Y = 0$ (position of eyes after rigid registration). Next, these initial positions are adjusted using the techniques mentioned before: use of additional cutting-planes, rotations and searches in the neighbouhood on the given point.

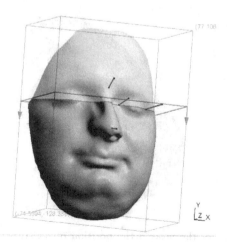

Fig. 8. Detection of the markers defining width of the eyes

5   Elastic Registration of Human Faces

As soon as the definition of the boundary curves (face contour) and the coordinates of the markers are known, elastic registration of the 3D data might be performed. Principal Component Analysis requires the same topology for all the objects in the input database. This prerequisite might be achieved by the use of one, base mesh for all the individuals in the database, deformed such a way, that the nodes of that mesh lay on the surface of a given individual face.

This might be done by mesh deformation method, e.g. basing on spring analogy (using Finite Element Method [7]) or Inverse Distance Weighting [6,5].

In this method, the markers of the reference face (base mesh) are snapped to the corresponding markers on the registered mesh and the coordinates of the remaining nodes from surrounding areas are interpolated basing on the weighting functions w_i:

$$x^\kappa = \sum_{i=1}^{n} x_i w_i, \tag{2}$$

where

$$w_i = \frac{d_i^{-p}}{\sum_{j=1}^{n} d_j^{-p}}. \tag{3}$$

In the above equations p is an arbitrary positive real number, n is a number of markers and nodes on boundary curves and d_i (d_j) is a distance between interpolated and i-th (j-th) known coordinate.

In the finishing stage, for all the nodes translated using Inverse Distance Weighting the nearest neighbours on the surface of new (registered) face are searched using kd-tree algorithm [9], and the coordinates of these nodes are adjusted so as to lie on the surface of a new face.

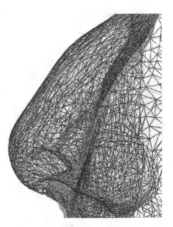

Fig. 9. The base mesh of the nose in the position of registered face, before finishing stage and after it (right)

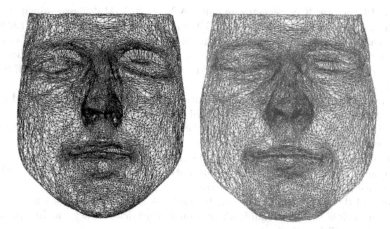

Fig. 10. Base mesh of the reference face (left) and the deformed base mesh stretched to the mesh of registered face (right)

This step leads to a better matching of the meshes in the areas that are not described by the characteristic points, such as the cheeks and forehead, and the areas lying between the markers - for example, the curvature of the nose (fig.9).

The example of whole 3D registration procedure is depicted in the fig.10, where the same, base mesh is representing reference face (left) and registered face (right).

6   Summary

The effect of accurate registration is a deformed mesh of the reference face, describing the geometry of the registered face, and introduced into the database.

In the present paper a method for automatic detection of characteristic points (markers) on the surface of the face is described. This method allows to perform accurate registration (eg elastic) of scanned face, leading to a triangular mesh of the same topology as in the case of previous (base) mesh.

This approach is a key enabler of further analysis of scanned faces, for example using statistical analysis or moda decomposition using Principal Component Analysis.

References

1. Lumley, J.L.: The structure of inhomogeneous turbulent flows. Atmospheric Turbulence and Radio Wave Propagation, 166–178 (1967)
2. Rychlik, M., Stankiewicz, W., Morzynski, M.: Application of modal analysis for extraction of geometrical features of biological objects set. In: BIODEVICES 2008: Proc. 1st Int. Conf. Biomed. Electronics and Devices, vol. 2, pp. 227–232 (2008)
3. Hoffmann, H.: Kernel PCA for Novelty Detection. Pattern Recognition 40, 863–874 (2007)

4. Lu, H., Plataniotis, K.N., Venetsanopoulos, A.N.: MPCA: Multilinear principal component analysis of tensor objects. IEEE Trans. Neural Netw. 19(1), 18–39 (2008)
5. Stankiewicz, W., Roszak, R., Morzynski, M., Noack, B.R., Tadmor, G.: Continuous Mode Interpolation between Multiple Operating and Boundary Conditions for Reduced Order Modelling of the Flow. AIP Conference Proceedings 1389(1), 94–97 (2011)
6. Shepard, D.: A two-dimensional interpolation function for irregularly-spaced data. In: Proceedings of the 1968 ACM National Conference, pp. 517–524 (1968)
7. Dhondt, G.: The Finite Element Method for Three-Dimensional Thermomechanical Applications. Wiley (2004)
8. Geuzaine, C., Remacle, J.F.: Gmsh: A 3D finite element mesh generator with built in pre and post processing facilities. International Journal for Numerical Methods in Engineering 79(11), 1309–1331 (2009)
9. Kennel, M.B.: KDTREE 2: Fortran 95 and C++ software to efficiently search for near neighbors in a multi-dimensional Euclidean space. arXiv preprint physics/0408067 (2004)

Gamification in the Development of Accessible Software

Andreas Stiegler and Gottfried Zimmermann

Responsive User Interface Experience Research Group, Stuttgart Media University,
Stuttgart, Germany
`mail@andreasstiegler.com, gzimmermann@acm.org`

Abstract. This paper describes a theoretical framework covering game design, game mechanics and game engines, linking examples from actual commercial games with a gamification application. The goal of the framework is to develop an online platform for software developers to aid them in designing accessible applications, finding help on the topic etc. A software stack will be derived taking a typical game development project as an example. We will further identify process requirements for implementing crucial game design rules, like immediate feedback. Finally, an outlook on the final project will be given and possible evaluation metrics will be described.

Keywords: Gamification, Game Development, Serious Games.

1 Introduction

Gamification has become a popular term in management, application design and usability in the last few years. Gamification refers to the application of methodologies and design patterns from game design to other contexts [3], such as the design of a business application. The idea behind this approach is to bring a possibly repetitive, non-rewarding work-task closer to tasks as performed in games, which are usually considered fun and entertaining. One has to be careful, though, on how to apply gamification, since the question how to apply it to its best effect is neither trivial nor straightforward. Game development is often split into three important fields: game design, dealing with the meta-level of a game, such as its topic, general approach, setting or features. Game mechanics are, roughly speaking, the rule sets that implement the game design into an actual game, which includes describing how characters move, what attributes an object has and what the action space of a game is. Finally, the actual game engine is the implementation of the game mechanics into executable code, including a renderer, a physics engine, artificial intelligence and more. Each of these three layers comes with its own requirements and restrictions and offers new challenges. Gamification is often described as just using metaphors and approaches from game design, which never happens in actual game development, as game design, game mechanics and the game engine are closely tied together. An effective approach of gamification will therefore have to take all of them into consideration and adapt them to a business scenario.

C. Stephanidis and M. Antona (Eds.): UAHCI/HCII 2014, Part I, LNCS 8513, pp. 171–180, 2014.

2   Gamification

The term gamification is used in various contexts with different definitions. [3] defines gamification as "the use of game design elements in non-game contexts". Other definitions classify certain design approaches as gamification, leading to games themselves being gamified if they include systems like achievements or badges [5]. While the definition of [3] is more generic, it also covers the evolution of gameplay and game mechanics best. Typical cooperative or competitive reward systems like avatar upgrades in the form of player levels were used in the very first games [11] and are commonly adopted in gamification, while other reward systems, like badges and medals, were used in internet forum software a lot more frequently, before they became mainstream in computer games. Both game design and game mechanics are evolving and changing over time and there is also a flow back from non-game applications into games. Recent "blockbuster" titles like Battlefield 4, for example, use a web page with a browser plugin as their game menu, only launching the actual game application when a player picks a game server to participate. Thereby most of the avatar development like configuring weapons and checking unlocked rewards are moved into the browser. Typical non-game design patterns are used in this context and the game closely ties into social media. There is also a tablet application for Battlefield 4 that uses typical design patterns for the mobile platform. This is a good example of adopting non-game design patterns in games, beyond the very basics of user interactions.

Gamification became a popular research topic in human-computer interaction, starting in the 1980s with work by [8]. Today, computer games are becoming a social phenomenon. Massively multiplayer online role-playing games (MMORPG) like World of Warcraft® are attracting player bases of several millions and eSport is becoming more and more popular. Research in gamification aims to identify the metaphors and methods used to make games successful and apply them in a work or educational context. In general, gamification not only applies to computer software, but also to physical real-world examples [7], although this paper will focus on digital game development and derives patterns from these applications.

We will follow the gamification definition of [3]. Gamification is not a single method that can be applied to a specific problem, unlike, for example, a software design pattern that can be applied when certain problem criteria are met and that offers a path to solve the problem. Instead, gamification describes the repurposing of many different "game design elements", which themselves vary greatly from genre to genre and even from title to title [4].

2.1   User Interface

The most obvious "game design elements" taken from games are interface design patterns [1]. A typical game interface looks different from the average software application at first glance. While the basic interface elements are the same, particularly in more interface-intensive game genres like massively multiplayer online role-playing games or real-time strategy games, their visual design differs greatly. Figure 1 shows the most important part of the Diablo® III user interface, the action bar, where players can find the most vital information about their character: the current experience gathered to advance to the next character level is displayed as a conventional progress bar (small orange bar, center). The character's health (red globe, left) and resource to use abilities (purple globe, right) are both represented as slightly different (non-linear) progress bars, as the fill level of the globe represents the current status of the respective resource. Due to the different volume distribution of spheres along an axis, a 90 percent fill state of the health sphere does not represent 90 percent of the maximum health points. This suits gameplay well, as players see larger visual drops in their fill level when their character has only few health points left and is close to death. The ability buttons (bottom center) are an array of buttons that grant access to selected abilities. When an ability is used, the button also displays the cool down until the spell is ready for use again, as well as the hotkey binding. Small conventional buttons to the right grant access to other important parts of the user interface, such as the character sheet or the inventory screen.

Fig. 1. Diablo III Action Bar

The user interface also includes purely aesthetic elements like the demon and angel figure (very left and right) which serve no game play purpose, but still are quite prominent and about the size of the most vital health-globe and even overlap them. Game user interfaces also follow the "five E's" principle of interface design [10]: Efficient, Effective, Engaging, Error tolerant, and Easy to learn. Yet, comparing a typical office application to a game shows that their weights and goals for these categories differ.

The "Engaging" criterion is probably the most obvious one. In a game, this category also includes weaving the interface into the setting and atmosphere of the game. This aspect is very crucial for games, as the user interface is often the primary interaction channel for a player: if a game's goal is to achieve immersion, the very interaction channel has to transport the setting and atmosphere of the game, just as much as the 3D graphics on the rest of the screen. This results in a large portion of the interface being concerned with reassembling symbols of the game setting, like demons and angels in the case of Diablo III.

The "Effective" criterion is another user interface aspect in games that often differs in weight and goals. Obviously, the user interface has to be effective to fulfill the goals assigned to it. Yet, in a game, these goals themselves are restricted. Consider the example of Diablo III again, compared to a typical office application like Microsoft Excel®. Introducing a "Solve Problem" button to Excel that automatically solves any problem encountered in a spreadsheet (for simplicity, let us assume there is a very advanced artificial intelligence running in the background that can solve any problem you might encounter) would actually be a great benefit to the application and a superior selling point on advertisements. In a game like Diablo III, a "Solve Problem" button replacing the action bar would ruin gameplay, as combining abilities and using them in correct order is one of the basic principles of the game. This difference originates in a popular concept known as flow [2]. Flow describes matching the challenge of a game to the skill level of the player. If the game challenges are too low for the skills of the player, he may become bored. On the other hand, if the challenges are too hard, the player may become frustrated. Including a deliberate challenge, even if there would be automated solutions, is a very important aspect of games [6].

Another aspect of user interface design that game developers are particularly concerned in is symbolism. Unlike most applications, many games have quite complex virtual 3D worlds, where navigation and user interaction are more difficult to handle than on a flat 2D plane. Though most gamified applications will not require offering a 3D world for interaction, there are certain principles used in 3D interaction design that can be transferred to 2D environments. Symbolism, i.e. using the same iconic object for any instance of a respective interaction possibility, is already well established in application design. A game example from Diablo III would be the reward chests hidden in dungeons sharing the same visual appearance, no matter in which dungeon the player is.

Another method, which is less frequently used in gamified applications, is color coding. A typical example can be seen in Figure 2, showing a game scene from Mirror's Edge. The game features a vast, light-colored environment, where players have to navigate through a city using procuring techniques. Certain interactive game elements are colored in bright red. Color coding can be a very effective method to achieve navigation, but comes with obvious accessibility constrains. One could imagine pattern coding or similar approaches to achieve the same effect without relying on color perception.

Fig. 2. Mirror's Edge Color-Coding

A gamified application might be limited in purpose and screen estate, and may lack opportunities for adding aesthetic elements to the user interface. Yet, in the context of a certain gamification metaphor – e.g., displaying a road map as an actual map that developers uncover while fulfilling milestones – it can help to underline this metaphor by adding additional visual elements, e.g. wrinkled map edges.

An often-neglected aspect of game user interfaces is that they should be usable and accessible for as many users as possible, including those with disabilities. Game accessibility guidelines, e.g. [9], and software frameworks, e.g. [12], can support the game designer in achieving this goal. It is obvious that some games cannot be made accessible to all users without changing core features. For example, a person who is blind will not be able to play a game in which flying a fighter jet in real-time is a requirement. However, with some creativity, it may be possible to deliberately change the game to include alternative (and more inclusive) playing modes beyond the "traditional path". For example, an "auto pilot" function could be added to the game, and the challenge for the user would be to continuously adjust the parameters of the auto pilot in such a way that the fighter jet performs best in the current situation.

The inclusive approach in designing for gamification is important since we want all users to benefit from the gamification features, not just a subgroup. Games sometimes deliberately address a specific user group only, e.g. young persons with good vision and quick reaction; or older persons who need to jog their brains to prevent dementia to progress. However, if we apply gamification to an application that is used by a broad variety of users, we need to make sure that it is for the benefit of all these users.

2.2   Game Play

In game development, game play is often compared to the script of a movie. Game play describes the high-level design aspects of the game, like the genre, the story, the environment, and setting, what important goals a player should pursue, what aspects of the game should be the most relevant for a player, how social interaction with other player works etc. Notably, game play does not define the actual rules that implement these goals. This is a major difference to application design, where the rules of the underlying business logic often dictate closely what the application should look like.

Challenge, is a very basic principle of game design. In order to design for flow, the game play often specifies what kind of challenges a player can expect and how they scale along a players experience and increasing skill. A gamified application has to offer some kind of challenge to its users, as most established gamification mechanisms, such as reward systems or competitive comparison become meaningless if there is no challenge involved. This requirement might actually contradict the efficiency of the application, which is often very crucial for business applications. Yet, in the context of an educational or communicational application, challenge might actually benefit the goal of the application and should be planned carefully from the very beginning of development. It might be worth reducing efficiency for offering a meaningful challenge to the user, as the overall contribution of a user having fun with an application is increased.

Another important aspect of game play is replayability, i.e. describing methods that make a replay of the game entertaining for the player. This might involve challenge considerations, as a challenge already mastered is usually a lot easier than an unseen one, as in puzzles.

Game play development is very specific not just to a particular genre but also to a particular game. Different real-time strategy games, for example, differ greatly in their game play. Therefore, metaphors from game play cannot be transferred in a straightforward way to a gamified application. Yet, including a "game play" development step in the design phase of a gamified application, planning for challenge or replayability (or repetitive tasks in a gamification context) is an important advice for designing a gamified application. Adaptable vs. adaptive system

We call a system *adaptable* if it lets the user adjust its user interface aspects by dedicated user actions, e.g. in a configuration dialog, or by activating a button or menu item. A system is *adaptive* if it automatically adapts some aspects to the current context of use; which may involve asking the user for confirmation of the suggested change. In brief words, a system is adaptable if the adaptation is user-initiated, and it is adaptive if the adaptation is system-initiated.

Oftentimes, systems are both adaptable and adaptive. This will typically result in mixed dialogs in which a user changes some aspect of adaptation, and the system will react upon this by proposing to change another (complementary) aspect to the user.

	Example: chess	Example: StarCraft® II
Game play	Two players/sets of pieces, turn-based game on limited piece of terrain, focus on tactical and strategic usage of figures. Goal: capture the enemy king, ...	Three distinct alien races, real-time game on limited piece of terrain, two resources to gather to produce units, focus on tactical usage of units and economy, clear visuals to support eSport, ...
Game mechanics	How the figures move, 8x8 squares, how to take a figure, rules for win/loose/draw, ...	Damage and hitpoints of units, unit categories, techtree layout, economy and costs, ...
Game engine	(the actual physical figures)	Component-based engine, deferred rendering, ...
Game content	(the actual physical figures)	3D models for units, voice recording, cinematics, ...

Fig. 3. Game examples: Chess and StarCraft II

2.3   Game Mechanics

The game mechanics of a game describe its set of rules implementing the goals and design concepts of the game play. Figure 3 shows a non-virtual example illustrating the difference between game play, game mechanics, and the game engine, although the latter is quite artificial in the context of a physical game. While the game play of a game specifies the more abstract rules, goals, and the setting of a game, the game mechanics implement it into actual rules, though these rules are still not implemented in code.

Two crucial aspects in game mechanics are difficulty and balancing. While those are rather generic terms, they are usually referred to balancing the action space of a player against either the environment and non-player characters (difficulty) or against other human players in a multiplayer game (balancing). For gamification, game mechanics mean to select appropriate tools for the user to achieve a certain goal, for example a badge system or avatar improvement. Yet, balancing or difficulty are often ignored in the process, though they are crucial for most games (there are examples of games where difficulty and balancing are hard to identify, for example Tetris® or many puzzle games in general).

Difficulty ties closely with flow, as it describes how challenging it is for a player to beat a certain portion of the game. Optimizing a game for flow would mean to linearly increase the difficulty of the game as the player's skills improve. This is a difficult if not impossible task, as it is neither possible to measure the skill of a player effectively, nor to measure how difficult a certain portion of the game is for a certain player. Many games therefore offer optional, explicitly challenging levels, which players can attempt to beat. Doing so increases the reward a player would usually get (like experience or a golden badge). Gamification could offer similar difficulty approaches, such as adding extra time to an imminent deadline, if a developer manages to reach an important milestone.

Balancing is always relevant when a game offers a multiplayer mode. It is of particular importance in eSport games, like StarCraft II, where a game should be perceived as "fair" even though the players may have differing skills. This can be achieved by offering the same chances of winning for all players, although their methods to reach victory might differ. In the context of accessibility and gamification, balancing becomes a crucial task. Accessible gamification cannot be limited to the user interface layer, which is trying to display the chosen interface elements in a way that they can be perceived, operated and understood by anybody. Gamified accessibility will also have to respect balancing, where the deployable methods per participant can vary greatly. This obviously influences game play decisions, as not any possible game play can be implemented with game mechanics that take this requirement into account.

2.4   Game Engine

The game engine, finally, is the technical implementation of the game mechanics in executable code. This is probably the clearest difference between serious games and gamification, as serious games use the same underlying technology as a common game, while gamification usually builds on different software stacks, like the Web or an office application. In game development, there is an important feedback channel from the engine development to both game play and game mechanics, since no game mechanics – and therefore game play concepts – about what can be implemented. The game play goal of vast and continuous game worlds to explore will clash with the technical requirement of a rendering system that may require a maximum visible distance or a limited complexity of the game world.

Game content is an only vaguely defined term, used in game development to describe material that is used by the game engine to implement the game mechanics. While the game engine contains a rendering system that is capable of drawing a space ship on the screen, the actual model of the space ship would be the game content. Roughly speaking, everything that is supplied by an artist or not required for the engine to run without errors could be regarded as content. Yet, this definition becomes a bit unclear when thinking about scripting languages. These are often used in game engines to allow developers to work on difficulty and balancing without having to compile the whole game engine over and over again. Such scripts may define how the weapons and engines of the star ship work. These scripts are no longer technically part of the code of the game engine, as they are interpreted at run-time, but they are still required to get a meaningful game running. For the purpose of gamification, however, the game engine and game content can be construed as a single module.

Just as with game engines, the software stack of a gamification project varies greatly from project to project. There may be external constraints, like having to use a certain software framework or having to run in the browser. These constrains are not different from constraints that game engines have to face, for example having to get a certain rendering technique to run on consoles and PCs alike. A great difference between game development and a gamification project, however, is that game engines are usually the first thing that are specified and developed in a game project. This could either happen because parts of the game engine, like the rendering system or the physics simulation, are middleware, or because developing a game engine from scratch is both expensive and risky. This leads to game studies knowing very precisely what their technology is capable of when designing game play and game mechanics. In addition, if a certain game play or game mechanics concept seems worth it, the game engine can be extended to cover the new technological requirements. This is very different from many gamification projects that either start with requirements like "gamify this application" or just deliver design guidelines as their outcome.

In the first case, where the task is to gamify an existing application, the underlying software stack – the whole game engine and content – is set into stone, and there are only few successful game titles that build entirely on existing code. If gamifying an existing application is the goal, it is important to closely analyze the existing software and make changes to the code if necessary. Gamification is not an add-on that can be installed any time.

In the second case, gamification is used on a purely theoretical level and only delivers mock-ups or concepts on how to gamify a certain usage metaphor. This is similar to an experience that most enthusiastic young game developers have to go through, i.e. when they first realize that their "splendid" game design and game mechanics they came up with are actually not implementable given the external constraints (usually runtime performance). Gamification cannot be done on a theoretical level and then be expected to run under the technological requirements.

2.5   From Game Development to Gamification Development

Above, we gave an overview over the three fundamental modules in game development: game design, game mechanics and the game engine. While all three of them have their unique aspects to cover, they also have clear and strong influences on each other. A successful game cannot be developed while ignoring one of these modules. Development in each of these modules can have impact on the development of the other two, requiring all three of them to be under continuous observation until the very end of the development phase – and even afterwards as maintenance (patching) is vital in today's gaming communities.

Gamification development shares many of the fundamental requirements of game development. The game engine may be very different, but both game mechanics and particularly game play are very similar. There is no reason – and no excuse – for not taking the challenge of developing all three of them continuously when creating a gamification solution. This is a significant challenge, but a challenge that the games industry has learned to master. It is neither easy nor are there any recipes granting success.

But at the end of the day, challenges reward golden badges.

3   Application and Outlook

Within the Prosperity4All project, we will create a gamified online platform for software developers to collaborate and learn about deploying accessibility in software. Care will be taken to make the platform suitable to use for all developers, including those with disabilities. The platform will link with popular developer sources like Stack Overflow and offer libraries, coding tools and tutorials on how to integrate into GPII and build software allowing integration of accessibility solutions. This platform will use gamification approaches derived from actual game development as described above in both its development phase and implementation. Evaluation of the described gamification approach is one of the key goals of the project.

Acknowledgments. The research leading to these results has received funding from the European Union Seventh Framework Programme (FP7/2007-2011) under grant agreement n° 610510, Prosperity4All ("Ecosystem infrastructure for smart and personalised inclusion and PROSPERITY for ALL stakeholders"). This publication reflects only the authors' views and the European Union is not liable for any use that may be made of the information contained herein.

References

1. Crumlish, C., Malone, E.: Designing social interfaces: Principles, patterns, and practices for improving the user experience. Yahoo Press (2009)
2. Csikszentmihalyi, M.: Flow and the Psychology of Discovery and Invention. Harper Perennial, New York (1997)
3. Deterding, S., Dixon, D., Khaled, R., Nacke, L.: From game design elements to gamefulness: defining gamification. In: Proceedings of the 15th International Academic Mind Trek Conference: Envisioning Future Media Environments, pp. 9–15. ACM (September 2011)
4. Elverdam, C., Aarseth, E.: Game Classification and Game Design Construction Through Critical Analysis. Games and Culture 2(1), 3–22 (2007)
5. Hamari, J., Eranti, V.: Framework for designing and evaluating game achievements. In: Proc. DiGRA 2011: Think Design Play, vol. 115, pp. 122–134 (2011)
6. Johnson, D., Wiles, J.: Effective affective user interface design in games. Ergonomics 46(13-14), 1332–1345 (2003)
7. Juul, J.: Half-real: Video games between real rules and fictional worlds. MIT Press (2011)
8. Malone, T.W.: Heuristics for designing enjoyable user interfaces: Lessons from computer games. In: Proceedings of the 1982 Conference on Human Factors in Computing Systems, pp. 63–68. ACM (1982)
9. Ossmann, R., Miesenberger, K.: Guidelines for the development of accessible computer games. In: Miesenberger, K., Klaus, J., Zagler, W.L., Karshmer, A.I. (eds.) ICCHP 2006. LNCS, vol. 4061, pp. 403–406. Springer, Heidelberg (2006)
10. Quesenbery, W.: The five dimensions of usability. Content and Complexity: Information Design in Technical Communication, 81–102 (2003)
11. Salen, K., Zimmerman, E.: Rules of play: Game design fundamentals. MIT Press (2004)
12. Vickers, S., Istance, H., Heron, M.J.: Accessible gaming for people with physical and cognitive disabilities: a framework for dynamic adaptation. In: CHI 2013 Extended Abstracts on Human Factors in Computing Systems, pp. 19–24. ACM (April 2013)

User Models, Adaptation
and Personalisation

A Tool to Support the Collection of User Preferences and Device Characteristics to Enable UI Adaptability in Web 2.0 Applications

Philip Ackermann, Carlos A. Velasco, and Evangelos Vlachogiannis

Fraunhofer Institute for Applied Information Technology FIT
Schloss Birlinghoven, 53757 Sankt Augustin, Germany
{philip.ackermann,carlos.velasco,
evangelos.vlachogiannis}@fit.fraunhofer.de

Abstract. We present in this paper a tool that supports the collection of user preferences within the set of components developed in the i2web project to enable UI adaptability of web 2.0 applications. The tool (called Model Management System, MMS) is based upon a semantic web modelling framework to describe user preferences and device capabilities, combined with state-of-the-art models of web applications. This work builds upon previous efforts of the authors [1] leveraged with the use of the semantic framework Composite Capability/Preference Profiles (CC/PP [2]). The MMS gathers information on user preferences and supports user and application providers in discovering the characteristics of the device utilized by the user when accessing the application.

1 Introduction

The web is not any more a static hypertext system and has evolved into a platform for distributed and ubiquitous applications that emulate the functionality of desktop applications. These applications are known as Rich Internet Applications (RIAs) [3,4]. The concept is known as well, depending on architectural considerations, as cloud computing and web 2.0 applications.

This trend poses severe obstacles to accessibility. The absence of semantics in the custom graphical components often prevent assistive technologies from proper rendering. Several accessibility issues of RIAs are identified in [5]: lack of semantic cues and metadata in HTML content, its re-purposing for formatting and presentation, the lack of keyboard access, etc. These issues have been addressed in the previous years by adding semantic annotations to (X)HTML via WAI-ARIA [6], which adds roles, states and properties to its DOM elements. These enhancements are partially obsolete by the enriched semantics of the new HTML5 [7] elements.

The participative nature of web 2.0 complicates this landscape, where users can aggregate and combine themselves content and applications via mashups, creating a myriad of possibilities (described as 2^W in [8]).

C. Stephanidis and M. Antona (Eds.): UAHCI/HCII 2014, Part I, LNCS 8513, pp. 183–190, 2014.
© Springer International Publishing Switzerland 2014

From a socio-economic standpoint accessibility and usability issues are becoming critical, considering the demographic change worlwide. When we add to these figures the percentage of the population afflicted with a disability, we get an idea of the relevance of the problem.

The paper is organized as follows. Section 2 briefly reviews the state of the art in this area. Section 3 describes the modeling framework used in the project. Section 4 presents the Model Management System per se. Section 5 briefly discusses the user evaluation results. And finally, section 6 presents our conclusions and future work.

2   State-of-the-Art

The state-of-the-art of the different modeling perspectives for users, devices and web applications is reviewed in detail in [1]. More recent approaches like those of the Cloud4all and Prosperity4all projects [9] are by far more complex and they do not define an explicit modeling framework that can be used by the different actors (users, developers, content providers, etc.) and how the components can interoperate with each other. In the authors' opinion that may hinder a wider adoption by industry.

The approach followed by us diverges from those described there because do not focus on the description of the user physical or cognitive abilities, but on the description of the user preferences and the device capabilities of the dispositive utilized to access the application.

3   Modeling Framework

Our modeling framework is based upon the Composite Capability/Preference Profiles (CC/PP) 2.0 [2] RDF framework [10]. CC/PP allows to construct user and device profiles as a two level hierarchy: a profile with a number of components, which have a number of attributes. The attributes of a component may be included directly in a profile document, or may be specified by reference. This simple framework allows an efficient processing of profiles without the parsing overhead of semantic models based on OWL, for instance. In the following, we describe shortly the main components of our framework. The architecture of the framework is described in more detail in [1].

One of the novelties of our approach was the definition of a decoupled Web Technology model,[1] which could be used by any other component of the framework. This approach offers several advantages:

(i) it allows the expression of device capabilities for either hardware or software components;

---

[1] Available at: http://i2web.eu/ns/2012/technology#

(ii) it allows the expression of user preferences; and

(iii) it simplifies the expression of matching rules for adaptation with different granularities, ranging from top components like, i.e., images or movies to HTML elements and attributes, or CSS properties, for instance.

Device modeling started to acquire relevance as ubiquitous and mobile computing became mainstream. The most relevant industrial application has been the User Agent Profile (UAProf [11]), which provided a framework for describing capabilities of mobile devices until the middle of the previous decade. This vocabulary became obsolete because its applicability to the recent generations of smart phones is minimal. Although our approach for the device model is similar to that of UAProf, we decided not to extend it but to design our own vocabulary,[2] denoting a semantic equivalence or difference where appropriate.

As mentioned earlier, we focused on the modeling of the user preferences and not on the modeling of her physiological characteristics. On that way, we could focus on transforming different UI components to enable adaptivity. Our work is based upon the CAMELEON Unified Reference Framework [12,13], which *"...is a framework that serves as a reference for classifying user interfaces supporting multiple targets, or multiple contexts of use in the field of context-aware computing."* Furthermore, following the work of the SERENOA project [14], we have newly introduced a semantic container that holds categories of pre-defined transformations, which can be mapped to algorithms similar to those of the library of algorithms for advanced adaptation logic defined by SERENOA. Due to the abstraction level introduced by the Web Technology model, we can avoid redundancies in their classification due to different content-types.[3]

Application modeling generally involves three major aspects: architecture, implementation and interaction. Ensuring a good level of accessibility for an application is a task that has impacts on all the three aspects. Accessibility obviously affects the user interaction, but it affects also the implementation and architectural choices, because sophisticated and adaptive user interaction can scale only if the underlying architecture and implementation patterns are appropriate. Since it is realistically impossible to impose architectural and implementation patterns that adapt to all application types, the i2web application models are a set of guidelines that implement application modeling best practices for incorporating accessibility into a Web application. The model is based upon the WAI-ARIA recommendation [6], concentrates on the semantics of the application and does not contain any domain-dependent information. This approach was validated by expert and user tests.

With this approach we have been able to generate successfully inference rules customized to three industrial-size web applications: a multiplatform e-banking framework; a multiplatform e-government application; and a multimedia content management system.

---

[2] Available at: http://i2web.eu/ns/2012/devicemodel#

[3] The user preferences model is available at: http://i2web.eu/ns/2012/usermodel#

4   Model Management System

The Model Management System (MMS) of the i2web project is an assistive system with two main functions:

(i) support the user in configuring her preferences when interacting with different web applications; and

(ii) extend the functionality of standard web browsers (user agents) to facilitate the communication with the different web applications so that they receive information on the user's device, her assistive technology and her preferences.

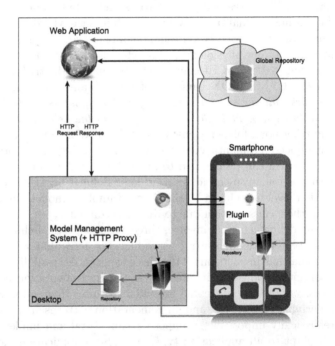

Fig. 1. General overview of the Model Management System (MMS)

Fig. 1 presents a high level overview of the system. The target is that the MMS is able to run in different devices (desktop, smart phone, etc) and at the same time, it takes care of the synchronization of the user preferences between them and the global repository (which location does not need to be necessarily on the cloud). The MMS also supports the user in deciding which preferences fit her needs.

Additionally, it provides to the user's device a HTTP proxy so that the anonymized profile location is transmitted via HTTP headers to the web application. The web application communicates with the global model repository and provides to the user an adapted web application. This HTTP proxy component defines clearly an interaction sequence between the user agent in the corresponding client device and the web application at the server-side. This sequence consists of six stages (see Fig. 2):

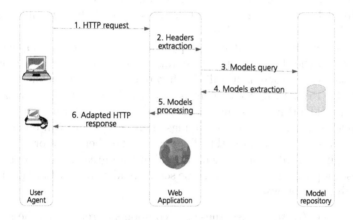

Fig. 2. Client-server interaction sequence diagram

1. The client device sends in addition to the normal HTTP requests, two supplementary headers that represent pointers to model instances of the user preferences and her device profile.
2. These headers are extracted by the web application.
3. The server queries the global models' repository to receive the relevant information for the web application.
4. The global models' repository sends the requested profiles.
5. The web application processes this information and prepares the corresponding adapted response.
6. The HTTP response is sent to the client.

It must be highlighted that due to the asynchronous nature of modern web 2.0 applications, this sequence is transparent to the user and a great effort was invested to avoid performance penalties.

Fig. 3 presents an overview of the architecture of the system via a layered diagram. Its main components are:

- Cross-cutting Infrastructure Layers: these are components related to common functionalities (e.g., logging services or security/authentication) or with third-party services (like communication with the semantic repositories).
- User Interface Layer: this component includes interactions with end users in regard to the configuration of their preferences and of the client.
- Service Interfaces Layer: components related to different applications services.

– Application Layer: these components include the core functionality of the MMS and have 4 elements:

  • HTTP Server Controller: client-side HTTP server with small memory footprint responsible of controlling the local web application utilized by the user to configure the system among other tasks.
  • Model Interpreter: component responsible of bidirectionally "translating" modeling information.
  • Operating System Native Components: set of specific components tailored to the different operating systems to detect relevant information to the MMS, such as installed software and assistive technology.
  • HTTP Proxy: this component is responsible of inserting at runtime the i2web HTTP headers that contain the relevant information of the user preferences and her device settings. This component can be used in two versions, as a standard HTTP proxy at the client side or as a browser plug-in. This dual implementation allowed a great flexibility in the user testing phase. For instance, some screen readers do not function properly with given browsers.

– Data Sources/Data Access: these are components related to the storage of information, be it the semantic models representing device information or user preferences or authentication information that protects the privacy of the users.

These components are developed in a service-oriented architecture and communicate with each other via REST-based services.

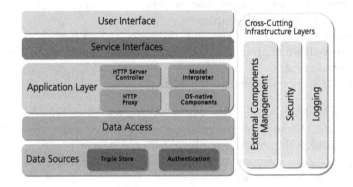

Fig. 3. Layered architecture diagram of the MMS assistive system

5 User Evaluation

The user interface went through 4 design iterations, which included 3 expert and end-user evaluations. It has been conceived as a wizard application that supports the user to configure her system in a step-by-step manner. In the different versions of this interface, major changes were introduced only in the sequence/number of steps, the amount of information displayed to the user, and improving the automatic detection of system characteristics to hide from the user any complexity. The key steps identified were:

- authentication,
- detection of previous configurations,
- operating system detection,
- user agent (browser) detection,
- assistive technology detection, and
- preferences configuration.

After these steps were complete, a submission to the persistence layer is done by the system to store the changes and inform the proxy of those changes.

The final user evaluation was in general very positive and the users were able to use and manage the system autonomously. Due to resources and time constraints, the system offered a limited set of adaptations to the end user. It is expected in the near future to widen these elements, so that the user had at her disposal more choices for this adaptation process.

6   Conclusions and Future Work

As mentioned earlier, we have successfully tested the whole framework in several environments from the technical perspective and with end users. For its applicability to a larger scale, the repository needs to include more instances of devices capabilities and user preferences. To that end, it is necessary first to extend the MMS to support different mobile devices and to test the framework with more users with special needs.

Acknowledgements. Parts of this work have been undertaken within the framework of the Inclusive Future-Internet Web Services (i2web) project, co-financed by the 7th Framework Programme of the European Commission under its ICT Programme (Grant Agreement number 257623).[4]

References

1. Ackermann, P., Velasco, C.A., Power, C., Mohamad, Y., Pullmann, J.: Developing a Semantic User and Device Modeling Framework that supports UI Adaptability of Web 2.0 Applications for People with Special Needs. In: Proceedings of the International Cross-Disciplinary Conference on Web Accessibility, Lyon, France, pp. 12:1–12:4. ACM (2012)
2. Kiss, C. (ed.): Composite Capability/Preference Profiles (CC/PP): Structure and Vocabularies 2.0, W3C Working Draft 30 April 2007. World Wide Web Consortium, W3C (2007)

---

[4] http://i2web.eu/

3. Allaire, J.: Macromedia Flash MX — A next-generation rich client. Technical Report March, Macromedia, Inc., San Francisco (March 2002)
4. Duhl, J.: Rich internet applications. Technical report, IDC, Framingham (November 2003)
5. Pappas, L., Schwerdtfeger, R., Cooper, M. (eds.): WAI-ARIA 1.0 Primer - An introduction to rich Internet application accessibility challenges and solutions, W3C Working Draft. World Wide Web Consortium, W3C (September 16, 2010)
6. Craig, J., Cooper, M. (eds.): Accessible Rich Internet Applications (WAI-ARIA) 1.0, W3C Proposed Recommendation . World Wide Web Consortium, W3C (February 6, 2014)
7. Berjon, R., Faulkner, S., Leithead, T., Navara, E.D., O'Connor, E., Pfeiffer, S., Hickson, I. (eds.): HTML5 - A vocabulary and associated APIs for HTML and XHTML, W3C Candidate Recommendation World Wide Web Consortium, W3C (February 4, 2014)
8. Raman, T.V.: Toward 2^W, beyond web 2.0. Communications of the ACM 52(2), 52–59 (2009)
9. Vanderheiden, G.C., Treviranus, J., Chourasia, A.: The global public inclusive infrastructure (gpii). In: Proceedings of the 15th International ACM SIGACCESS Conference on Computers and Accessibility. ASSETS 2013, pp. 70:1–70:3. ACM, New York (2013)
10. Brickley, D., Guha, R. (eds.): RDF Vocabulary Description Language 1.0: RDF Schema, W3C Recommendation. World Wide Web Consortium (W3C) (February 10, 2004)
11. Open Mobile Alliance: User Agent Profile – Approved Version 2.0. Technical report, Open Mobile Alliance (February 6, 2006)
12. Calvary, G., Coutaz, J., Bouillon, L., Florins, M., Limbourg, Q., Marucci, L., Paternò, F., Santoro, C., Souchon, N., Thevenin, D., Vanderdonckt, J.: The CAMELEON Reference Framework. Technical report, CAMELEON Project, IST-2000-30104 (2002)
13. Calvary, G., Coutaz, J., Thevenin, D., Limbourg, Q., Bouillon, L., Vanderdonckt, J.: A unifying reference framework for multi-target user interfaces. Interacting with Computers 15(3), 289–308 (2003)
14. Motti, V.G.: Algorithms for Advanced Adaptation Logic. Deliverable 4.2.1, SERENOA project (2011)

Personalizing Interfaces
Using an Inclusive Design Approach

Dana Ayotte, Joanna Vass, Jess Mitchell[*], and Jutta Treviranus

Inclusive Design Research Centre, OCAD University, Toronto, ON, Canada
{dayotte,jvass,jmitchell,jtreviranus}@ocadu.ca

Abstract. The Web is ubiquitous and yet many potential users are unable to access it at all or to access it in a way that works well for them. As more daily activities become tied to digital systems it becomes imperative that we design these systems for everyone to use. Personalized interfaces have the potential to help marginalized digital users overcome barriers to access and participation in an increasingly digital world. Interfaces that meet users where they are, adapt to their unique preferences, and empower them to participate are a necessity for many to "get in the digital door."

By using the rich tools and techniques afforded by the web, combined with the inherent mutability of the digital, we can design tools that allow users to customize their digital interaction. Below are details of an inclusive design approach to create preference management tools that allow portable interface personalization.

Keywords: Inclusive design, digital accessibility, user interface design, personalization, preference management tools, user needs and preferences.

1   Introduction

The Web is ubiquitous and yet many potential users are unable to access it at all or to access it in a way that works well for them. As more of our daily activities become tied to digital systems (kiosks, ticket machines, ATMs, library terminals, etc.) it becomes imperative that we design these systems for everyone to use. Personalized interfaces have the potential to help marginalized digital users overcome barriers to access and participation in an increasingly digital world. Interfaces that meet users where they are, adapt to their unique preferences, and empower them to participate by putting the personalization decisions in their hands are not only possible, but they are a necessity for many to "get in the digital door."

Users are unique, and the situations where users interact with technology are diverse. These complex and unpredictable combinations mean we can't take a one-size-fits-all approach to creating interfaces, and yet this is the current state of most digital interactions. Where solutions currently exist, they are often too specialized or apply to only a single application or web browser. By using the rich tools and techniques af-

---

[*] Corresponding author.

C. Stephanidis and M. Antona (Eds.): UAHCI/HCII 2014, Part I, LNCS 8513, pp. 191–202, 2014.
© Springer International Publishing Switzerland 2014

forded by the web, combined with the inherent mutability of the digital, we can design tools that allow users to customize their digital interaction to fit their specific contexts, needs, and preferences.

Through work on the Global Public Inclusive Infrastructure (GPII) carried out through the following projects (Cloud4All, Prosperity4All, Floe Project, and Preferences for Global Access) [1, 2, 3, 6], the design team has used an inclusive design approach to create preference management tools that allow portable interface personalization. This approach focuses on the full range of human diversity and aims to meet that diversity with flexible and transformable tools that are easy to use and understand.

2   Background

Design processes are often a negotiation between values and practice where values define overall goals and practice is the methods used to achieve the goals. An inclusive design approach's goal is to design interfaces that are inclusive of the full range of human diversity.

2.1   Values: Designing for Human Diversity

An inclusive design approach starts with a re-definition of disability as a mismatch between a given technology and the needs and preferences of the user in a particular context [7]. Working from this definition, accessibility becomes a match between the user's needs and the ability of the interface to meet or exceed those needs. This simple perspective shift reframes accessibility as a design and development problem that impacts all of us.

The common assumption that designing for accessibility is limited to addressing the needs of a limited number of "extreme" users or users "on the margins" motivates many designers to avoid addressing accessibility issues. Based on this assumption designers believe it is not worth the trouble or cost to try to meet the needs of so few users as they believe they can't address these "special" needs within a single, mainstream design. As a result designers miss rich and important input into the design process and users are delivered interfaces that suffer from inherent limitations in usability and personalization [8].

By considering disability as a momentary and/or contextual mismatch between technology and user needs we take on the challenge of addressing accessibility in all of our designs; in this way technology becomes more useable for everyone. The design problem becomes: how can we create flexible tools that adapt to an overwhelming diversity of needs and preferences?

This big picture helped the design team at IDRC think more broadly and keep an open perspective on context, individuals, cultures, ages, abilities and circumstances, and it presents a larger opportunity for all designers to broaden their perspective and improve their designs. In this paper we detail how the design team used an inclusive, one-size-fits-one approach to address this problem through the design of tools that afford user interface personalization.

2.2   Practice: Making Flexible Tools

The design team focused on creating a tool that allows users to declare their needs and preferences and to create their own one-size-fits-one interfaces. It became clear that declaring needs and preferences first required an awareness or familiarity with the notion of adjusting settings in the digital environment – an awareness that cannot be assumed for all users. The challenge, then, was to conceive of a preference management tool that could enable and promote the discovery, adjustment and application of user preferences.

The team started by thinking extensively about the circumstances for realistic uses of the tools. To address a broad range of unique needs, the preference management tool must be inherently flexible and adaptable. The team also concluded that to be truly inclusive, the tool must meet each person wherever he or she is in any particular context.

Though it would be practically impossible to enumerate all of the potential contexts within which a user might encounter a digital interface, it is useful to put some thought to the various types of contexts that can have a significant impact on a user's ability to use an interface. The following are just a few of the many unique individual and contextual factors the team considered when thinking through user interactions with digital systems:

- Environment (noisy bus station, bright sunlight shining on a screen, etc.)
- Unique user abilities (age, digital literacy, comfort with technology, mobility, dexterity, preferred and necessary means of computer interaction, cognitive needs, etc.)
- Operating system and application variability
- Learning approaches (preferred ways of consuming content)

This list helped the design team keep the breadth and depth of contextual complexities in mind while conceptualizing interfaces for addressing user needs.

Meeting users where they are is fundamental to an inclusive design approach and requires consideration of a broad range of users from those who are not comfortable with technology at all to power-users who are technology savvy. To take the design thinking further, the team fleshed out use cases and associated scenarios to begin to understand these realistic uses and workflows. User testing (currently being conducted) will further help to guide the direction of the design process.

To fully meet users "wherever they are," we concluded that the tool must meet users both in the context of their current task (simpler for quick "on-the-fly" adjustments), as well as in full-featured applications that users can access at their leisure. It became clear that the design team needed to consider multiple tools to allow diverse users to discover, adjust, and apply needs and preferences. The preference management tools must allow for a range of users: first-time users getting in the door, users exploring new preferences that might meet their needs, and technology-savvy users making advanced refinements for specific customizations. The tools must also allow users to move through levels of complexity as they become more comfortable with the idea and process of setting preferences.

The ultimate vision for these tools is that they will allow users to customize any interface they might encounter by exploring and then declaring preferences, saving them to the cloud, and applying them to devices (both private and public). This personalization meets users wherever they are and adapts the interface to their needs and preferences, getting users in the door and making their interaction with technology as painless and as enjoyable as possible.

2.3   Applications

The work described in this paper was done under the Global Public Inclusive Infrastructure (GPII), a project of Raising the Floor. This work applies to multiple projects including Preferences for Global Access (PGA), Cloud4All, Prosperity4All, and Floe Project.

The designs presented in this paper are works in progress and are at various stages of development. At the time of writing this paper the Preferences for Global Access project has completed Phase I (Knowledge Building and Design), and the Cloud4All project is about to complete a second round of reviews and user testing on the latest preference editing tools.

3   Methodology

In working on this project three interrelated methods emerged as the most relevant and useful to the design process. The team developed their own approach to using these methods, which included mind-mapping, use cases and wireframes. The team cycled through these methods, iterating repeatedly as the designs developed. With each iteration, the team revisited early assumptions and added greater layers of detail and granularity.

Mind-mapping allowed the design team to tackle the big picture early on in the design process, and revealed many possibilities and questions about a desired preference editing workflow. While working on the mind-maps it became clear that the team needed a way to evaluate how realistic the workflow was and to consider user behavior in more detail. As a result the team began to develop a number of detailed use cases and related scenarios in order to consider realistic situations and user needs that needed to be addressed by the preference editing tools. At the same time, the team began to sketch wireframes in order to zero in on a level of granularity of the interface and interactions and to consider the levels of complexity of user needs.

3.1   Mind-Maps

The space of preference discovery and declaration is quite complex. Early in the design process the team developed a number of graphical mind-maps for thinking through the complex workflow of someone using the preference management tools.

Sketching out these mind-maps allowed the design team to begin to visualize interface flows and to identify open questions related to workflow of the tools. The development of mind-maps quickly led to the need for use cases and wireframes to consider user behavior and contexts and to demonstrate the variety of interactions at each stage of the workflow.

Over the course of the design process the team returned to these mind-maps several times to refine the workflow, consider alternate workflow options, and to tweak the corresponding wireframes.

3.2   Use Cases and Scenarios

Use cases provide a way for the design team to consider the many situations and contexts in which users might encounter and use the preference management tools. Through the development of these use cases and scenarios the team began to understand both the breadth of requirements for the tools design as well as the specifics of how to meet individual users' needs. By their very nature these use cases are limited in that they cannot cover the full spectrum of potential users, and in no way do they replace the need for user testing. However they provided a starting point for the design team to map out various scenarios in which the preference management tools might be used and thus provided a starting-point for interface and interaction design. The use cases allowed the design team to consider a broad range of potential users including first-time computer users, power users, and users with and without assistance.

The following use case example was developed under the Cloud4All project. The details described in the scenarios refer to specific design concepts related to preference management. The use case shown here is partial only. For more detailed use cases please refer to the following wiki page:

http://wiki.fluidproject.org/display/fluid/%28C4A%29+Use+Cases [5].

Use Case Example – Sam .

> Sam is an artist and an instructor at a local art college. She teaches three classes per week, and spends approximately 20 hours outside of teaching marking papers, preparing lectures, and updating the online forums for her classes. Outside of her teaching duties she dedicates about 15 hours per week to her art practice, including online research.
> Sam usually goes to the coffee shop every day around 9:00 am. She likes to avoid the early morning rush of people on their way to work, since when the coffee shop is too crowded she finds it difficult to maneuver freely in her wheelchair. This morning Sam has some emails she needs to respond to. After she gets her coffee and wheels over to her table, Sam gets out her laptop from the pouch at the side of her chair. Once on the table she slides the laptop out of its sleeve and

sets it up. Sam gets out her type-aid from the side pocket of the sleeve and straps it to her right hand. The type-aid allows her to type on the keyboard more quickly and with better accuracy than would be possible with her hand alone. When she is using her laptop she relies on keyboard input as she does not use a mouse. Sam prefers to use speech recognition rather than typing, but isn't comfortable doing it in a public place. She also occasionally likes to use text-to-speech because she likes to give her eyes and neck a break from looking up at the monitor, especially when reading long research papers.

Scenarios

Scenario 1: Creation of Base Set (Preferences Management Tool)
Sam recently used her desktop computer to register her Cloud4all account and set up her base preference set. When she logged into the preference management tool she was asked if she wanted to create her base preference set from the device settings, using the editor, or with a step-by-step guided setup. She chose to create her base preference set using the device settings on her desktop computer, as she already had it set up the way that she likes it.

The following settings were detected in the preference management tool:
- **speech recognition turned on** (gathered from system preferences)
- **optional text to speech turned on** (gathered from system preferences)
  - sub-settings including voice selection, speaking rate, and customized control keys
- **slow keys turned on** (gathered from system preferences)
  - with medium-short delay setting
- **mouse control** (gathered from system preferences)
  - double-click speed set to slow
  - cursor movement set to "no inertia"

Based on the detected settings, the Cloud4all system recommended that sticky keys also be turned on. Sam had tried the sticky keys setting in the past but had not found it to be helpful to her, so she declined the recommendation and reviewed her detected preferences in the overview. Since everything looked good to her, she confirmed her settings and her base preference set was saved. She then exited the preference management tool and carried on with her work. [5]

3.3   Wireframes

As the mind-maps became more detailed the team began to sketch wireframes of the interface designs corresponding to stages in the workflow for different preference editing tools. Several iterations of wireframes were developed as the team returned to the mind-maps and use cases repeatedly. For examples of wireframes see http://wiki.fluidproject.org/display/fluid/Preference+Editing+Tools+Design [4].

3.4   User Testing

At the time of writing this paper user testing has not been completed on the PGA or Cloud4All designs. However, much of this design work is based on the foundation laid by the work done under UI Options and related user testing results.

A user testing protocol for the Cloud4All tools is under development and will address both broad issues as well as granular questions about the designs. Broader questions include:

- When (in a user's workflow) are settings changed?
- Where do users go to make changes to settings/preferences (website, browser, operating system, hardware)?
- How does the process of changing settings vary across different circumstances?
- What do users view as a preference?
- Do users distinguish between temporary preference and a permanent preference? This relates to saving preferences - when and how?

More granular questions for testing include measuring the ease of use of the search bar, relevance of curated categories, switching between preferences and presets, adjuster design variations, tool panels layout, etc.

4   Results – Tool Design for Personalization

Throughout the process of sketching out mind-maps, creating wireframes and writing use cases, several design questions emerged. These questions presented interesting and complex design problems that the team grappled with in an effort to create an inclusive solution to the challenge of personalizing interfaces. Through the grappling, the team came up with unique, inclusive approaches to each challenge detailed below. These design concepts have been gathered into four sections that broadly define the range of user actions: discovering preferences, declaring preferences and saving preferences.

4.1   Discovering Preferences

How does a user discover preferences and preference tools? For someone who has never changed their system settings how can preference management tools most effectively be presented to them? How can a user be encouraged to explore and discover preferences in ways that are engaging and simple while at the same time minimally obtrusive? These considerations are essential to address the needs of users who are not already using a computer or other device, or who are not comfortable with technology. The novice user or the user with cognitive needs must be supported in determining what is necessary in order for them to be able to use the computer (or other devices) at all. To ensure that users can access these tools it must be possible to use them in a variety of ways from the start, including visually, aurally, with mouse control, with keyboard-only control, in any language, etc.

> "...how can we create a computer-based tool to help novice users set up their first preference sets if they cannot perceive, operate, or use the computer? Accessibility solutions must be flexible and responsive enough to balance the need to overcome serious barriers to entry with the need to showcase diverse preference possibilities to users who are interested in them."[1]

Methods of Preference Discovery

The team considered different ways that a user might discover preferences. "Learning to learn" was the starting point for many aspects of the tools design, particularly on the Preferences for Global Access project. A user may come to the preference editing tools with little or no previous experience in changing their settings and/or with little knowledge of what settings and preferences exist – one goal of the tools is to help users discover what preferences work for them and in so doing they learn about themselves and about their preferred ways to learn or to consume digital content. As a result the team considered preference exploration-based tools as well as various features within more advanced and/or complex tools that would allow for this discovery: for example the option of a guided "wizard" and the presentation of preference bundles or "starter combos".

The idea of "learning to learn" also precipitated discussion about whether and how to use evaluation and inference to determine a user's needs. The team aimed to design the tools to make the learning to learn process as playful and engaging as possible. In its simplest form such a tool or features of a tool could allow the user to try things out in a safe and enjoyable way, rather than putting the user in a position of being evaluated or having their preferences prescribed to them.

Guide
Preference management tools may include the option of a step-by-step guide or "wizard" to walk a new user through the steps of setting up an account, choosing and adjusting preferences, and saving preferences to a set.

Primary Preferences
Basic or common preference may be shown to the user when they first enter the tool (see Figure below). Adjusters are set to default values and may be accepted as-is or modified by the user. The user is also given the option to explore related preferences (in this case by selecting the gear icon) or they can search for other preferences.

Starter combos
Starter combos or "presets" are preference activation bundles and contain a group of preferences, related through a particular user need, which are activated all at once. They provide a means of "getting in the door" for users unfamiliar with modifying their settings or users who cannot access the tools as-is.

When a starter combo is turned on, it activates all associated preferences and automatically sets the preferences to pre-determined values. Starter combos get the user to a "good enough" place, thus allowing them to use the tools to further modify their preferences, or to carry on with the task at hand. For example, selecting a "No mouse" starter combo might activate Mouse Keys and Sticky Keys as well as set the Repeat Key settings to pre-determined values. Selecting a "Speak" starter combo might turn voice over on as well as set the words spoken per minute and volume settings to default values.

Explore Tool
One design solution that the team explored is an in-context tool aimed at encouraging and allowing users to explore the idea of setting preferences as well as to explore the effects of specific preferences. With this tool users are encouraged to try new preferences and combinations of preferences. A successful exploration will allow users to try things without fear of permanently losing their current level of access (e.g. by providing a clear way to undo changes). Users should also be confident that once they find preferences they like, they will be able to save them for future sessions. A functional demo of an explore tool can be found at: http://build.fluidproject.org/ prefsEditors/demos/explorationTool/

Inference/Recommendations
One example of inference would be to have the system recommend preferences related to those selected or adjusted by the user, at the moment that they make the adjustment. Common preferences may also be suggested, or preferences indirectly related to a search term.

Preference Organization
The design team considered various ways of organizing preferences to determine what might provide the highest level of findability for users and the greatest ease of navigation through the preferences. Curated categories provide one way of organizing preferences. Categories organize all available preferences into

their broadest groupings; they are containers for related preference families e.g. the "visual alternatives" category might include the Text size preferences, Speak text preferences Contrast preferences, Cursor size preferences, and Text style preferences. Search-based categories are temporary categories that appear in search results and which contain preference families that are related through a search term.

4.2   Declaring Preferences

When a user knows what they want or is comfortable with the idea of preference-setting, how can they declare their preferences? The design team aimed to provide a number of different ways of allowing users to declare preferences to try to meet them where they are in different situations.

Ingest
If a user is already using a computer that they have set up to their liking, their current settings can be used as a starting point to create a preference set. When the user first logs into the preference management system, they can be offered the option to ingest the current device settings.

Adjust
This activity involves providing the user with the ability to easily adjust a single preference, or adjust multiple preferences. This also allows users to: a) adjust the setting of a preference (i.e. change the size of the text for a text enlargement preference); b) undo previous settings; and c) instantly apply changes to content that the user is viewing (independent of whether or not the user saves or stores their settings for later application to other devices).

Share & Sync
A user may want to apply preference sets that have been created by others with similar needs, or a teacher may want to create preference sets for her students and then share these sets with multiple students. Sharing sets would allow users who aren't familiar with changing their settings or who aren't sure which preferences might help them to try out preferences recommended by other users.

"On-the-fly" Adjustments
The team discussed the need to support adjustments that a user would make frequently and temporarily, which would be applied to their device immediately and which they wouldn't necessarily want to have stored in a preference set (for example, volume and brightness). Preferences could be determined by the user (manually "favourited"), they may be inferred by the system (based on most frequently made adjustments), or they may be determined by an implementer who wishes to limit the functionality of the tool(s) – for example a museum kiosk which does not allow saving to the cloud and which is intended only to provide temporary and basic settings to be adjusted.

4.3   Saving Preferences

The question of how and when preferences should be saved relates to many other aspects of the tools including the complexity of an "on the fly" tool as well as the concept of preference sets. Which tools should allow saving? How should this be presented to the user? Should adjustments be saved locally only, until the user chooses to add them to a preference set which applies to multiple devices? Should adjustments be saved automatically with an option to undo? This concept of the "stickiness" of settings/adjustments came up frequently in the design process. It presents a challenge to meeting the needs and expectations of diverse users.

5   Discussion

In addressing the issue of a one-size-fits-one solution to digital accessibility, the design team developed both a methodology for inclusive design as well as designs for flexible and adaptable preference management tools. To see the latest designs as well as all iterations and design artifacts from the project visit the team wiki workspace at http://wiki.fluidproject.org/display/fluid/Preference+Editing+Tools+Design [4].

6   Conclusion

With a clear problem statement and an approach that focuses on human diversity the design team designed preference management tools that empower users to personalize their experience, adapting the interface to their own unique needs and preferences.

Since no one interface will meet the needs of all users, the design team produced interfaces that adapt to individual user needs. And since the situations where users will encounter these interfaces are as diverse as users themselves, the team produced a number of tools for those different contexts.

Acknowledgments. The authors would like to thank the larger community of designers, developers, volunteers, testers, and users for their contributions to this work. In particular thanks to the GPII User Experience team and the team from Preferences for Global Access. Thanks to The William and Flora Hewlett Foundation (Floe Project), 7th Framework Programme of the European Union (Cloud4All and Prosperity4All), U.S. Department of Education (Preferences for Global Access).

References

1. Petrides, L., McLaughlin, L., Jimes, C., Brennan, M., Treviranus, J., Schwerdtfeger, R., Rothberg, M., Vanderheiden, G., Tobias, J., Trewin, S., Clark, C., Mitchell, J.: Preferences for Global Access Design Report: Profile Creation Support for Cloud-based Accessibility. Unpublished manuscript, submitted to the U.S. Department of Education's Office of Special Education and Rehabilitative Service (2013)
2. Cloud4All Project, http://wiki.gpii.net

3. FLOE Project, `http://floeproject.org`

4. Vass, J., et al.: Preference Editing Tools Design,
   `http://wiki.fluidproject.org/display/fluid/`
   `Preference+Editing+Tools+Design`

5. Ayotte, D., et al.: Use Cases, `http://wiki.fluidproject.org/display/`
   `fluid/%28C4A%29+Use+Cases`

6. Global Public Inclusive Infrastructure, `http://gpii.net`

7. Treviranus, J.: Inclusive Design Research Centre, What is Inclusive Design? (2013),
   `http://idrc.ocad.ca/index.php/about-the-idrc/`
   `49-resources/online-resources/articles-and-papers/`
   `443-whatisinclusivedesign`

8. Treviranus, J.: The Value of the Statistically Insignificant. Educause Review, 46–47
   (January/February 2014), `http://www.educause.edu/ero/article/value-`
   `statistically-insignificant`

Using a Common Semantic Structure to Provide Comparable Contextual Models of Users and Technology

Matthew Bell, Colin Machin, and Roger Stone

Loughborough University, Loughborough, Leicestershire, LE11 3TU, UK
{m.j.bell,c.h.c.machin,r.g.stone}@lboro.ac.uk

Abstract. The accessibility solution that is appropriate for an individual in a given situation may be provided through variations in the choice of device, assistive technologies (AT) and adaptations used. Profiles can be created to represent users and technology, however, owing to trade-offs between profile specificity and transportability, there is currently no universally accepted method for creating profiles for holistic interaction.

This paper describes an approach which represents both user and technology in symmetrical (hierarchical) recursive profiles, using a vocabulary that moves from device-specific to device-agnostic capabilities. Through the use of semantic relationships, capabilities can be attributed —and accessibility comparisons made—at varying (appropriate) levels of granularity, using contextually comparable data.

Where accessibility problems are identified, they are described in terms of the gap between the capabilities of the user and technology, inherently providing a functional description of the support required. Speculative augmentation can then be used to evaluate different solutions in order to maximise accessibility for the individual.

Keywords: Evaluation of Accessibility, Usability, and User Experience, User and Context Modelling and Monitoring, Semantics.

1 Introduction

The accessibility solution that is appropriate for an individual in a given situation may be provided through variations in the choice of device, assistive technology (AT) and adaptations used (Sloan *et al.* 2010). Different devices are often used in different contexts or for different tasks owing to their individual characteristics. A desktop computer may be used at work or for creating documents, a Smart TV used at home or for consuming online media, and a tablet used 'on the move' or for checking emails. ATs can then be used to augment the capabilities of devices or users in order to improve their accessibility. Screen readers may be used to provide an audio version of a device's visual content and a hearing aid may be used to increase the range of sounds that a user can perceive. Finally, adaptations can be used as micro-ATs, providing personalisation that increases the range of users who are able to access content (Vanderheiden

C. Stephanidis and M. Antona (Eds.): UAHCI/HCII 2014, Part I, LNCS 8513, pp. 203–214, 2014.

2008). By moving closer to a screen a user can improve their ability to see its contents; the same result can also be achieved by increasing the size of the text on the screen. As they are intended for customisation, many adaptations are not labelled as accessibility options, however device-specific settings are increasingly being included in profiles describing accessibility needs.

In order to maximise accessibility, a model is therefore required that can compare between profiles representing the user and their device, as well as any ATs and adaptations they are using. The variety in interaction paradigms results in a need for specificity in order to capture the nuances of each particular device, interface or control. However, as users frequently interact with multiple technologies there is also a need for profiles that are generic enough to be transportable.

This paper will provide a framework for identifying accessibility problems by moving between device-specific and device-agnostic profiling through the logical structuring of profiles. The approach provides flexibility during both profile acquisition/maintenance and the matching process. Dynamic comparison of profiles at varying (appropriate) levels of granularity allows discovery of accessibility issues to be performed efficiently. In addition it is also possible for contextual information to be represented using the same structure, providing a measure of the applicability of data to a given situation.

2   Background

The presence (or absence) of accessibility issues between a user and a piece of technology can be predicted by simulating their interaction using representative models and profiles. Given the variety found within users, technologies and interaction paradigms, there is no universally accepted method of modelling any aspect of the simulation. This is due in part to the range of hierarchical levels and functional layers of abstraction for which simulations are created. Levels of abstraction describe the way that higher-level tasks can be built up from lower-level ones (e.g. hand-eye co-ordination). Layers of abstraction describe the way that data can be viewed in multiple frames of reference; with lower layers providing structural information and higher layers storing specific contextualised measurements.

Biswas & Robinson (2010) describes the issue of fidelity and the resulting trade-off between low-level (high-fidelity), and high-level (low-fidelity models). A similar problem is observable when contrasting between low-layer (low-fidelity) and high-layer (high-fidelity) models. The greater the fidelity of a simulation, the more accurately it is able to represent the situation under investigation. This accuracy is however gained at the expense of transportability, resulting in an inability to reuse the simulation to model other situations. Reducing the fidelity of the simulation increases its transportability, whilst decreasing its ability to accurately represent a situation.

As demonstrated by the generation of a glossary of terms in Peissner et al. (2012), this has resulted in a lack of consensus on the components that are

required within a simulation. Some common components include models or profiles describing:

User: A representation of the user in terms of a number of variables describing
his/her various characteristics.

Device: A representation of the device with which the user wishes to interact
describing its various characteristics. The device may be a piece of hardware
or software.

Task: A representation of the task to be simulated. It can be used to dictate
the structure and contents of the other models by indicating the level of
abstraction of the simulated interaction.

Environment: The context in which the interaction takes place. The environment can affect accessibility by interfering with interaction and its importance is dependent on the layer of abstraction at which the simulation is
targeted.

At a high level, accessibility simulation is a comparison between user and
technology (or task). In order for a comparison to take place, the respective
profiles must be described in compatible vocabularies. In the field of Knowledge
Representation a "domain model" contains the vocabulary and structural information necessary to describe a particular problem domain. A domain model
for a generic accessibility problem will contain information about the user and
technology in order to allow a comparison to be made. There are two main vocabularies that are used to facilitate this description: technology-focused preferences
and human-focused capabilities. Competing standards have been developed that
use each of the vocabularies respectively.

ISO 24751 deals with the provision of individualised adaptability and accessibility in the context of e-learning. It is a three-part standard, which describes the
user and application profiles separately. Currently under revision, it is based on
a fixed vocabulary of technology-focused needs and preferences. Preferences refer
to device or software settings that can be specified to improve accessibility (e.g.
font size). As they are device specific, they provide an accurate representation
of the needs of the user in terms of the technology-focused preferences required
in order for a device to be accessible. As above however, this specificity reduces
the transportability of a user's profile owing to a need for mappings between all
related preferences across devices.

ISO 24756 uses Common Accessibility Profiles (CAPs) to allow direct comparison between the needs and capabilities of users, systems and their environment (Fourney & Carter 2006). It views accessibility in terms of channels
of communication that are facilitated by human-focused capabilities. CAPs are
constructed from a series of Interacting Components which are able to either
input or output via a fixed vocabulary of modalities (e.g. visual acuity). Unlike
preferences, the approach provides a static vocabulary against which any device
setting may be mapped (Atkinson *et al.* 2010). Human capabilities provide the
transportability required to compare a single user profile against multiple device
profiles. Their generalisability, however, comes at the expense of the extra effort

required in terms of describing device settings and adaptations in terms of their corresponding human-focused capabilities.

It is possible to link the two vocabularies by modelling higher-level technology-focused preferences in terms of their lower-level human-focused capabilities. The resulting multi-level models lead to improved transportability while still allowing specific situations to be simulated. This type of simulation is called Hierarchical Task Analysis (HTA) and can be found in the GOMS family of models which break tasks down into a series of sub-tasks. Those sub-tasks can then be evaluated based on their constituent Motor, Cognitive and Perceptual elements.

Hierarchical structures can be found in models related to both accessibility and the personalisation of knowledge-based adaptive systems. Kaklanis *et al.* (2012) describes a framework for simulating accessibility evaluations. It uses hierarchical structures both within the organisation of its user-profile and during the simulations that are based on them. Data is firstly stored under a series of parameter types (Cognitive, Behavioural, Physical, Kinematic and Geometric), within those types a hierarchy is then developed based on the structure of the human body. During simulation, higher-level tasks are built from lower-level primitives, which are computed from the bio-mechanical data in the profile. Whilst the framework is hierarchical in nature, it is reliant on a fixed lowest level, from which higher levels are computed.

Sosnovsky & Dicheva (2010) describes the widespread use of hierarchical modelling within web-based adaptive systems. The article describes the Adaptive Web as focused on the personalisation of information and many of the systems are knowledge-based recommenders. The featured user models are all based on ontologies, which provide a hierarchical structure allowing the systematic storage and creation of new knowledge. Once again, higher-level knowledge can be inferred from its lower-level constituents. Through the use of stereotyping however, the models can also provide top-down inference.

Efforts have also been made to standardise the data structures used to expose profile data. Peissner *et al.* (2012) describes a number of formats based on XML and RDF. The Semantic Web is a collection of standards (including RDF) that allows data to be shared and reused across application, enterprise, and community boundaries[1]. By storing data in terms of its relationships to other data, networks can be formed to produce machine-readable information. Semantic technologies have already been used to produce an implementation of the CAP (Sala *et al.* 2011), and the CC/PP (Klyne *et al.* 2004) provides an RDF structure for defining the technology-focused accessibility needs of individuals and is therefore directly compatible with ISO 24751.

3   Approach

Two trends are visible in the previous section:

- The need for a standard vocabulary to describe both users and technology in order to expose profile information for comparison, and

---

[1] http://www.w3.org/2001/sw/

– The need to provide abstraction within profiles in order to cater for the diversity found in real life.

The approach taken builds on existing profiling techniques by providing a series of standard semantic relationships which allow both users and technology to be described using a symmetrical (hierarchical) recursive structure.

Taking the high-level view that accessibility simulation is a comparison between user and technology, there is little to differentiate between their resulting profiles. Rather than modelling them differently, they are both considered as 'actors' taking part in an interaction. Various elements within the interaction model can be standardised, as seen in figure 1. A vocabulary based on interaction capabilities allows accessibility to be described using a functional assessment of the abilities and requirements that are being compared. The abilities and requirements are stored in a common 'internal structure' and exposed via a standard 'external interface'. If a match is observed between the capabilities of the user and technology then interaction is possible using those matching capabilities. When a mis-match is observed, a description of the required assistance is provided in terms of the gap that must be bridged and the capabilities that are available to do so. Rather than relying on the presence of specific technology-based preferences or assistance targeted at a specific labelled impairment, a solution could involve re-routing interaction via alternate (matching) capabilities.

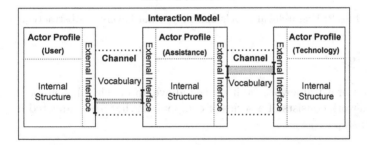

Fig. 1. Standardisation of Elements Within the Interaction Model

Where alternate matching capabilities are not available, assistance can be chosen based on its ability to bridge the gap between available capabilities. The use of a common internal structure allows capabilities to be linked internally and exposed in a predictable way via a standard external interface. The format is able to represent both users and technology (including hardware, software, assistive technology and adaptations) with chains of actors being used to represent the route that information takes. This provides the potential for automation as profiles can be stored in a machine-readable format allowing matching algorithms to be developed.

Profiles are also able to contain data at various levels and layers of abstraction[2]: from low-level human-focused capabilities to high-level technology-focused preferences, and from generic low-layer descriptions of abilities to specific high-layer contextualised ability recordings. This allows direct matching between profiles at the appropriate level of abstraction rather than requiring reference to a fixed (low) reference level as seen in existing models. In addition, a measure of the confidence of a match can be estimated based on the similarities between the highest layer at which information is provided. This approach reduces the rigidity suffered through the application of either of the themes mentioned above in isolation. Figure 2 shows the use of both levels and layers of abstraction within a profile as well as a channel of communication between two actors.

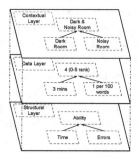

Fig. 2. Hierarchical Levels and Functional Layers of Abstraction

4   Design

The design of a framework built on the above approach will now be described. The framework consists of a series of components that are connected by a series of relationships.

4.1   Actors

Actors describe the entities (users and technologies) that are able to take part in interactions. Within the framework, profiles are built up using a nested series of actors, which may possess several sub-actors, describing their components. Sub-actors are actors in their own right (demonstrating the recursive nature of the framework) and can be viewed either as autonomous entities, separate to other actors at their level, or as constituents of higher-level actors. This mirrors the real-life construction of users, as demonstrated through the hierarchical VUMS profiles in Kaklanis *et al.* (2012).

---

[2] As describe in section 2.

The metaphor is even more useful when modelling technology, as individual actors can potentially be placed inside or separated from their higher-level actors, mirroring the modular nature of technology. A device like a desktop computer is actually a composite of several sub-devices (a screen, keyboard, mouse and speakers), each of which can be purchased separately and removed for use within another computer system. In the same way software is represented as an actor, which can be placed within numerous higher-level actors to represent its use within different devices.

An actor can also be used to represent the environment within which an interaction is taking place. Comparison between different environments (or the same environment at time times) can then be made based on their sub-actors. As an example, the environmental conditions of an open-plan office and a small home office may vary in terms of the number of people present, the type of light bulbs used, the weather outside the window and the ergonomy of furniture available.

This method of representation inherently identifies the abstract level at which comparisons should initially be made. For example, a simulation could be developed to describe a user interacting with a mobile phone. As the actors are defined at a high level, the initial comparison would focus on the high-level assessment of whether "the user can use the phone" (and whether the phone can be used by the user). The result of this comparison is a function of lower-level comparisons between the sub-actors of each actor (e.g. the user's eyes versus the phone's screen), which are in turn dependent on their sub-actors (e.g. the user's visual cones versus the phone's colour sub-pixels).

Through investigation of the sub-actors that are involved in an interaction, it is possible to identify which parts of the user and technology are responsible for its success or failure ('problem actors'). This form of assessment allows problem actors to be avoided, either by re-routing communication, or putting assistance in place to cope with the actor's deficiencies. For technology-based actors, replacement and upgrading are also possible.

4.2   Capabilities

Actors are able to interact with each other via capabilities, which are organised in the same hierarchical fashion as actors. Capabilities are described in terms of their direction, modality and a measure of their bandwidth, allowing channels of communication to be built and investigated between actors. An actor may have more than one capability, which allows it to take part in communication in either one or both directions. Processing functions provide links between capabilities allowing an actor to receive information via one capability and transmit it via another. An actor also inherits the capabilities of all of its sub-actors, (which are likely to be its own capabilities' sub-capabilities). A finger is an actor with capabilities to both input and output via the tactile medium. Output is provided through the capabilities of its muscles (sub-actors) to generate movement and input is provided through its nerves which are able to sense pressure, texture and temperature.

Capabilities share the same hierarchical structure as actors with higher-level capabilities being inferred by (reliant upon) the presence of lower-level capabilities. Where a mismatch is found between two capabilities, investigation of their sub-capabilities can indicate its source by identifying the constituent capabilities that are causing the problem. Where a gap is identified, its effects will propagate upwards, affecting the interaction of any higher-level capabilities that rely on it. As described previously, higher-level capabilities are likely to be task-focused with a vocabulary moving towards human-capabilities as focus is moved further down the capability hierarchy. Figure 3 depicts a low-layer (structural) view of a series of actors, sub-actors and their related capabilities. It provides a limited example of a number of pieces of technology that are all dependent on one of the capabilities provided by a finger (1-D Movement). At a higher-level, each capability would have data attached, describing a measurable ability and the context in which it was collected.

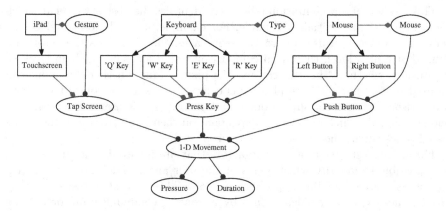

Fig. 3. A graphic representation of the hierarchical nature of physical actors and their capabilities (see figure 4 for key.)

4.3   Context

Capability data is constrained by the context within which it is collected (Peissner *et al.* 2012). User and device capabilities fluctuate throughout the day and their resulting abilities may be based on the presence of a number of factors. Multiple data items may therefore be stored against a single capability, providing information about an actor's capabilities in different contexts. Environments can be modelled using the same structure and vocabulary as any other actor. Interference (e.g. background light or noise) can be described as capabilities of the environment and exposed in a format compatible with a user's (or technology's) abilities to perceive them. As data is collected, information about its context can be stored by defining a relationship between the data and an actor representing its context. This again demonstrates the recursive nature of the framework.

5   Implementation

By defining flexible relationships rather than dictating rigid data structures, the (theoretical) design is not dependent on any specific technology or file format. The use of a graph-based representation (as seen in figure 4) does however bias implementation towards pattern-based representation and matching technologies. Development has been carried out using the semantic languages RDF and OWL for data storage and the graph-based logic language Prolog to provide reasoning capabilities. Figure 4 is a generic graph describing some of the relationships that have been defined and used in the framework.

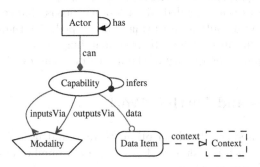

Fig. 4. A graph representing the elements of the framework and their relationships

Interaction is modelled in terms of a series of actors, with capabilities, that can be measured to provide data, which can be stored in context. Users, technology and context are all modelled as actors made up of one or more sub-actors ('HAS'). An actor may also have capabilities allowing them to interact with each other ('CAN'). Capabilities share the same hierarchical structure as actors with higher-level task-focused capabilities being inferred by lower-level human-focused ones ('INFERS'). Capabilities are compared based on their modality ('INPUTSVIA' and 'OUTPUTSVIA') and can be measured to produce data that is collected in context.

Any two actors are able to sustain interaction when they have compatible capabilities with:

Opposite Directions: In order to communicate with each other one must transmit a message which is received by the other.

The Same Modality: Measured in the same units (or be convertible).

Overlapping Abilities: The two capabilities must share a common range within the modality.

Measured in Context: The ability measurements should be based on a common context (which is similar to that displayed in the current environment).

As the quality of a match is dependent on all of the above factors, adherence to the list can be used as a measure of the probability that two capabilities are compatible.

The framework has also been designed to support a modular implementation. The multi-layered approach taken to data storage allows the separation of vocabulary specification, the selection of data storage mechanisms and the development of matching algorithms. This provides the potential for different modules to be used based on the needs of a particular situation. Low-level capabilities related to transmitting or receiving sound could for example be described using a frequency response graph, with associated matching functions being used to predict their resulting accessibility.

This allows specific implementations of the framework to be developed to suit different interaction needs while providing the potential for integration through the definition of appropriate relationships. Gradual upgrades can be made available as vocabularies are extended, data storage needs change, algorithms are improved or improved context capturing is developed. Alternately "low-power" variants could be produced which restrict matching to lower layers, providing less information about the quality of the match or accuracy of the simulation.

6   Challenges and Further Work

This paper is focused on the description, storage and use of profile data, the success of the approach is therefore dependent on a number of other areas that are the subject of current research:

Semantic Web Technologies. are not yet fully realised, meaning there are still issues to be overcome before they can be widely adopted. A lack of accepted standards at the upper levels of the technology stack has resulted in the need for additional technologies to be used in order to achieve the functionality described at present. There are also outstanding questions regarding the scalability of graph-based data storage.

As they are researched further, many of these issues will disappear, assuming the further development and widespread use of semantic technologies. In addition, the identification of current deficiencies can be used to inform new research and development efforts. In terms of scalability, the modular and multi-layered design of the framework can be used to take advantage of pre-processing techniques that only present the data that is needed to evaluate a particular situation.

Data Acquisition. is a particular challenge with the problem being twofold: (1) initial population may require a bootstrapping procedure, and (2) information would need to be kept up-to-date. ISO 24756 for example, relies on the user (or other human agent) to create and update CAPs. However for mass adoption, the user cannot be relied upon either because (1) they may be unwilling, or (2) the information they provide may be unreliable (Godoy & Amandi 2005).

The framework is therefore reliant on the availability of agents that are able to populate user profiles. Given the nature of their task, current agents are highly specialised and tend to be developed as part of standalone systems (e.g. Hurst 2009). The intention of this framework is to allow agents to expose their data and as a result allow it to be used as part of a more holistic profile.

Context. can have a large effect on the usability of data, as described previously. At present the framework is able to model context and use it to determine the probability that a match is accurate. Where there is a lack of data to describe an actor's capabilities in a given context it is currently not possible to infer it (other than finding the closest possible match or using a stereotype). This concern can be addressed via inference back to human capabilities and the ability to model the environment as an actor. As interference (e.g. background light or noise) is stored as a capability in a format compatible with the users abilities to perceive them, it should be possible to determine the effect that a particular contextual capability has on an actor's capabilities. Known capabilities/contexts could then be used to extrapolated capabilities in other contexts.

Matchmaking Algorithms and Assistance Delivery Mechanisms. are, like data acquisition agents, are outside of scope given the focus of this research on data representation and storage. They are however required in order for the approach provided in this paper to be realised. Work aimed at developing a Global Public Inclusive Infrastructure is however providing research in this area (Vanderheiden & Treviranus 2011).

7   Discussion

The approach presented in this paper provides a flexible method of profiling users and technology, enabling direct matching between their capabilities at various hierarchical levels and functional layers of abstraction. The suggested relationships allow capabilities defined in various open and proprietary standards to be used together through attribution to an individual within a single profile. In addition contextual information can be included, providing a measure of applicability of data to a situation.

The accessibility of interaction between two actors can be assessed by matching their capabilities and the potential to include contextual information allows a measure of the accuracy of the resulting prediction to be provided. Where higher-level capability data is unavailable for a match to be made, inference can be used to recursively find a lower level at which matching constituent capabilities are available. As contextual data is stored in the same format as users and technology, contextual matching can also use similar algorithms.

Where a match is not possible owing to incompatible capabilities, an alternate route can be identified. Alternately, speculative augmentation of actors with representative sub-actors can used to identify the effect of different potential forms of assistance. As an example, both hearing-aids and text-to-speech functionality can be described in terms of the way they re-route and transform the existing channels of communication. Software can then be modelled on different devices by placing its highest representative actor within the actor describing each device.

References

Atkinson, M.T., Bell, M.J., Machin, C.H.C.: Towards ubiquitous accessibility: capability-based profiles and adaptations, delivered via the semantic web. In: Vigo, M., Abascal, J., Lopes, R., Salomoni, P. (eds.) Proceedings of the International Cross-Disciplinary Conference on Web Accessibility. W4A 2012, pp. 14:1–14:4. ACM, New York (2012)

Atkinson, M.T., Li, Y., Machin, C.H.C., Sloan, D.: Towards Accessible Interactions with Pervasive Interfaces, Based on Human Capabilities. In: Miesenberger, K., Klaus, J., Zagler, W., Karshmer, A. (eds.) ICCHP 2010, Part 1. LNCS, vol. 6179, pp. 162–169. Springer, Heidelberg (2010)

Biswas, P., Robinson, P.: A brief survey on user modelling in HCI. In: International Conference on Intelligent Human Computer Interaction, IHCI (2010)

Fourney, D., Carter, J.: A Standard Method of Profiling the Accessibility Needs of Computer Users with Vision and Hearing Impairments. In: Conference & Workshop on Assistive Technologies for People with Vision & Hearing Impairments (2006)

Godoy, D., Amandi, A.: User profiling in personal information agents: a survey. The Knowledge Engineering Review 20(11), 329–361 (2005)

Hurst, A.: Automatic assessment and adaptation to real world pointing performance. ACM, New York (2009)

Kaklanis, N., Moschonas, P., Moustakas, K., Tzovaras, D.: Virtual user models for the elderly and disabled for automatic simulated accessibility and ergonomy evaluation of designs. Universal Access in the Information Society, 1–23 (2012)

Klyne, G., Reynolds, F., Woodrow, C., Ohto, H., Hjelm, J., Butler, M.H., Tran, L.: Composite Capability/Preference Profiles (CC/PP): Structure and Vocabularies 1.0. W3C Recommendation, W3C (January 2004)

Peissner, M., Dangelmaier, M., Biswas, P., Jung, Y.M.C., Kaklanis, N.: White Paper: Virtual User Modelling Public Document. Tech. rept. 1.0. VUMS Cluster (June 2012)

Sala, P., Fernandez, C., Mocholí, J.B., Presencia, P., Naranjo, J.C.: Implementation of the ISO/IEC 24756 for the Interaction Modeling of an AAL Space. In: Stephanidis, C. (ed.) Universal Access in HCI, Part III, HCII 2011. LNCS, vol. 6767, pp. 210–219. Springer, Heidelberg (2011)

Sloan, D., Atkinson, M.T., Machin, C., Li, Y.: The potential of adaptive interfaces as an accessibility aid for older web users. In: Proceedings of the 2010 International Cross Disciplinary Conference on Web Accessibility (W4A). W4A 2010, pp. 35:1–35:10. ACM, New York (2010)

Sosnovsky, S., Dicheva, D.: Ogntological technologies for user modelling. Int. J. Metadata Semant. Ontologies 5(1), 32–71 (2010)

Vanderheiden, G.C.: Ubiquitous Accessibility, Common Technology Core, and Micro Assistive Technology: Commentary on "Computers and People with Disabilities". ACM Trans. Access. Comput. 1(2), 10:1–10:7 (2008)

Vanderheiden, G., Treviranus, J.: Creating a Global Public Inclusive Infrastructure. In: Stephanidis, C. (ed.) Universal Access in HCI, Part I, HCII 2011. LNCS, vol. 6765, pp. 517–526. Springer, Heidelberg (2011)

Exploiting Inclusive User Model
for an Electronic Agriculture System

Pradipta Biswas[1,*], Jaya Umadikar[2], Patrick M. Langdon[1],
Arti Kashyap[3], and Suma Prashant[2]

[1] University of Cambridge, Cambridge, UK
[2] RTBI, Chennai, India
[3] Indian Institute of Technology, Mandi, India
pb400@cam.ac.uk

Abstract. User model can be defined as a machine-readable representation of user characteristics of a system. We have developed a user model that considers users with physical, age-related or contextual impairment and can be used to personalize electronic interfaces to facilitate human machine interaction. This paper presents a case study of exploiting this Inclusive User Model to personalize an electronic agriculture application. The e-agriculture system aims to help farmers in reporting crop diseases electronically and getting help from experts. We have integrated the user model with this application so that it can be used by users with a wide range of perceptual, cognitive and motor impairment. Once users signed up to the user modeling system, their profile is carried with them regardless of the type of device they are using. The paper presents brief detail of both the user model and the e-Agriculture system along with description of a user study conducted on the system.

1   Introduction

This paper presents an inclusive design technique through user modelling. We have described an electronic agriculture system to help farmers in rural India and UK. The system will be used by both agricultural experts and farmers through a variety of devices ranging from low-end mobile phones to high end computers. The range of abilities of users and contexts of use will also be different considering the vast geographic stretch and cultural differences of India and UK. Tackling such diversity demands a new type of inclusive design where interfaces can be customized based on user and context profiles.

Precision agriculture is an innovation strategy that has been proposed to cope with the problem of environment sustainability. It centres on the use of technology to increase the agricultural efficiency through urgent forecasting and early warning system. The e-Agriculatue system supports early warning and disease identification through two applications

---

* Corresponding author.

C. Stephanidis and M. Antona (Eds.): UAHCI/HCII 2014, Part I, LNCS 8513, pp. 215–223, 2014.

The Pest-Disease Image Upload (PDIU) application will be used by farmers to upload images of infested crops, while they are in the field. The uploaded images will automatically be sent to remotely located experts, who will advise farmers about remedy. The application will run on low-end mobile phones or smart phones. It not only makes it easy for farmers who have difficulty in operating a keypad but also accommodates those suffering from poor vision or cognitive impairments.

A web-based Dashboard system that runs on a personal computer and used by experts to advice farmers. Experts can be across all age levels and it is therefore important to design a user interface that takes into account impairments of different kinds that an expert might possibly be dealing with.

Any information regarding modern agricultural trends and practices being delivered to farmers should be aligned with their actual needs and their existing experience and knowledge base. In other words, the information has to be as personalized and interactive as much as possible. Our user modelling system [3] first developed a simulator to predict perceptual, cognitive and motor abilities of users with a wide range of abilities. The simulator embodies both internal state of an application and machine learning models for visual and auditory perception systems, cognitive module and motor action system. We used the simulator along with a user survey on Indian population to develop a user modelling web-service and an adaptation algorithm to personalize user interfaces for the eAgriculture system. Figure 1 and 2 demonstrate different rendering of the eAgriculture system for different user profiles.

The user modelling system is itself application agnostic. A demonstration version of the simulator can be downloaded from

http://www-edc.eng.cam.ac.uk/~pb400/CambridgeSimulator.zip

A demonstration version of user modelling web services can be found at the following links.User Sign Up: This application creates a user profile,

http://www-edc.eng.cam.ac.uk/~pb400/CambUM/UMSignUp.htm

User Log In: This application predicts interface parameters and modality preference based on the user profile,

http://www-edc.eng.cam.ac.uk/~pb400/CambUM/UMLogIn.htm

Adaptation Example: This application renders a single webpage differently based on user profiles.

http://www-edc.eng.cam.ac.uk/~pb400/CambUM/UMStyleSelect.htm

Video demonstration: http://youtu.be/MiYp-d6rSXM

A couple of similar approaches are the Global Public Inclusive Infrastructure (http://gpii.net/) and the EU Cloud4All project [4]. However these projects do not have a user performance simulation and works mainly based on users' explicitly stated preferences. The use of the performance simulation with sufficient validation will help to cover a wider range of users than existing systems and reduce the development time for any new interface as designers can run initial validation without conducting long user trials. Additionally, our system considers wider range of applications and users than existing system with respect to ethnicity and socio-economic context of use.

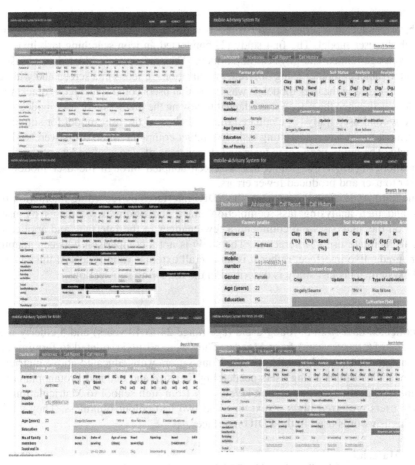

Fig. 1. Different renderings of the Dashboard application

Fig. 2. Different renderings of the PDIU application

User Studies

We have conducted a series of user trials to validate the adaptive interfaces generated through the user model. The first study [1] conducted an icon searching task involving users with age-related and physical impairment. The study was conducted on a desktop PC and a Tablet computer using different organizations of icons in a screen and with and without integrating the user model. It was found that users could select icons quicker and with less error when the screen was adapted following the prediction of user model.

The second user study [2] evaluated the prediction of the user model for situational impairment using a text searching task on a tablet computer while users were walking in a field. The study used same texts and dimensions of screen elements of the PDIU application. Again it was found that a screen adapted through the user model was quicker to user and produced fewer errors.

The third study aimed to improve the PDIU interfaces by recording interaction patterns and then analysing task completion times and wrong key presses by users. Based on the analysis we recommend a few changes in the interface and application logic to facilitate users' interaction. The study is not a comparison between adaptive and non-adaptive interface, rather it is an overall external validity test of the adaptive PDIU system. This last study is described in the following sub-sections.

1.1   Participants

We collected data from 5 young users (age range 24 to 40 years) and 5 elderly users (age range 56 to 65 years) from Mandi. They were all male, related to farming profession and use low-end mobile phones. Young users were educated above matriculation level. One of the young users needed big font size and one had Protanopia colour blindness. Elderly users' education levels vary from high school to Matriculation. All elderly users preferred biggest text size and two had colour blindness. They can all read English words used in the PDIU interfaces.

1.2   Material

The study was conducted on a Nokia 301 mobile phone.

1.3   Procedure

The task involved taking photographs of three leaves arranged on a desk using the PDIU application. At first they were registered to the application. The system then asked their preferred font size and conducted the Ishihara Colour Blindness Test [5] using the plate number 16. Based on their response, the application adapted itself and users were asked if they found the screen legible. Then they were demonstrated the task of taking photographs and after they understood it, they were requested to do the same. The experimenter recorded a video of the interaction. During the task, users needed to go through the screenshots shown in figure 1 below. The sequence of actions were as follows

Select PDIU from PDIU home screen (figure 1a)
Scroll down to Open Camera under Image 1 (figure 1b)
Select OpenCamera and take a photograph
Scroll down to Open Camera under Image 2 (figure 1b)

Select OpenCamera and take a photograph
Scroll down to Open Camera under Image 3 (figure 1c)
Select OpenCamera and take a photograph
Press Menu (figure 1c)
Scroll Down to Save option (figure 1c)
Select Save (figure 1c)

After they completed the task, we conducted a general unstructured interview about their farming experience and utility of the system.

a. PDIU Home Screen   b. Open Camera Screen   c. Menu Screen

Fig. 3. PDIU interfaces used in the study

2   Results

The following graphs (figures 2 and 3) plot the task completion times for the operations involving taking three pictures and saving them. In these figures, C1 to C5 stands for young participants while P1 to P5 stands for their elderly counterpart. An one factor ANOVA found a significant effect of type of tasks among all 10 participants [$F(3, 36) = 4.05$, $p < 0.05$]. Users took only 21.9 seconds on average to record the first image while they took 51.2 seconds on average to record the second image, 48.4 seconds on average to record the third image and 50.7 seconds on average to go to the Menu and press Save button.

We also analysed all instances of wrong key presses and Table 1 lists them with respect to each participant. In Table 1, C1 to C5 stands for young participants while P1 to P5 stands for their elderly counterpart.

During the open structured interview it emerged that they belonged to different sections of the society. They were farmers, land lords, part-time farmers of their ancestral agrarian land pursuing another profession like bus driving. They mostly harvested crops like corn, maize, bajra, wheat and so on. One of their   major problems was the quality of grains. One of them reported problem with harvesting corn, which often suffered from disease resulting white ends and less grains than usual. Another one complained about wheat, which suffered from a disease causing dried stalks. They face massive problems on farming, as they do not get enough modern equipment for harvesting good quality crops. One of them reported about a help centre in their capital town, but it was nearly a hundred kilometres away from their farming place with no good public transportation available. So they hardly could get help from them.

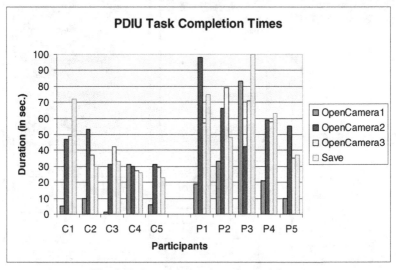

Fig. 4. Task completion times for participants

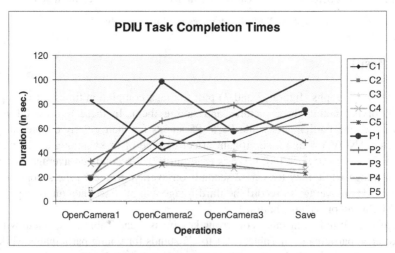

Fig. 5. Task Completion Times for each operation

Table 1. Lists of wrong Selection

Participants	Wrong Key Presses
C1	Went back from OpenCamera2 to OpenCamera1, scrolled up instead of down, recovered himself Cancelled Save option, was confused but then recovered and finished successfully
C2	Pressed middle button to select the PDIU in home screen Selected OpenCamera1 second time instead of scrolling to OpenCamera2
C3	No wrong key press
C4	Scrolling up instead of scrolling down before reaching Open-Camera buttons
C5	Pressed Submit instead of selecting Save, had trouble between selection and scroll down buttons
P1	Scrolling up instead of scrolling down before reaching Open-Camera buttons Pressed Back button instead of Selecting OpenCamera2 Pressed Back button again in the PDIU home screen Pressed Back button again instead of Selecting OpenCamera2 Could not scroll down to Save button in Menu items
P2	Pressed middle button of Scroll Button instead of selecting Capture in OpenCamera2 Pressed Menu instead of going to OpenCamera3
P3	Pressed Back button in PDIU Home Screen Presesed Back Button from the OpenCamera Screen Presesed Back Button again from the OpenCamera Screen Pressed Left button instead of Middle button in one system message screen Pressed OpenCamera1 second time instead of scrolling down to OpenCamera2 button Pressed Back button instead of Capturing image in OpenCa-mera3 Scrolled up to OpenCamera2 from OpenCamera3

Table 1. (*continued*)

	Scrolled down from Save button but then get back to Save button
P4	**Pressed middle button instead of Capture button in OpenCamera2**
P5	**No wrong key press**

3   Discussion

The farmers found the system useful and the interfaces were legible and comprehensible to them. However some of them especially the elderly ones faced problem in scrolling and recovering from error. It seemed to us a simpler interface will be more useful to the elderly users. Based on the study and list of errors we propose the following recommendations.

Initial focus on OpenCamera Screen
This initial focus can alleviate a few scrolling errors as users will understand that they need to scroll down to select the open Camera buttons.

Only one OpenCamera button with automatic Save option
The ANOVA shows that users were significantly slower in taking the second or third photograph and saving them. If there is only one OpenCamera button which automatically saves or submits the picture, a lot of scrolling errors can be avoided and the overall task completion time will also reduce significantly.

Confirmation of Back action in middle of interaction
We found users were often confused if they pressed the back button. It may be useful to add a confirmation dialog if they press the back button in the middle of taking a photograph or saving it.

Overridden buttons while capturing images
Users pressed the middle button to capture image which is a common feature in most mobile phones with a camera. It will be a good idea to let users do so making the system more intuitive.

4   Conclusions

This paper presents of a case study of personalizing an application using user model. The user model helps to render an interface differently for different users based on user profiles. Users do not need to manually change settings of browser, mobile phone or download applications. Once signed up to the user modeling web service, their profile is carried with them regardless of the type of device they are using. However our user trial also points out that the user model can not alone optimize interaction; rather a set of guidelines or recommendation about application logic is complementary to user model.

Acknowledgement. This research was sponsored by the DST, Government of India and the UK EPSRC.

References

1. Biswas, P., Langdon, P.: Validating User Modelling Web Service. W3C User Modelling for Accessibility (UM4A) Online Symposium
2. Biswas, P., Langdon, P., Umadikar, J., Kittusami, S., Prashant, S.: How interface adaptation for physical impairment can help able bodied users in situational impairment. In: Joining Usability, Accessibility, and Inclusion. Springer (2014)
3. Biswas, P., Robinson, P., Langdon, P.: Designing inclusive interfaces through user modelling and simulation, International Journal of Human-Computer Interaction 28(1) Print ISSN: 1044-7318
4. Cloud4All Project, http://cloud4all.info/ (accessed on December 14, 2013)
5. Colour Blindness Tests (2008), http://www.kcl.ac.uk/teares/gktvc/vc/lt/colourblindness/cblind.htm (accessed on August 12, 2008)

Accessibility through Preferences: Context-Aware Recommender of Settings[*]

Andrés Iglesias-Pérez[1,**], Claudia Loitsch[2], Nikolaos Kaklanis[3],
Konstantinos Votis[3], Andreas Stiegler[4], Konstantinos Kalogirou[5],
Guillem Serra-Autonell[6], Dimitrios Tzovaras[3], and Gerhard Weber[2]

[1] R&D Department, Fundosa Technosite
Technosite C/Albasanz 16, 3-B 28037 Madrid. Spain
aiglesias@technosite.es, andresip@gmail.com
[2] Technical University of Dresden, Germany
claudia.loitsch@tu-dresden.de
[3] Information Technologies Institute, Centre for Research and Technology Hellas, Greece
[4] Stuttgart Media University, Germany
[5] Hellenic Institute of Transport, Centre for Research and Technology Hellas, Greece
[6] Barcelona Digital Technology Centre, Spain

Abstract. A proposal for merging context-awareness and user preferences in the same software system is provided. Several modules from the on-going CLOUD4All project (European Commission Seventh Framework Programme) are enhanced with Context Awareness, including the Semantic Matching Framework, the RuleBased Matchmaker (with new rules) and the Statistical Matchmaker (with new features to be used as predictors). Some other components are created exclusively to deal with context features, as the Context Aware Server (to add context from motes) and the Minimatchmaker (to save computation and network resources for well-known situations)

Keywords: e-Inclusion, Personalization, Context-awareness for universal access.

1 Introduction

Daily life in urban environments tends to force the user to interact with a plethora of machines, each with its own User Interface (UI). Most probably even getting into the workplace will involve checking the smartphone in the morning for email and ToDo lists, getting a ticket to the metro or bus in a Ticket Vending Machine (TVM), reading on a tablet while in transit and finally opening the desktop computer on arrival. Currently, the personalisation of all of these systems would delay users, so they are likely to use systems under suboptimal conditions, because users rarely make any changes

---

[*] Results presented in this paper have been researched within the Cloud4all project. Cloud4all is an R&D project that receives funding from the European Commission under the Seventh Framework Programme (FP7/2007-2013) under grant agreement n° 289016.

[**] Corresponding author.

C. Stephanidis and M. Antona (Eds.): UAHCI/HCII 2014, Part I, LNCS 8513, pp. 224–235, 2014.

on the UI, especially when the interaction becomes more complicated, as when noise and light conditions vary.

Several approaches [1][2][3][4] have addressed the task of improving the interaction between a user and a computer by means of adding knowledge about the surrounding environment. However, not all of them employ the user needs and preferences about the HCI as a source of data on its own. This hinders the possibility of generating personalised UIs, which are especially important for people with disabilities, as it involves auto-activating Assistive Technologies (AT). On the other hand, researchers [6][7][8][9] have produced fruitful results when adapting the UI to the user needs, whether in automatic or semi-automatic fashion, Nevertheless, in these cases the adaptation of the UI is focused on user needs leaving the context reduced to the device that the user is employing [10]. A good universal design [5] on the server side plus the correct AT with the best configuration of settings on the client side will allow individuals with disabilities to complete tasks without the intervention of third persons, providing full accessibility even in environments that are not owned by the user.

2   Related Work

Several approaches and projects investigated semantic context-aware reasoning techniques towards accessibility in the past. [18] motivated the potential of semantic web reasoning in terms of user interface adaptation recently. Beyond that, they propose a general reasoning architecture to support adaptivity of web-based services. Thereby abstract user interface design is translated into a concrete user interface by considering user (e.g. disability, web familiarity, language) and context attributes (e.g. input-output devices, screen capabilities) as well as interaction data (e.g. user actions, navigation paths) represented in OWL and OWL_DL ontologies. A reasoning module and rule engine undertake decision-making about selecting appropriate and concrete interaction elements. Accessible TV applications through adaptive user interfaces, for instance, have been developing in the GUIDE[19] project. After initial adaptation according to the user capabilities have been calibrated, run-time adaptation is performed by rules. Capability-based reasoning, delivered by semantic information has been recently proposed by [20] Ubiquitous devices, adaptable applications and service-based content are targeted. Even if the reasoning approach fits into the matchmaking approach described in this paper, details about the process are not given. Kadouche`s [21] work based on semantic matching between an environmental model (environmental effectors) and a user model (human factors) to provide assistive user-environment interaction and services. Context information from sensors and a user profile are processed to identify potential handicap situations for users by Description Logic (DL) inference reasoning. The context query engine delivers environment effectors that lead to a handicap situation which can be resolved by assistive environment services. A further, not-directly linked domain knowledge approach is presented by [22] Based on a user model (user capabilities), a UI model (information, content, navigation, and styles) and existing guidelines (principles on web accessibilities e.g WCAG2), represented as ICF and WCAG ontologies, semantic matching through a GOAL model is created and specific guideline rationales are determined. Accessibility rationales are considered within the user context, e.g. capabilities or task. The approach does not perform personalization directly but is interesting as origin for specific contextual adaptations.

3   Methodology

The presented proposal bridges the gap between Context-Awareness and UI Personalisation by orchestrating a layered matching between a) user needs and preferences and b) device/platform settings. (a) is subdivided into a.1) common terms such as brightness or volume level, a.2) preferred applications e.g.: choose NVDA over JAWS, a.3) application-specific settings e.g.: choose voice "Jorge" when employing Loquendo TTS Engine or place keyboard on top-left corner when employing VirtualKeyboard ; whereas (b) deals with constrains "dpA" (device-platform-application) like b.1) physical constrains of the device, e.g: screen-witdht, maximum volume level or camera availability,   b.2) type of architecture (Windows, MacOS, AOSP…) , b.3) available solutions for that architecture. In the Figure 1 the "Preferences Server" deals with (a) and the "Device Manager" and "Solutions Registry" deal with (b). The source of knowledge represented as "Context Manager" is actually provided by two modules that are the Minimatchmaker and the Context Aware Server, explained below.

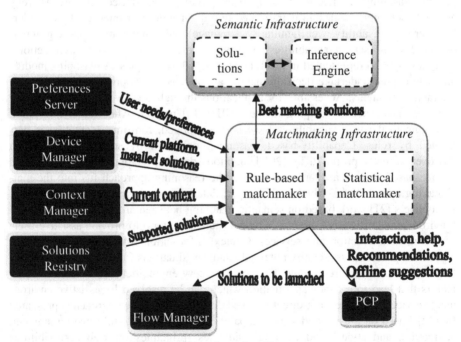

Fig. 1. Rule-based matchmaking strategy

Matchmaking is then the process of adapting a user's preference set to a given context to configure the available solution in a way that matches the preferences of the user [23]. Considering the different kinds of context that one could encounter, this task becomes quite challenging [24].There are two matchmaking strategies working together 14: a statistical approach to infer settings from previous uses of systems and a rule-based approach that exploits the knowledge of the Semantic Framework [13] to gain insights from experts on the domain of AT selection, both of them being able to fetch data from the Preferences Server that users can update thanks to the Preferences Management Tool (PMT) 15. In the device there is also a reasoning module that stores what-if conditions to save computing and network resources. The Flow Manager [16] is responsible for the communication between the modules. The Matchmakers output is divided into

Decision+Interaction Help+Recommendation+OfflineSuggestion.

- *Decision*: some ATs are automatically applied to ensure accessibility.
- *Interaction* Help: decisions to automatically apply AT aims to ensure accessibility but might entail difficulties in utilize, i.e. if the user is not aware of short cuts provided by a screen reader. Important operations are delivered to the user in addition to a decision.
- *Recommendation*: the proposed AT setup is presented in the Personal Control Panel (PCP), a module that acts as a PMT on the user's device. E.g.: preferred speech rate for screen readers.
- *OfflineSuggestion*: When new AT are available and could benefit a specific user, the Matchmakers send an to inform about the new choices.

Help

We have never launched **NVDA** for you before.
The following information about shortcuts might be helpful for you.

Shortcuts

General commands

	Desktop layout	Laptop layout
Report title	NVDA+t	NVDA+t
Voice Settings	NVDA+control+v	NVDA+control+v
Modifier Key	INSERT	INSERT
Report Status Bar	NVDA+end	NVDA+shift+end
Preference menu	NVDA + N	NVDA + N

Default short cuts of general commands for **NVDA**.

Review commands

	Desktop layout	Laptop layout
Previous line in review	numpad7	NVDA+upArrow
Say all in review	numpadPlus	NVDA+shift+a
Current character in review	numpad2	NVDA+.
Next character in review	numpad3	NVDA+rightArrow
Previous word in review	numpad4	NVDA+control+leftArrow
Current word in review	numpad5	NVDA+control+.
Current line in review	numpad8	NVDA+shift+.
Next word in review	numpad6	NVDA+control+rightArrow
Previous character in review	numpad1	NVDA+leftArrow
Next line in review	numpad9	NVDA+downArrow

Fig. 2. Interaction help example

Although the system is designed to let the user apply the settings he/she agrees, the Decision part seems to be unavoidable, as some AT (e.g., screenreader) have to be applied to let the system ask for further conformance. The Recommendation is not applied automatically, to let the user decide on this part, and the OfflineSuggestion is performed only if the user consented through the PMT.

3.1 Rule-Based Matchmaker

The Rule-based matchmaker can resolve cases where the adjustments preferred by the user cannot be directly applied due to limitations of the current system/device. Typical problematic cases include the following: a) user has application-specific preferences for a solution that is not currently available, b) user has application-specific preferences for two or more different solutions of the same type (ex. screen readers) and all of these solutions are currently available. In both cases, the Rule-based Matchmaker exploits the knowledge and the inference capabilities of the Semantic Infrastructure, in order to find the best alternative solution, or to select the most suitable solution between the available solutions of the same type, respectively. The selected set of solutions to be launched is then passed to the Flow Manager.

Beyond that a user feedback loop is triggered by passing information about matchmaking results to the Flow Manager which will be presented to users allowing them to keep control about automatically applied configurations, benefit from additional recommendations, and get useful information as well as interaction help about assistive solutions that have been launched and adjusted. Apart from information representations, users shall be able to alter and assess decisions or apply recommendations on settings and solutions directly. Figure 2 illustrates interaction help information that will be presented for solutions that user has never used before.

Table 1 shows an example of a Jena rule executed by the Rule-based MatchMaker. According to this rule, if user has specific preferences for two different solutions of the same type and the first solution is installed while the second is available but not installed (e.g. it may be accessed through the internet), the installed solution is selected as the most appropriate for launching. Context is embodied in the Rule-Based Matchmaker as a set of rules to be executed before any other reasoning. This execution allows the final decision to take into account that under suboptimal conditions the final access mode may differ from the one stated by the user in the "Preferences Server" hence the access mode is weighted to give a chance to other solutions that work on different access modes. It also have a subset of rules dealing with perfomance, the surrounding environment changes very often (light, noise conditions) but not every little change in context drives a change on access mode, so some rules are needed to stop checking for different solutions. Table 2 below shows a JENA environment rule, when a sensors detects a change in the environment variable [25]. Two use cases were defined at [26] highlighting the contextual changes: adquiring the contextual data directly from the sensors embedded in the device or from ambient motes. As an example of the first one the user Märta that has problems seeing the screen of the devices she uses, when the luminosity changes, so when she logs in she will have a visual, white on black scheme. So, when the luminosity changes, Märta would like to automatically have some of the following changes at the interface of her devices. When the brightness of the environment reaches a certain threshold, she will receive a black on white scheme. When the brightness reaches another threshold (higher) she will receive an auditory UI.

Table 1. Jena rule example – Installed solutions have priority over available solutions

```
[InstalledSolutionsTakePriorityOverAvailableSolutions:
(?tmpUser rdf:type ns:TempUsers)
(?tmpUser ns:TempUsers_hasSpecificPreferencesForSolutions
?tmpSolutionsIDOneForWhichUserHasSpecificPreferences)
(?tmpUser ns:TempUsers_hasSpecificPreferencesForSolutions
?tmpSolutionsIDTwoForWhichUserHasSpecificPreferences)
notEqual(?tmpSolutionsIDOneForWhichUserHasSpcificPrferences,
?tmpSolutionsIDTwoForWhichUserHasSpecificPreferences)
(?tmpSolutionsIDOneForWhichUserHasSpecificPreferences
rdf:type ?tmpSolutionClass)
(?tmpSolutionsIDTwoForWhichUserHasSpecificPreferences
rdf:type ?tmpSolutionClass)
(?tmpEnvironment rdf:type ns:TempEnvironment)
(?tmpEnvironment ns:TempEnvironment_installedSolutions ?tmpSo-
lutionsIDOneForWhichUserHasSpecificPreferences)
(?tmpEnvironment ns:TempEnvironment_availableSolutions ?tmpSo-
lutionsIDTwoForWhichUserHasSpecificPreferences)
-> (ns:InstalledSolutionsTakePriorityOverAvailableSolutions
rdf:type ns:TempSolutionsToBeLaunched)
(ns:InstalledSolutionsTakePriorityOverAvailableSolutions
ns:TempSolutionsToBeLaunched_IDs ?tmpSolutionsIDOneFor-
WhichUserHasSpecificPreferences)]
```

Table 2. If sensors detect changes in the environment variables, then trigger a further step

```
[apply_New_Value_On_Trigger:
    (?tmpEnvironment rdf:type ns:TempEnvironment)
    (?tmpEnvironment ns:Temp_environment_ContextChange
              ?tmpContextChange)
    (?tmpEnvironment ns:Temp_environment_ContextProperty
    ?tmpContextProperty)
(?tmpContextProperty ns:Temp_environment_ContextProperty
?val1)
(?val1 rdf:type ns:Temp_environment_ContextProperty)
equal(?tmpContextChange, "true"^^http://www.w3.org/2001/XMLSche
ma#boolean)
  equal(?tmpContextProperty , ?val1)
-> (?val2 rdf:type ns:Temp_environemnt_ContextProperty)
(?tmpContextProperty ns:Temp_environment_ContextProperty
?val12) ]
```

3.2   Statistical Matchmaker

There is no simple way to automatically translate application specific settings into the context of another application. While it would be possible to state a transformation of a setting from one application to another, it is difficult to automatically find these relations with algorithms. Font size, for instance, might be relatively easy to measure, so it would be possible to create a transformation expressing that operating system A always renders text five percent smaller than operating system B. Yet, both operating systems come with individual metaphors and UI styles that a matchmaker should try to maintain. Operating system B might always come with a relatively dense user interface, so font size should be even larger to make the information easier to read and separate. These subjective requirements cause an offset in the target configuration we want to infer. The goal is not just to reconstruct settings of application A for application B, but to infer settings for application B that make it 'feel and look like' application A. The strong subjective influence of 'feel and look like' is hard to describe with automated mathematical algorithms. Figure 3 illustrates this problem. A direct translation of user preferences from one application to another is possible if you can define a mathematical mapping. A very simple example would be that the font size rendering on Operation System A is 25 percent larger than rendering it on Operation System B (ignoring other influences on the actual physical font size in this example, like the display pixel density). Yet, those objective transformations will not always match what a user desires, as there are other influences to the "perceived clarity" of text items in an operation system. Operation System B might have a very clutter style, so that a user might want a larger font size for representing the same information. This also illustrates that those "subjective transformations" are user-specific.

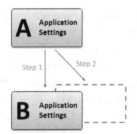

Fig. 3. Application Settings Transformation. Step 1 represents a direct transformation. Step 2 visualizes the offset originating in subjective requirements.

The task of the statistical matchmaker is to find a transformation that is as close to Step 2 in Figure 3 as possible. To solve this task, the statistical matchmaker deploys statistical inference. This process is based on recommender systems [27] and consists of several steps, subdivided in an offline and online section.The offline section of the statistical matchmaker, called the Statistical Inference module, iterates over all preferences sets known to the system and clusters them. This step is necessary, as the runtime section, running on a specific client device, might not have access to the preference servers at all. Further, there are obvious security limitations in User A accessing the preferences of User B.The idea behind the statistical matchmaker is to benefit of adaptations of other users that have similar preferences. If we continue the library example from above, the system might be able to infer a meaningful transformation, if it is able to find users that have similar settings for their smartphone, but also include settings for the library pc. Or, to put it more general: The statistical matchmaker tries to find preference sets of users that are similar for seen contexts, but also include settings that are close to the unseen context. Figure 4 illustrates this process.

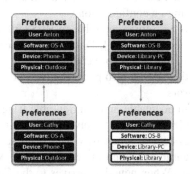

Fig. 4. Statistical Preference Matching

The offline clustering step takes care of reducing the amount of preference sets to measure against.The system starts with the preferences for user Cathy specific to her smartphone (preferences bottom left) and the target context it is supposed to infer to (Black on white context bottom right). In the first step, it compares the preference set to the known clusters of user preferences, trying to find a preference set that is close to Cathy's preferences for the smartphone. From all these preference sets that are close to Cathy's, those are extracted that also contain preferences for a context that is close to the target context. In this example, User Anton is found. It is now possible to either use Anton's preferences directly for Cathy's preference set, or to infer the transformation it required to get from Anton's smartphone preferences to Anton's library pc preferences and apply the same transformation to Cathy's preferences. Either process should generate a preference set that brings the system into a state so Cathy can interact with it and adjust it. Her adjustments will then serve as preferences for further inferences, just as Anton's just did.

Context in the Statistical Matchmaker is both simpler and more complex to embody. The simple part is that the context data is just added as more features in the feature vector. The complex one is that the ability of predicting the correct settings for a bigger feature vector [28] requires more samples or a better feature selection to be part of the predictor set [29.]

3.3   Context Aware Server

The context mechanism for fetching data from sensors might vary depending on the use cases. A first case is when the device that interacts with the user has itself the sensors – such as smartphones –, the second use case is when the device that the users interacts with, has not sensors to gather data – such as ATM –, then data is provided by motes around the device, collected and aggregated using a Context Aware Server platform.

The Context Aware Server (CAS) is developed in NodeJs provides a platform that collects, stores and process the data from sensors and when some triggers are fired it sends the processed data to a client in JSON format. Configuration, Sensors and Users are stored in MongoDb and new data is cached in Redis and it can be eventually saved to MongoDb depending on configuration.

The CAS is designed to be fully compatible to RESTful architectural design. It's structured in four main APIs: Sensor API, Device API, User API and Configuration API. The Sensor API offers the means for sending streams of new data from sensors and getting data stored in the CAS, it also permits advanced searching of data and the retrieval and search of sensors.

The CAS implements an adaptable and configurable triggering system that avails the definition of basic collection, aggregation and triggering rules that are applied when new user is in the system or when new data from sensor is received. All the triggering system is configurable through the configuration API and the Trigger API and it's applied in real time. When new data arrives to the Context awareness server, it fires an "onNewData" event. Afterwards, a listener gets the sensor configuration from the database.

Table 3. Sensor RESTful API (excerpt)

Command	Parameters	Response sample	Description

GET /sensors/:id	?populate	{
		  "__v": 0,
		  "_id": "524abe89d34ac49f24000001",
		  "_last": {
		    "value": 4,
		    "at":"2013-10 03T14:18:49.554Z"
		  },
		  "devid": "1",
		  "type": "light"
		}
			Gets sensor using the :id from database. _last references the last retrieved data stream, devid it's the internal sensor id (related to device) and type it's the type of sensor. ?populate=true parameter will populate the sensor with _last data timestamp and value.

GET /sensors/:id/ **data**	None, ?all, ?new,	[{
		  "at": "2013-04-22T00:35:43.12Z",
		  "value": 1
		},{
		  "at": "2013-04-22T00:55:43.73Z",
		  "value": 2
		}]
			If the parameter is ?new, it retrieves new data since last POST operation from sensor :id, otherwise or with ?all parameter, retrieves all data from sensor :id.

3.4   Minimatchmaker

The Minimatchmaker is a component able to execute simple if-then-else software code. It is named after the Matchmakers but it doesn't share their computational power. The Minimatchmaker receives a series of "what-if" [30] rules from the real Matchmaker that allow it to react to minor changes in the environment.

Recognised Environment:When the data sent by the Environmental Reporter can be managed by the Minimatchmaker, there is no need for querying an external Matchmaker. The information with the new adaptation is composed inside the Minimatchmaker and sent to the Settings Handler.

Unrecognised Environment: Sometimes the data sent by the Environmental Reporter cannot be managed by the Minimatchmaker. In these cases the Minimatchmaker communicates to the internal flow manager (The orchestrator) that it is not able to find a set of settings to respond to the changes in the context, and the orchestrator sends the same context data to the Cloud Flow Manager through a http proxy (HTTP Client). What happens in the cloud is transparent to the components inside the user device architecture, but nowadays the Flow Manager send the data to the Matchmaker module, which is composed by a series of different Matchmakers, including a Rule Based Matchmaker, a Statistical Matchmaker and a Flat Matchmaker. The response from the http proxy is formed by the new settings plus a new set of rules to deal with the context internally. The settings are directly sent to its handler (System Settings Handler) while the rules are passed to the MiniMatchmaker. The MiniMatchmaker erases any previous set of rules and stores those that are being received.

4   Results and Discussion

After a manual pre-load of the desired response of the MMM for the users, the lab tests had the following setup: 1) two separate devices were held by the user's assistant, one configured with a visual-magnified UI and the other one with an auditory UI. 2) the auditory one was given to the user, and he starts an interaction to get a trip ticket from the UI. 3) the observer switches on a music player with loud volume; when the MMM receives this noise, it produces a speech "switching to visual UI". 4) the assistant switches the mobile with the user, and the user ends the ticket purchase.

The test comprised a generic concept validation questionnaire and specific questions about the perceived usefulness of the solution and the level of satisfaction of the user. One of our main concerns is to make sure that the adaptation capabilities of the system developed does not conflict with Nielsen's first usability heuristic (the user has to be always in control of the interaction), specific questions were asked regarding this issue. One out of three expressed their concern that the system autoadapting without their permission may be annoying, and that changes in the UI should be configured by users. Nevertheless, three users considered the autoadaptation capabilities as useful (mean 4 in a 5-point Likert scale) and considered that, if they can configure the adaptations they may use it in the long term (mean 3,67 in a 5-point Likert scale).

A prospective implementation on Android can be found at 17 though it lacks integration with the Flow Manager but served to ask users for general acceptance and notion of control issues. These questions were refined during the second pilot stage of the Cloud4all project and as soon as the processed responses are available, the matchmaking mechanism will be updated accordingly.

The Context weighting mechanism has the drawback of a loss of performance, tighter integration at the ontology level is being tackled to decrease response time. Finally new algorithms are being explored to improve the hybrid approach that is employed to decide which of the matchmakers provides the final output.

References

1. Dey, A.K.: Understanding and Using Context. Personal and Ubiquitous Computing 5, 4–7 (2001)
2. Dey, A.K., Abowd, G.D., Salber, D.: A Conceptual Framework and a Toolkit for Supporting the Rapid Prototyping of Context-Aware Applications. Journal Human Computer Interaction 16, 97–166 (2001)
3. Zimmermann, A., Lorenz, A., Oppermann, R.: An operational definition of context. In: Kokinov, B., Richardson, D.C., Roth-Berghofer, T.R., Vieu, L. (eds.) CONTEXT 2007. LNCS (LNAI), vol. 4635, pp. 558–571. Springer, Heidelberg (2007)
4. Zimmermann, A., Lorenz, A., Specht, M.: Applications of a Context-Management System. In: Dey, A.K., Kokinov, B., Leake, D.B., Turner, R. (eds.) CONTEXT 2005. LNCS (LNAI), vol. 3554, pp. 556–569. Springer, Heidelberg (2005)
5. Stephanidis, C.: Designing for All in Ambient Intelligence Environments: The Interplay of User, Context, and Technology. Intl. Journal of Human-Computer Interaction 25, 441–454 (2009)
6. Karim, S., Tjoa, A.M.: Towards the Use of Ontologies for Improving User Interaction for People with Special Needs. In: Miesenberger, K., Klaus, J., Zagler, W.L., Karshmer, A.I. (eds.) ICCHP 2006. LNCS, vol. 4061, pp. 77–84. Springer, Heidelberg (2006)
7. Gajos, K.Z., Weld, D.S., Wobbrock, J.O.: Automatically Generating Personalized User Interfaces with SUPPLE. Artificial Intelligence 174, 910–950 (2010)
8. INREDIS. Project website, http://wiki.inredis.es
9. ISO/IEC 24752-3:2008. Information technology – User interfaces – Universal remote console – Part 3: Presentation template (2008)
10. Iglesias-Pérez, A., Linaje, M., Preciado, J.C., Sánchez, F., Gómez, E., González, R., Martínez, J.A.: A Context-Aware Semantic Approach for the Effective Selection of an Assistive Software. In: Proceedings of IV International Symposium of Ubiquitous Computing and Ambient Intelligence, pp. 51–60 (2010)
11. SERENOA. Project website, http://www.serenoa-fp7.eu
12. Iglesias-Pérez, A., Peinado, I., Chacón, J., Ortega-Moral, M.: Frontiers in Context Modelling to Enhance Personalisation of Assistive Technologies. In: Assistive Technology: From Research to Practice – Proceedings of AAATE 2013. IOS Press (2013), doi:10.3233/978-1-61499-304-9-829
13. Koutkias, V., Kaklanis, N., Votis, K., Tzovaras, D., Maglaveras, N.: An Integrated Semantic Framework Supporting Universal Accessibility to ICT. Universal Access in the Information Society. Special Issue: 3rd generation accessibility: Information and Communication Technologies towards universal access, Springer

14. Loitsch, C., Stiegler, A., Strobbe, C., Tzovaras, D., Votis, K., Weber, G., Zimmermann, G.: Improving Accessibility by Matching User Needs and Preferences. In: Assistive Technology: From Research to Practice – Proceedings of AAATE 2013. IOS Press (2013), doi:10.3233/978-1-61499-304-9-1357

15. Melcher, V., Krüger, A., Chalkia, E.: Managing Preferences in the Cloud – Requirements and UI Design. In: Assistive Technology: From Research to Practice – Proceedings of AAATE 2013, IOS Press (2013), doi:10.3233/978-1-61499-304-9-1372

16. Clark, C., Basman, A., Markus, K., Zenevich, Y.: A Cloud-Scale Architecture for Inclusion: Cloud4all and GPII. In: Assistive Technology: From Research to Practice – Proceedings of AAATE 2013. IOS Press (2013), doi:10.3233/978-1-61499-304-9-1366

17. Iglesias-Pérez, A., Peinado, I., Chacón, J., Ortega-Moral, M.: Architecture for Adding Context-Aware Capabilities to Preferences-Oriented User Interfaces. In: Proceedings of DRT4All, 5th edn. Fundación ONCE, Madrid (2013)

18. Partarakis, N., Doulgeraki, C., Leonidis, A., Antona, M., Stephanidis, C.: User Interface Adaptation of Web-Based Services on the Semantic Web. In: Stephanidis, C. (ed.) UAHCI 2009, Part II. LNCS, vol. 5615, pp. 711–719. Springer, Heidelberg (2009)

19. Jung, C., Hahn, V.: GUIDE–Adaptive user interfaces for accessible hybrid TV applications. In: Second W3C Workshop Web & TV (2011)

20. Atkinson, M.T., Bell, M.J., Machin, C.H.C.: Towards Ubiquitous Accessibility: Capability-based Profiles and Adaptations, Delivered via the Semantic Web, pp. 2–6

21. Kadouche, Mokhtari, M., Giroux, S., Abdulrazak, B.: Semantic approach for modelling an assistive environment using description logic, pp. 222–231 (2008)

22. Ponsard, C., Beaujeant, P., Vanderdonckt, J.: Augmenting Accessibility Guidelines with User Ability Rationales. In: Winckler, M. (ed.) INTERACT 2013, Part I. LNCS, vol. 8117, pp. 579–586. Springer, Heidelberg (2013)

23. Wassermann, B., Zimmermann, G.: User Profile Matching: A Statistical Approach. In: CENTRIC, pp. 60–63 (2011)

24. Middleton, S.E., De Roure, D.C., Shadbolt, N.R.: Capturing knowledge of user preferences: ontologies in recommender systems. In: Proceedings of the 1st International Conference on Knowledge Capture, K-CAP 2001, New York (2001)

25. Serra, G., Iglesias, A., Kalogirou, K., Montalvá, J.: Context-related profile adaptation algorithms, Cloud4all deliverable, p. 52 (2013)

26. Iglesias, A., Peinado, I., Kalogirou, K., Chalkia, E.: Rule sets for the automatic adaptation of the user profile to context-related features, Cloud4all deliverable, pp. 20–22, pp. 31–41 (2013)

27. Hofmann, T., Schölkopf, B., Smola, A.J.: Kernel Methods in Machine Learning. The Annals of Statistics 36(3), 1171–1220 (2008)

28. Ahonen, T., Hadid, A., Pietikäinen, M.: Face recognition with local binary patterns. In: Pajdla, T., Matas, J(G.) (eds.) ECCV 2004. LNCS, vol. 3021, pp. 469–481. Springer, Heidelberg (2004)

29. Gomez-Verdejo, V., Martinez-Ramon, M., Arenas-Garcia, J., Lazaro-Gredilla, M., Molina-Bulla, H.: Support Vector Machines With Constraints for Sparsity in the Primal Parameters. IEEE Transactions on Neural Networks 22(8), 1269 (2011)

30. Chaudhuri, S., Narasayya, V.: AutoAdmin "what-if" index analysis utility. In: Proceedings of the 1998 ACM SIGMOD International Conference on Management of Data, SIGMOD 1998, pp. 367–378. ACM, NY (1998)

A Semantic Framework for Assistive Technologies Description to Strengthen UI Adaptation

Nikolaos Kaklanis, Konstantinos Votis,
Konstantinos Giannoutakis, and Dimitrios Tzovaras

Information Technologies Institute, Centre for Research and Technology Hellas,
Thessaloniki, Greece
{nkak,kvotis,kgiannou,Dimitrios.Tzovaras}@iti.gr

Abstract. The present paper presents the Semantic Framework for Content and Solutions, an ontological framework that enables the classification of various assistive technologies (both software and hardware) according to well-known accessibility standards, such as the ISO 9999 standard, and also the description of all the supported adjustments/settings and their alignment with similar settings of other technologies. This semantic framework is a key component of the whole Cloud4all/GPII infrastructure and strengthens the UI adaptation process as it enhances the inference capabilities of the Rule-based Matchmaker, another component of the Cloud4all/GPII infrastructure that tries to match user needs with the corresponding configurations of different assistive technologies using rules.

Keywords: Semantic alignment, ontology, assistive technologies, application classification.

1   Introduction

Ontologies can play a very crucial role in strengthening the accessibility of user interfaces (UIs). The appearance of the parts of a UI as well as their functionalities may be directed by ontologies. If both UI elements and user needs and preferences are defined within ontologies, a reasoner can determine the appearance that fits user needs best [12]. The mapping between user impairments and user interface characteristics can be also expressed semantically [8].

A typical problem that often appears in ontology-based systems includes the lack of interoperability between other similar systems or even sub-components of the same framework, due to different representations of identical terms. Ontology alignment in the sense of identifying relations between individual elements of multiple ontologies is a necessary precondition to establish interoperability between agents or services using different individual ontologies [3]. Moreover, the semantic alignment enables the searching or browsing of the knowledge represented in numerous ontologies in a transparent way for the end-users.

C. Stephanidis and M. Antona (Eds.): UAHCI/HCII 2014, Part I, LNCS 8513, pp. 236–245, 2014.
© Springer International Publishing Switzerland 2014

Even if many approaches have been proposed for improving the visualization [13] and interaction capabilities [4, 6] of user interfaces by using ontologies, there is a need for an ontological framework that will enable the classification of the most common assistive technologies (both software and hardware) according to well-known accessibility standards and also the description of all the supported adjustments/settings and their alignment with similar settings of other technologies. The present paper presents the Semantic Framework for Content and Solutions (SEMA) developed within the premises of the Cloud4all FP7 EC project that fulfills the aforementioned requirements. The SEMA is a key component of the whole Cloud4all/GPII infrastructure and strengthens the UI adaptation process as it enhances the inference capabilities of the rule-based matchmaker, another component of the Cloud4all/GPII infrastructure that tries to match user needs with the corresponding configurations of different assistive technologies using rules.

2 Related Work

There are several efforts towards the direction of defining ontological concepts and architectures for the semantic representation of ICT solutions, devices and platforms within the area of e-Inclusion and personalised interfaces. These efforts try to cover adequately the personal requirements of the end users, under an ICT artifact specific perspective. For example, besides user modeling, the ontologies developed in ACCESSIBLE [16] and AEGIS[1] incorporate the semantic description of solutions, applications and user interaction terms targeting users with functional limitations. Also the INREDIS Knowledge Base [11], stores all the ontologies that collect formal descriptions of the elements in the INREDIS domain (e.g. users, AS, devices, software requirements, etc.) and its instances.

Castro et al. [2] proposed the use of metadata and meta-reasoning to address the design challenges encountered when building an ontology repository for an application framework devoted to assistive technologies that can be browsed and queried in a highly heterogeneous and expressive way. They analyzed how metadata can be used in the context of open repositories of ontologies, and how it can and needs to be extended in various ways. More specifically, they studied a redesign of the Ontology Metadata Vocabulary (OMV) [5] by restructuring and enriching it with the ABC ontology [9] and domain-specific categories for assistive technologies.

The WWAAC EU project launched also an effort to use semantic web technologies for providing a generic solution for integrating the assistive technology, the web, and the signs and symbol language used traditionally by people with communication problems for text interpretation. Within the premises of the WWAAC project, the Concept Coding Framework (CCF) [10] was defined as a means to break down the isolation and barriers between different augmentative and alternative communication (AAC) symbol vocabularies by defining an open technology for connecting these vocabularies to other vocabularies and to standard lexical resources. The CCF included a plain

---

[1] http://www.aegis-project.eu/index.php?Itemid=65

concepts list called Concept Code Definitions, the Base Reference Ontology (concepts mapped from WordNet3 to used symbols) and the Complementary Reference Ontology specifying missing concepts.

In the current work, our main purpose is to provide a high-level modeling of content-related information of ICT solutions, platforms and devices by extending and integrating previous ontological implementations. A framework that enables the semantic representation of assistive technologies is proposed, in order to encourage and enable all potential stakeholders (e.g. assistive technology owners, retailers, etc.) to use the same terms when describing the same things. Moreover, the proposed framework provides a common interface to all interested vendors, providers, etc. that intend to include their applications/solutions in the Cloud4all/GPII infrastructure [14, 15].

3   The Semantic Framework for Content and Solutions (SEMA)

The main component of the SEMA is the solutions ontology[2], which aims at maintaining relevant information and metadata regarding solutions/applications, platforms, devices and their specific settings along with detailed information regarding vendors or implementers of the assistive technologies supported by the Cloud4all/GPII infrastructure. The terms inside the solutions ontology are classified according to the ISO 9999 standard [7].

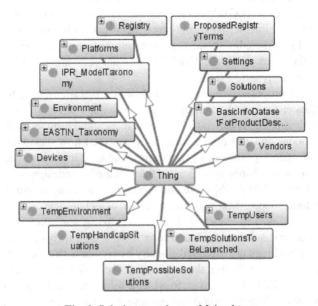

Fig. 1. Solutions ontology – Main classes

---

[2] The solutions ontology is publicly available at: http://160.40.50.183/cloud4all/

Fig. 1 presents the main classes of the solutions ontology, which are the following:

- The *Devices* class: The *Devices* class and their subclasses represent in a hierarchical way the devices on which applications can run. The classification per each of the supported devices has implemented according to their domain (e.g. PC, PDA, mobile phone devices, etc.).
- The *EASTIN_Taxonomy* class: The *EASTIN_Taxonomy* class and its subclasses are used to categorize each solution according to the taxonomy proposed by the European Assistive Technology Information Network[3] [1] (EASTIN), the biggest and most comprehensive information service on assistive technology serving older and disabled people, their families and careers across the globe.
- The *Environment* class: The *Environment* class and its subclasses describe the environment (ex. at home, at work) in which a solution is launched.
- The *IPR_ModelTaxonomy* class: The *IPR_ModelTaxonomy* class and its subclasses are used to describe Intellectual Property Rights (IPR), cost and trust aspects of services and applications.
- The *Platforms* class: The *Platform* class and their subclasses, represent in a hierarchical way the platforms on which solutions/applications run (e.g. Windows, Linux). A solution can be either an application or a network/cloud based service. Thus, a platform can refer either to a specific operating system on which an application runs, or to a web execution platform for web based applications and web services.
- The *Registry* class: The *Registry* class is used to store the common terms of the Registry. The Registry of common terms is a vocabulary describing common applications settings. Each instance of the class contains the definition of a Registry term.
- The *ProposedRegistryTerms* class: This class is used to store the common terms proposed by solution owners/vendors/retailers. The administrator of the SEMA finally decides if a suggested common term will be finally added in the Registry of common terms or it will be rejected.
- The *Settings* class: The term *setting* refers to each unique setting aspect of each solution, platform or device that can be customized according to the needs and preferences of the user. Thus, the *Settings* class tries to capture in a semantic manner all possible solution -, platform - and device – specific settings that could provide more added value to the personalization and adaptation process based on semantics.
- The *Solutions* class: The *Solutions* class and their descendant classes aim to classify in a semantic manner solutions/applications supported and surveyed in the Cloud4all process. The semantic classification of solutions is also based on the ISO standard 9999 "Assistive Products for Persons with Disability" 7 and includes the "subdivisions" (i.e. a refinement of the ISO 9999 standard) defined in the ETNA

---

[3] http://www.eastin.eu

project[4]. This has been selected in order to support the integration of well-known databases of ATs and accessible applications like the EASTIN.

- The *BasicInfoDatasetForProductDescription* class: The *BasicInfoDatasetForProductDescription* class is used to store some extra information such as the country of the manufacturer or the logo for each solution.
- The *Vendors* class: The *Vendors* class aims to capture and represent information about application-, platform-, and device- vendors or implementers. The *Vendors* class has the following subclasses: *DeviceVendors*, *PlatformVendors* and *SolutionVendors*.

The solutions ontology includes also a set of auxiliary classes that are essential for the proper execution of the Rule-based Matchmaker, a component of the Cloud4all/GPII infrastructure that tries to match user needs with the corresponding configurations of different assistive technologies using rules. These rules use classes and properties defined within the solutions ontology. As the rules, additionally to the solution-specific settings, take also into account the needs and preferences of the current user as well as the current environment, the following 5 auxiliary classes had to be defined in the solutions ontology, in order to work as basic containers for storing the corresponding instances of the corresponding user and the environment.

- The *TempEnvironment* class: The *TempEnvironment* class works as a temporary container for storing the details of the user's current environment.
- The *TempHandicapSituations* class: The *TempHandicapSituations* class works as a temporary container for the description of the current problematic situations (e.g. cases where there is user preferences cannot be fully fulfilled due to the current environment/context).
- The *TempPossibleSolutions* class: The *TempPossibleSolutions* class works as a temporary container of the description of possible solutions proposed by the Rule-based Matchmaker for the settlement of the current problematic situations.
- The *TempSolutionsToBeLaunched* class: The *TempSolutionsToBeLaunched* class works as a container for storing the list of solutions that have to be launched, according to the needs/preferences of the current user and the current environment/context.
- The *TempUsers* class: The *TempUsers* class contains the corresponding temporary description of the current user

For all the 5 aforementioned auxiliary classes there are no predefined instances in the solutions ontology. Instead, temporary instances are automatically created by the Rule-based Matchmaker to enable the proper execution of the rules and they are automatically deleted after the execution of the Rule-based Matchmaker.

A variety of Datatype properties and Object properties are used to describe the instances of each class of the solution ontology in detail as well as to define relationships between different instances.

---

[4] http://www.etna-project.eu/

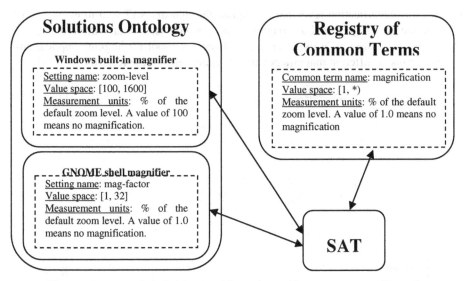

Fig. 2. Alignment of application-specific settings with common terms - Example

Different applications of the same type (e.g. screen readers) usually have similar settings expressed with different names (e.g. speech-rate, voice-speed, etc.) and different value spaces (e.g. words per minute, phonemes per second, etc.). The relationship between these similar settings can be described through another component of the SEMA, the Semantic Alignment Tool[5] (SAT). The SAT is a tool that acts as a middleware between the solutions ontology and the solutions/applications that are stored in the Cloud4all federated repositories and offered by different vendors. The tool's primary role is to provide a common interface to all interested vendors, providers, administrators, etc., that intend to add/modify the description of their applications/solutions as well as to align their application-specific settings with the corresponding common terms of the Registry (Fig. 2). The Registry of common terms is a vocabulary describing common applications settings (e.g., magnification factor, speech rate, font size, etc.) used to encourage and enable all stakeholders to use the same terms when describing the same things (the same concept and value range) with regard to user needs and preferences.

An application-specific setting is a setting used by a specific application while a common term of the Registry is a term that has been chosen as generic terms for a particular concept. For instance, the "magnification level" setting, which is a common setting for screen magnifiers, is defined in a different way in the Windows built-in magnifier compared with the corresponding setting of the GNOME Shell Magnifier. More specifically, the magnification level for the Windows built-in magnifier has the ID "Magnification", is an integer with value space [100, 1600] and its default value is 200. The magnification level for the GNOME Shell Magnifier has the ID "mag-factor", is an integer with value space [1, 32] and its default value is 2. Both these

---

[5] The Semantic Alignment Tool is publicly available at: http://160.40.50.183:8080/

settings for magnification level can be aligned through the SAT tool to the common term of the Registry with ID "magnification", which is a float with value space [1.0, ..*]. Fig. 3 presents a usage example of the SAT tool for aligning application-specific terms of different magnifiers with common terms of the Registry.

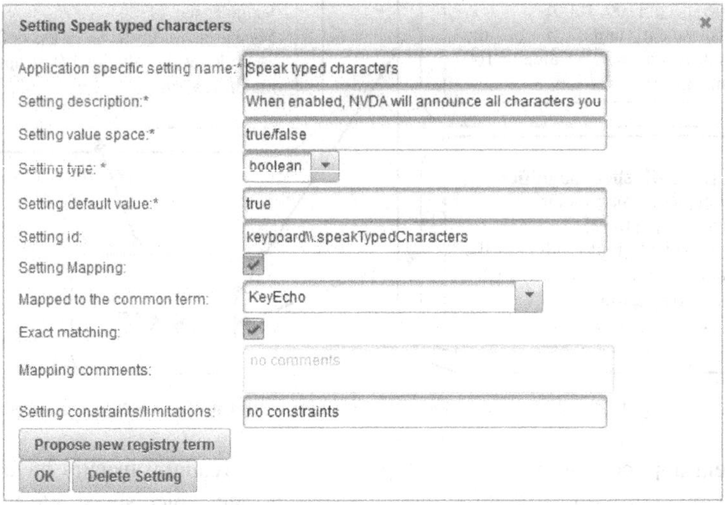

Fig. 3. Align an application-specific term to a common term of the Registry

As the manual alignment of an application-specific term with a common term of the Registry is not always a trivial task for an end user, a mechanism has been developed inside the SAT that helps user identify similar terms by performing automatic lexicographical analysis.

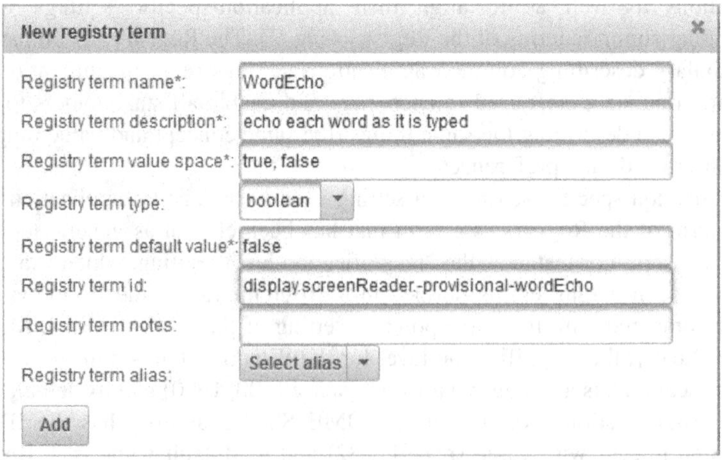

Fig. 4. Proposing a new Registry term

Moreover, through the SAT tool, a solution owner/vendor can propose new terms to be included in the Registry of common terms, as presented in Fig. 4. Then, the SEMA administrator can decide if the proposed terms should be finally included in the Registry Fig. 5.

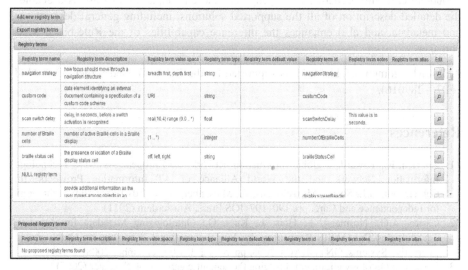

Fig. 5. Managing the Registry of common terms through the SAT tool

4   Preliminary Results

Currently, all the application-specific settings of the applications that were tested during the first pilot phase of the CLOUD4all project as well as the ones that will be tested during the second pilot phase have been included in the solutions ontology. Moreover, the alignment of the aforementioned settings with common terms of the Registry has been performed through the SAT tool. This knowledge was found to enhance the inference capabilities of the rule-based matchmaker and further enforce the whole process of UI adaptation for people with special needs and preferences.

5   Conclusions

In the present paper the Semantic Framework for Content and Solutions, a framework that enables the semantic high-level modeling of content-related information of ICT solutions, platforms and devices, was presented. The proposed framework enables the categorization of assistive technologies according to the ISO 9999 standard, the detailed description of their settings as well as the alignment between similar terms among different technologies. Moreover, it enables the integration of information coming from various external sources, such as the EASTIN databases. The SEMA provides a common interface to all interested vendors, providers, etc. that intend to include their applications/solutions in the Cloud4all/GPII infrastructure. Moreover, it aims at encouraging all potential stakeholders (e.g. assistive technology owners, retailers, etc.) to use the same terms when describing the same things. The Semantic Framework for Content and Solutions is a key component of the whole Cloud4all/GPII infrastructure and strengthens the UI adaptation process as it enables the detailed description of all the supported solutions, including general descriptions and metadata, and also enhances the inference capabilities of the Rule-based Matchmaker.

Acknowledgements. This work is supported by the EU co-funded project Cloud4all (FP7 – 289016).

References

1. Andrich, R.: Towards a global information network: the European Assistive Technology Information Network and the World Alliance of AT Information Providers. In: Gelderblom, G.J., Soede, M., Adriaens, L., Miesenberger, K. (eds.) Everyday Technology for Independence and Care, pp. 190–197. IOS Press, Amsterdam (2011)
2. Castro, A.G., Normann, I., Hois, J., Kutz, O.: Ontologizing Metadata for Assistive Technologies-The OASIS Repository. In: First International Workshop on Ontologies in Interactive Systems, ONTORACT 2008, pp. 57–62. IEEE (September 2008)
3. Ehrig, M.: Ontology alignment: bridging the semantic gap, vol. 4. Springer (2007)
4. Guarino, N., Masolo, C., Vetere, G.: Ontoseek: Content-based access to the web. IEEE Intelligent Systems and Their Applications 14(3), 70–80 (1999)
5. Hartmann, J., Sure, Y., Haase, P., Palma, R., Suárez-Figueroa, M.D.C.: OMV–ontology metadata vocabulary. In: ISWC 2005 Workshop on Ontology Patterns for the Semantic Web (November 2005)
6. Hildebrand, M., Van Ossenbruggen, J.: Configuring semantic web interfaces by data mapping. In: Visual Interfaces to the Social and the Semantic Web (VISSW 2009), vol. 443, p. 96 (2009)
7. ISO 9999:2011, Assistive Products for Persons with Disability – Classification and Terminology (2011)
8. Karim, S., Tjoa, A.M.: Towards the use of ontologies for improving user interaction for people with special needs. In: Miesenberger, K., Klaus, J., Zagler, W.L., Karshmer, A.I. (eds.) ICCHP 2006. LNCS, vol. 4061, pp. 77–84. Springer, Heidelberg (2006)
9. Lagoze, C., Hunter, J.: The ABC ontology and model. Journal of Digital Information 2(2) (2006)
10. Lundälv, M., Derbring, S.: AAC Vocabulary Standardisation and Harmonisation. In: Miesenberger, K., Karshmer, A., Penaz, P., Zagler, W. (eds.) ICCHP 2012, Part II. LNCS, vol. 7383, pp. 303–310. Springer, Heidelberg (2012)
11. Miñón, R., Aizpurua, A., Cearreta, I., Garay, N., Abascal, J.: Ontology-Driven Adaptive Accessible Interfaces in the INREDIS project. In: Procs. of the Int. Workshop on Architectures and Building Blocks of Web-Based User-Adaptive Systems, Haway, pp. 37–39 (2010)
12. Paulheim, H., Probst, F.: Ontology-enhanced user interfaces: A survey. International Journal on Semantic Web and Information Systems (IJSWIS) 6(2), 36–59 (2010)

13. Potter, R., Wright, H.: An ontological approach to visualization resource management. In: Doherty, G., Blandford, A. (eds.) DSVIS 2006. LNCS, vol. 4323, pp. 151–156. Springer, Heidelberg (2007)
14. Vanderheiden, G., Treviranus, J.: Creating a global public inclusive infrastructure. In: Stephanidis, C. (ed.) Universal Access in HCI, Part I, HCII 2011. LNCS, vol. 6765, pp. 517–526. Springer, Heidelberg (2011)
15. Vanderheiden, G.C., Treviranus, J., Chourasia, A.: The global public inclusive infrastructure (GPII). In: Proceedings of the 15th International ACM SIGACCESS Conference on Computers and Accessibility, p. 70. ACM (October 2013)
16. Votis, K., Lopes, R., Tzovaras, D., Carriço, L., Likothanassis, S.: A Semantic Accessibility Assessment Environment for Design and Development for the Web. In: Stephanidis, C. (ed.) UAHCI 2009, Part III. LNCS, vol. 5616, pp. 803–813. Springer, Heidelberg (2009)

Tailored versus Prioritized Configuration towards Accessibility – A Study on Weighted Preferences

Claudia Loitsch[1], Eleni Chalkia[2], Evangelos Bekiaris[2], and Gerhard Weber[1]

[1] Technical University of Dresden, Germany
{claudia.loitsch,gerhard.weber}@tu-dresden.de
[2] Hellenic Institute of Transport, Centre for Research and Technology Hellas, Greece
{hchalkia,abek}@certh.gr

Abstract. We present the results of a user study on human factors towards personalization and accessibility which was conducted with 97 participants (cognitive impaired, dyslexic, low digital literacy, visual impaired and elderly). Amongst others, the presented results gave insights on user weightings of requirements as well as on difficulties in customizing accessibility features of ICT products.

Keywords: User Experience, User Preferences, Personalization, User Interface Adaptation for universal access, Accessibility.

1   Introduction

By utilizing assistive technologies and customization capabilities of main stream ICT products, in particular settings such as color contrast options, font adjustments, or zoom capabilities, individuals with disabilities or reduced capabilities (also situational impairments) can access and interact with most software or devices if they are configured according to their needs and preferences. However, it presumes (1) user`s knowledge and awareness of assistive technologies and assistive settings, (2) that users know how to configure a product, and (3) that they know which customization capabilities suit best to their individual needs.

Personalization of ICT products can automatically deliver tailored configurations on certain devices or software applications according to user's needs, capabilities, tasks and contexts. However, it requires that ICT products supply the customization features and adaptation capabilities allowing tailoring the user interface as well as, input and output characteristics even if the current situation is changing. Both dimension, the individual`s characteristics on the one hand and the technical customization/adaptation capabilities of ICT products on the other hand are itself heterogeneous. For this reason, existing personalization approaches and technologies towards accessibility focus on certain aspects, domains or user groups and are typically referred to as universal or aiming at all people.

A new entire approach for ensuring accessibility through auto-personalization from Needs and Preferences (N&Ps) has been developed in the Cloud4all project.

C. Stephanidis and M. Antona (Eds.): UAHCI/HCII 2014, Part I, LNCS 8513, pp. 246–257, 2014.
© Springer International Publishing Switzerland 2014

Cloud4all is a project funded by the European Commission that builds a new architecture for accessible computing through auto-configuring public, as well as private, devices to match individual N&Ps of people with disabilities. The entire concept of Cloud4all is included in the general idea of the Global Public Inclusive Infrastructure (GPII) [11]. Through matchmaking, user preferences will be inferred, translated, selected, or modified to customization capabilities of different ICT products. Details of that process dependent on a certain matchmaking implementation which can be, for instance, of statistical or rule-based nature [7]. Moreover, components to enable cross-platform configuration [2] as well as user interfaces to create or modify preferences [9] are components of the Cloud4all architecture.

1.1 Tailored Versus Prioritized Configuration

Inherent to Cloud4all/GPII scope is the problem of matching the users' preferences to the customization/adaptation capabilities of devices, operating systems, assistive technologies and other ICT solutions [7]. For several reasons, users' preferences used in Cloud4all neither allow explicit inferences on disabilities, nor classify users into groups due to the definition that a preference consist of properties and values that refer to system characteristics, not to user characteristics. Hence, Cloud4all personalization can deliver tailor-made user configurations on each device, following the "one size fits one" concept. Apparently, no user preference can be perfectly mapped and applied on any system. For instance, a preference about the amount of punctuation, a user wants to be spoken, can be successfully applied by various screen readers on Windows or Linux but, TalkBack for Android does not support this feature. Moreover, preferences about verbosity settings of screen readers might be less important for users than not having text-to-speech and Braille output configured on a current device. Launching and configuring a self voicing application on a new device might result in adequate matches according to verbosity preferences of a user, but could even mean a mismatch when the user is familiar with interacting by a screen reader instead. Thus, the entirety of user`s preferences describe a tailor-made configuration if applicable on the device a user is using, mainly in a private environment. If a user need requires a specific accessibility setting which is not supported by a product, tailored configuration cannot be delivered directly. Prioritized configuration, thereby, describes the auto-configuration of high weighted settings on arbitrary devices allowing users to interact with it. This will appear mainly on public devices, such as internet kiosks, in libraries, ATMs, or computer labs which might be characterized by certain customization/adaptation limitations. New personalization approaches need to detect and overcome barriers triggered by the inadequacy of the technical environment, limitations of software products and their capabilities, or environmental conditions such as lights or noise that might constrain the current usage in a certain context.

1.2 Characteristics of Users

User N&Ps are a core concept in personalized systems to describe user characteristics which are applied and/or translated into tailor-made adaptations. There are several approaches and standards describing user characteristics, i.e. classified into disabilities [1, 10], capabilities [4, 12] or preferences [6]. Each of them is currently limited to a specific application domain and none of them matches entirely the essential requirements for the kind of personalization that is targeted by Cloud4all, which supports that "each size fits one" and we should not cluster the needs and preferences into profiles, since each individual has its own characteristics. The origin for Cloud4all personalization is a set of needs and preferences that describe which kind of accessibility features, assistive technologies, or applications are either required or preferred by users to interact with ICT. The international standard ISO/IEC 24751-2 provides a common model of needs and preferences divided into three categories display, control and content. Additionally, the standard incorporates a priority rating (required, preferred, optionally, prohibited) for configurations or technology settings. Likewise, generic preferences and specific, product unique preferences, users may wish to apply, are distinguished. Thereby, the ISO/IEC 24751-2 constitutes a sustainable fundament for expressing user needs and preferences among the diversity of devices, software products and contexts. However, insights on individual needs and preferences, problems that users are facing when using various devices in specific situations, or barriers triggered by the technical environment have not been sufficiently researched while that information is important to the design of the personalization developed in Cloud4all.

1.3   Purpose of the User Study

The user study presented in this paper aims at collecting qualitative data about the requirements and difficulties of a broad variety of individuals when using ICT products in their daily live. To point this out clearly, the scope of this study does not focus on receiving user feedback on how to personalize specific devices, applications, or services to each one individually. We rather concentrate on a kind of snap shot of current difficulties and limitations users are facing when assistive technologies or customized accessibility settings are needed, which we want to overcome by personalization. Beyond that, we are investigating if users can actually specify their needs and preferences to get insights which specific considerations need to be addressed by personalization approaches towards accessibility as we are developing in Cloud4all.

2   User Study on Human Factors towards Accessibility

The results of the user study described in this paper include qualitative data on needs and preferences of users when interacting with information technologies, and characteristics as well as difficulties in the usage of ICT products that participants are facing in their daily live. 97 participants with various kinds of impairments, elderly as well as individuals with low digital literacy participated in the study. The main research questions of the presented user study are:

1. Can users specify their needs and preferences?
2. What are general accessibility settings that are needed or preferred among the various groups?
3. What are characteristics and difficulties according to the needs and preferences of the participants?

The second research question relates to the first and focus on analyzing sets of high and low weighted accessibility settings required by users.

2.1 Procedure and Participants

The study consists of a two-staged process. Initially we conducted interviews with a small group of blind and visual impaired people (n=6). Participants of those interviews had good digital literacy. They are familiar with their computer systems and have good knowledge about accessibility. The main goal of these interviews was to figure out, if asking users with disabilities about their needs and preferences is a sufficient approach and that it results in meaningful data according to our research questions, which was the case. Hence, we continued our approach with a larger amount of participants with various characteristics or disabilities through questionnaires that have been answered during the first pilot evaluation of Cloud4all. The distribution of all participants is summarized in Table 1.

Table 1. Distribution of participants

	Initial Interviews	Questionnaires
Participants	Total: 6	Total : 91
	Blind: 6	Blind: 29
	Low vision: 2	Low vision: 29
		Elderly: 16
		Cognitive disabilities: 6
		Dyslexia: 5
		Low digital literacy: 5
Method	Structured Interviews	Questionnaires

Based on the purpose of the study to capture real requirements and difficulties of participants instead of opinions or expectations from personalization, we ask users to answer two open questions:

1. "What are your needs (Needs are settings, without which you might not be able to work with the system, i.e.: speech output, magnification, high contrast and large font, etc.)
2. "What are your preferences? Preferences are settings that improve your experience of working with the system, i.e.: speech output when reading long texts, individual colors for background of applications, individual speech rate when reading individual literature, etc."

This simple approach has been chosen as we assumed beforehand that many users do know little about ICT products, possible configurations, and what they want to be applied when and how. With particular caution, we did not provide a broad variety of options to reduce complexity and to allow users to answer as free as possible. Within the initial interviews we figured out users are able to understand the meaning of both questions and, if they require an accessibility setting at all or in specific situations, they know it. Only 1 of 97 participant of our user study replied not to understand the questions by saying "I do not know and cannot see what this is all about". The experiences from the initial interviews disclosed as well, the two questions we ask the participants were sufficient to receive insights on certain weighting of the individual needs and preferences. The weighting consists, at first, in 1 (high weight) for answers to the first question and 0 (low weight) for answers to the second questions. The answers to both questions have been collected and written down by the test facilitators. Afterwards, all raw data have been sighted, structured and coded.

2.2   Results

Results of our study comprise a set of high weighted accessibility settings that are required by the participants to interact with ICT products as well as a set of lower weighted accessibility settings that are additionally desired to be applied immediately on ICT products or in various contexts (Table 2). Due to the design of the study which allows participants to give free answers, we received a broad variety of answers which have been coded into common settings, grouped according to perception, input and specific content characteristics (Table 2). Due to limited space, the following accessibility settings presented in Table 2 are summarized:

- **Font adjustments** include remarks on type face, font size and font weight.
- **Simplification** regards information and navigation.
- **Alternative content** include the following remarks: more icons in relation to text; screen elements presented in lists or grids; alternatives for pop-up information.
- **Change settings easily** regards: zoom level; recover cursor by short cuts; speech rate; individual short gestures/short cuts for punctuation and language.

Remarks from participants according to needs and preferences for specific contexts are presented in Table 3.

High Weighted Accessibility Settings
Answers we received to the first question "What are your Needs [...]?" are presented in columns with headings N of Table 2. Data includes all settings, mentioned by participants, which they want to be configured immediately when ICT products are used or which are required in specific contexts and without having it available, interacting with information technologies would be worst or impossible. The data presented combine the results from initial interviews and questionnaires from the pilots study.

All blind participants (N=35) named at least one accessibility setting that is required. TTS, Braille or combinations are prerequisites by these participants but some blind participants necessitate visual settings as well. Only few settings according to text-to-speech (tts), e.g. speech rate or voice adjustments, have been mentioned to be essential. Likewise, all participants (N=31) with low vision specified at least one high weighted accessibility setting according to visual perception, especially screen enlargement, e.g. magnification or zoom, and text enhancements related to fonts and text have been named. In contrast to blind participants, settings relating to visual perception vary stronger than for blind participants. Several participants stated that they need different screen enlargement options for different contexts. Only 1 participant with cognitive impairments (n=6) specified a need when using ICTs, 5 replied that they have no specific demand when they interact with computer technology. Similar results apply for participants with low digital literacy (n=5) and dyslexic (n=5). Only 2 participants in each case specified accessibility settings to be required. 5 elderly participants (n=16) mentioned requirements as well.

Low Weighted Accessibility Settings
Answers according to the second question "What are your Preferences [...]?" are presented in columns with heading P in Table 2. Data include all settings, mentioned by participants, which they wish to be configured on ICT products, or which are used in specific contexts. In contrast to strongly weighted accessibility settings, usage in general would be still feasible for participants if these accessibility settings are not adopted. However, performance with tasks would be affected.

Additionally to strongly weighted accessibility settings, blind participants named further settings related to tts. For instance, voice adjustments, speech rate, punctuation, and echo are important preferences. Likewise, participants with low vision specified several settings that detail a basic need. If, for instance, magnification was named as a need, users specified related preferences as magnifier position or tracking options. Preferences from other groups then visual impaired and blind are distributed broadly. In general, we received rather unspecified remarks from the majority of these participants which will be still discussed.

Required Accessibility Settings for Specific Contexts
27 of 97 participants from the interviews and the questionnaires gave additional remarks on further weightings of accessibility settings by means of when they need or prefer accessibility options to be applied. We call these conditional weighting of a specific need or preference. Even if the given examples of the participants varied broadly, they can be summarized in a small set of conditions which is presented in Table 3. It can be differentiated between: activating accessibility settings always or conditionally; preferences of specific assistive technology products; dependencies between preferences.

Table 2. Total amount of (1) high weighted settings required to interact with ICT from the beginning or in specific contexts (**N = Needs**) and (2) low weighted settings additionally preferred from the beginning or in specific contexts (**P = Preferences**). CD = Cognitive disability; LL = Low digital literacy; D =Dyslexic; E=Elderly; LV = Low vision; B=Blind.

	CD		LL		D		E		LV		B		Total	
Accessibility settings	N	P	N	P	N	P	N	P	N	P	N	P	N	P
Non-visual perception														
TTS					2				7	10	32	1	41	10
Braille											11	5	11	5
voice adjustment			1							1	1	12	2	13
speech rate						2				2	3	19	3	23
punctuation											1	8	1	8
echo												6		6
pitch						1						2		3
announce capital												1		1
permanent reading												3		3
synthesizer												1		1
short mode												2		2
Visual perception														
magnification							1		19	7	3	2	23	9
magnifier position										1				1
cursor/caret tracking										2				2
various zoom options									2	3		1	2	4
high contrast							1		2	1	3	1	6	2
individual colors		1						2		3				6
word spacing						1								1
color inversion									1	2	1		2	2
font adjustments	1	1		2	1	1	3	5	6	6	2		13	15
large icons or images	1					1			2				3	1
brightness											1		1	
screen resolution									2				2	
Audio perception														
volume						2		1				2		5
Pointing and typing														
simplified keyboard			1									1		
keyboard layout					1							1	1	1
single hand control			1									1		
mouse pointer adjustments									1	4		3	1	7
Input														
speech input										1		2		3
Content														
simplified information			2	2			1	1					3	3
captions and subtitles								2						2
alternative content							1	1		1			1	2
Others														
change settings easily										3		3		6
None	5	4	3	3	3		9	8	3	8		5	23	28
Question unclear							1	1					1	1
Total	7	6	7	7	8	9	17	20	45	55	40	81		

Table 3. Conditions for applying accessibility settings coded into condition classes given with examples based on statements of the participants

Condition Class	Examples (statements of participants)
Activate accessibility setting always	TTS required from the beginning;
	Braille required from the beginning;
	TTS and/or Braille required from the beginning.
Activate accessibility setting conditional upon:	
content attributes	Braille is required when reading **large texts**.
	Voice and speech adjustments are required dependently on the **content language** (quickly configurable).
	Individual speech rate for **tables** as it is easier to read.
	Permanent reading (screen readers) only for **books**, else line-by-line reading is preferred.
	Speech synthesizer selectable based on the **language** quality (one synthesizer is good for English but is bad for Greek).
	Alter volume when watching **videos** (e.g. YouTube).
	Captions and subtitles for **videos.**
	High contrast when information is presented on **white background**.
applications	TTS only required for playing games.
	Simplified information on web pages.
devices attributes	TTS only preferred on mobile phones.
	Browser zoom if screen greater than 14 inch.
Preferred AT products	ZoomText is preferred for magnification.
Dependent preferences	Brightness of screen off if TTS is used to save battery.
	Never launch TTS and Magnification combined.

To give one additional example of a remark; we received, for instance, from a participant with low vision who does not need specific accessibility configurations but usually uses a screen reader, the following comment: "If voice is not appropriate for me, I read it visually as I can do it." He further noted that "If web sites are not accessible, then I use zoom the screen (two finger options as ctrl + mouse wheel or ctrl + "+") without a magnifier". Even if the given example is not very specific it illustrates the challenges that need to be addressed by personalization approaches. Examples given in Table 3 include more specific statements of participants.

2.3   Discussion

A profound result of the user study was that there are, on the one hand, individuals who really know what they require to use information and computer technologies and, on the other hand, individuals that have no specific requirements. It shall be emphasized again, that the results reflect current user opinions as that was intended to investigate in the study. Results do not allow implications whether or to which degree assistive technologies or accessibility settings are refused or not helpful for users.

Can Users Specify Their Needs and Preferences?

Related to our first research question, results of our study show that in particular visual impaired participants, including low vision and blindness, have a basic understanding of the assistive technologies and accessibility settings they require to interact with their ICT products. Based on the collected data it can be proved that we need to differentiate between the need of an accessibility setting to be applied consistently across applications and devices or in specific contexts, and additional preferences of accessibility options that are preferred for specific conditions as 96 of the 97 participants gave different answers to both questions Table 2. Therefore there is a basic weighting of 1 with relates to a need and a weighting of 0 which relates to a preference. That implies that personalization approaches, as for instance developed in Cloud4all/GPII, need to provide solutions for circumstances where a mapping between a user's need, e.g. TTS, and the capabilities of current technical environment cannot be handled directly, e.g. if an assistive technology is not installed, if more than one assistive technologies of the same type are installed, at which level (OS, browser, application, etc.) accessibility settings needs to be applied. Inferences to overcome such barriers need to be performed automatically, e.g. through launching a cloud-based solution or automatically trigger the re-installation of a screen reader to grant that the need is fulfilled. In the contrary, situations, where preferences cannot be fulfilled by customization or adaptation capabilities of the technical environment, might be acceptable by users if no proper accessibility option could be applied. Specific weights have not been considered explicitly in the user study as simplicity in the questionnaires has been aspired. Users might be confused, answers might be wrong or user might be misleading by asking them whether they either prefer or want to use a feature optionally as, for instance, specified in ISO/IEC 24751-2. However, results of our study gave insights on additional weightings of needs and preferences especially in terms of specific conditions according to content, applications, devices, preferred products and dependencies between preferences which have been presented in Table 3.

Results of our study show also a tendency that bootstrapping as well as recommendations of accessibility settings will become important in the personalization approach of Cloud4all/GPII or similar approaches. Participants with cognitive disabilities, low digital literacy, dyslexic or even elderly know relatively few options related to accessibility that might improve their work. In contrast to information we received from visual impaired participants, only few precise accessibility settings could be extracted for other groups as presented in table 2 and 3. The majority (62%) of participants of groups other than visual impaired indicated that they have no specific need, 46% indicated that they have no specific preferences. These participants usually live with the ICT products as they are. They have less knowledge and experience what might improve their handling of computers and electronic devices. They were not aware on what they want to change and how to do it. However, it is has been already researched early [8] that there are barriers for users to customize and that there are sticking points to grapple with computer technologies by what those comments were expected in our study. Hence, these participants were rather able to indicate their problems or difficulties instead of naming requirements as consequence or solution to the problem itself. Comments we received were, for instance: *"I do not know many things about PCs but*

I would like the access to be simpler with just pressing a few buttons or talking to the PC". Another participant stated: *"Zoom is ok [...]. I cannot spend much time on PC because it is tiring. If someone shows me speech activation then it would be less tiring"*. As a consequence, selective recommendations of convenient accessibility options, enclosed in the personalization and/or in the profile initialization process, can help them to find solutions to their difficulties, simplify computer tasks, and even lower barriers with ICT in general. In an early concept study [5] we showed that recommending accessibility settings can impact the user`s awareness of ways that might improve their work when it will be implemented properly. Recommendations of accessibility can also be a solution to a potential drawback which is that personalization approaches can negatively impact the user`s overall awareness of software features [3]. A balance between automatic performed personalization from preferences, recommendations of new preferences, and user interfaces to explore and control resulting tailor-made customization capabilities should be sought and further researched.

What Difficulties Need to be Addressed by Personalization?
Apart from the condition classes that could be extracted from the collected data, there are specific characteristics that have been commented by participants. Blind users that usually depend on oral information stated language constitutes a main barrier. This means that even if they have the proper AT installed in their devices, they may not be able to use some applications if they are not in a familiar language to them. In addition, people who are blind are used in the usage of a specific screen reader with specific shortcuts. Without being familiar with the screen reader's shortcuts blind people are unable to use it.

In terms of screen enlargement options several characteristics have been highlighted as well. Participants with low vision mentioned that they combine various magnifications and zooming options as one single solution does not suit the requirements. For instance, a user with low vision specified the need of magnifier, however, he also stated the complexity of magnify and zoom options. He pointed out 2 important issues. Firstly, he mentioned an orientation and navigation problem triggered by magnifiers: *"Magnifiers do not give quick overview of web pages that are busy in colors and graphics; videos are the worse."* He further highlighted that magnifying web content is complex compared to just reading text documents: *"Magnification is not needed for all elements of a web page and not the same zooming is effective for all parts of a web page."*. Similar statements relating to web page magnification have been given by another participant with low vision. Although he replied to the question on his needs with *"I read what I need to read. The need is covered by Windows."*, his answer according to the preferences differed: *"[...] depend on complexity and type of information and how it is presented to me what I will end up achieving to read and/or see. Magnifying should be based on type of information received or wanted to search for. [...]"*. These characteristics need to be addressed by the personalization from preferences that we are investigating.

Additionally, there is a requirement for modeling preferences whether assistive technologies or accessibility settings shall be launched automatically (always or under certain conditions) or whether users want to have preferred accessibility options (all or subsets; always or under certain conditions) available that they can be activated or adjusted easily and individually. Participants stated that they want to change important settings easily. That implies also to allow users quickly to kill applications, to launch it again, or to activate other preferred accessibility option that have been expressed for the current context. For instance, one participant commented: "The option should be all theses configurations to be able to change very easy [...] with keyboard short cuts". That requires that, apart from the auto-personalization, tailored adjustment and control options should be given to the user.

3   Conclusion

Personalization from preferences as developed in Cloud4all/GPII, show great promise for improving accessibility by delivering tailor-made auto-configuration of assistive technologies and accessibility settings across a complexity of information technology usage in an individual's daily live. Within that research field, new approaches are significant to match an individual's needs and preferences to the technical environment and its adaptation capabilities which includes to overcome limitations and barriers triggered by heterogeneities of information technologies. We are contributing to that topic with a user study that gives insights in the needs and preferences of individuals and we report on challenges that individuals are facing when interacting with user interfaces. Our research questions comprise if users can specify their needs and preferences, what are general accessibility settings and their weightings and what are characteristics according to these factors. The design of the study focuses on data capturing about what users actually know and we avoid grappling users with expectations they might have from personalization. Results presented reveal that further investigation on preference representations is relevant to express needs and preferences on a more fine level of granularity for certain contexts or to convey demands of users when and in which way they wish specific preferences quickly be applied and while being still adjustable. A large amount of individuals can benefit from future work on recommending suitable accessibility settings which implies user interface design on presenting these recommendations providing that awareness of technology features can be increased and that aspects in usage can be improved.

Acknowledgements. We thank all participants who took part in our interviews and user study. Beyond that we thank all test facilitators in Germany (SDC and HDM), Greek (CERH) and Spain (Technosite) for undertaking the Cloud4all pilots and asking our research questions. We received meaningful feedback for future development and research. Results presented in this paper have been researched within the Cloud4all project. Cloud4all is an R&D project that receives funding from the European Commission under the Seventh Framework Program (FP7/2007-2013) under grant agreement n° 289016.

References

1. Abou-Zahra: How People with Disabilities Use the Web. W3C (MIT, ERCIM, Keio) Status: Draft Updated (2012), http://www.w3.org/WAI/intro/people-use-web/Overview
2. Clark, C., et al.: A Cloud-Scale Architecture for Inclusion: Cloud4all and GPII. In: Assistive Technology: From Research to Practice – Proceedings of AAATE 2013. IOS Press (2013)
3. Findlater, L., McGrenere, J.: Beyond performance: Feature awareness in personalized interfaces. International Journal of Human-Computer Studies 68(3), 121–137 (2010)
4. Frydyada de Piotrowski, A.M., Tauber, M.J.: Benutzerprofile von Menschen mit Beeinträchtigungen/Fähigkeiten. In: Mensch & Computer: Grenzenlosfrei!?, pp. 33–42. Oldenburg Verlag, München (2009)
5. Hille, D.: Analysis and design of user-friendly interaction mechanism with a feedback system for personalisation. TechnischeUniversität Dresden. Dept. of Computer Science, IAI, 67 p. (2013) (Study Thesis)
6. ISO/IEC 24751. Information technology - Individualized adaptability and accessibility in elearning, education and training — Part 2: "Access for all" personal needs and preferences for digital delivery (2008)
7. Loitsch, C., et al.: Improving Accessibility by Matching User Needs and Preferences. In: Assistive Technology: From Research to Practice – Proceedings of AAATE 2013. IOS Press (2013)
8. Mackay, W.E.: Triggers and barriers to customizing software. In: Proceedings of the SIGCHI Conference on Human Factors in Computing Systems, pp. 153–160. ACM (1991)
9. Melcher, V., Krüger, A., Chalkia, E.: Managing Preferences in the Cloud – Requirements and UI Design. In: Assistive Technology: From Research to Practice – Proceedings of AAATE 2013. IOS Press (2013)
10. Ruth-Janneck, D.: MultidimensionaleKlassifizierung von Barrieren in Webanwendungen. In: Mensch & Computer: Grenzenlosfrei!?, pp. 13–22. Oldenburg Verlag, München (2009)
11. Vanderheiden, G., Treviranus, J.: Creating a global public inclusive infrastructure. In: Stephanidis, C. (ed.) Universal Access in HCI, Part I, HCII 2011. LNCS, vol. 6765, pp. 517–526. Springer, Heidelberg (2011)
12. WHO. International Classification of Functioning, Disability and Health (ICF). WHO Press, Geneva (2009)

Improving the Accessibility of Public Digital Terminals through Personalisation:
Comparison of Direct and Indirect Interaction Modes

R. Ignacio Madrid[1], Kathrin Schrader[2], and Manuel Ortega-Moral[1]

[1] Fundosa Technosite, ONCE Foundation, Madrid, Spain
{nmadrid,mortega}@technosite.es
[2] SoVD-Landesverband Niedersachsen e.V, Hannover, Germany
kathrin.schrader@sovd-nds.de

Abstract. The APSIS4all project has developed and evaluated two different approaches to improve the accessibility of Public Digital Terminals (PDTs). The first one implements the approach called 'direct interaction', by using an online tool to collect users' needs and preferences and use them to provide personalised PDT interfaces. The second one implements the approach called 'indirect interaction', by using a smartphone make the operations and receive and 2D code to finalise the service in the PDT. This paper analyses and compares the results of the trials with both approaches, focusing on the impact of accessible and personalised services in the user experience of different user groups.

Keywords: Accessibility, Personalisation, User Experience, Public Digital Terminals, Automated Teller Machines, Ticket Vending Machines.

1 Introduction

1.1 Accessibility of Public Digital Terminals (PDTs)

Public Digital Terminals (PDTs), also known as self-service terminals (such as automated teller machines (ATMs), ticket vending machines (TVMs), virtual kiosks, etc.), play a key societal role by providing autonomous access to essential services on a 24/7 basis. Moreover, their presence in the urban environment is increasing, showing the trend towards a self-serving economy. For example, there were 435,000 ATMs in the EU at the end of 2012 [1].

However, a wide range of users found barriers that mean some citizens are unable to access PDT services, thus limiting people's ability to fully participate in society. Barriers that are frequently mentioned include the lack of speech output, the complexity of interfaces or difficulties for handling physical controls [2-3]. In many cases, there are not alternative methods for accessing the services when citizens cannot use the terminal and many of them are not supervised. In order to cope with these barriers, different standards, accessibility guidelines and solutions (e.g. speech technology or high-contrast interfaces) have been developed during the last years [4-5]. Despite all

C. Stephanidis and M. Antona (Eds.): UAHCI/HCII 2014, Part I, LNCS 8513, pp. 258–269, 2014.
© Springer International Publishing Switzerland 2014

these valuable initiatives, the accessibility status of PDTs is still moderate in European countries, as well as other countries as Australia or USA [6].

1.2   The APSIS4all Project

APSIS4all [7] is a pan-European consortium of industry partners, research institutes and organisations which represent disability groups with the goal of making PDTs more accessible and usable. This includes adaptive interfaces offering users a personalised service adapted to their needs and preferences, and thereby overcoming the existing accessibility barriers.

Within APSIS4all, and with the aim to validate, in real life settings, the impact of providing customised interaction modes, a pilot on Automated Teller Machines (ATMs) for banking services and a pilot on Ticket Vending Machines (TVM) for transport services is taking place in Spain and Germany respectively. During these pilots, two different approaches are being implemented and tested:

Direct Interaction. Users specify their needs and preferences by using a web application. They are able to change the text size, background colours, include voice output options, add help content or simplify the interaction, among other features. This information is coded (according to specification EN 1332-4 [8]) and stored in a user device such as a contactless smartcard. Because it is based on standards, the PDT will retrieve the user's needs and preferences, regardless of the service provider, and display the most suitable interface available. See Fig. 1.

Fig. 1. Diagram representing the user journey with the direct interaction mode

Indirect Interaction. This second approach shifts the PDT operation to the Internet, so users can operate on their laptop or smartphone which is already configured according to their needs and preferences and have the corresponding assistive technologies installed when necessary. The user requests the desired service and the system generates an identification item, such as a 2D-barcode, which is transmitted to the customer's mobile phone. Finally, the user presents the 2D-barcode in the PDT and finish the payment process to obtain the service. See Fig. 2.

Fig. 2. Diagram representing the user journey with the indirect interaction mode

2   Methodology and Tools

2.1   Evaluation Framework

The development and implementation of both direct and indirect approaches has followed a Human Centered Design (HCD) process, during which near 300 users belonging to different user groups (i.e. blind, low vision, deaf, hearing impaired, motor impaired, people with intellectual disabilities, elderly people or people without disabilities) have participated in evaluation activities as surveys, usability testing and interviews (See [9-10] for a detailed description of previous user research activities).

As an important part of the HCD process, different user experience (UX) evaluations were performed in pilot sites. The evaluation framework adapted state-of-the-art techniques and questionnaires for assessing five dimensions tapping user experience with PDTs: ease of use, learnability, satisfaction, expectations and fulfillment of human needs [11-12]. By averaging the score on these individual measures, a combined single UX metric was also computed to summarize and make comparisons between user profiles. The UX metric score can range from 0 to 100, considering scores between 50-70 points as '*Just OK*', between 70-80 points as '*Good*' and above 80 points as an '*Excellent*' user experience. Together with this UX metric, both quantitative and qualitative data have been collected over the trials in APSIS4all through interviews and facilitator diaries.

2.2   Description of the APSIS4all Solutions

The Direct Interaction Approach. Direct interaction requires implementing a user modeling process where the needs, preferences and the most appropriate interfaces are covered. Along this process, the users should interact with two different solutions.

Collecting Tool of Needs and Preferences (CTNP)
A web application was designed to gather information about users' capabilities in order to define the *User's Needs and Preferences Profile* that will be later on coded and stored in the user smart card. The CTNP shows an interactive questionnaire that the users have to fill in after getting registered in the system webpage [13].See Fig. 3.

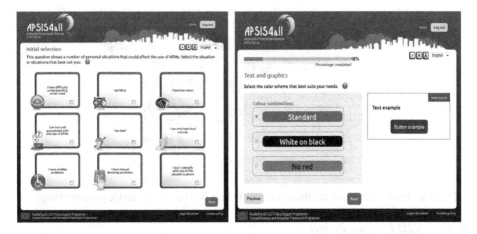

Fig. 3. Screenshots of the Collecting Tool of Needs and Preferences (CTNP)

Personalised ATM Interfaces
The accessible ATMs map the users' profiles with personalized user interfaces that take into account user requirements. Some of the available options include the use and configuration of screen readers, different high contrast interfaces, keyboard or touch screen use, simple interfaces or sign-language avatars (see Fig. 4 as an example).

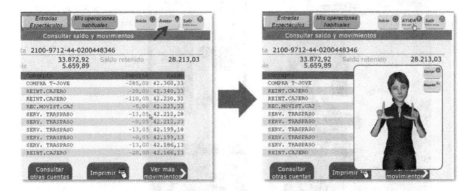

Fig. 4. Screenshot of the personalized ATM interface with sign-language avatar

Indirect Interaction Approach. In the indirect interaction approach, the users should first use their own smartphone to purchase the travel ticket through a Mobile web app, and then go to the TVM to finalize the service.

Mobile Web App
An accessible mobile web allows buying tickets and predefining the user preferred travel destinations as favorites. After that, the user receives a 2D-barcode that should be presented in the TVM to finalize the service and get his/her ticket.

Fig. 5. Screenshot showing the list of favorite tickets (left) and the barcode generated (right)

TVM with 2D Barcode Reader

The main interaction element of the TVM in this trial is the 2D barcode reader that is used to read the barcode that have been previously created with the Mobile web app. After reading the barcode and finalizing the service, the TVM will produce the travel ticket (See Fig. 6).

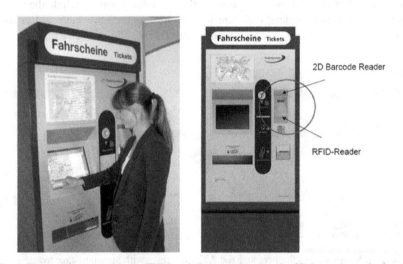

Fig. 6. Picture of a user with the TVM and diagram showing the 2D barcode reader location

2.3   Participants

Table 1 shows the distribution of users that participated in research activities (field studies and user testing) for the direct interaction (ATMs, in Spain) and indirect inte-raction (TVMs, in Germany) approaches. There were participants from the following user groups: blind (B), visually impaired (VI), deaf (D), hearing impaired (HI), motor impaired (MI), cognitively impaired (CI), elderly people (E) and non-disabled people below 65 years old (ND). Overall, near 300 people participated in field studies and more than 200 in user testing activities during trials.

Table 1. Distribution of participants per user groups and test site

	(B)	(VI)	(D)	(HI)	(MI)	(CI)	(E)	(ND)	All
D.Int. (ATMs)									
Field studies	18	29	14	11	33	16	20	43	166
CTNP testing	16	16	15	7	14	13	10	9	100
ATM testing	4	4	4	4	4	4	6	4	34
I.Int. (TVMs)									
Field studies	10	15	13	11	16	12	25	34	125
TVM testing	3	3	3	3	3	3	6	5	29

3   Direct Interaction with Automated Teller Machines (ATMs)

3.1   Previous Experiences with ATMs and Existing Accessibility Barriers

Frequency of Use. ATMs are widely used in Spain. However, 22,23 % of the users participating in field research claimed not to use them. The lack of use of ATMs was more important for certain user groups (e.g. 50% cognitively impaired or 30% of elderly people never use ATMs, against 14% of non-disabled people younger than 65).

Usability and Accessibility Barriers. Considering the whole user sample, the most frequent problems found are the unclear and difficult to understand interfaces (experienced by 22,6% of the users) and the mismatch between ATM options and user needs (experienced by 14,4% of the users). Some of the barriers affecting specific users groups include the impossibility of reading screen content (38,9% of the blind and 60% of the visually impaired users), the inadequate functioning of the keyboard or other technical elements (33% of the motor impaired users) and the lack of instructions on the procedure (28,9% of the elderly people and 19% of the cognitively impaired users). Interestingly, it should be noticed that some of the difficulties was claimed by more than 35% of the non-disabled, younger than 65 years people. This suggests that the benefits of usability and accessibility improvements are not limited to people with disabilities and are extensive to a wider population of users.

Previous Experiences and Expectations for Future APSIS4all ATMs. The user experience with existing ATMs cannot be considered as 'Good', but at least 'Just OK' taken into account the whole sample of participants (M=57; SDE=2,54). However, a closer look at the results showed poor user experience of specific user groups as the motor impaired (M=27,35;SDE=7,72) and blind people (M=49,3;SDE=5,58).

The expected user experience with the future APSIS4all ATMs was also measured after experiencing the CTNP. The results showed a general improvement on UX scores in comparison with the existing ATM systems (M=82,44;SDE=1,70), which means that users values the APSIS4all concept and expect to have an 'Excellent' user experience when using future systems. See Fig. 7.

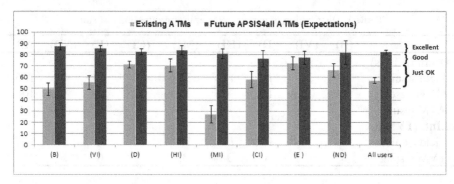

Fig. 7. Overall user experience with ATMs (existing vs. personalised) for each user profile

3.2   User Experience with the CTNP

The development of the CTNP followed a Human Centered Design approach through different design iterations, which led to improvements in the user experience in comparison with first prototypes. The process and full results are described in [9].

Results from UX questionnaires, summarized in Fig. x, have shown that the CTNP was very positively valued by the participants (M=79.06; SDE=1.84) without big differences between user groups (See Fig. 8).

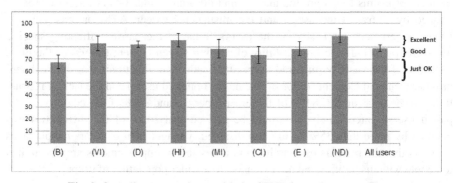

Fig. 8. Overall user experience with the CTNP for each user profile

During the evaluation process, some interesting insights were gathered while interviewing and observing users, which will help the project to improve the CTNP:

Reduce the Number of Questions. In early prototypes, users answered more than 8 questions on average to produce a complete set of user needs and preferences. However this required much effort from the users to make selections that could be inferred directly by the tool. To improve this, the current version show a reduced set of questions that can be complemented later on if needed through an 'Advanced settings' section.

Include Previews. In order to answer some questions, the users need to know what will be the consequences in the final ATM interface (e.g. How a sign-language avatar looks like? Where will it appear in the interface?). Example screenshots and animated graphics are shown in the CTNP to illustrate the aim of questions.

Limit the Number of Personalisation Options. Personalisation options are potentially unlimited. Early prototypes of the CTNP allowed choosing between 8 different colour combinations of the interface. However, this placed a burden in the user that had doubts about which of the interfaces would be the best for him/her. The current version of the CTNP offer a limited number of personalisation options based on previous user selections (e.g. if the user have problems with certain colours, it is possible to choose between a 'black&white' or 'avoid red" interface).

3.3   User Experience with ATMs

The analysis of results from questionnaires showed that, in general, the UX with APSIS4all ATMs can be considered as good (M=82.11; SDE=3.92). Results for each of the user groups were very valuable to identify future improvements, but should be taken carefully due to low number of participants per group (See Fig. 9).

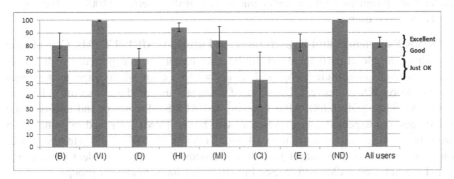

Fig. 9. Results on user experience with ATMs for each user profile

The 34 participants completed the user testing tasks without finding remarkable barriers. Some interesting ideas were expressed that are useful to improve the accessibility of ATM interfaces:

Accessibility Features Should Not Interfere with the Usability of the Interface. For example, in early prototypes the continuous appearance of the sign-language avatar caused confusion for some deaf participants. The current sign-language interface can be activated and deactivated by the user on-demand.

Remove Severe Barriers First. Some problems can even impede the use of PDTs and when these are overcome other barriers seem easier to get over. For example, participants with dexterity problems acknowledged the advantages of using a contactless card, since they hardly could reach and handle the card slot with other ATM models. Even the use of cursor navigation needed some practice they successfully completed all the tasks.

4   Indirect Interaction with Ticket Vending Machines

4.1   Previous Experiences with TVMs and Existing Accessibility Barriers

Frequency of Use. Taking into account survey responses from all user groups, 35,2% of the participants claimed not to use TVMs. Certain user groups had higher percentages of lack of use (e.g. 60% of elderly people, 58,3% of the cognitively impaired or 40% of blind people never use TVMs, against 12% of non-disabled people younger than 65). In order to interpret this data properly it has to be noticed that some user groups with severe disabilities can use public transportation for free in Germany, which surely explain their low use rates.

Usability and Accessibility Barriers. Considering the whole user sample, the most frequent problems found with TVMs are related with menu navigation and the mismatch between the available options and user needs. Some of the barriers affecting specific users groups include poor touch-screen sensitivity (63,9% of the motor impaired) and problems with the understandability of the interface (100% of the cognitively impaired users).

Previous Experiences and Expectations for Future APSIS4all TVMs. Considering the whole sample of participants, it can be said that previous experience with TVMs was perceived as sufficient (M=65.19; SDE=3.15), even when some user groups showed lower UX scores (e.g. UX score of the motor impaired users seems to be very poor; M=33.5; SDE=8.68). After knowing the APSIS4all concept and testing some prototypes, the expected user experience with future TVMs improved in comparison with the existing ones in more than 10 points (M=75.59; SDE=1.98). However, data on previous experiences didn't include impressions from blind or deaf participants who have not used TVMs before. See Fig. 10 with data from all user groups.

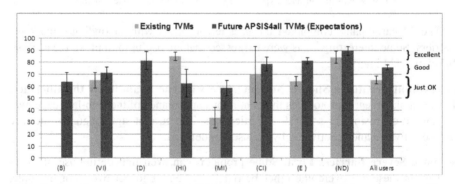

Fig. 10. Overall user experience with TVMs (existing vs. personalised) for each user profile

4.2   User Experience with the Mobile Web App

In general, the Mobile app was rated as excellent in terms of user experience according to responses to questionnaires (M=85.06; SDE=3.75). Fig. 11 shows differences between users groups that seem to be not big.

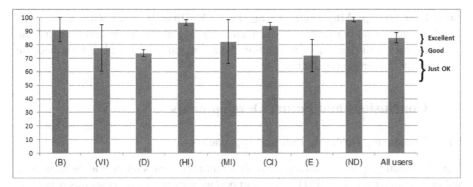

Fig. 11. Overall user experience with the mobile app for each user profile

User experience evaluations were also performed regarding the ease of use of the scanning of the 2D barcode in TVMs. This task received medium scores on average but had a wider variability between user groups (M=60.4; SDE=7.38). See Fig. 12.

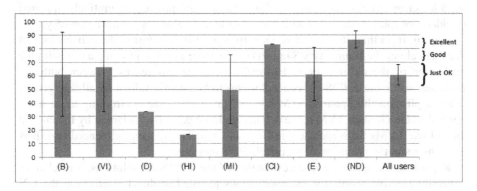

Fig. 12. Ease of use of the scanning procedure in TVMs for each user profile

The following considerations can be extracted when looking at specific user groups:

Scanning Bar Codes Requires Some Training. All participants used the Mobile web app without problems. However, for most of the users it was the first time scanning barcodes and for some of them it was very difficult to find the right angle or place under the scanner.

Blind People were the More Enthusiastic User Group. Many blind people have an accessible smartphone (e.g. iPhone with voiceover function), that they use for many different tasks in daily life. Since most of these users had not previous experiences with TVMs (i.e. because they have free access to public transport) and frequently find barriers in similar PDTs, the use of mobile phones was valued very positively.

Some User Groups May Prefer Using the TVM Directly. Even when some users may have not found big problems when using the Mobile web app and scanning the barcodes, they still can prefer a traditional way of interacting with TVMs because they already master the procedure.

5   Conclusions and Future Developments

5.1   Comparing Direct vs. Indirect Approaches

The APSIS4all project is evaluating two different approaches for providing accessible and personalized access to PDTs. As an important step in this process, this paper has described field studies and user testing conducted to evaluate the direct interaction approach (using first an online tool and then operating directly with ATMs) and the indirect interaction (using a Mobile web app to operate indirectly with TVMs).

First of all, user research has shown that there are several accessibility barriers affecting both the users of existing ATMs and TVMs. This fact is partially responsible for a lower use rate in both contexts for some user groups (e.g. cognitively impaired or elderly people) if compared with people without disabilities younger than 65 years.

Starting from this situation, it is not surprising that, in general, the expectations of the users about the future APSIS4all PDTs are more positive in comparison with the evaluation of the existing ones. However, there are differences between both approaches: while the APSIS4all concept seems to be equally valued by all user groups when applied to the Spanish ATM context, there are some confronting ideas when applied to the German TVM context. This could be partially explained by the current lack of use TVMs for some users in Germany, which may have influenced their perceptions about the provision of accessible PDT services.

Regarding the user experience evaluation of the APSIS4all solutions, it resulted in generally positive scores for the applications tested. For direct interaction, the UX scores obtained can be considered as 'Good' for the CTNP and 'Excellent' for the ATM interfaces. For indirect interaction, the Mobile web app obtained UX scores that can be considered as 'Excellent', but the ease of use of the barcode scanning process was rated as 'Just OK' on average, with high variability between user responses. This suggests that the indirect interaction mode may be not suitable for all type of users.

5.2   Next Steps in APSIS4all

Using the results of the evaluation procedure described here, the APSIS4all solutions used in the direct and indirect interaction modes have been improved before the project pilots in real environments.

The Spanish pilot implements the direct interaction in 1000 ATMs by the Spanish bank "la Caixa" in Madrid and Barcelona, whereas the German pilot will tests both the direct and the indirect interaction approaches in 24 machines deployed by TVM manufacturer Hoeft & Wessel and used by the Padersprinter transport company in Paderborn. Up to 3,000 customers are expected to use them during the pilot period which has been running for six months since the end of 2013.

References

1. European Central Bank, Payment Statistics (2012),
   http://sdw.ecb.europa.eu/reports.do?node=100000760_ALLPDF
2. Kouroupetroglou, G.: Universal Access in Public Terminals: Information Kiosks and ATMs. The Universal Access Handbook, 48.1–48.19 (2009)
3. Schreder, G., Siebenhandl, K., Mayr, E., Smuc, M.: The Ticket Machine Challenge: Social Inclusion by Barrier-free Ticket Vending Machines. In: Loos, E.F., Haddon, L., Mante-Meijer, E. (eds.) Generational Use of New Media, pp. 129–148. Ashgate (2012)
4. Fundació Barcelona Digital, Adaptability of Cashpoints for the Disabled (Normalization proposal) (2006)
5. ETSI EG 202 116 V1.2.2 Human Factors (HF); Guidelines for ICT products and services; "Design for All" (2009)
6. Monitoring eAccessibility in Europe: 2011 Annual Report, Technosite for the European Commission (2011),
   http://www.eaccessibility-monitoring.eu/researchResult.aspx
7. APSIS4all: Accessible Personalised Services in Public Digital Terminals for All, http://www.apsis4all.eu/
8. EN1332-4 Identification Card Systems-Man-Machine Interface-Part 4: Coding of user requirements for people with special needs
9. Madrid, R., Turrero, M., Ortega-Moral, M.: Applying Human-Centred Design to create a collecting tool of needs and preferences for the personalisation of ATMs. In: Assistive Technology: From Research to Practice, pp. 380–385,
   doi:http://dx.doi.org/10.3233/978-1-61499-304-9-380
10. Graf, C., Hochleitner, C., Tschelig, M.: How to Design Accessible TVMs for Older Adults. In: Proceedings of the 7th Nordic Conference on Human-Computer Interaction, NordiCHI 2012, Copenhagen, Denmark, October 14-17 (2012)
11. Tullis, T., Albert, W.: Measuring the user experience: Collecting, analyzing, and presenting usability metrics. Morgan Kaufman, San Francisco (2008)
12. Sauro, J., Lewis, J.R.: Quantifying the user experience: Practical Statistics for User Research. Morgan Kaufmann, Burlington (2012)
13. APSIS4all Collecting Tool of Needs and Preferences,
    https://cajerofacil.apsis4all.eu/
14. Padersprinter Mobile Web App, http://www.padersprinter.de/app_eu-projekt?__sid=e4450fddd30424f866a63f1ad36a10a9

Future Challenges of User Modelling for Accessibility

Yehya Mohamad[1], Christos Kouroupetroglou[2], and Pierre T. Kirisci[3]

[1] Fraunhofer FIT. Germany
[2] Caretta-Net Technologies, Greece
[3] University of Bremen, Germany

Abstract. User models are abstract representations of user properties including their needs, preferences, knowledge, as well as physical, cognitive, and behavioral characteristics. These characteristics are usually represented by variables. User models are instantiated by the declaration of these variables for a particular user or group of users. Such instances of user models are called user profiles. A user profile captures the kind of information about an individual user that is considered by an adaptive system to adapt to aspects of a certain situation and preferences of different users.

Complimentarily the process of user modelling can be applied to enhance the accessibility of user interfaces by generating or adapting them according to the particular user needs and preferences represented in the user profiles. In spite of the different approaches in this area, further research and development is necessary, particularly in addressing the need for standards to support the interoperability and portability of user models across implementations. More specifically, one of the main challenges of user modelling is the lack of a common approach for integrating user profiles that support different user models within individual implementations, and for migrating profiles from one implementation to another. This can be attributed to the broad variety of user profiles and the incompatibilities that can occur among them. For example, differences in user profiles can occur due to differences in scope of the modelling, source of information for the modelling, time sensitivity and update methods of the model (static vs. dynamic model). In this paper a thorough review of the latest developments in the area of user modelling for accessibility is presented. Further, in the core of the paper future potentials and challenges that this technology has to face in order to gain significant traction and adoption from wider audiences is analyzed.

Keywords: user model, user profile, adaptivity, simulation, context awareness, interoperability.

1 Introduction

User modeling is a technology used in a variety of domains in order to model specific attributes and characteristics of a system's user. The quantitative values and qualitative properties for such characteristics are stored within user profiles which could refer to a specific user or user group, allowing this way the system to adapt according to the respective users' needs. Obviously accessibility to products and systems could

C. Stephanidis and M. Antona (Eds.): UAHCI/HCII 2014, Part I, LNCS 8513, pp. 270–278, 2014.

benefit largely from such adaptive mechanisms since it would allow for systems to adapt to specific needs that e.g. people with physical and cognitive disabilities possess. In summary, the process of user modelling aims to:

offer different ways to access the content (rights, devices, user agents etc.),
allow for different access to the functionalities provided by the system (roles),
maintain the preferences affecting the results of the user operations,
differentiate the output based on the context of the user.

Recently a number of research programs and standardization actions have emerged in order to exploit the potentials of user modelling for accessibility purposes. However, the usage of the technology in real world scenarios still in its early stages and there are a number of issues and challenges that lie ahead in order for research and development in the area to be taken up into wide adoption [35].

The area of user modelling for accessibility is an active one, so research, development and standardization actions are being carried out. Many user modelling for accessibility projects were funded in the frame of the European research program FP7, e.g.:

The projects VICON (http://vicon-project.eu/) and VERITAS (http://www.veritas-project.eu/index.html) focused mainly on the question: How user modelling is used for simulation purposes in projects that aim to simulate human behavior using virtual user models

The projects
GUIDE (http://www.guide-project.eu/) ,
MyUI (http://www.myui.eu/),
CLOUD4ALL (http://cloud4all.info/)

focused on how user modeling is used for adaptations of user interfaces at runtime. The project I2Web (http://i2web.eu) developed user models based upon existing accessibility standards combined with an analysis of user requirements for people with special needs and older people in relation to ubiquitous Web 2.0 applications. As a result of the above mentioned projects Table 1 summarizes the areas and challenges that lie ahead in the future of user modelling for accessibility technology.

Table 1. Areas and challenges of user modelling

Area	Challenges
User needs research	For which groups of people with disabilities is more research required, so that their specific needs can be better understood and covered by user modeling technology?
Privacy issues	What has to be done in order to ensure privacy of user profiles, secure and transparent exchange of information between sources, control of user over their user profile information?
Modelling approaches	What are the advantages and disadvantages of storing user characteristics or preferences in a user profile and how can these two main apporaches be merged?

Table 1. (*continued*)

design and user experience practices	What kind of user experience and design techniques exist that could help in building more accurate user profiles and get more advanced and sophisticated batter feedback from users?
Standardization	What standards exist in terms of user modeling for accessibility and how could they develop a critical mass of usage so that they enable quicker innovation in the area of design for accessibility?
advanced contextual models	How important is to model contextual information in order to achieve better adaptive systems and what kind of information is currently available for modeling aspects of situations and how could these exploited?

There exist many standards and standardization actions in the area of user modeling for accessibility e.g. "Individualized Adaptability and Accessibility for Learning, Education and specification for the User Modelling software Training" (ISO/IEC 24751 1:2008) (http://www.iso.org/iso/ iso_catalogue/catalogue_tc/catalogue_detail.htm?csnumber=41521) and its part 2, which specifies a model dividing the personal needs and preferences of the user into three categories (ISO/IEC 24751 2, 2008): (a) Display (b) Control and (c) Content. The IMS Learner Information Package Accessibility for LIP Information Model (ACCLIP) provides a means to describe how learners can interact with an online learning environment based on their preferences and needs (IMS Global Learning Consortium, 2003). The standard is meant to serve the needs and preferences of all users, not only those with a disability. In particular, through its information model, accessibility extends beyond disability to benefit users in learning situations that require alternative modes of use. The user preferences defined aim to aid the user in displaying learning material in the style best suited to their particular needs and in specifying an interface that they can interact with effectively which allows the accessible display and control of the learning material.

Virtual Human Modelling

The purpose of Virtual human modelling (VHM) as well known as (digital human modelling DHM) or VUM (Virtual user Modelling) reduces the need for the production of real prototypes, thus applying these approaches can even make the generation of prototypes partially obsolete [9, 11]. During the past years, research interest in using digital human modelling for ergonomics purposes increased significantly [10]. Lamkull et al (2009) [11] performed a comparative analysis on digital human modelling simulation results and their outcomes in the real world. The results of this study show that ergonomic digital human modelling tools are useful for providing designs of standing and unconstrained working postures.

Researchers worked on modelling various body parts, including face [12][13], neck [14], torso [15], hand [16], and leg [17]. In particular, many researchers [18][19] [20][21][22] concentrated on the biomechanical analysis of the human upper limb. Hingtgen et al (2003) [31] constructed an upper extremity (UE) model for application in stroke rehabilitation to accurately track the three-dimensional orientation of the trunk, shoulder, elbow, and wrist during task performance.

In the area of accessibility a previous case study was presented, the HADRIAN system, based on the SAMMIE CAD [24], which tried to detect accessibility issues during the interaction between users and ATM machines.

Sapin et al (2008) [25] reported a comparison of the gait patterns of trans-femoral amputees using a single-axis prosthetic knee that coordinates ankle and knee flexion's with the gait patterns of patients using other knee joints without a knee–ankle link and the gait patterns of individuals with normal gait. Prince et al (1997) [26], reviewed spatio-temporal, kinematics, kinetics and EMG data as well as the physiological changes associated with gait and aging. Coluccini et al (2007) [27] assessed and analyzed upper limb kinematics of normal and motor disabled children, with the aim to propose a kinematic based framework for the objective assessment of the upper limb, including the evaluation of compensatory movements of both the head and the trunk. Ouerfelli et al (1999)[28] applied two identification methods to study the kinematics of head-neck movements of able-bodied as well as neck-injured subjects. As a result, a spatial three-revolute joint system was employed to model 3D head-neck movements.

In other related areas there are tools and frameworks available, which provide designers with the means for creating virtual humans with different capabilities and use them for simulation purposes. DANCE [29], for instance, is an open framework for computer animation research focusing on the development of simulations and dynamic controllers, unlike many other animation systems, which are oriented towards geometric modelling and kinematic animation. SimTk's OpenSim is also a freely available user extensible software system that lets users develop models of musculoskeletal structures and create dynamic simulations of movement. There are also many tools such as JACK from Siemens, RAMSIS from Human Solutions, or Santos from University of IOWA. Human Builder is the virtual user model for CATIA, Enovia and Delmia from Dassault Systems, offering considerable benefits to designers looking to design for all, as they allow the evaluation of a virtual prototype using virtual users with specific abilities.

As described above significant effort has been made in physical user modelling and many tools use virtual humans for simulation purposes. However, there is no widely accepted formal way for the description of the virtual users, being able to also describe users with special needs and functional limitations, such as the elderly and users with disabilities. This divergence hinders cooperation between research projects and slows down innovation in the area.

2   User Involvement in Product Development

One challenge of recent product development is the inclusion of customer-oriented needs in product design addressing as much user groups of population as possible. Existing methods of user involvement range between „Design for-" and "Design by-" approaches [32].

Kaulio presented a review on selected methods of user involvement and compared 7 different methods [1]. (1) Quality function deployment [4] describes an analytical approach for first design phases with involvement of end users by extraction of consumer demands into quality characteristics. (2) User-oriented product development [4] focuses upon the involvement after first prototype generation. (3) Concept testing [4] uses first sketches in an evaluation with customers. (4) Beta testing [5] refers to prototype evaluation with customers. (5) Customer-idealized design [13] involves customers by transferring product design into a group exercise. (6) Lead user method lets single representatives of a target group solve design problems and issues.(7) Participatory ergonomics involves different groups of product development into the process. Eventually all 7 methods have pros and cons for physical end products, according to the level of involvement (Design for-, with-, and by-) but also to the creativity of design and technological advancement. The challenge for user modeling technologies in this area lays in the question whether user models could be used in combination with some of the aforementioned methods and whether this combination could make some of the methods easier to apply.

3   User Adaptive Systems

Frameworks for the generation of user-adaptive systems [33] are used in different domains and contexts e.g. ergonomics, simulation, e-commerce, e-learning, tourism, cultural heritage, digital libraries, etc. A user-adaptive system adapts its content, structure and interface according to the user features contained in the user model. The user model typically maintains user characteristics such as preferences, interests, behavior, knowledge, goals and other facts that are deemed relevant for a user-adaptive application [7, 8]. As a result, the user model is a key component of an adaptive system. In fact, the quality of personalized services provided to the user largely depends on the characteristics represented in the user model, like its accuracy, the amount of data it stores, whether such data are up to date, etc.

There are many modelling areas and approaches related to the user modelling, so e.g. task modelling and application modelling [30]. Task models describe how to perform activities to reach users' goals. The need for modelling is most acutely felt when the design aims to support system implementation as well. If there are only informal representations (such as scenarios or paper mock-ups) available to developers, they would have to make many design decisions on behalf of their own, likely without the necessary background, to obtain a complete interactive system. Task models represent the intersection between user interface design and more systematic approaches by providing designers with a means of representing and manipulating an abstraction of activities that should be performed to reach user goals.

The application modelling is a multifaceted approach; one can address the topic from different perspectives: architecture design, implementation design or interaction design, part of this research is the area of Model-Based User Interface design (MBUID), which aims at identifying high-level models for the specification and analysis of interactive applications from a semantic perspective. Under this umbrella, the more interesting approach is the CAMELEON Unified Reference Framework [2].

Furthermore the SERENOA project,[1] introduced a semantic container that holds a library of algorithms for advanced adaptation logic. The I2Webproject extended this approach and focused on the research area of Model-Based User Interface design, which aims at identifying high-level models for the specification and analysis of interactive applications from a semantic perspective [34].

4   Conclusions and Future Work

The majority of research projects were so far targeted towards modelling of persons without disabilities. The few projects, which targeted towards disabled people, were concerned with physical disabilities such as visual, hearing and motor. Some of the research efforts are also covering some cognitive disabilities. Sophisticated user models need to cover all aspects of disability to really make a significant difference. Some user models consider visual and motor disabilities and do not involve other disabilities as hearing or cognitive disabilities. The extension of user models to become complete models covering all disabilities implies further work in user studies and statistical analysis.

Having said that, it is obvious that one of the basic challenges for user modelling for accessibility is how can a standard for user models be established so that it covers a wide spectrum of disabilities (physical and cognitive), user needs and preferences. A critical aspect of such a standard would also be the definition of the importance and necessity for each possible adaptation and their prioritization based on each user.

Given the above challenge and the variety of attempts in the area so far a question that rises is how could a user model standard such as the one developed within the VUMS cluster be further extended and matured in order to establish a critical mass of supporters and stimulate adoption. This critical mass is what is missing in most of the attempts so far. Given that, an already existing solution could mature and transform into the standards that the area is missing.

Apart from a common standard however the area of user modelling for accessibility is also split in between two different approaches discussed earlier (characteristics based and preferences based). Therefore, another challenge that is presented is how the strengths of these well-established and recognized user modelling approaches can be integrated in order to establish a seamless link between user characteristics and user preferences. This combination would benefit largely the product development process. One of the possible technologies that could help in that direction is machine learning, thus user modelling should probably invest on that area.

Machine learning could also benefit user modelling helping current VUM to extend in order to evolve to "dynamic virtual user models" which are characterized by dynamic properties in order achieve a concise integration of usage and context data provided e.g. through real-time monitoring of interactions with user interfaces and consumer products.

---

[1] http://www.serenoa-fp7.eu/

Most of the challenges discussed so far are mostly technical but there is a very critical aspect for user modelling technologies in order to reach wider audience adoption. Privacy especially for people with disabilities and elderly is paramount and this is a very complex issue that needs to be addressed. It involves (a) the development of protocols and mechanisms for exchange of user profiles between various sources (b) the control of users on their user profile information and its exposure and (c) the control and awareness of data gathering mechanism (e.g. eye-tracking, mouse-tracking, etc.) so that users feel comfortable and safe when using such technologies.

References

1. Kaulio, M.A.: Customer, consumer and user involvement in product development: A framework and a review of selected methods. Total Qual. Manag. 9, 141–149 (1998)
2. Calvary, G., Coutaz, J., Thevenin, D., Limbourg, Q., Bouillon, L., Vanderdonckt, J.: A Unifying Reference Framework for multi-target user interfaces. Interacting with Computers 15(3), 289–308 (2003)
3. Kirisci, P.T., et al.: Supporting inclusive design of user interfaces with a virtual user model. In: Stephanidis, C. (ed.) Universal Access in HCI, Part II, HCII 2011. LNCS, vol. 6766, pp. 69–78. Springer, Heidelberg (2011)
4. Kirisci, P.T., Thoben, K.D., Klein, P., Modzelewski, M.: Supporting inclusive product design with virtual user models at the early stages of product development. In: Proceedings of the 18th International Conference on Engineering Design (ICED 2011), vol. 9, pp. 80–90 (2011)
5. Lawo, M., Kirisci, P., Modzelewski, M., O'Connor, J., Fennell, A., Fiddian, T., Gökmen, H., Klann, M., Geissler, M., Matiouk, S., Mohamad, Y.: Virtual User Models – Approach and first results of the VICON project. In: Echallenges E-2011 Conf. Proc. (2011)
6. Marshall, R., Case, K., Summerskill, S., Sims, R., Gyi, D., Davis, P.: Virtual Task Simulation for Inclusive Design. In: Duffy, V.G. (ed.) Digital Human Modelling, HCII 2009. LNCS, vol. 5620, pp. 700–709. Springer, Heidelberg (2009)
7. Brusilovsky, P., Millán, E.: User models for adaptive hypermedia and adaptive educational systems. In: Brusilovsky, P., Kobsa, A., Nejdl, W. (eds.) Adaptive Web 2007. LNCS, vol. 4321, pp. 3–53. Springer, Heidelberg (2007)
8. Brusilovsky, P.: Methods and techniques of adaptive hypermedia. User Model. User-Adap. Inter. 60(2-3), 87–129 (1996)
9. Kobsa, A.: Generic user modeling systems. User Model. User-Adap. Inter. 11, 49–63 (2001)
10. Cappelli, T.M., Duffy, V.G.: Motion Capture for Job Risk Classifications Incorporating Dynamic Aspects of Work. In: Digital Human Modeling for Design and Engineering Conference, Lyon, July 4-6. SAE International, Warrendale (2006)
11. Lamkull, D., Hanson, L., Ortengren, R.: A comparative study of digital human modelling simulation results and their outcomes in reality: A case study within manual assembly of automobiles. International Journal of Industrial Ergonomics 39, 428–441 (2009)
12. Porter, J., Case, K., Freer, M.T., Bonney, M.C.: Computer-aided ergonomics design of automobiles. In: Automotive Ergonomics. Taylor and Francis, London (1993)
13. DeCarlo, D., Metaxas, D., Stone, M.: An anthropometric face model using variational techniques. In: Proceedings of the 25th Annual Conference on Computer Graphics and Interactive Techniques, SIGGRAPH 1998, pp. 67–74. ACM, New York (1998)

14. Kähler, K., Haber, J., Yamauchi, H., Seidel, H.P.: Head shop: Generating animated head models with anatomical structure. In: ACM SIGGRAPH/EG Symposium on Computer Animation, pp. 55–64 (2002)
15. Lee, S.H., Terzopoulos, D.: Heads up! Biomechanical modeling and neuromuscular control of the neck. ACM Transactions on Graphics 25(3), 1188–1198 (2006); Proc. ACM SIGGRAPH 2006
16. DiLorenzo, P.C., Zordan, V.B., Sanders, B.L.: Laughing out loud: Control for modeling anatomically inspired laughter using audio. ACM Transactions on Graphics 27(5), 125:1–125:8 (2008)
17. Van Nierop, O.A., Van der Helm, A., Overbeeke, K.J., Djajadiningrat, T.J.: A natural human hand model. The Visual Computer 24(1), 31–44 (2008)
18. Komura, T., Shinagawa, Y., Kunii, T.L.: Creating and retargeting motion by the musculoskeletal human body model. The Visual Computer 16(5), 254–270 (2000)
19. Pennestrì, E., Stefanelli, R., Valentini, P.P., Vita, L.: Virtual musculo-skeletal model for the biomechanical analysis of the upper limb. Journal of Biomechanics 40(6), 1350–1361 (2007), http://www.sciencedirect.com/science/article/pii/S0021929006 001679 ISSN 0021-9290, 10.1016/j.jbiomech.2006.05.013
20. Koo, T.K., Mak, A.F., Hung, L.K.: In vivo determination of subject-specific musculotendon parameters: applications to the prime elbow flexors in normal and hemiparetic subjects. Clinical Biomechanics 17(5), 390–399 (2002) ISSN 0268-0033, 10.1016/S0268-0033(02)00031-1
21. Garner, B.A., Pandy, M.G.: Estimation of Musculotendon Properties in the Human Upper Limb. Annals of Biomedical Engineering 31, 207–220 (2003)
22. Choi, J.: Developing a 3-Dimensional Kinematic Model of the Hand for Ergonomic Analyses of Hand Posture, Hand Space Envelope, and Tendon Excursion. PhD thesis, The University of Michigan (2008)
23. Holzbaur, K.R.S., Murray, W.M., Delp, S.L.: A model of the upper extremity for simulating musculoskeletal surgery and analyzing neuromuscular control. Annals of Biomedical Engineering 33, 829–840 (2005)
24. Marshall, R., Case, K., Summerskill, S., Sims, R., Gyi, D., Davis, P.: Virtual Task Simulation for Inclusive Design. In: Duffy, V.G. (ed.) ICDHM 2009. LNCS, vol. 5620, pp. 700–709. Springer, Heidelberg (2009)
25. Sapin, E., Goujon, H., de Almeida, F., Fodé, P., Lavaste, F.: Functional gait analysis of trans-femoral amputees using two different single-axis prosthetic knees with hydraulic swing-phase control: Kinematic and kinetic comparison of two prosthetic knees. Prosthetics and Orthotics International 32(2), 201–218 (2008)
26. Prince, F., Corriveau, H., Hebert, R., Winter, D.A.: Gait in the elderly. Gait and Posture 5(2), 128–135 (1997)
27. Coluccini, M., Maini, E.S., Martelloni, C., Sgandurra, G., Cioni, G.: Kinematic characterization of functional reach to grasp in normal and in motor disabled children. Gait & Posture 25(4), 493–501 (2007) ISSN 0966-6362, 10.1016/j.gaitpost.2006.12.015
28. Ouerfelli, M., Kumar, V., Harwin, W.S.: Kinematic modeling of head-neck movements. IEEE Transactions on Systems, Man and Cybernetics, Part A: Systems and Humans 29(6), 604–615 (1999), http://ieeexplore.ieee.org/stamp/stamp.jsp?tp=&arnumber=798064&isnumber=17313, doi:10.1109/3468.798064
29. Shapiro, A., Faloutsos, P., Ng-Thow-Hing, V.: Dynamic animation and control environment. In: Proceedings of Graphics Interface 2005, pp. 61–70 (2005)

30. Annett, J., Duncan, K.: Task analysis and training design. Occupational Psychology 41, 211–227 (1967)
31. Hingtgen, B.A., McGuire, J.R., Wang, M., Harris, G.F.: Design and validation of an upper extremity kinematic model for application in stroke rehabilitation. In: Proceedings of the 25th Annual International Conference of the IEEE Engineering in Medicine and Biology Society, September 17-21, vol. 2, pp. 1682–1685 (2003)
32. Herstatt, C., Von Hippel, E.: From experience: Developing new product concepts via the lead user method: A case study in a "low-Tech" field. J. Prod. Innov. Manag. 9, 213–221 (1992)
33. Jena 2 Inference Support (2011), `http://jena.sourceforge.net/inference/#rules` (accessed 2014)
34. Ackermann, P., Velasco, C.A., Power, C.: Developing a Semantic User and Device Modeling Framework that supports UI Adaptability of Web 2.0 Applications for People with Special Needs. In: Proceedings of the International Cross-Disciplinary Conference on Web Accessibility (W4A 2012). ACM, New York (2012), doi:10.1145/2207016.2207018
35. Velasco, C.A., Mohamad, Y., Gilman, A.S., Viorres, N., Vlachogiannis, E., Arnellos, A., Darzentas, J.S.: Universal access to information services | the need for user information and its relationship to device proles. Universal Access in the Information Society 3(1), 88–95 (2004)

Personalized Multimodal Geo-visualization through Inclusive User Modelling

Sanat Sarangi[1], Pradipta Biswas[2], Patrick M. Langdon[2], and Subrat Kar[1]

[1] Indian Institute of Technology, Delhi, India
[2] University of Cambridge, Cambridge, UK
sanat.sarangi@ieee.org, subrat@ee.iitd.ac.in,
{pb400,pml24}@cam.ac.uk

Abstract. This paper presents a geo-visualization system that can be personalized based on range of abilities of users and contexts of use. The personalization features uses the Inclusive User Model which simulates interaction and uses those to adapt interfaces based on perceptual, cognitive and motor abilities of users. For example, the proposed visualization system will automatically adjust font size and colour contrast based on perceptual capability of users. It also adjusts spacing between interactive screen elements based on motor abilities of users and context of use. A preliminary user study confirmed that the personalization feature can enhance the usability experience of users.

Keyword: Personalization.

1 Introduction

This paper presents a geo-visualization system that can be personalized based on range of abilities of users and contexts of use. The personalization features uses the Inclusive User Model [4] which simulates interaction and uses those to adapt interfaces based on perceptual, cognitive and motor abilities of users.

Interface personalization is well explored in the domain of content personalization and developing intelligent information filtering or recommendation systems based on user profiles. In most of those systems content (or information) is represented in a graph like structure (e.g. ontology or semantic network) and filtering or recommendation is generated by storing and analyzing users' interaction patterns. Little research work has been done beyond content personalization. A few representative and significant projects on interface personalization are the SUPPLE project at University of Washington [6, 11], and AVANTI project [9] for people with disabilities. The SUPPLE project [11] personalizes interfaces mainly by changing layout and font size for people with visual and motor impairment and also for ubiquitous devices. However, the user models do not consider visual and motor impairment in detail and thus work for only loss of visual acuity and a few types of motor impairment. The AVANTI project [9] provides a multimedia web browser for people with light, or severe motor disabilities, and blind people. It distinguishes personalization into two

C. Stephanidis and M. Antona (Eds.): UAHCI/HCII 2014, Part I, LNCS 8513, pp. 279–287, 2014.
© Springer International Publishing Switzerland 2014

classes - static adaptation which is personalization based on user profile and dynamic adaptation that is personalization following the interaction pattern (e.g. calculating error rate, user idle time etc. from usage log) with the system.

The lack of a generalized framework for personalization of users with a wide range of abilities affects the scalability of products as the existing systems work only for a small segment of the user population. For example, there are numerous guidelines [12] and systems for developing accessible websites but they are not always adequate to provide accessibility. Moreover designers often do not conform to the guidelines while developing new systems and design non-inclusive applications. It is also difficult to change existing systems to meet the guidelines. There are a few systems (e.g.: IBM Web Adaptation Technology, AVANTI Web browser [9] which offer features to make web sites accessible but either they serve a very special type of user (motor-impaired for AVANTI) or there is no way to relate the inclusive features with the particular need of users. The Global Public Inclusive Infrastructure (http://gpii.net/) and the EU Cloud4All projects [5] work mainly based on users' explicitly stated preferences though it is still not clear how exhaustive this set of preferences are and how these preferences were collected from users at the first place.

We have identified a set of human factors that can affect human computer interaction and formulated models [4] to relate those factors to interface parameters. We have developed the inclusive user model, which can adjust font size, font colour, inter-element spacing (like line spacing, button spacing and so on) based on age, gender, visual acuity, type of colour blindness, presence of hand tremor and spasm of users. The model is more detailed than GOMS model [7], easier to use than Cognitive Architecture based models [1, 8], and covers a wider range of users than existing user models for disabled users. The user profile is created using a web form and the profile is stored in cloud. Once created, this profile is accessible to the user irrespective of application and device. We have conducted a series of user trials [2-4] involving people with different range of abilities to validate the user modelling system. We have already integrated this user modelling system with a digital TV framework (EU GUIDE system [10]) and an electronic agriculture system [3]. The present paper exploited this model for a Wisekar [13] based geo-visualization system for sensor networks.

2   Configuring Wisekar for the Geo-visualization System

Wisekar (**Wi**reless **Se**nsor **K**nowledge **Ar**chive) [13] is an Internet of Things (IoT) based repository developed at IIT Delhi for archival of sensor-derived information. While allowing both manual and automated contribution of information, Wisekar offers a flexible structure to represent this information in a variety of standards, for example in the OGC-defined SensorML. Furthermore, information based on multiple XML-derived standards can co-exist in Wisekar which facilitates the integration of this information with the Semantic Web. Geo-visualization of sensor node- and event-related information in Wisekar is convenient due to its hierarchical structure. Also, a RESTful API for event-contribution makes it possible for all kinds of sensor-enabled devices, from sensor nodes to mobile phones, to transfer their data to Wisekar over the HTTP protocol which is not restricted by firewalls.

Initially, web-based repositories developed to archive research data used a form-based interface for data-contribution. For example, the UCI machine learning repository (developed in 1998) [14] contains datasets for evaluation of machine learning algorithms. CRAWDAD (2005) [15] captures network data in datasets. In 2006, Sensorbase.org [16] was developed at UCLA to allow events to be streamed from sensor networks over HTTP in Environment Markup Language (EML), where EML is a standard defined on XML. SenseWeb [17] from Microsoft Research is a peer produced sensor network that offers a SOAP-based Web Service API for contribution of sensor events. A visualisation tool Sensormap is used to create mashups from Sense-Web data. A SOAP web-service requires a SOAP library at the client-end to consume the service. This led to the increasing popularity of REST-based web-services where the HTTP url along with methods GET, POST, PUT and DELETE could be used to invoke and use the services. Cosm [18], now Xively, is an IoT repository that offers a RESTful API for contribution of data formatted in Extended Environments Markup Language (EEML). However, other XML-based standards to describe sensor-based data also exist, such as the Open Geospatial Consortium (OGC) defined SensorML. To accommodate data described in multiple standards, IoT repository Wisekar has been developed which offers a RESTful web-service interface for data contribution. Wisekar allows multiple XML-defined standards to co-exist and also permits contributors to describe the structure of their data in XML.

A subdomain of Wisekar – Wisekar/home (http://wisekar.iitd.ac.in/home) – is used to archive research datasets on pervasive sensor environments. We develop a web-application for geo-visualization of Weather data, which uses one of the Wisekar/home datasets called *WorldWeather* as the data-source. The objective of this application is to use the world map as the visualization platform to present all weather information logged in *WorldWeather*. This information consists of temperature and humidity levels reported regularly for various places around the world.

Each node in the *WorldWeather* dataset corresponds to a place for which the temperature and humidity levels are monitored. Every node contains a sequence of events with the temperature and humidity values for the place over a period of time. After creating the *WorldWeather* dataset through a form-based interface, each node in *WorldWeather* is created using the Wisekar/home *POST node* API method:

POST node:
http://wisekar.iitd.ernet.in/api/home/resource.php/resource/node?key=<key>&datasetId=<datasetId>&localId=<localId>&nodeName=<name>&nodeDesc=<desc>&lat=<lat>&long=<long>

In the *WorldWeather* dataset, we create four nodes - New Delhi, Cambridge, Sao Paulo, and San Fransisco - by assigning appropriate values to the various fields, notably to <name>, <lat> and <long>. Wisekar/home generates a *node Id* for every node successfully added to it. To add events to the node, the *POST event* API method shown below is used.

POST event:
http://wisekar.iitd.ernet.in/api/home/resource.php/resource/event?key=<key>&nodeI
d=<nodeId>&typeId=<typeId>&status=<temp>,<hum>

In the *POST event* method, <nodeId> is the unique *node Id* generated by Wisekar/home for this node as discussed earlier, <typeId> is the *Wisekar Glossary type* which indicates that the status fields contain temperature and humidity.

3   Wisekar Based Geo-visualization System

The geo-visualization web-application presents the dataset information on the map by adding a marker for each place (node). The information obtained from the latest five events logged in the dataset for each node is available in a chart that shows up when the marker is clicked. Three fields are presented for each event - *Reporting Time, Temperature and Humidity. Node name* and *Node Id* are presented on the top of the chart. The node and event details are visible on clicking the appropriate links on the chart.

Figure 1 below shows four different renderings of the web-application for people with different range of visual and motor impairment. All these figures are reporting temperature and humidity data of different cities with possible extension to show pollution data as well. The system changes the foreground colour to blue and background colour to yellow for users having red green colour blindness (Figure 1b). It uses bigger font size and turns on high-contrast for people having blurred or distorted vision due to myopia, macular degeneration or diabetic retinopathy (Figure 1c). Finally the system also adjusts the default zooming level if the user has tremor or spasm in hand. A higher zooming level separates screen elements to reduce chances of wrong selection (Figure 1d).

4   User Trial

The following user trial reports a controlled experiment on the web-based Wisekar application. It compared users' objective performance and subjective preference for an adaptive and a non-adaptive version of the weather monitoring system. We purposefully used two different devices for signing up and using the application to highlight the notion of transporting user profile across multiple devices.

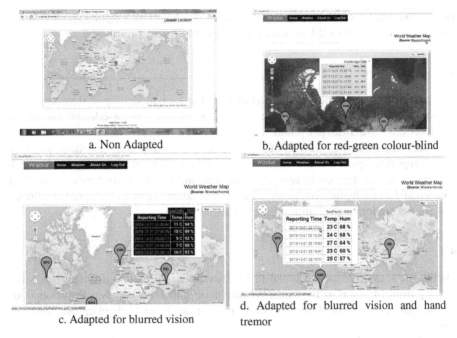

a. Non Adapted

b. Adapted for red-green colour-blind

c. Adapted for blurred vision

d. Adapted for blurred vision and hand tremor

Fig. 1. Personalized Wisekar System

4.1 Participants

We collected data from users with age-related visual or motor impairment. Table 1 below furnishes details of participants.

Table 1. List of Participants

Participants	Age	Gender	Impairment
P1	60	Male	Plus 2.5 Dioptre power
P2	57	Male	Minus 2.5Dioptre power
P3	59	Male	Plus 2.5Dioptre power
P4	42	Male	5/6 vision
P5	50	Female	Plus 1Dioptre power
P6	57	Male	Recently operated cataract, blurred vision
P7	59	Male	Plus 1.5Dioptre power

4.2 Material

We have used a Windows 7 HP computer with 54 cm × 33 cm monitor having 1920 x 1080 pixels resolution to record users' performance with the weather monitoring system. We used a standard Logitech mouse for pointing. Users signed up using a HP Tx2 laptop with 30 cm × 20 cm screen and 1280 × 800 pixels resolution.

4.3   Procedure

The participants were initially registered with the user modelling system using the Laptop. The sign-up page can be accessed at www-edc.eng.cam.ac.uk/~pb400/CambUM/UMSignUp.htm

After that participants were briefed about the weather monitoring system. The task was to report temperature and humidity of cities on a specific date (Figure 2). Each participant was instructed to report temperature and humidity six times for each of adapted and non-adapted conditions. The order of adapted and non-adapted conditions was altered randomly to eliminate order effect.

4.4   Results

During the sign up stage we found that different users preferred different font sizes ranging from 14 points to 18 points. We also noticed that one user was Protanomalous colour blind and he read 45 instead of 42 in the plate 16 of Ishihara colour blindness test.

During use of the weather monitoring system, we measured the time interval between pressing the left mouse button on the bubble with the city name (green transparent round shape in Figure 3a) and reporting of the required temperature and humidity data (Figure 3b).

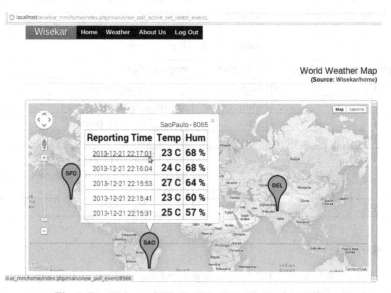

Fig. 2. Screenshots of Wisekar Weather monitoring system

| a. The screenshot shown to user for selecting city | b. The weather reporting screen |

Fig. 3. The experimental task

In total we analysed 84 tasks from seven participants (42 for adapted and 42 for non-adapted).. We found that users took less time in adapted condition (average 8.25 secs, std dev 3.1 secs) than non-adapted condition (average 9.75 secs, std dev 3.63 secs). All participants were already familiar with mouse and also practiced the system before the actual trial. So we assumed that each pointing task is independent to each other. Under this assumption, the difference is significant in a two-tailed paired t-test with $p < 0.05$ and with an effect size (Cohen's d) of 0.44 (Figure 4).

Without this assumption, the difference to significant in Wilcoxon signed-rank test $(Z = -2.89, p<0.05)$.

We conducted a subjective questionnaire to understand users' subjective preference. All users noticed bigger font and preferred it. One user was colour-blind and he preferred the change in colour contrast too.

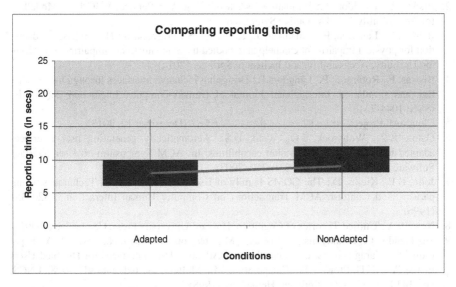

Fig. 4. Comparing weather reporting times

4.5   Discussion

The user study shows that users prefer different font sizes and colour contrast even for a simple system. The study also confirms that even for a simple text searching task, users performed and preferred an adaptive system that can automatically adjust font size, line spacing and colour contrast. The user modeling system successfully converted users' preference across two different devices having different screen resolutions. Future studies will collect data from more users and will use more complicated tasks than the present study.

5   Conclusion

This paper presents a personalized geo-visualization system based on a sensor network. A preliminary user study confirmed that the personalization feature can enhance the usability experience of users. The Sensor network already provides pollution data in the form of amount of Carbon-Dioxide in air and in future can be integrated to more versatile type of sensors. The whole system will have a plethora of applications like in Ambient Assistive Living (AAL) system, Weather monitoring and reporting system and even for visualizing sensor data in automobile and aircrafts. Future research will investigate these new applications of the system.

References

1. Anderson, J.R., Lebiere, C.: The Atomic Components of Thought. Lawrence Erlbaum Associates, Hillsdale (1998)
2. Biswas, P., Langdon, P.: Validating User Modelling Web Service, W3C User Modelling for Accessibility (UM4A) Online Symposium
3. Biswas, P., Langdon, P., Umadikar, J., Kittusami, S., Prashant, S.: How interface adaptation for physical impairment can help able bodied users in situational impairment. In: Joining Usability, Accessibility, and Inclusion. Springer (2014)
4. Biswas, P., Robinson, P., Langdon, P.: Designing inclusive interfaces through user modelling and simulation. International Journal of Human-Computer Interaction 28(1) Print ISSN: 1044-7318
5. Cloud4All Project, http://cloud4all.info/ (December 12, 2013)
6. Gajos, K.Z., Wobbrock, J.O., Weld, D.S.: Automatically generating user interfaces adapted to users' motor and vision capabilities. In: ACM Symposium on User Interface Software and Technology, pp. 231–240 (2007)
7. John, B.E., Kieras, D.: The GOMS Family of User Interface Analysis Techniques: Comparison And Contrast. ACM Transactions on Computer Human Interaction 3, 320–351 (1996)
8. Newell, A.: Unified Theories of Cognition. Harvard University Press, Cambridge (1990)
9. Stephanidis, C., Paramythis, A., Sfyrakis, M., Stergiou, A., Maou, N., Leventis, A., Paparoulis, G., Karagiannidis, C.: Adaptable and Adaptive User Interfaces for Disabled Users in the AVANTI Project. In: Campolargo, M., Mullery, A. (eds.) IS&N 1998. LNCS, vol. 1430, pp. 153–166. Springer, Heidelberg (1998)

10. The GUIDE Project, `http://www.guide-project.eu/` (accessed on March 23, 2013)

11. The SUPPLE Project, `http://www.cs.washington.edu/ai/supple/` (accessed on March 23, 2013)

12. WAI Guidelines and Techniques, `http://www.w3.org/WAI/guid-tech.html` (accessed on December 4, 2012)

13. Sarangi, S., Kar, S.: Wireless Sensor Knowledge Archive. In: International Conference on Electronics, Computing and Communication Technologies (IEEE CONECCT 2013), Bangalore, January 17-19 (2013)

14. Frank, A., Asuncion, A.: UCI machine learning repository (2010), `http://archive.ics.uci.edu/ml`

15. Kotz, D., Henderson, T.: Crawdad: A community resource for archiving wireless data at dartmouth. IEEE Pervasive Computing 4(4), 12–14 (2005)

16. Chang, K., Yau, N., Hansen, M., Estrin, D.: A centralized repository to slog sensor network data. In: International Conference on Distributed Computing in Sensor Systems, San Francisco, CA, USA (June 2006)

17. Grosky, W., Kansal, A., Nath, S., Liu, J., Zhao, F.: Senseweb: An infrastructure for shared sensing. IEEE Multimedia 14(4), 8–13 (2007)

18. Cosm, `https://cosm.com/` (accessed on March 23, 2013)

Simulation-Based Accessibility Evaluation
of Graphical User Interfaces Using Virtual User Models

Athanasios Tsakiris, Ioannis Paliokas, and Dimitrios Tzovaras

Centre for Research and Technology Hellas-CERTH, Information Technologies Institute-ITI,
6th km Charilaou-Thermis, 57001, Thessaloniki, Greece
{atsakir,ipaliokas,tzovaras}@iti.gr

Abstract. Accessibility assessment for ICT software products and human-machine interfaces is rapidly gaining increasing significance within the research and development (R&D) cycle of new products, as the population of aging users increases. Through VERITAS automatic simulation framework, we evaluated both Virtual User Models (VUMs) and the simulation framework and its results by conducting a series of pilot tests that involved elderly users using user interfaces in Infotainment and Games. The followed methodology and simulation results are presented with respect to the scores of actual users performing the same tasks as VUMs. Finally, the comparison between the actual user's and virtual models performance is used for VUM optimization.

Keywords: Virtual User Models, Accessibility Assessment, Infotainment.

1 Introduction

Accessibility assessment for ICT software products and human-machine interfaces is rapidly gaining increasing significance within the R&D cycle of new products, as the population of aging users increases. To that effect, under the VERITAS EU-funded research project [2] [8] we have developed Virtual User Models (VUM) that reflect elderly users' capabilities and impairments, simulation models that reflect the major aspects of a User Interface (UI) as well as the interaction parameters that define it in a similar manner to other research efforts in this area [3] [4].

The history of user modeling has been through modeling of reflective behaviors to conceptual (and not computational) models of 80's, and most modern approaches which used physical body and cognitive processors [7]. In the most recent projects, VUM-based solutions for inclusive design are based on simulation testing on early phases of the product development. Such an approach is VICON which also supports designers in interface development having the evaluation phase to offer qualitative and quantitative design recommendations [6]. GUIDE offer designers a software framework to create adaptive tv interfaces (emerging Web & TV platforms and services) for the elderly and moderately impaired users [5]. On the other hand, MuUI project collect user profiles, social constructs and context information for interface customization [1].

C. Stephanidis and M. Antona (Eds.): UAHCI/HCII 2014, Part I, LNCS 8513, pp. 288–298, 2014.
© Springer International Publishing Switzerland 2014

Our automatic simulation framework can test several accessibility aspects of user interfaces and identify problems in the early design stage without the need to involve real user trials. In order to evaluate both our VUMs, as well as our simulation framework and validate our approach and its results, we have conducted a series of pilot tests that involved elderly users using a Metaverse interface.

2   Analysis of the Methods

The proposed method can be divided into five major phases, each one divided into discrete steps. The followed methodology is discussed in more detail in the following sections with respect to the order each phase appears in Figure 1. Note that after the Preparatory phase which comes first, the Metaverse interface assessment using VUMs (Phase 2) and the one using actual users (Phase 3), together with the redesign of the interface (Phase 4) are making a loop. This study describes the two first cycles which are considered enough to conclude about which design characteristics the Metaverse interface should have in order to be accessible, following the design-for-all-principle.

2.1   Preparatory Phase

Second Life, as a popular socially-aware virtual environment (Metaverse) was chosen as the testing application to apply VERITAS methodology for the infotainment application area. The OpenSim server was used to create a virtual environment which would allow distant visitors to create content, meet others, exchange messages and share files on a SecondLife implementation (island) which run independently of others. A new SecondLife viewer was engineered to be the Metaverse testing interface. It consisted of a simulated virtual world being viewed through a 3D interactive view and common GUI widgets like menus, buttons, panels and windows.

The accessibility assessment of the Metaverse viewer was performed by VUMs and actual users who executed sets of well-defined tasks called 'scenarios'. During the scenario development, common everyday tasks were group together such as enter the Metaverse (user authentication), change outfit, create, pan and rotate a 3D object, perform near and far avatar navigation, met other visitors, initiate chatting and share files and folders.

Automatic accessibility evaluation using the simulator (VERITAS Simulation Core) requires that one or more VUMs will be used to perform the tasks described in scenarios. Virtual User Models (VUMs) were created using a custom-made tool which takes as input the percentile of an elderly or impaired person (the corresponding level of similarity to the targeted group, e.g. Parkinsonians), the visual, acoustic or motor impairment and exports a persona file with anthropometrics. For this study, four (N=4) VUMs were created: Elderly at the 50th percentile, Elderly at the 90th percentile, Parkinson's disease at the 50th percentile, Parkinson's disease at the 90th percentile and Stroke at the 50th percentile. To apply the 'design for all' principle in industrial design, simulating cognitive and behavior mechanisms have been considered critical. VUM creation was based on ACT-R architecture (from Carnegie

Mellon University), which has provided us a conceptual framework for creating models of how people perform tasks.

The recruitment of elderly persons who would test the Metaverse interface was made after some basic inclusion criteria were applied. Such criteria included age over 60, a good health status, basic computer driving skills, personal willingness to participate and schedule availability.

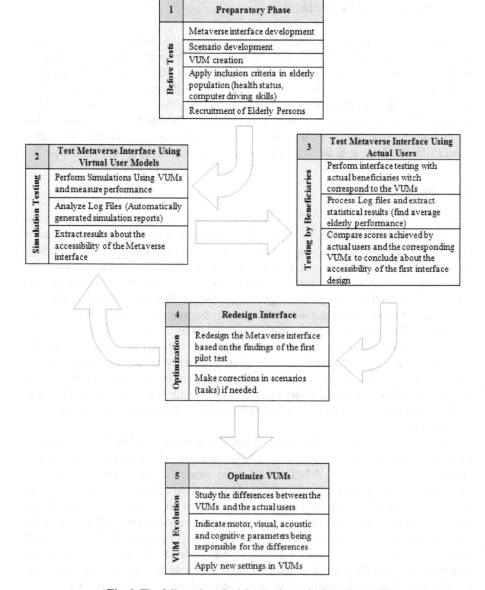

Fig. 1. The followed methodology schematically presented

2.2   Test the Metaverse Interface Using Virtual User Models

The metrics to be used to determine performance primarily were the scenario duration, that is the time needed to complete all the tasks included in a given scenario and the total number of interaction events during a session. The reports produced by the simulator extracted the success rate, number of interaction events and duration. Figure 2 presents the duration results per scenario and per VUM category. The highest completion time were recorded on T13 where VUMs needed 165 sec on average. This, along with sharing folder with another user (T20) and uploading a file (T07T08T09) constitute the most time-consuming scenarios. Elderly had an error rate of 0.711, while Parkinsonians had 0.337. Scenarios which require long interaction times are more likely to fail given the error rates stated previously. Thus, redesign of the GUI towards associability should start from the most sensitive areas which are menu item selections in 2D and 3D object manipulation in the immersive part of the screen (3D Metaverse window).

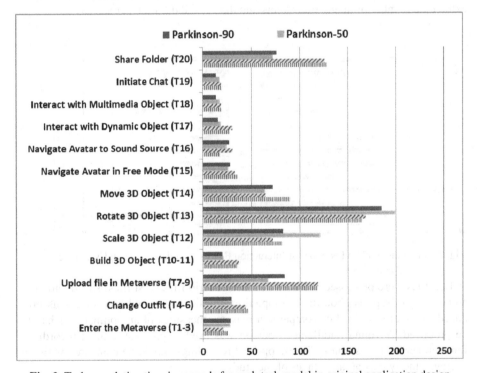

Fig. 2. Task completion time in seconds for each task model in original application design

2.3   Test the Metaverse Interface Using Actual Users

This phase is about conducting pilot tests on the same interface design with actual elderly users that correspond to the models used in the previous step. The group of testers consisted of twenty elderly persons (N=20). Half of the participants were

54-74 years old with an average of 66.25. Both genders were equally represented (50% males-50% females). At the time of the interview, the 88.24% implied no specific illness and the rest preferred not to say. The most common impairment mentioned was the low vision by 45.83%. Regarding the use of computers and the level of their confidence, the 55% of the users said they feel average computer users and the rest 45% consider themselves novice computer users.

After a short introduction on the scopes of the project and the procedure to be followed during the pilot tests, participants were demonstrated by research personnel all tasks involved in the infotainment scenarios. With printer instructions in hand, the elderly testers performed the same tasks while their activity was recorded in log files. By interaction events it is meant the input device activity, made on GUI elements and captured in the Operating System layer. Events raised in the Metaverse interface by user activity (such as mouse clicks, keystrokes and/or joystick events) were captured by a custom-made tool developed to offer automatic and uniform logging of user's performance. The Log files produced by the capturer were statistically processed to extract the number of interaction events and the overall duration per scenario.

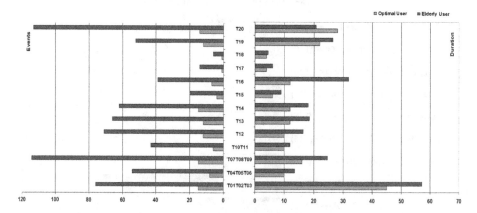

Fig. 3. Durations (sec) and Number of Interaction Events recorded by the OpUs and the elderly

Log files were processed according to the scenario files (USI files) specification to come up with reports about task completion times, number and kind of events produced by input devices. For comparison reasons, measures of an optimal user had to be produced. A young middle-aged person was used to produce optimal recordings for each performing scenario. Those optimal recordings should be compared with the average elderly user at later stages of the study.

In overall, an average difference of 554.69% in duration between the OpUs and the average elderly was calculated by all scenarios. Similarly, the difference on the number of events was calculated equal to 44.45%. Among the most strained scenarios was those dealing with 3D objects manipulation. For example, apply 90 degrees rotation on 3D objects along the three axes (indicated in the immersive window as Green, and Red axes as seen in Figure 4).

Fig. 4. The Metaverse interface: the first design (left) and the second design (right)

2.4   Redesign the Interface Towards Accessibility

Generally speaking, the first GUI design was found to have distracting features and the fact that there were a plethora of controls over layered windowed dialogs was possible to create information overload to the elderly testers. The elderly's deflected attention could be caused by the density of the GUI visual components. Results of the first pilot study with beneficiaries showed that there is enough room for making the features of the Metaverse interface more accessible for the target audiences studied so far. During the redesign phase, emphasis was given on the controls and interface features which were involved in the most strained scenarios. A visual comparison between the old and the new interface can be made on Figure 2. The 3D object manipulation dialogs and the visual indicators (handles) involved in 3D operations were redesigned to give wider areas of interaction. For example, it was assumed that the thicker rotation rings (Figure 4) could help elderly testers to handle 3D objects in more confidence and make more accurate actions. Also, all visual controls (like buttons and menu items) were scaled up by a factor of 50% and separated enough in space so as to have some empty space in between to eliminate fault mouse clicks.

2.5   Second Iteration of Pilot Tests

After the redesign of the Metaverse interface, a second testing cycle (indicated as phases 2, 3 and 4 in Figure 1) should confirm or reject the changes made in the interface. The results of every pilot test provide the GUI designers with feedback about the most recent changes and how those changes enhance the accessibility of the interface.

Figure 5 presents the results of the VUMs performing the same scenarios on the second interface design. Parkinsonians, in both percentiles (50% and 90%), still need more time in 3D object manipulation tasks than the healthy elderly (T12 and T13). On the other hand, they were slightly faster in 3d object contruction (T10-22) and moving (T14) and apparently faster than the elderly in content sharing (T20). Figure 6 shows the differences in VUM scores between the first and the second iteration of pilot tests.

There is substantial improvement both on the average completion times of the tasks carried out using the improved design over the initial one. With larger UI elements, fonts and 3D objects, the interaction becomes easier and the virtual users perform the tasks faster. The size increment in all UI elements to the 140% of their original size has resulted in an average improvement of 46% less errors through all task, as well as around 44% less time required to complete the scenarios.

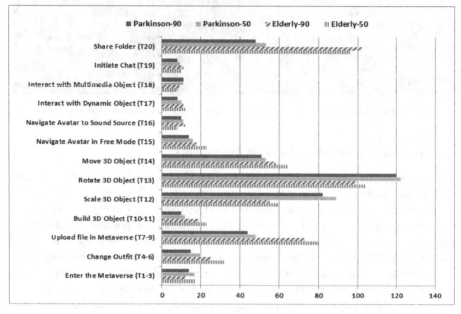

Fig. 5. Task completion times of VUMs using the new GUI design (in sec)

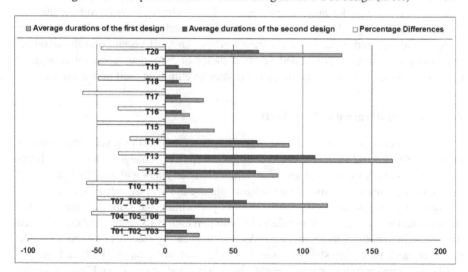

Fig. 6. Comparison results of the VUM's time scores (in sec) between the 1ˢᵗ and the 2ⁿᵈ test

A second iteration of pilot test using actual users was also needed to make safe conclusions. The majority of the testers (N=20) had already taken part in the first pilot test and they were familiar with the evaluation procedures. Others were invited by phone using day care organizations and local social networks, as in the first pilot study. Finally, the 70% of participants were returning testers. The results of the second test (second design) are presented in Table 1 in comparison with those of the first one. The negative sign in percentage differences indicate a positive result as the durations required to complete the scenarios are decreased in the case of the improved GUI design. Figure 7 graphically presents the differences between the two pilot tests, while the Optimal User is mentioned as a reference.

In general, apart from T14, which seems to have been stayed almost unchanged during the second test, all other scenarios were performed faster in the second GUI design. The T20, which was one of the most difficult and complex scenario, appears to have been benefited the most. In all scenario average, the duration of tasks was reduced by 14.09% and the number of interaction tasks was varying. It appears that moving a 3D object (T14) required more interaction in the second design than in the first one, but similar results can explained by the fact that elderly users were trying to achieve more accuracy in certain scenarios (especially on moving and rotating 3D objects) during the second pilot test.

Table 1. Results of the second design using real elderly users

Scenarios	Overall Duration in sec			Number of Interaction Events		
	1st Iteration	2nd Iteration	Diff%	1st Iteration	2nd Iteration	Diff%
T01T02T03	72,00	67,00	-6,94	57,19	56,84	-0,61
T04T05T06	54,00	47,00	-12,96	13,60	13,60	0,00
T07T08T09	114,00	103,00	-9,65	24,68	26,80	8,59
T10T11	43,00	36,00	-16,28	12,00	12,43	3,58
T12	71,00	62,00	-12,68	16,50	16,05	-2,73
T13	66,00	64,00	-3,03	18,47	21,47	16,24
T14	62,00	64,00	3,23	18,06	25,70	42,30
T15	20,00	15,00	-25,00	8,90	7,75	-12,92
T16	39,00	33,00	-15,38	31,90	30,30	-5,02
T17	14,00	9,00	-35,71	6,05	4,85	-19,83
T18	6,00	5,00	-16,67	4,45	5,05	13,48
T19	52,00	45,00	-13,46	26,47	26,63	0,61
T20	113,00	92,00	-18,58	40,67	39,33	-3,29
	Avg. Duration diff.%		-14,09	Avg. Events diff.%		3,11

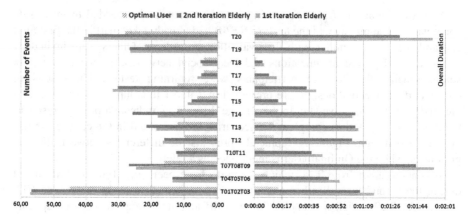

Fig. 7. An overall comparison chart: Scenario durations (elderly scores in sec) for the first and the second GUI design (Optimal User's scores are presented as a reference)

2.6   Optimize VUMs and Simulation Framework

The helix which appears in the middle of the VERITAS methodology and involves phases 2, 3 and 4 serves in redesigning the products before testing them and also in optimization of the VUM themselves. The philosophy behind virtual model development is to design models which can be reusable in testing of a wide range of products and in varying use case scenarios. Following a deterministic approach, the VUM scores of every previous test is used to predict in more accuracy the behavior of the actual end users in future. The way to perform this VUM optimization process is described below.

The outcome of each pilot test which was based on a revised version of the interface include measures of the VUM and actual testers performance. By comparing the scores of actual users and VUMs we can make VUMs to be better predictors of the corresponding target group. The proposed method to eliminate the expected differences in future tests, and thus to maximize the VUMs reusability and the quality of the results, is to apply the right settings in the VUM parameters. Solving the inverse error estimation problem, we finally compute which motor and cognitive parameters should be updated and by which factor in order to eliminate the differences to the scores of the actual elderly users.

The optimization process in the studied infotainment example gave strong fixing in time scores. Table 2 is a comparison between the scores of the actual users and the corresponding virtual user models recorded during the two iterations of pilot tests. Indeed, the average difference between actual users and VUMs was reduced from 64.48% to 41.17%. If more testing cycles would have been performed, then the prediction quality of the VUMs could be even better. In most cases, two or three iterations of the testing process (involving the same interface design when targeting in VUM optimization only) is enough to make VUMs effective predictors of the end user's behavior on new interfaces.

Table 2. Differences between the time scores of elderly and their corresponding VUMs (in sec)

Scenario	1st Iteration			2nd Iteration		
	Actual	VUM50	Diff	Actual	VUM50	Diff
T01-T03	72	25	65,28	67	17	74,63
T04-T06	54	47	12,96	47	32	31,91
T07-T09	114	118	3,51	103	80	22,33
T10-T11	43	35	18,60	36	23	36,11
T12	71	82	15,49	62	60	3,23
T13	66	165	150,00	64	104	62,50
T14	62	90	45,16	64	64	0,00
T15	20	36	80,00	15	23	53,33
T16	39	18	53,85	33	8	75,76
T17	14	28	100,00	9	12	33,33
T18	6	19	216,67	5	8	60,00
T19	52	19	63,46	45	10	77,78
T20	113	128	13,27	92	96	4,35
	Average Difference		**64,48**	Average Difference		**41,17**

3   Conclusion

Using Virtual User Models (VUMs) in interface accessibility assessment will help GUI designers to evaluate their drafts and first prototypes, and be suggested what to avoid when designing products for all. The discrete steps of the proposed methodology were described, having SecondLife as an infotainment case study in a practical guide. The interface design of 3D and 2D UI elements of a custom-made SecondLife Viewer was modified according to changes indicated by the scores of VUMs over stated qualities (total scenario duration and number of interaction events). The VUM results were confirmed by real elderly users after two iterations of pilots tests in good accuracy.

The comparison between results of the first and second pilot iterations with real users showed that most users prefer the bigger UI and 3D GUI elements, like the rotation rings and translation arrows and stronger contrast on colours in most cases. Tests with VUMs, as well as with real elderly users gave smaller completion times in the second GUI design.

Repeating the helix in the test-and-redesign method can achieve better accuracy in predicting end user's performance in future tests. Possibly, there always will be some noise in experimental data and limitations regarding VUM prediction expectations. Prediction accuracy based on a set of metrics is not a panacea as only the positive or negative sign in percentage differences of scores between two pilot tests can be interpreted by the interface designer. Numerical values can show the strength of the positive or negative indicator.

Figure 5 presents the results of the VUMs performing the same scenarios on the second interface design. Parkinsonians, in both percentiles (50% and 90%), still need more time in 3D object manipulation tasks than the healthy elderly (T12 and T13). On the other hand, they were slightly faster in 3d object contruction (T10-22) and moving (T14) and apparently faster than the elderly in content sharing (T20). Figure 6 shows the differences in VUM scores between the first and the second iteration of pilot tests.

There is substantial improvement both on the average completion times of the tasks carried out using the improved design over the initial one. With larger UI elements, fonts and 3D objects, the interaction becomes easier and the virtual users perform the tasks faster. The size increment in all UI elements to the 140% of their original size has resulted in an average improvement of 46% less errors through all task, as well as around 44% less time required to complete the scenarios.

Our main area of improvement in the future is to develop an army of VUMs for all motor, hearing and cognitive impairments and also for age-related inclinations, taking into consideration factors other than those related to the health status. For example, various psychological parameters (e.g. the level of stress), the social context, and the interests of the target audiences.

Acknowledgement. This work is supported by the EU funded project VERITAS (FP7 247765).

References

1. Edlin-White, R., Cobb, S., Floyde, A., Lewthwaite, S., Wang, J., Riedel, J.: From guinea pigs to design partners – involving older people in technology design. In: Langdon, P., Clarkson, J., Robinson, P., Lazar, J., Heylighen, A. (eds.) Designing Inclusive Systems - Designing Inclusion for Real-world Applications, ch. 16, pp. 155–164. Springer, London (2012)
2. Kaklanis, N., Moschonas, P., Moustakas, K., Tzovaras, D.: Virtual user models for the elderly and disabled for automatic simulated accessibility and ergonomy evaluation of designs. Universal Access in the Information Society, pp. 1–23 (2012)
3. Korn, P., Bekiaris, E., Gemou, M.: Towards Open Access Accessibility Everywhere: The ÆGIS Concept. In: Stephanidis, C. (ed.) Universal Access in HCI, Part I, HCII 2009. LNCS, vol. 5614, pp. 535–543. Springer, Heidelberg (2009)
4. Picking, R., Robinet, A., Grout, V., McGinn, J., Roy, A., Ellis, S., Oram, D.: A Case Study Using a Methodological Approach to Developing User Interfaces for Elderly and Disabled People. The Computer Journal 53, 842–859 (2009)
5. Langdon, P., Gonzalez, M.F., Biswas, P.: Designing studies for requirements and modelling of users for an accessible set-top box. In: Sharkey, P.M., Sánchez, J. (eds.) 8th Intl Conf. on Disability, Virtual Reality and Assoc. Technologies, pp. 203–212 (2010)
6. Modzelewski, M., et al.: Creative Design for Inclusion using Virtual User Models. In: Miesenberger, K., Karshmer, A., Penaz, P., Zagler, W. (eds.) ICCHP 2012, Part I. LNCS, vol. 7382, pp. 288–294. Springer, Heidelberg (2012)
7. Nakata, T., Simo, A., Kitamura, K., Kanade, T.: Human Operational Errors in a Virtual Driver Simulation. In: 11th Int. Conference on Human-Computer Interaction, p. 754 (2005)
8. Tsakiris, A., Moschonas, P., Kaklanis, N., Paliokas, I., Stavropoulos, G., Tzovaras, D.: Cognitive Impairments Simulation in a Holistic GUI Accessibility Assessment Framework, Association for the Advancement of Assistive Technology in Europe. In: 12th European AAATE Conference, Vilamoura, Algarve, Portugal (2013)

Towards Deep Adaptivity – A Framework for the Development of Fully Context-Sensitive User Interfaces

Gottfried Zimmermann[1], Gregg C. Vanderheiden[2], and Christophe Strobbe[1]

[1] Responsive User Interface Experience Research Group, Stuttgart Media University,
Stuttgart, Germany
gzimmermann@acm.org, strobbe@hdm-stuttgart.de
[2] Trace R&D Center, University of Wisconsin-Madison, USA
gv@trace.wisc.edu

Abstract. Adaptive systems can change various adaptation aspects at runtime, based on an actual context of use (the user, the platform, and the environment). For adaptable systems, the user controls the adaptation aspects. Both adaptivity and adaptability are pre-requisites for context-sensitive user interfaces that accommodate the needs and preferences of persons with disabilities. In this paper, we provide an overview of the various adaptation aspects and describe a general framework consisting of six steps for the process of user interface adaptation. Based on the framework, we describe our vision of combining the GPII and URC technologies to achieve fully context-sensitive user interfaces.

Keywords: Adaptive user interface, adaptable user interface, user interface adaptation, user interface adaptation aspect, context-sensitive user interface, abstract user interface, Universal Remote Console (URC), Global Public Inclusive Infrastructure (GPII), Cloud4all.

1 Introduction

Systems that adapt their user interfaces in one or more aspects (e.g. font size, navigation structure, closed captions) have been around for a while. However, existing systems tend to focus on selected aspects of adaptations, addressing only the needs of a particular user group. For fully context-sensitive user interfaces it is important to cover the full range of adaptations that is required to address the wide range of needs and preferences of all users, including those that are ageing and those with disabilities.

The remainder of this paper is structured as follows: Section 2 introduces basic concepts of user interface adaptation and a 3-layer model of user interface adaptation aspects. Section 3 looks at selected previous work with varying coverage of user interface adaptation (based on the 3 layers of user interface adaptation aspects). The main contribution of this paper is presented in section 4, where we describe a six-step framework for the development of fully context-sensitive user interfaces. Section 5 describes how a combination of the Global Public Inclusive Infrastructure (GPII) and the Universal Remote Console (URC) framework can produce fully context-sensitive user interfaces with all six steps involved. Finally, section 6 provides a conclusion.

C. Stephanidis and M. Antona (Eds.): UAHCI/HCII 2014, Part I, LNCS 8513, pp. 299–310, 2014.

2   User Interface Adaptation Terms and Concepts

In this section, we define basic terms and concepts that are necessary for a common understanding on the topic of this paper.

2.1   User Interface Adaptation

We define user interface adaptation as a process spanning development time (i.e. when the application is developed and its user interface is designed) and runtime (i.e. when the user interface is shown to the user and the user interacts through it with the application). The activities in this process serve the purpose of preparing and instantiating a user interface in which at least some aspects are tailored (adapted) to the specific context of use at runtime. We will come back to the question what these user interface aspects are in section 2.5.

2.2   Context of Use

The context of use reflects the specific conditions under which the user interacts with the application through the user interface. It consists of the following components:

1. A *user model* describing the needs and preferences of the user at the time of user interaction.[1] A user model may include static information such as the need for a special contrast theme, or the need for sticky keys to be enabled. However, even static information may change over the lifetime of a user, e.g. when the user's abilities change due to ageing. The user model may also include dynamic information that is changed quite often, even during the course of user interaction. Such dynamic information may include the user's current level of attention, or their current mood.
2. A *platform model* comprising information about the user's interaction device (hardware) and the software platform the user interface runs on. This may include the size and resolution of the visual display, the type of a keyboard (e.g. physical, onscreen) or the availability of a runtime engine (e.g. JavaScript) and version.
3. An *environment model* holding information on the specific situation in which the user interaction occurs. This may include the location of the user interaction, levels of ambient light and ambient noise, or the current screen orientation (portrait vs. landscape) that depends on how the user is holding their mobile device.

Due to the heterogeneous nature of the context of use, its information cannot be prepared at full before runtime. Rather it needs to be assembled from various sources of information, sometimes upon demand only. However, some parts of the context of use are rather persistent over time, such as the static part of the user model, and the platform model (only if the user does not change their device). Also, some locations may

---

[1] In GPII, we explicitly focus on the user's needs and preferences only (see section 5). We do not try to model the users themselves.

always have the same conditions of light and noise. These parts can be set up once, stored safely at a dedicated place, and retrieved any number of times to be used as readily available components of a context of use.

The format in which the context of use is represented varies over different systems. Common formats include nested structures, key-value pairs, and formal ontologies. However, many applications use proprietary formats.

2.3   Adaptable vs. Adaptive System

We call a system *adaptable* if it lets the user adjust its user interface aspects by dedicated user actions, e.g. in a configuration dialog, or by activating a button or menu item. A system is adaptive if it automatically adapts some aspects to the current context of use; which may involve asking the user for confirmation of the suggested change. In brief, a system is adaptable if the adaptation is user-initiated, and it is adaptive if the adaptation is system-initiated.

Oftentimes, systems are both adaptable and adaptive. This will typically result in mixed dialogs in which a user changes some aspect of adaptation, and the system will react upon this by proposing to change another (complementary) aspect to the user.

2.4   User Interface Integration vs. User Interface Parameterization

In general, there are two ways of building adaptability and adaptivity into systems:

1. *User interface parameterization:* The user interface is "tweaked" along predetermined parameters (e.g. font size) at runtime. The capability for tweaking may be part of the user interface code, or be provided by the runtime platform (e.g. browser buttons for changing the font size). In any case, the designer needs to make sure that their user interface design is suitable for presentation with a variety of user interface parameter settings.
2. *User interface integration:* A user interface is assembled from a set of user interface resources (e.g. dialogs, icons, fonts, labels, videos, captions) at runtime, based on the specific context of use or the user's configuration. Usually, user interface resources have to be prepared by humans at development time, although in some cases they can be generated by sophisticated automatic systems (e.g. YouTube can automatically create closed captions for English video clips, but the quality is usually not as good as when done by humans). Unfortunately, at development time the specific context of use is not known. Therefore, usually a set of user interface resource variants are created for a variety of (projected) contexts of use. If, however, user interface resources can be swiftly generated on demand, the creation of the resources and the user interface integration can both happen at runtime, thus resulting in a user interface that can explicitly address the peculiarities of the context of use at hand.

Most adaptable and adaptive systems today employ user interface parameterization as a means for adaptation. If user interface integration is involved, it is usually done

manually at development time, fully automated (with automatically generated resources) at runtime, or provided by the runtime platform (e.g., the browser on an
iPhone replaces a pull down menu on web pages by a drum). Although quite flexible
and convenient for developers, automatically generated user interfaces sometimes
have the drawback of being designed with functional rather than aesthetic goals in
mind.

2.5   User Interface Adaptation Aspects

We divide a user interface and its aspects into three layers, stacked on top of each
other. This notion is inspired by the layered human-computer interaction model by
Herczeg [1]. We describe our model of user interface adaptation aspects with its
layers from top to bottom (see **Error! Reference source not found.**).

- *Presentation & input events layer:* Presentational aspects (i.e. related to information output to the user) can easily be changed at runtime, usually by user interface
  parameterization. Examples include visual presentation aspects such as text size,
  zoom factor, contrast theme (for text), letter spacing, line spacing, and button size;
  auditory presentation aspects such as speech volume, pitch and speech rate; and
  tactile presentation aspects such as Braille mode (6 or 8 dots) and Braille grade
  (contraction level). User interface aspects for receiving information from the user
  address input events, including the mapping of user actions to the application's operations. Examples include keyboard shortcuts, keyboard settings (sticky keys,
  repeat keys, toggle keys), mouse speed and acceleration, and gesture alphabet.

- *Structure & grammar layer:* This layer includes aspects of the information architecture, input and output modalities, and widget substitution. For example, the
  navigation structure may be modified based on the available screen space (e.g.
  desktop version vs. mobile version of a Website). The standard grouping of a user
  interface may change into a "wizard mode" in which the novice user is walked step
  by step through a set of dialogs. Widgets may get replaced by variants which better
  suit the particular user or platform (e.g. a set of big push-buttons may be better
  suited for a user with hand tremor than a drop-down menu). A screen reader may
  augment the output modality from visual presentation to speech output. The input
  modality may switch from using the keyboard for text input to speech input.

- *Content & semantics layer:* The "deep" aspects of user interface adaptation involve
  changes in content and semantics. Information may be presented in alternative
  languages, including sign languages. Text may be rephrased and shortened to make
  it easier to read, and images may be changed to simplified versions. Additional
  content may be provided to assist some users in using the user interface and the
  functionality of the application. Alternative images may be needed for accommodating a user's or device's limitations on the use of color and color coding. For multimedia, captions, audio descriptions and sign language interpretation may get
  displayed with the video in a synchronized fashion.

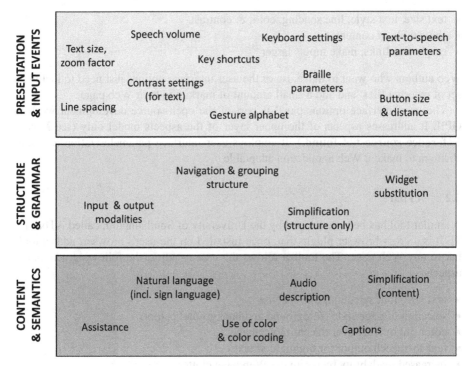

Fig. 1. A 3-layer model of user interface adaptation aspects, populated with sample aspects

Aspects in the upper layer (presentation & input events) are typically handled by user interface parameterization, or alternate presentation modes built into a browser or player/viewer, that take effect at runtime. Aspects in the middle layer (structure & grammar) and lower layer (content & semantics) usually involve user interface resources that have to be prepared at development time, with the resulting user interface integration happening at runtime.

3   Previous Work

Based on the three-layer model of user interface adaptation aspects, in this section we briefly describe some selected systems and tools that address one or more layers of aspects. For the purpose of this paper, we focus mainly on technologies in the area of Global Public Inclusive Infrastructure (GPII) and Universal Remote Console (URC). For a more elaborated review of related work in the field of adaptive user interfaces, refer to [9].

3.1   Fluid User Interface Options

The Fluid user interface options panel [2, 5] is a JavaScript library that can be integrated into any Web page or Web application to allow the user to adapt the Web content in the following aspects:

- text size, text style, line spacing, color & contrast
- show table of contents
- emphasize links, make inputs larger

Web authors who want to make use of the user interface options just need to include a set of external files, and add a small amount of markup to their Web page.

The user interface options panel is part of the open-source development work in GPII. It addresses aspects of the upper layer of the aspects model only (see **Error! Reference source not found.**). It employs user interface parameterization as a mechanism to make a Web application adaptable.

3.2   ATbar

A similar tool has been developed by the University of Southampton, called ATbar [6, 8]. It is a cross-browser plugin that, once installed on the user's browser, adds a toolbar to any Web page. The toolbar allows the user to adjust the following adaptation aspects:

- text size, font selection, line spacing
- selection of page style (foreground and background colors)
- color tint overlay over the entire webpage
- text-to-speech output for highlighted text
- increased readability by removing Web page clutter

In addition to these aspects, the ATbar provides the following functions:

- report an encountered accessibility issue on a Web page to volunteers who will bring them to the website owners ("fix the web" function)
- highlight a word and call its definition from Wiktionary
- word prediction and spell checker for user input into forms

ATbar addresses some aspects of the top and middle layer of the aspects model (see **Error! Reference source not found.**), but no content-related aspects (lower layer). It employs user interface parameterization[2] as a mechanism to make a Web application adaptable.

3.3   URC Pick-An-Interface

The URC framework [3] is a technology for pluggable user interfaces for the control of electronic devices and services (*Targets*). In its most commonly installed architecture, a gateway called Universal Control Hub (UCH) [10] connects any number of controllers with any number of Targets. Supplemental user interfaces and pertaining resources (for projected contexts of use) may be created by any party and deployed to a *Resource Server* that acts as a market place for pluggable user interfaces. If multiple

---

[2]   Except for the text-to-speech function which represents a user interface integration mechanism using an automatically generated resource (the speech output).

user interfaces are available for a Target and the controller platform, the user can select one from the pick-an-interface screen [4].

In the URC framework, user interface resources typically need to be prepared at development time, marked with metadata describing their suitability for specific contexts of use, and are then deployed to the Resource Server. At runtime, a suitable user interface can be assembled by the UCH by pulling together the resources that are most suitable for the current context of use.

In general, URC-based user interfaces can cater for all layers of adaptation aspects. However, due to the specific architecture of URC and its focus on user interface integration, it is most commonly used for adaptations on deeper adaptation aspects, i.e. the lower and middle layer of the three-layer model (see **Error! Reference source not found.**). For example, the set of available user interfaces for a home media system may include a simplified version that displays only the most common functions. The URC framework defines a special resource type for describing a grouping structure which makes it easy to prepare alternative navigation structures for different contexts of use.

Current URC-based implementations are adaptive based on the platform model. However, the user needs to pick their preferred user interface, i.e. they are also adaptable for the user's preferences.

3.4   Summary of Previous Work

Each system described above caters for a part only of the whole set of adaptation aspects. Today's GPII implementations are adaptable and focus on the shallow adaptation aspects. The ATbar is similar in its concept, with some deeper aspects included, and some extra functions. The URC framework addresses the medium deep and deep adaptation aspects, and provides both adaptability and adaptiveness (although in a limited manner for each).

It can be seen that, if we combine the GPII and the URC approach, it is possible to cover the full range of adaptation aspects, across all three layers (see **Error! Reference source not found.**). The combination results in a framework for fully context-sensitive user interfaces that are both adaptable and adaptive based on the full range of the context of use (i.e. the user model, platform model and environment model[3]). Before we further elaborate on the combination of GPII and URC, we introduce a generic framework for user interface adaptation that will be the basis for describing our vision on such a combined system.

4   A Six-Step Framework for User Interface Adaptation

In general, the process of user interface adaptation (which results in fully context-sensitive user interfaces) is composed of six steps (see Fig. 2). Note that the first three steps occur at development time, and the last three steps at runtime.

---

[3]   Current GPII and URC implementations don't address adaptations based on the environment model, but this is not due to conceptual constraints. The Cloud4all project is currently working on the accommodation of the environment model.

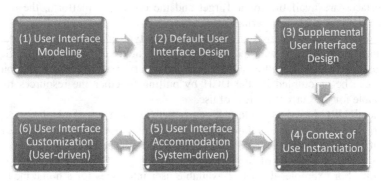

Fig. 2. The six steps of user interface adaptation

We describe the six steps in the following sub-sections. Note that we provide a "canonical" description of the framework; concrete implementations may vary. For example, steps may be executed by automatic systems or humans, and they may be combined or performed in a different order. However, if a step is completely omitted, this will result in a decrease of user interface adaptation capabilities.

4.1   User Interface Modeling

The first step in the user interface adaptation process is for the application developer to describe the user interface in an abstract fashion. This step happens at design time. There are many forms of abstract user interface descriptions, including task models, user interface models, Web service interface descriptions (WSDL), descriptions of an Application Programming Interface (API), or ontological descriptions of a user interface's functionality.

Sometimes, a supplementary user interface model (or parts thereof) is created as an annotation to the default user interface (see section 4.2). In this case, the default user interface is designed first, and then its model is "bolted on" by the designer or another person. For example, the WAI-ARIA [7] markup extends HTML (and other markup languages) by semantic annotations that support user interface adaptation, and would otherwise not be available in the host language.

It is a common mistake to completely omit user interface modeling in the design process. This happens quite often when design is directly aimed (on purpose or unintentionally) at the "typical user" who does not have a conceived need for user interface adaptations. Usually, this results in visual user interfaces with no or only a low level of adaptation.

4.2   Default User Interface Design

The second step is about the design of the default version of a concrete user interface which is usually done at development time by a user interface expert or designer. Typically, aesthetics and corporate identity play an important role in this step.

However, some systems automatically generate the (default) user interface on demand at runtime, tailored to a concrete context of use. In this case, there is no supplemental user interface design, and the third step is omitted (see section 4.3).

The default user interface is based on the abstract description of an application's user interface (see section 4.1). The design of the default user interface includes pertaining resources such as icons, textures, labels, audio clips and videos.

4.3   Supplemental User Interface Design

In the third step, alternative user interfaces or parts thereof are designed. This usually happens at any time between development time and runtime, and is done by the designer of the default user interface, or other designers, possibly by third parties. As the default user interface, supplemental user interfaces are based on the abstract description of an application's user interface (see section 4.1).

Supplemental user interfaces or supplemental user interface resources are created to extend or replace the default user interface and/or its resources (see section 4.2). They are tailored for a particular context of use, and marked as such. They are typically deployed to a resource repository, acting as a "market place" for supplemental user interfaces and pertaining resources that can be downloaded on demand at runtime. However, some systems store supplemental user interfaces locally, and therefore are usually not open for third party contributions. This restricts user interface adaptations to "officially sanctioned" user interfaces, and can lead to inaccessible user interfaces for some non-accommodated user groups.

4.4   Context of Use Instantiation

The fourth step is for the runtime platform to identify and instantiate the context of use (user model, device model and environment model, see section 2.2). This is useful for adaptable systems, and required for adaptive systems. For adaptable systems, the system may have the user's previous settings stored in order to restore them at the next time when the same or a similar context of use is encountered. For adaptive systems, the system-driven accommodation is for the specific user, device and environment which are encountered.

Things can get more complicated for more sophisticated systems that can adapt user interfaces in the course of a user sessions, in response to dynamically changing values of the context of use. For example, the user may change the orientation of a hand-held device (from portrait to landscape mode or vice versa), or the lighting conditions may vary over time.

If this step is omitted (i.e. there is no notion of context of use), the system can only be adaptable by user-driven customization (see section 4.6), and not be adaptive by system-driven accommodation (see section 4.5).

4.5   User Interface Accommodation (System-Driven)

The fifth step is the accommodation of the user interface by the system, adapting the user interface to best match the particular context of use at runtime. This step is required for adaptive systems. It is a good habit, though, to give the user final control over what user interface aspects are adapted in which way, by letting the user confirm or reject system-derived suggestions.

This step can involve both user interface integration and user interface parameterization.

Oftentimes, user interface accommodation is a continuous process, involving multiple iterations of refinements in the course of a user session, e.g. when reacting to dynamic changes in the context of use, or to user-initiated adaptations (see section 4.6).

4.6   User Interface Customization (User-Driven)

The sixth step occurs when the user changes a user interface aspect at runtime, by customizing the user interface by user operations that are either provided by the user interface or by the runtime platform. This step is required for adaptable systems.

As for user interface accommodation, user interface customization can involve both user interface integration and user interface parameterization.

User-initiated customizations may be stored (e.g. in the user model) to make them permanent for the user and the particular context of use. However, this is not sufficient to be called an adaptive system.

Care must be taken for adaptable systems in the design phase (steps 2 & 3) to accommodate for changes on the full range of user interface aspects that the user can control at runtime. For example, if a Web designer ignores the implications of the browser's zooming function, content may get distorted at runtime, or require constant horizontal scrolling, when the user selects an unusual zoom level.

User interface accommodation (see section 4.5) and user interface customization can be used together in an interwoven fashion. For example, the system may react to a user increasing the font size, by suggesting to also modifying the contrast theme to make it easier to read. This can go back and forth, in a mixed dialog negotiation to find the best possible adaptation for a particular context of use.

5   GPII + URC: A Vision for User Interface Adaptation

Taken together, GPII and URC provide the concepts and ingredients for a technology that can fill all gaps in the six-step adaptation framework described above (see section 4). With its abstract user interface and user interface integration concepts, URC provides the means for the preparation and deployment of (manually or automatically) designed user interface resources at development time. At runtime, these resources are selected and/or assembled to provide a "good match" for the particular context of use. Now, GPII with its user interface parameterization approach can further fine-tune the user interface to make it into a "best match" for the particular context of use, ready to also react to changes during runtime, if necessary.

With a combination of the GPII and URC technologies, the six steps of user interface adaptations (see section 4) can be annotated as follows:

1. **User interface modelling:** If suitable (in particular for the control of devices), a user interface model is created as a URC "user interface socket description". If a full-fledged user interface socket is not appropriate (e.g. for information-oriented Web applications), the user interface model can consist of some additional markup (dubbed "URC Light") embedded in the default user interface.
2. **Default user interface design:** The Personal Control Panel (a component for letting the user control the adaptation aspects) is embedded into the default user interface. This is the basis for user interface parameterization, and for adaptability.
3. **Supplemental user interface design:** Alternative user interfaces and supplemental resources are designed by any party (including automatic systems), marked with metadata regarding their suitability, and deployed to the openURC Resource Server. This is the basis for user interface integration.
4. **Context of use instantiation:** A standard format for the description of the context of use is currently being developed in the GPII project Cloud4all. In GPII, the user model is called *personal preference set* since it contains only the user's preferences with regard to user interface aspects rather than a functional description of the user.
5. **User interface accommodation (system-driven):** Based on the specific context of use and the available supplemental user interface resources, the runtime engine assembles a user interface (user interface integration). It then fine-tunes the user interface by user interface parameterization. These steps are reapplied if the context of use changes significantly at runtime.
6. **User interface customization (user-driven):** The user can explicitly change selected adaptation aspects by operating the Personal Control Panel. The user interface is then immediately updated to reflect the change. The system remembers the user's preferred settings together with the context of use at hand, and learns from it. Next time, the preferred settings will be activated as part of the user interface accommodation.

6   Conclusion

User interface adaptation needs to be understood as a process spanning development time and runtime. If done properly, this will result in fully context-sensitive user interfaces, thus accommodating users with varying needs and preferences, hardware and software platforms with varying features and constraints, and environmental constraints that can change dynamically.

In this paper we have described our vision on combining the GPII and URC technologies, and we have shown how this can result in fully context-sensitive user interfaces that are capable of the full range of adaptations, including deep adaptations related to content & semantics. The combination of GPII and URC has already been considered in the development of GenURC [9], and is currently being implemented as *URC Light* technology in the Cloud4all Online Banking Demo application[4].

---

[4]   The Online Banking Demo application is described in a separate paper of this conference titled "A Showcase for Accessible Online Banking".

Acknowledgments. This work has been funded by the US Dept of Education, NIDRR, under Grant H133E080022 (RERC on IT Access), and by the European Commission, under FP7 Grant Agreement 289016 (Cloud4All). The opinions herein are those of the authors and not necessarily those of the funding agencies.

References

1. Herczeg, M.: Interaktionsdesign: Gestaltung interaktiver und multimedialer Systeme. Oldenbourg, München (2006)
2. infusion, Tutorial - User Interface Options - Infusion Documentation - Fluid Project Wiki (2014), http://wiki.fluidproject.org/display/docs/Tutorial+-+User+Interface+Options (retrieved February 4, 2014)
3. ISO/IEC, ISO/IEC 24752-1:2008. Information Technology - User Interfaces - Universal Remote Console - Part 1: Framework. International Organization for Standardization, ISO (2008)
4. openURC Alliance, iUCH client for UCH (2013), http://www.openurc.org/tools/iuch-ios-3.0/ (retrieved February 4, 2014)
5. Treviranus, J.: You say tomato, I say tomato, let's not call the whole thing off: the challenge of user experience design in distributed learning environments. On the Horizon 17(3), 208–217 (2009), doi:10.1108/10748120910993231
6. University of Southampton (n.d.). ATbar, https://www.atbar.org/ (retrieved February 4, 2014)
7. W3C, WAI-ARIA Overview (2014), http://www.w3.org/WAI/intro/aria (retrieved February 10, 2014)
8. Wald, M., Draffan, E.A., Newman, R., Skuse, S., Phethean, C.: Access toolkit for education. In: Miesenberger, K., Karshmer, A., Penaz, P., Zagler, W. (eds.) ICCHP 2012, Part I. LNCS, vol. 7382, pp. 51–58. Springer, Heidelberg (2012)
9. Zimmermann, G., Jordan, B., Thakur, P., Yuvarajsinh, G.: Abstract User Interface, Rich Grouping and Dynamic Adaptations - A Blended Approach for the Generation of Adaptive Remote Control User Interfaces. In: Assistive Technology: From Research to Practice, vol. 33, pp. 1289–1297. IOS Press, Vilamoura (2013), doi:10.3233/978-1-61499-304-9-1289.
10. Zimmermann, G., Vanderheiden, G.: The Universal Control Hub: An Open Platform for Remote User Interfaces in the Digital Home. In: Jacko, J.A. (ed.) HCI 2007. LNCS, vol. 4551, pp. 1040–1049. Springer, Heidelberg (2007), doi:10.1007/978-3-540-73107-8.

Natural, Multimodal
and Multisensory Interaction

Multi-modal Target Prediction

Pradipta Biswas and Patrick M. Langdon

University of Cambridge, Cambridge, UK
pb400@cam.ac.uk

Abstract. Users with severe motor impairment often depends on alternative input devices like eye-gaze or head movement trackers to access computers. However these devices are not as fast as computer mouse and often turn difficult to use. We have proposed a Neural-network based model that can predict pointing target by analyzing pointing trajectory. We have validated the model for standard computer mouse, eye-gaze and head movement trackers. The model is used to develop an adaptation system that can statistically significantly reduce pointing times.

Keywords: Multi-modal, Target prediction.

1   Introduction

Users with severe motor impairment find existing computer interaction devices hard to use as their body movements are often limited to only few muscles. These users can access computers using alternative interaction devices like eye-gaze tracker or head movement tracker. However these devices are pretty slow and difficult to use even with the state-of-the-art hardware and software interfaces. This paper proposes a model that can reduce pointing times for eye-gaze and head trackers as well as standard computer mouse. The model implements a target prediction technology and uses it to adapt software interfaces.

Researchers already worked on algorithms to reduce pointing time through determining the difficulty of a task using Fitts' Law [6], increasing target size [8, 13], employing larger cursor activation regions, moving targets closer to cursor location, dragging cursor to nearest target, changing CD ratio[18] and so on. It is certain that these algorithms will perform even better in the existence of a target prediction algorithm so that only correct or most probable targets could be dynamically altered. With this in mind, researchers proposed target or end-point prediction methods.

One of the first algorithms for target prediction was suggested by Murata [14], which calculates the angle deviation towards all possible targets and select the target with minimum deviation. The results show that pointing time can be reduced by 25% using this algorithm [14]. Asano and colleagues [1] pointed out that having more than one target on a particular movement direction results in poor performances of Murata's algorithm, especially when dealing with targets located far away. They used previous research results about kinematics of pointing tasks and showed that peak velocity and target distance has a linear relationship. They predicted the endpoint through linear regression involving peak velocity and total distance to endpoint [1].

C. Stephanidis and M. Antona (Eds.): UAHCI/HCII 2014, Part I, LNCS 8513, pp. 313–324, 2014.
© Springer International Publishing Switzerland 2014

Lank and colleagues also employed motion kinematics where they assume minimum jerk law for pointing motion and fit a quadratic function to partial trajectory to predict endpoint [11, 15]. Ziebart and colleagues [20] used inverse optimal control equations to predict target and compared its performance with other polynomial equations modeling cursor trajectory.

Cursor movements vary in characteristics for motor impaired users since they experience tremor, muscular spasms and weakness [9]. The velocity profile includes several stops and jerky movements. This needs to be taken into account when applying target prediction. State space filtering techniques, in particular particle filters are found to be promising [10] in estimating intended targets as well as smoothing cursor trajectories. However there are not much reported work on target prediction for motor impaired users except Godsill's work [7] on particle filter and Wobbrock's work [18] on Angle Mouse. There are also almost no attempt to use target prediction algorithms for novel interaction devices like eye-gaze, gesture or head tracking systems. This paper reports three user studies where we used a neural network based target prediction system for elderly users using a computer mouse and able-bodied users using a head tracker involving Brain-Computer Interface (BCI) and an eye-gaze tracking based system.

2   Theory

2.1   Feature Calculation

We have used the following features as input to our models for target prediction. This section explains the features in detail.

Velocity. We have recorded the pointer position using the getCurrentPosition() API, which records pointer position in every 15 msecs. The velocity is measured as the ratio of the Euclidian distance between two consecutive readings to the difference in timestamp in msec.

Acceleration. The ratio of two consecutive velocity readings to the time difference between them in msec.

Bearing Angle. This is calculated as the angle between two vectors (figure 1) - first being the previous cursor position to current cursor position and the other one is the current cursor position to target position.

2.2   Target Prediction Model

Pointing tasks are traditionally modeled as a rapid aiming movement. In 1887, Woodsworth [19] first proposed the idea of existence of two phases of movements in a rapid aiming movement, main movement and homing phase, which was later formulated to predict pointing time by Paul Fitts. Fitts' law [6] study has been widely used in computer science to model pointing movement in a direct manipulation

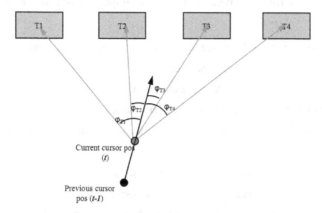

Fig. 1. Bearing Angle Calculation

interface though its applicability for users with motor impairment is still debatable. However the existence of main movement and homing phase is generally accepted among all users' groups [2].

Once a pointing movement is in homing phase, we can assume the user is pretty near to his intended target. The present algorithm tries to identify the homing phase and then predict the intended target. Previous work on analyzing cursor traces of users with a wide range of abilities concentrated on angle, velocity and acceleration profiles [9, 18]. So we consider velocity, angle and acceleration of movement and with the help of a back-propagation neural network, try to identify the homing phase.

We used the simplest model available that can classify a dataset non-linearly. Neural Network is a mathematical model containing interconnected nodes (or neurons) inspired by biological neurons used as a classifier and pattern recognizer for complex data set. Before using this model, we tried to fit different functions to predict homing phase from velocity, acceleration and bearing angle using two different curve-fitting software and found higher-order polynomial equations work in most cases though having different coefficients for different devices and users. So we used a model that can automatically learn new polynomial equations. The neural network model was trained using the standard backpropagation algorithm which was coded by authors. Even after prior training, the neural network keeps training itself during interaction. As a user undertakes a pointing task, the model trains itself. If the user hovers on the target area without clicking, it trains itself for homing phase, otherwise it trains itself for the main movement. At the same time the model is run to get prediction. If it predicts a homing phase, we change colour or enlarge the target. We have used a three layer Backpropagation network for this study. After the neural network predicts the homing phase, we predict the nearest target from current location towards the direction of movement as intended target. Our previous work [3] has already compared Neural Network model with a Kalman filter based model and

Neural network is found to perform better. A simple version of the algorithm is as follows:

```
For every change in position of pointer in screen
     Calculate angle of movement
     Calculate velocity of movement
     Calculate acceleration of movement
Run Neural Network with Angle, Velocity and Acceleration
     Check output
     If output predicts in homing phase
          Find direction of movement
          Find nearest target from current location towards
direction of movement
```

2.3   Eye-Gaze Tracker

We used a Tobii X120 eye tracker [17] and the Tobii SDK is used to read raw coordinates of eye gaze movement. Eye movement is different from a mouse movement as it does not smoothly move in a continuous space as a mouse. The eye gaze rather follows a spotlight metaphor and the saccade focuses at the regions of interest. The raw reading from the eye tracker results in jerky movement of the pointer in the screen and it never stays steady at a single location, which makes it difficult to make a selection. We record the eye gaze positions continuously and average the pixel locations in every 400 msec to estimate the region of interest or saccadic focus points. We simulate the eye movement using a Beizer curve [16] that smoothes the cursor movement between two focus points. We push the focus points into a stack and the Beizer curve algorithm interpolates points in between two focus points. The user needs to blink his eyes to make a selection,. The system can classify between intentional and non-intentional eye blinks and only recognizes the intentional ones through dwell time adjustment.

2.4   Head-Movement Tracker

Head movement tracking was conducted using a Emotiv Epoch Brain-Computer Interface Headset [4]. The headset has an internal gyroscope that can detect head-movement. The Emotiv SDK was used to extract raw co-ordinates from head movement and a Beizer curve [16] was used to smooth cursor movement in screen. We used an eye-blink to make a selection. The Emotiv Headset [4] can detect a blink from EEG measurement without any prior training of participants. We developed software that smoothes up the cursor movement following head movement and make a mouse click if the user blink his eyes.

3   Evaluation Criteria

Once we have a working algorithm that can predict intended target, we need to evaluate its performance so that we can compare and contrast its performance with prior research. So far there is not much consensus on the evaluation criteria for target prediction algorithms. We have defined the following three parameters to evaluate the quality of a target prediction algorithm.

Availability. In how many pointing tasks the algorithm makes a successful prediction.

For example, say a user has undertaken 10 pointing tasks. An algorithm that correctly predicts target in 7 of them is better than another one which is successful in predicting correct target in 5 pointing tasks.

Accuracy. Percentage of correct prediction among all predictions. Any target recognition algorithm keeps on predicting target while the user is moving a pointer in a screen. It may happen that within a single pointing task, an algorithm initially predicts a wrong target but as the user gets closer to the intended target, the algorithm finds the correct target. So if an algorithm predicts an intended target 100 times among which 70 are correct, its accuracy will be 70%.

This metric complements the previous metric. For example, say we have an algorithm that predicts the nearest target from current pointer location as the intended target. This algorithm will have 100% availability as it will fire in all pointing tasks but pretty low accuracy while there are multiple targets available on the path of pointer.

Sensitivity. How quickly an algorithm can detect intended target. For example, an algorithm that can find the intended target while the user crossed 90% of target distance or pointing time is less sensitive than an algorithm that can predict correct target after the user crosses only 70% of target distance or pointing time.

4   Implementation and Validation

We have implemented a bank of neural networks considering all possible combinations of three movement properties (bearing, velocity and acceleration of movement). We have used supervised learning to detect users' movement phases from movement features. Initially we trained the neural networks with a multiple distracter task. Later we used the same task to evaluate the networks following our evaluation criteria. Our training and test set of participants were different.

We conducted three user trials involving three different input modalities:

1. The first trial involved people with age related and physical impairment and they used a standard computer mouse

2. The second trial involved a head tracker and Brain Computer interface used by able-bodied users who never used similar system before.
3. The third trial involved an eye-gaze tracker used by able-bodied users who never used similar system before.

We described these trials in the following sections. Besides the target prediction system we also present an analysis of cursor trajectories for the head and eye-gaze tracking systems.

5   User Trials

Participants. We have collected data from 23 users using mouse. The users used to operate computer everyday and volunteered for the study. The group of participants included users with a wide range of abilities in terms of visual and motor impairment. Age related impaired users were more than 60 years old and physically impaired users suffer from Cerebral Palsy or Spinabifida.

We trained the neural networks with 13 users among which five have age related or physical impairment (like cerebral palsy). Then we test the system with 10 participants among which five have age related visual and motor impairment. The gender was balanced to nearly 1:1 in both training and test cases.

The head tracking system was evaluated by eight able-bodied users (5 male, 3 females) aged between 20 and 35. They never used any head tracking system before.

The eye tracking system was evaluated by eight able-bodied users (5 male, 3 female) aged between 20 and 45. They never used the eye tracking system before. They did not have any trouble in using the experimental set up.

Material. The study was conducted using a 21" screen (435 mm × 325mm) with 1600 × 1200 pixels resolution. and a standard computer mouse. The head tracking was conducted using a Emotiv Epoch Brain-Computer Interface Headset [4] while a Tobii X120 eye tracker [17] is used for eye tracking.

Procedure. The task was like the ISO 9241 pointing task with multiple distractors on screen (figure 2). We tried to strike a balance between the complete natural interaction scenario of Input Observer system [5] and the controlled single target task [6] of traditional Fitts' Law analysis. We developed software to conduct this task which automatically records mouse locations and mouse events on screen every 16 msec.

Users need to click the button at the centre of the screen and then the target button appears with other distractors. We used five different target sizes (20, 40, 30, 50, 60 pixels) and source to target distances (100, 140, 180, 240, 300 pixels). The participants using mouse were instructed to click target for 10 minutes after they were briefed about the procedure.

For the head tracking based system, we used five different target sizes (40, 50, 60, 70, 80 pixels) and source to target distances (100, 160, 220, 280, 350 pixels). The participants were instructed to click target for 5 minutes after they were briefed about the procedure.

We calibrated the eye tracking system with 9 dots before start of trial with each participant. The system was kept on calibrating until the Tobii SDK did not need any further recalibration. Users need to click the button at the centre of the screen and then the target button appears with other distractors. We used five different target sizes (60, 70, 80, 90 and 100 pixels) and source to target distances (160, 220, 280, 350, 400 pixels). We have to change the target size and amplitude than the head tracking system as it was too difficult even for the developer to select target less than 60 pixels wide using the eye tracking system. The participants were instructed to click target for 5 minutes after calibration.

Fig. 2. Multiple Distractor task

Results. Figure 3 plots the average percentage of availability and accuracy in different systems. In figure 3, different combinations of features are plotted in X-axis while the average Availability and Accuracy is plotted in Y- axis. The model only fires (or turns available) when it detects a change in movement phase. In the availability graphs, green bars show the percentage when it correctly identified target, the red bar shows when it could not. In certain occasions it fails to detect this change of movement phases and so the availability is not always 100% (white bars).

Figure 4 plots the sensitivity of the system. The x-axis shows the fraction of pointing time spent in a scale of 100. The y-axis represents the probability of correct target prediction. We found that velocity and bearing of movements have highest availability for mouse and eye-gaze tracking system while the combination of all parameters have highest availability of head tracking system. Velocity and bearing also have the highest accuracy for all systems. The sensitivity is found to be rather same for all possible combinations of parameters.

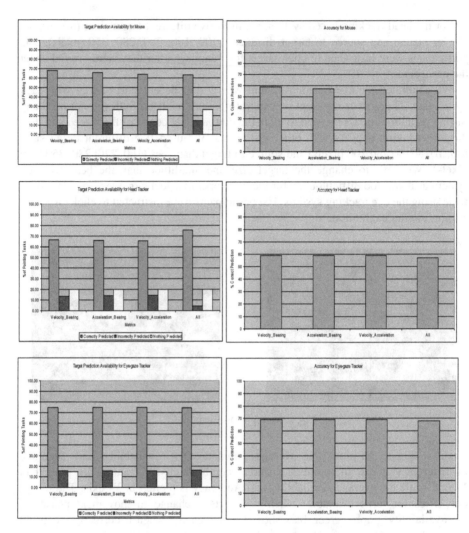

Fig. 3. Availability and Accuracy of Target Prediction system

Video demonstrations of the multiple distractor task is available at http://youtu.be/QsxDxcccwAw and target prediction system is available at http://youtu.be/p9YOKj59TiY

Discussion. This study proposes a new model for target prediction based on Neural Network, and applied this model in two different scenarios. The model accurately detects change in pointing phase in more than 70% of the pointing tasks for head and eye-gaze trackers and 65% for mouse used by people with age-related or physical impairment. The accuracy of target prediction is nearly 60% for all cases, however it reaches more than 90% as the user reaches near the target as shown in the Sensitivity graph (figure 4).

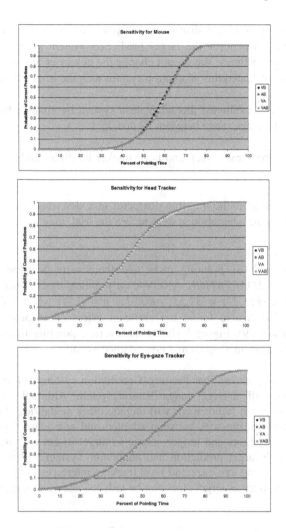

Fig. 4. Sensitivity of target prediction system

6   Adaptive System

The main purpose of developing the target prediction system is to reduce pointing times. After validating the target prediction model, we tested its performance again as an adaptation algorithm. We have developed an adaptation system that enlarges a target whenever it is predicted as a probable target. Recent work by Hwang [8] already found similar technique can reduce pointing times for older adults in a single target task though Lee [12] did not find a significant reduction of pointing times in multiple distractor task.

We used the similar multiple distractor set up as our previous studies described above. In this study, whenever the target prediction system predicts a target, we increased its size by 1.5 times. We do not change the colour or any other property of the target. We have evaluated this adaptation system with the head tracker system.

Participants. We have evaluated this adaptation system by six able-bodied users (4 male, 2 female) with an age range between 22 and 45.

Material. We used the same screen and head tracker hardware and software for this study.

Procedure. It was same as the multiple distractor task described above, participants were not trained with the adaptation system before the trial, they were using it for first time.

Results. We recorded 181 pointing tasks and there were 5 instances of wrong selection. A *SIZE × ADAPTATION* ANOVA on pointing times found a significant effect of adaptation $(F(1,27) = 31.53, p<0.01, \eta^2 = 0.54)$ while a *DISTANCE × ADAPTATION* ANOVA also found a significant effect of adaptation $(F(1,31) = 30.05, p<0.01, \eta^2 = 0.49)$. Figure 5 shows the average pointing times for different target sizes and distances in adapted and non-adapted versions.

Discussion. This study shows that the target prediction system can reduce pointing time when coupled with a target magnification system. Although this study only evaluated head tracker but future work will include other modalities of interaction. It can be noted that the differences between adapted and non-adapted pointing times increases for smaller targets and longer source to target distances. We can assume that presence of such target prediction and adaptation system will not only reduce pointing times for existing eye-gaze and head tracking interfaces but also allow better utilization of screen space as target sizes can be reduced and more targets can be used in a single screen.

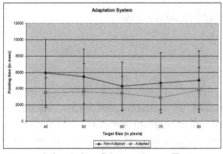

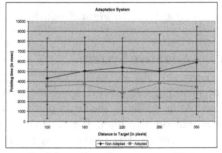

a. Adaptation System w.r.t. Target Size

b. Adaptation System w.r.t. Target Distance

Fig. 5. Adaptation system based on target prediction

7   Conclusions

This paper aims to facilitate human machine interaction through target prediction technology for severely motor-impaired users who have to depend on eye-gaze or head tracking based interfaces. We proposed a framework to evaluate target prediction algorithms and then formulated an algorithm based on a Neural Network based model. We compared the performance of the algorithm for people with a wide range of abilities and three different input modalities and obtained more than 60% accuracy of prediction in all cases. Finally we combined the target prediction system with a target magnification algorithm that statistically significantly reduced pointing times.

References

1. Asano, T., Sharlin, E., Kitamura, Y., Takashima, K., Kishino, F.: Predictive Interaction Using the Delphian Desktop. In: Proceedings of the 186th Annual ACM Smposium on User Interface Software and Technology (UIST 2005), New York, pp. 133–141 (2005)
2. Biswas, P., Langdon, P.: Developing multimodal adaptation algorithm for mobility impaired users by evaluating their hand strength. International Journal of Human-Computer Interaction 28(9) (2012) Print ISSN: 1044-7318
3. Biswas, P., Aydemir, G.A., Langdon, P., Godsill, S.: Intent Recognition Using Neural Networks and Kalman Filters. In: Holzinger, A., Pasi, G. (eds.) HCI-KDD 2013. LNCS, vol. 7947, pp. 112–123. Springer, Heidelberg (2013)
4. Emotiv Epoch Headset, http://www.emotiv.com/ (accessed on: August 31, 2013)
5. Evans, A.C., Wobbrock, J.O.: Taming Wild Behavior: The Input Observer for Obtaining Text Entry and Mouse Pointing Measures from Everyday Computer Use. In: Proceedings of the ACM Conference on Human Factors in Computing Systems (CHI 2012), Austin, Texas, May 5-10, pp. 1947–1956. ACM Press, New York (2012)
6. Fitts, P.M.: The Information Capacity of The Human Motor System In Controlling The Amplitude of Movement. Journal of Experimental Psychology 47, 381–391 (1954)
7. Godsill, S., Vermaak, J.: Models And Algorithms For Tracking Using Variable Dimension Particle Filters. In: International Conference on Acoustics, Speech and Signal Processing (2004)
8. Hwang, F., Hollinworth, N., Williams, N.: ACM Transactions on Accessible Computing (TACCESS) 5(1) (2013)
9. Keates, S., Hwang, F., Langdon, P., Clarkson, P.J., Robinson, P.: Cursor measures for motion-impaired computer users. In: Proceedings of the Fifth International ACM Conference on Assistive Technologies – ASSETS, New York, pp. 135–142 (2002)
10. Langdon, P.M., Godsill, S., Clarkson, P.J.: Statistical Estimation of User's Interactions from Motion Impaired Cursor Use Data. In: 6th International Conference on Disability, Virtual Reality and Associated Technologies (ICDVRAT 2006), Esbjerg, Denmark (2006)
11. Lank, E., Cheng, Y.N., Ruiz, J.: Endpoint prediction using motion kinematics. In: Proceedings of the SIGCHI Conference on Human Factors in Computing Systems (CHI 2007), New York, NY, USA, pp. 637–646 (2007)
12. Lee, D., Kwon, S., Chung, M.K.: Effects of user age and target-expansion methods on target-acquisition tasks using a mouse. Appl. Ergonomics 43(1), 166–175 (2012)

13. McGuffin, M.J., Balakrishnan, R.: Fitts' law and expanding targets: Experimental studies and designs for user interfaces. ACM Transactions Computer-Human Interaction 4(12), 388–422 (2005)
14. Murata, A.: Improvement of Pointing Time by Predicting Targets in Pointing With a PC Mouse. International Journal of Human-Computer Interaction 10(1), 23–32 (1998)
15. Ruiz, J., Lank, E.: Speeding pointing in tiled widgets: Understanding the effects of target expansion and misprediction. In: Proceedings of the 15th International Conference on Intelligent User Interfaces (IUI 2010), pp. 229–238. ACM, New York (2010)
16. Salomon, D.: Curves and Surfaces for Computer Graphics. Springer (August 2005), ISBN 0-387-24196-5
17. Tobii X120 Eye Tracker, http://www.tobii.com/en/eye-tracking-research/global/products/hardware/tobii-x60x120-eye-tracker/ (accessed on: August 31, 2013)
18. Wobbrock, J.O., Fogarty, J., Liu, S., Kimuro, S., Harada, S.: The Angle Mouse: Target-Agnostic Dynamic Gain Adjustment Based on Angular Deviation. In: Proceedings of the 27th International Conference on Human Factors in Computing Systems (CHI 2009), New York, pp. 1401–1410 (2009)
19. Woodworth, R.S.: The accuracy of voluntary movement. Psychological Review 3, 1–119 (1899)
20. Ziebart, B., Dey, A., Bagnell, J.A.: Probabilistic pointing target prediction via inverse optimal control. In: Proceedings of the 2012 ACM International Conference on Intelligent User Interfaces (IUI 2012), pp. 1–10 (2012)

A Skirt for Well Aged Ladies with Cognitive Loss

Alma Leora Culén and Sisse Finken

University of Oslo, Department of Informatics, Gaustadalléen 23 B
Oslo, Norway
{almira,finken}@ifi.uio.no

Abstract. In this paper, we consider design of skirts for well-aged ladies with cognitive loss. In line with recent trends, a graduate student project, which we supervised, focused on monitoring solutions for those suffering from dementia. The result of the project was a skirt. We found ourselves intrigued by the proposed solution and started unpacking, using a phenomenological approach, the meaning of the skirt, when losing cognition. Our conclusion is that skirts for dement ladies should never be viewed as unimportant, or as the new interfaces for assistive technology. Rather, they may be viewed as an opportunity for design to support body, mind and emotions of the person whose cognition is weakening. Aesthetically appealing garments, which improve self-image, designed for ease of dressing, engaging hands, may provide comfort. From the ethical standpoint, embedding skirts or other garments with technology, should be consented to prior to loosing the ability to reason well.

Keywords: interfaces, elderly, dementia, ethics, body.

1 Introduction

A persistent increase in the ageing population may be seen as both a challenge and an opportunity for human-computer interaction researchers and designers wishing to find technological solutions enabling elderly to retain independent living for as long as possible. Elderly suffering from dementia have received special attention. Dementia is a chronic, progressive illness, affecting persons memory, judgment and ability for abstract thinking [19]. It inevitably leads to a loss of autonomy. Currently, there is little that can be done to prevent it. Research, such as [1], shows that the ability to perform activities of daily living is the main factor affecting quality of life for people suffering from dementia. On the other hand, [13] shows that persons with dementia are likely to have decreased ability to manage everyday technology, including technology that should assist everyday living. The ability to manage technology is thus important to consider when assessing ability to perform everyday activities [5,6]. Further, [2] have examined a host of technologies aiming at improving the quality of life and the quality of care for patients with dementia. These authors were able to identify very few (3) clinical studies involving people with dementia, concerned with evaluation and use of assistive technologies. Although this number might have increased since this paper was published, evaluation of technologies offered to dement people is still an opportunity for researchers in HCI. The use of participatory

C. Stephanidis and M. Antona (Eds.): UAHCI/HCII 2014, Part I, LNCS 8513, pp. 325–336, 2014.

approaches in designing for and with elderly is considered to be the correct approach by many researchers [18]. In [16], the authors have, with full participation from people with dementia, provided a "wish list" of technologies that elderly would like use; some of these items were a simple music player, window on the world, and conversation prompter. In [20], the authors have identified activities in daily life that could be supported by technology: dressing, taking medication, personal hygiene, preparing food, and socializing.

In this paper, we discuss design of clothing, in particular skirts, for ladies with cognitive loss. A departure point for the work is a graduate student project entitled "Skirts with Meaning" [12], which we supervised in the context of an interaction design class [7]. The project involved design of skirts with sensors for elderly ladies. In the aftermath of the project, we had one skirt that intrigued us, and we wanted to further explore its design and considerations around embedded GPS sensor. Can skirts be used as the next interface for ladies with cognitive loss? We had good help from four people who are either medical professionals, or have a mother who is suffering from dementia. In our discussions with the participants, we have used the skirt from the project, and some other simple prototypes, in order to really get into the subject of skirts and dementia. Through this process we have started to gain better understanding of what it means to design clothes (with or without technology) for ease of dressing, support sense of aesthetics, well-being and increase self-esteem. This paper, thus, is about sharing lessons learned on this journey, which we believe is just the beginning of thinking about clothing as a support for those suffering from dementia.

In our paper [6], on the use of a smart gym by elderly, we have observed that there was a need to support both cognitive and bodily mastery through design for the smart gym. One would think that talking about a skirt would be easier, but that did not turn out to be the case. We will argue now, there are three equally important dimensions that need to be accounted for in design efforts when designing for elderly ladies: body, mind and emotions.

In research like this, ethical challenges permeate many aspects of the work. Design for and with users who may be considered vulnerable [8,18] is distinguished by increased need for sensibility, empathy and care for ethical concerns.

The paper is structured as follows: in the next section, we discuss the making of the skirt. In Section 3, we present our own experiences with the use of the skirt, and excerpts from interviews with the four above-mentioned participants in this research. In Section 4, we discuss our findings. We conclude in Section 5.

2   Skirts with Meaning

Wellbeing and self-esteem are linked to personal appearance. Clothes and what one wears matters a whole lot, we found out, also when one can no longer remember one's own clothes, even the favorite ones. Aging alone brings problems in terms of dressing oneself, regardless of whether one has dementia or not. Putting stockings on becomes harder, if not impossible. However, when cognition is affected, people may start to suffer from dressing apraxia, and forget how and in which order to put the pieces of clothes on. Dressing processes can thus become stressful and frustrating. At the same time, the act of dressing is a very private experience. Conducting research in homes about such a topic is difficult. Schulte, a fashion knitwear and knitted textiles design student, describes her interest in designing garments for dementia in [15]. Her study is motivated by direct experience with her grandmother, who suffered from apraxia. This made her think how to design clothes that are simple to put on, require minimum assistance, yet extend the sense of beauty and dignity.

A group of three graduate students taking our interaction design course were inspired by this work, as well as [4], Fig. 1. However, being in the computer science department, they wanted to experiment with embedding sensor technology into skirts. Design thinking, with rapid prototyping, focus on empathy and abductive reasoning, was used to explore. No users were involved, in part due to the format of the course, and in part, strict regulations from the Norwegian ethics board. The outcome of the their project work are 'skirts with meaning', one of which was designed for ladies with dementia, see the students' blog for further information [12].

Fig. 1. The students discussing skirts as a technology interface, on the left, a skirt with a proximity sensor (a working prototype made), and an idea for a skirt with QR code, light and sound. Photos: Finken and Culén.

The students made a skirt, Fig. 2, paying attention to the visual load (choosing a solid color) and cognitive processing (simple wrap around style with Velcro closure, for the ease of putting it on and taking off). A solid, blue color was chosen. The skirt has lining for comfort in wear and so that the technology based components could be placed between the two layers of fabric. The panel made of stringed Styrofoam balls, which was placed between the lining and the outer fabric, was a surprising design element for us. The students got inspiration from existing products – the 'ball duvet' and the 'ball vest' – both having small balls inside. When the students presented their project in class, before showcasing their work at the Student Faire, they explained that the small balls were meant as sensory stimuli, which *"may reduce anxiety and provide a sense of security"*. Also, they pointed out that the panel, in the skirt, might have other benefits, such as providing a light massage or simply an interesting surface to engage hands of elderly. Indeed, the Styrofoam balls were pleasant to touch.

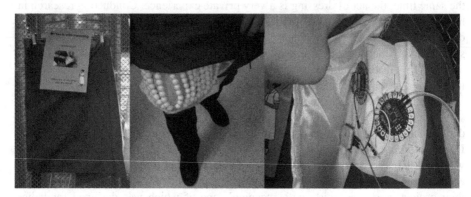

Fig. 2. The final concept for the skirt: simple wrap-around style with Velcro closure, balls for comfort and GPS sensor for motion tracking. Photos: Culén.

The panel with a GPS sensor and two Lilypads was sawn on the side, at the upper part of the skirt close to the belt, and closed with Velcro fasteners. The technology was, in terms of wearing it, unnoticeable. The students developed a tracking solution to be used by caretakers on the iPad. However, it was not possible to use the GPS in the building in which the department is located, and thus, a simulation was used for demonstration purposes.

The skirt and the tracking demo on the iPad were exhibited at the annual faire. The purpose of the Faire is to present various research groups within the institute of informatics, and to present to students a range of local ICT companies.

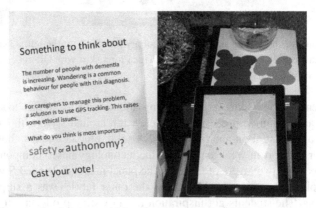

Fig. 3. The voting stand: visitors could try the skirt and the GPS simulation and then cast orange token for safety and the purple one for autonomy. Photo: Culén

The students have used the opportunity to collect some votes on ethical dilemma: should one worry more about person's safety, or their autonomy, see Fig. 3. The people who voted were predominantly students, some researchers and guests for the day. Nobody was in the target group. So the results indicate only how young, technology-oriented people view this question today: 65 % thought security was the most important, while 35% opted for autonomy. The exhibit was the final point for this student project, and we were left with an intriguing piece of clothing to work with further. Was it really a skirt with meaning?

3   Constructing the Meaning

There were two elements of the skirt that we wanted to examine closer. The first one was the panel of Styrofoam balls. We could not find any related scholarly papers. The second element was the GPS, and much has been written and said about that. We give two examples where researchers try to evaluate the usefulness of GPS. In [3], the authors have studied monitoring of people inside homes and concluded that some of the positive aspects of using the GPS include peace of mind, feeling of safety and increased medical compliance. The negative aspects had to do with complying with demands of the technology in terms of wearing it or filling diaries, the glitches it may have, and, most importantly, privacy issues. In [14], the authors asses GPS based technology in terms of out of home wandering. Their study is inconclusive in terms of overall usefulness of GPS, indicating that while some people view use of GPS as loss of autonomy, other people with dementia view it as a means to increase the autonomy, due to the feeling of safety. Searching literature for more conclusive studies did not give results.

We opted for a phenomenological, embodied cognition approach to this issue. Speaking about embodied cognition, Varela states in [17]: "Perception and action, sensorium and motorium, are linked together as successively emergent and mutually selecting patterns". These successively emergent and mutually selecting patterns are formed also in the relation to the environment, in particular, environmental features that are directly relevant to the action that the body is currently performing. One's knowledge of the world is gained through ones experiences within the world and these experiences in turn, are constrained by person's sensorimotor functionality. When there is impairment, the person's experience of the world is affected on multiple levels, since sensorium and motorium are mutually dependent.

An outside observer can never know with certainty how it feels in the mind and the body of another. The best we could do then is to try ourselves. How does it feel to wear this skirt? What does it do to my body? What kind of sensory perception it gives?

One of the authors took the skirt home to wear over a couple of days. The very first observation that could be made was that the students did not take into account aging bodies: the skirt was made for a really thin person, and while students who wore it could easily wrap it around, the same thing was not possible in this case. In fact, a long pin had to be used to keep the skirt secure. The Styrofoam balls felt OK while sitting, but awkward and heavy while walking. As the skirt was not sitting right on the body, this effect was just increased. Furthermore, the fabric was synthetic, both the lining and the outer layer, and it was utterly uncomfortable from this perspective, too. As soon as the GPS component was truly forgotten, and the wearer threw herself on the sofa, she jumped up fast to check if all the components were undamaged. The skirt did not need to be worn the second day. It felt more like an evidence of how well minded designers compromise aesthetics, functionality and privacy, all in one piece of clothing (this even without considering washing the garment, glitches of technology, etc.).

It was easy to reject the concept of the skirt as it was. Yet, the questions around dementia and skirts persisted and we wanted to further explore the issue. The questions were no longer about concrete design solutions (for example, placing the GPS on a belt, which does not get washed). Rather, we concerned with exploring how fabric, materials, photos, etc. can support body, mind and emotions in designing new textile-based interfaces for ladies with dementia.

Both authors have experience with dementia. One of us had summer jobs when younger, working as a home care person, were she encountered people with dementia [10]. The other has a person in early stage of dementia in the immediate family.

We have decided to broaden our experiences by inviting four people to in-depth interviews about dementia and skirts. The first person interviewed is a woman, 72 years old, with an education in sensory perception from 1960's Berlin. Her mother died recently, 106 years old, suffering from dementia for the last 20 years of her life. The second person is a male psychiatrist, 74, chosen also because of his keen sense for ethical issues. The third interviewee is a clinical psychologist aged 54, whose mother is in early stages of dementia. The last interviewee is a 50-year-old woman whose parents very recently chose to live in smart nursing home, because her mother is suffering from both dementia and Parkinson's disease. The last two women were interviewed together. The interviews were conducted in English, Norwegian, and Danish, sometimes mixing the three languages in one interview. Thus, for the purpose of this paper, we have written up the interviews in English, summarizing their content.

In order to offer a richer starting point than just the one skirt, we also included other prototypes shown in Fig. 4. The purpose with these was to have tangible objects that can create engaging discussions, Fig. 4.

Fig. 4. The jeans skirt with transparent pockets into which different objects from a person's life can be placed. Beads attached to the pocket. Next, a wool skirt with contrasting texture pockets, a wool skirt with elastic waist and trim, or pocket with different texture and fur. Photos: Culén.

Fig. 5. The interviewee trying on a skirt, and materials of different textures. Photo: Culén.

4   Analysis and Discussion

How are we to design for supporting sensory perception? What is considered important to support and how should such support come about? In the following we present excerpts from interviews, were we touched upon topics related to body, mind, and emotions. These topics are considered equally important and need to be taken into consideration when designing skirts for people suffering from dementia.

4.1   Body, Mind, and Emotions

At the first interview we brought the original prototype made by the students and told about the idea behind the concept. The interviewee's first action was to try the skirt on. This made her comment on the size of the skirt, both in relation to waistline and length; it was way too tight and too short when not hanging on the hips. This made her remark that young people do not have an idea about what happens to the human body when it matures (in line with the experience by the author who brought the skirt home). In addition, the skirt did not appear aesthetically pleasing. The blue color reminded her of old school uniforms. On a later occasion, another interviewee backed up this observation, suggesting brighter colors, like red. Personal appearance, we learned in the process, is important not just for one's own wellbeing and self-esteem, but also in relation to how others treat you. Another interviewee told that her mother always got more attention when her hair and clothes were well done: *"How one looks like has influence on what kind of care they receive, because people are more attentive to people who look nice and they interact with them more"*.

In relation to other sensory perceptions, beyond color and shape, the first interviewee was keen on touching the fabric, turning the skirt, pulling it open to make the technology visible, sitting on the Styrofoam balls, turning them to the front, and/or 'fiddling' with them. We conversed about hands and how her mother's were always restless: *"My mothers hands were always slightly fiddling. The hands go because they were used to do things and the mind is not there and the energy goes to hands"*. We talked about the GPS, and the way in which it was embedded in the skirt, Fig. 2, and how loose threads most likely would be pulled out, just like her mother had repeatedly pulled out her hearing aid: *"As for the GPS, if there is any threads or anything, my mother would pull them out. She used to do that the whole time with her hearing aid"*.

In the first interview, sensory perceptions for triggering memory were directed towards music, photos, and flowers. In relation to such memory triggering we talked about how *"Pockets with things that would make good associations are great"*.

At the interview we got valuable insights on what worked well and what could be re-designed in terms of positively supporting the sensory apparatus of people suffering from dementia. The size of the skirt was an issue, so were loose threads, or other items that could be pulled at. However, it was considered important to provide for keeping the hands busy (support of the body), and within this, support of bodily memories. By bodily memories we mean things that the body does, and the mind has forgotten. A touching example is reported in [11] where a women, at a local center for elderly, repeatedly made a cradling movement. She did not speak, and nobody understood her behavior. It turned out that she had saved a baby from dying during the war, and the body remembered it as an important event from her life.

Summarizing the findings from the interviews, aesthetics were considered vital (support of emotions), so was the triggering of good associations (support mind). In order to bring further these ideas, we made some new prototypes that incorporated a broader spectra of tangibles to support sensory perceptions, herein transparent pockets that could hold pictures for triggering the memory, beads for keeping the hands busy, and different kinds of fabrics for emotional support, see Fig. 4 and Fig. 5. We were interested to learn how the new prototypes of skirts for supporting sensory perceptions were perceived. Thus, these prototypes we brought to the other interviews, were we got the following feedback and further insights on what it means to live with dementia.

4.2   The Interviews – A Discussion

The fabrics and texture on the skirts prompted different meanings. All interviewees really liked the red, very soft to touch imitation fur, Fig. 5, whereas the fur on Fig. 4 last image, was considered problematic. One interviewee remarked that it could have a negative effect: *"If there is any paranoid ideation which one may have with Alzheimer's, it could be threatening. Hallucinations are also frequent. Things like fur may seem threatening and experienced as an animal, the person may want to take it off. If it is part of the garment, they can not."* The interviewee further suggested designing a blanket or a stole so that the garment could easily be put away, if something suddenly becomes distressing: *"I would suggest a blanket or a stole, they can simply be thrown away if there is anything suddenly disturbing on the blanket"*.

Similar observations, concerning color, texture, and emotions, are reported in a study on sensory gardens for people with dementia [9]. Here plants and their ability to afford sensory is considered with respect to such concerns: *"Plants provide sensory, but non-confrontational, stimulation for all the senses through colours, structures, scents, tastes, forms and sometimes by sounds. Sensory stimulation is important for people suffering from dementia since it can improve orientation, trigger memory, prevent emotional outbursts and facilitate connectedness in individuals with dementia"*, [9:4].

Nature was also a topic mentioned in the interviews. Especially, we talked about it in relation to photos that could be carried in transparent pockets. Such photos were considered beautiful and calming, thus suitable for people who are suffering from dementia: *"Pictures of nature, beautiful and calming are good."* However, instead of pictures of nature, we had placed photographs of people as a means of triggering good memories, Fig. 4. Rather than being welcomed by the interviewees, this feature created much discussion. Other interviewees mentioned that carrying portraits (and other items) in this way, could be distressing as it could be difficult to figure out who was portrayed on the photo: *"People would pick at things and it could be distressing because there is an object or a photo they may recognize and wonder why are these people on my skirt?"* and *"Peoples photos are distressing as they can not figure out who it is and they know they should know who it is."* Another interviewee commented that some might perceive it as *"an insult to carry around memory on the outside"*. A suggestion from this interviewee was to try out different methods to see how they were perceived.

While the feature of carrying around portraits was debated, the attached beads were welcomed. One interviewee said that *"repetition with beads is good, picking is diminished"*. Another mentioned sensory qualities of beads, they had a *"suiting sound"* to them. This interviewee was attentive towards the feel of the beads also: *"The brown is too cold. So is the yellow. The white is nice"*.

During all the interviews, ethics was also a topic of discussion, especially regarding the GPS. Privacy issues in relation to use of such technology are important to discuss in situations of cognitive loss. Herein, it is essential to take into account the relationship between automation and autonomy when, on the one hand, independency of an individual is considered important, while, on the other, wandering might be a concern. At the interviews the interviewees had different and interesting viewpoints on this issue. One talked about the GPS in terms of wandering, safety, and autonomy, and considered the technology a supporting device: *"The GPS might be a good thing for a person alone. But in the center situation, there may be many to monitor at the same time, more room for problems. In principle, an ok solution"*. Yet another interviewee was particular about the relationship between patients, family, and medical staff. It was noted that a patient might be more sensitive towards having doctors and nurses knowing where the patient is. Thus, it was considered important to *"talk about it with the family, preferably the ones with whom there is a good relationship"*.

In coming to an end of the article we present our findings from the interviews in a table summarizing different thoughts around supporing the mind, the body and emotions when designing for ladies who suffer from dementia, Table 1.

Thus, what we have learned from this process is that a designed garment for people suffering from dementia should cater to mind, body, and emotions. Also, it is important to take into consideration the flexibility of use (easy to put on and away), in addition to colors and textures of both fabrics and other materials. Neither aesthetics nor ethics should be forgotten or compromised, in particular if including sensors or memory triggering objects as design elements.

Table 1. Diverse ways to support the mind, the body or the emotions of people with dementia

Activate the mind	Support the body	Support emotions
Photos	Balls	Soft fury materials
Flowers	Beads	Velvet
Jewellery	Trims	Colours
Musical buttons		Shape, e.g., blanket

We conclude with a quote from Alanna Shaikh's *How I'm preparing to get Alzheimer's* talk on TED: *"The more things my hands know how to do, the more things that I can be happy and busy doing when my brain's not running the show anymore"* , [22].

5   Conclusion

In this paper, we have started unpacking possibilities of skirts or other garments embedded with sensors such as GPS to support ladies with genitive loss. While opinions on this topic vary, we have come to the conclusion that the choice between autonomy or safety, offered by GPS monitoring, is a very personal issue, best taken care of while the person still has faculties to make decisions. Other aspects of clothing were then looked at, through series of interviews with tangible props, such as a skirt with a panel of Styrofoam balls or clear fabric pockets containing memorabilia. The main lessons learned are that skirts need to support mind, body and emotions, that is, aim for the simplicity of taking them on and off, use them to engage hands, and make those aging mothers thrive in them, as well as look good! Clothing for dement people should never be seen as a new interface for assistive technology. Rather, it should be seen as an opportunity for design of aesthetically appealing garments improving self- image, feeling good etc. which have a potential to offer more through technology, if the person allows it.

Acknowledgments. First and foremost, we thank the "Skirts with Meaning" project team: Anja Simonsen, Sylvia Saxlund and Rita Johnsen. You have started something really interesting! Thanks are also due to the rest of the participating students: Henrik Kjersem, Lena Risvik, Paria Tahaee, and Ingrid Arnesen, Lena Risvik, Agnethe Heggelund and Rebekka Castro. This research is part of the project *Autonomy and Automation in an IT society for All,* funded by The Norwegian Research Council, grant number 193172.

References

1. Andersen, C.K., Wittrup-Jensen, K.U., Lolk, A., Andersen, K., Kragh-Sørensen, P.: Ability to perform activities of daily living is the main factor affecting quality of life in patients with dementia. Health and Quality of Life Outcomes 2(1), 52 (2004)
2. Bharucha, A.J., Anand, V., Forlizzi, J., et al.: Intelligent assistive technology applications to dementia care: current capabilities, limitations, and future challenges. The American Journal of Geriatric Psychiatry: Official Journal of the American Association for Geriatric Psychiatry 17(2), 88 (2009)
3. Bradford, D., Freyne, J., Karunanithi, M.: Sensors on My Bed: The Ups and Downs of In-Home Monitoring. In: Biswas, J., Kobayashi, H., Wong, L., Abdulrazak, B., Mokhtari, M. (eds.) ICOST 2013. LNCS, vol. 7910, pp. 10–18. Springer, Heidelberg (2013)
4. Charlesworth, J.: Wearables as "relationship tools". Ai & Society 22(1), 63–84 (2007)
5. Culén, A.L., Bratteteig, T.: Touch-Screens and Elderly users: A Perfect Match? In: The Sixth International Conference on Advances in Computer-Human Interactions, ACHI 2013, pp. 460–465 (2013)
6. Culén, A.L., Finken, S., Bratteteig, T.: Design and Interaction in a Smart Gym: Cognitive and Bodily Mastering. In: Holzinger, A., Ziefle, M., Hitz, M., Debevc, M. (eds.) SouthCHI 2013. LNCS, vol. 7946, pp. 609–616. Springer, Heidelberg (2013)
7. Culén, A.L., Mainsah, H.N., Finken, S.: Design Practice in Human Computer Interaction Design Education. In: The Seventh International Conference on Advances in Computer-Human Interactions, pp. 300–306, ThinkMind (2014)
8. Culén, A.L., van der Velden, M.: The Digital Life of Vulnerable Users: Designing with Children, Patients, and Elderly. In: Aanestad, M., Bratteteig, T. (eds.) SCIS 2013. LNBIP, vol. 156, pp. 53–71. Springer, Heidelberg (2013)
9. Edwards, C.A., McDonnell, C., Merl, H.: An evaluation of a therapeutic garden's influence on the quality of life of aged care residents with. Dementia 12(4), 494–510 (2013)
10. Finken, S.: Public care in private homes. In: Chandler, J., Barry, J., Berg, E. (eds.) Dilemmas for Human Services 2012. Papers from the 15th International Research Conference, London, September 1-2, pp. 32–39 (2011)
11. Gummer, R.: Et skvulp I glemslens hav. Weekendavisen #9, Ideer, pp. 1–3 (2011)
12. Johnsen, R., Saxlund, S., Simonsen, A.: Skirts with Meaning (2013), http://skirtswithmeaning.wordpress.com/
13. Malinowsky, C., Almkvist, O., Kottorp, A., Nygård, L.: Ability to manage everyday technology: a comparison of persons with dementia or mild cognitive impairment and older adults without cognitive impairment. Disability and Rehabilitation. Assistive Technology 5(6), 462–469 (2010)
14. McKinstry, B., Sheikh, A.: The use of global positioning systems in promoting safer walking for people with dementia. Journal of Telemedicine and Telecare 19(5), 288–292 (2013)
15. Schulte, B.F.: Designing Guiding Garments for People Affected by Dementias. In: Holzinger, A., Ziefle, M., Hitz, M., Debevc, M. (eds.) SouthCHI 2013. LNCS, vol. 7946, pp. 657–663. Springer, Heidelberg (2013)
16. Sixsmith, A.J., Gibson, G., Orpwood, R.D., Torrington, J.M.: Developing a technology 'wish-list' to enhance the quality of life of people with dementia. Gerontechnology 6(1), 2–19 (2007)
17. Varela, F.J.: The Embodied Mind: Cognitive Science and Human Experience. MIT Press (1991)
18. Vines, J., McNaney, R., Lindsay, S., Wallace, J., McCarthy, J.: Special topic: Designing for and with vulnerable people. In: Interactions XXI, pp. 44–84 (2014)

19. Wallace, J., Wright, P.C., McCarthy, J., Green, D.P., Thomas, J., Olivier, P.: A design-led inquiry into personhood in dementia. In: Proceedings of the SIGCHI Conference on Human Factors in Computing Systems, pp. 2617–2626. ACM (2013)
20. Wherton, J.P., Monk, A.F.: Technological opportunities for supporting people with dementia who are living at home. International Journal of Human-Computer Studies 66(8), 571–586 (2008)
21. How I'm preparing to get Alzheimer's. Alanna Shaikh's TED talk, http://www.ted.com/talks/alanna_shaikh_how_i_m_preparing_to_get_alzheimer_s.html

Recommendations for Gesture-Based Residential Interactive Systems Inspired by Diversity

Ana Carla de Carvalho Correia[1], Leonardo Cunha de Miranda[1], Heiko Hornung[2], and Juvane Nunes Marciano[1]

[1] Department of Informatics and Applied Mathematics,
Federal University of Rio Grande do Norte (UFRN), Natal, Brazil
{anacarla,juvane}@ppgsc.ufrn.br, leonardo@dimap.ufrn.br,
[2] Institute of Computing, University of Campinas (UNICAMP), Campinas, Brazil
heix@gmx.com

Abstract. Gestural interaction is becoming an important mode of interaction with residential systems, be it with or without using physical artifacts such as remote controls or cell phones. When constructing respective gestural vocabularies social implications need to be considered. The importance of the residential environment to users and the heterogeneity of user profiles make the theme diversity an important concern in the development of these applications. Therefore, the main goal of this paper is to describe the recommendations for diversity that support the inclusive design of residential interactive systems based on gestures.

Keywords: accessibility, usability, domotics, gesture-based interaction, smart home, home automation.

1   Introduction

One of the first challenges of developing residential interactive systems based on gestures is the requirements elicitation. The search of a more unobtrusive integration of the technology into the environment has led to an increase of the use of perceptual technologies [11] for residential applications. Analyzing publications in this context (e.g. [7,13,20,25,27]), we noticed that the development of these systems is primarily focused on technological requirements, and that there are few studies on user interaction with the system [3].

Due to the heterogeneity of users that are part of this context, the inclusion of concerns about diversity in the development of residential applications becomes an important aspect. From this perspective, going beyond the technological requirements, we found that usability and accessibility of user interaction with the system are only considered in a limited way in literature. Norman and Nielsen [19] already mentioned the need for further exploration and study.

In previous work [3], we reported on Human-Computer Interaction (HCI)-related challenges in the context of gestural interaction with residential applications. In this paper we report on the recommendations that can mitigate these challenges by

C. Stephanidis and M. Antona (Eds.): UAHCI/HCII 2014, Part I, LNCS 8513, pp. 337–345, 2014.

considering requirements for a development oriented to diversity, such as issues related to culture [12], ergonomics [18], and gender [1,21], among others.

Considering the questions related to diversity that inform the inclusive design for residential interactive systems based on gestures, the construction of these recommendations is based on two important topics for any system in development, i.e. usability and accessibility. A goal of this paper is to support developers during the requirements elicitation phase.

The paper is organized as follows: in Section 2, we present the description of the recommendations for diversity; in Section 3, we present a real usage scenario; in Section 4, we discuss our proposal; in Section 5, we present the conclusion.

2   Recommendations for Diversity

Different authors found that traditional usability models, methods, or guidelines have to be revisited for gestural interaction, especially in the context of residential applications [3,19]. Similarly, accessibility guidelines need to be reevaluated. We did not find guidelines or recommendations for smart homes that specifically consider gestural interaction. However, already existing guidelines for smart homes (e.g. [8,24]) might be built upon, and existing general usability or accessibility standards and guidelines, e.g. [9,10,26] might be adapted. Furthermore, we follow the argument of Chi [2] and acknowledge that accessibility and usability should not be considered as two separate or dichotomous concepts.

The construction of this set of recommendations is not specified to any graphical of visual interfaces or technologies that allow gestural recognition. The recommendations allow specifying the context of use in a systematic way, also simplifying the process of describing the context and thus reducing reliance on specialists.

Analyzing usability and accessibility literature [5,6,14,15,16,17,18,19,23], we realize that diversity regarding gestural interaction is still an underexplored topic. We did not find scientific literature about diversity-specific recommendations or guidelines. for gestural interaction with residential applications and hence focused on literature in the area of Web applications. In Table 1 we describe recommendations inspired by user diversity regarding physical, perceptual and cognitive abilities, using the following coding: (C)ognitive, ph(Y)sical, and (P)erceptual.

Table 1. Recommendations for gesture-based residential interactive systems

Recommendation	Description	Ability
Help	The system should provide means to aid the user to deduct or remember how to use the system and its gestures	C
Confidence	The system has to provide confidence to the user in performing a command	C
Memorization	Property of construction of gestural vocabulary guided by the memorization capacity of the gestures of its users	C
Satisfaction	System's ability to produce comfort, relaxation and enjoyment to the user	C

(**Table 1.** *Continued.*)

Recommendation	Description	Ability
Effort	Ability of the system to be used with the minimum physical and mental effort from the user	C & Y
Stress	The system should avoid psychic disturbances on the functioning of the system, derived from repetitions of unnecessary commands, complex interaction flow, misinterpretation of commands, inappropriate gestures or feedback out of context	C & Y
Discomfort	The gestures should be designed so that even with many repetitions, they can be used without causing discomfort to users	C & Y
Progressive learning	Mechanisms that guide the user of the simplest tasks to the most complex, encouraging continuous learning	C, Y & P
Culture	Appropriateness of gestures to cultural habits in which they are immersed	C, Y & P
Feedback	Various informational output resources to the user	C, Y & P
Gender	Ability of the system to adjust its functioning considering particularities that differentiate users of different genders	C, Y & P
Customization	Property of the system to allow the users to configure their gestural commands the way they prefer to	C, Y & P
Metaphorical property	Metaphoric property of gestures to express their functionality	C, Y & P
Learnability	The system should help the users through mechanisms that can help them understand and apply the gestures	C & P
Completeness	The gestural interaction must have commands that are complementary to additional features of the application, for example, open/close and on/off	C & P
Predictability	Property of navigation in the system that induces the sequence of gestures used for a given task, i.e., the sequence of gestures used should be predictable to the user	C & P
Coordination	The sequence or number of members used in the gestures must comply with the coordinative ability of its users	Y
Balance	The gestures should be designed so that even during its execution, users do not lose balance	Y
Explosion	Ability of users to execute commands with variations in speed and intensity	Y
Tension	Gestures should not keep the muscles tight during execution	Y
Ergonomics	Related to characteristics of the human anatomy, anthropometry, physiology and biomechanics, in building gesture	Y & P
Accuracy	Property of the system to recognize the gestures to a certain degree of tolerance	Y & P
Efficiency	System property that determines how efficiently the human and automation resources are used by the application	P
Operability	Property that expresses how much operational is the gestural vocabulary of the application, in terms of its construction and ease of setup/configuration	P

Fig. 1 graphically illustrates these items of recommendations, highlighting the contemplated skills and embracing in an inclusive way the diversity that the group of users needs in the physical, perceptual and cognitive framework.

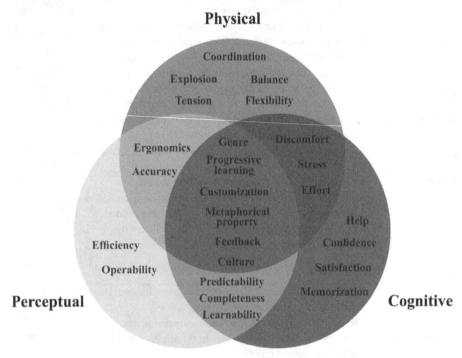

Fig. 1. Recommendations classified by physical, perceptual and cognitive skills

Some items of recommendations might influence others. Consider for example memorization. If each interaction object has a unique gesture, the gestural vocabulary of the application is extensive and people will probably not learn the commands easily. But what would be the "ideal" amount of commands for an application with respect to diversity? As we do not yet have that answer, some steps can be performed as in the reuse of gestures itself. To give a concrete example: a gesture of farewell or goodbye to turn off a TV might also be used to turn off a stereo system or a fan. We can also use other metaphorical properties for each given service, or, still, use completeness to help memorization. That is, to additional features, their gestures are also performed in complementary way, for example, open and close the arms.

Feedback can facilitate progressive learning displaying messages of how the gestural command is performed, which are the options that the user can perform, or help messages that may also be gradually hidden from the application. The variety of ways to externalize the information includes acoustic, haptic, or visual feedback. Feedback should be given directly by the application since a user is not necessarily near a controlled device where the effect of the action could be directly perceived.

Other recommendation that are beyond the usual field of usability and accessibility have been added to this set, for example, culture, which refers to a study of the cultural context in which the application is deployed. Since we know that there are particular gestures in different cultures or with different meanings in each of them. Although today there is still no explicit evidence of what the ethnic differences of gesticulation are, considering cultural aspects avoids gradually decrease the cultural identity of certain user groups within the context of an application [12].

Another important item of recommendations is gender. There are still many open research questions. In addition, an important factor is the large number of men in Information and Communications Technology (ICT)-related professions that may be implicitly bring a bias towards the development of products that not adequately consider gender-related aspects [1,21]. Coordination, balance, tension, explosion and discomfort are recommendations that should influence directly and mainly the construction of the gestural vocabulary of the application. All presented recommendations are intended to provide a reflection for the application development.

3   Usage Scenarios

The recommendations is large and complex enough to possibly pose a barrier to developers that would like to employ this set. Specific studies on each category of the recommendations are necessary to facilitate understanding of respective impacts on application design, evaluation and use.

Knowledge of these recommendations helps developers to adequately consider diversity in their designs. To illustrate the recommendations, we presented the recommendations (Table 1) to a group of undergraduate and graduate computer science students who were involved in a research and development project in the area of gesture-based residential systems. The group identified four items to be explicitly addressed in their project.

The group's research and development project was at an initial stage. The most prominent idea in the group was developing a system that targets diversity. Another feature already defined was that the application would be perceptual, i.e. would not use any physical device to aid the recognition of gestures for the application. Thus, a goal was to enable the user to control doors, lights, air conditioning and other features seen as basic in a residential application from any location within the house. The development team had prior knowledge of usability and accessibility.

In this scenario, the recommendations already supported the requirements elicitation for the system. Exposing the recommendations to the development team, it was perceived that all members identified new requirements. The additional recommendations were related to customization, memorization, discomfort and metaphorical property: **customization**, since the physical skills of the users may interfere in the gestures performance; **memorization**, due to the need to relate functionalities with gestures; **discomfort** because of the gesture repetitions; **metaphorical property** because of similarities among chosen gestures and static or animated graphical interface elements.

Regarding customization, the user can assign gestures to the services that the application provides. When designing the graphic interface, the number of commands for navigation in the system was reduced to five, i.e. horizontal movements (right/left and left/right), vertical movement (up/down), selection (forward motion), and back (rearward movement). While the up/down movement appeared, the down/up movement was eliminated from the gestural vocabulary due to the use of a carrousel widget. The gesture for interacting with a carrousel widget has a metaphoric quality. To decrease the discomfort of the execution of the gestures, they were limited to the trunk region of the body, allowing users to use the application while sitting.

The team implicitly used other concepts, such as: completeness in the horizontal movement; confidence, clearly stating to the user that the requested service has been properly executed or not; decreased effort; flexibility in the choice of gestures and precision, seeking to improve the representation of gestural commands to be better recognized by the application.

4   Discussion

There are several attributes of a house that make it a home, which is much more than a physical entity [22]. According to Dovey [4] a house is an object and home is an emotional and significant relationship between people and their houses, that is, the house is where the experience of home occurs. This definition shows the importance and complexity of the context, and resonates well with approaches in HCI consider issues beyond the technological nature of residential systems.

A contribution of this paper are the recommendations that resulted from an analysis of the interaction with gesture-based residential applications. These recommendations promote the consideration of diversity during the development of residential applications as well as reflections about gesture-based interaction in these applications. The identified recommendations go beyond accessibility and usability and include aspects such as accuracy, stress, culture, genre, flexibility, balance, coordination, ergonomics, tension, discomfort, completeness, explosion and metaphorical properties. In the present stage of this research, developers might be supported in the step of eliciting the requirements of application.

Current visions of gestural interaction design do not consider diversity sufficiently. Diverse perspectives on these applications should be investigated so that the impact of technological immersion on user's lives and family relationships can be evaluated. Correia et al. [3] identified the visual, haptic and acoustic resources in residential applications to support gestural interaction. These features can help the user to utilize the functionalities the application provides.

Another important point to this discussion is the requirement of customization, which is a means to promote diversity and facilitate the access of users with or without disabilities. By offering customization, users can define or adapt gestures that match their personal preferences or capabilities.

Gestural interaction, even if informed by the recommendations presented in this paper, might be inadequate for certain users; for example, quadriplegics are limited to performing movements above the neck. Even considering memorization, predictability of gestures or through the mechanisms of continuous learning, the controlling of many remote devices in a house with many rooms might exert a large cognitive load on the user. Thus, we emphasize the need to other mechanisms to mitigate this kind of problems, such as multimodal interactions, or visual interfaces.

Although the presented recommendations are not exhaustive, they contribute to making explicit and reflecting about some important values of designing residential systems. Besides being used during requirements elicitation, e.g. in form of a questionnaire, the list of recommendations also serves to broaden the discussion and research about gestures used in these applications.

5   Conclusion

This paper presented recommendations for residential systems with gestural interaction, grounded in the points of view of usability and accessibility. Besides adapting concerns of these two areas of study other recommendations were added to best suit the diversity of users. The main contribution of this research includes identifying key recommendations that aim to support the inclusive design of residential applications of gestural interaction.

We also presented a scenario of real use, along with the classification of the recommendations according to physical, perceptual and cognitive abilities. The tabulation of these recommendations allows the study of methodological grounding of development, contextualizes the conceptual visions of accessibility and usability found in the literature for domotic and gestural contexts, and instigates reflections about building applications' gestural commands.

As future work, we will apply the proposed recommendations during requirements elicitation process of design projects, e.g. through questionnaires. These experiences will contribute to refining and validating our recommendations. Since many recommendations have interdependencies, another step will be to articulate requirements derived from the recommendations with design values in order to support prioritizing requirements.

Acknowledgements. This work was partially supported by the Brazilian Federal Agency for Support and Evaluation of Graduate Education (CAPES), by the Brazilian National Council of Scientific and Technological Development (CNPq grant #163408/2012-2), by the Institute of Computing at University of Campinas (IC/UNICAMP), and by the Physical Artifacts of Interaction Research Group (PAIRG) at Federal University of Rio Grande do Norte (UFRN), Brazil.

References

1. Bardzell, S., Churchill, E., Bardzell, J., Forlizzi, J., Grinter, R., Tatar, D.: Feminism and Interaction Design. In: CHI Conference on Human Factors in Computing Systems, pp. 1–4. ACM (2011)
2. Chi, E.H.: The False Dichotomy Between Accessibility and Usability. In: 10th International Cross-Disciplinary Conference on Web Accessibility, pp. 1–2. ACM (2013)

3. de Carvalho Correia, A.C., de Miranda, L.C., Hornung, H.: Gesture-Based Interaction in Domotic Environments: State of the Art and HCI Framework Inspired by the Diversity. In: Kotzé, P., Marsden, G., Lindgaard, G., Wesson, J., Winckler, M. (eds.) INTERACT 2013, Part II. LNCS, vol. 8118, pp. 300–317. Springer, Heidelberg (2013)
4. Dovey, K.: Home and Homeless. In: Home Environments, pp. 36–61. Plenum Press (1985)
5. Eason, K.D.: Towards the Experimental Study of Usability. Behaviour and Information Technology 3, 133–143 (1984)
6. Gabbard, J.L.: A Taxonomy of Usability Characteristics for Virtual Environments. Masters Thesis, Virginia Tech. (1997)
7. Gandy, M., Starner, T., Auxier, J., Ashbrook, D.: The Gesture Pendant: A Self-Illuminating, Wearable, Infrared Computer Vision System for Home Automation Control and Medical Monitoring. In: 4th IEEE International Symposium on Wearable Computers, pp. 1–8. IEEE (2000)
8. Guidelines for Design of Smart Homes, http://www.johngilltech.com/guidelines/guidelines_list.htm
9. ISO 9241. Ergonomics Requirements for Office Work with Visual Display Terminals (VDTs). Part 11: Guidance on Usability (1998)
10. ISO/IEC 9241. Ergonomics of Human-System Interaction - Part 110: Dialogue Principles (2006)
11. Karam, M., Schraefel, M.C.: A Taxonomy of Gestures in Human Computer Interactions. Technical Report ECSTR-IAM05-009, University of Southampton (2005)
12. Kita, S.: Cross-Cultural Variation of Speech-Accompanying Gesture: A Review. Language and Cognitive Processes 24, 145–167 (2009)
13. Kleindienst, J., Macek, T., Serédi, L., Šedivý, J.: Vision-Enhanced Multi-Modal Interactions in Domotic Environments. In: 8th ERCIM Workshop "User Interfaces For All", pp. 1–8 (2004)
14. Madan, A., Dubey, S.K.: Usability Evaluation Methods: A Literature Review. International Journal of Engineering Science and Technology 4, 590–599 (2012)
15. Mosqueira-Rey, E., Alonso-Ríos, D., Moret-Bonillo, V.: Usability Taxonomy and Context-of-Use Taxonomy for Usability Analysis. In: IEEE International Conference on Systems, Man and Cybernetics, pp. 812–817. IEEE (2009)
16. Nielsen, J., Loranger, H.: Prioritizing Web Usability. New Riders Press (2006)
17. Nielsen, J.: Usability Engineering. Academic Press (1993)
18. Nielsen, M., Störring, M., Moeslund, T.B., Granum, E.: A Procedure for Developing Intuitive and Ergonomic Gesture Interfaces for HCI. In: Camurri, A., Volpe, G. (eds.) GW 2003. LNCS (LNAI), vol. 2915, pp. 409–420. Springer, Heidelberg (2004)
19. Norman, D.A., Nielsen, J.: Gestural Interfaces: A Step Backward in Usability. Interactions 17, 46–49 (2010)
20. Rahman, A.S.M.M., Saboune, J., Saddik, A.E.: Motion-Path based in Car Gesture Control of the Multimedia Devices. In: 1st ACM International Symposium on Design and Analysis of Intelligent Vehicular Networks and Applications, pp. 69–76. ACM (2011)
21. Rode, J.A.: A Theoretical Agenda for Feminist HCI. Interacting with Computer 23, 393–400 (2011)
22. Saizmaa, T., Kim, H.C.C.: A Holistic Understanding of HCI Perspectives on Smart Home. In: 4th International Conference on Networked Computing and Advanced Information Management, pp. 59–65. IEEE (2008)

23. Shackel, B.: Usability-Context, Framework, Definition, Design and Evaluation. In: Shackel, B., Richardson, S. (eds.) Human Factors for Informatics Usability, pp. 21–38. Cambridge University Press (2011)
24. Smart Home Guidelines,
http://www.tiresias.org/research/guidelines/smart_home.htm
25. Wahlster, W., Reithinger, N., Blocher, A.: SmartKom: Multimodal Communication with a Life-Like Character. In: 7th European Conference on Speech Communication and Technology, pp. 1547–1550 (2001)
26. Web Content Acessibility Guidelines (WCAG) 2.0., http://www.w3c.org/TR/WCAG20
27. Wilson, A., Shafer, S.: XWand: UI for Intelligent Spaces. In: SIGCHI Conference on Human Factors in Computing Systems, pp. 545–552. ACM (2003)

MuBiks: Tangible Music Player
for Visually Challenged

Apurva Gupta, Aditi Padhi, Keyur Sorathia,
Surbhit Varma, and Bhasker Sharma

Department of Design, Indian Institute of Technology, Guwahati,
Assam, India
{g.apurva,p.aditi,keyur,surbhit,d.sharma}@iitg.ernet.in

Abstract. MuBiks is a novel tangible music player, designed for visually challenged to create and manipulate music playlists. Users can manipulate musical controls to play, pause and increase-decrease volume through rotating different sections of MuBiks. We followed a user-centered-design approach to understand user behavior towards existing human-machine interactions. Contextual inquiry in the form of semi-structured interviews among teachers and students were conducted across three blind schools in Assam and Madhya Pradesh in India. A series of tasks was given to users to understand patterns of existing communication through texture and size identification. Heavy dependence on memory and secondary help[1], easy recognition of texture, shape, size and sound and extensive use of hands were observed during the study. Identified insights were referred and accommodated to design proposed music player.

Keywords: Tangible User Interface, Music player, Visually challenged, User-centered design.

1   Introduction

With technology getting cheaper, smaller and smarter, it has opened a new dimension for incorporating different interaction modalities for digital systems. One such relatively new and emerging area is Tangible User Interface (TUI) [34]. TUIs have seen a lot of developments over the past few years across sectors like entertainment [6, 9, 13, 16, 21], education [10, 20, 26, 28, 31], various other complex applications such as urban planning [5, 8, 14] as well as music and performance. Studies show that a host of research explorations has also been undertaken in musical interfaces [1, 19, 23, 24]. Music is an entity that has no cultural or social barriers and can be enjoyed equally by all. Through this project, we have tried to enhance the experience of music for one specific section of the society vis-à-vis visually challenged. India accounts for 20 per cent of the 39 million blind populations across the globe [8] which comes close to 7.8 million blind people. Visually impaired students make use of physical artifacts

---

[1] help taken from others to perform any task.

C. Stephanidis and M. Antona (Eds.): UAHCI/HCII 2014, Part I, LNCS 8513, pp. 346–356, 2014.

like cubes etc. to form active mental models of the physical world around [28]. The interactions with such artifacts are strictly hands-on. Moreover, people with visual disabilities have been found to have well developed tactile and auditory senses [33, 35] as compared to rest of the population. Several technological and sociological improvements have aided visually challenged people in their everyday life activities [18, 29] such as helping them to navigate without additional help, improving their communication with personal computers, learning character shapes and handwriting, and to track and locate lost objects. Tangible User Interfaces like MICOO [25] and Touch Your Way [18], have lessened the need for manual intervention and enabled independent discovery on the part of visually challenged. However, making music tangible for visually challenged is a relatively unexplored domain. Since, TUIs have the inherent quality of engaging user's perception of the world and thus his sensory and motor skills, they could be used effectively to couple the enhanced sensitivity of the visually challenged user population.

MuBiks is a tangible music player that enables visually challenged to create and manipulate playlists from a database of songs. The playlist is manipulated using familiar interactions identified during user study. Contextual inquiries with semi-structured interviews were conducted across three blind schools in Guwahati, Assam and Bhopal, Madhya Pradesh with teachers and students. The design of MuBiks is based on findings from user study. We developed a low fidelity prototype using arduino board, potentiometers, gyroscope and bump sensors to demonstrate the feasibility of the system. We explain related work in next section, followed by methodology and concept generation. Further, details of low fidelity prototype are explained in prototyping section, followed by discussion for future research work.

2   Related Work

Music applications are one of the oldest and most popular areas for TUIs which have become both ubiquitous and popular around the millennium. Over the past few years, there have been various attempts to develop TUIs for sound and music. Block Jam [12] controls a dynamic polyrhythmic sequencer using 26 physical artifacts as input device for manipulating an interactive music system and interprets the user's arrangement of the blocks as meaningful musical phrases and structures. Cubed [1] is yet another music sequencer integrated into a Rubik's Cube where users generate different sounds by manipulating colors on the cube. Audiopad [17] aims to combine the modularity of knob-based controllers with expressive character of multidimensional tracking interfaces. Table top interface allows users to manipulate volume and effect controls to present associated digital information. While these projects largely involve content generation and manipulations, [23, 24] enable user to access and control musical contents. Music cube [24] is a wireless cube-like object, which uses gestures to shuffle music and a rotary dial with a button for song navigation and volume control. The tangible music player [23] uses a shape of a shelf placed on a wall, where user interacts with different items kept on the shelf to control the player functionality such as play, pause, change volume and tracks. In [19], the author explores various concepts in making digital music more tangible and expressive such as use of physical metaphors, music rhythm visualization multifunctional control, spoken song description and use of gesture control.

In addition to its diverse applications in music interfaces, physically challenged section of the society also has been focused. [3] summarizes how tokens representing frequently used words are used to teach basic concepts of language and space to children with disabilities. While [4] presents a new method to engage people with hearing impairment in interactive storytelling, [30] proposes a system that helps the visually challenged navigate around in an unfamiliar environment. Further, [25, 32] use auditory output to teach statistics and graphs to the visually challenged by series of tokens. However, relatively few tangible interfaces have been developed for visually impaired users in the domain of music. Those developed have been mostly on music sequencing or music education rather than for enjoying and listening to music [11, 27, 36]. Moreover, even though a variety of application domains have been explored in TUI's, the methodology has been mostly data-centric relying heavily on designer's perceptions and understanding of the interactions and affordances with the system. The system is evaluated with users at a later stage, unlike in user-centric approach. MuBiks is one such attempt to integrate the experience of listening to songs with TUIs. It is inspired from the form of Rubik's cube and effectively combines users' auditory and tactile senses, allowing them to multitask with other ongoing activities.

3   Methodology

We followed a user-centered design approach and began with a preliminary study to understand the aspirations and motivations of target users. We conducted semi-structured interviews to understand their everyday behavior, tasks and actions associated with each task. We recorded our insights and designed a few tasks to understand how users interacted with everyday objects. We studied their modes and methods of interaction with the music. Finally, we conceptualized the design and interaction model for MuBiks based on the inferences and conclusions drawn from the user study.

3.1   User Study

Contextual inquiries were conducted at the Guwahati Blind School in Guwahati, a state run blind school in Bhopal and Aarushi, an NGO based in Bhopal. We conducted semi-structured expert interviews with a music teacher, who was himself visually impaired, the director of Aarushi and students at the blind schools. Later, task based analysis was done with 5 students at the Guwahati Blind School.

Expert Interviews. Teachers were interviewed to understand different methods of teaching that they employed. Insights were drawn regarding the equipment used and daily interactions of students with their surroundings. Familiarity with existing technology was analyzed and we inferred that users had heightened tactile and auditory senses.

We drew following major inferences from the expert interviews:

1. Users could identify small subtleties in objects. The music teacher at Blind School in Bhopal mentioned that students could differentiate between two different local newspapers despite having same texture as one of them had a small cut at the bottom of each page.
2. Any new object was identified through exploration of texture and sound. Users identified any new object by understanding its texture or the sound it makes.
3. It was easier for them to remember objects by arranging them in a particular order. One of the helpers at the blind school mentioned that students arranged spices in kitchen in a specific order for easy remembrance for later usage.
4. Students were familiar with computers and mobile phones. Specific software with audio feedback helped them navigate through the system.
5. They learned using digital audio books.
6. They mostly listened to music on media players and were familiar with the use of buttons.

We noted the insights and designed a few tasks aimed at understanding the interaction of the target users with the physical objects in the surroundings and their current music usage pattern.

Contextual Task Analysis. We conducted contextual user enquiry among 5 users at Guwahati blind school, all of whom were males aged between 15-21 years of age, to understand their behavior patterns towards everyday interactions. The students were asked to perform a set of given tasks. After the task, each student was interviewed to understand how he felt while doing the task, what was his approach to finish the task and if he enjoyed doing it. The actions used by them to identify and interact with new objects, or memorize new concepts were recorded.

Users were given different objects such as plastic cubes, cylinders made of mud, wooden cuboids, Jigsaw pieces and magnified Lego blocks [22]. They were asked to perform the following tasks:

— Task 1: Identify texture/material of given objects.
— Task 2: Differentiate between two objects of different shape, size or texture.
— Task 3: Slide an object horizontally and vertically on the table.
— Task 4: Rotate an object.
— Task 5: Place a different face of an object on the table.
— Task 6: Join two Lego blocks.
— Task 7: Solve a Jigsaw puzzle (or try to join two jigsaw pieces).
— Task 8: Play and pause a song (on mobile phone).
— Task 9: Change a song (on mobile phone).
— Task 10: Increase and decrease volume of a song (on mobile phone).

Fig. 1. User differentiating between two cubes for a given task

The tasks were not timed and were given to the user one-by-one, in the order mentioned above. Their actions were both video recorded and noted. The insights that were drawn from the user study are as follows:

- **Shape, size, texture and sound recognition:** It was observed that users were able to easily identify objects based on their texture and sounds. Additionally, it was easier for users to distinguish between objects made of mud and plastic than between objects made of different types of plastic. Similarly, it was easier for them to differentiate between spherical and cubical items. One user could even point out the difference in size between two similar objects by aligning their bases together (Figure 1). However, it was difficult for most of them to distinguish through size unless the difference was significant.

- **Ease of rotary motion:** It was observed that users were comfortable rotating them, as compared to sliding them horizontally or vertically on a surface. When asked to horizontally/vertically move an object on the table, most users turned the face of the object or rotated it. It was also noted that it was difficult for them to comprehend the idea of linear motion.

- **Extensive use of hands:** Users were comfortable manipulating objects with their hands, without using any surface (tabletop). It was noted that they preferred fiddling with them in their hands, rather than placing them on any surface. When asked to identify a wooden cuboid, a user first tried to recognize the texture by manipulating it with his hands and then tapped it with his fingers to make out its sound.

- **Difficulty in solving puzzles:** Users were found to easily point out at any unevenness on object's surface; however it was difficult for them to connect the depressions in one object to the elevations in another. They were asked to fit Lego blocks together and except for one user, none of them could connect the blocks appropriately. It was also observed that the level of difficulty increased when the blocks were replaced by Jigsaw pieces.

- **Memory and secondary help:** It was found that visually challenged users relied heavily on memory and secondary help from different individuals. They did not use any software application to remember the order of songs, instead remembered through individuals' memory. Similarly, before using a new system or product, they needed help of another individual to get acquainted with its manipulation controls and interactions.

- *Music usage:* Mobile phones were found common for listening to songs. Visually challenged users used existing gadgets like radios, music players and computers to listen to music (Figure 2). Additionally, it was observed that, listening to songs was never a stand-alone primary activity for the users. They generally listened to music after classes in their leisure time.

Fig. 2. User listening to songs on mobile phone

4   Concept Generation

The insights drawn from user study helped us to define the form and interactions of the system. We drew mind-maps and affinity diagrams to consolidate the collected data. Personas, tasks and interactions were also defined based on the analysis. We came up with the following design guidelines for the system after iterative and exhaustive brainstorming sessions:

1. Considering the users' familiarity with identification of shapes, sizes and textures, it should be beneficial to use these material properties to incorporate familiar interactions.
2. Since users were found to be comfortable with rotating objects, the affordance of rotation should be beneficial in the proposed design.
3. The final design should be portable because users were found to be comfortable with hands-on activities, and at the same time, multi-tasking while listening to music.
4. Since users were heavily dependent on memory and secondary help, the system should try to address these issues and be relatively easy to understand from the usage point of view.

4.1   Persona Creation

Once the system goals were defined, the user persona was defined as follows:

"Nihar is 23 years old, living at the Guwahati Blind School and has been visually impaired since birth. His day starts with attending morning prayers at the school followed by attending classes of Mathematics, Science and English. He is very

passionate about music and plays the piano after classes. He and his friends listen to music using their mobile phones while walking, and singing in the corridors of the school's hostel. He loves to listen to Bollywood music and is a big fan of Sonu Nigam. He sometimes browses through the net and reads online digital audio books with the help of audio-feedback software pre-installed in the system."

4.2   System Tasks

System tasks and flow of information was drafted by analyzing the user persona. These included adding songs to the playlist, playing songs, pausing songs, changing the current song, increasing the volume and decreasing the volume.

4.3   Interactions

We referred back to the tangible interface frameworks [34] to incorporate tangible design features and characteristics into the system. We faced the challenge of limiting the number of tokens and imparting portability to the system. Analysis of user study helped us to identify possible list of tokens and relevant interactions:

1. There should be at least two similar tokens, differing in shape or size. One token would contain the database of songs while the rest would be used to create playlists.
2. Both the tokens should be able to perform the following tasks: add songs from database to playlist, play songs, pause songs, change song, increase volume and decrease volume.

5   System Overview

The system consisted of two cubical tokens or MuBiks differing in size. The smaller MuBiks was a playlist (p-MuBiks) while the bigger one contained a song database (d-MuBiks).

Since users were more familiar with the act of rotation, inspiration was taken from the form of a Rubik's cube. Each MuBiks consisted of three horizontal sections (Figure 3). The middle section was fixed whereas the top and the bottom sections could freely rotate along the Z-axis only. The two rotating sections could be differentiated through textures. For instance, the top section was covered with cloth whereas the bottom section was made of metal. The middle section was made relatively smaller in size to help users to hold the cube.

Rotating top section of MuBiks clockwise played a song whereas rotating it anti-clockwise paused it. Similarly, rotating the bottom section clockwise increased the volume while rotating it anti-clockwise decreased the volume. Shaking the MuBiks changed a song. If a song was being played from the database, it could be transferred to the playlist by simply touching the two MuBiks (Figure 4). The confirmation of transfer was given in the form of auditory feedback.

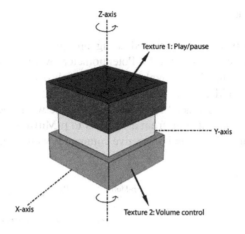

Fig. 3. Sections of MuBiks

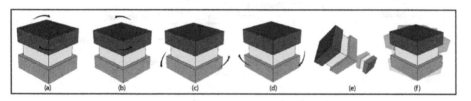

Fig. 4. (a) Rotate top section clockwise to play song; (b) Rotate top section anti-clockwise to pause song; (c) Rotate bottom section clockwise to decrease volume; (d) Rotate bottom section anti-clockwise to increase volume; (e) Add song from d-MuBiks to p-MuBiks; (f) Change current song

Fig. 5. Low-fidelity prototype of MuBiks

6   Prototyping

A low-fidelity prototype was developed using arduino board [2], potentiometers, gyroscope and bump sensors (Figure 5). Potentiometers were set-up inside upper and lower sections of the MuBiks to toggle volume and play/pause controls. Gyroscope was set-up to detect rapid change in motion while shaking the MuBiks to change the songs. Bump sensors were placed to detect collision between the two MuBiks and initiate transfer of the current song from d-MuBiks to p-MuBiks. All the sensors were connected to the arduino board and respective commands were executed (Figure 6).

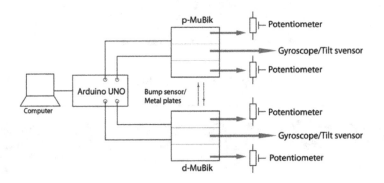

Fig. 6. Schematic diagram of prototype

7   Future Work

The paper introduced a novel interactive way to re-define the experience of listening to music for the visually impaired. The system is yet to be tested to evaluate usability issues. Further improvements could to be done with respect to the shape and form of MuBiks and the kind of feedback received. For instance, instead of a cubical form we can have a truncated pyramidal or frustum like shape. Additionally, the surface could include letters in Braille to identify different playlists or functions. The system could also be made ubiquitous by networking it with external speakers or other music systems and devices. On a broader perspective, the same player, with additional research on its features and functionality, could be imitated for the general population and developed as an accessory-cum-interactive music player. The concept opens wide avenues for further research and exploration.

Acknowledgments. We thank the Guwahati Blind School and Aarushi, Bhopal for permitting us to carry out interviews and user study with their students. The insights thus gained were very crucial to the development of MuBiks.

References

1. Abstract machine,
   http://www.abstractmachine.net/blog/abstractmachinev87d6/
2. Arduino, http://www.arduino.cc/
3. Hengeveld, B., Hummels, C., Overbeeke, K., Voort, R., van Balkom, H., de Moor, J.:
   Tangibles for Toddlers Learning Language. In: Proceedings of the Third International
   Conference on Tangible and Embedded Interaction (TEI 2009), Cambridge, UK, February
   16-18 (2009)
4. Parton, B.S., Hancock, R.: Interactive Storybooks for Deaf Children,
   http://prezi.com/bvxjkyvcdx5w/interactive-storybooks-for-
   deaf-children-by-becky-sue-parton-and-robert-hancock/
5. Huang, C.J., Yi-Luen Do, E., Gross, M.D.: MouseHaus table. In: Proceedings of CAAD
   Futures (2003)
6. Magerkurth, C., Memisoglu, M., Engelke, T., Streitz, N.A.: Towards the next generation
   of tabletop gaming experiences. In: Graphics Interface 2004 (GI 2004), pp. 73–80. AK
   Peters (2004)
7. Colella, V., Borovoy, R., Resnick, M.: Participatory simulations: using computational
   objects to learn about dynamic systems. In: CHI 1998 Conference Summary on Human
   Factors in Computing Systems. ACM (1998)
8. Deccan Herald, http://www.deccanherald.com/content/240119/india-
   accounts-20-per-cent.html
9. van Loenen, E., Bergman, T., Buil, V., van Gelder, K., Groten, M., Hollemans, G.,
   Hoonhout, J., Lashina, T., van de Wijdeven, S.: EnterTaible: A solution for social gaming
   experiences. In: Tangible Play: Research and Design for Tangible and Tabletop Games,
   Workshop at the 2007 Intelligent User Interfaces Conference, Honolulu, Hawaii, USA, pp.
   16–19 (2007)
10. Raffle, H.S., Parkes, A.J., Ishii, H.: Topobo: A constructive assembly system with kinetic
    memory. In: Proceedings of the ACM CHI 2004, pp. 647–654. ACM, NY (2004)
11. Haenselmann, T., Lemelson, H., Adam, K., Effelsberg, W.: A tangible MIDI sequencer for
    visually impaired people. In: Proceedings of the 17th ACM International Conference on
    Multimedia, pp. 993–994. ACM (October 2009)
12. Newton-Dunn, H., Nakano, H., Gibson, J., Jam, B.: A Tangible Interface for Interactive
    Music. In: Proceedings of the 2003 Conference on New Interfaces for Musical Expression
    (NIME 2003), Montreal, Canada (2003)
13. Leitner, J., Haller, M., Yun, K., Woo, W., Sugimoto, M., Inami, M.: IncreTable, a mixed
    reality tabletop game experience. In: Proceedings of the 2008 International Conference on
    Advances in Computer Entertainment Technology, pp. 9–16. ACM, NY (2008)
14. Patten, J., Ishii, H.: Mechanical constraints as computational constraints in tabletop
    tangible interfaces. In: Proceedings of CHI 2007, pp. 809–818. ACM, NY (2007)
15. Underkoffle, J., Ishii, H.: Urp: a luminous-tangible workbench for urban planning and
    design. In: Proceeding CHI 1999 Proceedings of the SIGCHI Conference on Human
    Factors in Computing Systems, pp. 386–393 (1999)
16. Zigelbaum, J., Horn, M., Shaer, O., Jacob, R.: The tangible video editor: Collaborative
    video editing with active tokens. In: Proceedings of TEI 2007, pp. 43–46. ACM, NY
    (2007)
17. Patten, J., Recht, B., Ishii, H.: Audiopad: A Tag-based Interface for Musical Performance.
    In: Proceedings of the 2002 Conference on New Interfaces for Musical Expression, NIME
    2002, pp. 1–6 (2002)

18. Song, J.-W., Yang, S.-H.: Touch Your Way: Haptic Sight for Visually Impaired People to Walk with Independence. In: CHI 2010: Work-in-Progress (Spotlight on Posters Days 1 & 2), Atlanta, GA, USA, April 12-13 (2010)
19. Zimmerman, J.: Exploring the Role of Emotion in the Interaction Design of Digital Music Players. In: Proc. DPPI 2003 (2003)
20. Ryokai, K., Cassell, J.: StoryMat: A play space for collaborative storytelling. In: Proceedings of CHI 1999, pp. 272–273. ACM, NY (1999)
21. Ryokai, K., Marti, S., Ishii, H.: I/O brush: Drawing with everyday objects as ink. In: Proceedings of CHI 2004, pp. 303–310. ACM, NY (2004)
22. Lego, http://www.lego.com/en-us/
23. Hjulström, M., et al.: Tangible Music Player, Chalmers University of Technology (2009), http://web.student.chalmers.se/groups/idp09-1/#
24. Alonso, M.B., Keyson, D.V.: MusicCube: Making Digital Music Tangible. In: Proc.CHI 2005 (2005)
25. Manshad, M.S., Pontelli, E., Manshad, S.J.: MICOO (Multimodal Interactive Cubes for Object Orientation): A Tangible User Interface for the Blind and Visually Impaired. In: Proc. ASSETS 2011 (2011)
26. Zuckerman, O., Arida, S., Resnick, M.: Extending tangible interfaces for education: Digital montessori-inspired manipulatives. In: Proceedings of CHI 2005, pp. 859–868. ACM, NY (2005)
27. Omori, S., Yairi, I.E.: Collaborative music application for visually impaired people with tangible objects on table. In: Proceedings of the 15th International ACM SIGACCESS Conference on Computers and Accessibility, p. 42. ACM (October 2013)
28. Frei, P., Su, V., Mikhak, B., Ishii, H.: Curlybot: Designing a New Class of Computational Toys. In: Proceedings of CHI 2000, pp. 129–136. ACM, NY (2000)
29. Guy, R.T., Truong, K.N.: Crossing Guard: Exploring Information Content in Navigation Aids for Visually Impaired Pedestrians. In: CHI 2012, Austin, Texas, USA, May 5-10 (2012)
30. Willis, S., Helal, S.: RFID Information Grid for Blind Navigation and Wayfinding. In: Ninth IEEE International Symposium on Wearable Computers, ISWC 2005, pp. 34–37 (2005)
31. Sorathia, K., Servidio, R.: Learning and experience: teaching tangible interaction & edutainment. In: International Educational Technology Conference IETC. Social and Behavioral Sciences, vol. 64, pp. 265–274 (2012)
32. Tangible Graph Builder, http://www.youtube.com/watch?v=iELy-hws5u8
33. The Journal of Neuroscience, http://www.jneurosci.org/content/31/33/11745.short
34. Ullmer, B., Ishii, H.: Emerging frameworks for tangible user interfaces. IBM Systems Journal 39(3-4), 915–931 (2000)
35. US National Library of Medicine and National Institutes of Health, http://www.ncbi.nlm.nih.gov/pmc/articles/PMC544930/
36. Yairi, I.E., Takeda, T.: A music application for visually impaired people using daily goods and stationeries on the table. In: Proceedings of the 14th International ACM SIGACCESS Conference on Computers and Accessibility, pp. 271–272. ACM (October 2012)

A CPML-Signwriting Interpreter: A New form to Generate the Graphical Symbols of Signwriting

Carlos E. A. Iatskiu[1], Laura Sánchez García[1], Diego Roberto Antunes, and André Luiz Pires Guedes[1]

Federal University of Paraná, Curitiba PR, Brazil
{ceaiatskiv,laurag,diegor,andre}@inf.ufpr.br

Abstract. The Brazilian Sign Language is the natural language used by deaf people in Brazil to communicate between themselves and with the society, as well as it is part of culture and tradition. Despite this importance, the record of Libras is still one difficulty, because many existing tools do not support their needs for plain appropriation. This paper presents, through SignWriting, a new way to generate graphical symbols correspondents do Libras Signs in order to make possible the Libras recording for the members of the deaf communities . . .

Keywords: Human-Computer Interaction, Deaf Culture, Social Inclusion, Computational Tools for Citizenship, SignWriting, Computational Phonological Model.

1 Introduction

The Brazilian Sign Language (Libras) is the "sine qua non" tool for deaf people in Brazil to have access to communication, information and education for achieving the plain citizenship.

Though the Brazilian Sign Language is official by law, deaf people still find difficulties in relation to its use in different contexts, like in communication between them and with other people, information storage and retrieval and knowledge building.

Information systems and technological artefacts in general are of great usefulness for minimize these difficulties, but, instead of being useful, they frequently are themselves a barrier to information access for deaf people.

One of the limitations consists on the unnatural interaction process, since the communication does not occur in Libras, their mediation language for all purposes, considered by linguistics to be their first language, even if it is not chronologically the first.

In Brazil there are 5.7 millions of people with some degree of deafness and approximately 3% of them are considered deaf, according to the official demographic census IBGE [8]. This part of the population suffers continuously of lack

C. Stephanidis and M. Antona (Eds.): UAHCI/HCII 2014, Part I, LNCS 8513, pp. 357–368, 2014.

of opportunities. In this sense, these communities need tools to help them to communicate between them and with other people of their society.

Within all the necessities of these communities, one that emerges with evidence is the difficulty in the graphic registering of their language (Libras) or, in other words, of the writing itself. No natural language survives without a writing system, since languages evolve along with time and, without an adequate register, part of them can be lost. The deaf communities in Brazil use Libras for inside communication, but at the moment they need some record, they need to appeal to written Portuguese.

There are several different writing systems for the set of existent sign languages, this causing additional trouble for the deaf communities. Among them, SignWriting, is the most well-known one. Never-the-less, the available tools to support this system are rather inadequate and insufficient to facilitate its use. This is in fact one of our hypothesis for the low use of sign languages writing systems by deaf people.

There is a lack of proper support for deaf culture and few research results to inform designers about how to built technological artefacts to promote the social inclusion and the citizenship for deaf people. In this context, this research group of *Universidade Federal do Paraná* (Federal University of Parana State, in Brazil) took for itself the responsibility of building an integrated approach between research and practice which had as its main basis two architecture models, one in three layers (basic software, tools - some of which could be also applications and applications), and the other an integrated functional one that has been proved, up-to-now, to be adequate as an important ally of deaf communities in their search for communication and access to information and knowledge building possibilities.

In conjunction with this architecture, the group developed a Computational Model of the Phonology of Libras (CMPL). This model has supported and will support the development of the majority of the modules of the functional architecture, such as the Natural Language Processing part of the Portuguese-Libras translator and the avatar generator. All these tools and basic software have there main purpose making the computer human interaction in Libras possible.

Faced to all these needs of deaf communities, their problems with the sign language writing, the inefficiency of available tools and having the architecture and the model already built as support, the present work began to solve the problem of developing a WEB service for the interpretation (mapping) of the sign descriptions by the Computational Model of the Libras Phonology to the graphic elementary symbols that compose the SignWriting system.

This service consists one more contribution for the set solutions that the architecture will offer. It receives an XLM description of a Libras sign according to the Model of Libras Phonology and produces the corresponding set of Sign-Writing components.

2   The Relevance of Writing

For many centuries, the writing has helped the human beings. Is is with us in the caves since 8,000 years B.C., since the first civilizations in the World. It emerged form the necessity of humans to register and storage data between peoples of different civilizations.[9]

We have several manners of communicate with each other, as the speech or the gestures, but these two, in particular, are considered volatile, because while passing from a person to other one it carries the risk of it sense be changed and it's meaning modification. The need for the Libras, as for any other language, written registration follows naturally.

"The relevance of writing for History and for records maintenance comes from the fact that it allows for the storage and the propagation of information not only between individuals but also between generations as well. By means of the writing, we find possibilities of situating the current Man in contact with the Man of the past, rescuing facts that, when analysed from an innovative perspective, surely will gain benefits for human existence" [9]

From the perspective of the Deaf Culture, the use of the writing code of the oral language of the country as the unique writing possibility determines problems not only in the personal relationships between the contemporary deaf individuals of a community but also in the relationship between deaf persons that are spatially distant and, even worst, between the current deaf communities and the ancient ones, since they were mediated and registered in a language that was not their natural one, what implies, necessarily, an external intervention on the information or knowledge available.[3]

3   Writing Systems for Sign Languages

Several writing systems for sign languages exist all around the World trying and solve the graphic representation of signs. Never-the-less, this is seen as a additional problem for deaf communities that, unable to know which is the most adequate system to use, appeal to the written form of the oral language of their country, not without significative effort. In the present section some available writing systems for sign languages will be presented, with emphasis to Sign-Writing, which, having be considered the most complete one, was chosen to be used in the Interpretation Service described in the present paper.

3.1   Sistema de Stokoe

Apart from being the precursor of the legitimate of the linguistic character of sign languages, Stokoe[1] created a notation to represent the sign languages based on its observed parameters: hand configuration (10), location (12 positions), action movements (22) and hand orientation(4). The aim of his notation was to respond to the himself necessity in the registration and the study of sign languages. In this way, the notation did not have, as one of its purposes, the use of the written code by the deafs themselves.[7]

The Stokoe's System was the first notation to represent the "phonological" (by the level equivalence to oral languages analysis) components of the American Sign Language by graphic symbols. The original notation was composed by 55 symbols, but afterwards, researchers modified this set as a consequence of the proper live language.[7].

3.2   The François Neve's Notation

Being a researcher at the University of Liége (1996), François Neve expanded the Stokoe's notation, complementing it. Along with the modifications, the François Neve notation made the enumeration and the computational treatment of the signs possible. The written representation is done by means of columns from up to down (in a single column when the dominant hand signalizes or in two columns for both hands)[1].

Both in Stokoe's and in Neve's notations, one can perceive the phonological aspects specified up to that moment. The notations also had the basic elements needed to represent non-manual expressions (face, body and head, between others), indispensable components of sign languages as seen before.

3.3   HamNoSys

The HamNoSys (Hamburg Sign Language Notation System) [2] is a phonological linear transcription system with a greater scope than Stokoe's that defines about 200 symbols for the representation of the parameters: hand configuration, orientation, locations in the head and in the trunk and the movements by means of iconic representations easily perceived and recognized. An innovation of this representation was the inclusion of the non-manual expressions.

From this writing system, a computational system for sign transcription was developed and this helped to propose some tools for deaf people.

The SiGML (Signing Gesture Markup Language) [4] is a transcription model based on HamNoSys, built by means of XML (the eXtensible Markup Language) and a flexible alternative for representing sign language signs constituents in a computational way.

3.4   SignWriting

The SignWriting is a graphic written notation of sign languages. Its components allow for any sign language to be represent visually, or, in other words, the writing system allows for representing the phonological structure of sign languages in a graphic manner.

According to Capovilla & Raphael (2001)[5], the SignWriting has as its objective more than a scientific simple sign notation system, having as an additional aim being a practical system for sign writing capable of assuring fast, safe and error-free written communication between deaf people in their everyday activities.

This writing system was developed by Valerie Sutton in 1981 as an extension of a movement notation system, the Sutton Movement Writing & Shorthand, that aimed at being able to represent, in a systematic way, any movement of dance, sports, physiology between others.[5]

SignWriting is a robust system capable of representing, graphically, any sign language, acting as an alphabetic system in which the graphic units correspond to the minimal elements that compose the sign. [4] In Brazil, the use of SignWriting is still restricted, but many authors defend its use as a means of amplifying the scope Libras use and registrations. This writing system is not well known among the deaf communities, mostly because great part of the information and knowledge legacy is represented in other languages, frequently in the written form of the oral ones, in our case, Portuguese. Additionally, there are few tools for Libras that offer support for SignWriting use. In this context, the developing of technological artefacts that can propel SignWriting use and legitimation as a writing system for Libras by which the deaf communities can produce and register this knowledge emerges as critical.

In Capovilla & Raphael work (2001)[5], it is possible to perceive that SignWriting has a fundamental role in sign languages in general, since it helps the deaf people to understand efficiently each detail of the sign composition by means of the written correspondent. Parameters as location, movement, orientation, facial expressions can be easily visualized with SignWriting.

Even being SignWriting a graphic code for signs writing, some important parameters such as velocity, frequency, sequentiality marks, between others, are not available. For human use, sometimes, these are perceived in a natural and unconscious form by sign language users. Never-the-less, for adequate computational treatment, a more detailed sign phonological components description is needed.

The writing systems presented here are seen as interesting alternatives for helping in signs registration. SignWriting, mainly, is a proper written system with all the potentiality to be used with Libras, by the reasons discussed above. This justifies its choice as the basis for the WEB service for the Model Interpretation to a writing signs system in question.

Further differential of SignWriting to other similar systems refers to the broad existent documentation. This system is the unique one that presents characteristics related to simultaneity so clearly and that utilizes a precise spacial description.

4   Conceptual Bases

In this section the Architecture [13] and the Phonological Model [12] for adequate Libras treatment, fundamental stones for the present WEB service, are presented.

4.1   The Computational Architecture to Support the Social Inclusion of Deaf Communities in Brazil

The proposed architecture can be described trough two main elements: the abstract four general layers hierarchy (with special relevance of the basic interface structure built) and the integration model, which shows all the modules and their identified interrelations that give support for the execution of the abstract architecture. Figure 1 presents an abstract of the proposed HCI Architecture, in its four levels.

The surface layer is responsible for providing adequate applications, mainly in the axes of i) giving adequate support to Deaf natural language (i.e. Sign Language) acquisition and registration (as occurs traditionally in the written codes of any oral language); ii) supporting teaching-learning processes of Libras itself and of written Portuguese as their second language (i.e. literacy); and, what is self- explaining of the situation of real severity level, iii) supporting knowledge acquisition of every other area, considered the hypothesis of the Sign Language acting as the mother language for the Deaf in any interpretation process.

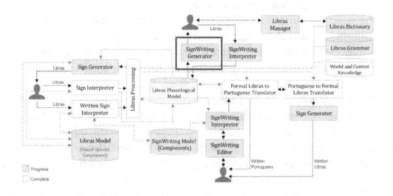

Fig. 1. Proposed HCI Architecture with developed and in progress modules and bases. Adapted from [13]

The services needed referred specially to those associated to language itself, starting by dictionaries, thesaurus and translators. Though being themselves applications, they can be seen and even more they are critic as tools to allow for plain applications for Deaf communities. The interface between the services and the internal APIs has as its principal function providing correct frameworks for both tools layers being built scientifically sound. Finally, the internal level is responsible for the Computer Science subareas knowledge and technology necessary for the several tools and applications.

After presenting the overall architecture, we proceed to describe the integrating model. This representation makes explicit all the modules and bases involved, and their necessary interrelations. Figure 1 shows it, together with the modules instantiated (developed/in progress) up to the present moment.

The work described in the present paper - the WEB service for the interpretation of the sign descriptions by means of the computational model of Libras phonology to SignWriting symbols - is situated within the described architecture as indicated in Figure 1, in the SignWriting Generator, since it receives the computational phonological description of a sign components and produces for the user, the graphic representation components of the sign in SignWriting.

4.2   Computational Description Model of Libras

This Research Group present a computational representation model based on a compilation and adaptation of phonological models that aggregates a high degree of details for sign description. Such finesse in describing the signs render the model presented as adequate for computational treatment of SL. Figure 2 shows an adaptation of the basic structure of the model with some of its main parameters. For example, one can see in figure 1 that a Sign is composed by a Hold, a Non-Manual Expression and a Movement (that may be combined in different levels to represent simultaneity and sequentiality. Each element, by turn, are roots of tree that expands down to the leaf level, where the actual values of the required parameters are enumerated (e.g. the element of quality may be defined by the extension, tension, velocity and other temporal aspects of the movement). The proposed structure (its use and the degree of computational details of signs) is important to solve a series of problems thus far encountered in SL recognition, building signs (3d), written signs, among others.

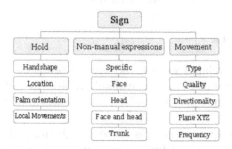

Fig. 2. Conceptual Structure of Sign Computational Representation. Adapted from [10] and [11]

The proposed model is a compilation of several phonological models existing in the literature, and it extends these models in various aspects: it allows for simultaneity, sequentiality; non-manual expressions etc. The model has a high degree of detailed parameters and values that could be attributed to such parameters. Additionally, the proposed model allows for adoption of new expressions, parameters and values, which is a powerful feature in the model to support new discoveries in SL.

This completudeness is important for the processing (use of the knowledge as described by the model for image recognition, translation etc.) and for the execution (e.g. to generate 3D interpreters). Additionally, the proposed model includes the non-manual expressions, that may be used in the intensity, sentence formation, semantics and in the singular characterization of a sign. This singular characterization often occurs in disguised signs. These expressions aggregate facial. The proposed model is an important element of a conceptual Human-Computer Interaction (HCI) architecture previously cited that takes several aspects of the deaf needs into consideration.

Such model is necessary, for example, to aid Computer Vision (CV) to better train algorithms for sign recognition, with the correct set of representative signs and descriptions. Most CV studies, for example, rely on the use of gloves for recognition. A glove limits the natural signing of the SL and does not consider, in most cases, very important aspects as non- manual expressions, locations, among others.

To assist CV in the recognition process, the creation of an adequate sign base (not random or isolated) with descriptions of the signs according to phonology is all important. Thus, CV will have a representative set of signs and their recognition will be the elements of phonology. This way you can retrospectively identify any other signs not present at the base, because recognition is for their formation parameters. Thus, will possible the create tools that allowing the search signals by the elements of phonology and the real support of the translators.

This model is of extreme importance for the work in question, since from its rules for sign components description, in a high level of detail, it allows for the automatic generation of the graphic symbols.

5   Related Work

During the study of related work found several problems that justify the lack of use, by deaf communities, of the available tools. Most of them are based on inadequate input/output paradigms for the production of SignWriting graphic symbols.

Incorrect input/output paradigms cause a high time for the generation of a unique sign graphic symbols. Additionally, sometimes, available systems seem to have been built for a non-representative portion of deaf communities, namely the one that are himself called hearing impaired and understand its country official oral language. The tools revised were the following: SignNet [3], SW-Edit[6] and SignPuddle [14].

6   The Developed Service and Some Results

The WEB service developed is situated within the architecture as described, and can be used in two ways: for the automatic interpretation of XML to the Sign-Writing graphic symbols, and, also, for an intelligent search for graphic symbols. As can be observed in Figure 3, the system reads the Libras sign description

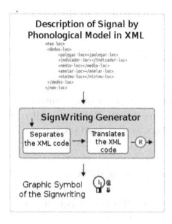

Fig. 3. Abstraction of the proposed system

in the Phonological Model in XML and the user receives as output the graphic symbols components of SignWriting that correspond to the input sign.

In Figure 3 the reader can see in a more detailed way the service operation. The main difference from it to the other tools available comes from the fact that it does not make a conversion from a sign to an unique pre-existent Sign-Writing correspondent symbol but, instead, converts each piece of XML describing the primitives that compose the sign (dominant hand, movement,...) to the correspondent SignWriting sign component.

Only after having converted every piece of XML to the correspondent one, the SignWriting sign spelling process is completed. In this way, the developed service allows for the written sign partial and gradual composition of the writing sign, through a search for the sign construction in an inverse manner of the one used by others available tools.

Fig. 4. Graphic sign of yellow color in SignWriting

In Figure 4, we can see the Libras sign for the Portuguese world "amarelo" (yellow). In order to understand the way in which the system interprets each piece of XML code and forms the written symbols we can observe Table I, which shows the movement in Libras Phonological Model of Figure 4.

Table 1. Table with the XML description of the movement of the sign "amarelo'" in Libras - Adapted from [12]

```
<movement sequence="1">
  <dominantHand>
    <type>
      <contour>rectilinear</contour>
      <unidirectional>down</unidirectional>
      <contact>rub</contact>
    </type>
    <quality>
      <velocity>normal</velocity>
    </quality>
    <frequency>simple</frequency>
  </dominantHand>
</movement>
```

As we can observe in this Table, the service reads each described XML chunk in an independent manner for the SignWriting symbols generation. In this way, every existent (or non-existent yet, if represented in the Model) Libras sign can be generated from its primitives description. The system's databases composed of each elementary component described by the Libras Phonological Model, and not by the correspondence sign-SignWriting symbols like other available tools do. This makes the system managing possible, since along the language evolution, it will not be necessary to enter each new sign created, because its elementary components will be already storage.

The second functionality of the service presented here acts in a similar way as other available tools do, with the difference that it uses as input the same XML code with the sign description in the first capacity or use of the service described above. The output for the user consists on the set of all the signs that have that chunk as a component. The service is all being developed for the WEB platform in order to be available for deaf communities. Meanwhile it expects to be integrated within a non-distant future, to the whole working architecture.

6.1   Results

A concrete result can be observed in Figure 5, which shows the execution of the developed service doing a convertion from the Libras XML sign description and produces the graphic SignWriting symbols.

In the same Figure, we can see a chunk of XML code that refers to the hand configuration for the sign in Libras for "deaf". Some details can be stated: the thumb: contact form and in which other finger, the adjacent and parallel thumb rotations, the other fingers (indicator, medium, ring and little) disposition and junction, only the indicator is open and the others closed, all fingers are united and the thumb contact is the pad of the back of the middle finger.

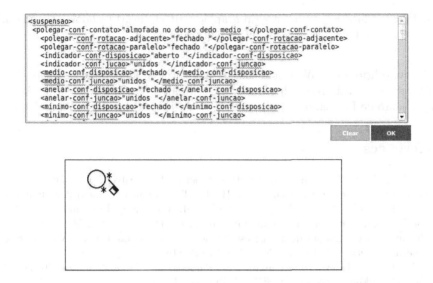

```
<suspensao>
  <polegar-conf-contato>"almofada no dorso dedo medio "</polegar-conf-contato>
    <polegar-conf-rotacao-adjacente>"fechado "</polegar-conf-rotacao-adjacente>
    <polegar-conf-rotacao-paralelo>"fechado "</polegar-conf-rotacao-paralelo>
  <indicador-conf-disposicao>"aberto "</indicador-conf-disposicao>
  <indicador-conf-jucao>"unidos "</indicador-conf-juncao>
  <medio-conf-disposicao>"fechado "</medio-conf-disposicao>
  <medio-conf-juncao>"unidos "</medio-conf-juncao>
  <anelar-conf-disposicao>"fechado "</anelar-conf-disposicao>
  <anelar-conf-juncao>"unidos "</anelar-conf-juncao>
  <minimo-conf-disposicao>"fechado "</minimo-conf-disposicao>
  <minimo-conf-juncao>"unidos "</minimo-conf-juncao>
```

Fig. 5. Service Web Interface

Faced to these results, we can consider that the automatic generation of the graphic SignWriting symbols for the Libras signs representation is viable and innovative, and can bring useful benefits for deaf communities in Brazil. The written code, that will be storaged and searched for, can be seen as potentially global for this problem solution, since sign languages share most of their "phonological" constituents. In this way, the service developed can be seen as a promissory step for the solution of the written sign language edition problem.

7   Conclusions and Future Work

The necessity of any natural language writing is critical, for it not to be lost along time. The deaf communities needs are clear, mainly when we talk about access to information without the country oral language mediation. In this sense, the work presented here has potentiality to represent a significative contribution to solve a relevant technical problem with clear social results. This service presented here is relevant part of an alternative output of the writing Portuguese - translator module under developing.

The principal question to be treated in future work is the generation of Sign-Writing symbols of a sign within it's proper spacial. It refers to the conversion of the written version of our oral language (Portuguese) into the corresponding XML Libras description by the Phonological Model built within the research group. disposition.

This capability will be one of the bases for the automatic translation from written Portuguese to Libras that will give the Brazilian deaf communities the possibility of having easy access (in graphic written form) to books, classroom notes, films and any other academic or cultural content.

Acknowledgments. We would like to thank the students and teachers that collaborated to this research. This work is funded by Coordenação de Aperfeiçoamento de Pessoal de Nível Superior - CAPES and Fundação Araucária.

References

1. Stokoe, W.C.: Sign Language Structure. Linstok Press, Silver Spring (1978)
2. Prillwitz, S., Leven, R., Zienert, H., Hanke, T.: Hamnosys version 2.0: Hamburg notation system for sign languages: An introductory guide. International Studies on Sign Language and the Communication of the Deaf, pp. 195–278 (1989)
3. Stumpf, M.R.: Língua de sinais: escrita dos surdos na internet. In: V Congresso Ibero Americano de Informática Educativa (2000)
4. Elliott, R., Glauert, J., Kennaway, J., Parsons, K.: Sigml definition. Technical report working document. ViSiCAST Project (2001)
5. Capovilla, F., Raphael, W.: Dicionário Enciclopédico Ilustrado Trilíngue da Língua de Sinais Brasileira, vol. I. Sinais de A à L. Editora da Universidade de São Paulo, São Paulo (2001)
6. Torchelsen, R., Costa, A.: Aquisição da escrita de sinais por crianças surdas através de ambientes digitais. Escola de Informática, Universidade Católica de Pelotas (2002)
7. Stumpf, M.R.: Aprendizagem de Escrita de Língua de Sinais pelo Sistema SignWriting: Línguas de Sinais no Papel e no Computador. Tese de Doutorado, Universidade Federal do Rio Grande do Sul (2005)
8. Fernandes, S.F.: Avaliação em língua portuguesa para alunos surdos: algumas considerações. Universidade Federal do Paraná (2007)
9. Azevedo, D.: A importância da escrita na sociedade contemporânea. Universidade Estácio de Sá (2010)
10. García, L., Guimarães, C., Antunes, D., Trindade, D., da Silva, A.: Structure of the Brazilian Sign Language (Libras) for Computational Tools: Citizenship and Social Inclusion. World Summit on the Knowledge Society 112, 365–370 (2010)
11. García, L., Guimarães, C., Antunes, D., Trindade, D., da Silva, A., Miranda Jr., A.: Techonological Artifacts for Social Inclusion: Structure of the Brazilian Sign Language (LIBRAS)- Gestures for Citizenship. In: IADIS International Conference on WWW/Internet, vol. 1, pp. 267–271 (2010)
12. Antunes, D.: Um Modelo da Descrição Computacional Da Fonologia Da Língua de Sinais Brasileira. Dissertação de Mestrado - Universidade Federal do Paraná (2011)
13. García, L., Guimarães, C., Antunes, D., Fernandes, S.: HCI Architecture for Deaf Communities Cultural Inclusion and Citizenship. In: ICEIS (2013)
14. SignWriting.org.: Oficializado Alfabeto Internacional do SignWriting (2013)

A Universal Assistive Technology with Multimodal Input and Multimedia Output Interfaces

Alexey Karpov[1,2] and Andrey Ronzhin[2]

[1] University ITMO, St. Petersburg, Russia
[2] St. Petersburg Institute for Informatics and Automation of RAS (SPIIRAS), Russia
{karpov,ronzhin}@iias.spb.su

Abstract. In this paper, we present a universal assistive technology with multi-modal input and multimedia output interfaces. The conceptual model and the software-hardware architecture with levels and components of the universal assistive technology are described. The architecture includes five main interconnected levels: computer hardware, system software, application software of digital signal processing, application software of human-computer interfaces, software of assistive information technologies. The universal assistive technology proposes several multimodal systems and interfaces to the people with disabilities: audio-visual Russian speech recognition system (AVSR), "Talking head" synthesis system (text-to-audiovisual speech), "Signing avatar" synthesis system (sign language visual synthesis), ICANDO multimodal system (hands-free PC control system), and the control system of an assistive smart space.

Keywords: Assistive Technology, Multimodal User Interfaces, Multimedia, Universal Access, Audio-Visual Speech, Assistive Applications.

1 Introduction

A lot of people around the world are limited in their possibilities because of hearing, vision, speech, motion dysfunctions and mental impairments. For the help, support and rehabilitation of these people there are various governmental programmes in many countries like e-Accessibility, e-Inclusion, Ambient Assisted Living (AAL) [1].

In the last years, Russian government also pays more attention to the problems of life of people with disabilities. In May 2012, the President of Russia has ratified the Convention on the Rights of Persons with Disabilities [2], which was accepted several years ago by the General Assembly of the United Nations. The key points of this Convention state that countries must create conditions for maximal integration of disabled people into the social life on all its levels (including education and information society). Also, the State Programme "Accessible Environment" [3] intended for 2011-2015 has recently started in Russia. This program supports adaptation of work of governmental, educational, social organizations and information services (including electronic services) for needs of persons with disabilities, as well as provision of information accessibility and computer means for disabled people, creation and embedding of new means of interaction and development of new goods and services that

C. Stephanidis and M. Antona (Eds.): UAHCI/HCII 2014, Part I, LNCS 8513, pp. 369–378, 2014.

apply special interfaces and devices for various groups of people with special needs. Moreover, on December 30th 2012, The President of Russia has confirmed important changes to the law "On social defense of people with disabilities in the Russian Federation" that has essentially increased the status of Russian sign language, which is an official language of Russia now. According to the Ministry of Health of Russia, in the country there are more than 13 million people with disabilities (almost 10% citizens of the Russian Federation), including above 700 thousand children with disabilities. And each year there are up to one million people getting disability that is caused by a lot of reasons (ecological, medical, psychological, etc.).

Nowadays assistive technologies are known as any technical devices, tools or services that increase, maintain or improve functional capabilities of people with disabilities. It is known that the term "Assistive technology" was firstly used in the USA in the state document "Technology-Related Assistance for Individuals with Disabilities Act of 1988 (The Tech Act)" [4], and now it is widely used. At that assistive technology may have electronic, software, mechanical, optical, biological nature, etc.; they are, for example (not limited to), wheelchairs, prostheses, hearing aids, optical glasses, television subtitles, robot-assistants and telepresence robots, wheelchair lifts, sounds of traffic lights, guide dogs with the appropriate equipment and more other.

Among various assistive technologies we may highlight special information technologies that can assist people in human-computer interaction, information access, electronic learning, communication, etc. Therefore, we define the new term "assistive information technology", which is special software and/or hardware that improves information accessibility and communication means for people with disabilities and special needs.

Usually assistive technologies are adapted to disabilities of concrete users, i.e. specific technologies are used for blind people (for instance, speech and haptic interfaces), deaf (e.g. sign language-based interfaces), dumb people (textual interfaces), motor disabled (e.g. hands-free interfaces) and mentally handicapped persons (e.g. touch-screens with simple graphical user interfaces). However, universal assistive technologies are rarely developed. One example of such technology is a computer system that supports natural communication between blind and deaf persons [5, 6]. Some other examples of multimodal human-computer interfaces for universal access framework are presented in [7-11].

The given paper presents a conceptual model (Section 2) and an architecture of software-hardware complex (Section 3) of a universal assistive technology both with multimodal input and with multimedia output user interfaces. At that a modality is considered as a way (process) of producing some information and a media is a process of receiving some information by a human being during human-computer interaction [12].

2   Conceptual Model of the Universal Assistive Technology

The conceptual model of the universal assistive technology is shown in Figure 1. A computer complex is placed in the center of this model, and it is able to hear and see users by microphones and video-cameras, as well as it can output multimedia information by a display with touch-screen and loudspeakers. A layer of methods and functions of automatic processing (audio, visual and textual information recognition and synthesis) is placed farther from the center and then a layer of user interfaces, which are used for multimodal human-computer interaction. These user interfaces are based on speech recognition, automatic lip-reading, video-based head tracking, text-to-speech synthesis, machine text processing, manual gestures and speech synthesis, which are combined in four assistive multimodal systems for:

1. Automatic audio-visual speech recognition.
2. Text-to-audiovisual speech synthesis ("Talking head").
3. Sign language visual synthesis ("Signing avatar").
4. Multimodal hands-free computer control.

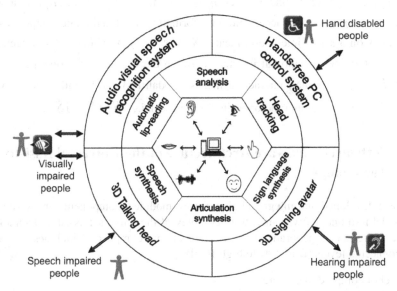

Fig. 1. The conceptual model of the universal assistive technology with multimodal input and multimedia output interfaces

The proposed conceptual model of the universal assistive technology includes only developed or studied by the authors assistive technologies, however, there are some other prospective systems and technologies, not covered in this research, for example, gesture and sign language recognition [13], eye tracking [14], brain-computer interfaces [15], haptic interfaces [16] and so on, which can also be integrated in this framework.

User interfaces for human-computer interaction in assistive technologies must meet some principal requirements of potential users. They should be: universal, multimodal, natural (intuitive), usable (ergonomic), friendly, effective and reliable. Also there are some basic types of cooperation between modalities: transfer, specialization, equivalence, redundancy, complementarity and concurrency [12].

The proposed assistive information technology is universal one because it is aimed for different categories of users with sensory and physical disabilities: blind people can rely on audio man-machine interface based on speech/sound recognition and synthesis, deaf people focus on text and sign language-based interface, motor disabled people can use multimodal hands-free PC control interface, whereas regular able-bodied users may interact using multimedia (mainly audio-visual) information.

A crucial advantage of multimodal user interfaces is that they provide several alternative ways of human-computer interaction at the same time, and the user may choose how he/she wants (or may) to communicate with information systems. Besides, lacking communicative abilities of a human being can be compensated by some other modalities without any loss of application functionality. At that a set of abilities $P^u = \{p_1^u,...,p_k^u\}$ of a concrete user $u_i \in U$ (where $U = \{u_1,...,u_l\}$ is a set of potential users), which are accessible for information input and output, imposes some restrictions on a set of interaction means $S = \{s_1,...,s_n\}$ of the assistive technology, that determines an optimal interface between the user and the computer system: $I^u = P^u \bigcap S$. At that, interaction means (modalities) can be either input S^I or output S^O for the system (and opposite for the user), i.e. $S = S^I \bigcup S^O$.

3   Software-Hardware Architecture of the Universal Assistive Technology

We have developed and integrated all software modules, components and systems of the model into one software-hardware complex of the universal assistive technology. Figure 2 presents a generalized architecture of this complex; it includes five main interconnected levels (from low to high-level):

1. Level of computer hardware.
2. Level of system software (middleware).
3. Level of application software of digital signal processing.
4. Level of application software of human-computer interfaces.
5. Level of software of assistive information systems.

The low level of computer hardware includes available on the computer market information input sensors and output devices connected to one server: microphones (both stationary ones and portable headset), video cameras (digital camcorders, web-cameras and high speed camera JAI), display (with a touch-screen), and loudspeakers.

The level of system software includes operational system (Microsoft Windows family), drivers of microphones and sound board (provided by manufacturers), drivers of video cameras (provided by manufacturers), computer vision library (OpenCV), computer graphics libraries (OpenGL, DirectX), sound processing libraries (HTK, Julius), and an Internet browser (Microsoft Internet Explorer).

The level of application software of digital signal processing has the modules for voice activity detection, audio and video signals processing/analysis, information fusion, audio and video information synthesis.

The level of application software of human-computer interfaces contains modules for speech and audio events recognition, automatic lip-reading, text-to-speech synthesis, articulation and mimics video synthesis, sign language video synthesis, video-based head tracking, and user fall detection.

The high level of software of assistive information systems includes an audio-visual Russian speech recognition system (AVSR), "Talking head" synthesis system (text-to-audiovisual speech synthesis), "Signing avatar" synthesis system (sign language visual synthesis), ICANDO multimodal system (hands-free PC control system), and a control system of an assistive smart space.

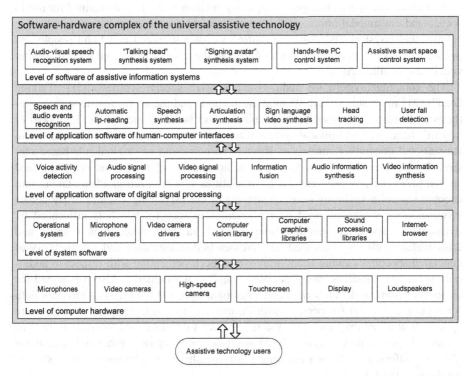

Fig. 2. The architecture of levels of the software-hardware complex of the universal assistive technology

All proposed methods, modules and systems have been implemented as software by C/C++ programming language in Microsoft Visual Studio toolkit using some free available and commercial libraries and software (OpenCV, OpenGL, DirectX, HTK, Julius, MFC, etc.) that works under control of Microsoft Windows operational systems (32/64 bit).

The system for audio-visual Russian speech recognition (AVSR) fuses mathematical models, methods and tools for automatic recognition of auditory speech and reading speech by lips movements [17-19]. The audio-visual system recognition system allows simultaneous processing both audio signal and visual speech (lips articulation) using an information fusion method based on asynchronous Coupled Hidden Markov Models (CHMM) [20] with weights of informativity of these speech modalities depending on audio noises. The recognition approach based on Coupled Hidden Markov Models of the first order allows making information fusion of feature vectors on the level of states of joint probabilistic CHMMs. It provides a possibility to take into account asynchrony (some time lag) between streams of elements of audio speech (phonemes) and visual speech (visemes), which is natural for human's speech production. The bimodal speech recognition system allows increasing accuracy and robustness of automatic speech recognition in noisy environments. It is also aimed for use in speech and multimodal interfaces for human-computer interaction with people having sensory and physical disabilities, including visually impaired and blind people and people with speech disabilities, for example, in the case of whispered speech without vocalization ability, etc.

The computer system for audio-visual Russian speech synthesis (3D "Talking head") [21] integrates virtual 3D models, methods and means for text-to-speech synthesis and video synthesis of lips articulation and facial mimics of the 3D model of human's head. The multimodal system allows processing entered texts and phrases in Russian and generating continuous Russian speech using an original rule-based method for synchronization and fusion of audio and visual modalities of synthesized speech [22]. The proposed method for modalities synchronization allows taking into account natural asynchrony between streams of corresponding visemes of phonemes (visemes always take the lead over phonemes in speech), which is influenced by dynamics of speech production (inertance of human's articulation organs) and co-articulation effects. This method increases both naturalness and intelligibility of generated speech. "Talking head" improves speech perception with respect to audio-only speech synthesizers, and especially in noisy environments. Also it is aimed for creation of human-like embodied conversational agents (ECA) [23] and avatars both for regular users and for persons with disabilities, for example, people with severe speech disabilities may use this system in order to replace own speech, as well as visually impaired people may rely on acoustic modality of synthesized speech for obtaining information from a computer). Multimedia demonstration of this system is available in the Internet [24].

The multimodal system for sign language and speech synthesis (3D "Signing avatar") integrates virtual models, methods and tools for video synthesis of elements of Russian sign language, visual speech (articulation), and audio synthesis of Russian speech [25, 26]. The main components of this system are: a text processor that takes text as an input to generate phoneme and viseme transcriptions, and sequences of HamNoSys (Hamburg Notation System) [27] codes for hand description of manual gestures; text-to-speech module that generates audio speech with time labeling corresponding to the entered text; virtual 3D model of human's head with controlled lips articulation, mimics and facial expressions; control unit for the talking head that synchronizes and integrates lips movements with synthesized audio signal; virtual 3D model of human's upper body, which is controlled by HamNoSys codes; audio-visual multimodal user interface that synchronizes output audio and visual speech and gesture modalities, integrates all the components for automatic generation of auditory speech, visual speech (articulation and facial expressions) and avatar's gestures of Russian sign language and fingerspelling, as well as outputs multimedia information. "Signing avatar" is aimed for organization of universal human-computer interaction both with regular users, who can perceive multimedia audio-visual-textual information, and with handicapped people, who have severe hearing disabilities or deaf, by generating manual gestures of Russian sign language and fingerspelling, as well as synthesizing visual speech (which is an obligatory component of any sign language), and audio-based verbal communication with visually impaired and blind people. Multimedia demonstration of this system is available in the Internet [28]. There was also some research on automatic recognition of Russian sign language and fingerspelling [29, 30]; however, we have only preliminary results with a prototype of such system.

The multimodal system for hands-free computer control ("ICANDO – Intellectual Computer AssistaNt for Disabled Operators") [31, 32] assembles methods, tools and sub-systems for automatic speech/voice commands recognition in Russian, English and French, video-based user's head tracking in order to interact with the graphical user interface of a PC without use of hands. Instead of use of standard information input devices (such as a keyboard, mouse, touch-screen, touch-pad, etc.) the system proposes to utilize head movements (head gestures) and speech commands. 40 voice commands ("Start", "Escape", "Double click", "Scroll down", etc.) for controlling virtual devices of mouse and keyboard compose system's vocabulary. This system is aimed for organization of multimodal user interface for hands-free human-computer interaction both for regular users (for instance, in edutainment applications, computer games, presentations, in the case when user's hands are busy) and for people with severe hand disabilities (for example, for persons with paralyzed hands or without hands). Demo-version and multimedia demonstration of this system is available on-line [33].

The control system of the assistive smart space [34] combines methods, tools and sub-systems for automatic recognition of speech commands and non-speech audio events (e.g., cry, cough, fall, etc.), which is aimed for analysis and monitoring of audio information in the assistive smart space, and video-based user fall detection, that allows the system to detect involuntary falls of persons inside the assistive smart space, determine extraordinary situations and notify on it. The assistive smart space (assisted living environment) is aimed to help single elderly people and persons with disabilities in independent living. In the case of an extraordinary situation with the user (e.g. at an involuntary fall of the person on the floor, his/her cry or a verbal appeal for help) the control system can detect this and inform a dispatcher service. The scaled-down model of the assisted smart space is equipped with microphone and video-camera arrays, as well as includes developed software modules and tools.

The proposed universal assistive technology is aimed for organization of novel ways of human-computer interaction for support, rehabilitation and education (including electronic learning [35]) of persons with disabilities and special needs, as well as for improving socio-economical integration of disabled people into the information society and increasing their independence from other persons.

4   Conclusion

We have presented the conceptual model and the architecture of the software-hardware complex of the universal assistive technology. It integrates several multi-modal systems: audio-visual Russian speech recognition system, text-to-audiovisual speech synthesis system ("Talking head"), sign language visual synthesis system ("Signing avatar"), multimodal hands-free PC control system (ICANDO), and the control system of the assistive smart space. The proposed universal assistive technology is aimed for organization of novel ways of human-computer interaction for support, rehabilitation and education of individuals with disabilities (visually impaired, deaf people, persons with dysfunctions of hands), and it is useful for regular able-bodied users as well.

Acknowledgements. This research is partially supported by the Russian Foundation for Basic Research (Project № 12-08-01265-a), by the Russian Humanitarian Scientific Foundation (Project № 12-04-12062), and by the Government of Russian Federation (Grant 074-U01).

References

1. Ambient Assisted Living Joint Programme, http://www.aal-europe.eu
2. The Convention on the Rights of Persons with Disabilities of the United Nations, http://www.un.org/disabilities/convention/conventionfull.shtml
3. The Russian State Programme "Accessible Environment", http://zhit-vmeste.ru
4. Tech Act, http://www.ok.gov/abletech/documents/Tech%20Act-Individuals%20with%20Disabilities.pdf
5. Argyropoulos, S., Moustakas, K., Karpov, A., Aran, O., Tzovaras, D., Tsakiris, T., Varni, G., Kwon, B.: A Multimodal Framework for the Communication of the Disabled. Journal on Multimodal User Interfaces 2(2), 105–116 (2008)
6. Hruz, M., Campr, P., Dikici, E., Kindirouglu, A., Krňoul, Z., Ronzhin, A., Sak, H., Schorno, D., Akarun, L., Aran, O., Karpov, A., Saraclar, M., Železný, M.: Automatic Fingersign to Speech Translation System. Journal on Multimodal User Interfaces 4(2), 61–79 (2011)
7. Stephanidis, C., Akoumianakis, D., Sfyrakis, M., Paramythis, A.: Universal accessibility in HCI: Process-oriented design guidelines an tool requirements. In: Proc. 4th ERCIM Workshop on User Interfaces for All, Stockholm, Sweden, pp. 19–21 (1998)
8. Savidis, A., Stephanidis, C.: Unified user interface design: designing universally accessible interfaces. Interacting with Computers 16(2), 243–270 (2004)
9. De Marsico, M., Kimani, S., Mirabella, V., Norman, K.L., Catarci, T.: A Proposal toward the Development of Accessible e-Learning Content by Human Involvement. Universal Access in the Information Society 5(2), 150–169 (2006)
10. Obrenovic, Z., Abascal, J., Starcevic, D.: Universal Accessibility as a Multimodal Design Issue. Communications of the ACM 50(5), 83–88 (2007)

11. Oviatt, S., Cohen, P.: Perceptual user interfaces: multimodal interfaces that process what comes naturally. Communications of the ACM 43(3), 45–53 (2000)
12. Martin, J.-C.: Towards "intelligent" cooperation between modalities. The example of a system enabling multimodal interaction with a map. In: Proc. IJCAI 1997 Workshop on Intelligent Multimodal Systems, Nagoya, Japan (1997)
13. Ong, S., Ranganath, S.: Automatic Sign Language Analysis: A Survey and the Future beyond Lexical Meaning. IEEE Transactions on Pattern Analysis and Machine Intelligence 27(6), 873–891 (2005)
14. Grauman, K.: Communication via Eye Blinks and Eyebrow Raises: Video-Based Human-Computer Interfaces. In: Grauman, K., Betke, M., Lombardi, J., Gips, J., Bradski, G. (eds.) Universal Access in the Information Society, vol. 4, pp. 359–373 (2003)
15. Graimann, B., Allison, B., Pfurtscheller, G.: Brain–Computer Interfaces: A Gentle Introduction. In: Brain-Computer Interfaces. The Frontiers Collection, pp. 1–27. Springer (2010)
16. Colwell, C., Petrie, H., Kornbrot, D., Hardwick, A., Furner, S.: Haptic Virtual Reality for Blind Computer Users. In: Proc. Annual ACM Conference on Assistive Technologies, ASSETS 1998, Marina del Rey, CA, USA, pp. 92–99 (1998)
17. Karpov, A., Ronzhin, A., Markov, K., Zelezny, M.: Viseme-Dependent Weight Optimization for CHMM-Based Audio-Visual Speech Recognition. In: Proc. INTERSPEECH 2010 International Conference, ISCA Association, Makuhari, Japan, pp. 2678–2681 (2010)
18. Karpov, A., Ronzhin, A., Kipyatkova, I., Zelezny, M.: Influence of Phone-viseme Temporal Correlations on Audiovisual STT and TTS Performance. In: Proc. 17th International Congress of Phonetic Sciences, ICPhS 2011, Hong Kong, China, pp. 1030–1033 (2011)
19. Karpov, A., Markov, K., Kipyatkova, I., Vazhenina, D., Ronzhin, A.: Large vocabulary Russian speech recognition using syntactico-statistical language modeling. Speech Communication 56, 213–228 (2014)
20. Nefian, A., Liang, L., Pi, X., Xiaoxiang, X., Mao, C., Murphy, K.: A Coupled HMM for Audio-Visual Speech Recognition. In: Proc. International Conference on Acoustics, Speech and Signal Processing, ICASSP 2002, Orlando, USA, pp. 2013–2016 (2002)
21. Karpov, A., Tsirulnik, L., Krňoul, Z., Ronzhin, A., Lobanov, B., Železný, M.: Audio-Visual Speech Asynchrony Modeling in a Talking Head. In: Proc. INTERSPEECH 2009 International Conference, Brighton, UK, pp. 2911–2914 (2009)
22. Karpov, A., Tsirulnik, L., Zelezny, M., Krnoul, Z., Ronzhin, A., Lobanov, B.: Study of Audio-Visual Asynchrony of Russian Speech for Improvement of Talking Head Naturalness. In: Proc. 13th International Conference SPECOM 2009, St. Petersburg, pp. 130–135 (2009)
23. Morales-Rodriguez, M.L., Pavard, B.: Embodied Conversational Agents: A New Kind of Tool for Motor Rehabilitation? In: Proc. 11th Annual International Workshop on Presence, PRESENCE 2008, Padova, Italy, pp. 95–99 (2008)
24. Multimedia demonstration of "Talking head" for audio-visual Russian speech synthesis, http://www.spiiras.nw.ru/speech/demo/th.avi
25. Karpov, A., Krnoul, Z., Zelezny, M., Ronzhin, A.: Multimodal Synthesizer for Russian and Czech Sign Languages and Audio-Visual Speech. In: Stephanidis, C., Antona, M. (eds.) UAHCI 2013, Part I. LNCS, vol. 8009, pp. 520–529. Springer, Heidelberg (2013)
26. Karpov, A., Železný, M.: Towards Russian Sign Language Synthesizer: Lexical Level. In: Proc. 5th International Workshop on Representation and Processing of Sign Languages at the LREC 2012, Istanbul, Turkey, pp. 83–86 (2012)

27. Hanke, T.: HamNoSys - Representing sign language data in language resources and language processing contexts. In: Proc. International Conference on Language Resources and Evaluation, LREC 2004, Lisbon, Portugal, pp. 1–6 (2004)
28. Multimedia demonstration of 3D "Signing avatar" for Russian sign language synthesis, http://www.spiiras.nw.ru/speech/demo/signlang.avi
29. Kindiroglu, A., Yalcın, H., Aran, O., Hruz, M., Campr, P., Akarun, L., Karpov, A.: Automatic Recognition of Fingerspelling Gestures in Multiple Languages for a Communication Interface for the Disabled. Pattern Recognition and Image Analysis 22(4), 527–536 (2012)
30. Kindiroglu, A., Yalcın, H., Aran, O., Hruz, M., Campr, P., Akarun, L., Karpov, A.: Multilingual Fingerspelling Recognition in a Handicapped Kiosk. Pattern Recognition and Image Analysis 21(3), 402–406 (2011)
31. Karpov, A., Ronzhin, A., Kipyatkova, I.: An Assistive Bi-modal User Interface Integrating Multi-channel Speech Recognition and Computer Vision. In: Jacko, J.A. (ed.) Human-Computer Interaction, Part II, HCII 2011. LNCS, vol. 6762, pp. 454–463. Springer, Heidelberg (2011)
32. Karpov, A., Ronzhin, A.: ICANDO: Low Cost Multimodal Interface for Hand Disabled People. Journal on Multimodal User Interfaces 1(2), 21–29 (2007)
33. Demonstration of multimodal hands-free PC control system (ICANDO), http://www.spiiras.nw.ru/speech/demo/assistive.html
34. Demiröz, B., Ari, I., Ronzhin, A., Çoban, A., Yalçın, H., Karpov, A., Akarun, L.: Multimodal Assisted Living Environment. Report on research project at eNTERFACE-2011 Summer Workshop on Multimodal Interfaces, Pilsen, Czech Republic (2011), http://www.cmpe.boun.edu.tr/~ari/files/demiroz2011enterface.pdf
35. De Marsico, M., Sterbini, A., Temperini, M.: A Framework to Support Social-Collaborative Personalized e-Learning. In: Kurosu, M. (ed.) HCII/HCI 2013, Part II. LNCS, vol. 8005, pp. 351–360. Springer, Heidelberg (2013)

Multi-sensor Technology and Fuzzy Logic for Dancer's Motion Analysis and Performance Evaluation within a 3D Virtual Environment

Alexandros Kitsikidis[1], Kosmas Dimitropoulos[1],
Erdal Yilmaz[2], Stella Douka[3], and Nikos Grammalidis[1]

[1] Informatics and Telematics Institute, ITI-CERTH,
1st Km Thermi-Panorama Rd, Thessaloniki, Greece
{ajinchv,dimitrop,ngramm}@iti.gr
[2] KANAVA Tech, Turkey
erdal.yilmaz@kanavatech.com
[3] Department of Physical Education and Sport Science,
Aristotle University of Thessaloniki, Greece
sdouka@phed.auth.gr

Abstract. In this paper, we describe a novel methodology for dance learning and evaluation using multi-sensor and 3D gaming technology. The learners are captured during dancing, while an avatar visualizes their motion using fused input from multiple sensors. Motion analysis and fuzzy-logic are employed for the evaluation of the learners' performance against the performance of an expert. Specifically, a two level Fuzzy Inference System is proposed which uses as input low level skeletal data and high level motion recognition probabilities for the evaluation of dancer's performance. Tests with real dancers, both learners and experts, dancing Tsamiko, a very popular traditional Greek dance, are presented showing the potential of the proposed method.

Keywords: Kinect, fuzzy inference system, dance performance evaluation, Unity.

1 Introduction

As traditional dances are forms of intangible cultural heritage, there is always a risk that certain elements of this culture could die out or disappear if they are not safeguarded and transmitted. ICT technologies can play an important role in their preservation, e.g. in the form of virtual learning systems, assisting in the transmission of dancing knowledge. Such systems employ various sensors to capture the movements of the learner, analyse the movement and provide a feedback, thus facilitating the learning procedure [1]. Automatic performance evaluation in the form of scoring and visual feedback through a 3D virtual environment can significantly improve the competency of the learner.

C. Stephanidis and M. Antona (Eds.): UAHCI/HCII 2014, Part I, LNCS 8513, pp. 379–390, 2014.
© Springer International Publishing Switzerland 2014

Detection, classification and evaluation of dance gestures and performances are active topics of research [2], while commercial products also exist, such as the Harmonix' Dance Central video game series [3], where a player tries to imitate the motion demonstrated by an animated character. Many research projects have been conducted on the topic of dance assistance and evaluation employing various sensor technologies. Saltate![4] is a wireless prototype system to support beginners of ballroom dancing. It acquires data from force sensors mounted under the dancers' feet, detects steps, and compares their timing to the timing of beats in the music playing, thus detecting mistakes. Sensable project [5] also employs wireless sensor modules, worn at the wrists of dancers, which capture motions in dance ensembles. The VR-Theater project [6] allows choreographers to enter the desired choreography moves with a user-friendly user interface, or even to record the movements of a specific performer using motion capture techniques. Also, different kinds of augmented feedback (tactile, video, sound) for learning basic dance choreographies are investigated in [7].

Markerless motion capture based on real-time depth sensing systems have recently emerged with the release of Microsoft Kinect [8] and other similar depth cameras like Asus Xtion [9]. These sensors offer a cost-effective alternative to more expensive inertial and optical motion capture systems. In [10], evaluation of dance performance is conducted against the performance of a professional using skeleton tracking data captured by Kinect sensor, visualized within 3D virtual environments.

In this paper, we propose a dance evaluation system, which offers two novel features. First, a multi-Kinect acquisition system is used, where synchronized skeletal data from each sensor are fused in order to improve the quality of the final skeletal tracking, based on our previous work [11]. Secondly, we propose a scoring system based on fuzzy inference. The reasons for choosing fuzzy inference are the following: i) the ability to produce realistic and less predictable reactions, ii) the ability to capture a real human knowledge-base and use it extensively with minimal coding and iii) the use of an AI technique that is more suitable to model complex virtual behaviour.

The evaluation of a dancer is performed based on low level and high level features. Low level features are the fused skeletal tracking data and high level features are the motion recognition probabilities are used by the 3D virtual environment for the evaluation of the dancer's performance against an expert's performance and the generation of visual feedback. The 3D environment is based on Unity 3D engine [12], which is a popular multiple platform gaming and visualization solution among the graphics and gaming community.

2   Methodology

The architecture of the proposed system is illustrated in Fig. 1. Specifically, for capturing we use several Kinect sensors placed around the dancer. Captured skeletal data consists of 3D position and rotation data (relative to a reference coordinate system centred at the origin of each sensor) of 20 predefined skeletal joints of the dancer's body, along with the confidence level of tracking of each joint. A skeletal fusion procedure is proposed to combine the data obtained from multiple sensors onto a single fused skeleton (described in section 2.1), which is then used for motion analysis of the dancer. Subsequently, the evaluation of the dancer's performance takes place. The low level features are extracted to calculate the distance metrics (section 2.2). In addition, the motion analysis module performs motion recognition to extract high level features (section 2.3). Those features are subsequently provided to the Fuzzy Inference System, where the final evaluation of the dancer takes place (section 3). Moreover, the visualization module provides a 3D environment for the learner to examine his performance along with the numerical and textual performance grading. The visualization module is implemented in Unity and takes input from the fused skeletal animation data. The resulting animation screenshots are shown in Fig. 2.

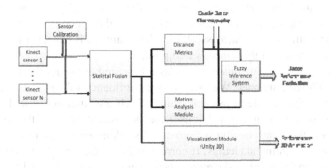

Fig. 1. System architecture overview

Fig. 2. Visualisation of an expert dancing the tsamiko dance. A 3D avatar wearing a traditional costume is animated in Unity 3D using the fused skeletal animation data acquired during the recording session.

2.1 Skeletal Fusion

Skeletal fusion is the process of combining skeletal data captured by multiple sensors into a single, more robust skeletal representation. It allows to reduce occlusion and self-occlusion problems and to increase the total area of coverage. Prior to fusion, sensor calibration procedure must take place in order to estimate the rigid transformation between the coordinate systems of each sensor and the reference sensor. We use

Iterative Closest Point algorithm [13] implementation found in the Point Cloud Library (PCL, http://pointclouds.org/) [14] to estimate the rigid transformation (Rotation-Translation) which is subsequently used to register the skeleton captured by each sensor in the reference coordinate system.

The skeletal fusion is performed on registered skeletons, i.e. the representations of each skeleton transformed to the coordinate system of the reference sensor. This is accomplished by multiplying the skeleton joint positions by the corresponding RT matrix, estimated in the calibration process. Then, a skeletal fusion procedure is used to combine these registered skeletons into a single skeleton representation (**Fig. 3**) according to a specific fusion strategy.

The proposed fusion strategy is applied on joint positional data, which can be easily extended on joint rotations as well. Initially, the sum of all joint confidence levels per skeleton is computed and the skeleton with the highest total is selected. Since this is the skeleton with the most successfully tracked joints, it is expected to be the most accurate representation of the dancer's real pose.

We consider the joints of this skeleton as a base and construct the fused skeleton joints in the following manner. We examine the confidence values of each joint of the base skeleton. There are three possible values: high, medium and low. If the confidence of the base joint is high, it is left as is for the fused skeleton. If the confidence is medium or low, the joint position is corrected by taking into account the position of this joint in the remaining skeletons. If corresponding joints with high confidence are found in any of the remaining skeletons, their average position is used to replace the position value of the joint. Otherwise, the same procedure is applied for joints containing medium confidence values. Finally, if only low confidence joints are present, their average is used as a position value of the fused joint.

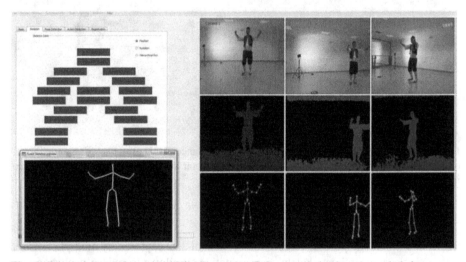

Fig. 3. Fused skeleton from three Kinect sensors. Color maps, depth maps and skeleton previews of each sensor along with the resulting fused skeleton are displayed.

As a last step, a stabilization filtering is applied in order to overcome problems due to the rapid changes in joint position from frame to frame, which may occur because of the use of joint position averaging in our fusion strategy. We use a time window of three frames, to keep the last three high-confidence positions for each joint. The centroid of these three previous positions is calculated and updated for each frame. If the Euclidean distance between a joint position and this centroid is higher than a certain threshold, then we replace the joint position with the value of the centroid, so as to avoid rapid changes in joint positions. The thresholds are different for each joint, since it is expected that some joints (hands and feet) move more rapidly than others. In our experiments of Tsamiko dance these thresholds were set to 40cm for the feet joints and 20cm for the remaining joints.

2.2 Distance Metrics

To evaluate the performance of a dancer, specific metrics should be defined for measuring the motion similarity between a learner and an expert. Taking into account that in Tsamiko dance leg movements constitute the key element of the choreography, in this paper we propose two metrics for measuring the motion accuracy of the dancer. Specifically, we define the knee-distance D_K and the ankle distance D_A for each frame as (Fig. 4 A):

$$D_K = |K_L - K_R| \tag{1}$$

$$D_A = |A_L - A_R| \tag{2}$$

However, both distances heavily depend on the height of the dancer that is their values change from dancer to dancer. To ensure the invariance of the proposed metrics (in terms of dancer's height), a specific normalization process is proposed. More specifically, we calculate the normalized distances by dividing the proposed metrics by the distance of the path connecting the joints. For the normalized knee-distance $\widehat{D}_K$, the path is computed by dividing the distance between the knee joints by the sum of the distances between the *Left Knee, Left Hip, Root, Right Hip* and *Right Knee* joints:

$$\widehat{D}_K = \frac{D_K}{|K_L - H_L| + |H_L - R| + |R - H_R| + |H_R - K_R|} \tag{3}$$

The normalized ankle distance $\widehat{D}_A$ is calculated in a similar manner:

$$\widehat{D}_A = \frac{D_A}{|A_L - K_L| + |K_L - H_L| + |H_L - R| + |R - H_R| + |H_R - K_R| + |K_R - A_R|} \tag{4}$$

The estimation of the above metrics is repeated in each time instant, i.e. frame, resulting in the creation of time series like the ones presented in Fig. 4 B. To compare the similarity of these time series we introduce the use of two motion accuracy scores S_K and S_A, which are computed by calculating the maximum correlation coefficient between the testing subject's normalized distances ($\widehat{D}_K t$) and the reference subject's normalized distances ($\widehat{D}_K r$). The maximum correlation coefficient is computed by iteratively shifting the testing signal by one sample at a time, with respect to the reference signal and by computing the maximum correlation coefficient over all these shifts. The shifting step ranges from 1 sample to 250 samples, which is approximately the duration of a single dancing cycle of Tsamiko dance. The correlation coefficient is defined as:

$$R = \frac{\sigma_{x,y}}{\sqrt{\sigma_x * \sigma_y}} \quad (5)$$

Where:

$$\sigma_{x,y} = E[(x - E[x])(y - E[y])] \quad (6)$$

$$\sigma_x = E[x^2] - \mu_x^2 \quad (7)$$

$$\sigma_y = E[y^2] - \mu_y^2 \quad (8)$$

where $E[\ ]$ is the expected value and μ is the mean value.

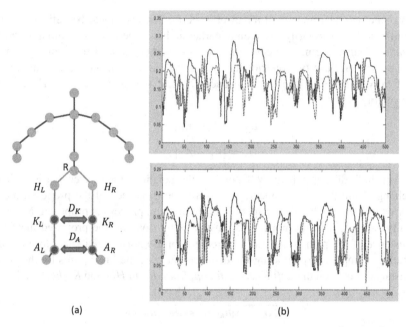

(a)   (b)

Fig. 4. a) The knee distance and the ankle distance metric b) Time series of $\widehat{D}_K$ and $\widehat{D}_A$ of two dancers.

2.3   Motion Analysis

The motion analysis subsystem (Fig. 5) performs the detection of the basic motion patterns, in our case, the three dance movements of the Tsamiko dance. The correct choreography of this dance consists of sequential repetition of these three moves. Thus, we derive a choreography score S_{Ch} which is the precision of the correct detection of those motion patterns by the motion analysis subsystem.

A pre-processing step for motion analysis is a view-invariance transform of the skeleton, by translating each joint position relative to the root joint and subsequently rotating the skeleton around the y axis so that it is facing towards the positive z direction. Next, the skeleton is split into five parts: torso, left hand, right hand, left foot and right foot, each consisting from a root and children joints. For each skeleton part we generate a feature vector consisting of positions of joints relative to the root joint of the part. In fact, those feature vectors constitute a representation of a dancer's posture. For each skeleton part, a codebook of k basic postures is defined using k-means clustering in a large set of postures obtained from recorded training sequences. A multiclass SVM classifier is used to classify each incoming feature vector as a specific posture from this posture codebook. Thus, each motion sequence is transformed to a sequence of symbols of this codebook, one sequence per body part. Those sequences are fed to the final stage of the motion analysis subsystem, which consist of a Hidden-state Conditional Random Fields classifier (HCRF).

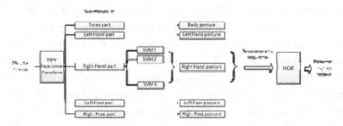

Fig. 5. Motion analysis module

HCRFs [15][16] are a class of statistical modelling method (discriminative undirected probabilistic graphical model) often applied to pattern recognition problems and machine learning in general. HCRFs are a generalization of / is alternative to Hidden Markov Models and are popular in natural language processing, object recognition and motion recognition tasks. We use multi-class HCRF model trained on a set of M basic motion patterns (the three dance moves of Tsamiko). For the training of the HCRFs we use labelled sequences described in the previous paragraph. For the detection phase HCRFs classifier provides a probability of the model of the HCRF fitting the observed sequence, thus it is labelled accordingly.

3   Fuzzy Inference System

For the evaluation of the dancer's performance against an expert's performance a two level Fuzzy Inference System (FIS) was designed. FIS is a way of mapping an input space to an output space using a collection of fuzzy membership functions and rules i.e. linguistic statements in the form of *if....then* that describe how the FIS should make a decision. The proposed FIS system is based on Mamdani method [17], which is widely accepted for capturing expert's knowledge and allows the description of the domain knowledge in a more intuitive, human like manner.

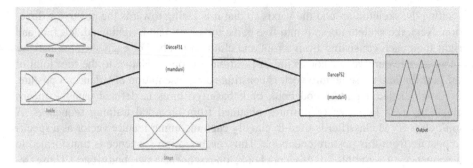

Fig. 6. The structure of the two-level fuzzy inference system

Low level features obtained from raw skeletal tracking data and high level motion recognition probabilities are used as input to the two-level FIS for the evaluation of the dancer's performance. The proposed FIS architecture is illustrated in Fig. 6. The estimated maximum correlation coefficients between the normalized joint distances (knee distance and ankle distance) S_K and S_A of the expert and the learner dancer are fed as input to the first FIS to generate the motion accuracy index. While this index contains meaningful information about the motion of the dancer, little information is provided regarding the proper execution of the choreography e.g. it is difficult to discriminate whether the dancer cannot follow the choreography or he/she cannot be synchronized with the music. To address this issue, besides the output of the first FIS i.e. the motion accuracy index, the percentage of the correct identified motion patterns of the learner dancer (the choreography score S_{Ch} provided by the motion analysis module) is also fed as input to the second FIS. The final output is converted into human understandable messages (defuzzification), such as low, medium and high performance score.

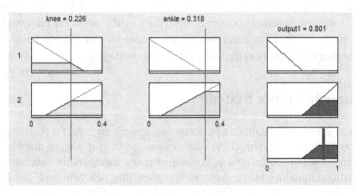

Fig. 7. The output of the first FIS in the case of high motion accuracy scores leading to high motion accuracy index.

The set of rules used for building the fuzzy inference of the first FIS are described below together with the example of an output Fig. 7:

- If S_K is High and S_A is High then 'motion accuracy index' is High
- If S_K is Low and S_A is Low then 'motion accuracy index' is Low

Similarly, the set of rules used for building the fuzzy inference of the second FIS are described below:

- If 'motion accuracy index' is High and 'choreography score' is High then 'dancing performance' is High
- If 'motion accuracy index' is Low and 'choreography score' is Low then 'dancing performance' is Low
- If 'motion accuracy index' is Low and 'choreography score' is High then 'dancing performance' is Medium

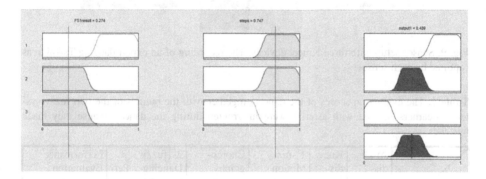

Fig. 8. The output of the second FIS in the case of low motion accuracy index and high choreography accuracy

Fig. 8 illustrates an example of low motion accuracy index and high choreography accuracy. In this case, while the dancer can follow the choreography i.e. the expected motion patterns are identified accurately, he/she cannot be synchronized with the music and, therefore, a low motion accuracy index is produced. Since, the above case is satisfied by the third fuzzy rule, the performance of the dancer is considered as medium.

4   Experimental Results

For the evaluation of our methodology we recorded a performance of an expert along with performances of experienced dancers and learners of the Greek traditional Tsamiko dance. Tsamiko is a popular traditional folk dance which follows a strict and slow tempo. The steps are relatively easy to execute but must be precise and strictly on beat. We captured the movements of the dancers using a setup consisting of three

Kinect sensors, placed in front of a dancer. The reference sensor was placed directly in front, and the other two at the sides, creating an arc topology (Fig. 9). This setup allowed for the dancers to have a freedom of movement of about 2,5 meters along a straight line.

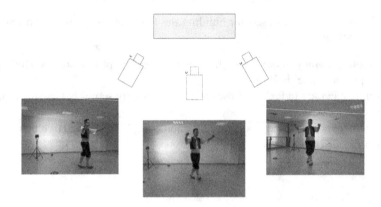

Fig. 9. Sensor setup with three Kinect devices. The recording of an expert dancing Tsamiko as captured by each sensor.

Table 1. The evaluation scores of the dancers together with the outputs of the two fuzzy systems. Learners marked with asterisk were interrupted during the dance because they made mistakes.

	Ankle distance score	Knee distance score	1st fuzzy Motion Accuracy index	Choreography precision score	2nd fuzzy Dancing Performance index	Performance Evaluation Low: <0.4 Medium:0.4-0.6 High: >0.6
Experienced dancer 1	0,28	0,26	**0.7244**	**100%**	**0.8500**	**High**
Experienced dancer 2	0,33	0,33	**0.8270**	**100%**	**0.8608**	**High**
Learner 1	0,19	0,29	**0.7243**	65%	0.5000	Medium
Learner 2	0,22	0,13	0.4221	68.42%	0.3411	Low
Learner 3 *	0,13	0,11	0.2821	70.58%	0.3146	Low
Learner 4	0,18	0,13	0.3788	**77.78%**	0.500	Medium
Learner 5	0,14	0,08	0.1969	40%	0.1414	Low
Learner 6	0,13	0,13	0.3358	55.56%	0.1575	Low
Learner 7	0,17	0,15	0.4044	66.67%	0.2319	Low
Learner 8 *	0,17	0,15	0.4031	66.67%	0.2258	Low

There were two recording sessions performed using the same setup. During the first session the expert and two experienced dancers were captured, and during the second session eight students of different level of experience participated in the experiments. Each person was recorded for the duration of a single dance (approx. 4

minutes). The performance of all dancers was compared against that of an expert, who is considered as a reference. First, the motion accuracy scores S_K and S_A were computed by comparison to the expert. Then, the recorded sequences were manually annotated and fed to the motion classifier, which detected the three motion patterns of Tsamiko dance. The choreography score S_{Ch} was then computed as the percentage of the motion patterns that are identified correctly, i.e. the precision of the recognition. Those were provided as input to the FIS to obtain the final performance evaluation score.

The results obtained are illustrated in Table 1. As expected, both experts received high score in their performance evaluation, since they had high motion accuracy scores and also perfect choreography precision. The learners, on the other hand received medium and low scores. Learner 1 had high motion accuracy but relatively low choreography precision, while for student 4 the opposite is true. They both were graded as medium by the system. The rest of the learners received low rating, with varying performance indexes (they were not equally bad), since they had both motion accuracy and choreography scores low.

5   Conclusions and Future Work

This paper presents a methodology for automatic dance evaluation, intended to be used in dance learning systems. The learners are captured during dancing, while an 3-D avatar is used to visualize their motion. The main contributions are the use of a multi-Kinect motion capture and the definition of a new scoring system based on fuzzy inference. Based on the obtained experimental results, the system seems to properly distinguish between the varying levels of dance expertise, so it is suitable to be used as a tool to assess the learners dancing performance. In the future, a feedback can be provided to the user, based on this performance evaluation, together with a visualization of both user and expert performances, which could significantly assist dance learning.

Acknowledgement. The research leading to these results has received funding from the European Community's Seventh Framework Programme (FP7-ICT-2011-9) under grant agreement no FP7-ICT-600676 "i-Treasures: Intangible Treasures - Capturing the Intangible Cultural Heritage and Learning the Rare Know-How of Living Human Treasures".

References

1. Essid, S., Alexiadis, D., Tournemenne, R., Gowing, M., Kelly, P., Monaghan, D., Daras, P., Drimeau, A., O'connor, N.: An Advanced Virtual Dance Performance Evaluator. In: IEEE International Conference on Acoustics, Speech and Signal Processing (ICASSP 2012), Kyoto, Japan, March 25-30 (2012)
2. Raptis, M., Kirovski, D., Hoppe, H.: Real-time classification of dance gestures from skeleton animation. In: Proceedings of the 2011 ACM SIGGRAPH/Eurographics Symposium on Computer Animation, Vancouver, British Columbia, Canada, August 5-7 (2011)

3. Dance central, http://www.dancecentral.com/
4. Drobny, D., Weiss, M., Borchers, J.: Saltate! - A Sensor-Based System to Support Dance Beginners. In: CHI 2009: Extended Abstracts on Human Factors in Computing Systems, pp. 3943–3948. ACM, New York (2009)
5. Aylward, R.: Sensemble: A Wireless Inertial Sensor System for InteractiveDance and Collective Motion Analysis. Masters of Science in Media Arts and Sciences, Massachusetts Institute of Technology (2006)
6. VR-Theater project, http://avrlab.iti.gr/HTML/Projects/current/VRTHEATER.htm
7. Drobny, D., Borchers, J.: Learning Basic Dance Choreographies with different Augmented Feedback Modalities. In: CHI 2010: Extended Abstracts on Human Factors in Computing Systems. ACM Press, New York (2010) .
8. Kinect for Windows | Voice, Movement & Gesture Recognition Technology (2013), http://www.microsoft.com/en-us/kinectforwindows/
9. Asus Xtion PRO, http://www.asus.com/Multimedia/Xtion_PRO/
10. Alexiadis, D., Kelly, P., Daras, P., O'Connor, N., Boubekeur, T., Moussa, M.: Evaluating a dancer's performance using kinect-based skeleton tracking. In: Proceedings of the 19th ACM International Conference on Multimedia (MM 2011), pp. 659–662. ACM, New York (2011)
11. Kitsikidis, A., Dimitropoulos, K., Douka, S., Grammalidis, N.: Dance Analysis using Multiple Kinect Sensors. In: VISAPP 2014, Lisbon, Portugal, January 5-8 (2014)
12. Unity, http://unity3d.com
13. Besl, P., McKay, N.: A Method for Registration of 3-D Shapes. IEEE Trans. on Pattern Analysis and Machine Intelligence 14(2), 239–256 (1992)
14. Rusu, B., Cousins, S.: 3D is here: Point Cloud Library (PCL). In: 2011 IEEE International Conference on Robotics and Automation (ICRA), May 9-13, pp. 1–4 (2011)
15. Wang, S., Quattoni, A., Morency, L.-P., Demirdjian, D., Darrell, T.: Hidden Conditional Random Fields for Gesture Recognition. In: Proceedings of the IEEE Conference on Computer Vision and Pattern Recognition (June 2006)
16. Quattoni, A., Collins, M., Darrell, T.: Conditional Random Fields for Object Recognition. In: Neural Information Processing Systems (2004)
17. Mamdani, E.H., Assilian, S.: An experiment in linguistic synthesis with a fuzzy logic controller. International Journal of Man-Machine Studies 7(1), 1–13 (1975)

A Detecting Sensor as Interface for Children with Severe Physical Disabilities

Chien-Yu Lin

Department of special education, National University of Tainan, Tainan, Taiwan
`linchienyu@mail.nutn.edu.tw`

Abstract. Children with cerebral palsy and physical disabilities could not control the standard device, thus the purpose of this study was to redesign the interactive effect for children with physical disabilities. This study extended Makey Makey and scratch software to evaluate the possibility of operate interactive game with a high resistance switching system, whether two children (one is cerebral palsy ,the other is severely physical disabilities) would be able to participant actively by using open source software. This study was following single-subject research using ABAB designs in which A indicated the baseline and B indicated intervention. The data showed that two children with different physical disabilities significantly increased their scores on normal game. From the study, they could execute better performance during the intervention phases.

Keywords: physical disabilities, cerebral palsy, conductive substance, interface, intuition.

1 Introduction

In recent years, with technological advances, there has been using technology for special need [1],but, one of the challenges in human–computer interaction is to design systems that are not only usable but also appealing to users [2], through assistive technology for people with disabilities , those studies are very encouraging the possibility of students with multiple disabilities to request and choose among environmental stimulation with the help of microswitch and computer technology [3]. In order to run such systems effectively, efficiently and safely, much research has been developed taking into account human performance, technological possibilities [4], a computer task-based screening test could be useful for this purpose.

The adapted keyboards may have different shapes and sizes or may include keyguard covers (i.e., to facilitate the motor responses required for the writing activity and guide such responses to target one letter at a time). In spite of their facilitative features, the overall effectiveness of these keyboards may be negligible and/or their use may be very tiring for participants who present particularly serious motor disabilities [5], although many multi-screen has change the method of operate the interface, only use finger or body move to sent to information to computer and control it, special participation in more leisure activities has been shown to improve participants' physical fitness and adjustment to a life with disabilities, the majority available for

C. Stephanidis and M. Antona (Eds.): UAHCI/HCII 2014, Part I, LNCS 8513, pp. 391–397, 2014.

people with severe physical limitations is often extremely with different barriers ,so it is not useful for people with severe physical disabilities.

People with physical disabilities experience limitations in fine motor control, strength, and range of motion. These deficits can dramatically limit their ability to perform daily tasks independently, such as dressing, hair combing, and bathing. In addition, these deficits can reduce participation in community and leisure activities [6]. Participation in leisure activities is a fundamental human right and an important factor of life quality. Many people with intellectual disabilities also have physical difficulties which prevent them from using standard computer control devices. Custom made alternative devices for those with special needs expensive and the low unit turnover makes the prospect unattractive to potential manufacturers [7].

Just as the art games on console systems such as Microsoft Xbox, Nintendo Wii or Sony PlayStation see a recent review. It's not only for fun ,but also applied in rehabilitation treatment, depend on the therapeutic systems could leverage the games available [8]. Recently, efforts have been made to assess new sensors (A conductive substance). MaKey MaKey is an invention kit. MaKey MaKey is a printed circuit board running by Arduino Leonardo firmware [9]. It uses the human interface device (HID) protocol to communicate with the computer, and it can send keypresses. The use of Makey Makey board create a novel game controller to control different types of Flash or scratch games.

With the progress of technology, the input interface from relied on the mouse and keyboard gradually transfer to touch screen. Although the special character of touch screen is focus on learned and operated more easily by the user [10], but it could not be suit for people with physical disabilities. The MaKey MaKey uses high resistance switching to detect when you've made a connection, even though materials aren't very conductive. This study used aids on children with disabilities, compare with the expert device, the advantage is this kit could be redesign the relative conductive substance for children with physical disabilities to extent their activities.

2   Material and Methods

2.1   Participants

Participant A is an 8th grader, 14 years old, female. Her disabled condition is severely physical disabilities along with severely mental disabilities, belongs to severely multiple disabilities, type of cerebral palsy convulsions. Because of cerebral palsy convulsions, she only has operated ability on his left hand. Her right hand and both legs cannot operate mouse and bottom because of convulsions cause by tension. When she sits on kinder chair, if you don't tie on her H-suspenders, her body will suddenly tilt forward. Her upper arm and forearm have moving ability; all of her joints can move normally, and the balance of her body cannot be remaining for a long time.

Participant B is an 6th grader, 12 years old, male. His disabled condition is severely physical disabilities along with moderately mental disabilities. All of his limbs are involuntarily twitch so he needs to sits on customization Kinder chair. He cannot operate mouse and keyboard with his hands and feet. He can only control his head to move in the whole body, thus he can't join ordinary activity.

2.2   Material and Setting

The computer presented the interactive effect and recorded data. The game was de-sign by scratch software. The input device used in this study is aluminum foil . The goal for participants was to acquire the touch of any part of aluminum foil. Participant A could control the standard keyboard, but because her high tension, the standard is not a good input tool for her. Participant B could not control the standard keyboard, he can only move a part of his hand, others could not be moved, so this study design two aluminum foil blocks stick on both his ears' side of   his wheelchair seat back.

The computer was put on the table, and the participant sat in a chair(or wheel-chair), facing the computer screen.

2.3   General Procedure

This study focuses on discussing the effect of adjusted keyboard and interactive com-puter game training on operate computer in helping people with physical disabilities.

In the design of interactive effect, this study used Scratch as the software. From Scratch software, designer can create their own interactive stories, games, and anima-tions [11]. This study was focus on how to use touch conductive substance to operate whether there are response , at the beginning ,there is a black dot on the screen, the original design is when the black dot on the right, press the right arrow of the key-board, the black dot received signal and moved to the left of the screen, the operator also got score as feedback , because the participants are people with physical disabili-ties and they response slower than normal people relatively, so the operate process time is set to 1 minute.

The input device is standard keyboard. Fig. 1.illustrates the computer screens. The research adopted scratch software technology [12]. To control the experiment, this study decrease the variables. The screen was white background and a black dot. When the participant press   the right arrow key 1 time, the black will move to the right side(Fig. 1 left), then press the left arrow key 1 time, the black will move to the left side right(Fig. 1 right).

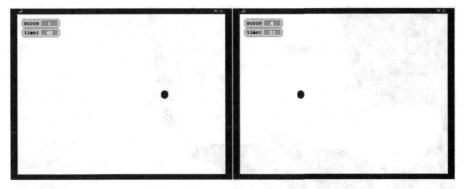

Fig. 1. Scratch interface and experiment design

The experimental design adopted ABAB reversal design for single-subject research, in which A (baseline phase) was followed by B (intervention phase), a return to baseline phase, and then a final intervention phase. The presented intervention phases while the via Makey Makey system.

The decision to limit the baseline was based on previous observation suggesting that the participants were not able to or difficult to press the button of standard keyboard. In intervention phase, The input device is adjusted aluminum foil and use Makey Makey as a connect tool between aluminum foil and computer. In this phase, worth 3 or more points, the interactive technology is introduced. Intervention I, to collect at least three points or more, and make sure the data of participant's touch the aluminum foil to maintain at least three points. A total of 6 points was achievable in this phase.

3   Results

The results from this study are based primarily on descriptive and qualitative analyses of data processing, and also participant interviews to ascertain differences between the use of interactive technological games with standard keyboard or adjustment substance. The data collected from the 4 phases were used to create a graph, where the x-axis indicates the 4 different phases and points scored while the y-axis represents the times that the participant press the correct press so get the feedback.

3.1   Participant A

Participant A, taking and operating items from left hand side is difficult. The area which is much easier for her hand to work is 20cm in front of his chest, which is about 25cmX25cm. When she operates her fingers, her thumb, ring finger and little finger will shrink back involuntarily. As the function of her hand, when she operates the keyboard, her basic ability to grab and hold is poor. Though she can still grab items which sizes are like beads, the accuracy is poor, which needs to try many times to do this. As her cognitive ability, when the questions are easy, she can express her feeling. She can also understand basic oral and gesture instructions, just as Fig. 2.

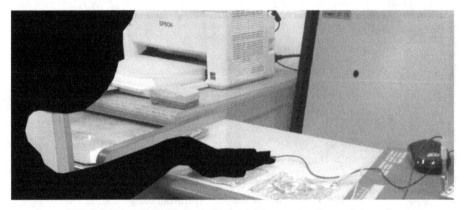

Fig. 2. intervention phases via Makey Makey system for participant A

Fig.3.shows A's data. In baseline I, The correct press scores' range is 4-11 in a minute; the average at baseline I scores was 8.

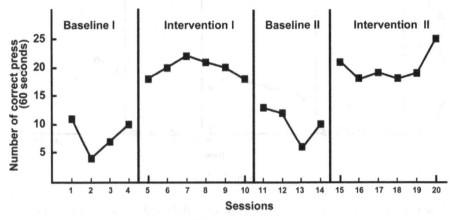

Fig. 3. A's data

3.2 Participant B

Our study adjust the original Kinder chair, installing aluminum foil at both sides of the part of B's head of the Kinder chair, and make sure that there are some space between the aluminum foil and both his ears' side. When head is at the middle, it will not be connected into any aluminum foil and lead to electric conduction. When the experiment start, B looks at the screen first, and tilt his face to the right hand side, let his face touch the aluminum foil, this is the same as operate the right arrow key , get the point. And then tilt his face to the left hand side, let his face touch the aluminum foil, this is the same as operate the left arrow key, just as Fig. 4.

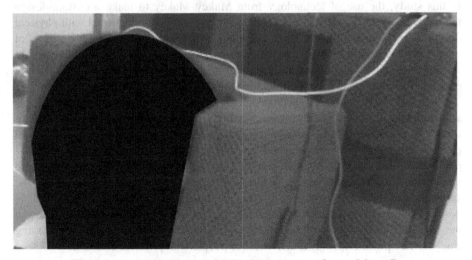

Fig. 4. intervention phases via Makey Makey system for participant B

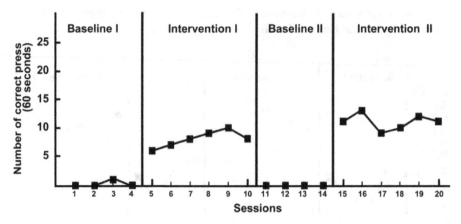

Fig. 5. B's data

Before the experiment, we told B to touch the right and left arrow key can have a interaction with the items in the screen, and show it to him for one time. When the experiment starts, put keyboard in front of him, at the site his hands can touch. At the process of the baseline experiment, he can't move his hands to the right and left arrow key on the keyboard, so most of that didn't get point. The point he get is because his hands touch the whole keyboard and accidently touch the right arrow key.

At the process of the intervention experiment, from the experience intervention I, he found if he let his head in a higher position, his cheek could be touch the aluminum foil easier, just as Fig.5.

4   Discussion

In this study, the use of technology from Makey Makey to make a custom-design interactive basic program was investigated for an individual diagnosed with physical disabilities. The use of Makey Makey interactive technology is to provide a variety of input substance, such as fruits, water, hairs and other electrically conductive substance in helping overcome barriers from physical disabilities, extending the different effect on different game and rehabilitation treatment.

After this study, the researchers design an activity in a daycare center for people with mind or physical disabilities, it only revise the input signal components to fit users' needs and made it be adjusted in accordance with the user's obstacles. Partial patients with paralysis but clear consciousness , muscle and nerve damage, limb hypoplasia, spinal cord injury, the elderly, and gradually freeze people have limb movement disorder, these patients still could move on some parts of their limb, the application of the results of this study could be develop interactive hardware interface design for the part of the limb that still active. Just use the same concept to redesign the device, let the limb   move and touch the conductive substance instead of pressing single switch process that bring activities for people with physical disabilities.

Acknowledgements. This work supported by Taiwan, NSC 100-2410-H-024-028-MY2.

References

1. Kagohara, D.M., Sigafoos, J., Achmadi, D., O'Reilly, M., Lancioni, G.: Teaching children with autism spectrum disorders to check the spelling of words. Research in Autism Spectrum Disorders 6, 304–310 (2012)
2. Bonnardel, N., Piolat, A., Bigot, L.L.: The impact of colour on Website appeal and users' cognitive processes. Displays 32, 69–80 (2011)
3. Lin, C.Y., Lin, M.C., Shih, L.J., Hu, W.H.: Application of low-cost interactive floors on special education and assistive technology. International Journal of Elementary Education 1(1), 1–7 (2013)
4. Carvalho, P.V.R., dos Santos, I.L., Gomes, J.O., Borges, M.R.S., Guerlain, S.: Human factors approach for evaluation and redesign of human–system interfaces of a nuclear power plant simulator. Displays 29, 273–284 (2008)
5. Lancioni, G.E., Singh, N.N., O'Reilly, M.F., Sigafoos, J., Green, V., Oliva, D., Lang, R.: Microswitch and keyboard-emulator technology to facilitate the writing performance of persons with extensive motor disabilities. Research in Developmental Disabilities 32(2), 576–582 (2011)
6. Chang, Y.J., Chen, S.F., Huang, J.D.: A Kinect-based system for physical rehabilitation: A pilot study for young adults with motor disabilities. Research in Developmental Disabilities 32, 2566–2570 (2011)
7. Standen, P.J., Camm, C., Battersby, S., Brown, D.J., Harrison, M.: An evaluation of the Wii Nunchuk as an alternative assistive device for people with intellectual and physical disabilities using switch controlled software. Computers & Education 56(1), 2–10 (2011)
8. Ding, Q., Stevenson, I.H., Wang, N., Li, W., Sun, Y., Wang, Q., Kording, K., Wei, K.: Motion games improve balance control in stroke survivors: A preliminary study based on the principle of constraint-induced movement therapy. Displays 34, 125–131 (2013)
9. Aron, J.: Makey Makey DIY circuit board makes bananas musical. New Scientist 214, 22 (2012)
10. Wu, F.G., Lin, H., You, M.: The enhanced navigator for the touch screen: A comparative study on navigational techniques of web maps. Displays 32, 284–295 (2011)
11. Monroy-Hernández, A., Resnick, M.: Feature: empowering kids to create and share programmable media. Interactions 15(2), 50–53 (2008)
12. Resnick, M., Rosenbaum, E.: Designing for Tinkerability. In: Honey, M., Kanter, D. (eds.) Design, Make, Play: Growing the Next Generation of STEM Innovators, pp. 163–181 (2013)

Depth-To-Audio Sensory Substitution for Increasing the Accessibility of Virtual Environments

Shachar Maidenbaum[1], Daniel Robert Chebat[1,2],
Shelly Levy-Tzedek[1,2], and Amir Amedi[1,2]

[1] Department of medical neurobiology, Institute for Medical Research Israel-Canada,
Faculty of Medicine
[2] The Edmond and Lily Safra Center for Brain Research
The Hebrew University of Jerusalem, Hadassah Ein-Kerem, Jerusalem, Israel
amira@ekmd.huji.ac.il

Abstract. As most computerized information is visual, it is not directly accessible to the blind and visually impaired. This challenge is especially great when discussing graphical virtual environments. This is especially unfortunate as such environments hold great potential for the blind community for uses such as social interaction, online education and especially for safe mobility training from the safety and comfort of their home. While several previous attempts have increased the accessibility of these environments current tools are still far from making them properly accessible.We suggest the use of Sensory Substitution Devices (SSDs) as another step in increasing the accessibility of such environments by offering the user more raw "visual" information about the scene via other senses. Specifically, we explore here the use of a minimal-SSD based upon the EyeCane, which uses point depth distance information of a single pixel, for tasks such as virtual shape recognition and virtual navigation. We show both success and the fast learned use of this transformation by our users in these tasks, demonstrating the potential for this approach and end with a call for its addition to accessibility toolboxes.

1 Introduction

1.1 Motivation

Virtual worlds and environments are increasingly gaining importance in our lives. They can be used for a wide variety of purposes ranging from games through education, navigation and scientific research to simply general social interaction.

Yet as these virtual worlds are mainly built around visual information, they are almost completely inaccessible to the blind. This is especially unfortunate as such environments hold great potential for the blind community for uses such as social interaction and online education from the safety and comfort of their own home.

Furthermore, the main potential of these virtual environments for the visually impaired lies in the field of mobility, which poses some of their greatest everyday challenges. Since it is well established that spatial information can be transferred between virtual and real-world environments both for the general population [1,2] and

C. Stephanidis and M. Antona (Eds.): UAHCI/HCII 2014, Part I, LNCS 8513, pp. 398–406, 2014.
© Springer International Publishing Switzerland 2014

for the blind [3,4], they can be used for familiarization with an environment virtually through freely available virtual worlds (for example, Google Street-View) before visiting it in the real world. This is far safer than learning to navigate through them in the real world [5], and as this can be done alone at one's own leisure, it spares the cost and availability problems of personal instructors.

1.2 Related Work

Unfortunately, current generic tools for making computerized graphic information accessible to the blind are still far from adequate for virtual environments.

Commonly, these tools are Text-based, such as Screen-Readers. They read the textual information to the blind user and thus make it accessible non-visually. However, such tools are simply not relevant for the transfer of graphical spatial information.

Other common tools substitute the visual information by mapping different virtual objects to text or auditory cues. This approach has birthed many attempts at creating dedicated virtual environments for the blind [see review in [6]. However, none of these attempts has graduated past the research stage as they suffer from the dual problem of interfacing the graphic information to the user and the initial creation of these tags, which involves either heavy automatic pre-processing or labor-intensive human tagging which makes them impractical on a large scale or for the existing virtual environments.

It should be noted that several tools exist to increase the accessibility of specific environments and have achieved impressive results [7,8], but even they are still far from being decreed accessible.

1.3 Sensory Substitution for Increasing Accessibility and the Virtual - EyeCane

A different potential approach, which we utilize here, is the use of Sensory Substitution Devices (SSDs). In this approach, the visual information in the scene is transferred to the user via alternative senses. SSDs rely on the ability of the brain to reinterpret this information coming through a different sense and then transform and process it for its original task. SSDs such as the vOICe and Brainport have been used to obtain impressive results both in the real world (reviewed in [9]), and in laboratory settings (for example [10-12]). However, SSDs have several known problems limiting their wide adoption. Mainly, they require long periods of training to master their use and are hard to use in noisy real-world environments [13].

As one of the first steps upon this path we explore the use of a minimal-SSD which transfers a single point of information. Specifically, we use a virtual version of the EyeCane [14]. The EyeCane augments the traditional white cane using sensors to detect obstacles from a greater distance (5m) and transforms this information into a simple auditory cue (the user hears a series of beeps, where the closer the object the user is pointing at, the higher the frequency of cues).

The Virtual-EyeCane, which we describe here, gives the same sensory output as the real-world EyeCane. This feature has the potential of easing the transfer of learning from the virtual environment to the real one. Additionally, as this simulation relies only on the distance between the participant and the object they are pointing at, it can be easily calculated in any 3D mesh which is the foundation of nearly every virtual environment.

We will present our recent results [14,15] showing the fast-learned practical use of this algorithm by blind and blindfolded-sighted participants for navigation in simple virtual environments, and for recognizing 2D and 3D shapes after less than 10 minutes of training.

We will then present for the first time results showing the feasibility of using this approach to enable successful navigation in more complex virtual indoor environments including rooms and corridors with multiple decision points. Additionally, we will present new results showing the shape identification task can be performed online after self-training with comparable results to those achieved with an instructor.

2   General Methods

2.1   Participants and Ethics

The experiment was approved by the Hebrew University ethics committee, and all participants signed informed consent forms.

2.2   Experimental Setup

We created dedicated virtual environments using Blender 2.49, and Blender-Python modules using python 2.6.2. The environments produce a graphical output of the virtual environment. However, it was not available to the participants in this experiment, who were either blind or blindfolded. The software automatically logs any activity within the virtual environments.

The environments are controlled using a standard keyboard and a mouse.

2.3   The Virtual EyeCane

In the real world, the EyeCane uses a set of IR sensors to sense the distance to the object it is pointed at. This distance is then transformed to sound such that the shorter the distance the higher the frequency of sounds [14]. The Virtual EyeCane calculates the distance using Blender's standard Ray-Casting algorithm (which calculates the distance to the object the virtual device is directly pointed at, much like the sensors of the EyeCane) and links it to a sound file recorded from the EyeCane's auditory output, which the user than uses to perceive the distance. Distances within the environment are set so that each "blender meter" correlates to a real world meter so that the EyeCane and virtual-EyeCane give identical outputs at the same distance.

3   Task 1 – Virtual Shape Recognition in the Lab and Online

3.1   General and Previous Work

As a first step we tested [15] whether our participants could use this approach to recognize simple 2D & 3D virtual shapes. This experiment was conducted with no training at all, to explore the concept's simplicity.

We found there that participants (n=26, 23 sighted & 3 blind, 11 Male, aged 25.1±5.3) were indeed able to correctly recognize 2D shapes (61.1%±12.9%(SD), p<5E-9, standard t-test. Square, triangle & circle) and 3D shapes (81.1%±17.8%, p<3E-13. Pyramid, Half-Pipe, Ball & Bowl).

The next step, reported here for the first time, was to explore the ability of users to learn this transformation by themselves without supervision from an instructor. To test this, and to expand the pool of participants, we created an online version of this experiment and opened it to public access.

3.2   Methods

Participants. 41 users completed this study. No additional data was collected about them.

Training. Users had access to a training task which consisted of 2 training levels and included being told the correct answer as feedback and been allowed to try again until success.

Experimental Paradigm. Both the 2D and 3D tasks each included 8 levels with 4 different shapes (see fig 1a-b). No information about the shape was presented visually on the screen, forcing them to rely on the information from the virtual-EyeCane. The experiment is online at http://brain.huji.ac.il/online_games/Default.aspx (note that the experiment and instructions are in Hebrew).

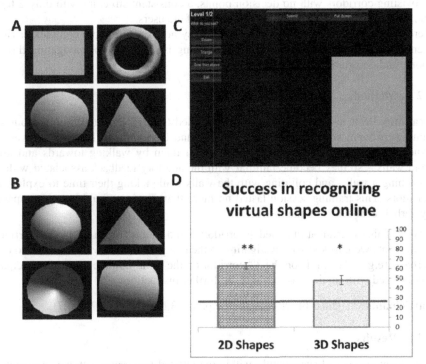

Fig. 1. Online shape recognition (A) 2D shapes: Square, Circle, Ring, Triangle (B) 3D shapes: Ball, Cone, Pyramid, Cylinder (C) Screenshot of a level with the shape displayed (D) Results for shape recognition in 2D and 3D shapes.

3.3   Results

Participants correctly recognized 2D shapes with a significant success rate of 63.1%±20.3%(mean±SD) (p<5E-12, standard t-test) and the 3D shapes with a significant success rate of 47.9%±30.0% (p<5E-3). These results fall within the range of the results reported in [15]. See graph in figure 1d.

4   Task 2 – Simple Virtual Navigation

4.1   General and Previous Work

We have recently explored [14] whether blind and blindfolded users can navigate down a virtual twisting corridor using only the Virtual-EyeCane's single point distance parameter, after only a few minutes of training. We found there that all participants (n=23, 20 sighted & 3 congenitally blind, 9 Male, Aged 27.6±8.4) were able to complete all levels while significantly shortening the required time, path length and number of collisions over repeated trials.

Those results showed that all participants were indeed able to navigate all routes successfully following minimal training.

However, these results were obtained in very simple environments, which consisted of twisting corridors with no decision points, a consistent structure with only 2 turns, and with constant walls spaced on both sides of the users.

Here, we expand these results to show that they hold even in more complex environments, specifically that similar minimal training is sufficient for navigating through rooms and corridors with decision points.

4.2   Methods

Training. Prior to the task participants travelled through 2 virtual training routes to familiarize them with the keyboard controls and environment. Participants were instructed and encouraged to experiment within them by walking towards and away from walls – so they become familiar with the auditory feedback associated with approaching a wall - and colliding with the walls while taking their time to explore the corridors. This training session lasted no more than 7 minutes and was accompanied by verbal feedback from the instructor.

Levels. This experiment included 4 corridors and 5 rooms (fig 2a-b). In the Corridors, participants were tasked with navigating to the end point which was described to them verbally (e.g. "The exit is on the 3rd corridor on the right"). In the Rooms, participants were tasked with finding the exit with no further instructions.

Participants. 7 sighted-blindfolded participants (3 Male, Aged 27.9±6.7).

4.3   Results

Participants navigated successfully within the allotted timeframe with a success rate of 64.2±6.8 for corridors and 94.2±3.4 for rooms (figure 2c). These results are significant as without any assistive device there is no way for the user to complete these mazes.

Fig. 2. Virtual navigation. (A) The virtual corridors (B) The virtual rooms (C) Results for success in the virtual navigation tasks.

5   Discussion

5.1   General

These results suggest that the approach of using virtual canes in virtual environments is both feasible and beneficial to potential users, and enables them to perform virtual tasks which are otherwise impossible for them. Our results show that even using such a simple feedback parameter as distance to an object, and even using only it, can enable the blind to perform tasks otherwise impossible to them, thus incrementally improving the accessibility of online 3D environments and objects in a way that can easily be combined with other state-of-the-art tools for accessing other types of computerized information such as screen-readers.

A key point of our method is that it is easily usable without the need to computationally pre-process a specific scene, but rather relies on data that a customized plugin to almost any virtual environment will be able to supply. Thus, instead of having to create each scene with a virtual world, the user would only need to download a plugin for the specific environment (such as WoW, Google-Earth etc.).

Another factor enhancing our method's accessibility is that it does not rely on any special equipment, but rather only on standard hardware – a sound output source (speaker/headphones) and input devices (mouse/keyboard).

This success with even a minimal-SSD indicates the potential of more complex SSDs such as the EyeMusic [16-17] or the vOICe [18] for increasing accessibility in a far more significant fashion, as they offer whole-scene information and parameters such as shape, location and color.

5.2   Training

The results from the online task indicate that users can indeed train themselves with this tool, potentially enabling a solution to the cost and lack of availability of personal instructors required by other tools. It will be important to explore whether this result can indeed hold for more complex tasks and transformations.

5.3   Gamification and Positive User Experience

Participants treated the Virtual-EyeCane experiments as games, and often requested to continue playing with them after the experiment ended (all participants volunteered to participate in future experiments). This echoes previous successful reactions to other online game-based tools for the blind [4], and demonstrates the efficacy of the current popular trend of using gamification for general research and education in the general public.

5.4   Lack of Vestibular and Proprioceptive Information

One of the main difficulties users had was the lack of vestibular & proprioceptive information as they navigated through the environments, especially when turning, which often caused confusion. This is a common problem with all virtual simulations of motion. It would be interesting to explore this question in the future using full body control instead of a keyboard interface and see the effect of such information. It should be noted that without vision such orientation is often harder than we one would expect [19].

6   Conclusion

We have shown here that using our method it is both feasible and simple to perform virtual tasks such as shape recognition and navigation using single-point depth information for both blind and blindfolded-sighted individuals, a task which is impossible for them without such a method.

This approach has several advantages such as simplicity and extendibility to existing virtual environments, thus increasing their accessibility to the blind. The use of identical stimuli in the virtual world from the Virtual-EyeCane to that given by the EyeCane in the real world may potentially increase the efficiency of its use in novel real-world scenarios learned virtually.

We call on further research to test whether SSD can indeed be used for enabling the visually impaired to accomplish further, more complex, tasks in virtual environments, and for making these environments more accessible in general. Additionally, we believe this ability will be extended significantly when used together with other devices such as the EyeMusic.

Acknowledgements. We would like to thank Shlomi Hanassy and Sami Abboud for their help in developing the EyeCane, upon which the virtual EyeCane is based, Itay Ariel for his help in developing the online system and experiment, and Ori Lavi for her help in running the experiment. This work was supported by a European Research Council grant to A.A. (grant number 310809); The Charitable Gatsby Foundation; The James S. McDonnell Foundation scholar award (to AA; grant number 220020284); The Israel Science Foundation (grant number ISF 1684/08); The Edmond and Lily Safra Center for Brain Sciences (ELSC) Vision center grant (to AA) and an ELSC fellowship (to SL & DRC); The Azrieli Foundation fellowship award (to DRC).

References

1. Witmer, B.G., et al.: Virtual spaces and real world places: transfer of route knowledge. International Journal of Human-Computer Studies 45(4), 413–428 (1996)
2. Foreman, N., et al.: Spatial information transfer from virtual to real versions of the Kiel locomotor maze. Behavioural Brain Research 112(1), 53–61 (2000)
3. Lahav, O., Mioduser, D.: Exploration of unknown spaces by people who are blind using a multi-sensory virtual environment. Journal of Special Education Technology 19, 15–24 (2004)
4. Merabet, L.B., et al.: Teaching the Blind to Find Their Way by Playing Video Games. PloS One 7(9), e44958 (2012)
5. Manduchi, R., Kurniawan, S.: Watch Your Head, Mind Your Step: Mobility-Related Accidents Experienced by People with Visual Impairment. Tech. Rep. UCSC-SOE-10-24, University of California, Santa Cruz (2010)
6. Lahav, O.: Improving orientation and mobility skills through virtual environment for people who are blind: past research and future potential. In: ICDVRAT 2012, Laval (2012)
7. White, G.R., Fitzpatrick, G., McAllister, G.: Toward accessible 3D virtual environments for the blind and visually impaired. In: Proceedings of the 3rd International Conference on Digital Interactive Media in Entertainment and Arts, pp. 134–141. ACM (September 2008)
8. Trewin, S., Hanson, V.L., Laff, M.R., Cavender, A.: PowerUp: an accessible virtual world. In: Proceedings of the 10th International ACM SIGACCESS Conference on Computers and Accessibility, pp. 177–184. ACM (October 2008)
9. Maidenbaum, S., Amedi, A.: Applying plasticity to visual rehabilitation in adulthood. In: Jennifer Steeves, L.R.H. (ed.) Plasticity in Sensory Systems. Cambridge University Press (2012)
10. Striem-Amit, E., Guendelman, M., Amedi, A.: 'Visual' acuity of the congenitally blind using visual-to-auditory sensory substitution. PloS 1 (2012)
11. Chebat, D.R., Schneider, F.C., Kupers, R., Ptito, M.: Navigation with a sensory substitution device in congenitally blind individuals. Neuroreport 22(7), 342–347 (2011)
12. Chebat, D.R., Rainville, C., Kupers, R., Ptito, M.: Tactile-'visual' acuity of the tongue in early blind individuals. Neuroreport 18(18), 1901–1904 (2007)
13. Reich, L., Maidenbaum, S., Amedi, A.: The brain as a flexible task machine: implications for visual rehabilitation using noninvasive vs. invasive approaches. Current Opinion in Neurology (2011)
14. Maidenbaum, S., et al.: Increasing Accessibility to the Blind of Virtual Environments, Using a Virtual Mobility Aid Based On the EyeCane. PloS One 8(8), e72555 (2013)

15. Maidenbaum, S., et al.: Virtual 3D shape and orientation discrimination using point distance information (2012)
16. Abboud, S., Hanassy, S., Levy-Tzedek, S., Maidenbaum, S., Amedi, A.: EyeMusic: Introducing a "visual" colorful experience for the blind using auditory sensory substitution. Restorative Neurology and Neuroscience (2014)
17. Levy-Tzedek, S., Novick, I., Arbel, R., Abboud, S., Maidenbaum, S., Vaadia, E., Amedi, A.: Cross-sensory transfer of sensory-motor information: visuomotor learn (2012)
18. Meijer, P.B.: An experimental system for auditory image representations. IEEE Transactions on Biomedical Engineering 39(2), 112–121 (1992)
19. Loomis, J.M., Klatzky, R.L., Giudice, N.A.: Representing 3D space in working memory: Spatial images from vision, hearing, touch, and language. In: Multisensory Imagery, pp. 131–155. Springer, New York (2013)

Seeing through the Kinect: A Survey on Heuristics for Building Natural User Interfaces Environments

Vanessa Regina Margareth Lima Maike[1], Laurindo de Sousa Britto Neto[1,2],
Maria Cecília Calani Baranauskas[1], and Siome Klein Goldenstein[1]

[1] Institute of Computing, State University of Campinas (UNICAMP), Campinas, Brazil
[2] Departament of Computing, Federal University of Piauí (UFPI), Teresina, Brazil
vanessa.maike@gmail.com, laurindoneto@ufpi.edu.br,
{cecilia,siome}@ic.unicamp.br

Abstract. The idea of interacting with technologies through touch-less and body-based interfaces has caused great excitement amongst users, but for the designers it has created various new challenges. Usability encompasses part of these challenges, and there have been attempts at creating heuristics for NUIs design. However, most of these heuristics consider using a device such as Kinect for the recognition of gestures, not people or objects. Therefore, in this paper we investigate the subject by presenting a systematic literature review aimed at finding heuristics for the design and evaluation of NUIs. Our analysis focuses on the scenario of helping people with visual disabilities in their daily activities. By looking at the state of the art, we intend to verify how many and which heuristics fit in this context.

Keywords: Human-Computer Interaction, HCI, Accessibility, Assistive Technologies.

1 Introduction

Consider a scenario in which a blind professor is working in her office facing the computer while leaving her office door open. Meanwhile, a Microsoft® Kinect, a camera capable of capturing videos with color and depth information, faces the door and is connected to the computer As soon as someone walks into the room, the system recognizes the person as one of the professor's coworkers or students, and signals in accordance to some prior configuration, such as saying the person's name or chiming a person-based sound snippet. Later that day, someone walks by the office and waves at the professor. The system recognizes the gesture as a way of saying hello, and tells the professor someone in the corridor has sent a greeting.

This scenario describes some of the possible uses for the new paradigm in Human Computer Interaction (HCI) that has become known as Natural User Interfaces (NUIs). The idea of interacting with technologies through touch-less and body-based interfaces has caused great excitement amongst users, but for the designers it has created various new challenges [14]. Usability encompasses part of these challenges, and there have been attempts at creating heuristics for NUIs design [7, 19]. However,

C. Stephanidis and M. Antona (Eds.): UAHCI/HCII 2014, Part I, LNCS 8513, pp. 407–418, 2014.
© Springer International Publishing Switzerland 2014

most of these heuristics consider using a device such as Kinect for the recognition of gestures, not people or objects. For instance, [7] propose guidelines for touch-less gestural interaction, looking to the gestures as specific commands, not as day-to-day actions that need to be interpreted. Therefore, in this paper we investigate the subject by presenting a systematic literature review aimed at finding heuristics for the design and evaluation of NUIs. Our analysis, however, will be focused in the context of helping people with visual disabilities with their daily activities, such as walking, translating textual information (e.g. signs, symbols, plaques...), or recognizing people and objects. By looking at the state of the art, we intend to verify how many and which heuristics fit in the scenario described previously.

The paper is organized as follows: section 2 will summarize a previous systematic review made about the use of the Kinect as an assistive technology; section 3 will detail the methodology applied in this systematic review; section 4 will present the main results; finally, section 5 will discuss these results and conclude.

2   Kinect as an Assistive Technology

Previous to the review presented in this paper, we conducted a preliminary systematic review, with the purpose of answering the research question: *"How is the Kinect being used to assist people with visual impairments?"* A search was conducted by applying the keywords "Kinect" and "blind" in both ACM and IEEE digital libraries. This search returned 105 results, from which only 19 were relevant to answer the research question. The publication years of these 19 papers ranged from 2011 to 2013.

The analysis of the obtained papers involved characterizing the participants and the devices used in the studies. The review included papers that either showed work involving the Kinect assisting users with some sort of disability, or other device used to assist visually impaired people. Papers that did not meet these criteria or that did not present user evaluation were discarded. The following list summarizes the types of data that were extracted from the 19 selected papers, and then Table 1 summarizes the actual data that was extracted using these questions.

1. What was the device used in the study?
2. Where does the user place the device?
3. How does the device provide feedback to the user?
4. Can the user send commands or feedback to the device?
5. What is the type of disability that the study deals with?
6. Did the user evaluation involve users with disabilities?
7. Are the test users people with real or simulated disabilities?
8. How many test users were involved?
9. How many test scenarios were applied?
10. Was the impact of the proposed solution measured by comparing it with other solutions?

Table 1. Data extracted during the first exploratory systematic review

Data	Summary of Extracted Data
Device used	**Kinect:** 55%; **iPad:** 10%; **Wii Mote:** 10%; **Others:** 25% (include robot, interactive map, TOF camera, and wearable haptic devices)
Location of the Device	**Head:** 31%; **Waist:** 15%; **Hand:** 23%; **Table:** 31%
Feedback provided	**Sound:** 32%; **Tactile:** 47%; **Other/None:** 21%
Does User interact?	**Yes:** 33%; **No:** 67%
Disability type	**Visual:** 88%; **Cognitive:** 12%
Are Users with disabilities involved?	**Yes:** 47%; **No:** 53%
Are disabilities real or simulated?	**Real:** 46%; **Simulated:** 23%; **Both:** 15%; **None:** 8%; **Unspecified:** 8%
# Test users	**Average:** 7; **Minimum:** 2; **Maximum:** 28
# Test scenarios	**Average:** 2; **Minimum:** 1; **Maximum:** 4
Is the study compared with other solutions?	**Yes:** 32%; **No:** 68%

This data helped in understanding the current scenario in the research field of using NUIs for assisting people with disabilities. The characteristics extracted from the studies represent what we believe are the key points to pay attention to when developing a new solution for assistive technology. Thus, three specific aspects lead to important conclusions. First, the data shows a clear tendency towards tactile feedback. Also, amongst the studies that used sound feedback, none utilized 3D sound, which is an interesting form of feedback to explore since it provides a sense of direction and angle. Furthermore, a combination of two types of feedback (tactile and sound) could be explored. Second, the extracted data shows that many studies involved only users with simulated disabilities (e.g., blindfolded people instead of real blinds) in the evaluation phase. Working with real users is extremely important, because they already have their own strategies to deal with their disabilities, which may conflict or not be supported by the proposed solution. On the other hand, users with simulated disabilities are representing users with a recently acquired disability, i.e., a completely different category of user. Therefore, it is important to involve both types of users in the design process of any novel assistive technology. Third, the very low number of studies that had solutions in which users could somehow interact with the system, instead of just receiving feedback, can be a consequence of the novelty of this research field. Most papers were about solutions driven almost exclusively to very specific tasks – an indicative that they are being tested in limited contexts, instead of wide ones. This allows the specialization of the solution, perfecting it for its intended task, but it also limits its applications and possibility of usefulness to real users.

Therefore, the current scenario of NUIs as technologies for assisting people with disabilities is still in its early stages. To push the research field forward and develop solutions that are truly helpful to visually impaired people, it is important to involve real users throughout the design and evaluation process. Prior to that, however, it is essential to better understand the current Natural User Interfaces; what are their strengths and their limitations, and how they can best be used. Therefore, a set of heuristics for NUIs could help designers and developers in creating solutions that best explore this new category of interface. The next sections show how we came to a set of heuristics for NUI, with the scenario of assisting visually impaired users in mind.

3   Research Methodology

In this paper we adopted the PRISMA statement [10] to organize a systematic review in which we tried to answer the research question: *"What heuristics for NUIs could inform the design and evaluation of assistive technology for visually impaired people?"* The audience considered in this work was that of technology users, including visually impaired people (blind and low vision). The intervention to be created is a set of heuristics (guidelines) for the design and evaluation of Natural User Interfaces (NUIs) as an assistive technology for users with visual impairments. The control group is the already established usability, design and evaluation heuristics for computer interfaces [13]. The expected results are the aforementioned set of heuristics, and they are expected to be useful for both NUI designers and HCI researchers.

3.1   Eligibility Criteria

The inclusion (I) and exclusion (E) criteria for the papers were the following:

- (I) It presents design or evaluation of novel NUIs;
- (I) It presents information that might be relevant to establish heuristics for NUIs;
- (E) It does not present relevant information regarding heuristics for NUIs;
- (E) Its publication date is older than 2004.
- (E) Its search result was related to entire proceedings or magazines, not to specific entries;

The last criterion was created because there were many search results, especially from the ACM digital library, that included generic references to conference proceedings or entire magazines, without specifying any article. It was decided that these results could be discarded after realizing that the specific item within the proceedings or magazine that met the search criteria would also show up as an individual search result, eliminating the need to search through the entire proceedings or magazine. The language restriction for the selection of studies was papers written in English or in Brazilian Portuguese. There were restrictions regarding type of study or what Liberati et al. [10] refer to as PICOS.

3.2   Information Sources and Search

The last search was performed on January 2014. The sources of information utilized were the following digital libraries: ACM, IEEE, Springer, Science Direct and Scopus. Manual search was not immediately discarded, but ultimately it was not used. The ACM Digital Library (http://dl.acm.org) comprehends all publications from the

Association for Computing Machinery (ACM), a total of 402,435 full papers (as of early 2014). The IEEE digital library (http://ieeexplore.ieee.org) contains the 3,675,903 (as of early 2014) publications from the Institute of Electrical and Electronics Engineers (IEEE). The Springer digital library (http://link.springer.com) contains over 8 million resources published by Springer Science+Business Media, the majority consisting of articles and book chapters. Science Direct (http://www.sciencedirect.com) is a full-text scientific database that offers journal articles from more than 2,500 journals and book chapters from almost 20,000 books, making a total of over 12 million resources. Finally, Scopus (http://www.scopus.com/) is an abstract and citation database of peer-reviewed literature, covering more than 50 million records, 21,000 titles and 5,000 publishers from the fields of science, technology, medicine, social sciences and arts and humanities.

There were two search terms used in parallel: "NUI Usability" and "NUI Heuristics". Except for the search results from Springer, in all other sources the title, abstract and keywords of every search result were read. In the case of Springer, before reading these informations, two search filters were applied: first, the chosen "Discipline" was "Computer Science", and second, the "Subdiscipline" was "HCI" (Human-Computer Interaction).

3.3   Study Selection and Data Collection

The first step in the strategy for study selection was to identify duplicated search results, since multiple search engines were used. After that, the inclusion and exclusion criteria were applied by reading the title, abstract and the keywords and by looking at the publication year of the papers that came up as search results.

A data extraction form was created to apply to each selected study. The following table details the contents of this form.

Table 2. Data extraction form for the systematic review

Field Name	Type	Options
Type of study	Pick many list	Qualitative Research Quantitative Research Others
Heuristics Proposal	Pick one list	Proposes heuristics and evaluates them Only evaluates heuristics proposed by others Only proposes heuristics Does not propose heuristics directly but allows inference Does not propose heuristics and does not allow inference
User Testing	Pick many list	Visually impaired users Users with other types of disabilities Users without disabilities Users with simulated disabilities Does not have user testing

Table 2. *(continued)*

Device Test-ing	Pick many list	Kinect Other devices Does not use specific devices
Heuristics drawn from this study	Text	-

The adopted strategy was to first skim each paper, looking for sections in which there would probably be either heuristics proposals or information that suggests heuristics (such as design decisions, learned lessons, or user evaluation strategy and results). Then, these sections were carefully read searching for these kinds of information, which were annotated in the last field of the extraction form. The remaining fields would then be filled either during the skimming or the careful read. However, if that did not happen, then a new skim would be made on the paper, now looking for the missing information.

3.4   Risk of Bias in Individual Studies

It is very common in HCI papers that present a novel design to first present the design, then describe a user evaluation, apply a statistical analysis to it and assume the numbers prove the design was successful. Although this is a valid method, it carries great risk of bias, especially depending on which aspects of the user evaluation the authors applied their quantitative analysis. Therefore, during the data extraction step of this systematic review, most of the information was taken from design decisions, qualitative analysis or discussion of results. Quantitative analysis was considered, but only when directly related to a specified heuristic being evaluated or when this quantitative data was associated with some qualitative assessment.

3.5   Summary Measures

The heuristics drawn from each selected study presented patterns, either by the use of identical words in different papers (such as comfort or fatigue), or by reporting similar issues or recommendations regarding NUIs (even with NUIs that were related to different devices and interaction methods). Therefore, as the data extraction process progressed, the drawn heuristics were gradually being separated into categories.

3.6   Synthesis of Results

The data extraction forms utilized were embedded in the tool used for this systematic review, named StArt (http://lapes.dc.ufscar.br/tools/start_tool). This allowed for automatic generation of statistics, at least for the selection step of the systematic review and for the analysis of the first four fields of the data extraction form. As for the last field ("Heuristics drawn from this study"), the analysis process was manual and gradual, as the data extraction occurred. When all data was gathered, a final organization was necessary to remove redundant or inconsistent information.

3.7 Risk of Bias Across Studies

We tried to avoid publication bias by selecting what we believed were the main digital libraries currently available. Even so, there may be two types of bias in this systematic review. First, the filters applied in the Springer search engine may have removed studies that were either incorrectly categorized or that were not from the field of HCI but provided useful information for the establishment of NUI heuristics. Second, as explained in section 3.5, the strategy adopted for data extraction was to skim the papers. This may result in important information being overlooked or neglected, especially if the paper mixed heuristics or qualitative information with technical information.

3.8 Additional Analyses

Additional analysis was necessary to evaluate the obtained heuristics through the perspective of accessibility and assistive technologies. This means assessing which heuristics apply to every kind of user and which do not apply or apply only to users with disabilities. However, Universal Accessibility was kept in mind to provide, as much as possible, heuristics that did not discriminate types of users.

4 Results

The database search returned a total of 457 results. The following graph shows the percentage of studies that were duplicated, rejected and accepted to the data extraction phase. Next, Table 3 shows the heuristics drawn from this systematic review.

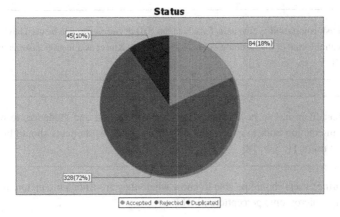

Fig. 1. Numbers for the selection phase

Table 3. Categorized heuristics for NUI

Interaction
1. **Operation modes:** provide different operation modes, each with its own primary information carrier (e.g., text, hypertext, multimedia…).. Also, provide an explicit way for the user to switch between modes and offer a smooth transition. [8, 9, 21]
2. **"Interactability":** selectable and/or "interactable" objects should be explicit and allow both their temporary and permanent selection. [1, 3, 9]
3. **Accuracy:** input by the user (e.g., gestures) should be accurately detected and tracked. [1, 4, 13, 19, 16]
4. **Responsiveness:** the execution of the user input should be in real time. [3, 4, 13]
5. **Identity:** sets of interaction metaphors should make sense as whole, so that it is possible to understand what the system can and cannot interpret. When applicable, visual grouping of semantic similar commands should be made. [1]
6. **Metaphor coherence:** interaction metaphors should have a clear relationship with the functionalities they execute, requiring a reduced mental load. [3, 4]
7. **Distinction:** interaction metaphors should not be too similar, to avoid confusion and facilitate recognition. [19]
8. **Comfort:** the interaction should not require much effort and should not cause fatigue on the user. [1, 3, 4, 5, 12, 18]
9. **Device-Task compatibility:** the tasks for which the NUI device is going to be used have to be compatible with the kind of interaction it offers (e.g., using the Kinect as a mouse cursor is inadequate). [3, 19, 21]
Navigation
10. **Guidance:** there has to be a balance between exploration and guidance, to maintain a flow of interaction both to expert and novice users. Also, shortcuts should be provided for expert users. [1, 6, 9, 18]
11. **Wayfinding:** users should be able to know where they are from a big picture perspective and from a microscopic perception. [9, 18]

Table 3. *(continued)*

12. **Active Exploration:** to promote the learning of a large set of interaction metaphors, a difficult task, active exploration of this set should be favored to enhance transition from novice to expert usage. [1, 2]
13. **Space:** the location in which the system is expected to be used must be appropriate for the kinds of interactions it requires (e.g., full body gestures require a lot of space) and for the number of simultaneous users. [8, 19]
User Adoption
14. **Engagement:** provide immersion during the interaction, at the same time allowing for easy information acquiring and integration. [8, 9]
15. **Competition:** in comparison with the equivalent interactions from traditional non-NUI interfaces, the NUI alternative should be more efficient, more engaging and easier to use. [17, 18, 19]
16. **Affordability:** the NUI device should have an affordable cost. [18]
17. **Familiarity:** the interface should provide a sense of familiarity, which is also related to the coherence between task and device and between interaction metaphor and functionality. [1, 3, 13]
18. **Social acceptance:** using the device should not cause embarrassment to the users. [3, 5, 19]
19. **Learnability:** there has to be coherence between learning time and frequency of use; if the task is performed frequently (such as in a working context), then it is acceptable to have some learning time; otherwise, the interface should be usable without learning. [2, 10, 19]
Multiple Users
20. **Conflict:** if the system supports multiple users working in the same task at the same time, then it should handle and prevent conflicting inputs. [1, 2, 8, 10, 13, 19]
21. **Parallel processing:** enable personal views so that users can each work on their parallel tasks without interfering with the group view. [2, 13]

Table 3. *(continued)*

22. Two-way communication: if multiple users are working on different activities through the same interface, and are not necessarily in the same room, provide ways for both sides to communicate with each other. [21]
23. Learning: when working together, users learn from each other by copying, so it is important to allow them to be aware of each other's actions and intentions. [2]

5   Discussion

In this section we present a brief analysis of the obtained heuristics from the perspective of accessibility and universal access, and finalize with our concluding remarks.

5.1   NUI Heuristics and Accessibility

The set of 23 heuristics shown in Table 3 was compiled bearing in mind two key aspects: embracing any NUI technology and following universal access. For this reason, we avoided using any terms that are specific to certain interfaces, such as "gesture" and "screen". Although the studies that served as theoretical basis did, in most cases, present works and conclusions based upon certain NUIs, we tried to look at their proposed guidelines, learned lessons and recommendations from an impartial perspective. This is a double-edged blade, as it may lead to heuristics that do not apply to every NUI (especially to NUIs that were not invented yet), but at the same time is meant to be of help to any NUI designer or HCI researcher.

Regarding universal access, we believe all heuristics are adequate to any kind of user, although some heuristics have a more evident contribution to assistive technologies. This last remark is especially true if we consider the scenario depicted in section 2. The lack of proposed solutions that do not allow for users to send interactions to the system can be remedied by heuristic 1 in Table 3. Providing different modes of operation with distinct information carriers implies offering not only multiple forms of communication (system to user and vice-versa), but also different types of feedback that can each be suitable to a kind of disability. Furthermore, all the heuristics in the "User Adoption" group are essential when thinking of new assistive technologies. First, because users who already live with their disabilities in a long time already have their own strategies to dealing with it, so a new technology must offer really good advantages to them. Second, because many solutions are developed keeping in mind only the novelty of the technology behind it, and not necessarily if it will actually be acceptable to users in their daily lives.

5.2   Conclusions

This paper presented the methodology adopted to make a systematic review with the goal of answering the research question *"What heuristics for NUIs could inform the design and evaluation of assistive technology for visually impaired people?"* It also presented a set of 23 heuristics for NUIs, resulting of this literature review.

This set of heuristics is intended to help both designers and HCI researchers working with NUIs. They represent an interpretation of the designs and user evaluation results of several researches from the last 10 years. Therefore, they are not to be taken as a rigid set of rules, but a guide to design NUIs that can care to all types of users.

Acknowledgements. We would like to thank the Institute of Computing (IC) from UNICAMP, Microsoft®, Fundação de Amparo à Pesquisa do Estado de São Paulo (Fapesp), Coordenação de Aperfeiçoamento de Pessoal de Nível Superior (CAPES) and the Departament of Computing from the Federal University of Piauí (UFPI) for their support in the development of this work.

References

1. Bailly, G., Müller, J., Lecolinet, E.: Design and evaluation of finger-count interaction: Combining multitouch gestures and menus. Int. J. Hum. Comput. Stud. 70, 673–689 (2012)
2. Block, F., Wigdor, D., Phillips, B.C., Horn, M.S., Shen, C.: FlowBlocks: A Multi-Touch UI for Crowd Interaction. In: Proceedings of the 25th Annual ACM Symposium on User Interface Software and Technology, UIST 2012, pp. 497–508. ACM, Cambridge (2012)
3. Cox, D., Wolford, J., Jensen, C., Beardsley, D.: An evaluation of game controllers and tablets as controllers for interactive tv applications. In: Proceedings of the 14th ACM International Conference on Multimodal Interaction, ICMI 2012, p. 181. ACM Press, New York (2012)
4. Cuccurullo, S., Francese, R., Murad, S., Passero, I., Tucci, M.: A gestural approach to presentation exploiting motion capture metaphors. In: Proceedings of the International Working Conference on Advanced Visual Interfaces, AVI 2012, pp. 148–155. ACM Press, New York (2012)
5. Ertin, E., Stohs, N., Kumar, S., Raij, A., Al'Absi, M., Shah, S.: AutoSense: Unobtrusively Wearable Sensor Suite for Inferring the Onset, Causality, and Consequences of Stress in the Field. In: Proceedings of the 9th ACM Conference on Embedded Networked Sensor Systems, SenSys 2011, pp. 274–287. ACM, Seattle (2011)
6. Frisch, M., Heydekorn, J., Dachselt, R.: Diagram Editing on Interactive Displays Using Multi-touch and Pen Gestures. In: Goel, A.K., Jamnik, M., Narayanan, N.H. (eds.) Diagrams 2010. LNCS, vol. 6170, pp. 182–196. Springer, Heidelberg (2010)
7. Garzotto, F., Valoriani, M., Milano, P.: Touchless Gestural Interaction with Small Displays: A Case Study. In: Proceedings of the Biannual Conference of the Italian Chapter of SIGCHI - CHItaly 2013, pp. 1–10. ACM, Trento (2013)
8. Gomes, A., Oh, H., Chisik, Y., Chen, M.: Ilha Musical: a CAVE for nurturing cultural appreciation. In: Proceedings of the 11th International Conference on Interaction Design and Children, IDC 2012, Bremen, Germany, pp. 232–235 (2012)

9. Jankowski, J., Decker, S.: A Dual-Mode User Interface for Accessing 3D Content on the World Wide Web Categories and Subject Descriptors. In: Proceedings of the 21st International Conference on World Wide Web, pp. 1047–1056. ACM, Lyon (2012)
10. Klompmaker, F., Paelke, V.: A Taxonomy-Based Approach Towards NUI Interaction Design. In: TEI 2013, pp. 32–41. ACM, Barcelona (2013)
11. Liberati, A., Altman, D.G., Tetzlaff, J., Mulrow, C., Gotzsche, P.C., Ioannidis, J.P., Clarke, M., Devereaux, P.J., Kleijnen, J., Moher, D.: The PRISMA statement for reporting systematic reviews and meta-analyses of studies that evaluate healthcare interventions: explanation and elaboration. BMJ 6, 27 (2009)
12. Lin, S., Shie, C., Chen, S., Hung, Y.: AirTouch Panel: A Re-Anchorable Virtual Touch Panel. In: Proceedings of the 21st ACM International Conference on Multimedia, MM 2013, pp. 625–628. ACM, Barcelona (2013)
13. Nebe, K., Klompmaker, F., Jung, H., Fischer, H.: Exploiting New Interaction Techniques for Disaster Control Management Using Multitouch-, Tangible- and Pen-Based-Interaction. In: Jacko, J.A. (ed.) Human-Computer Interaction, Part II, HCII 2011. LNCS, vol. 6762, pp. 100–109. Springer, Heidelberg (2011)
14. Nielsen, J.: Usability Engineering (1994)
15. O'Hara, K., Harper, R., Mentis, H., Sellen, A., Taylor, A.: On the Naturalness of Touchless: Putting the "Interaction" Back into NUI. ACM Trans. Comput. Interact. 20, 1–25 (2013)
16. Oh, J., Jung, Y., Cho, Y., Hahm, C., Education, S.S., Sin, H., Science, C., Lee, J.: Hands-Up: Motion Recognition using Kinect and a Ceiling to Improve the Convenience of Human Life. In: CHI 2012 Extended Abstracts on Human Factors in Computing Systems, pp. 1655–1660. ACM (2012)
17. Sae-bae, N., Ahmed, K., Isbister, K., Memon, N.: Biometric-Rich Gestures: A Novel Approach to Authentication on Multi-touch Devices. In: Proceedings of the SIGCHI Conference on Human Factors in Computing Systems, CHI 2012, pp. 977–986 (2012)
18. Sanna, A., Lamberti, F., Paravati, G., Rocha, F.D.: A kinect-based interface to animate virtual characters. J. Multimodal User Interfaces 7, 269–279 (2012)
19. Shiratuddin, M.F., Wong, K.W.: Game Design Considerations When Using Non-touch Based Natural User Interface. In: Pan, Z., Cheok, A.D., Müller, W., Chang, M., Zhang, M. (eds.) Transactions on Edutainment VIII. LNCS, vol. 7220, pp. 35–45. Springer, Heidelberg (2012)
20. Wigdor, D., Wixon, D.: Brave NUI World (2011)
21. Yang, J., Dekker, A., Muhlberger, R., Viller, S.: Exploring Virtual Representations of Physical Artefacts in a Multi-touch Clothing Design Collaboration System. In: Proceedings of the 21st Annual Conference of the Australian Computer-Human Interaction Special Interest Group, OZCHI 2009, pp. 353–356. ACM, Melbourne (2009)

Affective Haptics for Enhancing Access to Social Interactions for Individuals Who are Blind

Troy McDaniel[1], Shantanu Bala[1], Jacob Rosenthal[2], Ramin Tadayon[1], Arash Tadayon[1], and Sethuraman Panchanathan[1]

[1] Center for Cognitive Ubiquitous Computing,
Department of Computer Science and Engineering, Arizona State University, Tempe, AZ, USA
[2] HeatSync Labs, Mesa, AZ, USA
{troy.mcdaniel,shantanu.bala,atadayon,rtadayon,panch}@asu.edu,
jakerosenthal@gmail.com

Abstract. Non-verbal cues used during social interactions, such as facial expressions, are largely inaccessible to individuals who are blind. This work explores the use of affective haptics for communicating emotions displayed during social interactions. We introduce a novel haptic device, called the Haptic Face Display (HFD), consisting of a two-dimensional array of vibration motors capable of displaying rich spatiotemporal vibrotactile patterns presented through passive or active interaction styles. This work investigates users' emotional responses to vibrotactile patterns using a passive interaction style in which the display is embedded on the back of an ergonomic chair. Such a technology could enhance social interactions for individuals who are blind in which emotions of interaction partners, once recognized by a frontend system such as computer vision algorithms, are conveyed through the HFD. We present the results of an experiment exploring the relationship between vibrotactile pattern design and elicited emotional response. Results indicate that pattern shape, duration, among other dimensions, influence emotional response, which is an important consideration when designing technologies for affective haptics.

Keywords: Affective haptics, emotions, vibrotactile stimulation, interpersonal interaction, assistive technology.

1 Introduction

Social interactions play an important role in our health and wellbeing: building and maintaining personal and professional relationships; achieving education and career goals; and shaping who we are as individuals. However, social interactions are still not universally accessible to individuals who are blind. Nearly 65% of information exchanged during a typical social interaction is nonverbal, and 72% of nonverbal communication is visual [1]. Visual nonverbal cues include facial expressions, eye gaze, body language, posture and appearance, which are largely inaccessible to individuals who are blind. Awkward and embarrassing situations are not uncommon for individuals who are blind during interactions with their sighted peers due to an

C. Stephanidis and M. Antona (Eds.): UAHCI/HCII 2014, Part I, LNCS 8513, pp. 419–429, 2014.
© Springer International Publishing Switzerland 2014

inaccessible visual channel through which most social cues are conveyed. Such situations can ultimately lead to social avoidance and isolation, and prevent individuals who are blind from fully participating in society.

Previously, we developed the Social Interaction Assistant (SIA) to sense, process and deliver specific visual nonverbal social cues to individuals who are blind using a wearable platform [2-6]. The social cues we targeted include the identity of a user's interaction partner; interpersonal distance between a user and interaction partner; and facial expressions of a user's interaction partner. Facial expressions are communicated through the sense of touch by displaying spatiotemporal vibration patterns on the back of the hand through a custom-made device called the VibroGlove [5-6]. Vibrations were chosen as the communication modality since audio output can obstruct a user's hearing, especially during a social interaction. The back of the hand was chosen for its impressive temporal and spatial acuity. While the palm and fingers are more sensitive (glabrous, hair-less skin), their backs were chosen for display to not limit the use of the hands during social interactions, especially social touch cues such as handshakes and pats on the back. Spatiotemporal vibrotactile patterns were designed to represent the following six basic emotions plus the neutral expression: happy, sad, surprise, anger, fear and disgust. Happy, sad and surprise are represented by displaying their respective common mouth expressions: vibrotactile shapes in the form of a U (smile), inverted U (frown), and circle. Anger, fear and disgust are represented by complex patterns found to evoke these emotions in the wearer of the VibroGlove.

While study participants could accurately distinguish between these patterns with minimal training and found them intuitive, individuals who are blind requested a richer display device. The device requested was one that could switch between symbolic representations to convey emotions being displayed by an interaction partner; and a literal representation that could allow users to feel the facial movements of interaction partners. To address these needs, in this work, we propose the Haptic Face Display (HFD)—an assistive technology to communicate emotions and facial expressions through rich spatiotemporal vibrotactile patterns displayed passively (back of a chair) or actively (tabletop). This technology also provides a useful research platform for exploring Affective Haptics—a subfield of computational science that explores how the emotional state of a user can be stimulated and influenced. As a first step, this work explores how affective haptics can be used to elicit the six basic emotions in a user to naturally communicate emotions of an interaction partner using symbolic vibrotactile patterns. Our implementation is a passive display on the back of a chair, which could be used during dyadic (one-on-one) social interactions. Our implementation, detailed later in this paper, can be easily transformed into a tabletop display for investigating active exploration of symbolic (or literal) vibration patterns.

The rest of the paper is organized as follows: Section 2 provides a literature review of research on affective haptics and communicating facial expressions/emotions to individuals who are blind. Section 3 introduces our proposed approach and technology. Section 4 presents the design and results of an Institutional Review Board-approved user study exploring the linkage between symbolic vibrotactile patterns and the emotions they naturally represent using a forced-choice paradigm. Section 5 concludes and presents possible directions for future research.

2   Related Work

Very little work has explored the presentation of facial expressions and emotions to enrich social interactions for individuals who are blind. Rehman et al. [7] proposed mapping the manifold of facial expressions to the back of a chair for vibrotactile rendering. To compute the manifold of facial expressions, they proposed an extended locally linear embedding (LLE) algorithm for analyzing the emotional content of facial expression videos in real-time. Their proposed vibrotactile display consisted of nine actuators arranged into three axes representing happy, sad and surprise where stimulation along one of three axes not only determines the type of emotion but also its intensity. While Rehman et al. have proposed a useful approach to mapping video-based facial expressions to vibrotactile renderings, their approach handles only three of the six basic emotions.

Leveraging existing work in affective haptics, the current work attempts to identify symbolic representations of vibrotactile patterns that evoke the six basic emotions in users by engaging the sense of touch. Existing work in affective haptics has focused mainly on two applications: enriched telepresence or movie viewing. Tsetserukou et al. [8] have proposed haptic devices to augment online and mobile interactions with enriched emotional experiences. Their haptic devices include HaptiHug, HaptiHeart, HaptiButterfly, HaptiShiver, HaptiTemper and HaptiTickler. HaptiHug simulates a hug by generating pressure around a user's chest and back. HaptiHeart conveys heartbeat patterns by generating heartbeat sensations on a user's chest. HaptiButterfly reproduces the sensation of "butterflies in the stomach" through vibrotactile stimulations delivered to a user's abdomen. HaptiShiver reproduces the sensation of "shivers up and down the spine" through vibrotactile stimulations. HaptiTemper reproduces the sensation of "chills up and down the spine" through temperature changes using fans and a Peltier. HaptiTickler simulates being tickled by generating random vibrotactile stimulations on a user's ribs.

To enhance immersion and emotions during movie viewing, Lemmens et al. [9] developed a body-conforming jacket consisting of 64 vibrotactile actuators distributed across the torso. Their proposed device allows the exploration of users' emotional immersion while watching movies and feeling stimulations from the jacket. Rich vibrotactile patterns can be conveyed through the jacket; in their study, they designed 40 vibrotactile patterns created from knowledge of touch behaviors in humans, common expressions (e.g., "butterflies in the stomach") and abstract patterns.

The aforementioned approaches have yet to explore a large set of vibrotactile patterns for conveying the six basic emotions of interaction partners during a dyadic interaction. As described in Section 1, such a system would be useful to individuals who blind, providing universal access to visual non-verbal cues, specifically facial expressions, during social interactions. In the next section, we present the implementation details of the Haptic Face Display. We then present a user study to explore a large set of symbolic vibrotactile patterns via the Haptic Face Display through the use of a forced-choice paradigm, in contrast to commonly-used open-response paradigms [10], to better identify emotional responses across patterns.

3   Haptic Face Display

The Haptic Face Display (HFD) is a research platform consisting of a two-dimensional array of vibration motors (eccentric rotating mass) for exploring haptic representations of facial expressions and emotions between interaction styles—passive or active—and at different levels of mediation—literal, semi-literal, semi-symbolic and symbolic. Examples of different levels of mediation are in Table 1.

Table 1. Literal, semi-literal, semi-symbolic and symbolic levels of mediation for haptic representation of facial expressions and emotions

Level of Mediation	Example
Literal	Facial features and fiducial points as is
Semi-Literal	Lip curved upwards, eye brow curved
Semi-Symbolic	Smile, eyes wide open
Symbolic	Happy

The current work explores the passive display of spatiotemporal vibration patterns represented at a symbolic level to elicit emotional responses. Patterns that naturally elicit emotional responses will be used as part of an assistive technology for individuals who are blind to improve universal access to visual nonverbal social cues during dyadic interactions. For this purpose, the HFD was embedded in the back of an ergonomic chair, depicted in Fig. 1(a). Vibration motors are attached to custom-designed boards, referred to as tactor strips. There are eight vibration motors per tactor strips, and tactor strips may be connected to build larger two-dimensional displays with adjustable spacing between tactor strips. Each tactor strip is embedded within the mesh backing of the chair, but vibration motors are placed on the outer mesh via Velcro for direct contact with the skin, depicted in Fig. 1(b). Horizontal inter-tactor spacing is 2 cm, and vertical inter-tactor spacing is 4 cm. A close-up of an individual tactor strip is depicted in Fig. 1(c).

3.1   Hardware Design

The HFD control module, which communicates with the tactor strips, is based on the Arduino platform for ease of prototyping and community support. The control module uses a custom shield design for the Arduino FIO, and can easily support a range of 10-20 vibration motors to be actuated at the same time. We have also developed and manufactured a custom control module to miniaturize its size and improve wearability for other related research projects. The control module connects to the tactor strips via the I^2C bus, which has an upper limit of 128 devices. Our current software protocol limits the number of devices to 64.

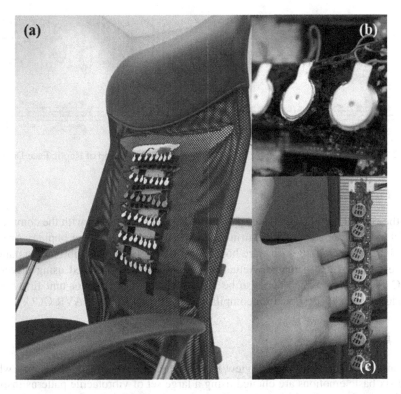

Fig. 1. Haptic Face Display (a) Tactor strips are embedded on the back of an ergonomic mesh chair to explore passive display of symbolic vibration patterns; (b) Close-up of vibration motors and how they attach to a chair; (c) Close-up of a tactor strip

The tactor strips are an extension of our previous work on developing vibrotactile belts [11-12]. As previously described, each tactor strip consists of a linear array of eccentric rotating mass vibration motors and an I²C extender. Each tactor unit of the tactor strip consists of a 3 V DC pancake vibration motor and an ATTINY88 microcontroller for processing communication and pattern commands with independent timing from the control module. The addition of the I²C extender removes bus capacitance, which allows us to approach the bus address device limit of 128. The tactor is implemented on a printed circuit board to maximize flexibility in spacing (as small as 18 mm apart) and placement of vibration motors. The design of the tactor strip is innovative by offering a completely modular solution, not only when combined to create large two-dimensional displays, but also at the level of individual tactor modules. Each tactor unit can be detached from the strip and extended out for larger spacing or reused as a standalone tactor module. The front and back of a tactor strip's circuit design for PCB manufacturing is depicted in Fig. 2. This design is intended to support ease of implementation and rapid prototyping, and has since been shared with the community as a *haptic construction kit*[1].

---

[1] http://hapticconstructionkit.com

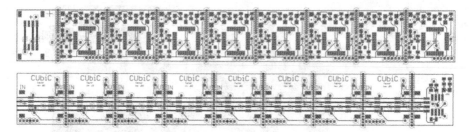

Fig. 2. Front (top) and back (bottom) of circuit design for tactor strip of Haptic Face Display

3.2   Firmware Design

Both the control module and tactor unit firmware has been shared with the community via github[2]. The control module firmware can be loaded using the popular Arduino IDE. Once connected, the firmware hosts a test mode where new vibrotactile patterns may be designed and actuated. Actuation scripts can be developed using drivers in both C and Python, which can also be found on github. The tactor unit firmware is lower level Atmel C designed for compilation via the open source AVR GCC.

4   Experiment

We conducted an Institutional Review Board-approved experiment to identify which of the six basic emotions are elicited using a large set of vibrotactile patterns inspired by existing vibrotactile designs for affective haptics [10]; existing designs that have been explored for possible use in a variety of other applications such as navigation [13]; common wisdoms/sayings such as "a chill down the spine"; and our own results from our previous work and pilot tests with the HFD. Identification of vibrotactile patterns that naturally evoke emotions will support the development of intuitive and easy-to-use social aids for individuals who are blind. The experiment involved 20 participants (10 males and 10 females) recruited from graduate students at Arizona State University. The age range of participants was 18 to 26 years old. Participants had no known visual or tactile impairments. The HFD described in Section 3, Fig. 1(a), was used during the study. Custom software was designed to fully automate the experimental procedure.

During the study, each participant sat in the HFD chair in front of a laptop while listening to white noise through headphones so that vibrations could not be heard. Each participant used the laptop to step through the study's forced-choice procedure using a custom software application created using the Python programming language, the Bootstrap GUI framework, and the serial interface to the HFD. The software presents 54 vibrotactile patterns in a random order. After feeling each pattern, participants select the emotion elicited ('happy', 'sad', 'surprise', 'anger', 'disgust', 'fear' or 'neutral'), intensity of elicitation (rated using a 5-point Likert scale from "Low"-1 to

---

[2] https://github.com/Haptic-Construction-Kit

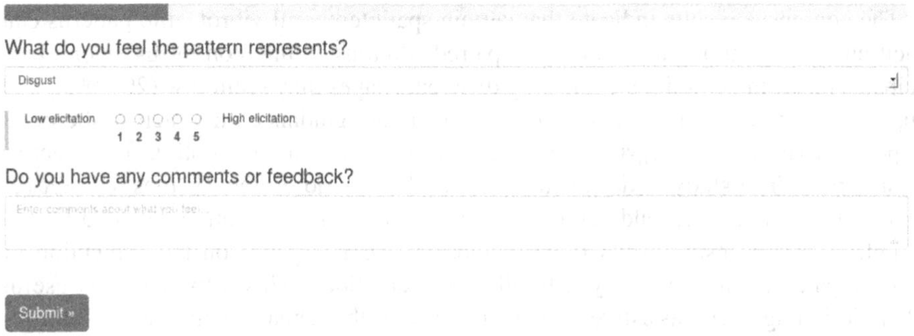

What do you feel the pattern represents?

| Disgust | ▾ |

| Low elicitation | ○ ○ ○ ○ ○ | High elicitation |
| | 1 2 3 4 5 | |

Do you have any comments or feedback?

Enter comments about what you feel...

Submit »

Fig. 3. Screenshot of software for prompting participants and collecting responses

"High"-5 elicitation) and provide further description through an open-ended comment box. Participants also have the option of selecting 'none at all' if no emotion was elicited. Fig. 3 depicts a screenshot of the software, which is implemented as a form in a web browser. The vibrotactile patterns are depicted in Fig. 4-19, and run from left to right. The basis of these patterns is 16 shapes each with 3 timing variations for 48 patterns. Timing variations include pulse widths of 250 ms, 500 ms and 1000 ms; gap width was kept constant at 50 ms. Six saltation [14] versions of the following patterns were also included in the pattern set: Snake (Horizontal), Snake (Vertical), Spiral (In), Spiral (Out), Spine (Up) and Spine (Down).

Certain shapes were more likely to elicit specific emotions compared to others. The following results are averaged across gender, vibration duration (three variations) and with/without saltation.

- Shoulder Tap (Fig. 8), elicited anger with a 22.4% consensus.
- Six Motor Burst (Fig. 9), elicited anger with a 26% consensus.
- Snake (Fig. 10-11), regardless of directionality, elicited happiness with a 28.1% consensus.
- Spine (Fig. 12-13), regardless of directionality, elicited happiness with a 27.2%.
- Spiral (Fig. 14-15), regardless of directionality, elicited neutrality with a 22.9% consensus.
- Wave (Fig. 16-19), regardless of directionality, elicited anger with a 20.9% consensus.

Considering duration variations, patterns of 1000 ms pulse width elicited sadness with 131.6% greater frequency compared to 250 ms; whereas shorter pulse widths were more likely to elicit positive emotions. Patterns of 250 ms pulse width were 103.6% and 23.7% more likely to elicit surprise and happiness, respectively, compared to 500 ms and 1000 ms pulse widths. Considering with/without saltation, those patterns utilizing saltation elicited anger or disgust 59.4% and 18.7% more often, respectively. Patterns without saltation elicited surprise or neutrality 36.5% and 19.2% more often, respectively.

The consensus results indicate that certain spatiotemporal vibrotactile patterns can elicit emotions without any training or paired stimulus. While consensus among participants regarding emotions elicited by different shapes may seem low (20-30%), it is important to note that participants are not given any guidance on which of the eight responses (happy, sad, surprise, anger, fear, disgust, neutral, no emotion) is correct or most correct. The study is designed such that there is no correct or most correct response; the response depends entirely on each user and the emotions elicited by the stimuli. The consensus results found demonstrate convergence on the perception of specific patterns and how they naturally elicit emotions. This information is useful when designing social assistive aids in such a way that enhances naturalness and reduces training times; for example, the proposed Snake pattern seems best for conveying happiness; the Six Motor Burst or a saltation design may be used to convey anger; and the Spiral pattern may be used to convey neutrality. Longer durations may be used to convey sadness whereas shorter durations may be used to convey happiness and excitement.

Fig. 4. Alternate (Left, Right)

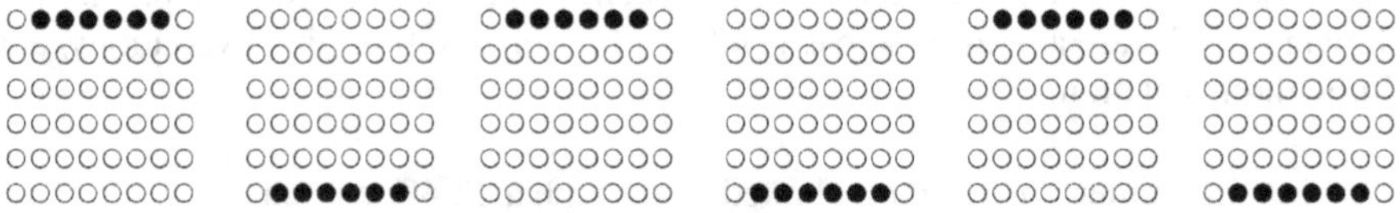

Fig. 5. Alternate (Top, Bottom)

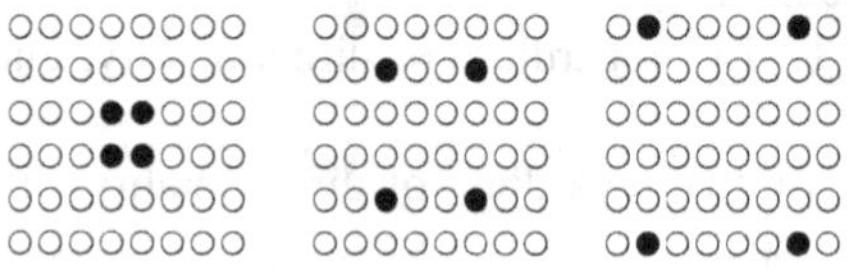

Fig. 6. Explode

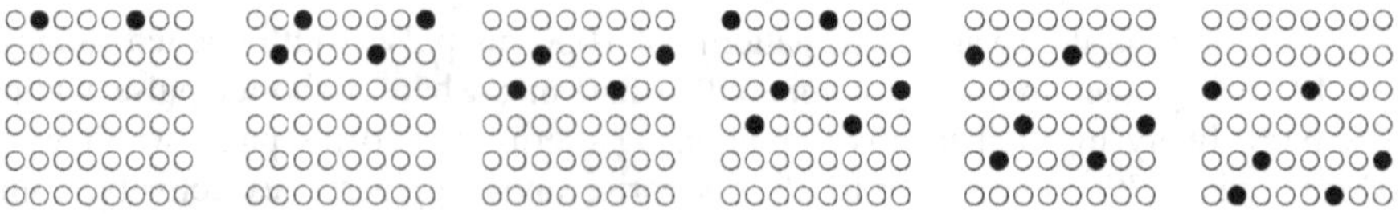

Fig. 7. Rain

Fig. 8. Shoulder Tap

Fig. 9. Six Motor Burst

Fig. 10. Snake (Horizontal)

Fig. 11. Snake (Vertical)

Fig. 12. Spine (Down)

Fig. 13. Spine (Up)

Fig. 14. Spiral (In)

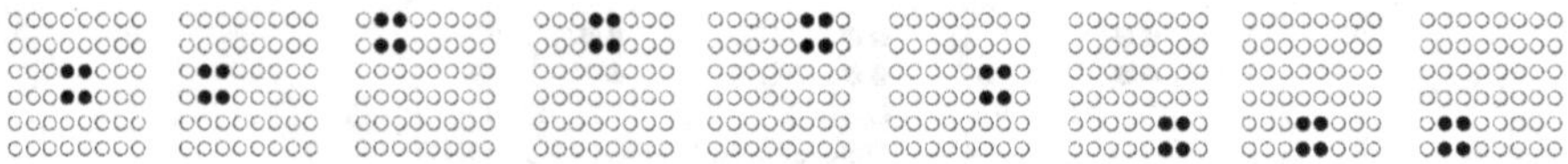

Fig. 15. Spiral (Out)

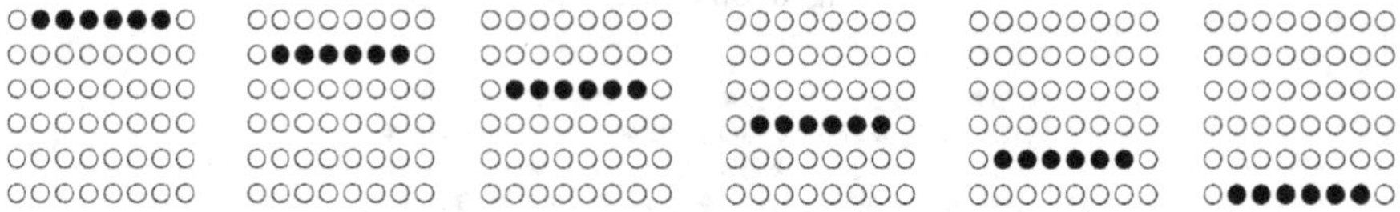

Fig. 16. Wave (Down)

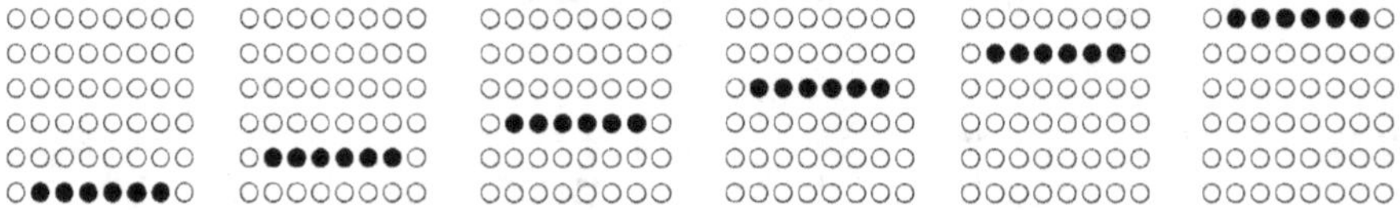

Fig. 17. Wave (Up)

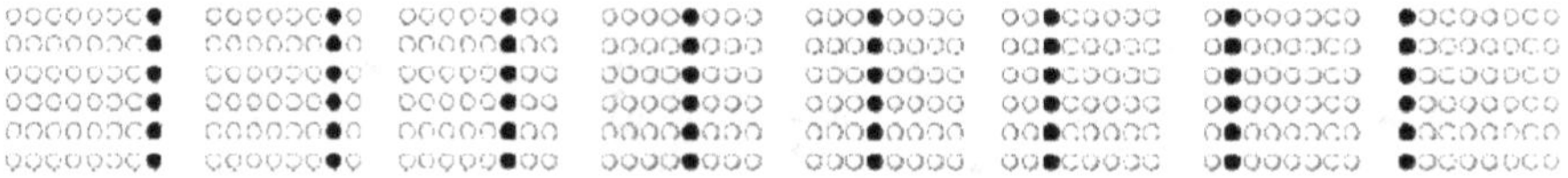

Fig. 18. Wave (Left)

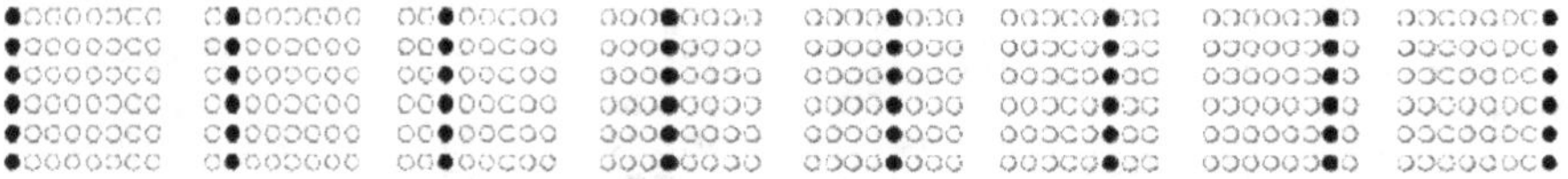

Fig. 19. Wave (Right)

5   Conclusion and Future Work

We have introduced a novel haptic display, called the Haptic Face Display (HFD), which serves as a versatile research platform to explore affective haptics among other applications in passive or active interaction styles. In this work, we have used the HFD to explore natural emotional responses to spatiotemporal vibrotactile patterns for eventual use in assistive social aids for individuals who are blind. As part of future work, we are using the HFD to explore different levels of mediation including semi-symbolic, semi-literal and literal haptic representations of emotions and facial expressions. We are also extending the design presented here to support multimodal presentation of emotions using other modalities of touch such as light to hard pressure and temperature variations.

Acknowledgements. We would like to thank the National Science Foundation and Arizona State University for their funding support. This material is partially based upon work supported by the National Science Foundation under Grant Nos. 1069125 and 1116360.

References

1. Knapp, M.L.: Nonverbal Communication in Human Interaction. Harcourt College Pub. (1996)
2. Krishna, S., Colbry, D., Black, J., Balasubramanian, V., Panchanathan, S.: A Systematic Requirements Analysis and Development of an Assistive Device to Enhance the Social Interaction of People Who are Blind or Visually Impaired. In: Proceedings of the Workshop on Computer Vision Applications for the Visually Impaired (CVAVI 2008), ECCV (2008)
3. McDaniel, T., Krishna, S., Balasubramanian, V., Colbry, D., Panchanathan, S.: Using a Haptic Belt to Convey Non-Verbal Communication Cues during Social Interactions to Individuals who are Blind. In: Proceedings of the IEEE International Workshop on Haptic Audio Visual Environments and Games, pp. 13–18 (2008)
4. McDaniel, T.L., Krishna, S., Colbry, D., Panchanathan, S.: Using Tactile Rhythm to Convey Interpersonal Distances to Individuals who are Blind. In: Proceedings of the CHI 2009 Extended Abstracts on Human Factors in Computing Systems, pp. 4669–4674 (2009)
5. Krishna, S., Bala, S., McDaniel, T., McGuire, S., Panchanathan, S.: VibroGlove: An Assistive Technology Aid for Conveying Facial Expressions. In: Proceedings of the CHI 2010 Extended Abstracts on Human Factors in Computing Systems, pp. 3637–3642 (2010)
6. Krishna, S., Bala, S., Panchanathan, S.: Exploring the Dorsal Surface of the Fingers for Visio-Haptic Sensory Substitution. In: Proceedings of the IEEE International Symposium on Haptic Audio-Visual Environments and Games (HAVE), pp. 1–6 (2010)
7. Liu, L., Li, H.: Manifold of Facial Expressions for Tactile Perception. In: Proceedings of the IEEE 9th Workshop on Multimedia Signal Processing, pp. 239–242 (2007)
8. Tsetserukou, D., Neviarouskaya, A.: iFeel_IM!: Augmenting Emotions during Online Communication. IEEE Computer Graphics and Applications 30(5), 72–80 (2010)
9. Lemmens, P., Crompvoets, F., Brokken, D., van den Eerenbeemd, J., De Vries, G.-J.: A Body-Conforming Tactile Jacket to Enrich Movie Viewing. In: Proceedings of the Third Joint EuroHaptics Conference and Symposium on Haptic Interfaces for Virtual Environment and Teleoperator Systems, pp. 7–12 (2009)
10. Benali-Khoudja, M., Hafez, M., Sautour, A., Jumpertz, S.: Towards a New Tactile Language to Communicate Emotions. In: Proceedings of the IEEE International Conference Mechatronics and Automation, pp. 286–291 (2005)
11. Edwards, N., Rosenthal, J., Moberly, D., Lindsay, J., Blair, K., Krishna, S., McDaniel, T., Panchanathan, S.: A Pragmatic Approach to the Design and Implementation of a Vibrotactile Belt and its Applications. In: Proceedings of the IEEE International Workshop on Haptic Audio Visual Environments and Games, pp. 13–18 (2009)
12. Rosenthal, J., Edwards, N., Villanueva, D., Krishna, S., McDaniel, T., Panchanathan, S.: Design, Implementation, and Case Study of a Pragmatic Vibrotactile Belt. IEEE Transactions on Instrumentation and Measurement 60(1), 114–125 (2011)
13. Piateski, E., Jones, L.: Vibrotactile Pattern Recognition on the Arm and Torso. In: Proceedings of the First Joint Eurohaptics Conference and Symposium on Haptic Interfaces for Virtual Environment and Teleoperator Systems, pp. 90–95 (2005)
14. Geldard, F.A., Sherrick, C.E.: The Cutaneous 'Rabbit': A Perceptual Illusion. Science 178(4057), 178–179 (1972)

Haptic Visualization of Real-World Environmental Data for Individuals with Visual Impairments

Chung Hyuk Park[1] and Ayanna M. Howard[2]

[1] Department of Electrical and Computer Engineering, School of Engineering and Computing
Sciences, New York Institute of Technology, U.S.A
[2] School of Electrical and Computer Engineering, College of Engineering,
Georgia Institute of Technology, U.S.A
ayanna.howard@ece.gatech.edu, chung.park@nyit.edu

Abstract. In this paper, we present a haptic visualization system that transforms visual perception of depth into a 3D tangible experience. This haptic interface is used to enable a user with visual impairments to explore a remote environment through touch feedback. Experiments with participants with/without visual impairments are constructed, and results are presented that show efficiency of the system as well as discuss responses from user interaction. Furthermore, a viable solution is described that utilizes the presented methodology of transforming image-based data into haptic representation for assisting in STEM education for students with visual impairments.

Keywords: Haptic exploration, haptic assistance for remote perception, haptic assistance for visual information transfer.

1 Introduction

It might be difficult to imagine what it would be like to live with a visual impairment; to imagine a situation where a person with a visual impairment (VI) must walk on public streets while heading to an, unknown, remote location or explore a new place such as a museum or a shopping center. However, most people realize that the most popular device or means within the last decade for assisting individuals with VI are still the guide cane and guide dog. At the same time, we notice that there are many new technological breakthroughs, such as telepresence and augmented reality, that are expanding our social boundaries, enabling us to visually explore remote places on our own or enabling immersion of oneself as an avatar in new environments.

Although many assistive devices have been developed to aid individuals in achieving their daily activities of living [1], the boundary conditions for operation are usually limited to the physical surrounding area for individuals with visual impairments. Recent assistive devices, including electronic Braille adaptors and computer-screen readers, have evolved to transfer more information to the user and have granted wider access to daily living for people with impairments, including education and employment [2, 3, 4]. However, most of these tools are designed to work passively

C. Stephanidis and M. Antona (Eds.): UAHCI/HCII 2014, Part I, LNCS 8513, pp. 430–439, 2014.
© Springer International Publishing Switzerland 2014

with predefined sources of information, and aid in mobility or manipulation to assist in daily living only in specific conditions. What can be added to this list of assistive devices? Which technology can be further developed to support individuals with visual impairments? Can an intelligent and multi-purpose assistive system help in this domain?

Based on the current status of assistive technology and advancements in robotics, we speculate that a mobile manipulation robotic platform will be a viable solution to serve as a multi-purpose assistive tool for people with visual impairments. Teleoperation and robotics technology, which are enabling remote operations and telepresence experience, can bring a new form of assistance that can expand the physical boundaries of living and provide new possibilities with multi-functional capabilities. If combined with robotic sensing capabilities (such as robotic vision) and multimodal interaction methodologies (such as auditory and haptic feedback), a robotic system can be further utilized as a gateway to providing multi-purpose assistance including sensory perception.

As such, in this paper, we discuss a method to increase the range of accessibility to a remote environment through robotic embodiment that enables tele-operation and tele-perception through haptic visualization. In developing the haptic visualization system, we also examine the linkage between control modality and haptic feedback as well as the effectiveness of the haptic visualization process on users with/without VI. The general concept of our system is illustrated in Fig. 1.

Taking a step further, once we develop the haptic visualization process, we anticipate that this system could be utilized in STEM (Science, Technology, Engineering, and Math) education for individuals with visual impairments. Due to the fact that learning material mostly rely on visual aids in STEM fields, it has been observed that the population of VI students entering colleges with STEM majors has far lower percentile than that of average students with disabilities [5]. We expect that our haptic visualization process will be also effective in generating tangible representation to convey visual materials in STEM-related curriculums. Thus, we will address this challenging issue and add our ideas toward more effective supports in STEM education for individuals with VI.

Fig. 1. The conceptual illustration of our telepresence robot with haptic visualization for individuals with visual impairments (VI) in exploring a remote environment

2   Haptic Exploration for Telepresence of Individuals with VI

2.1   Haptic Visualization Algorithm

With the recent advancement in 3D depth sensing with RGB-D sensors, point-cloud based depth data is found to be effective in enabling 3D haptic rendering [6] both in real-time [7] and in off-line applications [8]. In our prior work [9], we developed a method to provide real-time 3D perception for a remote environment to a user. By incorporating this method with the tele-operative controllability of a haptic interface, we have developed a bi-lateral telepresence system through 3D haptic exploration. The haptic 3D rendering module enables the user to gain 3D perception of the remote environment through real-time interaction, so the user can "explore" the remote environment through touch feedback while the telepresence robot smoothly follows the navigation control of the user.

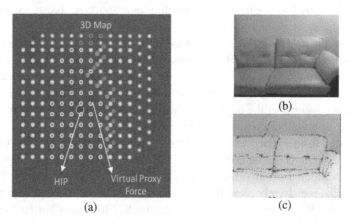

Fig. 2. Illustration of a virtual-proxy force calculation: (a) An illustration of a 3D point map of a bottle-shaped object for the generation of virtual-proxy force; (b),(c) Example of the haptic 3D visualization and trajectories of exploration on a real environment.

We utilize a RGB-D camera mounted on a telepresence robotic system to transfer information about the 3D scene to the remote user. For haptic feedback, an interface that includes a stylus for providing haptic feedback is used by the user, and we employ the Phantom Omni (now renamed with Geomagic Touch) as our haptic interface. Once the 3D scene is acquired through vision-based imaging, it is transformed into a 3D occupancy map (Fig. 2-(a)) that represents volumetric objects in the observed environment in the haptic workspace. This map can be updated in real time to handle the dynamic changes and movements of the telepresence robot as it navigates in the remote environment. Based on the user's movement using the haptic interface, virtual-proxy forces [10] can be calculated by finding the closest surface point of the object and the haptic interaction point (HIP) that penetrates the object on the 3D map. For estimating the penetration depth, we monitor the position of HIP in the haptic workspace and then find the optimal surface-normal vector (Pproxy) that can enable the user to feel the 3D shape of the region the user's haptic interface is touching. We employ a spring-damper model [11, 12, 13] for kinesthetic representation of the force feedback, as described in Equation 1. Given the position vector of the proxy Pproxy, a position vector of the probe Pprobe, and the velocities of the proxy and the probe, vproxy and vprobe, a virtual-proxy force-feedback ffeedback is composed of a penetration depth term (with a spring constant k) and a damping term (with a damping constant b). This real-world imagery data is extracted directly from the camera sensors embedded on the mobile robot.

$$f_{feedback} = k(P_{proxy} - P_{probe}) + b(v_{proxy} - v_{probe}) \quad (1)$$

2.2   Haptic Telepresence Robotic System for Individuals with VI

For our telepresence robotic platform, we incorporate a mobile manipulation robot as shown in Fig. 3-(a). The main hardware platform is composed of a robotic arm (Pioneer2 Arm) and a robotic mobile base (Pioneer 3AT), equipped with the Kinect depth sensor. The system interfaces with a user through a graphic-user-interface (GUI) for typical users and through a haptic interface for visually-impaired users. The visual and haptic view from the robot is displayed in Fig. 3-(b). The haptic interface also incorporates verbal feedback in its design.

The main control architecture is composed of three functional blocks: 1) vision-based depth perception module, 2) haptic interaction module, and 3) telepresence robot control module. The visual module perceives 2D color perception of the environment as well as 3D depth information in real time (30fps) and feeds this information into the haptic interaction module. The haptic interaction module governs both haptic force feedback to the user for 3D perception and haptic control input for teleoperation of the robot. The robot control module is composed of a finite-state-machine (FSM) that governs state changes and sub-module controllers [14]. As a side component of the architecture, there is also a verbal feedback block, which works synchronously with the haptic interface to present verbal feedback to the user. Details are explained in the following section.

(a) Robotic platform and the experimental setup   (b) Trajectories of haptic 3D exploration

Fig. 3. Experimental setup for our telepresence robot and the user's trajectories during haptic exploration

2.3   System Control Algorithms

3D Depth Sensor Processing. The Kinect sensor, despite its outstanding performances and cost-efficiency, has two characteristics that limit the quality of its sensory perception. First, since the depth is measured by the array of reflected lights emitted from a

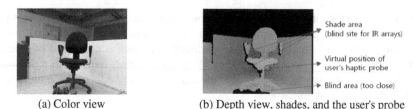

(a) Color view   (b) Depth view, shades, and the user's probe

Fig. 4. Haptic probing of a chair in a 3D map

small source emitter, the reconstructed 3D points inevitably contain large shading areas that degrade the quality of haptic representation (Fig. 4). Secondly, the inherent noise in the sensor data creates random noise in values, which can cause "dark spots" (missing depth values) and broken/rough surfaces in the constructed 3D map.

Since we seek fast algorithms to enable real-time implementation, we provide a solution to the above issues by using temporal filters. As Fig. 5 illustrates, the noisy Kinect depth data goes through a temporal filtering process to reduce the effects from the two issues. The temporal filter first finds the shaded regions, fills the shaded regions using distance-based smoothing, and then performs pixel-wise median filtering to reduce outliers ("dark spots") due to the sensory noise. Fig. 6 shows the difference between the raw depth data and the filtered depth data.

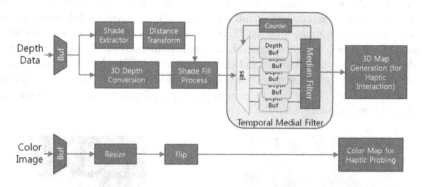

Fig. 5. Temporal filtering of Kinect sensor data

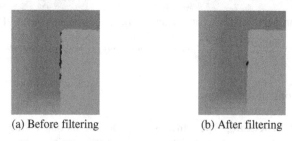

(a) Before filtering   (b) After filtering

Fig. 6. Result of the temporal filtering

Robot Controller and Haptic and Auditory Feedback. Based on the user's click on the button on the stylus of the haptic interface, the robotic system automatically iterates between three states of robot control: idle, static haptic exploration, and robotic navigation with haptic exploration (Fig. 7). In addition, the robotic navigation state can be configured with one of the following control options: manual control with keyboard or semi-autonomous navigation with the haptic interface. In manual control mode, the user can move the robot around with arrow keys, while in the semi-autonomous navigation mode (namely "AutoNav") the user can first explore the remote environment with the haptic interface and just click on a desired target location in the haptic workspace, which will activate the robot's autonomous navigation module to reach the goal location corresponding to the clicked-point in the haptic space.

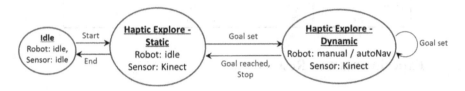

Fig. 7. Finite-state machine (FSM) for our telepresence robot control with haptic feedback. Goal is set by the user through touching on a virtual space corresponding to a point on a remote environment and clicking on the stylus.

Haptic force feedback is used to transfer information to the user through the user's force and tactile perception. The Virtual-Proxy force explained in Section 2.1 is the main haptic feedback source that is formed by the user's haptic exploration in the 3D space mapped from the robotic perception. As the user moves the stylus of the haptic interface in the free space (in the workspace of the device), the user will experience no force (if the HIP is exploring empty space of the remote environment) or virtual-proxy force feedback toward the surface of the volume space perceived by the depth sensor. To provide multi-modal information to assist in better perception, we also provide auditory feedback in the form of verbal notification.

The auditory feedback consists of verbal descriptions of color and distance information associated with an object the haptic probe is in contact with. It also consists of a brief verbal report on the status of robotic movements. The color and distance information is reported to the user when the haptic probe is interacting with an object in the 3D map (in other words, "penetrating" the virtual objects in the 3D map). The list of colors recognized by our system is shown in Table 1. The verbal description of the status of our robotic system consist of "forward", "left", "right", "backward", and "stop", and are reported only when the status changes. i.e. it does not keep reporting "forward" while moving forward but reports only once.

Table 1. List of colors available for verbal feedback.

1	aqua	18	gold	35	midnight blue	52	sea green
2	aquamarine	19	green	36	navy blue	53	sienna
3	black	20	green yellow	37	neon blue	54	sky blue
4	blue	21	grey	38	olive	55	slate blue
5	blue violet	22	hot pink	39	olive green	56	spring green
6	bronze	23	indian red	40	orange	57	steel blue
7	brown	24	ivory	41	orange red	58	summer sky
8	cadet blue	25	khaki	42	orchid	59	turquoise
9	charteuse	26	lawn green	43	pale green	60	violet
10	chocolate	27	light blue	44	pale violet	61	violet red
11	coral	28	light coral	45	peach	62	white
12	dark green	29	light gold	46	pink	63	wood
13	dark grey	30	light sky blue	47	plum	64	yellow
14	deep pink	31	lime green	48	purple	65	yellow green
15	deep sky blue	32	magenta	49	red		
16	dodger blue	33	maroon	50	royal blue		
17	forest green	34	mdeium purple	51	scarlet		

3   Experiments and Results

To evaluate the ability of the system in increasing the range of accessibility to a remote environment, we designed a set of experiments to evaluate the system performance as well as the user's experience. The experiments are performed given a common haptic input method for haptic exploration and two control mechanisms: manual control and haptically-aided semi-autonomous navigation. The goal for the user was to "find a blue/red ball and approach it."

We provided two scenarios. In Scenario 1, the participant was asked to use keyboard control to control the robot while utilizing the haptic interface for haptic exploration. The controls were defined as the traditional keyboard control of ↑ for making the robot move forward, ↓ for making the robot move backward, ← for making the robot turn left, → for making the robot turn right, and Ctrl-key for making the robot stop.

In Scenario 2, the participant was allowed to explore the remote environment with the haptic interface, and upon finding the target object, was instructed to click on the position in the haptic space to command the robot to approach that position autonomously.

A total of 10 human subjects (one female and nine male subjects) participated in our experiments. Among them, nine were sighted and one was fully blind. The age group was between 20 and 40. Each subject was given a tutorial of the system (about 5-10 minutes) and then given two scenarios.

To evaluate user performance in task solving with our telepresence system, we measured the control time for task achievement and the success rates for Scenarios 1 and 2. The average time taken for Scenario 1 was 58.2 sec, and 32.38 sec for Scenario 2. The median values and the variations are depicted as a bar plot in Fig. 8.

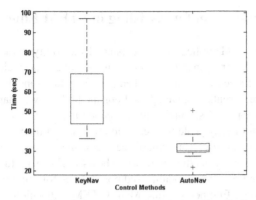

Fig. 8. Task time comparison between manual control and haptically-aided navigation

Table 2. Success rates of human subjects in achieving the tasks using different control methods. (O: success, X: failure)

Scenario \ Subjects	1	2	3	4	5	6	7	8	9	10
1 (KeyNav)	O	O	O	X	O	O	X	X	O	X
2 (AutoNav)	O	X	X	O	O	X	O	O	O	O

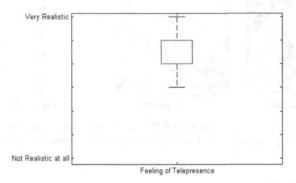

Fig. 9. Survey result of the question on the feeling of being tele-present

The success rates for Scenario 1 and 3 for the 10 participants were 60% and 70% respectively, as shown in Table 2. The average success rate of the participants with visual impairments was 100% for both scenarios, but the number of participants is small at this stage to draw a statistically reasonable conclusion. Based on these results, we can see that the control methods does not affect the performance in the success of the task, but significantly reduce the time for controlling the robot.

For qualitative evaluation, participants of our experiments were asked to answer a survey ([14]), and the result on the question "Did you feel like you are being tele-present in a remote place through the robotic system? How realistic was it, in the degree of 1 to 7 ? (7: Very realistic, 1: Not realistic at all)" is presented in Fig. 9.

4   Haptic Exploration for Assisting in STEM Education

As an additional real-world application, we expanded the ability of the system to enable haptic 3D rendering of more general geometric, mathematical, and scientific contents as illustrated in Fig. 10. Since our haptic visualization algorithm transforms depth information into 3D haptic representation, we applied our methodology to haptically transform geometric, mathematical, and scientific images (since many of them contain depth information in the form of gray-scale images) into a haptic 3D representation. With simple gray-scale images, the user can experience the shapes and properties through our haptic visualization instantly, as the trajectories shows in Fig. 10 – (a,d,e). We envision that this approach can bring new modality and possibilities for other opportunities, such as Science, Technology, Engineering and Math (STEM) education, especially for students with visual impairments.

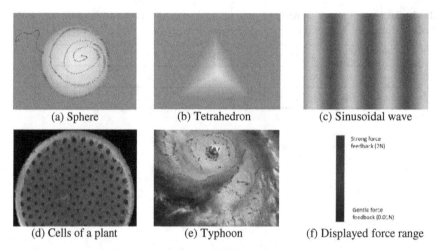

| (a) Sphere | (b) Tetrahedron | (c) Sinusoidal wave |
| (d) Cells of a plant | (e) Typhoon | (f) Displayed force range |

Fig. 10. Images for haptic visualization on STEM education. (a,d,e) contains trajectories of haptic forcefeedback during haptic exploration, with the force scale colorized as in (f).

5   Discussions

In this paper, we have presented a haptic-visualization system and its application for providing haptic-based perception of a remote enviornment, as well as possibilities in STEM data visualization. Our system can effectively represent vision-rich data (both spatial and informational data) to the user through haptic and verbal feedback. Based on feedback from the participants of our experiments, our next step of studies will focus on a much broader empasis in providing well-designed support for daily living. We believe, in the future, there will be additional ways for investigating and expanding on our research, and we plan to pursue this goal through more user studies and user adaptation of our system.

References

1. Hersh, M.A.: Assistive Technology for Visually Impaired and Blind People. Springer (2007)
2. Ludi, S.A., Reichlmayr, T.: Developing inclusive outreach activities for students with visual impairments. In: Proceedings of the 39th SIGCSE Technical Symposium on Computer Science Education, pp. 439–443. ACM (2008)
3. Pell, S.D., Gillies, R.M., Carss, M.: Relationship between use of technology and employment rates for people with physical disabilities in Australia: implications for education and training programs. Disability & Rehabilitation 19(8), 332–338 (1997)
4. Robinson, J.E.: Access to employment for people with disabilities: findings of a consumer-led project. Disability & Rehabilitation 22(5), 246–253 (2000)
5. National Science Foundation, Division of Science Resources Statistics, Women, Minorities, and Persons with Disabilities in Science and Engineering: 2002 (September 2003)
6. Salisbury, K., Conti, F., Barbagli, F.: Haptic rendering: Introductory concepts (2004)
7. Rydén, F., Chezeck, H.J., Kosari, S.N., King, H., Hannaford, B.: Using Kinect and a haptic interface for implementation of real-time virtual fixtures. In: Proceedings of the 2nd Workshop on RGB-D: Advanced Reasoning with Depth Cameras (in conjunction with RSS 2011) (2011)
8. Sreeni, K.G., Chaudhuri, S.: Haptic rendering of dense 3D point cloud data. In: Proceedings of IEEE Haptics Symposium (HAPTICS), pp. 333–339 (March 2012)
9. Park, C.H., Howard, A.M.: Real world haptic exploration for telepresence of the visually impaired. In: Proceedings of ACM/IEEE International Conference on Human Robot Interaction (HRI). IEEE (2012)
10. Ruspini, D.C., Kolarov, K., Khatib, O.: Haptic interaction in virtual environments. In: Proceedings of the IEEE-RSJ Int. Conf. on Intelligent Robots and Systems, pp. 128–133 (1997)
11. Colgate, J.E., Schenkel, G.: Passivity of a class of sampled-data systems: Application to haptic interfaces. In: Proceedings of IEEE American Control Conference, vol. 3, pp. 3236–3240 (June 1994)
12. Corso, J.J., Chhugani, J., Okamura, A.M.: Interactive haptic rendering of deformable surfaces based on the medial axis transform. In: Proceedings of Eurohaptics, pp. 92–98 (2002)
13. Mehling, J.S., Colgate, J.E., Peshkin, M.A.: Increasing the impedance range of a haptic display by adding electrical damping. In: Proceedings of First Joint World Haptics Conference, Eurohaptics Conference, and Symposium on Haptic Interfaces for Virtual Environment and Teleoperator Systems, pp. 257–262 (March 2005)
14. Park, C.H.: Robot-based haptic perception and telepresence for the visually impaired. Ph.D. thesis, School of Electrical and Computer Engineering, Georgia Institute of Technology (2012)

A Speech-To-Text System's Acceptance Evaluation: Would Deaf Individuals Adopt This Technology in Their Lives?

Soraia Silva Prietch[1], Napoliana Silva de Souza[1], and Lucia Villela Leite Filgueiras[2]

[1] Lic. em Informática/Sistemas de Informação, Universidade Federal de Mato Grosso (UFMT),
Rod. Rondonopolis-Guiratinga, KM 06 (MT 270). Sagrada Família,
Rondonopolis-MT, BR, 78735-901, Brazil
[2] Escola Politécnica, Universidade de São Paulo,
Av. Prof. Luciano Gualberto, trav. 3, n. 158. Sao Paulo-SP, BR, 05508-970,Brazil
soraia@ufmt.br, souzapoliana2@gmail.com, lfilguei@usp.br

Abstract. The problem observed was the difficulty of people who are Deaf or Hard of Hearing (D/HH) to know what is being said or informed in an environment, especially at schools, when sign language interpreter is absent. Thus, the main goal was to investigate which variables most influence on the acceptance of a Speech-To-Text system with regard to the different profiles of people who are D/HH. For the purpose mentioned, we conducted a pilot study in two distinct field researches, in which 11 D/HH volunteers participated. During this study, we used two models as inspiration, TAM and UTAUT, for data collection, which was concerned with: written communication, educational barriers, technology use, habit of using captions and subtitles, emotions, technology acceptance, social influence, empowerment and privacy. In the case of emotions, we used Emotion-LIBRAS, an instrument for people who are D/HH to identify positive, negative or mixed emotions towards technology.

Keywords: People who are Deaf or Hard of Hearing (D/HH), Automatic Speech Recognition (ASR), Technology acceptance, Mobile app, Emotions.

1 Introduction

Picture a place, in which there is only one person who is deaf signer among many hearing individuals who are non-signers. This is a common scenario in inclusive public high-schools in Brazil. Most of the time, deaf students are helped by sign language interpreters. However, interpreters are not always with them at schools. This situation is problematic for many reasons. Deaf students who are signers: (a) may tend to communicate only with a few individuals, mostly other deaf students, forming a segregated group; (b) may involve in a communication-dependency with interpreters, not only in classroom but in other school environments; and, (c) may not know how to follow classes if interpreters are not present. Coupled with these difficulties, also, in Brazilians mainstream public schools, we do not have note-takers; there are a small

C. Stephanidis and M. Antona (Eds.): UAHCI/HCII 2014, Part I, LNCS 8513, pp. 440–449, 2014.
© Springer International Publishing Switzerland 2014

number of interpreters to assist all deaf students; and, in some cities, only a small group of deaf persons are oralized and/or can do lip-reading.

Taking this information into account, you may note that we cannot generalize a specific characteristic of groups of people who are Deaf or Hard of Hearing (D/HH). They are a diverse community concerning with their communication skills. In Table 1, the combination of three types of communication that deaf individuals may use: sign language, text reading and writing, and orally speaking with lip reading. This combination resulted in eight modes of communication. Thus, someone might use sign language and written text, another might use three types, and so on.

Table 1. Profiles of people who are D/HH

Sign Language (SL)	Read and Write texts (RW)		Oralization and Lip reading (OL)
	Yes	No	
Yes	[Profile1] SL+RW+OL	[Profile5] SL+OL	Yes
Yes	[Profile2] SL+RW	[Profile6] SL	No
No	[Profile3] RW+OL	[Profile7] OL	Yes
No	[Profile4] RW	[Profile8] *Null*	No

This diversity has stimulated interest in research regarding the possibility of acceptance of a speech-to-text system. This research can bring up some controversial discussions, such as: reduction of jobs for interpreters, or the devaluation of the mother tongue of people who are D/HH. However, we are trying to offer one alternative for situations in which deaf individuals are at a disadvantage in an environment communicatively uncomfortable for them. The problem observed was the difficulty of people who are D/HH to know what is being said or informed in an environment, especially at schools, when sign language interpreter is absent.

Thus, the main goal was to investigate which variables most influence on the acceptability of a speech recognition system with regard to the different profiles of people who are D/HH (Table 1). For this purpose, we conducted a pilot study in two distinct field researches, in which 11 D/HH volunteers participated. During this study, we used two models as inspiration, TAM and UTAUT, for data collection, which was concerned with: written communication, educational barriers, technology use, habit of using captions and subtitles, emotions, technology acceptance, social influence, empowerment and privacy. In the case of emotions, we used Emotion-LIBRAS [7][8], an instrument for people who are D/HH to identify emotions towards technology.

The remainder of the paper is organized as follows. Section 2 describes the theoretical foundation on technology acceptance models; In Section 3, related works about educational use of STT systems concerning with deaf students are briefly described. In Section 4, methods and materials are presented; Section 5 report results and discussion; and, in Section 6, conclusions are evidenced.

2   Technology Acceptance Models

Elements from two technology acceptance models were used in this research; the first model is the Technology Acceptance Model (TAM) proposed by Davis, Bagozzi and

Warshaw [2] to understand information systems usage behavior, using 02 constructs as the main predictors: *perceived usefulness* and *perceived ease of use*; and, the second model, called Unified Theory of Acceptance and Use of Technology (UTAUT), was proposed by Venkatesh *et al* [12] in order to unify eight existent information technology acceptance models. UTAUT model concerns with 04 constructs: *performance expectancy, effort expectancy, social influence,* and *facilitating conditions.*

Pan *et al* [4] carried out a research using real-time transcription for computer-mediated communication tested with 24 Chinese university students who are non-native English speakers. Their model constructs included: (a) Response accuracy; (b) Participant's confidence of the answer's correctness; (c) User satisfaction; (d) Cognitive load; and, (e) Perception of speech recognition errors. Tests were conducted, by [4], considering three transcription conditions: no transcript, perfect transcript, and transcript with low recognition rate. As results, Pan *et al* [4] reported that (a), (b), and (c) were significantly better in perfect transcript condition than the others; with respect to cognitive load, it was not found significant user perceived task difficulty and that participants felt recognition errors caused interference in understanding.

Papadopoulos and Pearson [5] developed the Semantic and Syntactic Transcription Analysing Tool (SSTAT) in order to improve text transcription from automatic recognition systems, and conducted an acceptance evaluation of the system with 26 undergraduate and postgraduate students as participants (03 were D/HH). Research constructs used were: (a) Perception of transcription quality; (b) Perceived acceptance of transcripts; and, (c) Usefulness and perceived usability. As results, Papadopoulos and Pearson [5] informed general findings, not specifying by type of disability, in which constructs (a) and (b) are related to transcription accuracy; also participants found ASR useful (c) as an alternative of conventional note taking.

Rodríguez, Caminero and Van Kampen [11] proposed the SignSpeak, an assistive technology for people who are deaf, which recognize and translate continuous sign language to text. Authors refers to acceptance models (TAM, UTAUT and TPC), however results from an acceptance evaluation by people who are deaf are not shown.

3   STT System for Educational Use by Deaf Students

Motivated by Liberated Learning Project (LLP)[1], the sixteen following works investigated the use of STT systems in classroom settings by hearing students and students who are D/HH: Bain et al [1], Primiani, Tibaldi and Garlaschelli [9], Ranchal et al [10], Wald [13], Wald [14], Wald and Bain [15], Wald [16], Wald and Bain [17], Wald [18], Wald [19], Wald and Yunjia [20], and, Zhili, Wanjie and Cheng [21].

Among these works, only four ([10], [19], [20], [21]) actually carried out field researches with D/HH participants and used synchronized medias (videos and classes

---

[1] "In 1998, Saint Mary's University (SMU) in Nova Scotia, Canada, proposed a project [LLP] to create a more fully accessible learning environment. [...] In the resulting Liberated Learning courses, instructors use ASR [*Automatic Speech Recognition*] to display spoken language as text." ([1], p. 592).

slides) along with automatic speech transcription. In [10], [19], [20] target users were undergraduate and graduate students, carried out in U.S.A. and Canada; and in [21] were deaf students from primary and secondary special schools, conducted in China. With respect of acceptance evaluation, none of researches used any acceptance model.

Ranchal et al [10] used a SR-mediated lecture acquisition (SR-mLA) taking two situations into account: (a) real-time captioning (RTC); and, (b) post-lecture transcription (PLT) using synchronized media; during an entire semester. Comparing these two situations, with respect to: technical feasibility and reliability of classroom implementation, instructors' experiences, word recognition accuracy, and student class performance; PLT showed better results for all compared factors. Also, emotional feedback of some students was the sense of minimizing the concern during note taking and of relaxing to pay more attention to the teachers.

Wald [19]; and, Wald and Yunjia [20] have been evaluating Synote for note taking during classes and for content reviewing, since 2008. During 04 years, it was evidenced improvements on: learning, attention, motivation, pleasure, and obtaining results. Zhili, Wanjie and Jiacheng [21] reported that distractions occurred when transcribed texts contain errors, reducing enthusiasm. According to Bain et al [1], transcription errors can be barriers in acceptance of STT systems.

4   Methods and Materials

First, we defined research's hypotheses and technology acceptance model, which are presented in Fig. 1. We used TAM [2] as the model structure and some ideas of UTAUT [12]'s constructs to formulate hypotheses.

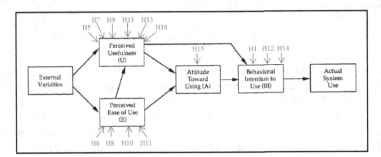

Fig. 1. Model and hypotheses of this research

Second, we prepared materials, specially elaborating questions (Pre-test (PeTQ) and Post-test (PoTQ) questionnaires[2]) taking hypotheses as the start point. Hypotheses are described in Subsection 5.1, where we report results and discussion. Third, materials were organized to be used in six stages of field research procedure. In Field research 1 and 2, the script followed the same order: (a) term of consent, explaining

---

[2]   Available in: `http://goo.gl/Qw6IRw`,
  file names: "Pre_test_PrietchSouzaFilgueiras.pdf" and "PostTest_and_EmotionLIBRAS.pdf".

research procedures and objectives, and asking for image authorization; (b) mood status sheet3, including 40 emoticons (with its respective words in Brazilian Portuguese), taken from Facebook ('How are you feeling?'); (c) pre-test questionnaire; (d) test, which consisted in a repetition the following three steps for each participant: one researcher read one phrase for audio capture and recognition processing, using a Samsung GalaxyNote GT-N7000; SampleVoiceApp from Nuance Dragon Mobile [3] deliver transcripted text; and, one participant read the transcripted text and communicate it in sign language what he/she understood without help; (e) Emotion-LIBRAS4, to identify emotions of participants concerning with experience of using a STT system; and, (f) post-test questionnaire was elaborated with inspiration in [2],[6],[12].

5   Results and Discussion

Table 2 refers to characteristics of pilot field researches, whose are displayed in. It is worth to inform that all questions and options of answers were read by the researcher and communicated in sign language by interpreters to participants. In Field research 2, participants responded in sign language and interpreters translated to oral Portuguese in order to assistants take note on paper.

Table 2. Characteristics of pilot Field research 1 and 2

	Field research 1	Field research 2
Date	October 7th of 2013	October 30 of 2013
Place	Computer Lab1 at UFMT	Alfredo Marien School5
Participants	05 (01 female, 04 males)	06 (01 female, 05 males)
Research team	01 interpreter, 02 assistants	02 interpreter, 03 assistants
Questionnaires type	Online (GoogleDrive Form)	Paper
Number of questions	PeTQ = 29, PoTQ = 14	PeTQ = 20, PoTQ = 14
Phrases	Average of 12.8 words	Average of 11.73 words

Answers from mood status sheet show, in total, 26 (19 positive and 07 negative) types of emotions selected. Top three positive emotions were: happy (09); great (05); and wonderful (05); and most voted negative emotions were: tired (04); and, indifferent/meh (02). P1-P5 and P10-P11 marked only positive emotions; in Field research 1, participants selected only one option each. In Field research 2, Participants P6 and P7 marked many types of emotions (13 and 19), however, they made confusing options, for example, <indifferent/meh> and <curious or amused>. Participants from P8 to P11 also marked many options (14 and 15), however they made sense, for example, P8 selected 12 positive and 02 negative, in which negative emotions were tired and lost, among happy, blessed, amused, and others. In general, deaf students were interested in participating of research, raising emotions such as, happiness; on the other hand, 06 of them (P4, P6-P8, P10-P11) never participated in researches involving technology before, raising emotions such as, feeling lost.

---

3   Available in: http://goo.gl/Qw6IRw, file name: "MoodStatusSheet.pdf".
4   Available in: http://goo.gl/Qw6IRw, file name: "EmotionLIBRAS.pdf".
5   This public regular school is specialized on youth and adult education (adult literacy).

Participants' age ranged from 17 to 43 years old, with average of 28; Among 11 participants, 04 are enrolled in primary school, 04 in high school, 02 concluded high school, and 01 is currently in higher education. From their self-report about modes of communication, in PeTQ, we identified profiles (Table 1) as follows: [Profile1] = 1 participant; [Profile2] = 4; [Profile5] = 3; [Profile6] = 3. Profiles 3, 4, 7 and 8 were not evidenced; none of these 04 profile types included sign language.

5.1   Responding Hypotheses

Each hypothesis[6] was tested using answers from pre-test and post-test questionnaires. Software used for statistical analysis was R[7]. In the case of hypotheses: H1-H3, chi-squared tests for independence were used, in order to understand the relation between categorical variables; for hypotheses: H4-H12, H14, H16, Kruskal-Wallis tests were conducted, since variable are ordinal; and, for hypotheses H13 and H15, Pearson Correlation Coefficient was used, in order to measure the level of correlation between variables, also the significance of the correlation was calculated. For all tests, we considered 10% of significance, in other words, null hypothesis was rejected when p-value turns out to be less than 0,10.

H1: "The level of hearing impairment is related to reading and writing texts as the favorite communication mode, independent of gender or age". It was observed a statistically significant relationship between 'level of difficulty to follow subtitles in movies' and 'level of hearing impairment' (p-value=0,06); also, even though we had a low number of participants, if we consider dependence by gender, it was found that among males this results are also significant (p-value=0,04). Another statistically significant relationship was found between 'level of confidence in signing documents without help' and 'level of hearing impairment' (p-value=0,08).

H2: "The higher the level of education, higher the written language proficiency, independent of communication mode". It was observed a statistically significant relationship between 'level of confidence in signing documents without help' and 'level of education' (p-value=0,06), indicating independence from deaf persons' profiles. Four participants enrolled in primary school and 03 high school students do not feel confident in signing written documents without help, indicating that in lower levels of education people who are D/HH tend to have more difficulty in these situations. During Field research 1 and 2, all participants needed interpreter's help to explain and to sign term of consent.

H3: "The higher the educational level of the D/HH person's mother, higher the influence on written language proficiency, independent of communication mode". In this case, it was not found any statistically significant relationships between variables. However, it is worth noting that 06 mothers of participants dropped out from primary school, 01 completed primary school, 01 dropped out from high school, 01 completed higher education, and 02 participants did not know the education level of their mothers. These information present a scenario that may not offer motivation for

---

[6]   Available in: http://goo.gl/Qw6IRw,
      file name: "Hypotheses_PrietchSouzaFilgueiras.pdf"
[7]   The R Project for Statistical Computing. Available in: http://www.r-project.org/.

mothers to help their children studying at home. The only one mother with completed higher education, her deaf son was one of most easy to communicate and to understand questions quickly, even though he is profoundly deaf.

H4: "Written language proficiency influences 'BI' of a STT system". It was verified that relation between 'in general, it is useful' and different intensity (yes, very much; and yes, sometimes) of 'frequency written language use with family' is statistically significant (p-value=0,02). From this, we conclude that people who are D/HH who communicate in written from with family tend to consider the STT app more useful, consequently raising behavioral intention to use, than those who do not use this mode of communication at home.

H5: "'U' of a STT system is more evident for D/HH adults, considering each of the profiles (Table 1)"; H6: "'E' of a STT system is more evident for younger people who are D/HH, considering profiles". In these cases, it was not found any statistically significant results; neither for total sample, nor for any type of profiles.

H7: "'U' of a STT system is more evident for D/HH males"; H8: "'E' of a STT system is more evident for D/HH females"; both considering profiles. It was noted statistically significant difference of perceived usefulness among gender only in Profile2 (p-value=0,08). Again, even though we had a low number of participants, this result shows that male participants find STT app more useful than do female participants, considering Profile2 (SL+RW).

H9: "'U' of a STT system is more evident for people who are D/HH in higher education levels, considering profiles"; H10: "'E' of a STT system is more evident for people who are D/HH in lower education levels, considering profiles". In these cases, it was not found any statistically significant results; neither for total sample, nor for any type of profiles.

H11: "'U' and 'E' of a STT system are more evident for people who are D/HH with advanced knowledge of computing, considering profiles". Only in the case of Profile2 (SL+RW), it was observed statistically significant difference of perceived ease of use between participants that use and those who do not use computer even if they do not have Internet connection (p-value=0,10). Participants who are D/HH who use computer even if they do not have Internet connection had higher ease of use perception of STT app. That means theses users may be more familiar to different kinds of systems, than those who just use computers for navigating on Internet.

H12: "Social influence influences 'BI' of a STT system by D/HH persons, considering profiles". It was not found any statistically significant differences.

H13: "Positive emotions influence 'U' of a STT system by people who are D/HH, considering profiles". For Profile2 and Profile6, it was observed high correlation, respectively, (r=1) and (r=-1), both are significant with p-value less than 0,0001. This means that the greater participants of Profile2 agree with the statement 'in general, it is useful', greater they feel satisfied (positive and significant correlation equal to 1); and, the opposite occurred for participants of Profile6, in which the greater they agree with the statement, lesser they feel satisfied, relaxed and amused (r = -1). Besides Emotion-LIBRAS, we also asked what level of 'positively surprised' participants felt during test conduction. In Field research 1, all participants answered to be extremely surprised; and, in Field research 2, 05 participants were extremely surprised and 01 felt very surprised. Also, we asked in what level they felt 'frustrated', answers were: 04 felt highly frustrated, 02 little frustrated, 01 average, 04 did not feel frustrated.

H14: "User empowerment influences 'BI' a STT system by D/HH persons, considering profiles". It was not found any statistically significant differences.

H15: "Privacy influences 'A' a STT system by people who are D/HH, considering profiles". For Profile2 and Profile6, it was observed high correlation, respectively, (r=1) and (r=-1), both are significant with p-value less than 0,0001. This means that the greater participants of Profile2 agree with the statement 'if someone's secret is transcripted, it can raise privacy issues', greater they worry about their own privacy (positive and significant correlation equal to 1); and, the opposite occurred for participants of Profile6, in which the greater they agree with the statement, lesser they worry about their own privacy (negative and significant correlation equal to -1).

H16: "The use of a STT system by people who are D/HH, considering profiles, can influence mitigation of educational barriers in classrooms". A statistically significant difference of means (p-value=0,08) was detected with respect to participants' understanding about 'It [a STT app] can favor understanding of classes, if teachers use it' and 'Group work's formation in school classroom'. This result shows that participants consider that group work statistically influence on how D/HH persons may think the use of a STT app in classroom can favor their understanding of classes.

5.2   Analysing Other Criteria of STT System's Acceptance

For pilot tests, SampleVoiceApp [3] was adjusted to recognize Brazilian Portuguese (pt_BR), and also was trained using the 30 selected phrases, taken from known authors, popular sayings or music pieces; and, for each participant a phrase was randomly designated. From Field research 1 to 2, new phrases replaced those 05 used before.

After pilot tests, video recordings were analyzed by two experienced interpreters[8] that, (#1) read the eleven original written Portuguese phrases (one phrase for each one of the eleven participants) and translate to a written Portuguese in LIBRAS structure; (#2) analyzed each participant video and write in Portuguese the translation from LIBRAS; and, (#3) compared results from step #1 and step #2 and assign a performance index[9] for each participant (Table 3).

Observing Table 3 we can notice that 09 participants (P2, P4-P7, P8-P11) were classified with indexes less than cutoff score (50%); 01 participant (P1) was classified with regular performance; and, 01 participant (P3) reached the higher index. However, it is important to highlight that, during the test in Field research 2, we noticed 08 phrases used metaphors and this kind of text is hard for people who are D/HH to understand. This perception was confirmed by interpreters when they analysed phrases

Table 3. Performance index of each participant

	P1	P2	P3	P4	P5	P6	P7	P8	P9	P10	P11
Interpreter1	C	D	A	E	E	E	E	D	D	E	E
Interpreter2	C	E	A	E	E	E	E	C	E	E	D

---

[8] *Interpreter1* and *Interpreter2* are certified by Pró-LIBRAS, a national SL exam, and, respectively, they have 10 and 05 years of professional experience.

[9] As a standard, we used Brazilian Academic Performance Index: A (Excelent) [90-100%]; B (Good) [80-89%]; C (Fair) [60-79%]; D (Fail) [50-59%]; E (Bad) [0-49%].

and videos afterwards. On the other hand, phrases translated by P6, P8 [Profile2], and P9 [Profile1] were the simplest ones, and they had a bad performance index; and, P3 (Profile5) translated a phrase containing metaphors and had an excellent performance.

Four participants that informed to feel highly frustrated using the STT app also were assigned to have bad performance index for translating phrases from Portuguese to LIBRAS; 02 of them were participants who marked most negative options in the mood status sheet at the beginning of procedures of Field research 2; and, 03 of them where classified as being in Profile2 (SL+RW) according to their answers about mode of communication preferences, which is inconsistent with their performance results.

None of participants knew any STT system before. They were very surprised and curious to see how it worked. Results were interesting to observe, such as: they were very interested in having the STT app "Where can I buy?", "How much does it cost?". After test, we gave them some time "to play" with the STT app and they liked to read what they spoke, they had an excited time (laughing and making fun of each other) when they found out that many words were transcripted differently from what they meant to say. In Field research 2, participants did not show such excitement as the group from Field research 1, but they expressed that this kind of STT system could be a great tool to practice pronunciation of words, improving oralization.

6   Conclusion

In total, only seven hypotheses (H4, H7, H8, H11, H13, H15, H16) had outcomes that showed statistically significant results. Our conclusion is that people who are D/HH, even though they have difficulties to understand written language, they are willing to adopt a STT system and have perception of its usefulness, not only at schools but in daily life, mostly because they considered it important as an alternative of communication and they like to use technological products. At least half of participants would have the STT app installed at the same date as researches happened. However, long-term, difficulties with written language may be a decision factor to discontinue using the STT app, after the excitement period using "the new toy" ends.

Since this paper reports pilot tests with a reduced number of participants, we could not study the total variety of deaf persons' profiles and also a representative number by gender. Also, we noticed that classifying participants in different profiles according their self-report of communication mode preferences is not the most suitable form. In future works, we intend to investigate a broader diversity and find other forms of classifying participants' profiles.

Acknowledgements. We thank FAPEMAT and CAPES, and everyone who made this research possible: deaf participants, Josimar da S. Cézar, Vanuza Leite, Elaine A. dos S. Campos, Shirley L. Maidana de Oliveira, Camila Sanchine, Cibele P. Pagno, Emili P. F. Pagno, Michael F. Pagno, Divino M. da Costa, Americo Talarico Neto, Daniel Oliveira.

References

1. Bain, K., Basson, S., Faisman, A., Kanevsky, D.: Accessibility, transcription, and access everywhere. IBM Systems Journal 44(3) (2005)
2. Davis, F.D., Bagozzi, R.P., Warshaw, P.R.: User Acceptance of Computer Technology: A Comparison of Two Theoretical Models. Management Science 35(8) (1989)

3. Nuance Dragon Mobile Developer (2013), `http://dragonmobile.nuancemobiledeveloper.com/` (access date: September 18, 2013)
4. Pan, Y.-X., Jiang, D.-N., Yao, L., Picheny, M., Qin, Y.: Effects of Automated Transcription Quality on Non-native Speakers' Comprehension in Real-time Computer-mediated Communication. In: CHI 2010, Atlanta, Georgia, USA, April 10-15 (2010)
5. Papadopoulos, M., Pearson, E.: Improving the Accessibility of the Traditional Lecture: An Automated Tool for Supporting Transcription. In: BCS HCI 2012, Birmingham, UK (2012)
6. Prietch, S.S., Filgueiras, L.V.L.: Assistive Technology in the Classroom Taking into Account the Deaf Student-Centered Design: the TApES project. In: EIST/CHI, Austin (2012)
7. Prietch, S.S., Filgueiras, L.V.L.: Developing Emotion-Libras 2.0: An Instrument to Measure the Emotional Quality of Deaf Persons while Using Technology. In: Emerging Research and Trends in Interactivity and the HCI, pp. 74–94. IGI Global, Portugal (2013b)
8. Prietch, S.S., Filgueiras, L.V.L.: Double Testing: Potential Website Resources for Deaf People and the Evaluation Instrument Emotion-LIBRAS. In: ChileCHI 2013, Temuco (2013c)
9. Primiani, R., Tibaldi, D., Garlaschelli, L.: Net4Voice – New Technologies for voice-converting in barrier-free learning environment. In: FECS 2008, Las Vegas, NV, USA (2008)
10. Ranchal, R., et al.: Using Speech Recognition for Real-Time Captioning and Lecture Transcription in the Classroom. IEEE Transactions on Learning Technologies (2013)
11. Rodríguez, M.C., Caminero, J., Van Kampen, A.: SignSpeak: Scientific understanding and vision-based technological development for continuous sign language recognition and translation. Research report, reviewer: Ruíz, G. M., Release version: V1.0 (2011)
12. Venkatesh, V., Morris, M., Davis, G., Davis, F.: User Acceptance of Information Technology: Toward a Unified View. MIS Quarterly 27(3), 425–478 (2003)
13. Wald, M.: Using Automatic Speech Recognition to Enhance Education for All Students: Turning a Vision into Reality. In: 34th ASEE/IEEE, Savannah (2004)
14. Wald, M.: Captioning for Deaf and Hard of Hearing People by Editing Automatic Speech Recognition in Real Time. In: Miesenberger, K., Klaus, J., Zagler, W.L., Karshmer, A.I. (eds.) ICCHP 2006. LNCS, vol. 4061, pp. 683–690. Springer, Heidelberg (2006)
15. Wald, M., Bain, K.: Enhancing the Usability of Real-Time Speech Recognition Captioning Through Personalised Displays and Real-Time Multiple Speaker Editing and Annotation. In: Stephanidis, C. (ed.) Universal Access in HCI, Part III, HCII 2007. LNCS, vol. 4556, pp. 446–452. Springer, Heidelberg (2007)
16. Wald, M.: Captioning Multiple Speakers Using Speech Recognition to Assist Disabled People. In: Miesenberger, K., Klaus, J., Zagler, W.L., Karshmer, A.I. (eds.) ICCHP 2008. LNCS, vol. 5105, pp. 617–623. Springer, Heidelberg (2008)
17. Wald, M., Bain, K.: Universal access to communication and learning: the role of automatic speech recognition. Univ. Access Inf. Soc. 6, 435–447 (2008)
18. Wald, M.: Developing Assistive Technology to Enhance Learning for all Students. In: Assistive Technology from Adapted Equipment to Inclusive Environments. IOS Press (2009)
19. Wald, M.: Important New Enhancements to Inclusive Learning Using Recorded Lectures. In: Miesenberger, K., Karshmer, A., Penaz, P., Zagler, W. (eds.) ICCHP 2012, Part I. LNCS, vol. 7382, pp. 108–115. Springer, Heidelberg (2012)
20. Wald, M., Li, Y.: Synote: Important Enhancements to Learning with Recorded Lectures. In: 12th IEEE International Conference on Advanced Learning Technologies (2012)
21. Zhili, L., Wanjie, T., Cheng, X.J.: A Study and Application of Speech Recognition Technology in Primary and Secondary School for Deaf/Hard of Hearing Students. In: 4th International Convention on Rehabilitation Engineering & Assistive Technology (2010)

A Computer Vision Based Web Application for Tracking Soccer Players

João Rodrigues[1,2], Pedro J.S. Cardoso[2], Tiago Vilas[2], Bruno Silva[3],
Pedro Rodrigues[2], Antonio Belguinha[2], and Carlos Gomes[2]

[1] Vision Laboratory, LARSyS, University of the Algarve, 8005-139 Faro, Portugal
[2] Instituto Superior de Engenharia, University of the Algarve, 8005-139 Faro, Portugal
[3] Inesting, S.A., 8005-146 Faro, Portugal
{jrodrig,pcardoso}@ualg.pt

Abstract. Soccer is a sport where everyone that is involved with it
make all the efforts aiming for excellence. Not only the players need to
show their skills on the pitch but also the coach, and the remaining staff,
need to have their own tools so that they can perform at higher levels.
Footdata is a project to build a new web application product for soccer
(football), which integrates two fundamental components of this sport's
world: the social and the professional. While the former is an enhanced
social platform for soccer professionals and fans, the later can be considered as a Soccer Resource Planning, featuring a system for acquisition
and processing information to meet all the soccer management needs. In
this paper we focus only in a specific module of the professional component. We will describe the section of the web application that allows
to analyse movements and tactics of the players using images directly
taken from the pitch or from videos, we will show that it is possible to
draw players and ball movements in a web application and detect if those
movements occur during a game.

Keywords: Applications, interfaces, soccer, web technologies, information system, computer vision.

1 Introduction

Soccer is a sport where everyone that is involved with it make all the efforts
aiming for excellence. Not only the players need to show their skills on the pitch
but also the coach, and the remaining staff, need to have their own tools so that
they can perform at higher levels. Granting both parts a multi-functional information system (IS), with the objective of minimizing the adverse effects from
the most critical and sensitive points of soccer. A match analysis, for example,
can generate a huge amount of data. Consequently, it is very important to have
a way to process that data, providing only the most important information to
the coach, as soon as possible.

Footdata [1] is a project in development by Inesting, S.A., the University of
the Algarve and the soccer coach Domingos Paciência. The goal is to build a web

C. Stephanidis and M. Antona (Eds.): UAHCI/HCII 2014, Part I, LNCS 8513, pp. 450–462, 2014.

application product for soccer, which integrates two fundamental components of this sport's world: i) a social network (FootData-Social), which provides the typical features adapted to the soccer reality, and ii) the professional component (FootData-PRO), which can be considered as a Soccer Resource Planning (SRP), featuring a system for acquisition and processing of information to meet all the soccer management needs. The latter includes (between other things) an automated platform to gather information from the teams. This platform will be based on a system that will process live images acquired on-site, using a single or a group of cameras placed together in the stands, or images gathered from a Full HD Handycam. One of the objectives is to add features which will allow the analysis of the soccer match structure, allowing rationalization and optimization of the team's actions regarding the occupation of spaces. All the application structure is supervised by the soccer coach Domingos Paciência.

There are a few commercial systems that partially integrate some of the components of this project, e.g., Kizanaro [3]. We can also find in the literature examples that explore some aspects of the project, like video technology for coaching [4] and computerized video analysis of soccer [5]. Even so, none of those integrate all the technologies and goals of the Footdata project. Please refer to [1, 2] for a more comprehensive review of the literature.

In this paper we will describe the design of part of the web application, tacking special focus on: (i) the needs and restrictions of the soccer coach, and (ii) on the computer vision based module for tracking and analyzing the soccer player(s) movements and teams tactics. The main contribution is this interconnection between the acquisition and analysis systems and the web interface for designing the movements and tactics. Furthermore, this module connected with the FootData-Social can give universal access to the inside of the statistics and performance in the soccer's world. Of course, all the information from the FootData-PRO is by default confidential and will need permissions from the actors (e.g., clubs, athletes and coaches) to be published in the social platform.

The remaining paper is divided as follows: a brief description of the FootData-PRO system and the involved technologies to implement it are presented in section 2, in section 3 we introduce one web interface of the application, sections 4 and 5 describes the ball and tracking of players and the game analysis, respectively. The final section presents conclusions and future work.

2   The System and The Technologies

Footdata-PRO [1] features an acquisition and information system divided in five main modules: (a) Field module, where the ball's and players' location in the pitch is done by computer vision. This information is sent through an Internet connection to a server, where the match tactical plans are verified, based on the information available from prepared tactical schemes, trainings, individual players, and collective information from each team. Supported in the above procedure, in the coach's (user) profile and in what is occurring in real-time in the field, selected information is sent to the coach's mobile device. (b) Center module, where all the data and the main computational procedures are congregated (including the processing and management of previously recorded videos). (c) Coach module, where the technical staff inputs and gets access to detailed information of every topic related to the soccer match, scouting, medical department, etc. (d) Player module, used to send specific information to the players, and the (e) Presentation module, where semi-automatic presentations are prepared for the players in preparation moments. An integrated web application, where usability is a key factor, will combine all the above features in a single place, including video manipulation tools, tactical planning/drawing tools, semi-automatic presentation tools, etc.

Being FootData-PRO a web application (inserted in a context of cloud-computing), the technologies employed to built the application discussed in this paper can be summarized to the following: The front-end has implemented using HTML5, CSS3 and JavaScript [9]. With regard to the back-end, this module has structured using Node.js [10] and Python. In both cases, we resorted to various JavaScript frameworks. In the latter case it was also used Django [7], which is a high-level Python web framework [12]. Python was also the programming language used to produce all the statistics as well to "decode" the drawn movements and team tactics (see Sec. 3) into code. The produce code is then used to compare the information sketched in those plans with the information retrieved from the tracking (Sec. 4) and achieve the game analysis (Sec. 5). The tracking system was implemented using C++ and OpenCV [16]. WebSockets [17] and Socket.IO [18] were used for the communication between the different modules. For the storage, necessary for the IS, we are at the moment using two NoSQL databases: a document oriented databased, MongoDB [8], and a graph database, Titan [11]. Finally, we can also refer Yeoman [6], which encompasses a number of frameworks (e.g., AngularJS), providing a development and production environment for a web application by automating some tasks related to the initialization, construction and testing of the application.

3   Interfaces

All the interfaces were projected having the best practices in consideration and bearing in mind three fundamental key points: (a) they must be user-friendly and very intuitive for the users (e.g., technical staff, players); (b) functional, i.e., they have to provide an easy way to add and edit text and shapes, along with some other functions (e.g., drag, resize, recolor or rotate); and (c) most of them had to "work" in a wide range of devices (e.g., mobile phones, phablets, tablets and personal computers), i.e., Responsive Design [13]. Furthermore, some of the interfaces have to show very dynamic situations since we want to make animations with the shapes we draw, while other have to show videos and allow to put layers of shapes and/or text over them. Bottom line, since almost all the interfaces were quite demanding in terms of design and usability, a Design Thinking approach [14] was used to create them.

In order to integrate the following sections, in this paper we only show a flavor of those interfaces. Figure 1 shows an example of a planification drawn in the

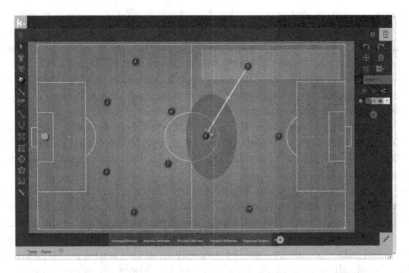

Fig. 1. Example of a planification drawn in Field Editor interface

Field Editor, a tool which targets the following generic points: (a) provide the coaches with a web platform where he can easily represent players movements to be applied in the training sessions and in matches; (b) provide an animation feature to help the coach to illustrate its intentions regarding a certain play or movement; (c) provide a way to extract data from a represented movement or action so it can be processed and analyzed later by matching it with the tracking obtained from a game. In this paper we will focus mostly in that last point. Using the Field Editor, the coach can draw a wide range of situations, from "static" players positions, e.g. a player or group of players appearing in a specific region of the field, to "animations," like the very simple one shown in the figure: player $\#_{tA}$ in region 1 passing ball to player $\#_{tB}$ in region 2. However, much more complex animations (movements, tactics) are also possible to edit, where all the team players are involved and different sectors of the team have to do different (tactical) movements in function of the moment of the game and the position of the ball. More information about this tool with the a alpha interface can be seen in [2]. The shown interface is in Portuguese, but all the main languages will be soon available. Also, due to the confidentiality agreement, some very specific parts of the interface are omitted.

4   Classification and Localization of Soccer Players and Ball

The tracking of the soccer players and ball is done in five stages: (1) the detection of the soccer pitch, (2) the detection of players and ball, (3) the assignment of players to their teams, (4) the tracking of players and ball, and (5) computation of their localization (in meters) in the pitch.

(1) **Soccer pitch detection** – let $I_{RGB}(x, y, t)$ and $I_{HSV}(x, y, t)$ represent a frame with dimensions $M \times N$, acquired for instance by a camera (typically an HandyCam) in the stands, where M is the width and N is the height of the image, t is the instant when the frame was acquired and RGB and HSV the color spaces [15]. The first step was the soccer pitch detection, which consists in (a) the segmentation of the green (grass) regions for each frame using I_{HSV}. This was done by a semi-automatic process, where selected pitch patches were used to compute the HSV thresholds intervals. For the pitch shown in Fig. 2 top, it was used the following thresholds levels: $H \in [0\%, 50\%]$, $S \in [12\%, 100\%]$ and $V \in [27\%, 100\%]$, which returns a binary image I_c, with $I_c = 1$ corresponding to the green pixels.

The next step has the purpose to eliminate the areas outside the pitch. This was carried out in several stages: First (b), in I_c was chosen a central point of the image as the seed (in most frames, the central area corresponds to the pitch, the exceptions are zooms to players or to the stands). The central point of I_c has to have a green color (see above), and recursively from this initial point, using 3×3 neighborhood, all central pixels that have all neighbors green are kept, $I'_c = 1$, the remaining are put to 0 ($I'_c = 0$). Over the last image, but only in areas where exists pitch, i.e. $I'_c = 1$, was applied (c) the Canny edge (I_{Ce}) detection [15] on I_{RGB}. After this, (d) the Hough transform [15] was applied over the I_{Ce}, in order to detect the lines (I_{Hl}) that limits the pitch. Finally (e), using I_{Hl} the most horizontal and vertical lines (left, right, up and down) are computed. Those lines correspond to the limits of the pitch, and everything outside these limits (lines) was removed. The final results consist only in the segmentation of the pitch (with some black blobs inside), I_{fj}.

(2) **Players and ball detection** – for the player detection it was used the I_{fj} image. In this image, most of the work for the players detection was already done, once the pitch area was delimited, the black blobs inside this area are likely players. Nevertheless, 3 major problems can arise: (a) blobs that are not players, e.g., areas with short grass, (b) players that almost disappear due to low image definition, or being partially equipped in "green," and (c) the overlap of various players. To solve these situations and to obtain only the contours of the players, morphological filters were applied, i.e., first it was applied the dilation filter (D) followed by an erosion filter (E) and finally a 9×9 medium filter (M). The result was an image, $I_{jf}(x, y, t) = M(E(D(I_{fj}(x, y, t))))$, where the players were better defined and specific noise regions were removed. After this, since some player still have more than one region (usually due to the equipment that they use) a vertical mask was applied to connect those regions.

The next step was the confirmation that each blob corresponding to a possible player (in I_{jf}) has at least one edge contour correspondence in I_{Ce}. Finally, it was checked if the final blob region of each player (in I_{jf}) doesn't had more than 10% of green pixels (using I_H). The final image after this validation was called I_f. To differentiate between players and the ball, all pixels with the "white color" (in I_V) inside I_f were detected. Those pixels can represent lines belonging to the pitch, the ball, and if it was the case, teams that had predominantly white equipments. For this purpose an threshold with $V \in [75\%, 100\%]$ was applied to I_V, returning a binary image, I_b, with all the white regions inside the pitch ($I_b = 1$). Combining the previous information with the size and shape of the blobs, the blob that corresponds to the ball can be classified. The first step, consists in detecting if the blob as more or less circular or oval shape, which was different from the player blobs that had (usually) a more "vertical-rectangular" shape. This way most of the players blobs were discarded. The second step, was to remove the areas corresponding to the pitch marks, eliminating the areas that correspond to the lines detected by the Hough transform in I_{Hl}. The final step consists in removing areas which exceed $M \times N/k$ pixels ($k = 100000$, this value was empirically determined). Figure 2 top shows the players delimited by rectangles, and the ball by a circle. Having the ball classified, it was necessary to classify the blobs as players from team A or B, referee or keepers.

(3) **Assignment of the players to their teams** – the players' classification to a team was based on the color of the equipment. Assuming that the video started at the beginning of the game, a group of 7 players on the right, and 7 players on the left of the middle field line were automatically selected. If the video didn't start at the beginning of the game, then a semi-automatic process selects the most probable 7 player from each team. Then for each team in separate, and using the blobs regions classified as players in I_f, the average of Hue using the I_H image was computed. Having the two average Hues values from team A and B, the middle threshold was computed to separate the teams.

The keepers were relatively easer to classify, once they correspond to the first blob that appear in the right and in the left of the image with significant difference from the two average Hues values computed for the teams (it is important to remember that the keepers use a different equipment from the teams). The referee was a major problem. If the video starts from the beginning of the game, the referee usually was very close to the middle field line. In those cases, the referee was a blob with a Hue different from the players near the middle line. If the video starts from a different position then a semi-automatic process is applied, i.e., the referee was considered the blob with the most different Hue (comparing with the Hues from the teams), and if by mistake was assigned as a team player, then a web tool (not shown in the paper) allows the user to manually change the player classified as referee and vise-versa.

All those Hues once detected were memorized by the system and adapted dynamically in function of the video conditions (e.g., light). The numbers assigned to the players were in function of the position they occupy in the pitch, and those numbers were associated to the real player number and name in function of the position posted in the game sheet (e.g., right-back). If necessary, this can be corrected later using the web tool mentioned above. Finally, obviously there is also the validation that it was impossible to assign more than 1 referee, 2 keepers and 10 players per team. Figure 2 shows the result of the player's assignment to a team and referee identification.

(4) **Players' positions in the pitch** – in order to make a correct analysis of a soccer game, it is important to know as accurate as possible the correct

Fig. 2. In the top, the result of the ball, referee and players detection and assignment to their respective team. Bottom, the representation of the players' position considering as the origin of coordinates system the interception between the middle field line and the top lateral line.

position of the players in the pitch. To calculate that position, a perspective transformation (homography) [15] from each frame to a normalized pitch was needed, see Fig. 2 bottom. For this purpose a set of references in the pitch was computed. Those were extracted from the lines detected in the Hough transform, I_{Hl}, and the pitch delimitations in I_f. On the other hand, for the position of the players, it was considered the middle point in the bottom line of the box that limits the players, which corresponds in most cases to the coordinates of the players' feet, see Fig. 2 top and the respective projection in the bottom.

Since the pitches have different sizes (weight and height), it was important to compute the size of a pixel (in our case, in meters). For this computation, in the first frames (or as soon as possible) the lines of the center circle, penalty area or goal areas had to be automatically detected to calibrate the value of a pixel in meters, using the fact that their dimensions are the same for all pitches. An automatic process was then applied every time there was a small zoom, or a zoom to a player.

(5) **Tracking of players and ball** – the players and ball tracking doesn't require the repeating for all frames of all the operations mentioned in steps 2 and 3. Though simple, the implemented tracking process was effective, except in situation of great confluence of player, such as corners or discussions with the referee. Nevertheless, the main focus of this framework is not to follow the players everywhere, but to compute the distances between players and from the players to the ball during open plays. The tracking was divided into five steps for each frame t: (a) the distance (in meters) was calculated between each player in the previous frame, $t - 1$, to the players in the current frame, t. Making the correspondence to the player that was closer. If there were two or more players at the same distance (non-overlapping) the player was assigned to the one that in the previous frame has the nearest Hue value. (b) If there was no players in frame t near to the position occupied by some player in frame $t - 1$ (few meters apart), then a player with the same color as the one in frame $t - 1$ was looked up in frame t, using circular areas with increasing diameters and centered in the original coordinates. Furthermore, it was used a trajectory computed from the previous 5 frames to limit within the circle the "sectors" of the search. (c) For situations in which a particular player was not tracked/located during a long frame set (2 seconds), this player was then searched from the position where he was "lost" using again circular areas with increasing diameters. The first blob found that was not tracked and has the same Hue value was assigned as the lost player. (d) It is important to note that in the majority of the frames, there was the possibility that some players were not detected because they are not in the field of view of the camera, e.g., at the beginning of the game, due to fact that the camera doesn't capture the entire pitch. Every player that appear at the left or right (top or bottom, depending if there has a zoom applied) was considered as new player to track, except if a player was "lost" on a previous frame in a nearby position. (e) Finally, it was also necessary to verify the existence of collisions. If after the above procedure (a-c), a player was not found, it was assumed that there was a collision (junction of two or more players). For those situations, all blobs that correspond to players, that were in positions very close and were lost, were associated with a single blob, assigning to 2 or more players that were tracked in $t - 1$ in a nearby position. When the collision ends (separation of two or more players) the Hue of each blob were checked and players reassigned.

After a collision there was always the possibility of players being wrongly identified, for instance when the collision was between two players of the same team. To solve this, the already mentioned web tool can be used to correct the the players assignment. The process of tracking the ball and referee is similar to the players. Having the players and ball tracked, i.e., the x and y coordinates of each one on the field, now we can compare/match the "draws" (tactics) done in the Field Editor and return the game analysis.

5   Game Analysis

In this paper we only focus on return: (1) heat, (2) passes and (3) ball losses maps, which can be a good resource to measure a player/team performance and a base to their improvement. More complex movements drawn in the Field Editor are also possible to be automatically analyzed, nevertheless: (a) movements from different coaches need to be drawn and tested for a complete validation of this tool and (b) due to the confidentiality agreement some of the tested tactics (game moments) are not allowed to be shown.

(1) **Heat maps** – the heat maps are graphical representation of data where the positions of the players are inserted into an incremental matrix which is then represented with colors. In sports, the heat map can have different uses. Depending on the sport, heat maps help to visually analyze which areas a team, a player, or a set of players preferably occupy. In the particular case of soccer, they can be used to infer if a player has a preferred side, area, or if the defense is occupying the expected positions.

In our case, the data structure behind the heat map is a matrix, HM, that has the same size as the image resolution used to draw it. HM is build using the data from the tracking system, that returns for each frame the players' and ball's positions in meters, $\{frame_{id} : t, team_A : \{player_1 : (x_1, y_1), player_2 : (x_2, y_2), \ldots\}, team_B : \{\ldots\}, ball : (x, y)\}$. Those positions are relative to the pitch top left corner and are obtained using an perspective transformation (see Section 4 – *Players' positions in the pitch*).

To compute HM we start by setting it to the null matrix, $HM = [0]$. Then for each frame a cross-multiplication is used to get the corresponding positions of the players in the pitch, (x, y), to their corresponding entry in HM matrix, (x', y'), and $HM_{x'y'}$ is incremented by one unit. Once all the frames and players are processed, the matrix is normalized, i.e., each entry of the matrix is divided by the matrix maximum element. Finally, the HM values (ranging from 0 to 1) are used to build the output image, by setting the color opacity of the pixels that form the heat map. Figure 3 (top left) sketches a team heat map from one minute of a soccer match. The heat map can also be filtered within different time intervals, and multiple or individual players (on the right).

(2) **Passes maps** – these maps are a graphical representation of the passes made by the players in the game. It shows the passing player's number and the receiver's number. The passes map is a tool which allows several analyses, like how a team organizes the attack or maintains the ball possession. Other statistics can also be inferred like who are the most important players in the teams' strategies, in the sense that they have more ball actions. The passes are detected using the following process: for every frame, (a) the distance between each player and the ball is calculated. (b) If the ball enters in a player's radius (the Field Editor tool sets to 3 meters by default; this value can be adjust for more/less precision on the pass detection) then that frame and player are tagged, and the ball's vectorial velocity and direction are calculated using the current position and its position five frames before. (c) If the ball leaves that player's radius then the vectorial velocity and direction are also calculated, considering the ball's

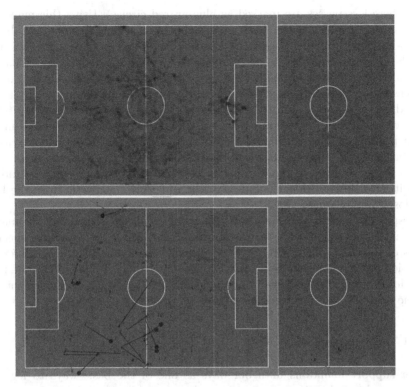

Fig. 3. Example of team heat map (top left), single player heat map (top right), teams passes/losses map (bottom left), and single player passes/losses map (bottom right) from one minute of a soccer match

current position and its position five frames after. (d) The velocity and direction values are then subjected to a set of conditions in order to probabilistically state if it is a pass or not, i.e, if there is a significant change in the ball's direction or velocity then it is probabilistically considered as a pass. Figure 3 (bottom) shows a passes map where it's possible to see all the passes made by both teams (bottom left) or by a single player (bottom right). Simultaneously, a passes log is built as the game is processed, containing a list with the intervening players numbers, teams and time of the pass execution and reception.

The passes can also be filtered using the Field Editor interface. For example, Fig. 1 illustrates a pass between two players. The drawn actions are converted using the (JSON) strings created from the Field Editor interface to another JSON document that contains the relevant information about the depicted movements. This structure is then used to create a set of coded functions (basically containing if-then-else statements) which are then matched to the tracking data, in order to detect the drawn movements (a more detailed explanation of this procedure is out the focus of this paper).

(3) **Ball loss maps** – similar to the passes maps, we have the ball loss maps that can also be filtered by time interval and by player/team (see Fig. 3 bot-

tom where loss passes are marked as blue an red circles). Using this map, it's possible to see which player loses more balls, or in which areas more ball are loss. Analyzing both the passes and loss ball map, we can have a general view about the players and teams performance, by seeing how many correct passes were made and how many balls were loss. The loss ball map is generated using the passes log as base. The passes algorithm counts the passes made by players from different teams, so that when a pass is made to a player of the other team we have a ball loss. Although, we have to distinguish two cases: ball loss made when passing or when dribbling. In order to distinguish between both cases, its considered the distance between the position where the pass was made and where it was received. If the distance is less than two times the player's radius then it is considered that the ball was lost while dribbling, otherwise the ball was lost while passing.

Despite the fact that this paper discusses only heat, passes and ball loss maps, much more movements can be drawn in the Field Editor. For example, specific zones of the field, player or group the players can be specified, even different situation of the game can be specify, this is only a small sample of can the tool do. More complex movements (game models) including dynamic movements of all the team are under the confidentiality agreement.

6   Conclusions

Paper support maintains until our days as one of the basic ways to log the player's and team's actions (e.g., passes, shots on target, ball possession, recurrent movements). At the end of the matches, those documents are statistically analyzed by elements of technical staff which in turn notify the coaches and the players about their actions. The log work is made by someone that is observing the game (live or recorded) and marking those moments by hand. This is a slow process and, in live games, can require more than one person to process all actions with an optimum precision.

This paper shows (a module of) an web application which is an alternative to that kind of work. In this case, we have shown a small part of the overall system that is being built to help coaches and technical staff in the improvement of their players and team's performance. The part of the system shown allows the user to draw a movement or a group of movements in a web application. After that, those movements can be detected automatically during the game, using the tracking data obtained from Full HD videos or, in a near future, on site in real time from live images acquired during a game. The returned data is then used to show individual or team actions. With this process, the information can be given in real time, allowing an instantaneous analysis of the players and teams actions, which gives to the technical staff the possibility to make in game adjustments, based on that information. As expected, knowing the opposite team performance is also possible with this system, which can give an extra advantage to those using these features.

The system is for now being optimized for soccer, but the difference to other ball sports is not big, which makes us believe that in a near future our system will be adapted to other sports.

The work presented is this paper is focused on the technical team. Nevertheless, different levels of accesses will be available inside each club for the entire Footdata-PRO web application. This FootData-PRO module is directly connected with FootData-Social, which will allow to give universal access to the non-confidential information (set by the users/clubs) retrieved by the system. In the future the consortium is studying how to use the information (e.g., from the position of the players, ball, heat maps, passes, ball losses) to develop applications for specific publics, to whom the system can explain in detail what is happening in the field, by automatically describe the game in several languages, e.g., in Braille to deaf people or as a complement to the traditional "narration" to blind people.

Acknowledgments. This work was partly supported by the Portuguese Foundation for Science and Technology (FCT), project LARSyS PEst-OE/EEI/LA0009 /2013 and project FootData QREN I&DT, n. 23119. We also thanks to project leader Inesting, S.A. [www.inesting.com], and the consultant soccer coach Domingos Paciência.

References

[1] Rodrigues, P., Belguinha, A., Gomes, C., Cardoso, P., Vilas, T., Mestre, R., Rodrigues, J.M.F.: Open Source Technologies Involved in Constructing a Web-Based Football Information System. In: Rocha, Á., Correia, A.M., Wilson, T., Stroetmann, K.A. (eds.) Advances in Information Systems and Technologies. AISC, vol. 206, pp. 715–723. Springer, Heidelberg (2013)

[2] Rodrigues, P., Cardoso, P., Rodrigues, J.M.F.: A Field, Tracking and Video Editor Tool for a Football Resource Planner. In: 8th Iberian Conf. on Information Systems and Technologies, Lisbon, Portugal, June 19-22, vol. 1, pp. 734–739 (2013)

[3] Kizanaro (2013), http://www.kizanaro.com

[4] Wilson, B.: Development in video technology for coaching. Sports Technology 1(1), 34–40 (2008)

[5] Duh, D.J., Chang, S.Y., Chen, S.Y., Kan, C.C.: Automatic broadcast soccer video analysis, player detection, and tracking based on color histogram. In: Juang, J., Huang, Y.C. (eds.) Intelligent Technologies and Engineering Systems. LNEE, vol. 234, pp. 123–130. Springer, Heidelberg (2013)

[6] Yeoman (2013), http://yeoman.io/

[7] Django (2013), http://www.djangoproject.com

[8] mongoDB (2013), http://www.mongodb.org/

[9] JavaScript (2013), http://www.w3schools.com/js/

[10] Node.js (2013), http://nodejs.org/

[11] Titan (2013), http://thinkaurelius.github.io/titan/

[12] Python (2013), http://www.python.org/

[13] LaGrone, B.: HTML5 and CSS3 Responsive Web Design Cookbook. Packt Publishing (2013)

[14] Lockwood, T.: Design Thinking: Integrating Innovation, Customer Experience and Brand Value. Allworth, New York (2010)
[15] Sebe, N., Lew, M.: Robust computer vision: Theory and applications. Kluwer Academic Publishers, The Netherlands (2003)
[16] OpenCV (2013), http://opencv.org/
[17] WebSockets (2013), http://www.websocket.org/
[18] Sockets.IO (2013), http://socket.io/

The Haptic Feedback Design of Augmented Reality Virtual Keyboard on the Air

Ho-Chih Yu and Fong-Gong Wu

Department of Industrial Design, National Cheng Kung University, Tainan, Taiwan
yuhochih@gmail.com, fonggong@mail.ncku.edu.tw

Abstract. With the promoting of the computing capacity system, the augmented reality (AR) technology has been gradually used in daily life application. And augmented reality on the hardware device can become smaller which is allowing user easy to carry. However, the location of virtual model in the AR technology on the reality just has air, which means people cannot touch the model actually. Therefore, augmented reality device still does not have ubiquitous haptic feedback equipment to give the user good haptic perception and operation experiment like other portable device such as mobile phone or tablet today. This study try to design the haptic feedback device for augmented reality virtual keyboard on the air, we use focus group to find the innovation idea of haptic feedback for augmented reality, and we create a simple and normal structure to achieve the goal without any high technology equipment. We hope this study cans give the reference for future study of augment reality haptic feedback and also influence the operate posture and interface of augmented reality device.

Keywords: haptic cognitive, focus group, ergonomics, human-computer interaction, Human-center Design.

1 Introduction

1.1 Development Trends of Augmented Reality

Since Boeing researcher Tom Caudell (1990) first coined the term "Augmented Reality"(AR),the computing capacity of AR technology system has been promoted and gradually used in life application [1]. With advances with technology, augmented reality on the hardware device can become smaller which is allowing user easy to carry. Augmented reality on the handhold mobile device is widely used in the daily life and has commercial value, such as smart phone or tablet can be used at anywhere after download the AR software program. Another example is head-mounted display (HMD) display device, which can show the virtual items and change while users turn their head, in order to provide user immersive experiment [2].More lightweight AR device can be mounted on the glasses, like the Google Glass. The iOptik is developed from military even can be installed on the contact lenses, that way the soldiers can see the aerial view of battlefield and focus on the battle situation at the same time[3].

C. Stephanidis and M. Antona (Eds.): UAHCI/HCII 2014, Part I, LNCS 8513, pp. 463–472, 2014.
© Springer International Publishing Switzerland 2014

Different kinds of device show that investors believe that augmented reality is worth to develop and has a bright future.

1.2   Interactive of Augmented Reality

Augmented Reality can project the virtual image onto the real world overlap each other instantly, allowing users to experiment the interaction between real and virtual world by various kinds of input and output device, and has been applied in various fields now. For example, the theme park "The Wizarding World of Harry Potter" use AR technology combines with the map. User can see a three-dimension virtual building on the flat map and interact with the virtual model by blowing into the microphone .Another example is the fashion business combine with AR and then develop the Virtual Fitting Rooms (VFRs), which let buyers know what they look like when they dress on the clothes. This technology not only increase sales but also reduces the number of return [4]. AR technology also can use on the medical, surgical physician use augmented reality to superimpose the virtual surgery video on the actual surgery to let two kinds of experiences assist and improve each other [5]. Interior designer use AR technology place the virtual furniture in the real space to simulate the decorated situation, in order to make change and adjustment with customer earlier [6]. Industrial Technology Research Institute use HMD and AR technology develop "Air touch" application to do navigate and other function [7].These cases show augmented reality can use on the diverse application and then give the people image the future value and contribution of AR technology.

1.3   Haptic Feedback Plays an Important Role in Portable Device

Haptic feedback means by item stimulating the skin, human can understand the characteristics of the object such as shape, texture, temperature, force and other information. A comfortable haptic feedback even can promote the willing of people to purchase the goods [8-9]. The literature also pointed out that smooth surface touch screen would cause fingertip lose the haptic message when the people use the virtual screen. The typing accuracy of people will reduce when the surface loss the haptic feedback including the reaction force and edge feel [10], and also the reaction time is longer than physical keyboard. The touch screen with haptic feedback does help reduce input error rate and increase the input speed, and also reduce the using cognitive load when it compare with the normal touch screen [11].Therefore, most of touch screen such as PDA, smart phone and tablet would add the haptic feedback device when they use virtual keyboard. Apple, Sony and other manufacturers also apply for a patent for their unique haptic feedback device also show that mobile device manufacturers think seriously of the haptic feedback.

1.4   Haptic Feedback on the New Developments in Mobile Devices

The normal mobile touch device use vibration equipment to produce haptic feedback, however, only vibration is not enough to give sufficient haptic information for people.

That way, various manufacturers are also actively developing new types of haptic feedback in recent year. NEC Corporation and Tokyo Institute of Technology co-design the touch screen with force feedback. The sensor can detect the direction of finger movement, and then use cable pull the screen in the opposite direction to allow user feel the elasticity and tension from the object [12]. Also, some haptic feedback study focus on the pressing behavior, such as Japan KDDI touch screen showed in CEATEC Japan 2011 Business Electronics Show, using a piezoelectric element to make the really pressed down feeling for user when they operate the tablet [13]. And in CES 2013 U.S. Commercial Electronics Show, Tactus Touch Screen display its microfluidics technology, which can float the bump from the screen to form the buttons when user need, and make the tablet has really physical buttons to provide better haptic feedback [14].

1.5   Summary

In recent year, the augmented reality technology try hard to combine with mobile device, hoping to extend to more applications. It means we will need better device to provide better haptic feedback for helping operate. However, the devices such as tablet right now still have basic haptic feedback because the material of screen that user touch can provide basic tactile and force feedback even without any haptic feedback equipment. But in the future the head-mounted displays and augmented reality technology would use frequently on the portable device, virtual item appear on the air which cannot be touch directly, user can not feel anything while interact with virtual item. Therefore, how to let the skin sensor the haptic feedback while operating the virtual item on the air, is what we are focus on.

2   Related Works

2.1   The Importance of Distinguish the Haptic Feedback

Haptic is a touch of science, derived from Greek ἁπτικός (haptikos), means "the feeling which can contact", and the response received from the object after touching the object is haptic feedback. Haptic feedback can divide into tactile, force feedback and proprioceptive feedback. Tactile let the people feel the texture, temperature and vibration. Force feedback show the direction of power, such as weight, inertia and object boundary. The proprioceptive feedback is related to location and postures [15], and in recent year study classifies the proprioceptive feedback as part of force feedback. Due to the design the virtual keyboard in the augmented reality would include tactile (keyboard vibration, buttons texture), force feedback (keyboard boundary and inertia) and proprioceptive feedback (control posture), finding which one is the mean type of feedback will significantly affect the design direction. That way, it is necessary to divide and understand different type of haptic feedback.

2.2   The Importance of Collect Concept

The design process has many kinds of judge criteria, and also it includes many intuitive behaviors to make the idea more diverse [16]. Therefore, collecting good idea is the key for create innovative design. In this time, we will use focus group to get the variety of new concepts. According to Jungk and Müllert (1996) argument, focus group consists of the following stages: (1) preparation phase, (2) judgment phase, (3) concept development stage, (4) implementation phase. The study uses focus group to get the inspiration and creativity of the haptic feedback from the user, evaluating and choosing feasibility structure to make the model by co-design with participate. Therefore, we delete the judgment phase.

2.3   Generating Haptic Feedback on the Screen Surface

The most basic idea of generating haptic feedback on the screen surface is making the surface changes with the image directly. With the movable array up and down, the surface can imitate the texture of the image [17-18]. The Tangible Media Group from MIT Media Lab also use movable array with different colors of light to make in-FORM, which can produce dynamic user interface, by changing the actual object to generate haptic feedback of the physical tips, constraints and operational for user [19]. Microsoft developed Light-induced Shape-memory Polymer Display Screen, which use different wavelengths of light to make the surface change for different texture [20]. These study include the force feedback and tactile feedback, however, these equipment are too huge and complicate to easy carry away.

The vibration that normal portable device used is belonging to the tactile. However, the tactile feedback message from the vibration is limit, so some study use voltage to create more detail feedback. Mallinckrodt found the Electrovibration phenomenon in 1954, which use electric current to generate an adjustable friction on the skin, and then imitate different texture by changing the voltage to let the user understand the object texture information [21]. In recent year, Disney Research Team use Reverse Electrovibration to build the REVEL, which use voltage stimulates the skin to create different friction coefficient. When user slide the finger, the surface would produce different friction to imitate other surface, to let the user has the illusion of touch different texture.

2.4   Generating Haptic Feedback Beyond the Screen Surface

Because of the public place need to keep clean and other health issues, the device which can generate haptic feedback beyond the screen surface is created. User can feel the feedback on the air when they in the action. The usual way is let the user wear the equipment with vibration device such as gloves or ring, and then give the user vibration alert in the right time which was analyzed by the system calculates, to allow user to understand their operation is valid or not. UltraHaptics focus ultrasound at a fixed distance and then become an operation point, let the user can feel the haptic feedback on the air, and also user can control the interface beyond the surface with the finger detect system [22]. The further design is to achieve surround haptic feedback by emitting directional air vortex from injection device. Making the skin feel different air pressure to create the haptic feedback is a famous direction of the haptic study. Due to the injection devices can install in different place, this design can reach the surround haptic feedback like surround sound, such as Disney Research Team create AIREAL [23] or Microsoft Research Team create AirWave [24].

2.5   Summary

Overall, the perception of haptic feedback for the augmented reality has a big breakthrough that the device is developed from normal vibrate alert to allow user feel the surface texture. But in the future direction of mobile devices, most of the equipment today is still too cumbersome, it would cause hard to control and unnatural in the operation. Also the technology demand of the haptic feedback is high to reach, it cannot rapid spread and use in the short term. Therefore, this study hope to design new haptic feedback way which use more concise device to break through the limit of huge equipment, increase the area that user can use. That way the device can reduce the burden of body carry and then it can break through the restriction of operate posture, and finally it would influence the innovation of the augmented reality interface.

3   Method

The research hopes to make innovation design modal for the haptic feedback of augmented reality keyboard on the air, breaking through the portable problem of the huge haptic feedback device to increase the control area and find the new operate posture. We try to create new type of haptic feedback technology by investigating the haptic feedback of physical keyboard and simulating the virtual keyboard operation process. The purpose of experiment is to find the simple, convenient and portable haptic feedback device, and discuss the future of the virtual keyboard interact with user. The main structure as follow:

3.1   Purpose

Due to the restriction of the equipment, human and time, we use focus group to co-design what kind of the haptic feedback is suitable for virtual keyboard in augmented reality, to find out the haptic feedback feeling that user really want. The purpose of the experiment is design the feasibility solution for haptic feedback device

3.2   Experiment Participants

The study default the student right now will become the haptic feedback device user in the next generation, so our experiment participants are students. In order to obtain the detail of information and advice, we choose the heavy internet users who use more than 28 hour per week (NOWnews.com, 2012) on the internet and use the keyboard, the ages between 20 to 30 years old.

3.3   Experimental Execution

Each meeting contains 6 to 8 participants in addition to the host and recorder. The focus group would focus on haptic feedback, and the focus group would do three times. The process as follow:

Preparation Phase. The host would rent the place for discussion and prepare the pen, paper and different kind of keyboards for use, and then prepare the interactive mode. After participant arrive, the host would explain the experimental purpose, descript the relative design of the haptic feedback, and then let the participant operate different kind of keyboards to know the different haptic feedback feeling.

Concept Development Stage. After participant try on different haptic feedback feeling, the host would invite them to associate with the question "Design a device that allows the fingers to feel the haptic feedback from the virtual button". The question asks participant to draw or write down what type of the haptic feedback they want to feel when they touch the virtual button in augmented reality, also they need to design the form and how to achieve the goal. In addition, the research hope to create light and portable device for human, therefore the question would have some limit for its specification. After participant finish the question, host would invite them discuss their thoughts and advance some new element or idea. After first question, the second question would ask participant "consider the feasibility, design a haptic feedback device system" according to the conclusion of the first question. And then do the discussion again and create the final concept.

Implementation Phase. After focus group, we would collect the concepts from each participate, and then review each concept achieve what types of the tactile or force feedback, and also evaluate with the feasibility for us, to finish the haptic feedback device for augmented reality virtual keyboard on the air.

4   Results

4.1   Analyze and Evaluation

After collect the concepts from each participate, we classify and integrate these concepts to the main 14 different kinds of types (see Table 1), and then we discuss the feasibility one by one to discuss what we can do next.

The first three concepts mention the tactile feedback of the temperature, and it is a good point for the haptic feedback because we do not notice before the focus group. However, the basic idea of temperature feedback is just let the user feel different temperature, so that means the device with low specific heat material is enough, the cooling or heating device is not necessary. The concept of use electric flow that we cannot

Table 1. Haptic feedback concepts and the required material

	Haptic Feedback Concept	Feedback Type	Material Use
1	The temperature of button is different with the finger to let the user feel the feedback	Tactile feedback	Low specific heat material
2	Take the heat of the finger away when finger touch the button	Tactile feedback	Thermoelectric Cooling
3	Infrared radiation to let the finger feel warm	Tactile feedback	Infrared device
4	Use the electric flow to simulate the finger	Tactile feedback	Electric circuit
5	Spin something to rub the finger	Tactile feedback	Motor
6	Accelerate something to hit the finger	Force feedback	Magnetic repulsion force
7	Inflate the small balloon when finger touch and then deflate immediately	Force feedback	Inflator
8	Give some suction or sticky feeling to let the user know he already touch	Force feedback	Sucker structure or sticky material
9	Use linkage to make a plane up when the finger push down	Force feedback	Anything can make a linkage
10	Use foldable physical tension plane for user	Force feedback	Plastic film
11	Make the user's body become a touch interface	Force feedback	User's body
12	Use Non-Newtonian Fluid for touch	Force feedback	Non-Newtonian Fluid
13	Vibrate the nail to let the user know they already touch	Force feedback	Ultrasound device
14	Use air vortex to make the skin feel the pressure	Force feedback	Air vortex emit device

do better than the REVEL created from Disney Research Team, so this concept is not consider in our design. The last two concepts also have been done by other research and we consider our technology cannot beyond them, so they are also not in consider of our design. Use Non-Newtonian fluid is a new idea for us. The property of Non-Newtonian fluid is it would become harder when it suffer from the greater force. But we are not sure whether we can handle it or not, we pass this interesting idea unfortunately.

The basic idea of 5 to 11 concepts is take a physical thing to touch the finger when user does the press button action, and these haptic feedback concepts are proposed for many times, so we try to design our model with these concepts seriously. After analyze these ideas in deep, we find that we can install a small portable button under the finger to give the user haptic feedback when their finger push down, and that means to generate the haptic feedback for augmented reality virtual keyboard on the air, the high technology is not necessary. We can use the simple and normal structure to solve this problem. Although we would still use other concept to try, we need evaluate these concepts first. The idea of make the user's body become a touch interface has already done by many research and study, so we cancel this concept into the design.

And the concept of spin something to rub the finger and inflate the small balloon when finger touch and then deflate immediately need to use the motor, but the motor is too big to stall it on the finger. That way, we also cancel these two concepts.

To sum up, we would use a low specific heat material in our device to add some tactile feedback for user, and try to add normal physical button on the device. We believe this evaluation can hope us innovation a new haptic feedback device for augmented reality virtual keyboard on the air.

4.2   Design Prototype

To use the simple and normal structure to achieve the haptic feedback device, we use LEGO brick, button switch and the metal gasket to create our prototype. We use LEGO brick on the main structure for easy to adjust with different length of finger, and we choose the button switch which is easy to press to increase the sensitivity of detection.   The metal gasket which is low specific heat material is added on the button to generate the tactile haptic of different temperature. The structure fix on the proximal phalanx and the button is below the fingertip. When the finger relaxes, the fingertip is free and would not touch anything.   When finger starts to operate the virtual keyboard, due to the displacement degree of distal phalanx and middle phalanx is more than proximal phalanx, the fingertip would touch the metal gasket and feel the haptic feedback just like using the physical keyboard.

4.3   Evaluation of New Design

The advantage of our new design show that the device does not need to use any electricity circuit, it means the user would not worry about the electromagnetic damage even he wear the device for all day. Also, the device can easy to product because it only has basic structure without any new technology or material. And no matter what posture of the hand, such as raise or lay down, the user still can feel the haptic feedback if they do the typing action. That means the posture of operate the augmented reality can be change, people would need to raise the arm while type the virtual keyboard on the air.   However, our design just shows one finger operate situation, the

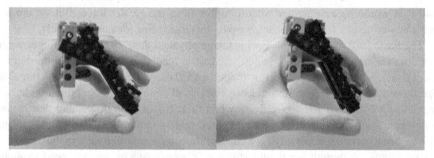

Fig. 1. Wear the prototype device in the relax situation and push action. The displacement degree of distal phalanx and middle phalanx is more than proximal phalanx obviously.

prototype now is still too big that the device would stuck each other if all the finger wear the device. Beside, the stability is not enough when finger push down, is has some offset problem on it.

5   Conclusion

To develop the haptic feedback device for augmented reality virtual keyboard on the air, we return to focus on people's feeling. We use focus group to find what kind of haptic feedback is user really wanted when they operate the augmented reality device. And we find a simple way to achieve the goal without electric to avoid the potential electromagnetic damage, and this idea can be produced easily because it does not use any high technology in it. Beside, our design can be used in different posture, we try to break through the limit of operate posture.

The next step we would simplify the structure to make the device lighter and more comfortable on the finger. And then we will expand the experiment from one finger to one hand, and use some method to compare the value between our design and physical keyboard, to improve the innovative device is really useful for operate the augmented reality virtual keyboard. Also, we would try other possibility concept from the focus group to find more possibility of haptic feedback. After the haptic feedback goal is achieved, our future development would focus on the new operate posture, try to find the new comfortable operate posture to let the user control augmented reality virtual keyboard easier.

References

1. Lee, K.: Augmented Reality in Education and Training. Techtrends: Linking Research & Practice To Improve Learning 56(2) (March 2012)
2. Rolland, J., Biocca, F., Hamza-Lup, F., Yanggang, H., Martins, R.: Development of Head-Mounted Projection Displays for Distributed, Collaborative, Augmented Reality Applications. Massachusetts Institute of Technology 14(5), 528–549 (2005)
3. Bernstein, J.A.: Invention Awards: Augmented-Reality Contact Lenses (May 06, 2012), http://www.popsci.com/diy/article/2012-05/2012-invention-awards-augmented-reality-contact-lenses (retrieved)
4. Pachoulakis, I., Kapetanakis, K.: Augmented Reality Platforms For Virtual Fitting Rooms. The International Journal of Multimedia & Its Applications (IJMA) 4(4) (2012)
5. Soler, L., Nicolau, S., Schmid, J., Koehl, C., Marescaux, J., Pennec, X., Ayache, N.: Virtual reality and augmented reality in digestive surgery. Mixed and Augmented Reality, 278–279 (2004), doi:10.1109/ISMAR.2004.64
6. Phan, V.T., Choo, S.Y.: Interior Design in Augmented Reality Environment. International Journal of Computer Applications (0975 – 8887) 5(5) (2010)
7. ITRI.HMD using Air Touch (November 6, 2013), https://www.youtube.com/watch?v=vpjPkEq-cYs (retrieved)
8. Grohman, B., Spangenberg, E.R., Sprott, D.E.: The influence of tactile input on the evaluation of retail product offerings. Journal of Retailing 83(2), 237–245 (2007)

9. Klatzky, R.L., Peck, J.: Please Touch: Object Properties that Invite Touch Roberta. IEEE Transactions on Haptics 5(2) (2012)

10. Rabin, E., Gordon, A.: Tactile Feedback Contributes to Consistency of Finger Movements During Typing. Experimental Brain Research 155(3), 362–369 (2004)

11. Brewster, S., Chohan, F., Brown, L.: Tactile feedback for mobile interactions. In: Proceedings of the SIGCHI Conference on Human Factors in Computing Systems, CHI 2007, pp. 159–162. ACM, New York (2007)

12. NEC, Tokyo Institute of Technology. Tactile Display with Directional Force Feedback #DigInfo (2012), http://www.youtube.com/watch?v=veP1BcdYrEY (retrieved)

13. Hornyak, T.: KDDI haptic touch screen pushes your buttons (October 5, 2011), http://news.cnet.com/8301-17938_105-20116256-1/kddi-haptic-touch-screen-pushes-your-buttons/ (retrieved)

14. Tactus Technology CES 2013: Tactus Touch Screen (MUST SEE!) (January 13, 2013), http://www.youtube.com/watch?v=A7ldnbLyr9s (retrieved)

15. Burdea, G.C.: Force and Touch Feedback for Virtual Reality (1996) ISBN-13: 978-0471021414

16. Akin, Ö.: An exploration of the design process. In: Cross, N. (ed.) Developments in Design Methodologies, pp. 189–208. John Wiley & Sons, New York (1984)

17. Iwata, H., Yano, H., Nakaizumi, F., Kawamura, R.: Project feelex: Adding haptic surface to graphics. In: Proceedings of ACM, ACM SIGGRAPH (2001)

18. Jansen, Y., Karrer, T., Borchers, J.: MudPad: localized tactile feedback on touch surfaces. In: UIST 2010 Adjunct Proceedings of the 23nd Annual ACM Symposium on User Interface Software and Technology, pp. 385–386 (2012), doi:10.1145/1866218.1866232

19. Follmer, S., Leithinger, D., Ishii, A.O.A.H.H.: inFORM: dynamic physical affordances and constraints through shape and object actuation. In: Proceedings of the 26th Annual ACM Symposium on User Interface Software and Technology, pp. 417–426. ACM (2013)

20. US 20100295820 A1, Erez Kikin-Gil, Microsoft Corporation, US 12/468,742 (November 2010)

21. Kaczmarek, K.A., Nammi, K., Agarwal, A.K., Tyler, M.E., Haase, S.J., Beebe, D.J.: Polarity Effect in Electrovibration for Tactile Display. IEEE Transactions on Biomedical Engineering 53(10) (October 2006)

22. Carter, T., Seah, S.A., Long, B., et al.: UltraHaptics: Multi-Point Mid-Air Haptic Feedback for TouchSurfaces. In: UIST 2013, St Andrews, United Kingdom, October 8-11 (2013), doi:10.1145/2501988.2502018

23. Sodhi, R., Poupyrev, I., Glisson, M., Israr, A.: AIREAL: Interactive Tactile Experiences in Free Air. ACM Trans. Graph. 32(4), Article 134, 10 pages (2013), doi:10.1145/2461912.2462007

24. Gupta, S., Morris, D., Patel, S.N., Tan, D.: AirWave: Non-Contact Haptic Feedback Using Air Vortex Rings. In: Proceedings of the 2013 ACM International Joint Conference on Pervasive and Ubiquitous Computing, pp. 419–428 (2013), doi:10.1145/2493432.2493463

Brain-Computer Interfaces

BNCI Horizon 2020 – Towards a Roadmap for Brain/Neural Computer Interaction

Clemens Brunner[1], Benjamin Blankertz[2], Febo Cincotti[3], Andrea Kübler[4],
Donatella Mattia[3], Felip Miralles[5], Anton Nijholt[6], Begonya Otal[5],
Patric Salomon[7], and Gernot R. Müller-Putz[1]

[1] Institute for Knowledge Discovery, Graz University of Technology, Graz, Austria
[2] Chair for Neurotechnology, Berlin Institute of Technology, Berlin, Germany
[3] Neuroelectrical Imaging and BCI Lab, Fondazione Santa Lucia, Rome, Italy
[4] Institute of Psychology, Biological Psychology, Clinical Psychology and Psychotherapy,
University of Würzburg, Würzburg, Germany
[5] Barcelona Digital Technology Centre, eHealth R&D, Barcelona, Spain
[6] Department EWI, Research Group Human Media Interaction,
University of Twente, Enschede, The Netherlands
[7] EnablingMNT GmbH, Berlin, Germany
clemens.brunner@tugraz.at

Abstract. In this paper, we present BNCI Horizon 2020, an EU Coordination and Support Action (CSA) that will provide a roadmap for brain-computer interaction research for the next years, starting in 2013, and aiming at research efforts until 2020 and beyond. The project is a successor of the earlier EU-funded Future BNCI CSA that started in 2010 and produced a roadmap for a shorter time period. We present how we, a consortium of the main European BCI research groups as well as companies and end user representatives, expect to tackle the problem of designing a roadmap for BCI research. In this paper, we define the field with its recent developments, in particular by considering publications and EU-funded research projects, and we discuss how we plan to involve research groups, companies, and user groups in our effort to pave the way for useful and fruitful EU-funded BCI research for the next ten years.

Keywords: Brain-computer interfaces, Horizon 2020, roadmap, Future BNCI, mental state monitoring, BCI publications, EU projects, BCI Society, user-centred design, ethical guidelines.

1 Introduction

Brain-computer interfaces (BCIs) have become a popular topic for research in recent years. A BCI is a communication device which allows people to control applications through direct measures of their brain activity. A BNCI (brain/neuronal computer interaction) system extends a BCI by including other physiological measures such as muscle or eye movement signals. The number of BCI research groups around the world, peer-reviewed journal articles, conference abstracts, and attendance at relevant

C. Stephanidis and M. Antona (Eds.): UAHCI/HCII 2014, Part I, LNCS 8513, pp. 475–486, 2014.
© Springer International Publishing Switzerland 2014

conferences are indicators of the rapid growth of this field. With dozens of companies and research groups actively participating in the development of BCIs and related technologies, collaboration, a common terminology, and a clear roadmap have become important topics. To provide a solution to these issues, the European Commission (EC) funded the coordination action Future BNCI in 2010/2011. This project was the first effort to foster collaboration and communication among key stakeholders. Furthermore, this project created a five-year roadmap for BCI research. In 2013, the EC decided to continue the efforts initiated by Future BNCI by funding the development of a more long-term roadmap within the new framework program Horizon 2020.

In this paper, we explain how BNCI Horizon 2020 will address and predict new developments in BNCI research, including new applications for people with motor, sensory, cognitive and mental disabilities, and people without these disabilities. The new roadmap will touch upon other key topics including ethics, societal needs for and acceptance of BNCI systems, user-centered approaches, evaluation metrics, and the transfer of technology from research labs to the market. A clear and comprehensive roadmap produced by BNCI Horizon 2020 will lay the foundations for, and impact on, a (continued) dominance and clear visibility of European research groups in the future. In addition, the roadmap will display opportunities, but also limitations and constraints, for the industrialization and commercialization of BNCIs. The aim of this paper is to inform the research community about this project and invite comments and involvement.

2   BCIs and BNCIs Definitions

According to the most commonly used definition, a brain-computer interface (BCI) is a communication device that classifies brain activity and controls a device such as a spelling application [1,2,3,4], a neuroprosthesis [5,6], a domestic environment [7,8], a wheelchair [9,10], a telepresence robot[11,12], an internet browser [13,14], computer games [15,16,17,18], or creative expression [19,20]. A BCI uses signals directly recorded from the brain, operates online, provides feedback, and relies on goal-directed behavior [21,22]. A more recent definition describes a BCI as follows [23]: "A BCI is a system that measures central nervous system (CNS) activity and converts it into artificial output that replaces, restores, enhances, supplements, or improves natural CNS output and thereby changes the ongoing interactions between the CNS and its external or internal environment." This definition includes BCIs that do not require intentional control, which are sometimes referred to as passive BCIs [24]. Other related terms include affective BCIs [25], emotional BCIs [26] or mental state monitors [27,28]. Figure 1 depicts the scheme of a BCI and lists possible applications.

The term brain/neuronal computer interaction (BNCI) was introduced by the European Commission (EC) without a clear definition at the beginning. However, the research community has adopted the convention that a BNCI differs from a BCI only in the used signals. Specifically, a BNCI does not only rely on direct measurement of brain activity, but also includes signals from other physiological activity such as eye

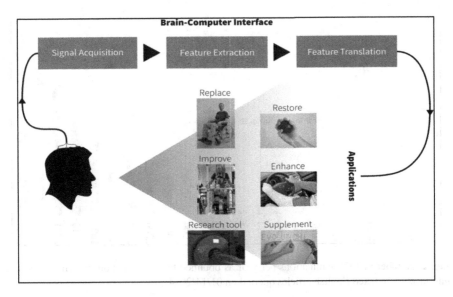

Fig. 1. BCI scheme and possible application scenarios (adapted from [23])

movement (electro-oculogram, EOG), muscle activity (EMG, electromyogram), or heart rate (HR, derived from the electrocardiogram, ECG). Furthermore, a device that combines a BCI with another input device is also known as a hybrid BCI [29,30] or a multimodal BCI [31].

3   BCI and BNCI Research Field

Research on BNCIs and BCIs started in the 80s of the last century (although first ideas date back to Vidal et al. in the 70s) and is currently transforming from a small field in its infancy to a large research effort across the globe. The number of scientific publications in this field is steadily increasing every year (see Figure 2). Another measure of progress is the attendance at international conferences; for example, the five Graz BCI conferences (organized by Graz University of Technology in Graz, Austria) in 2002, 2004, 2006, 2008, and 2011 were attended by 32, 52, 95, 116, and 236 people, respectively. The 5th International BCI Meeting in Pacific Grove, CA, USA, in June 2013 attracted more than 300 attendees.

While BCI research traditionally focused almost exclusively on applications for patients, the interest in developing non-medical applications has been growing recently; this targets a much larger user group. These applications include BCIs to control games [16,17], but also a plethora of other novel approaches are investigated [32]. EEG-based monitoring of workload can be used for example to mitigate workload in the case of overload in car/truck/train driving or aviation [33]. Similarly, monitoring the level of attention can be used to initiate counter-measures and thereby help to avoid hazardous situations in industrial workplaces [34,28]. Electrophysiology can

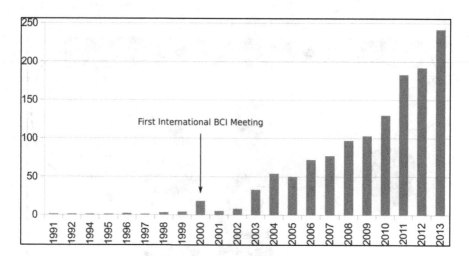

Fig. 2. Number of BCI publications per year as obtained by a PubMed query "brain-computer interface" in indexed English articles queried on 01/14/2014

also be exploited to detect precursors of braking intention and gives rise to a neuroergonomic approach to driving assistance [35]. Furthermore, many opportunities exist to improve human-computer interaction [24] using BCI systems by resorting to implicit information in the perceptual and cognitive processes. Examples include approaches based on (a) the possibility to extract subconscious processes from the EEG as exemplified in the detection of distortions in audio samples [36], (b) the EEG-based recognition of unexpected events [37], and (c) the quantification of the depth of processing [38].

Numerous companies are now active in the BCI sector. The roadmap developed in the EU-funded coordination action (CA) Future BNCI lists 39 companies working in and producing BCIs or related devices for different market sectors such as health and neurofeedback, assistive technology, education, safety and security, entertainment and performance, research, and financial and marketing. Within BNCI Horizon 2020, we have already identified more than 100 potential companies either directly developing BCIs or related devices, or aiming to integrate BCI-based technology into their product portfolio or upcoming market applications.

Several sources also indicate that commercial interest in BNCI research is increasing. Guger Technologies, a major supplier of amplifiers and other equipment for BNCI research, reports an increase in annual sales for BCI equipment of about 35% per annum since 2005. Other companies such as NeuroSky, Emotiv, InterAxon, and OCZ have heavily publicized new BNCIs for game control that did not exist a few years ago. These toys use very simple, inexpensive, sometimes single-channel systems aimed at healthy users for entertainment – instead of complex, expensive, often multi-channel systems aimed at severely disabled users for assistive technology. NeuroSky sold over one million chips in 2011 for BCI toys like the Necomimi Cat Ears and Star Wars Force Trainer [39]. Other companies like Advanced Brain Monitoring, Neuroelectrics, NeuroFocus and EmSense have developed more expensive BCIs that are also aimed at healthy users. These systems include devices to monitor alertness, sleep or anticipation. Healthy users seem to be a rapidly growing market for BNCIs. However, it is unclear which users, applications, companies or usage environments will be the strongest to emerge soon.

4   Relevant European Research Projects

The EU has funded several projects dealing with BNCIs within its Framework Programmes FP6 and FP7. Thirteen projects are part of a BNCI cluster within the e-Inclusion initiative, which consists of the following projects: TOBI (11/08-01/13), TREMOR (09/08-04/10), BRAIN (09/08-08/11), DECODER (02/10-04/13), BETTER (02/10-01/13), BrainAble (01/10-12/12), Future BNCI (01/10-12/11), As-TeRICS (01/10-12/12), MINDWALKER (01/10-12/12), MUNDUS (03/10-02/13), ABC (11/11-10/14), BackHome (01/12-06/15), and WAY (10/11-09/14). CONTRAST (11/11-10/14) and MindSee (09/13-08/16) are other ongoing EU-funded projects dealing with BCIs outside the BNCI cluster. Here, BCIs are used for feedback of EEG activity to improve general and specific cognitive functions (such as attention and inhibition) in stroke patients. Moreover, several researchers received individual European or national grants. Among these projects, Future BNCI was the first coordination action (CA) in this research field. Its main goals were (1) to foster collaboration between BCI researchers, (2) to develop a common terminology, and (3) to identify roadmaps and opportunities for the field of BCI research. The integrated project (IP) TOBI took over and continues to develop parts of the outcome of Future BNCI, in particular the roadmap.

5   Current Challenges

The field of BNCI research is growing rapidly, and there are no major coordination efforts in place to ensure efficient communication and collaboration between key stakeholders. For example, the field has still neither agreed upon common definitions of key terms, nor upon a common procedure concerning ethical issues, and opinions on promising future directions differ vastly. The fact that stakeholders address these issues individually not only wastes precious resources, but also translates to an excess expenditure, which could be reduced by a close and supported collaboration.

The synergy in efforts appears crucial to foster the translation of several BNCI research developments from the laboratories to real world scenarios, which include healthy and disabled end users [40,41].

The previous CA Future BNCI has successfully started to address these critical issues. However, these efforts were only the first steps toward our goal to identify and address current and future challenges and to create a coordinated research field including the foundation of a BCI Society, which would be a strong indicator of the maturation of the field.

On the whole, four major challenges can be identified: (1) *The growing need for standards is still unmet.* This challenge entails many aspects of standardization: terms and definitions for BCIs and BNCIs, guidelines for reporting key details of BCI articles, ethical guidelines for working with patients, and certifications for relevant personnel. There is still confusion and disagreement about what constitutes a BCI or BNCI. (2) *There is inadequate interaction within the BNCI community.* This makes it difficult to work together on standards, and also impedes collaboration for research and development. There is no central society or group that represents the BCI community and can foster interaction with policy makers, other stakeholders, the media and other groups. (3) *There is inadequate dissemination outside of the BNCI community.* Most doctors, patients, students, and the general public do not know about BCIs, or have unrealistic views based on how the technology is presented in the media and some news sources. Other research and development communities, particularly involving assistive technologies and patient care, do not interact enough with BNCI researchers. (4) *There is little agreement on the most promising future directions.* Since integrating BCIs with other BNCIs, other interaction paradigms, and other emerging technologies entails working with new people and new groups, the lack of interaction has made it difficult to objectively assess which technologies (and new combinations thereof) are promising. Companies, policy makers, medical decision makers, patients, and other groups without a BNCI background may find it especially difficult to identify the most promising products, directions, funding opportunities, and treatment options.

These four main challenges cannot be addressed without an effective coordination effort. It seems unlikely that any project can align constituencies and prepare future joint research and roadmaps when the relevant disciplines and stakeholders are not even clearly identified. The principal vision of BNCI Horizon 2020 is to address these challenges by establishing and supporting a thriving, efficient, and well-connected BNCI community.

6   Goals and Objectives

With BNCI Horizon 2020, we continue coordination efforts that were initiated by Future BNCI to ensure that progress is not impeded by a lack of infrastructure, lack of communication between key stakeholders, ambiguous terminology or an unclear roadmap of the research field. BNCI Horizon 2020 will develop a roadmap document, building on the results of Future BNCI and TOBI, but also on results of other past and current projects. The roadmap will serve as a guideline and will contain conclusions, recommendations, and a provision of ideas for future activities that will be supported by the EU framework program Horizon 2020. In the roadmap, we will identify new BNCI opportunities and synergies with existing fields, with respect to applications for people-with motor, sensory, and cognitive disabilities as well as for healthy users. We plan to identify these opportunities from a research, industrial, and end users' perspective.

The end users' perspective will embrace the principles of the user-centered design to address some of the future priorities in terms of BNCI applications in real world medical (i.e., assistive and rehabilitation field) and non-medical scenarios (i.e., entertainment and general purpose in healthy people).

The user-centered design was standardized in ISO-DIS-9241-210. It is focused on the concept of usability, i.e. "the extent to which a product can be used by specified users to achieve specified goals with effectiveness, efficiency and satisfaction in a specified context of use". The principles of this approach are adopted as an iterative process in the development of assistive technology (AT) devices as well as in the Human-Computer Interaction field, addressing the understanding and specification of users' needs and the context of use, and evaluation against the defined requirements.

In recent years, development of communication systems based on BNCI technology has started to take advantage of the AT design principles [18,19,41,42]. BNCI Horizon 2020 will capitalize on previous and current research and application experience to define standards for the efficient development and assessment of BNCI-based technologies taking in to account users' requirements and needs.

BNCI Horizon 2020 will encourage discussion and collaboration; the project will also disseminate knowledge and information among BCI researchers and the general public. Our main communication and dissemination channels are (a) workshops and conferences where we explain the aims of BNCI Horizon 2020 and collect feedback; (b) a dedicated community website, based on and incorporating information from the Future BNCI website (future-bnci.org), that will not only present results from the project, but will be a platform for BCI research in general and an information hub and community portal for researchers, reviewers, industrial partners, and the general public at large; (c) the creation of an open access database of BCI data sets on our website to foster competition and reproducibility of results. In addition, BNCI Horizon 2020 will actively support the foundation of an international BCI Society.

7   Coordination and Networking Efforts

First and foremost, a major result of the project will be a concise roadmap, a document that will build on the roadmap produced by the Future BNCI and TOBI projects. We will incorporate new findings to be generated within BNCI Horizon 2020 through the knowledge of its partners, their background, links to other projects, and by engaging with the relevant stakeholders (end user representatives, industry, and research) through questionnaires, workshops, and interviews. Roadmapping will be driven by interactive and iterative activities.

Based on the existing Future BNCI roadmap, initial application scenarios will be developed. These scenarios will be verified through the advisory board and updated throughout the project. The current state of the art (in all three areas research, industry, and end users) for these scenarios will be extracted from the existing roadmaps and updated with the latest knowledge.

User requirements and visions will be assessed from/with end users (e.g., focus groups) and visionary stakeholders. Initially, we will capitalize on previously established networking between a large community of end users (individuals, representative associations, assistive technology solution providers, and medical staff) and national and EU research projects. These requirements will be discussed with research and industry to check what is possible in 5-10 years from their view, which is then to be agreed with industry in terms of what is realistic and commercially feasible within this timeframe.

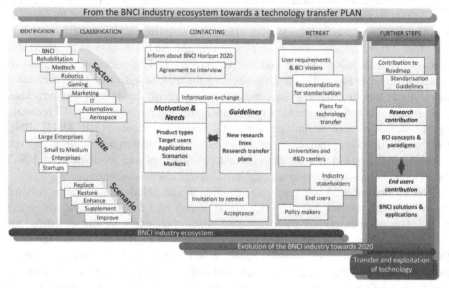

Fig. 3. From the industry ecosystem towards a technology transfer plan for the overall BNCI Horizon 2020 roadmap: coordination and networking efforts among academia, industry stakeholders, policy makers, and end users

The updated scenarios will again be discussed with end user representatives to verify if these ideas could actually add value for them and their stakeholders. The resulting technological challenges and the research needed to address them will then be assessed in joint discussions with industry and research representatives. Finally, a timeline can be drawn of technologies/research needed to address challenges and the possible results in terms of (commercial) products and services.

Additionally, we will collect and/or estimate data on numbers of users (EU- and world-wide) and calculate market data in terms of potential users of such devices to estimate the possible market and in general the possible impact of BCI technologies.

Other networking efforts include the organization of dedicated meetings with stakeholders, conferences, workshops, and special sessions.

Therefore, we will mainly focus on coordination and processing inputs from all identified industry stakeholders in BNCI and related domains to develop guidelines, recommendations, actions and plans about current and future products, application scenarios, markets and business models, with a strong focus on success stories, technology transfer, and exploitation avenues. We have been designing different strategies to acquire and process qualitative industry ecosystem data, and to manage a market analysis, in order to develop these guidelines and recommendations towards a technology transfer plan (see Figure 3).

Several steps prior to one of the main networking activities, the BNCI Horizon 2020 Retreat, correspond to the following coordination efforts: First, the *identification* of major industry stakeholders coming from the whole BNCI consortium. Second, the *classification* of those identified BNCI and new potential industry stakeholders from related domains. So far, we have already identified over 100 large enterprises, small to medium enterprises and startups, and defined the corresponding classification by company size, sector, location, potential BNCI scenarios, target users, and applications. Third, we have started to *contact* those main players and inform them about BNCI Horizon 2020 activities. Further, we try to engage them to participate by inviting them to the retreat and by asking them to answer questionnaires about their company in relation to BNCI motivations and needs. The first networking activity, the upcoming *retreat*, will enable us to engage in discussion sessions, surveys, and workshops. Thereafter, there will be a need to establish new procedures and methods to process all collected data from the research and academia contribution, the industry stakeholders' motivations and needs, and end users' new potential BNCI solutions and applications.

The overall BNCI Horizon 2020 roadmap will contain the analyzed material obtained from these major coordination and networking efforts. This will rely on qualitative market research, through the links to the industry, academia and end users coming from the whole consortium as well as from our advisory board and the upcoming BCI Society.

8   Conclusions

BNCI Horizon 2020 will impact the field of BNCIs in the following ways:

- We will provide a roadmap of the field of BNCIs for policy makers, politicians, researchers, companies, end user associations, end users, clinical staff, and the general public. This roadmap will clearly identify promising ideas for future BNCI activities that could be supported by the EU program Horizon 2020. The roadmap will display opportunities but also limitations and constraints for the industrialization and commercialization of BNCIs.
- We will investigate synergies with relevant fields. Fields that already impacted on BNCI research include assistive technologies, sensor technologies, robotics, information retrieval, neuroscience, machine learning, communication technology, human-computer interaction, ergonomics, and rehabilitation. One possible synergy from the field of machine learning could be an open database of BCI data sets and algorithms, which will increase competitiveness and reproducibility of results.
- The concepts of a user-centered design, specifically (but not exclusively) for people with motor, sensory, and cognitive disabilities will be more widespread, known, and understood.
- The involvement of industrial stakeholders throughout the duration of BNCI Horizon 2020 leads to a strong impact on a future BNCI market. For example by identifying possible products, new end user groups, and synergies with other fields. Similarly, we will actively involve end users throughout the duration of BNCI Horizon 2020, who will contribute feedback and influence the direction of our roadmap.
- BNCI Horizon 2020 will contribute to a foundation of a BCI Society through approaching key stakeholders, organization of meetings, targeted discussions, and

evaluation of possible scenarios to implement this society. A BCI Society will have a very strong impact on the whole field, because this would be the first time that people working with BCIs could speak with a common public voice.

- A common terminology and common standards for the evaluation of BNCIs promoted by our project will lead to stronger and more efficient research efforts and collaborations. We will create ethical guidelines for the use of BNCIs, and we will seek contact with the general public and address their questions, concerns, and ideas. This will benefit all people involved with the development and the (commercial) use of BCIs, including the general public.

Acknowledgments. This work was supported by EU FP7 CSA "BNCI Horizon 2020: The Future of Brain/Neural Computer Interaction", FP7-ICT-2013-10-609593.

References

1. Kübler, A., Neumann, N., Kaiser, J., Kotchoubey, B., Hinterberger, T., Birbaumer, N.: Brain-computer communication: self-regulation of slow cortical potentials for verbal communication. Archives of Physical Medicine and Rehabilitation 82, 1533–1539 (2001)
2. Scherer, R., Müller-Putz, G.R., Neuper, C., Graimann, B., Pfurtscheller, G.: An asynchronously controlled EEG-based virtual keyboard: improvement of the spelling rate. IEEE Transactions on Biomedical Engineering 51(6), 979–984 (2004)
3. Treder, M.S., Schmidt, N.M., Blankertz, B.: Gaze-independent brain-computer interfaces based on covert attention and feature attention. Journal of Neural Engineering 8(6), 066003 (2011)
4. Birbaumer, N., Ghanayim, N., Hinterberger, T., Iversen, I., Kotchoubey, B., Kübler, A., Perelmouter, J., Taub, E., Flor, H.: A spelling device for the paralysed. Nature 398, 297–298 (1999)
5. del R. Millán, J., Renkens, F., Mouriño, J., Gerstner, W.: Brain-actuated interaction. Artificial Intelligence 159(1-2), 241–259 (2004)
6. Müller-Putz, G.R., Scherer, R., Pfurtscheller, G., Rupp, R.: EEG-based neuroprosthesis control: a step towards clinical practice. Neuroscience Letters 382, 169–174 (2005)
7. Cincotti, F., Mattia, D., Aloise, F., Bufalari, S., Schalk, G., Oriolo, G., Cherubini, A., Marciani, M.G., Babiloni, F.: Non-invasive brain-computer interface system: towards its application as assistive technology. Brain Research Bulletin 75(6), 796–803 (2008)
8. Aloise, F., Schettini, F., Aricò, P., Leotta, F., Salinari, S., Mattia, D., Babiloni, F., Cincotti, F.: P300-based brain-computer interface for environmental control: an asynchronous approach. Journal of Neural Engineering 8(2), 025025 (2011)
9. Leeb, R., Friedman, D., Müller-Putz, G.R., Scherer, R., Slater, M., Pfurtscheller, G.: Self-paced (asynchronous) BCI control of a wheelchair in virtual environments: a case study with a tetraplegic. Computational Intelligence and Neuroscience 79642, 1–8 (2007)
10. Galán, F., Nuttin, M., Lew, L., Ferrez, P.W., Vanacker, G., Philips, J., del R. Millán, J.: A brain-actuated wheelchair: asynchronous and non-invasive brain-computer interfaces for continuous control of robots. Clinical Neurophysiology 119, 2159–2169 (2008)
11. Andersson, P., Pluim, J.P., Viergever, M.A., Ramsey, N.F.: Navigation of a telepresence robot via covert visuospatial attention and real-time fMRI. Brain Topography 26, 177–185 (2013)

12. Carlson, T., Tonin, L., Leeb, R., Rohm, M., Rupp, R., Al-Khodairy, A., del R. Millán, J.: BCI telepresence: a six patient evaluation. In: TOBI Workshop III: Bringing BCIs to End-Users – Facing the Challenge, pp. 18–19. University of Würzburg (2012)
13. Mugler, E.M., Ruf, C.A., Halder, S., Bensch, M., Kübler, A.: Design and implementation of a P300-based brain-computer interface for controlling an internet browser. IEEE Transactions on Neural Systems and Rehabilitation Engineering 18(6), 599–609 (2010)
14. Zickler, C., Riccio, A., Leotta, F., Hillian-Tress, S., Halder, S., Holz, E., Staiger-Sälzer, P., Hoogerwerf, E.-J., Desideri, L., Mattia, D., Kübler, A.: A brain-computer interface as input channel for a standard assistive technology software. Clinical EEG Neuroscience (42), 236–244 (2011)
15. Krepki, R., Blankertz, B., Curio, G., Müller, K.-R.: The Berlin Brain-Computer Interface (BBCI): towards a new communication channel for online control in gaming applications. Journal of Multimedia Tools and Applications 33(1), 73–90 (2007)
16. Nijholt, A., Oude Bos, D., Reuderink, B.: Turning Shortcomings into Challenges: Brain-Computer Interfaces for Games. Entertainment Computing 1(2), 85–94 (2009)
17. Plass-Oude Bos, D., Reuderink, B., van de Laar, B., Gürkök, H., Mühl, C., Poel, M., Nijholt, A., Heylen, D.: Brain-Computer Interfacing and Games. In: Tan, D., Nijholt, A. (eds.) Brain-Computer Interfaces: Applying our Minds to Human-Computer Interaction, pp. 149–178. Springer, London (2010)
18. Holz, E.M., Höhne, J., Staiger-Sälzer, P., Tangermann, M., Kübler, A.: Brain-computer interface controlled gaming: evaluation of usability by severely motor restricted end-users. Artificial Intelligence in Medicine 59(2), 111–120 (2013)
19. Zickler, C., Halder, S., Kleih, S.C., Herbert, C., Kübler, A.: Brain painting: usability testing according to the user-centered design in end users with severe motor paralysis. Artificial Intelligence in Medicine 59(2), 99–110 (2013)
20. Gürkök, H., Nijholt, A.: Affective Brain-Computer Interfaces for Arts. In: Nijholt, A., D'Mello, S., Pantic, M. (eds.) Affective Computing and Intelligent Interaction (ACII 2013), pp. 827–831. IEEE Press, New York (2013)
21. Kübler, A., Kotchoubey, B., Kaiser, J., Wolpaw, J.R., Birbaumer, N.: Brain-computer communication: unlocking the locked in. Psychological Bulletin 127, 358–375 (2001)
22. Wolpaw, J.R., Birbaumer, N., McFarland, D.J., Pfurtscheller, G., Vaughan, T.M.: Brain-computer interfaces for communication and control. Clinical Neurophysiology 113, 767–791 (2002)
23. Wolpaw, J.R., Winter Wolpaw, E.: Brain-computer interfaces: something new under the sun. In: Wolpaw, J.R., Winter Wolpaw, E. (eds.) Brain-Computer Interfaces: Principles and Practice, pp. 3–12. Oxford University Press, Oxford (2012)
24. Zander, T.O., Kothe, C.: Towards passive brain-computer interfaces: applying brain-computer interface technology to human-machine systems in general. Journal of Neural Engineering 8, 025005 (2011)
25. Mühl, C., van den Broek, E.L., Brouwer, A.-M., Nijboer, F., van Wouwe, N., Heylen, D.: Multi-modal affect induction for affective brain-computer interfaces. In: D'Mello, S., Graesser, A., Schuller, B., Martin, J.-C. (eds.) ACII 2011, Part I. LNCS, vol. 6974, pp. 235–245. Springer, Heidelberg (2011)
26. Garcia Molina, G., Tsoneva, T., Nijholt, A.: Emotional Brain-Computer Interfaces. International Journal of Autonomous and Adaptive Communications Systems (IJAACS) 6(1), 9–25 (2013)
27. Ferrez, P.W., del R. Millán, J.: Error-related EEG potentials generated during simulated brain-computer interaction. IEEE Transactions on Biomedical Engineering 55, 923–929 (2008)

28. Müller, K.-R., Tangermann, M., Dornhege, G., Krauledat, M., Curio, G., Blankertz, B.: Machine learning for real-time single-trial EEG analysis: from brain-computer interfacing to mental state monitoring. Journal of Neuroscience Methods (167), 82–90 (2008)
29. Pfurtscheller, G., Allison, B.Z., Brunner, C., Bauernfeind, G., Solis-Escalante, T., Scherer, R., Zander, T.O., Müller-Putz, G.R., Neuper, C., Birbaumer, N.: The hybrid BCI. Frontiers in Neuroscience 4(3) (2010)
30. Mueller-Putz, G.R., Breitwieser, C., Cincotti, F., Leeb, R., Schreuder, M., Leotta, F., Tavella, M., Bianchi, L., Kreilinger, A., Ramsay, A., Rohm, M., Sagebaum, M., Tonin, L., Neuper, C., del R. Millán, J.: Tools for Brain-Computer Interaction: a general concept for a hybrid BCI (hBCI). Frontiers in Neuroinformatics 5, 30 (2011)
31. Nijholt, A., Allison, B.Z., Jacob, R.K.: Brain-Computer Interaction: Can Multimodality Help? In: Bourlard, H., et al. (eds.) 13th International Conference on Multimodal Interaction, pp. 35–39. ACM, New York (2011)
32. Blankertz, B., Tangermann, M., Vidaurre, C., Fazli, S., Sannelli, C., Haufe, S., Maeder, C., Ramsey, L.E., Sturm, I., Curio, G., Müller, K.-R.: The Berlin Brain-Computer Interface: Non-Medical Uses of BCI Technology. Frontiers in Neuroscience 4, 198 (2010)
33. Kohlmorgen, J., Dornhege, G., Braun, M., Blankertz, B., Müller, K.-R., Curio, G., Hagemann, K., Bruns, A., Schrauf, M., Kincses, W.: Improving human performance in a real operating environment through real-time mental workload detection. In: Dornhege, G., del R. Millán, J., Hinterberger, T., McFarland, D., Müller, K.-R. (eds.) Toward Brain-Computer Interfacing, pp. 409–422. MIT Press, Cambridge (2007)
34. Martel, A., Dähne, S., Blankertz, B.: EEG Predictors of Covert Vigilant Attention. Journal of Neural Engineering (in press, 2014)
35. Haufe, S., Treder, M.S., Gugler, M.F., Sagebaum, M., Curio, G., Blankertz, B.: EEG potentials predict upcoming emergency brakings during simulated driving. Journal of Neural Engineering 8, 056001 (2011)
36. Porbadnigk, A.K., Treder, M.S., Blankertz, B., Antons, R., Schleicher, R., Möller, S., Curio, G., Müller, K.-R.: Single-trial analysis of the neural correlates of speech quality perception. Journal of Neural Engineering 10(5), 056003 (2013)
37. Schmidt, N.M., Blankertz, B., Treder, M.S.: Online detection of error-related potentials boosts the performance of mental typewriters. BMC Neurosci. 13, 19 (2012)
38. Venthur, B., Blankertz, B., Gugler, M.F., Curio, G.: Novel Applications of BCI Technology: Psychophysiological Optimization of Working Conditions in Industry. In: Systems, Man and Cybernetics (SMC 2010), pp. 417–421. IEEE Press, New York (2010)
39. Future BNCI: A Roadmap for Future Directions in Brain/Neuronal Computer Interaction. The Future BNCI Project (2012), http://bnci-horizon-2020.eu/images/bncih2020/FBNCI_Roadmap.pdf
40. Kübler, A., Mattia, D., Rupp, R., Tangermann, M.: Facing the challenge: brain-computer interfaces to end-users. Artificial Intelligence in Medicine 59(2), 55–60 (2013)
41. Kübler, A., Holz, E., Kaufmann, J.: A user-centered approach for bringing BCI controlled applications to end users. In: Reza-Fazel, R. (ed.) Brain-Computer Interface Systems – Recent Progress and Future Prospects. InTech, New York (2013)
42. Kübler, A., Zickler, C., Holz, E., Kaufmann, T., Riccio, A., Mattia, D.: Applying the user-centred design to evaluation of Brain-Computer Interface controlled applications. Biomedical Engineering / Biomedizinische Technik 58(suppl. 1) (2013), doi:10.1515/bmt-2013-4438

Braincontrol Basic Communicator:
A Brain-Computer Interface Based Communicator
for People with Severe Disabilities

Pasquale Fedele, Chiara Fedele, and Jarrod Fath

Liquidweb s.r.l., Siena, Italy
{p.fedele,c.fedele,j.fath}@liquidweb.it

Abstract. The "BrainControl Basic Communicator" (BrainControl BC) is an augmentative and alternative communication (AAC) system based on Brain-computer interface (BCI) technology. The system has been designed for patients with severe disabilities due to pathologies such as Amyotrophic Lateral Sclerosis (ALS), Multiple Sclerosis, ischemic or traumatic injuries.

The first prototype of the BrainControl BC was completed in mid 2012 and has been completed in the mid 2013. From 2012, 20 locked-in patients have been trained with success and in the last few months 12 of these patients are continuously using the system, as it represents the only possibility to communicate.

BrainControl BC is part of the BrainControl project, aiming to develop a BCI platform that allows people suffering from sever disabilities to overcome physical and communicative impairments. In particular, BrainControl can help patients suffering from diseases that paralyze the whole body or parts of the body, but who retain their intellectual abilities.

Future versions of BrainControl, which are currently under development, will include advanced communication and functionalities, home automation, the control of a wheelchair and robotics.

Keywords: Brain-Computer Interface (BCI), Augmentative and Alternative Communication (AAC), Assistive Technologies, Amyotrophic Lateral Sclerosis (ALS).

1 Introduction

Over 20 million people globally are completely paralyzed and/or have communication difficulties due to degenerative neuromuscular diseases (amyotrophic lateral sclerosis, multiple sclerosis, etc.) or ischemic or traumatic injuries.[1] The needs of at least 3.7 million of them (severe cases) are not met by assistive technologies currently on the market.

Degenerative neuromuscular or cerebrate-vascular disorders are characterized by a gradual loss of muscular function while retaining complete cognitive functions.

---

[1] Worldwide number calculated based on data from the Population Research Bureau, Christopher and Dana Reeve Foundation, Italian ALS Association, American ALS Association and American Multiple Sclerosis Association.

C. Stephanidis and M. Antona (Eds.): UAHCI/HCII 2014, Part I, LNCS 8513, pp. 487–494, 2014.

Amyotrophic lateral sclerosis (ALS) is a progressive neurodegenerative disease involving the motor neurons. It is pathologically characterized by progressive loss of upper and lower motor neurons. The disease duration is variable with a large spectrum of possibilities ranging from forms with mild conditions and a slower evolution to more severe forms with survival no more than 2.5 years and finally to very rapid forms with survival of less than 6 months. Clinically, ALS is characterized by a progressive complete destruction of the peripheral and central motor system but only affecting sensory or cognitive functions to a minor degree. The disease progresses until the patient loses control of the last muscular response, which is usually the eye muscle or the external sphincter. The resulting condition is called completely locked-in state. If rudimentary control of at least one muscle is present, we speak of a locked-in state. Other conditions leading to a locked-in state are subcortical stroke and other extended brain lesions, Guillain-Barre syndrome, some rare cases of Parkinson disease, and Multiple Sclerosis.

The principle assistive technologies for locked-in patients include residual movement controlled systems [1,2], voice-controlled systems, eye-tracking and brain-computer interface. Voice-controlled systems are based on speech recognition and speech-to-text, but cannot be used by the millions of patients who cannot speak due to the pathologies mentioned above. Eye-tracking systems follow the movement of the user's pupil, but they cannot be used by many patients. Brain-computer interface (BCI) technology interprets the electrical signals that correspond with certain brain activity and allows a computer or other external devise to be controlled with thoughts (Figure 1). [3, 4, 5, 6, 7, 8, 9, 10, 11, 12, 13, 14, 15, 16]

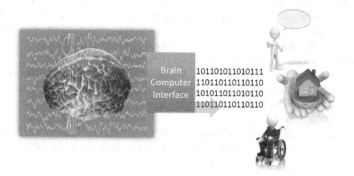

Fig. 1. Brain-Computer Interface

Over the past 20 years, research in the field of brain-computer interface (BCI) has led to significant results, driven by advances in our understanding of brain function and the evolution of computers and sensors. However, no sufficiently usable and robust solutions address the needs of people with severe physical and communication disabilities.

2   BrainControl Project Overview

BrainControl project aims to develop a usable and robust framework for assistive technologies based on BCI, by the use of low/reasonable cost, commercial available hardware (EEG headset and Tablet PC).

Fig. 2. BrainControl Architecture

The heart of BrainControl is a proprietary classifier of EEG patterns based on neural network technology and combined with an adaptive Bayesian algorithm for customizing different needs in different patients. The system works like a mental joystick, detecting 6 types of imagined movements (IM), push, pull, up, down, right, left, thus allowing a computer or other external devise to be controlled (Figure 2).

BrainControl's aim is to help users to overcome severe physical and communicative disabilities created by pathologies such as amyotrophic lateral sclerosis (ALS), multiple sclerosis, tetraplegia and various kinds of muscular dystrophies. In particular, BrainControl can help patients suffering from diseases that paralyze the whole body or parts of the body, but who retain their intellectual abilities. It will be possible for them to communicate feelings and needs, to move their own wheelchair, to interact with family and friends through social networks, email or SMS, to turn the lights on or off, and even open or close doors and windows.

A first prototype of the system, able to recognize pull/push imagined movements, was developed in fall the of 2010 [17]. It has been continuously developed between 2010 and 2012 and tested in the same period with more than 30 healthy volunteers providing excellent results and encouraging the development.

The first version of BrainControl, the Basic Communicator, was completed in the middle of 2013. It fills a technological void for patients in locked-in state who cannot use eye-tracking systems or other assistive technologies.

Future versions of BrainControl, which are currently under development, will include advanced communication and entertainment (virtual keyboard, text-to-speech, social networks, email,), home automation (lights, temperature, etc.), control of a wheelchair and robotics (Figure 3). BrainHuRo, a project that applies BCI to humanoid robots, has been started in 2013, partially funded by the Italian region of Tuscany (POR-CREO Fesr 2007-2013 – Le ali alle tue idee) and involving the University of Siena, Liquidweb s.r.l., Humanot s.r.l., Massimi Sistemi s.r.l. and Micromec s.r.l. [18].

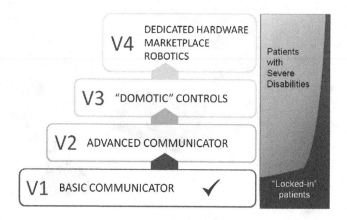

Fig. 3. Roadmap

3   BrainControl Basic Communicator

The BrainControl Basic Communicator has been designed around the needs of locked-in patients. It includes a "Yes/No/Don't know" Selector (Figure 4) and a "Sentence Finder" (Figure 5). The user interface uses a scanning mode to move between available options and utilizes just one movement-related thought to select the desired choice. The pre-defined sentences in the sentence finder are completely customizable, including the addition of images, audio feedback and the creation of sub-menus.

BrainControl BC utilizes proprietary software and commercially available hardware that has been made for the consumer market, including a non-invasive wireless EEG headsets Emotiv Epoc and a tablet PC.

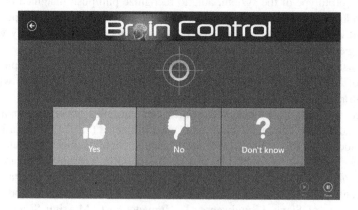

Fig. 4. Yes/No Mode

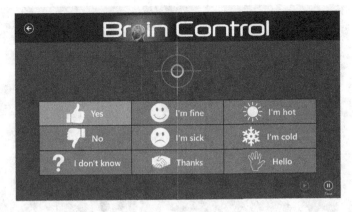

Fig. 5. Sentence Finder

Fig. 6. BrainControl Basic Communicator

The first prototype of the BrainControl BC has been released on mid 2012 and has completed in the mid 2013.

3.1   Training of Locked-In Patients

The training is carried out in one-hour remote sessions (video conference with remote desktop control). In many cases, one session is sufficient, but four sessions are generally scheduled during the first month.

During the first training the trainers explains to the patients how the system works, its functionalities and the training purpose, then he starts with multiple iterative sessions of calibration and tests. During the calibration phase, the software records the EEG data from the user witch was asked to stay focused for few seconds on the movement-related thought that will be used for controlling the system. The tests phases consists on asking the patients to select predefined sequences of choices.

This iterative session in conducted for 30-40 minutes and is replicated in the next 3 sessions during the first month.

If the user can select at least 5 predefined choices without errors during the test phase, the training is considered successful.

Fig. 7. Calibration

3.2 Results

In the period of August 2012 – January 2014 we carried out sessions training with two group of users:

   I)   30 healthy users;

   II) 21 patients with tetraplegia, 18 of them in locked-in state.

The training has been completed successfully for all the 30 users of the first group.

As for as the second group, the training has been completed successfully for 20 and failed for one of the patients in locked-in state.

12 patients of the second group are using continuously the system, as it represents the only possibility to communicate.

Aim of the future work is evaluating the use of the system in a long term period for patients affected by neurodegenerative diseases, after entering in a completed locked-in state.

4   Conclusion

The "BrainControl Basic Communicator" (BrainControl BC) is an augmentative and alternative communication (AAC) system based on Brain-computer interface (BCI) technology. The system has been designed for patients with severe disabilities due to pathologies such as Amyotrophic Lateral Sclerosis (ALS), Multiple Sclerosis, ischemic or traumatic injuries.

From 2012, 20 locked-in patients have been trained with success and 12 of these patients are using continuously the system, as it represents the only possibility to communicate.

BrainControl BC is part of the BrainControl project, aiming to develop a BCI platform that allows people suffering from severe disabilities to overcome physical and communicative impairments. In particular, BrainControl can help patients suffering from diseases that paralyze the whole body or parts of the body, but who retain their intellectual abilities.

Future versions of BrainControl, which are currently under development, will include advanced communication and entertainment functionalities, home automation, the control of a wheelchair and robotics.

References

1. Carlson, T., Demiris, Y.: Human-wheelchair collaboration through prediction of intention and adaptive assistance. In: Proceedings of the IEEE International Conference on Robotics and Automation, pp. 3926–3931 (2008)
2. Carlson, T., Monnard, G., Leeb, R., Millán, J., del, R.: Evaluation of Proportional and Discrete Shared Control Paradigms for Low Resolution User Inputs. In: Proceedings of the IEEE Intl. Conf. on Systems, Man, and Cybernetics, pp. 1044–1049 (2011a)
3. Carlson, T., Monnard, G., del R. Millán, J.: Vision-Based Shared Control for a BCI Wheelchair. International Journal of Bioelectromagnetism 13(1), 20–21 (2011b)
4. Carmena, J.M., Lebedev, M.A., Crist, R.E., O'Doherty, J.E., Santucci, D.M., Dimitrov, D.F., et al.: Learning to control a brain-machine interface for reaching and grasping by primates. PLoS Biology 1, E42 (2003)
5. Birbaumer, N., Ghanayim, N., Hinterberger, T., Iversen, I., Kotchoubey, B., Kübler, A., et al.: A spelling device for the paralysed. Nature 398, 297–298 (1999)
6. Buttfield, A., Ferrez, P.W., del R. Millán, J.: Towards a robust BCI: error potentials and online learning. IEEE Trans. Neural Sys. Rehab. Eng. 14, 164–168 (2006)
7. Birbaumer, N.: Breaking the silence: Brain-computer interfaces (BCI) for communication and motor control. Psychophysiology 43, 517–532 (2006)
8. Lebedev, M.A., Nicolelis, M.A.L.: Brain-machine interfaces: past, present and future. Trends in Neurosciences 29(9), 536–546 (2006)
9. Sitaram, R., Caria, A., Birbaumer, N.: Hemodynamic brain–computer interfaces for communication and rehabilitation. Neural Networks (2009)
10. Allison, B.Z., Wolpaw, E.W., Wolpaw, J.R.: Brain-computer interface systems: progress and prospects. Expert Review of Medical Devices 4(4), 463–474 (2007)
11. Dornhege, G., del R. Millán, J., Hinterberger, T., Müller, K.-R.: Toward Brain-Computer Interfacing. MIT Press (2007)
12. Van Gerven, M., Farquhar, J., Schaefer, R., Vlek, R., Geuze, J., Nijholt, A., Ramsey, N., Haselager, P., Vuurpijl, L., Gielen, S., Desain, P.: The brain–computer interface cycle. J. Neural Eng. 6 (2009)
13. Pfurtscheller, G., Allison, B.Z., Brunner, C., Bauernfeind, G., Solis-Escalante, T., Scherer, R., Zander, T.O., Mueller-Putz, G., Neuper, C., Birbaumer, N.: The Hybrid BCI. Frontiers in Neuroprosthetics 2, 3 (2010), doi:10.3389/fnpro.2010.00003
14. Zander, T.O., Kothe, C.: Towards passive brain–computer interfaces: applying brain-computer interface technology to human–machine systems in general. Journal of Neural Engineering 8 (2011)
15. George, L., Lécuyer, A.: An overview of research on "passive" brain-computer interfaces for implicit human-computer interaction. In: International Conference on Applied Bionics and Biomechanics, ICABB (2010)

16. Tonin, L., Carlson, T., Leeb, R., del R. Millán, J.: Brain-Controlled Telepresence Robot by Motor-Disabled People. In: Proceedings of the 33rd Annual International Conference of the IEEE Engineering in Medicine and Biology Society, pp. 4227–4230 (2011)
17. Fedele, P., Tavanti, M.: "BrainControl project" poster and demo. In: Mind Force Conference, October 7-8. Centre for the Study of Complex Systems, University of Siena, Siena (2010)
18. Casals, A., Fedele, P., Marek, T., Molfino, R., Muscolo, G.G., Tommaso Recchiuto, C.: A robotic suit controlled by the human brain for people suffering from quadriplegia. In: 14th Towards Autonomous Robotic Systems, TAROS 2013, St. Anne's College, Oxford, August 28-30. LNCS (LNAI), pp. 28–30. Springer (2013)

Eureka: Realizing That an Application is Responding to Your Brainwaves

Jonathan Giron and Doron Friedman

The Advanced Reality Lab, The Interdisciplinary Center, Herzliya, Israel
giron.jonathan@gmail.com, doronf@idc.ac.il

Abstract. We have conducted an experiment in which subjects controlled a brain-computer interface (BCI) without being aware that their brainwaves were responsible for events in the scenario. Ten subjects went through a stage of model training in steady state visually evoked potential (SSVEP)-based BCI, followed by three trials of an immersive experience where stars moved as a response to SSVEP classification. Only then the subjects were explained that they were using a BCI, and this was followed by an additional trial of immersive free choice BCI and a final validation stage. Three out of the ten subjects realized that they controlled the interface, and these subjects had better accuracy than the rest of the subjects and reported a higher sense of agency in a post study questionnaire.

Keywords: brain computer interface, steady state visually evoked potentials, electroencephalogram, agency.

1 Introduction

Brain-computer interface (BCI) has the potential to become the ultimate interaction paradigm, whereby user's intentions are automatically converted into actions. However, despite much progress in BCI in general and in SSVEP-based BCI specifically, the practice is very different. In order to achieve reasonable accuracy BCI users have to be very concentrated, avoid moving or blinking as much as possible, and often some period of training is required.

We have developed a system that naturally embeds electroencephalogram (EEG) steady state visually evoked potential (SSVEP) targets inside graphical scenes. Using our system any object in a 3D (or 2D) environment can be easily made into a BCI target, with the expectation of this leading to an improved user experience compared to most alternative paradigms. In this study we wanted to push the ease of use to its extreme and ask: would people be able to control an application using BCI without even being told that they are controlling the application? And if so, would people realize that they are affecting the application using their brainwaves?

We have conducted an experiment whereby ten subjects controlled a BCI without being instructed to control it. Our method uses the SSVEP paradigm, which is based on detecting occipital lobe activation that resonates with flickering visual stimuli.

C. Stephanidis and M. Antona (Eds.): UAHCI/HCII 2014, Part I, LNCS 8513, pp. 495–502, 2014.
© Springer International Publishing Switzerland 2014

The subjects experienced an immersive presentation of deep space, including stars flickering with different frequencies, while connected to the BCI system. Whenever the online classification indicated that the subject "selected" one of the stars, the star started to move, thus providing feedback to the subjects. The goal was to find out whether subjects would realize that the application is responding to their brain activity, and how this would affect their BCI performance and their overall experience.

2   Related Work

We suggest a distinction among three types of BCI control: i) implicit – the interface responds to the user's brainwaves but the user is not aware of it, ii) volitional – the user makes an aware mental effort to control the interface, and iii) the control of the BCI has become an automatic process, so the user knows that he is using a BCI but does not necessarily need to dedicate attention to that control. There has been some studies shedding light on the possible transition from volitional to automatic control (e.g., see [1] for a relevant review), but a very small number of studies regarding the differences between implicit and voluntary BCI control.

Shenoy and Tan [2] suggest a paradigm they call human-aided computing that uses an EEG device to measure implicit cognitive processing, processing that users perform automatically and may not even be aware of. They report two experiments whereby subjects were exposed to images for as briefly as 150ms and the category of the image was classified with some degree of success from the EEG patterns. Zander et al. [3,4] suggest a subclass of BCI systems that they call passive BCIs, which provide "easily applicable and yet efficient interaction channels carrying information on covert aspects of user state, while adding little further usage cost"[4]. Our study reported here suggests that SSVEP may similarly be used as a passive BCI.

3   Method

3.1   System

Our generic platform allows easily turning any object in a virtual environment into an SSVEP flickering target. We use the Unity 3D game engine (Unity Technologies, USA). The stimuli were presented in an immersive virtual environment displayed on a back projected large screen ("power wall") 182cm (height) by 256cm (width). Participants were asked to sit on an office arm chair positioned 180cm from the screen. The application was displayed using a 120 screen refresh rate projector at a screen resolution of 1280*768 using a high-end graphics card.

EEG recording, signal processing and algorithm classification were conducted on a laptop that sent the classification results through a user datagram protocol (UDP) over the local network to the computer running Unity. SSVEP classification was calculated using a well-known algorithm [5]. We recorded EEG signals at pO7, PO3, POz, PO4, PO8, O1, Oz and O2 locations according to the international 10-20 system. Reference

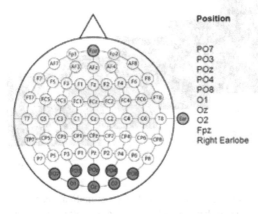

Fig. 1. Electrode locations on the scalp

electrode was positioned on the subject's left ear lobe and ground electrode was placed at Fpz location (Figure 1). EEG signals were recorded at 256Hz and amplification, analog filtering (5-100 Hz), and notch filtering at 50Hz were performed using the g.USBamp amplifier (Guger Technologies, Austria).

3.2   Experimental Protocol

Ten subjects participated in the experiment, aged 19-40, 8 females and 2 males. The experiment included three parts (Fig. 2): i) training, ii) free choice immersive BCI scenario, and iii) classification validation. Throughout the study we used five classes, four SSVEP frequencies: 8.57Hz, 12Hz, 15Hz, and 20Hz, and a null class.

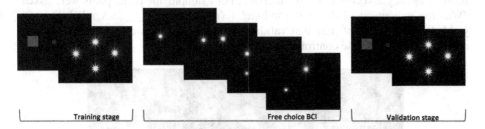

Fig. 2. The experimental protocol included three stages

In the first part (training), the system computed a classifier of the EEG patterns elicited by the stimuli (stars) (Fig. 3). Each of the training sessions included 20 stimuli, 5 times each frequency in pseudo-random order and location on the screen. A red square appeared before each stimulus that the subject was expected to attend to.

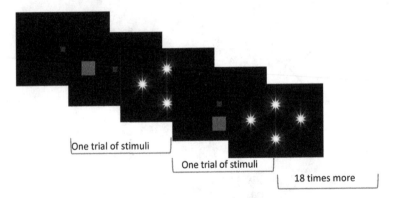

Fig. 3. The training stage claffication trial: before stimuli appearance a red square directs towards the location of the star that the participant needs to attend to in the following trial.

In the second stage (Fig. 4) the scene included an immersive experience of deep space with small stars moving towards the subject. Occasionally, larger stars would appear, all with the same texture, and each flickering at one of the four frequencies (there were up to four large stars simultaneously on the screen and never more than one with the same frequency). When an SSVEP response to a specific star has been detected in the participant's online signal, the star began moving towards the user. Each trial in this stage lasted 155 seconds of free choice BCI, and every participant went through four such trials.

In the first three trials the subjects were not told that the experience is responding to their brainwaves. After the first three trials and before the fourth trial the subjects filled in a questionnaire, and were then divulged about the nature of the interface and asked to do their best at moving the stars. The questionnaire included some demographic information as well as five questions on a 1-7 Likert scale that measured their sense of agency and control of the interface. For example, the participants were asked "Was the movement of the stars random? 1 (no) – 7 (yes) ___". A reliability test yielded a α-cronbach of .651 that validates the similarity between questions so they could be used as a single control measure.

Fig. 4. The experience: a subject controlling the star field using the BCI

During the online classification of the signals at the second part of the experiment, a 2-second running window was used for data collection. The algorithm computed a classification result 5 times per second (i.e., every 200ms). In order to decrease false positive classification errors a filter was applied to the stream of classification results: a total of 6 consecutive results (1 second) were required of the same class in order to activate a game object (star) command. Since we also used a sliding window of two seconds, the minimum possible response time of the stars (game objects) was 3 seconds.

In the free choice task we cannot provide accuracy measurements since we do not know the subject's intentions. However, we can provide an approximated metric as follows. Whenever the classifier indicated a non-zero class we could test whether a star with that frequency was present on screen at that moment or not; if it did this is considered a hit and if it did not we consider it a false positive. For the hits we do not know whether the subject intended to select that specific star or not, but the results are nevertheless of interest. Because the SSVEP has a residue duration reflected in the SSVEP even after the star has disappeared from the screen, we have ignored false positives in the first 3 seconds following the disappearance of a star.

In order to validate model fit the experiment included a third stage of validation for all subjects, which was constructed similarly to the training trial described above.

4   Results

Three subjects out of 10 realized that they were controlling the application, and the rest did not. We will refer to the first group as the Eureka group and to the second group as the non-Eureka group. Due to the small number of subjects in both groups statistical tests did not always reveal significant results, but we can see some clear trends.

In the validation stage the number of false positive classifications of the Eureka group was significantly smaller than that of the non-Eureka group ($t = 3.6$, $p = 0.03$) and the overall accuracy was nearly significantly higher in the Eureka groups than in the non-Eureka group ($t = 1.83$, $p = 0.066$) (Figure 5).

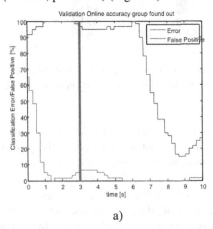

a)

Fig. 5. Accuracy (number of errors and false positive classifications) over time, averaged over all subjects in group (a) Eureka and (b) non-Eureka

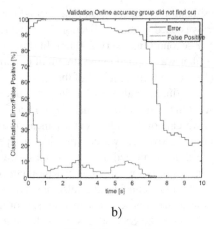

b)

Fig. 5. *(continued)*

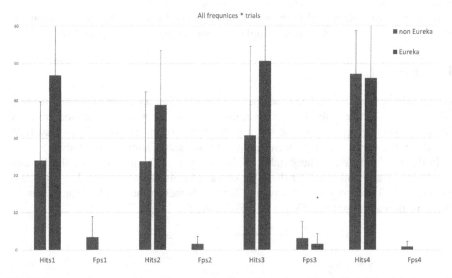

Fig. 6. A comparison between subjects who realized the task and those that did not, in terms of the number of hits and false positives of star classification in the free choice stage, over the four sessions

Figure 6 provides a comparison between the Eureka and non-Eureka groups in the four free choice sessions. We see that the number of false positives was always larger in the non-Eureka group than in the Eureka group; in the latter case there was only a small number of false positives in the third session. In addition, in the non-Eureka group the number of hits was smaller in the first three runs, when the subjects were not aware of their control, than the number of hits in the fourth run, after they have been notified about their control of the stars. In the Eureka group there was no such trend.

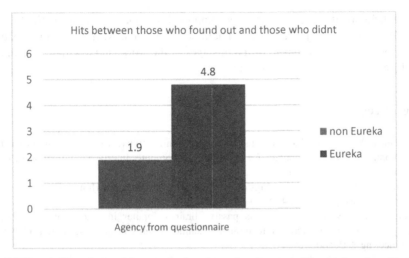

Fig. 7. Hits ratio between participants who found out they are controlling the interface (Eureka) and those who didn't (non eureka)

The subjects in the Eureka group reported a higher sense of agency (mean = 4.8) than in the non-Eureka group (mean = 1.9). Again the small number of the subjects prevents a statistical analysis but the difference seems substantial (Fig. 7).

5   Discussion

Our study shows that subjects can control an SSVEP BCI without being instructed at all. Only a small part (30%) of the subjects realized that the content of the display was responding to their brainwaves. Those subjects that did realize this were more successful in controlling the BCI and reported a significantly higher sense of agency.

Our study indicates that SSVEP, especially when embedded naturally inside 3D environments, can be used as a natural mode of interaction. Even those subjects that did not know that the content was responding to their brainwaves were able to perform the task much beyond chance levels.

Our hypothesis is that the relatively small number of subjects that realized that they were using a BCI is due to the high latency, of approximately 6 seconds between the appearance of the stimulus and the optimal point of classification. The neuroscience community assumes that a delay of 500 ms between stimulus and feedback already diminishes the sense of agency significantly (e.g.,[6]).

Finally, we see this early result as a trigger for two types of studies. First, we intend to further explore this paradigm and test whether implicit learning of such a BCI is possible. Second, we see this as an indication that SSVEP embedded naturally in the media is promising as a natural user interface, and hope to explore it in additional scenarios and experimental paradigms.

Acknowledgement. The project was supported by the EU project VERE (No 657295), www.vereproject.eu. The authors wish to thank Miri Segal and Beatrice Hasler for useful discussions in different stages of the work, and to Gilan Jackont and Yuval Kalguny for help with programming.

References

1. Curran, E.A., Stokes, M.J.: Learning to control brain activity: a review of the production and control of EEG components for driving brain–computer interface (BCI) systems. Brain and Cognition 51, 326–336 (2003)
2. Shenoy, P., Tan, D.S.: Proceedings of the SIGCHI Conference on Human Factors in Computing Systems, pp. 845–854. ACM (2008)
3. Zander, T.O., Kothe, C.: Towards passive brain–computer interfaces: applying brain–computer interface technology to human–machine systems in general. Journal of Neural Engineering 8, 025005 (2011)
4. Zander, T.O., Kothe, C., Jatzev, S., Gaertner, M.: Enhancing human-computer interaction with input from active and passive brain-computer interfaces. In: Brain-Computer Interfaces, pp. 181–199. Springer (2010)
5. Gollee, H., Volosyak, I., McLachlan, A.J., Hunt, K.J., Graser, A.: An SSVEP-based brain–computer interface for the control of functional electrical stimulation. IEEE Transactions on Biomedical Engineering 57, 1847–1855 (2010)
6. Tsakiris, M., Longo, M.R., Haggard, P.: Having a body versus moving your body: neural signatures of agency and body-ownership. Neuropsychologia 48, 2740–2749 (2010)

Cognitive Brain Signal Processing:
Healthy vs Alzheimer's Disease Patients

Vasiliki Kosmidou[1], Anthoula Tsolaki[2], Chrysa Papadaniil[3], Magdalini Tsolaki[4],
Leontios Hadjileontiadis[3], and Ioannis Kompatsiaris[1]

[1] Information Technologies Institute (ITI), Centre for Research & Technology Hellas, Greece
{kosmidou,ikom}@iti.gr
[2] Medical Physics Laboratory, Medical School, Aristotle University of Thessaloniki, Greece
tsolakianthoula@gmail.com
[3] Department of Electrical & Computer Engineering, Aristotle University of Thessaloniki, Greece
chrysa.papadaniil@gmail.com, leontios@auth.gr
[4] 3rd Department of Neurology, Aristotle University of Thessaloniki, Greece
tsolakim1@gmail.com

Abstract. Processing the brain functionality during certain perceptual stimuli or activities is beneficial to better understanding the lost abilities of a mind of a patient with cognitive impairment. Electroencephalogram (EEG) has been widely used as a tool for brain mapping. In this paper, we discuss the experimental setup and methods of the Cognitive Brain signal Processing (CBP) project towards this direction. High spatial resolution EEG (256 channels) is acquired, while the subject perform a series of cognitive tests with known expected response. Four tests from the CANTAB© Battery evaluating visual memory, spatial working memory and attention, a Sudoku puzzle and tasks with external visual and audio stimuli i.e., emotional (Ekman images) and audio event-related potentials (ERP) comprise the experimental protocol. Three groups of subjects are recruited, i.e., 30 healthy young adults 25-40 years old, 30 healthy adults of 65 years and older, and 30 patients with mild Alzheimer's disease (AD) aged 65 years and older. In the CBP project, the 2D vector field tomography (VFT) will be extended to the 3D space to create a novel tool to solve the inverse EEG problem towards source reconstruction and therefore brain mapping. The 3D VFT will be applied to the acquired data in order to facilitate the extraction of the cognitive states and the identification of dysfunctioning areas. The external stimuli will be correlated with the performance of the participants to verify which elements can be assistive and improve their performance. The results can be used to design intelligent assistive environments and help the communication of patients with AD in everyday life.

Keywords: brain mapping, Alzheimer's disease, EEG, 3D-vector field tomography.

1 Introduction

Alzheimer's disease (AD) is a neurodegenerative disorder that is characterized by cognitive deficits, disorders of Activities of Daily Living and behavioral disturbances.

C. Stephanidis and M. Antona (Eds.): UAHCI/HCII 2014, Part I, LNCS 8513, pp. 503–514, 2014.
© Springer International Publishing Switzerland 2014

Recent research is focused on defining methods for the earliest detection of AD, preferably in the preclinical stages [1]. However, research focusing on the way of brain functioning and the differences between healthy young and aged brains, as well as healthy and neurodegenerative brains may lead us to understand better the lost abilities of a patient's mind and improve their communication abilities.

The study of the human brain requires the use of specialized equipment. The modalities on which brain studies rely are either signal processing-based (Electro-Encephalography (EEG) and Magneto-Encephalography (MEG)) or tomographic imaging-based (Magnetic Resonance Imaging (MRI), functional MRI (fMRI) Positron Emission Tomography (PET), Computer Tomography (CT)), or, more recently, functional near infra red (fNIR), which uses optical signals. The use of EEG for advancing the comprehension of the underlying mechanisms during sensory stimulations or motor tasks against alternative brain mapping methodologies (e.g., MEG, fMRI) is justified in view of its excellent temporal resolution, low-cost, less sophisticated sensors employment and its overall facile applicability [2]. The engagement of advanced EEG equipment with high spatial resolution and increased clinical efficiency provides to the researchers a useful tool for in vivo studying of a "working" brain. An example of such equipment consists the EGI Geodesic EEG System 300 (GES300-www.egi.com) offering dense array EEG recordings of 256- channels, which measure the electrical activity in the brain using far more electrodes than in conventional EEG setups. In this vein, the increased spatial resolution allows researchers to see—in an intuitive topographic view—aspects of the EEG not visible with conventional EEG systems.

The use of EEG is based on the idea that by measuring the electromagnetic fields on the head surface, we may infer the distribution of the underlying current sources that give rise to these external fields, and thus, the brain areas that are activated during the task under study. For example, a subject may receive an audio, visual, or some other external sensory stimulation (evoked potentials), or s/he may execute a motor task (e.g., driving), or even be involved in a cognitive experience (e.g., concerning memory and language). The source reconstruction techniques have shown in some limited cases that decoding brain states using source level features can outperform an electrode level approach [3], [4]. The prevalent methodology for reconstructing the head model of the corresponding activated areas during a task is the representation of the underlying current distribution using a collection of discrete mathematical dipoles. The solutions for this inverse problem of EEG are categorized in the parametric and imaging methods [2]. In the parametric formulation, a number of dipoles is assumed to stand for the current sources and, using a non-linear method, the unknown dipole moments and locations are determined. To achieve this goal, the forward problem is initially solved, i.e., the potentials that the assumed dipoles would create on the scalp are estimated, and the presumed dipole parameters change until agreement is met between these estimates and the actual values recorded by the EEG sensors. The main drawback of this approach is that the number of dipoles has to be selected forehand, which frequently results in trying many models until data fitting is reached. Especially in cases of many sources, the pre-assumed models can be adjusted to satisfy any recording. On the other hand, imaging methods assume that current sources are typically distributed along the cortical surface, where a dense collection of dipoles is assigned. As the dipoles orientation is now restricted and their locations are known, the problem becomes linear, but involves a very large number of unknowns, leading to severe ill-posedness. Thus, weighting techniques between possible solutions, constraints schemes and regularization methods have to be imposed. Another aspect is that the choice of the best-fitting model is performed regardless of the data. Three imaging techniques (Low Resolution Electromagnetic Tomography (LORETA) [5], Local Auto-Regressive Averages (LAURA) [6], standardized LORETA (sLORETA) [7]) are implemented in GES300. In the interest of acquiring a unique solution, LORETA postulates that adjacent neurons are simultaneously and synchronously activated, while sLORETA performs brain source localization using images of standardized current density. These methods have been reported to fail in providing accurate localization when multiple sources were synchronously activated [8], [9]. In LAURA, brain activity at one point is connected to its neighbors based on a distance measure. The principle of LAURA is to produce estimates that justify the measured data, thus, presence of noise degrades its otherwise efficient performance [8]. Criticism on these parametric methods also includes the lack of physiological meaning in the adopted constraints.

In the "Cognitive Brain signal Processing" (CBP) project (http://cbp.iti.gr) described here, the problem of brain mapping is treated in a totally different way. Instead of trying to use a number of dipoles to model the millions of neurons of the brain, and instead of trying to use accurate tissue models to infer what exactly the electromagnetic properties of a particular brain are, mapping of the state of the brain in a systematic way to a set of "effective states" is adopted using vector field tomography (VFT). The most important difference here is that instead of using actively injected current, the natural sources inside the brain that create the potentials are observed. This novel methodology for the reconstruction of an irrotational field from boundary data has recently been proposed for the recovery of two dimensional irrotational vector fields, where the error bounds of the recovered solution have subsequently been defined [10]-[12]. VFT frames the methods used for recovering a vector field from integral data, a problem that is by definition underdetermined. According to the related investigation, a unique solution can be achieved when constraints are imposed, information about the kind of the field is available, or additional measurements are performed, which is possible in exceptional cases [13], [14]. Within CBP, this methodology is extended to three dimensions (3D) and the discretization process that can reconstruct an irrotational vector field is verified, in spite of the ill-posedness in the continuous domain [15]. Applying the theory of 3D-VFT to the inverse EEG problem, the effective brain states can be inferred and used to study the relationship between the electric activity of the brain and the cognitive states in order to associate the EEG measurements with certain perceptual stimuli or activities.

In this work, we present and discuss the experimental and medical protocol followed to meet the objectives of CBP research. A series of cognitive tasks and ones with evoked-related potentials of emotional and audio stimuli comprise the experiments conducted in the CBP project, involving EEG data acquisition from both a control group and a group of AD patients. The use of advanced acquisition equipment combined with the experimental setup will enable the attainment of the necessary data to better understand the cognitive processes in the brain and evaluate the performance of the brain when various stimuli occur. Therefore, the expected results may contribute to the brain-computer interaction research, with the ultimate aim to be used for assisting AD patients with their everyday activities.

2   Materials and Methods

2.1   Participants

Participants are volunteers from the Centre for Research & Technology Hellas, the dementia outpatient clinic of the 3rd Neurology department of Aristotle University of Thessaloniki as well as from personal inquiry and emails in social networks. Ninety participants are recruited, divided in three groups: a) 30 young healthy participants aged 25-40 years old, b) 30 healthy elderly greater than 65 years old and c) 30 mild AD patients aged greater than 65 years old. The study protocol has been approved by the Ethics Committee of the Centre for Research & Technology Hellas.

Exclusion criteria included any severe physical illness, current psychiatric or neurological disorder, history of drug or alcohol abuse, recent start (less than 15 days) of acethylcholinesterase inhibitors medication or other neuromodifying drugs and other types of dementia. Also, participants reported normal or corrected-to-normal vision and audition.

Prior to the experimental procedure all the participants undergo a short neuropsycological evaluation with MMSE [16], MoCA [17], TRAIL B [18], BDI [19], GDS [20], IADL [21], and FRSSD [22]. They are also subjected to blood tests and brain MRI. The diagnosis of mild AD or mild cognitive impairment is according DSM- V criteria [23]. The neuropsychological, medical and laboratory results are evaluated by a neurologist verifying the health or the disease status.

2.2   Stimulus Materials

The experimental protocol consists of a series of cognitive tasks, including tasks via the CANTAB® Battery, a Sudoku test, emotional triggering tasks and audio Event- Related Potential (ERP).The CANTAB® software comprises of 25 computerized neuropsychological tests specifically designed to examine areas of cognitive function and central nervous system disorder (http://www.camcog.com/cantab-tests.asp). We chose four of these tests to apply in CBP protocol, i.e., the Motor Screening Task (MOT), the Pattern Recognition Memory (PRM), the Spatial Working Memory (SWM) and the Rapid Visual Information Processing (RVP).

The MOT is actually an introduction, aiming to familiarize the subject with the tablet touch screen. Participants must touch a flashing cross shown in different locations on the screen. Two outcome features are measured: the participant's speed of response and the accuracy of the participant's pointing.

Through the PRM, the visual memory is evaluated by a 2-choice forced discrimination paradigm. The participant is presented with a series of 12 visual patterns, one at a time, in the center of the screen. These patterns are designed so that they cannot easily be given verbal labels. In the recognition phase, the participant is required to choose between a pattern already shown and a novel pattern. In this phase, the test patterns are presented in the reverse order to the original order of presentation. A second presentation set of 12 new patterns follows, with the corresponding recognition phase given after a 20 minute delay. This test has three outcome measures, including the number and percentage of correct trials, and the participant's speed of response.

Additionally, the participant's ability to retain spatial information and manipulate remembered items in working memory is evaluated through the SWM test, acting as a sensitive measure of frontal lobe and 'executive' dysfunction. The test begins with a number of squares shown on the screen. The aim of this test is that, by touching the squares and using a process of elimination, the participant should find one blue 'token' in each of a number of squares and use them to fill up an empty column on the right hand side of the screen. The number of squares is gradually increased to reach a total of eight squares. The position of the squares used is changed from trial to trial to discourage the use of stereotyped search strategies. The twenty-four outcome measures for SWM include errors (touching squares that have been found to be empty and revisiting squares which have already been found to contain a token), a measure of strategy and latency measures.

RVP is a test of sustained attention, sensitive to dysfunction in the parietal and frontal lobe areas of the brain and is also a sensitive measure of general performance. During the test, a box appears in the center of the computer screen, inside which digits, from 2 to 9, appear in a pseudo-random order, at the rate of 100 digits per minute. Participants are requested to detect target sequences of digits (i.e., 2-4-6, 3-5-7 and 4-6-8) and to register responses using the press pad. The nine RVP outcome measures cover latency, probabilities, sensitivity (calculated using Signal Detection Theory), hits, misses, false alarms and rejections.

Sudoku is a number puzzle game demanding high level cognitive processes. An easy 4-by-4 squares puzzle is engaged in order to allow the AD patients to understand the procedure and try to solve it. This task targets to identify the human brain activation during complex cognitive processes with the measure being the number of trials and the time needed to complete the test.

The emotional tasks include the Pictures of Facial Affect (POFA) (http://www.paulekman.com). The POFA collection consists of 110 black and white photographs of facial expressions [24], [25]. From this collection only the emotions of fear (13 images) and angriness (13 images) were used in the experiment. More specifically, the images were randomly projected for 5sec after a 5-sec black screen period, a 5-sec period in which countdown frames were demonstrated and an 1-sec projection of a cross shape in the middle of the screen to attract the sight of the subject. These two emotions were selected as the first was found to activate amygdala whereas the latter appeared to have no effect on this region of the brain [26]. The projection of each image is sent to the EEG acquisition system via a photocell and an audio-visual (AV) device to correctly map the brain functionality with the EEG recordings during each individual image. Since an LCD monitor is used, the stimulus is presented at actual time as an event in the EEG recordings.

The ERP is any stereotyped electrophysiological response to a stimulus. The stimulator is synchronized with the EEG, so the events and the caused response during the experiment can be efficiently correlated. Two different sounds, a high frequency (4000Hz) and a lower frequency (250Hz) sound, are used and the subject is asked to click the left or right button of a mouse with the right or left hand, respectively, each time s/he identifies the high frequency. 250 stimulus for each hand are produced and the target sound appears in a random order. The correct identification of the target sound, the use of the correct mouse button and the response time are measured. Again, the audio stimulus is sent with a maximum delay of up to 100 milliseconds through the AV device to the EEG acquisition system to be able to correlate the brain functionality with the recordings.

2.3   Experimental Procedure

Upon arrival in the laboratory the procedure is introduced and the participants read and sign a consent form, allowing them to stop at any time. The electrodes net is attached to the head of the participants and calibrated to ensure high quality data acquisition. The participants are then seated on a chair in a comfortable position, approximately 60 cm away from the monitor (resolution: 1280 × 960 pixel) and asked to move as little as possible (see Fig. 1). Following the preparation phase, participants are informed about the procedure and instructed about each following task, appearing on the computer monitor. Practice trials are presented before each of the main experimental task, in order to familiarize participants with the procedure. Overall, the experimental session lasts approximately 60 min.

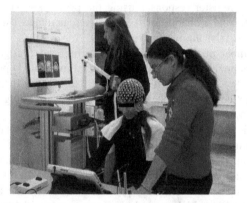

Fig. 1. Performing MOT test, while recording EEG with the GES 300 system, in the CBP lab

2.4   Data Acquisition and Preprocessing

EEG data are collected with the EGI 300 Geodesic EEG system (GES 300) using a 256-channel HydroCel Geodesic Sensor Net (HCGSN) and a sampling rate of 1 kHz. Electrodes are recorded according to the '256 HCGSN adult 1.0' montage system

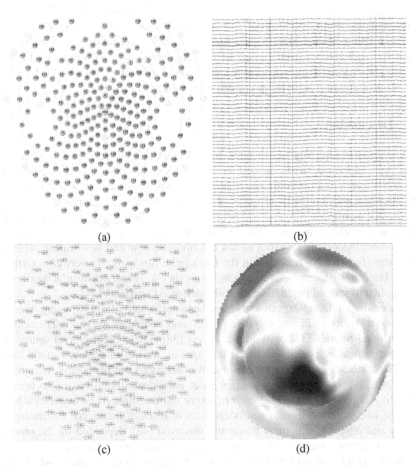

Fig. 2. (a) The 256 HCGSN adult 1.0 electrode placement montage (Source: Net Station Acquisition Manual, Electrical Geodesics, Inc., 2006, p. 215), (b), (c) and (d) a screenshot of the 256-channel EEG recordings acquired from a female healthy adult (27 years old) with the GES300 during the performance of the MOT task in a chart, a topographic plot and a topographic map view respectively.

(see Fig. 2(a)). EEG signals are recorded relative to a vertex reference electrode (Cz) and with AFz as the ground electrode. All the electrode impedances are kept below 50 kΩ as recommended [27] for the high-input impedance amplifier (NetAmps 300, Electrical Geodesics, Inc. (EGI), Eugene, OR, USA).

EEG data are analyzed offline and digitally filtered (IIR filter: high cut-off 30 Hz; low cut-off 0.1 Hz) using the Net Station 4.3 software (EGI). The continuous EEG signals are segmented using the task triggers and event stimulus timestamp. After the segmentation, artifact detection is conducted with Net Station artifact detection tool, which automatically detects eye blinks, eye movements and marks bad channels in the input file. In particular, a channel with more than 100μV peak-to-peak amplitude for a given segment is identified as a bad channel for that segment. A channel is marked as bad throughout the entire recording if it is marked bad for more than 10% of the segments. Signals from rejected electrodes are replaced using the 'bad channel replacement' algorithm in Net Station 4.3, which uses spherical splines to interpolate the signal of a bad channel from signals of the remaining channels. Figures 2(b)-(d) depict the 256-channel EEG recordings during the performance of the MOT task in a plain, a topographic plot and topographic map view, respectively.

3   Discussion

The biological complexity of the brain function and the physical "sum" effect of different brain electrical fields on surface EEG recordings make the understanding of EEG components and the source estimation a very difficult task, thus it still remains a high interest topic among neuroscientists. Performance in cognitive tasks has been studied with neurophysiological and neuroimaging studies. Visual memory tasks [28], [29], spatial working memory [30], [31] and attention [32], [33] are examples of recently neurophysiologic research issues examining linear and non- linear parameters of the brain functioning reflected in the EEG field. Studying the normal activity of a healthy brain in different ages is an ongoing process. However, similar studies have been applied to special population as well, such as AD patients [34].

Emotional stimulating experiments have been performed [35], [36] using mainly the International Affective Pictures System (IAPS) and POFA, as well as International Affective Digital Sounds [37] or WordNet Affect [38]. These experimental sources have been used in healthy population in various ages as well as in different morbid conditions. These studies came into various useful conclusions not necessarily in agreement in between [39], [40]. Sufficient studies about emotional stimuli have also been conducted to AD patients [41]. They aim to figure out the differences between a healthy brain and one suffering from a neurodegenerative disease. Emotional enhancement of memory and attention was most frequently observed [42], depended on the emotional stimulus. Literature suggests that pictures have greater emotional impact than words [43] and the combination of pictures with sounds have even greater one [44]. However, in each case there is a great variety of responses whether the emotional stimulus is positive, negative, or neutral [26], [45] and even unexpected outcomes with opposed combinations of stimulus [44] or with different types adopted [46]. The impaired cognitive functions of memory and attention in AD can be enhanced by emotional stimulus. However the emotional stimulus does not seem to have the exact same response both in healthy elderly and patients with AD. The results are not always as expected as the exact brain mechanisms serving them are still unknown. Consequently, more experiments are needed to understand better the human brain functionality.

Determining the equivalent current dipole techniques, LORETA, LAURA and sLORETA have been extensively used in brain localization research including a plethora of different pathologies or tasks under study and they compose valuable tools in the pursuit of understanding the human brain. Figure 3 depicts a screenshot of the output of the sLORETA algorithm when applied to the EEG recordings during the performance of the MOT task. However, the drawbacks of the methods indicated in the literature (computational cost, arbitrariness in choosing constraints, failure during simultaneous activation or presence of noise) lay the way open for the development of more efficient brain source localization methods. A key advantage of the 3D-VFT approach over the parametric methods is that it can disregard the complex electromagnetic field propagation through the different kinds of tissues that hold different electromagnetic properties that vary from one person to the other. By the uniform reconstruction suggested, the 3D-VFT method allows for simplicity and a generic model that can be used for all subjects. Moreover, the full field recovery is expected to raise the noted inefficiency of localization in the cases of more than one active source. The preconditions set for the formulation of the mathematical model of the 3D-VFT method accommodate the characteristics of the field inside the head, i.e., quasi static condition and irrotational property. Thus, the inverse EEG problem constitutes an ideal application for the method and on this ground is being under development to propose an original electrostatic field brain mapping scheme. The boundary data used in the latter method will eventually be the measurements obtained by the 256 electrodes of the GES300. Since we are dealing with a clinical system, the measurements are expected to be infiltrated with noise. In the specific application, noise may result from the acquired measurements by the sensors or from the lack of knowledge of the exact sensors locations. To account for this effect, noise tests that incorporate contaminated sensor measurements, displacement of the sensors and both kinds of noise are included in the formation of the method. The method seems to be slightly affected by inaccurate measurements and respond efficiently in the case of change in the sensors coordinates, which, given the fact that due to different head models, the electrode displacement is highly expected, is encouraging.

Applying the theory of 3D-VFT to the inverse EEG problem, the effective brain states can be extracted and used to study the correlation between the activity of the brain and the cognitive states in order to associate the EEG measurements with certain perceptual stimuli or activities. Being able to map the brain, the areas with dysfunctionalities in case of AD or other cognitive states can be identified. Using cognitive tasks with known expected response, the brain functionality can be evaluated and correlated with external stimuli (emotional, audio and/or visual). The role of the stimuli can be investigated towards the achievement of the maximum possible performance of the dysfunctioning brains. The results of this study can be used to design intelligent assistive environments to help patients with AD to outperform and improve their everyday activities.

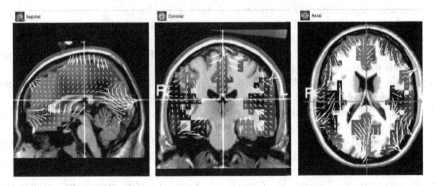

Fig. 3. An MRI view of the EEG recordings during performing the MOT task, using the sLORETA algorithm

Acknowledgments. This work was funded by the GSRT Research Excellent Grant ARISTEIA, within the 4th Strategic Objective of the operational programme "Education and Lifelong Learning" entitled 'Supporting the Human Capital in order Promote Research and Innovation', under grant agreement 440, project CBP: Cognitive Brain signal Processing lab, coordinated by the Information Technologies Institute - Centre for Research & Technology - Hellas.

References

1. Moretti, D.V., Frisoni, G.B., Fracassi, C., Pievani, M., Geroldi, C., Binetti, G., Rossini, P.M., Zanetti, O.: MCI patients' EEGs show group differences between those who progress and those who do not progress to AD. Neurobiology of Aging 32, 563–571 (2011)
2. Baillet, S., Mosher, J., Leahy, R.: Electromagnetic Brain Mapping. IEEE Sign Process. Mag. 18, 14–30 (2001)
3. Lotte, F., Lecuyer, A., Arnaldi, B.: FuRIA: an inverse solution based feature extraction algorithm using fuzzy set theory for brain-computer interfaces. IEEE Trans. Signal Process. 57, 3253–3263 (2009)
4. Grosse-Wentrup, M., Liefhold, C., Gramann, K., Buss, M.: Beamforming in noninvasive brain-computer interfaces. IEEE Trans. Biomed. Eng. 56, 1209–1219 (2009)
5. Pascual-Marqui, R., Michel, C., Lehman, D.: Low resolution electromagnetic tomography: a new method for localizing electrical activity in the brain. Int. J. Psychophysiol. 18, 49–65 (1994)
6. Grave de Peralta Menendez, R., Murray, M.M., Michel, C.M., Martuzzi, R., Gonzalez Andino, S.L.: Electrical neuroimaging based on biophysical constraints. Neuroimage 21, 527–539 (2004)
7. Pascual-Marqui, R.: Standardized low resolution brain electromagnetic tomography (sLORETA): technical details. Meth. & Find. Exper. & Clin. Pharm. 24D, 5–12 (2002)
8. Michel, C.M., Murray, M.M., Lantz, G., Gonzalez, S., Spinelli, L., Grave de Peralta, R.: EEG source imaging. Clinical Neuropsysiology 115, 2195–2222 (2004)
9. Wagner, M., Fuchs, M., Kastner, J.: Evaluation of sLORETA in the Presence of Noise and Multiple Sources. Brain Topography 16, 277–280 (2004)
10. Petrou, M., Giannakidis, A.: Full Tomographic Reconstruction of 2-D Vector Fields using Discrete Integral Data. The Computer J. 54, 1491–1504 (2011)
11. Giannakidis, A., Petrou, M.: Sampling bounds for 2D vector field tomography. J. of Math. Imag. and Vis. 37, 151–165 (2010)
12. Koulouri, A., Petrou, M.: Vector Field Tomography: Reconstruction of an Irrotational Field in the Discrete Domain. In: Proc. SPPR (2012)
13. Norton, S.J., Linzer, M.: Correcting for ray refraction in velocity and attenuation tomography: a perturbation approach. Ultrasonic Imag. 4, 201–233 (1982)
14. Braun, H., Hauck, A.: Tomographic Reconstruction of Vector Fields. IEEE Trans. on Sign. Proces. 39, 464–471 (1991)
15. Papadaniil, C.D., Hadjileontiadis, L.: Towards an Overall 3-D Vector Field Reconstruction via Discretization and a Linear Equations System. In: 13th IEEE Int. Conf. on BioInf. & BioEng. (2013)
16. Fountoulakis, K., Tsolaki, M., Chantzi, H., Kazis, A.: Mini mental state examination (MMSE): a validation study in Greece. JAD 15, 342–345 (2000)

17. Kounti, F., Tsolaki, M., Eleftheriou, M., Agogiatou, C., Karagiozi, K., Bakoglidou, E., Nikolaides, E., Nakou, S., Poptsi, E., Zafiropoulou, M., Papaliagkas, V., Kiosseoglou, G., Na, Z.: Administration of Montreal Cognitive Assesment (MoCA) test in Greek healthy elderly, patients with Mild Cognitive Impairment and patients with Dementia. In: Eur. Conf. on Psychol. Asses. & 2nd Int. Conf. of the Psychol Soc. of North Greece, vol. 129 (2007)

18. Armitage, S.G.: An Analysis of Certain Psychological Tests Used for the Evaluation of Brain Injury. APA J. 60, 1–48 (1946)

19. Beck, A.T., Ward, C.H., Mendelson, M., Mock, J., Erbaugh, J.: An inventory for measuring depression. Archives of General Psychiatry 4, 561–571 (1961)

20. Fountoulakis, K.N., Tsolaki, M., Iacovides, A., Yesavage, J., O'Hara, R., Kazis, A., Ierodiakonou, C.: The validation of the short form of the Geriatric Depression Scale (GDS) in Greece. Aging 11, 367–372 (1999)

21. Lawton, M.P., Brody, E.M.: Assessment of older people: self-maintaining and instrumental activities of daily living. The Ger. 9, 179–186 (1969)

22. Hutton, J.T., Dippel, R.L., Loewenson, R.B.: Functional Rating Scale for the symptoms of dementia. In: Gallo, J.J., Reichel, W., Andersen, L. (eds.) Handbook of Ger. Asses., pp. 77–80. Aspen Publishers, Rockville (1988)

23. American Psychiatric Association: The Diagnostic and Statistical Manual of Mental Disorders, 5th edn., Arlington (2013)

24. Ekman, P.: Are there basic emotions? Psychol Rev. 99, 550–553 (1992)

25. Ekman, P.: Strong evidence for universals in facial expressions: a reply to Russell's mistaken critique. Psychol. Bulletin 115, 268–287 (1994)

26. Fusar-Poli, P., Placentino, A., Carletti, F., Landi, P., Allen, P., Surguladze, S., Benedetti, F., Abbamonte, M., Gasparotti, R., Barale, F., Perez, J., McGuire, P., Politi, P.: Functional atlas of emotional faces processing: a voxel-based meta-analysis of 105 functional magnetic resonance imaging studies. J. Psychiatry Neurosci. 34, 418–432 (2009)

27. Ferree, T.C., Luu, P., Russell, G.S., Tucker, D.M.: Scalp electrode impedance, infection risk, and EEG data quality. Clin. Neurophysiol. 112, 536–544 (2001)

28. Lefebvre, C., Vachon, F., Grimault, S., Thibault, J., Guimond, S., Peretz, I., Jolicœur, P.: Distinct electrophysiological indices of maintenance in auditory and visual short-term memory. Neuropsychol. 51, 2939–2952 (2013)

29. Nenert, R., Viswanathan, S., Dubuc, D.M., Visscher, K.M.: Modulations of ongoing alpha oscillations predict successful short-term visual memory encoding. Front. in Hum. Neurosci. 6, 127 (2012)

30. Smyrnis, N., Protopapa, F., Tsoukas, E., Balogh, A., Siettos, C.I., Evdokimidis, I.: Amplitude spectrum EEG signal evidence for the dissociation of motor and perceptual spatial working memory in the human brain. Exp. Brain Res. 232, 659–673 (2013)

31. Störmer, V.S., Li, S.-C., Heekeren, H.R., Lindenberger, U.: Normative shifts of cortical mechanisms of encoding contribute to adult age differences in visual–spatial working memory. NeuroImage 73, 167–175 (2013)

32. Chang, Y.-C., Huang, S.-L.: The influence of attention levels on psychophysiological responses. Int. J. of Psychoph. 86, 39–47 (2012)

33. Ke, Y., Chen, L., Fu, L., Jia, Y., Li, P., Zhao, X., Ming, D.: Visual attention recognition based on nonlinear dynamical parameters of EEG. Biom. Mat. and Eng. 24, 349–355 (2014)

34. Ghorbanian, P., Devilbiss, D.M., Simon, A.J., Bernstein, A., Hess, T., Ashrafiuon, H.: Discrete wavelet transform EEG features of Alzheimer's disease in activated states. Conf. Proc. IEEE Eng. Med. Biol. Soc. 2012, 2937–2940 (2012)

35. Lang, P.J., Bradley, M.M., Cuthbert, B.: International affective picture system (IAPS): instruction manual and affective ratings. Tech. Rep. A-7 (Gainesville, FL: University of Florida) (2008)
36. Kujawa, A., Klein, D.N., Hajcak, G.: Electrocortical reactivity to emotional images and faces in middle childhood to early adolescence. Dev. Cogn. Neurosci. 2, 458–467 (2012)
37. Bradley, M.M., Lang, P.J.: The International Affective Digitized Sounds (2nd Edn. IADS-2): Affective ratings of sounds and instruction manual. Tech. Rep. B-3 (Gainesville, FL: University of Florida) (2007)
38. Strapparava, C., Valitutti, A.: WordNet-affect: an affective extension of WordNet. In: Proc. of the 4th Int. Conf. on Lang. Res. and Evaluation, Lisbon (2004)
39. Leclerc, C.M., Kensinger, E.A.: Neural processing of emotional pictures and words: a comparison of young and older adults. Dev. Neuropsych. 36, 519–538 (2011)
40. Mickley Steinmetz, K.R., Addis, D.R., Kensinger, E.A.: The effect of arousal on the emotional memory network depends on valence. NeuroIm. 53, 318–324 (2010)
41. Landré, L., Sava, A.-A., Krainik, A., Lamalle, L., Krolak-Salmon, P., Chainay, H.: Effects of Emotionally-Rated Material on Visual Memory in Alzheimer's Disease in Relation to Medial Temporal Atrophy. JAD 36, 535–544 (2013)
42. Schultz, R.R., de Castro, C.C., Bertolucci, P.H.F.: Memory with emotional content, brain amygdala and Alzheimer's disease. Acta Neurologica Scandinavica 120, 101–110 (2009)
43. Ally, B.A.: Using pictures and words to understand recognition memory deterioration in amnestic mild cognitive impairment and Alzheimer's disease: a review. Curr. Neurol. Neurosci. Rep. 12, 687–694 (2012)
44. Gerdes, A.B.M., Wieser, M.J., Bublatzky, F., Kusay, A., Plichta, M.M., Alpers, G.W.: Emotional sounds modulate early neural processing of emotional pictures. Front. in Psychol. 4, 741 (2013)
45. Perrin, M., Henaff, M.-A., Padovan, C., Faillenot, I., Merville, A., Krolak-Salmon, P.: Influence of emotional content and context on memory in mild Alzheimer's disease. JAD 29, 817–826 (2012)
46. Britton, J., Taylor, S., Sudheimer, K., Liberzon, I.: Facial expressions and complex IAPS pictures: common and differential networks. Neuroimage 31, 906–919 (2006)

A BCI Platform Supporting AAL Applications

Niccolò Mora, Valentina Bianchi, Ilaria De Munari, and Paolo Ciampolini

Dipartimento di Ingegneria dell'Informazione, Università degli Studi di Parma, Pal. 4,
Parco Area delle Scienze 181/A, 43124 Parma, Italy
niccolo.mora@nemo.unipr.it,
{valentina.bianchi,ilaria.demunari,paolo.ciampolini}@unipr.it

Abstract. Brain Computer Interface (BCI) technology can provide users lacking voluntary muscle control with an augmentative communication channel, based on the interpretation of her/his brain activity. Such technologies, combined with AAL (Ambient Assisted Living) systems, can potentially have a great impact on daily living, extending the scope of the ageing at home paradigm also to individuals affected by severe motor impairments, for whom interacting with the environment is troublesome. In this paper, a low cost BCI development platform is presented; it consists of a customized EEG acquisition unit and a Matlab-based signal processing environment. An application example using SSVEP paradigm is discussed.

Keywords: Brain Computer Interface (BCI), Ambient Assisted Living (AAL), Daily Living.

1   Introduction

Ambient Assisted Living (AAL) technologies aim at making the home environment more intelligent and cooperative, providing help in accomplishing daily living activities. So far, AAL techniques have been successfully applied for promoting and supporting independent life of elderly people: AAL, aims for instance, at providing safety-oriented services or smart, automated environmental control. Such solutions may also effectively support daily life of individuals affected by severe impairments, extending the AAL scope beyond the "ageing at home" paradigm. Such technologies, of course, are not to be regarded as substitutive of specialized care, but may support increased independence and autonomy in dealing with the home environment and thus foster a better quality of life. While useful "field" functionalities (e.g., lighting and climate control, opening/closing automated doors and windows, etc.) are easily implemented in conventional AAL systems, the main issue in bringing such solutions to users with impairments is related to the interface design: an effective and accessible interaction path towards the system is needed, suitable for overcoming specific difficulties in operating conventional user interfaces (based, for instance, on switches or touch panels).

For some classes of severe motion impairment, a possible solution can be found in Brain-Computer Interface (BCI) technology [1],[2]. A BCI is an alternative/augmentative

C. Stephanidis and M. Antona (Eds.): UAHCI/HCII 2014, Part I, LNCS 8513, pp. 515–526, 2014.

communication device that aims at providing the user (for instance lacking voluntary muscle control) with an interaction path, based on the interpretation of her/his brain activity; in this sense, a BCI can be regarded as an Assistive Technology (AT) device. BCI is being exploited since a relatively long time to support communication, and effective solutions have been developed, featuring high accuracy and processing speed. Such performances are obtained by exploiting sophisticated setups and powerful computing environments.

Introducing brain-computer interfacing into AAL environments, however, calls for quite peculiar specifications: the set of possible choices is generally reduced with respect, for instance, to typewriting or speech-synthesis applications; also, for AAL control purposes, data throughput is relatively less important.

"Conventional" BCI approaches may thus result somehow unfit (i.e., possibly outsized with respect to the application at hand), and inexpensive, lightweight and scarcely invasive devices are to be preferred. Interoperability with highly heterogeneous environments is also required.

In this paper, the development of a low-cost BCI module explicitly conceived for – even if not limited to – AAL control purpose is presented and discussed. The control target is CARDEA [3], a flexible and highly scalable ambient assisted living system, based on standard LAN technology. CARDEA was developed by the University of Parma, in an effort to bring AT and AAL services under a unique, convergent framework. In fact, besides common home automation tasks such as security, environmental control, smart energy management, several AT features are provided as well (e.g. fall detection, localization, vital sign monitoring[4]). CARDEA accounts for various user-interface systems, including button switches, touch-screen, vocal, remote internet control. CARDEA relies on a distributed-intelligence approach, in which most components have built-in processing power, this making the system more flexible and fault-tolerant. To introduce BCI into such a scenario, our goal is to develop a compact, standalone module, featuring local signal processing capabilities, suitable for integrating seamlessly into the system behaving as a plug-in, alternative control device. As stated above, looking at AAL control purposes allows to focus at relatively simpler tasks (with respect to most common BCI approaches), thus leaving room for lowering costs, user's effort and invasiveness. In [5],[6] the interaction scheme between CARDEA and a simple BCI is discussed; with respect to most literature works, the present approach aims at developing tools and methods for low-cost, standalone embedded BCI modules, making high-performance acquisition hardware or large computing powers unnecessary.

2   An Overview on BCI Technology

Among many possible brain signal acquisition techniques, Electroencephalography (EEG) is the most popular: EEG signals can be non-invasively acquired from the scalp, by sensing the electrical signal with skin-surface electrodes (dry or wet, the latter involving the use of conductive gels). More invasive scenarios involve direct access to the cerebral cortex (ECoG, ElectroCorticoGraphy [7]) or neural implants

[8]-[10]. Different bio-physical parameters were also investigated for noninvasive BCI purposes: for instance, techniques based on functional Magnetic Resonance Imaging (fMRI) exploit Blood Oxygen Level Dependent (BOLD) responses to map active brain areas [11],[12]. Similarly, NIRS (Near InfraRed Spectrography) [13]-[15] or PET (Positron Emission Technology) [16],[17] technologies can be exploited for monitoring brain activity induced by a stimulus or a voluntary modulation.

However apart from providing excellent spatial resolution and accuracy, such non-invasive methods involve bulky and expensive equipment, and typically feature time-domain resolution inadequate to environmental control applications. We therefore operate on EEG waveforms, which provide a fair tradeoff between spatial and temporal resolution, and imply simpler and less expensive equipment.

In order to operate a BCI, several features in the brain activity can be exploited to infer the user's will: the collections of such features, along with the (optional) external stimuli applied to the user, are called paradigms. Focusing on EEG-based BCI, several paradigms are currently exploited and, among the most common approaches, we can cite:

- Slow Cortical Potentials (SCP), i.e., potential shifts in the EEG waves voluntarily induced by user, who can learn to control them through biofeedback-like approaches [18].
- Event Related Desynchronization (ERD) and ER Synchronization (ERS) [19]-[22]: this paradigm exploits the brain response arising when preparing (or just imagining) to start a movement. In such conditions, neurons tend to de-synchronize from their idling state, to be allocated to motor processing, this reflecting in a decrease of spectral energy in the μ and β bands (8-12 Hz and around 20 Hz, respectively). After ERD, a pattern consisting in increase in the energy band after the completion of the motor task can also be observed (ERS).
- P300 [23]-[27]: when a rare target stimulus is presented to the user during a sequence of repetitive, non-target stimuli, a characteristic pattern can be observed in the EEG signals, approximately after 300 ms from the target stimulus appearance.
- Steady State Visual Evoked Potentials (SSVEP) [28]-[31]: this paradigm exploits brainwave features elicited by the involuntary response to a continuous, repetitive stimulus, such as a blinking LED. In particular, within a typical 4-40 Hz range, the blinking frequency reflects on the onset of a iso-frequency component in the brain signal spectrum.

In the following, we are going to focus on SSVEP, which was chosen as our primary operating paradigm. In fact, SSVEP responses are regarded as reliable features [32] for BCIs, given their inherent higher SNR (Signal to Noise Ratio). Moreover, SSVEP detection and classification can be carried out, in principle, without any calibration data at all [6],[32]: this makes SSVEP particularly attractive in terms of improved user comfort, fostering a plug and play type of interaction with the device. In fact, calibration sessions could be long and time consuming, and, in order to optimize the performance of methods relying on training data, periodic recalibration may be required. Considering the application we are targeting, i.e. enabling control of AAL

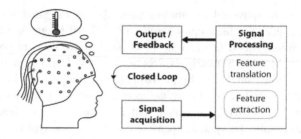

Fig. 1. Typical architecture of a BCI system

systems in daily living contexts, undergoing long training sessions for optimizing the system performance seems an overkill, given the more relaxed constraints on data throughput, as mentioned before. Finally, another advantage of the SSVEP paradigm is that it usually operates in the frequency domain, and no time synchronization between the stimulating unit and the acquisition unit is required. This allows to greatly simplify the BCI design, and to explore more compact and cost-effective solutions. This is in accord with our purposes, and simpler architectures and signal processing methods are more easily implementable on embedded systems, were computational resources are limited.

3   Brain.me: a Low-Cost Platform for Prototyping Embedded BCI Modules

In a typical BCI setup, three main units can be identified, shown in Fig. 1: *i)* an Analog Front End (AFE) for the acquisition of the EEG signal, *ii)* a digital signal processing unit, implementing feature extraction and classification and, *iii)*, an output/feedback unit for display and implementation of active controls.

We started from developing and testing a novel hardware AFE unit, aiming at a compact and inexpensive circuit. Signal processing and feedback units are currently

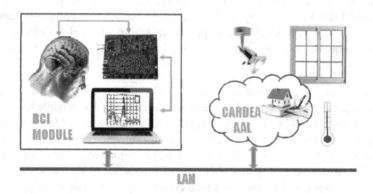

Fig. 2. Application example: control of ambient lighting through the CARDEA AAL system. The BCI module is seen by the AAL system as a simple remote control device

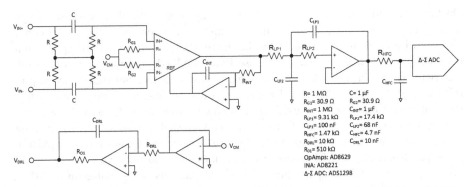

Fig. 3. Schematic of the custom AFE. The signal (AC-coupled) is amplified by a factor of 800 and low-pass filtered (f_{cut}=250 Hz) before being digitized by a 24 bit Σ-Δ ADC

implemented on a PC architecture, allowing for more flexibly testing and for better tuning performance. Even though the platform is actually suitable for dealing with all the aforementioned BCI paradigms, to begin with, we considered SSVEP responses and started researching efficient processing methods that are particularly suitable for implementation on low-cost, portable devices. Calibration-less operation is another important constraint we imposed on the system specifications.

In the following we present the several features of our platform with reference to a simple application, namely the control of ambient lighting through CARDEA (see Fig. 2). The BCI setup was the following: 4 healthy volunteers (age 23-26, two of them without any prior BCI experience, with normal or corrected to normal vision) were instructed to stare at one of the four simultaneously flickering LED in order to switch on/off a certain light. During the test, volunteers rested on an armchair at approximately 1m distance from the visual stimulus source. Each trial lasted for 6 s, and each LED presented a different stimulation frequency (16, 18, 20, 22 Hz); EEG was acquired at 250 SPS (Samples Per Second) from 6 scalp locations (namely O1, O2, P3, P4, P5, P6, according to the International 10-20 system), using standard 10 mm Ag/AgCl disk electrodes with conductive gel applied.

Even though this is a simple illustrative example, it is important to underline that the approach is general, and the BCI effectively plugs into the system as a conventional remote control device operating on a standard TCP/IP connection. In this sense, the BCI is a self-contained module, and system configuration just requires trivial mapping of BCI output onto CARDEA command space.

3.1   Analog Front End

Acquiring EEG signals, whose amplitude can be as low as a few µV, poses tight constraints on the electrical specifications of the acquisition system. However, high-end, clinical grade EEG equipments making use of a large number of electrodes are scarcely suitable for our particular application, and low-costs, small-size devices are to be designed, suitable for extracting basic information on brain activity. The adoption of low-cost, standard electronic components also fosters product interoperability.

On these grounds, the custom AFE circuitry has been realized. Low-noise design techniques were adopted, to ensure that the informative content of the signal is not corrupted by the noise contributed by the instrumentation. In the aimed application context, further sources of Signal to Noise Ratio (SNR) degradation may come from electrical and power line interference. While the use of active electrodes may help in mitigating those issues, the related higher costs and complexity made us opt (at this stage, at least) for the worst-case design, adopting passive electrode technology.

Fig. 3 shows the schematic of one of the six dedicated EEG channels, terminating with a multichannel, high resolution (24 bit) Σ-Δ Analog to Digital Converter (ADC). A Driven Right Leg (DRL) circuit was also introduced to improve common mode noise rejection [33]. Two spare, fully-differential channels are available on the AFE, and can be used, for example, for simultaneous recording of other bio-potentials, such as ElectroMyoGram (EMG).

Noise performance of the AFE was tested with input terminals shorted, extracting an input-referred noise lower than 1.8 µVpp, which is more than sufficient for our purposes. An example of a 18 Hz SSVEP power spectrum recorded with our AFE is given in Fig. 4.

Finally, it is worth mentioning that, at this stage of the research, the AFE is interfaced to a host PC via USB connection. An ARM-based microcontroller board (ARM Cortex-M4) takes care of proper AFE control and initialization, allowing acquisition parameters (e.g. individual input channel gain) control directly from the PC.

3.2   SSVEP Signal Processing

A first SSVEP classification algorithm, based on Power Spectral Density (PSD) estimation was first introduced in [6], with the aim of maximizing the accuracy of the BCI, i.e. the number of correct outputs. Essentially, the method proceeds as follows: at first, acquired data is digitally low-pass filtered for out-of-band noise reduction.

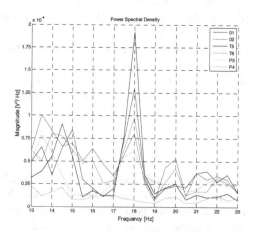

Fig. 4. An example of a 18 Hz SSVEP power spectrum, recorded with our AFE

PSD are then estimated by Welch's method: the window length can be tuned for different speed vs. accuracy tradeoffs, as shown in Table 1 (Information Transfer Rate, ITR, is also reported, as defined in [1]). The channel powers are equalized over a given pre-determined band of interest. Normalization is shown to slightly improve the classification performance, especially in case of a strong inter-channel imbalance, due to, for example, different electrode impedance; it improves the classification robustness by somehow self-adapting to such variable scenarios. The algorithm then exploits the a priori knowledge of the actual set of stimulation frequencies, checking the conditions only on such a set: the channel powers are summed for each target frequency. Candidate targets are selected whenever a given fraction (e.g., at least 50%) of the channels exhibit a local maximum in the PSD at the target frequency. If at least one candidate target exists, the sum of such powers are compared and the most probable frequency is picked, if larger enough (i.e., exceeding a given probability threshold). If no candidate targets were found in the previous step, comparison is made between the sum of powers at each frequency and classification is performed in the same way, accounting for a higher threshold.

The aforementioned algorithm privileges selection accuracy rather than speed: in strict terms of AAL systems control, where the number of choices is limited and the interaction between user and the system is not very frequent, this is the most important parameter, indeed. Nonetheless, we can think of developing a second algorithm, with the aim of improving selection speed, to provide the user with a more prompt, reactive interface. These apparently contrasting behaviors can actually converge into a cooperative vision, in which the interface adapts its speed in relation to the desired task: new functionalities that need higher speed can be added, such as, for example, typewriting. Another possibility is to operate with the faster algorithm as default and resort to the more accurate one when the estimated error rate is too high. In the following, a new algorithm, named MaxDeltaVar is presented and compared with other common SSVEP processing algorithms, such as Minimum Energy Combination (MEC) [34],Average Maximum Contrast Combination (AMCC) [35], Canonical Correlation Analysis (CCA) [36].

In general, the voltage time series of a single electrode $y_i(t)$, can be modeled as

$$y_i(t) = \sum_{k=1}^{Nh} a_{i,k} \sin(2\pi k f t) + b_{i,k} \cos(2\pi k f t) + E_i(t) , \qquad (1)$$

where the first term is the model of a SSVEP response corresponding to a stimulus frequency f (considering up to N_h harmonics), and $E_i(t)$ is a noise and nuisance signal. Given an EEG epoch of N_t samples, the input signals from the N_y electrodes can be represented as a matrix Y of size $N_t \times N_y$, whose columns are the potential readings from each electrode site. In the same way we can represent the SSVEP term in eq. 1 as a multiplication between a SSVEP information matrix X having size $N_t \times 2N_h$ and containing N_h (sin, cos) column pairs, and a weight matrix G of size $2N_h \times N_y$, containing all the $a_{i,k}$, $b_{i,k}$ coefficients. Eq. 1 then becomes:

$$Y = XG + E , \qquad (2)$$

with

$$X = \begin{bmatrix} \sin{(2\pi f t_1)} & \cos{(2\pi f t_1)} & \cdots & \sin{(2\pi N_h f t_1)} & \cos{(2\pi N_h f t_1)} \\ \vdots & \vdots & \vdots & \vdots & \vdots \\ \sin{(2\pi f t_{Nt})} & \cos{(2\pi f t_{Nt})} & \cdots & \sin{(2\pi N_h f t_{Nt})} & \cos{(2\pi N_h f t_{Nt})} \end{bmatrix} \quad (3)$$

MaxDeltaVar proceeds as follows: at first suitable filtering is applied to remove low frequency and out-of-band contributions. Then, input channels are normalized in order to have the same variance.. Projection on the space spanned by the sinusoidal components of X is performed to remove any potential SSVEP activity from the recorded signal:

$$\tilde{Y} = Y - X(X^T X)^{-1} X^T Y \quad (4)$$

$\tilde{Y}$ then approximately contains only noise, artifacts and background brain activity. We assume as (computationally inexpensive) features the difference in variance before and after projection, summing the contributes of all channels. The matrix X which induces the larger decrease in the overall variance is assumed to be the stimulus frequency. Performance of MaxDeltaVar and its comparison to other SSVEP processing is methods shown in Table 2, with all the algorithms being tested on the same recorded dataset, using a 1.5 s EEG segment (which implies up to 4x speed increase with respect to the first presented algorithm). Results show that our Algorithm 2, despite its simplified approach, performs close to, or better than, MEC and AMCC methods. It is worth noting, though, that MaxDeltaVar was explicitly designed for low-electrode count setups, and does not perform any dimensionality reduction as MEC or AMCC do. However, in our scenario, where the number of electrodes is intentionally low for cost and comfort constraints, computational demand is significantly lower, as shown in Table 3 (where execution time on a standard desktop PC, Intel® Core™ i5 @ 3.20 GHz, 8 GB RAM is taken as a simple indicator of computational efficiency and as a basis for comparisons). On the other hand, CCA has better accuracy and ITR than our method; in this case too, dimensionality reduction is also not taken into account in this method, and all the EEG channels are considered. Still, CCA is more computationally intensive than our algorithm.

Table 1. Accuracy and ITR (shown between brackets) of the PSD-based algorithm as a function of EEG window length

Subj.	3 s	4 s	5 s	6 s
1	90.0% (27.45)	83.3% (16.27)	86.7% (14.66)	90.0% (13.73)
2	91.7% (29.08)	91.7% (21.81)	100% (24.00)	100% (20.00)
3	87.5% (25.17)	95.0% (24.52)	92.5% (17.96)	97.5% (17.92)
4	94.1% (31.68)	94.1% (23.76)	94.1% (19.01)	91.2% (14.31)
Avg.	90.8% (28.35)	91.0% (21.59)	93.3% (18.91)	94.7% (16.49)

Table 2. Comparison of the MaxDeltaVar algorithm with respect to other SSVEP signal processing algorithms, as a function of accuracy and ITR (between brackets)

Subj.	MEC	AMCC	CCA	MaxDeltaVar
1	62.5% (18.05)	85.0% (46.10)	87.5% (50.33)	87.5% (50.33)
2	94.1% (63.32)	94.1% (63.32)	94.1% (63.32)	91.2% (57.23)
3	70.0% (25.73)	86.7% (48.94)	90.0% (54.90)	86.7% (48.94)
4	72.5% (28.62)	77.5% (34.97)	82.5% (42.14)	80.0% (38.44)
Avg.	**74.8%** **(33.93)**	**85.8%** **(48.33)**	**88.5%** **(52.67)**	**86.4%** **(48.74)**

Table 3. Comparison of mean execution time between the algorithms reported in Table 2

	MEC	AMCC	CCA	MaxDeltaVar
Mean time	9.65 ms	5.25 ms	1.13 ms	0.82 ms
Time reduction (proposed vs. others)	**-91.5 %**	**-84.4 %**	**-27.4 %**	–

It is important to highlight that both the presented algorithms operate on the basis of relative comparisons, thus virtually eliminating the need of calibration procedures. This could be a great improvement in the accessibility of such interface, resembling a plug and play device; of course, if we accept calibration steps, the performance of the BCI could be further improved. In addition, the optimized computation complexity of both methods better scales towards embedded implementation of the BCI.

4   Conclusions

In this paper, the development of a low-cost platform for BCI modules development was presented. The platform is built around a custom, versatile AFE board, whose main acquisition parameters can be directly controlled via software (connectivity is established via a USB 2.0 link). Noise performance of the module (below 1.8 µVpp) makes it suitable for BCI applications.

Besides flexibility and reconfigurability, main design focus was placed at enabling implementation of BCI solutions on small, low-cost embedded system. More specifically, the primary target was that of building a BCI-based controller suitable for (even though not restricted to) AAL system management.

A BCI prototype based on such board and exploiting the SSVEP paradigm was demonstrated. The whole control chain was implemented, including the BCI module into the CARDEA AAL system and allowing for actual control of ambient lighting. Of course, besides such an example, mapping of different AAL functions on the BCI controller is a trivial task and may straightforwardly be extended to many different and personalized actions.

In addition to a previously introduced algorithm [6], focusing at maximizing selection accuracy, a novel classification algorithm was presented, based on the SSVEP paradigm, aiming at improving ITR and responsiveness. Features of the algorithms include calibration-less operation and optimized computational effort, making it suitable for implementation on low-cost, embedded modules. Comparison with other reference SSVEP processing methods proved good results in terms of accuracy and computational efficiency.

Finally, an extension towards hybrid-BCI [37] is also being evaluated, exploiting some of the board's acquisition channels for surface EMG (ElectroMyoGraphy) and thus recording neuromuscular activity too. Such an approach seems to be particularly fit if daily-life support functionalities are targeted: the EMG additional channels can make the interaction scheme more flexible, reliable and customizable, and relieve the user from the stress of continuous BCI-based interaction. I.e., simpler tasks (or even switching on the BCI interface itself) can be activated by the less demanding and more comfortable EMG-based control.

Acknowledgements. The authors gratefully acknowledge partial support to this work provided by Provincia di Parma and Fondazione CaRiParma.

References

1. Wolpaw, J.R., Birbaumer, N., McFarland, D.J., Pfurtscheller, G., Vaughan, T.M.: Brain-computer interfaces for communication and control. Clin. Neurophysiol. 113(6), 767–791 (2002)
2. del R. Millán, J., Rupp, R., Müller-Putz, G.R., et al.: Combining Brain–Computer Interfaces and Assistive Technologies: State-of-the-Art and Challenges. Frontiers in Neuroscience 4(161) (September 2010)
3. Grossi, F., Bianchi, V., Matrella, G., De Munari, I., Ciampolini, P.: An Assistive Home Automation and Monitoring System. In: ICCE 2008, pp. 1–2 (January 2008)
4. Bianchi, V., Grossi, F., De Munari, I., Ciampolini, P.: Multi Sensor Assistant: A Multisensor Wearable Device for Ambient Assisted Living. Journal of Medical Imaging and Health Informatics 2, 70–75 (2012)
5. Mora, N., Bianchi, V., De Munari, I., Ciampolini, P.: Design for a low cost brain-computer interface for environmental and home control. Gerontechnology 11(2) (2012)
6. Mora, N., Bianchi, V., De Munari, I., Ciampolini, P.: A Low Cost Brain Computer Interface Platform for AAL Applications. In: AAATE 2013 Conf. Proc., Vilamoura, Portugal, September 19-22 (2013)
7. Leuthardt, E.C., Gaona, C., Sharma, M., Szrama, N., Roland, J., Freudenberg, Z., Solis, J., Breshears, J., Schalk, G.: Using the electrocorticographic speech network to control a brain–computer interface in humans. J. Neural Eng. 8(3) (2011)
8. Moran, D.: Evolution of brain–computer interface: action potentials, local field potentials and electrocorticograms. Current Opinion in Neurobiology 20(6), 741–745 (2010)
9. Sun, Y., Huang, S., Oresko, J.J., Cheng, A.C.: Programmable Neural Processing on a Smartdust for Brain-Computer Interfaces. IEEE Trans. Biomed. Circuits Syst. 4(5), 265–273 (2010)
10. Shahrokhi, F., Abdelhalim, K., Serletis, D., Carlen, P.L., Genov, R.: The 128-Channel Fully Differential Digital Integrated Neural Recording and Stimulation Interface. IEEE Trans. Biomed. Circuits Syst. 4(3), 149–161 (2010)

11. Andersson, P., Viergever, M.A., Pluim, J., Ramsey, N.F., Siero, J.: fMRI based BCI control using spatial visual attention at 7T. In: 4th International IEEE/EMBS Conference on Neural Engineering, NER 2009, April 9-May 2 (2009)

12. Sitaram, R., Lee, S., Ruiz, S., Birbaumer, N.: Real-Time Regulation and Detection of Brain States from fMRI Signals. In: Neurofeedback and Neuromodulation Techniques. Elsevier (2011)

13. Sitaram, R., Zhang, H., Guan, C., Thulasidas, M., Hoshi, Y., Ishikawa, A., Shimizu, K., Birbaumer, N.: Temporal classification of multichannel near-infrared spectroscopy signals of motor imagery for developing a brain–computer interface. NeuroImage 34(4), 1416–1427 (2007)

14. Sawan, M., Salam, M.T., Le Lan, J., Kassab, A., Gelinas, S., Vannasing, P., Lesage, F., Lassonde, M., Nguyen, D.K.: Wireless Recording Systems: From Noninvasive EEG-NIRS to Invasive EEG Devices. IEEE Trans. Biomed. Circuits Syst. 7(2), 186–195 (2013)

15. Choi, J.-K., Choi, M.-G., Kim, J.-M., Bae, H.-M.: Efficient Data Extraction Method for Near-Infrared Spectroscopy (NIRS) Systems With High Spatial and Temporal Resolution. IEEE Trans. Biomed. Circuits Syst. 7(2), 169 (2013)

16. Grafton, S.T., Arbib, M.A., Fatiga, L., Rizzolatti, G.: Location of grasp representations in humans by positron emission tomography. 2. Observation compared with imagination. Exp. Brain Res. 112(1), 103–111 (1996)

17. Fang, X., Brasse, D., Hu-Guo, C., Hu, Y.: Design and Integration of a High Accuracy Multichannel Analog CMOS Peak Detect and Hold Circuit for APD-Based PET Imaging. IEEE Trans. Biomed. Circuits Syst. 6(2), 179 (2012)

18. Hinterberger, T., Schmidt, S., Neumann, N., Mellinger, J., Blankertz, B., Curio, G., Birbaumer, N.: Brain-computer communication and slow cortical potentials. IEEE Trans. Biomed. Eng. 51(6), 1011–1018 (2004)

19. Pfurtscheller, G.: Event-related synchronization (ERS): an electrophysiological correlate of cortical areas at rest. Electroencephalography and Clinical Neurophysiology 83(1), 62–69 (1992)

20. Li, Y., Gao, X., Liu, H., Gao, S.: Classification of single-trial electroencephalogram during finger movement. IEEE Trans. Biomed. Eng. 51(6), 1019–1025 (2004)

21. Townsend, G., Graimann, B., Pfurtscheller, G.: Continuous EEG classification during motor imagery-simulation of an asynchronous BCI. IEEE Trans. Neural Syst. Rehabil. Eng. 12(2), 258–265 (2004)

22. Pfurtscheller, G., Brunner, C., Schlögl, A., Lopes da Silva, F.H.: Mu rhythm (de) synchronization and EEG single-trial classification of different motor imagery tasks. NeuroImage 31(1), 153–159 (2006)

23. Nijboer, F., Sellers, E.W., Mellinger, J., Jordan, M.A., Matuz, T., Furdea, A., Halder, S., et al.: A P300-based brain–computer interface for people with amyotrophic lateral sclerosis. Clinical Neurophysiology 119(8), 1909–1916 (2008)

24. Khan, O.I., Kim, S.H., Rasheed, T., Khan, A., Kim, T.S.: Extraction of P300 Using Constrained Independent Component Analysis. In: Annual International Conference of the IEEE EMBC 2009, September 3-6, pp. 4031–4034 (2009)

25. Zhang, J.-C., Xu, Y.-Q., Yao, L.: P300 Detection Using Boosting Neural Networks with Application to BCI. In: 2007 IEEE/ICME, May 23-27, pp. 1526–1530 (2007)

26. Salvaris, M., Cinel, C., Citi, L., Poli, R.: Novel protocols for P300-based brain-computer interfaces. IEEE Trans. Neural Syst. Rehabil. Eng. 20, 8–17 (2012)

27. Carabalona, R., Grossi, F., Tessadri, A., Castiglioni, P., Caracciolo, A., De Munari, I.: Light on! Real world evaluation of a P300-based brain-computer interface (BCI) for environment control in a smart home. Ergonomics 55(5), 552–563 (2012)

526   N. Mora et al.

28. Ortner, R., Allison, B.Z., Korisek, G., Gaggl, H., Pfurtscheller, G.: An SSVEP BCI to control a hand orthosis for persons with tetraplegia. IEEE Trans. Neural Syst. Rehabil. Eng. 19(1), 1–5 (2011)
29. Cecotti, H.: A Self-Paced and Calibration-Less SSVEP-Based Brain–Computer Interface Speller. IEEE Trans. Neural Syst. Rehabil. Eng. 18(2), 127–133 (2010)
30. Bakardjian, H., Tanaka, T., Cichocki, A.: Optimization of SSVEP brain responses with application to eight-command Brain–Computer Interface. Neuroscience Letters 469(1), 34–38 (2010)
31. Diez, P.F., Mut, V.A., Perona, E.M.A., Leber, E.L.: Asynchronous BCI control using high-frequency SSVEP. J. Neuroeng. Rehabil. 8(39) (2011)
32. Cecotti, H.: A Self-Paced and Calibration-Less SSVEP-Based Brain–Computer Interface Speller. IEEE Trans. Neural Syst. Rehabil. Eng. 18(2), 127–133 (2010)
33. Webster, J.G.: Medical Instrumentation Application and Design. Wiley (2009)
34. Volosyak, I.: SSVEP-based Bremen-BCI interface - boosting information transfer rates. J. Neural Eng. 8(3) (June 2011)
35. Garcia-Molina, G., Zhu, D.: Optimal spatial filtering for the steady state visual evoked potential: BCI application. In: 5th International IEEE/EMBS Conf. on Neur. Eng., pp. 156–160 (2011)
36. Lin, Z., Zhang, C., Wu, W., Gao, X.: Frequency recognition based on canonical correlation analysis for SSVEP-based BCIs. IEEE Trans. Biomed. Eng. 54, 1172–1176 (2007)
37. Leeb, R., Sagha, H., Chavarriaga, R., del R. Millán, J.: A hybrid brain-computer interface based on the fusion of electroencephalographic and electromyographic activities. J. Neural Eng. 8(2) (April 2011)

A BCI-Based Tool for Detection of Awareness and for Communication with Non-responsive Patients

Rupert Ortner[1], Arnau Espinosa[1], Javi Rodriguez[1], Steven Laureys[2], Zulay R. Lugo[2], Christoph Guger[1], and Günter Edlinger[1]

[1] Guger Technologies OG, Herbersteinstrasse 60, 8020 Graz, Austria
{ortner,espinosa,rodriguez,guger,edlinger}@gtec.at
[2] Coma Science Group, University of Liège, 4000 Liège - Belgium
{steven.laureys,zulay.lugo}@ulg.ac.be

Abstract. Imagine being able to think, hear, and feel - but not move or communicate. Over 40% of patients diagnosed as vegetative are reclassified as (at least) minimally conscious when assessed by expert teams. This publication presents a device that uses BCI (Brain-Computer Interface) technology for quick and easy assessment of patients suffering a disorder of consciousness, and even provides basic communication with some of them. A BCI detects changes in brain activity induced by the user's mental activity. The EEG is used to measure brain signals, which are automatically analyzed and classified on a standard laptop. As long as patients have enough cognitive functions to understand spoken messages, they can be trained to use different mental strategies to provide simple YES/NO answers to questions. The system combines three different BCI approaches within one tool: auditory P300, tactile P300, and motor imagery. These approaches work with patients who cannot see, and (in some cases) also cannot hear

1 Introduction

The process of diagnosing patients as being in a vegetative state (VS) or minimally conscious state (MCS) is difficult, and patients are often misclassified. A study in 2009 compared the accuracy of diagnosis between the clinical consensus versus standardized neurobehavioral assessment [1]. Out of 44 patients diagnosed with VS based on the clinical consensus of the medical team, 18 (41%) were found to be in MCS following standardized assessment with the Coma Recovery Scale-Revised (CRS-R). This result fits well with previous studies, which showed that 37% to 43% of patients diagnosed with VS demonstrated signs of awareness [2-3]. Classification scales are based on behavioral observations or assessment of auditory, visual, verbal and motor functions, as well as communication and arousal level. New technologies that can decode the brain's activity provide perfect tools to overcome the restrictions of behavioral rating scales. Even if patients cannot produce any voluntary movements, they may be able to modulate their brain activity to communicate.

In this publication, we present mindBEAGLE, a tool that uses Brain-Computer Interface (BCI) technology based on the Electroencephalogram (EEG) for assessment and communication with non-responsive patients and patients with Locked in

C. Stephanidis and M. Antona (Eds.): UAHCI/HCII 2014, Part I, LNCS 8513, pp. 527–535, 2014.

Syndrome (LIS). This is the first commercially available BCI that focuses on helping patients suffering from a Disorder of Consciousness (DOC).

2   System Architecture

Three BCI approaches are combined within mindBEAGLE - an auditory P300 approach, a vibrotactile P300 approach and a Motor Imagery (MI) based approach. These three BCIs can all operate in either of two modes: (i) assessment of consciousness and (ii) communication with patients. Fig. 1 shows an overview of the system and the electrode configuration. The patient wears an EEG cap with 16 electrodes, distributed over the scalp to provide data for all three BCI approaches. The mindBEAGLE laptop controls the paradigms, performs the signal processing and displays the results to the user. Three g.VIBROstim vibrotactile stimulators are used for the tactile P300 approach. Earphones are used for the auditory P300. The cues that are needed for the MI approach are also played via the earphones. Data are acquired with a g.USBamp (g.tec medical engineering GmbH, Austria) at 256 Hz.

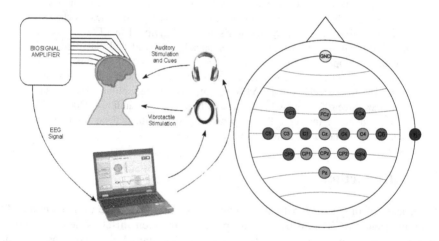

Fig. 1. Left: Block diagram of the mindBEAGLE device. Right: Electrode setup. The ground is placed on Fpz (yellow), the reference on the right earlobe (blue). The eight green positions are used for the P300 approaches. Sixteen positions (green and red) are used for the MI approach

mindBEAGLE allows two different types of communication: *YES- NO questions* and *YES questions*. A *YES - NO question* could provide two possible answers, either yes or no. If the system does not detect either of the two answers, then no answer is displayed. *YES questions* can result either in yes, or no answer. Hence, if a *YES question* provides no result, the user cannot assume a negative answer. The auditory P300 approach can be used for *YES questions* only. The vibrotactile approach can be used for *YES questions* and for *YES - NO questions*. The MI approach provides only *YES - NO questions*.

2.1   Auditory P300 Approach

This approach uses an auditory oddball paradigm, in which deviant stimuli (1000 Hz beeps) are randomly distributed within a train of more probable standard stimuli (500 Hz beeps). The probability of a deviant stimulus is 1/8; hence, there will be seven standard stimuli for each deviant stimulus. If the patient silently counts each deviant stimulus, these stimuli elicit several event-related potentials (ERPs), including the P300, a positive peak about 300 ms after stimulus onset (P300). Each beep lasts 100 ms, and the interval between the onset of each beep is randomly chosen between 540ms and 660ms. Data are bandpass filtered between 0.1Hz and 30Hz by applying a butterworth filter of 4th order. For each stimulus, a window of 100 ms before and 600 ms after the beep is stored for signal processing. The 100 ms pre-stimulus interval is used for baseline correction. A trend line is calculated via linear least square fitting and subtracted from trial data for detrending. Data is then downsampled by a factor of 12, resulting in 12 samples for the 600 ms of post-stimulus interval. Finally, all samples times channels features are entered into a Linear Discriminant Analysis (LDA), resulting in 12 x 8 = 96 features.

2.2   Vibrotactile P300 Approach

This approach also uses an oddball P300 paradigm, but the stimuli are delivered   via vibrotactile stimulators that are placed on the left and right wrist, and onto one leg. For YES questions, two tactors are used, while YES - NO questions use all three tactors. Each stimulus lasts 50 ms, and the inter-stimulus interval is randomly chosen between 198 ms and 242 ms. Filtering, detrending, baseline correction and selection of pre- and post-trigger intervals relied on the same methods described in section 2.1 above.

2.3   The MI Approach

In this approach, patients are asked to imagine moving either the left or right hand. Earphones are used to present auditory cues to start or stop the motor imagery. Data are bandpass filtered between 8Hz and 30Hz using a butterworth filter of 4th order. For better classification of MI via LDA, the EEG channels are spatially filtered with Common Spatial Patterns (CSP, see e.g. [4, 5]). This method yields a set of spatial filters designed to minimize the variance of one class while maximizing variance for the other class. The 4 most important CSP filters are applied, and the variance of each channel is calculated and normalized. Then the LDA classifier can be trained and applied to the data.

2.4   Assessment Mode

The assessment mode is designed to help an expert assess the level of consciousness within nonresponsive patients. In both P300 approaches, the patient needs to count the deviant stimuli. In the MI approach, patients are asked to follow a predefined sequence of left or right hand movements. After each run, evaluation plots are shown to the expert. Many trials need to be recorded within each session, providing data that is then evaluated offline. Because this may take up to twenty minutes, the expert can decide to pause any time during the procedure.

P300 Approaches. In each session of the auditory P300 assessment mode, 60 target stimuli and 60 x 7 (420) standard stimuli are presented to the patient. This results in 480 x 600 ms = 288s of data for each session. In the vibrotactile approach, 1200 stimuli are presented per session, resulting in 1200 x 220ms = 264s of data per session. Fig. 2 presents a final evaluation plot. The picture of a brain (left side) shows the distribution of highest P300 amplitudes over the single electrode positions. Each channel's color represents the maximum difference in amplitude between averaged deviant and standard trials, in a time window ranging from 250 ms after the stimulus to the end of the trial. Colors between channels are interpolated. The red color represents the highest peak, whereas the blue color shows the lowest peak. The plot on the top of the right side shows the time course of the evoked responses for averaged deviant and standard stimuli for one selected electrode. The electrode to be visualized can be chosen by a mouse-click. The green shaded areas indicate time periods of significant differences (p<0.05) between deviant and standard stimuli. If only the deviant stimuli elicit significant P300 peaks, then the user was presumably able to understand and follow the instructions, and hence was consciousness during the test. The evaluation of statistical significance uses the Mann Whitney U-test. The software creates a graph (bottom right of Fig. 2) that shows the BCI classification accuracy, ranging from 0-100%. This accuracy plot simulates an eight class P300 spelling experiment, and hence can reflect whether the patient could control a P300 speller.

Similar plots were also used in a previous publication testing a P300 speller on a group of people suffering motor impairments or LIS [6, 7]. The data from a stream of stimuli, which contain one deviant stimulus and seven standard stimuli, were shuffled and separated into two independent data sets of the same size. An LDA classifier was calculated from the first data set and then tested on the second data set. The plot evaluates how many stimuli (called flashes in Fig. 2) need to be presented to reach a certain level of control accuracy. The classifier is tested onto the first sequence of the data set. Each stimulus represents one class. Since the subject was asked to count the deviant stimulus, the brain activity from that stimulus should differ from the standard stimulus. The chance level of correct classification is 1/8, and the result is either correct or false. Then, the procedure is repeated with two sequences, while summing up the LDA distances for each class. Again, the classification could be correct or false. The number of sequences is increased step by step to get a classification for each number of flashes. After finishing, the whole data set is shuffled and separated again into two pools to repeat the calculations. This is done ten times to calculate an averaged accuracy, resulting in the plot shown in Fig. 2.

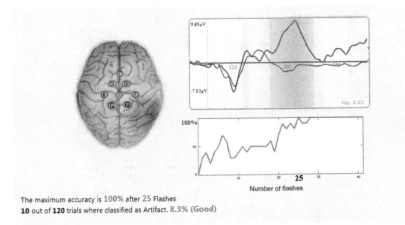

The maximum accuracy is 100% after 25 Flashes
10 out of 120 trials where classified as Artifact. 8.3% (Good)

Fig. 2. Evaluation plot of the auditory- or vibrotactile P300 approach for the assessment mode. The left panel shows the distribution of the highest and lowest P300 peak, the top right panel presents averaged deviant and standard stimuli from one channel, and the bottom right shows the classification accuracy across different numbers of counted stimuli.

MI Based Approach. The MI approach records 120 trials, each of which lasts eight seconds, separated by two second breaks. This results in 10s x 120 = 20 minutes overall session time, not counting any additional pauses that the expert adds. Each trial begins with a cue, presented via earphones, that instructs the subject to imagine moving either the left or right hand. The sequence of left and right-hand instructions is randomized. Fig. 3 presents an evaluation plot created after an assessment run with the MI based approach. The four maps on the top left side are time–frequency maps showing changes of Event Related De-Synchronization (ERD/ERS). The maps are calculated with a Laplacian derivation around sites C3 and C4 for left and right hand imagery. The maps are scaled from 8-30 Hz and present data from 8 seconds - 2 seconds before the cue and 6 seconds afterwards. ERD/ERS is calculated for bands of 2Hz with no overlap. The power in each band is compared with the power in each reference interval (time before stimulus), yielding an ERD (red color) when the power is lower and an ERS (blue color) when it is greater. On the top right side, the two most important patterns from the CSP calculation are mapped onto the picture of a brain. This shows the expert which brain regions were activated during imagination of left or right hand movements. On the bottom of Fig. 3, the accuracy plot shows the accuracy of the classifier over all trials. Again, the accuracy plot shows how well communication could work, and elucidates whether the user understood the instructions and could perform the desired MI task. Here, the time related classification accuracy of all tested trials is averaged and separated into the trials from left hand motor imagery (yellow line) and right hand motor imagery (blue line). The green line shows the averaged accuracy of both classes. In the example shown in Fig. 3, the user reached the highest accuracy level (94.4%) at about five seconds. The horizontal magenta line marks the level above which accuracy is significant ($p<0.05$).

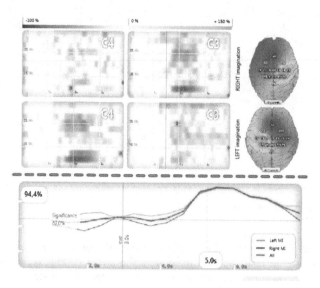

Fig. 3. The displays presented in the MI approach, further detailed in the preceding text

2.5   The Communication Mode

For the communication mode, a classifier needs to be loaded that was created in one of the previous assessment sessions. A user could load also a generic classifier that is created out of a pool of several sessions. Then, the experimenter explains the mode to the user. Before starting the procedure, the experimenter asks the user a question and waits to see if the device is able to detect an answer. In the two P300 approaches, a specific stimulus represents an answer. For the YES - NO questions, in the vibrotactile approach, three tactile stimulators are used. Two of them generate deviant stimuli and are usually placed on the left and right wrist of the patient. The third stimulator generates standard stimuli and could be placed e.g. on one of the patient's legs. Now, the patient can decide to concentrate on the stimulator on the left hand to convey the answer "yes", or to concentrate on the right hand stimulator to convey "no". Fig. 4 shows the display presented to the experimenter. The user in this example chose "yes", the classified answer is marked by a lens. The decision is made after classifying 15 sequences of deviant and standard trials, hence giving an answer requires about 44 seconds for the vibrotactile approach and 72 seconds in the auditory approach. For a YES question, only one type of deviant stimulus and one type of standard stimulus are presented. If the user concentrates on the deviant stimulus, and it is classified correctly, the displayed answer is yes. The word "Yes" will then be visualized in the middle of the computer screen. If the system does not show that the user counted deviant stimuli, then there is no answer displayed, and only the raw EEG and the brain showing the signal quality will be displayed on the screen. The visualization of YES - NO questions in the MI based approach looks the same.

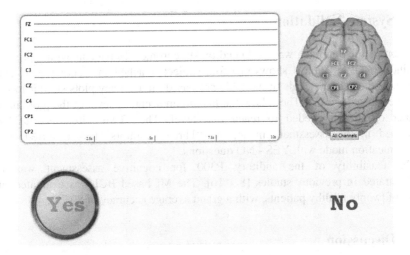

Fig. 4. Communication mode for *YES - NO questions*. The scope on the top left shows the raw EEG signal from all channels, and the brain on the right side depicts the EEG quality. The two possible answers (Yes and No) are presented on the bottom in green and red, respectively. The selected answer (Yes) is circled with a lens.

Table 1. Results from the vibrotactile approach in patients with two vibrators (left) and three vibrators (right), from Lugo et al. [6]

	Two Vibrators		Three Vibrators	
	Accuracy (%)	No of Stimuli	Accuracy (%)	No. of Stimuli
Patient 1	100	12	60	4
Patient 2	20	2	20	4
Patient 3	100	20	40	3
Patient 4	100	20	60	7
Patient 5	60	2	40	4
Patient 6	100	7	100	7
Average	80	10.5	55.3	4.8
Standard deviation	33.5	8.2	27.3	1.7

One decision is made after each eight second trial. Within the trial, data are classified each 0.5 seconds, beginning at 4 seconds at stopping at 8 seconds. The final "yes" or "no" answer is achieved via majority voting of the single classifications.

3   System Validation

The vibrotactile approach was evaluated on six chronic LIS patients with a prototype of mindBEAGLE. Table 1 shows that four subjects reached an accuracy level above chance. The accuracy levels in the table are based on accuracy plots similar to those described in section 2.4. They show the maximum accuracy level of the plot, and the number of stimuli needed to reach that level. The "Two Vibrators" task was performed in the assessment mode, the "Three Vibrators" task occurred in the communication mode with YES - NO questions.

The feasibility of the auditory P300 for cognitive assessment was also demonstrated in previous studies [8 - 10]. The MI based BCI was evaluated on a group of twenty healthy patients, with a grand average accuracy of 80.7%.

4   Discussion

This publication presented the first commercially available BCI system for assessment and communication with people suffering from DOC. It is important to emphasize that, if the system does not detect any EEG patterns that indicate consciousness, this does not mean that the patient is unconsciousness; it simply means that the system cannot detect it. Therefore, this tool is only designed to help with assessment, not provide an entire assessment. Further evaluation of the MI approach with patients is still to come. Future studies will evaluate all approaches within the mindBEAGLE system on both healthy users and patients.

References

1. Schnakers, C., Vanhaudenhuyse, A., Giacino, J., Ventura, M., Boly, M., Majerus, S., Moonen, G., Laureys, S.: Diagnostic accuracy of the vegetative and minimally conscious state: Clinical consensus versus standardized neurobehavioral assessment. BMC Neurology 9, 35 (2009), doi:10.1186/1471-2377-9-35
2. Childs, N.L., Mercer, W.N., Childs, H.W.: Accuracy of diagnosis of persistent vegetative state. Neurology 43(8), 1465–1467 (1993)
3. Andrews, K., Murphy, L., Munday, R., Littlewood, C.: Misdiagnosis of the vegetative state: retrospective study in a rehabilitation unit. BMJ 313(7048), 13–16 (1996)
4. Guger, C., Ramoser, H., Pfurtscheller, G.: Real-time EEG analysis with subject-specific spatial patterns for a brain-computer interface (BCI). IEEE Transactions on Neural Systems and Rehabilitation Engineering 8, 447–450 (2000)
5. Blankertz, B., Tomioka, R., Lemm, S., Kawanabe, M., Müller, K.-R.: Optimizing spatial filters for robust EEG single-trial analysis. IEEE Signal Processing Magazine 25, 41–56 (2008)
6. Lugo, Z.R., Rodriguez, J., Lechner, A., Ortner, R., Gantner, I.S., Kübler, A., Laureys, S., Noirhomme, Q., Guger, C.: A vibrotactile P300-based BCI for consciousness detection and communication. Clin. EEG and Neurosci. (2014)

7. Ortner, R., Aloise, F., Prückl, R., Schettini, F., Putz, V., Scharinger, J., Opisso, E., Costa, U., Guger, C.: Accuracy of a P300 Speller for People with Motor Impairments: a Comparison. Clin. EEG Neurosci. 42(4), 214–218 (2011)
8. Cipresso, P., Carelli, L., Solca, F., Meazzi, D., Meriggi, P., Poletti, B., Lulé, D., Ludolph, A.C., Silani, V., Riva, G.: The use of P300-based BCIs in amyotrophic lateral sclerosis: from augmentative and alternative communication to cognitive assessment. Brain Behav. 2, 479–498 (2012)
9. Kübler, A., Furdea, A., Halder, S., Hammer, E.M., Nijboer, F., Kotchoubey, B.A.: Brain-Computer Interface controlled Auditory Event-Related Potential (P300) Spelling System for Locked-In Patients. Ann. N. Y. Acad. Sci. 1157, 90–100 (2009)
10. Lulé, D., Noirhomme, Q., Kleih, S.C., Chatelle, C., Halder, S., Demertzi, A., Bruno, M.-A., Gosseries, O., Vanhaudenhuyse, A., Schnakers, C., Thonnard, M., Soddu, A., Kübler, A., Laureys, S.: Probing command following in patients with disorders of consciousness using a brain–computer interface. Clinical Neurophysiology 124, 101–106 (2013)

EEG-enabled Affective Human-Computer Interfaces

Olga Sourina and Yisi Liu

Fraunhofer IDM@NTU
Nanyang Technological University,
Singapore
{LiuYS,eosourina}@ntu.edu.sg

Abstract. Nowadays, the human computer interfaces can be designed to be adaptive and emotion-enabled. The recognized emotions of the user can help make the user's experience more complete, more engaging, less stressful or more stressful depending on the target of the applications. Such affective human-computer interfaces are getting more attention from researchers and engineers. EEG signals are used to recognize emotions of the user in real time. We describe a real-time emotion recognition algorithm that is used to personalize different applications according to the user's current emotions. The algorithm is subject-dependent and needs a training session before running the application. Two EEG-enabled games and one adaptive advertisement based on the algorithm are designed and implemented. One game is the "Bar" game where a difficulty level of the game is adapted based on the player's score and emotions. Another game is the "Girl Twins" one where the player's emotions are monitored in real time, and an emotional companion is implemented as the girl twins avatars whose behaviour changes according to the user's emotions. An adaptive advertising movie is designed and implemented as well. Here, the real-time emotion recognition algorithm is used to adjust the scenes of the advertisement based on the current emotion recognized.

Keywords: EEG, adaptive interfaces, emotion recognition, BCI, affective computing.

1 Introduction

Human-Computer interfaces can be adapted to the user's experience, knowledge, or even user's internal feelings. The recognized emotions of the user can help make the user's experience more complete, more engaging, less stressful or more stressful depending on the target of the application. It is useful to implement adaptive interfaces in many applications including games, medical applications, neuromarketing, etc.

Emotion is a mental state and an affective reaction towards an event based on subjective experience [1]. Emotions are involved in the human daily communications and are inevitable in human-computer interaction. Thus, it is important for computer "to feel" and "to understand" the user's mental state especially his/her emotions. Emotions can be recognized from the user's face expressions, speech, gestures and/or biosignals such as Electroencephalogram (EEG) or combination of biosignals (heart

C. Stephanidis and M. Antona (Eds.): UAHCI/HCII 2014, Part I, LNCS 8513, pp. 536–547, 2014.
© Springer International Publishing Switzerland 2014

rate, EEG, skin temperature, electrodermal activity, etc). In games, a combination of different types of bio-signals is often used for emotion recognition [2-6]. For example, pulse, respiration and skin conductance signals were used to detect the emotional states in the game [3]. In advertisement, emotional assessment can be done from verbal self-report, visual self-report, moment-to-moment rating, facial expression recognition, and biosignals [7]. There is less work done on emotion recognition through EEG signals only and on an integration of the corresponding affective interfaces in real-time applications. Since EEG devices become more affordable, portable, wireless and easy to set up, this technology can be used in emotion assessment of the user in human-computer interfaces. It is possible to adapt applications to the user by avoiding undesired emotions and by eliciting/maintaining the targeted emotions. The true feelings of the subject towards the application could be obtained in real time and could serve as an additional input and control in human-machine interfaces, for example, to adapt graphical user interface to the user's feeling or to change the game flow. It is possible to create adaptive games and advertising movies where some parameters of the scenes, for example, the difficulty level in the games are adjusted based on the recognized emotion or, for example, shapes, sizes, and colours of visuals are changed to induce emotions targeted by the advertisement or games. In [8], we proposed a real-time subject-dependent algorithm to recognize emotions from EEG. Combination of features such as statistical, Higher Order Crossings and fractal dimensions is proposed, and SVM classifier is applied. EEG signals are used to detect the current emotional states of the user. In this paper, we describe the algorithm and show that accuracy of the algorithm is better than other algorithms. The algorithm can recognize up to 8 emotions in three-dimensional Valence (Pleasure)-Arousal-Dominance emotion model proposed by Mehrabian and Russell in [9] and [10]. In this model, arousal dimension ranges from calm to excited, pleasure (valence) dimension ranges from negative to positive, dominance dimension ranges from a feeling of being in control during an emotional experience to a feeling of being controlled by the emotion [11]. The emotion labels can be located in the dimensional model, for example, anger and fear are both high arousal and negative states, but the anger has high dominance level and the fear has low dominance level. Based on the real-time subject-dependent algorithm we design affective interfaces and implement EEG-based emotion-enabled applications such as adaptive "Bar" and "Girl Twins" games, and an advertisement movie. The number of emotions used in the games depends on the game design. In the "Bar" game, two emotions based on 1-dimensional Valence scale are used. In the "Girl Twins" game, 8 emotions based on 3-dimensional Valence-Arousal-Dominance model are recognized and interpreted as the girl twins' behaviour. One adaptive advertisement is developed, and the advertisement is adjusted based on the user's real-time emotional feedback.

The paper is organized as follows. In Section 2, the real-time subject-dependent EEG-based emotion recognition algorithm is described. In Section 3, the real-time EEG based emotion recognition training system is introduced. In Section 4, the affective adaptive applications such as adaptive games and advertisement are described. At last, Section 5 concludes the paper.

2   Real-Time EEG-Based Emotion Recognition

Currently, most of the existing works on EEG-based emotion recognition are offline processing. [12] and [13] did a pioneer work on real-time EEG based emotion recognition, and fractal dimension features are used to detect the emotional states. The proposed algorithms are subject-dependent which means a classifier is trained for each subject.

The algorithm proposed in [8] is used in our games and emotion-adaptive advertisement movie. Fractal dimension, Higher Order Crossings (HOC) and statistical features are used as combined features, and Support Vector Machine is used as the classifier. Up to eight emotions such as happy, surprised, satisfied, protected, angry, frightened, unconcerned, and sad can be recognized. Only 4 channels are needed in the recognition to get adequate accuracy. 6 subjects' data from DEAP database [14] are used to validate the algorithm. 5-fold cross validation was used to calculate the accuracy. An accuracy of 53.7% is obtained for 8 emotions recognition and an accuracy of 83.73% is obtained for any 2 emotions recognition (Table 1). By using 32 channels the accuracy of the algorithm can be improved from 53.7% to 69.53% for the recognition of 8 emotions, from 56.24% to 71.43% for the recognition of 7 emotions, from 59.3% to 73.73% for the recognition of 6 emotions, from 63.07% to 76.53% for the recognition of 5 emotions, from 67.9% to 80% for the recognition of 4 emotions, from 74.36% to 84.41% for the recognition of 3 emotions, and from 83.73% to 90.35% for recognition of 2 emotions.

Although emotion processing is believed to be executed in frontal lobe [15-18], different brain areas may interact with each other. For example, the parietal lobe is proved to strongly interact with frontal cortex [19], and the amygdale co-activation of parietal cortex during emotion regulation is found in [20]. Mutual Information (MI) [21] was chosen to be investigated and to be compared with the proposed algorithm as it can measure the statistical dependency between different brain areas.

The Mutual Information (MI) features are extracted using the Moddemeijer's toolbox [22], where different distributions are estimated based on histograms, and the appropriate bin size is automatically determined. Since there are 32 channels in DEAP database, the total number of the MI features is 496. The obtained accuracy is shown in Table 1. It can be seen that the proposed combined features (HOC, 6 statistical, FD) with 32 channels outperform MI features by 20.15% in the recognition of 8 emotions, by 19.16% in the recognition of 7 emotions, by 18.19% in the recognition of 6 emotions, by 17.09% in the recognition of 5 emotions, 15.64% in the recognition of 4 emotions, 13.4% in the recognition of 3 emotions, and 9.35% in the recognition of 2 emotions.

Since the EEG-based emotion recognition algorithm is a subject-dependent one, a training session is needed for each subject before the recognition. The diagram of the algorithm is shown in Fig. 1. In the training session, firstly, the raw data labelled with emotions are filtered by a 2-42 Hz bandpass filter. Secondly, a sliding window with size of 512 and 75% overlapping is used to extract the Higuchi fractal dimension (FD) feature, HOC feature and 6 statistical features. By using the combination of these

Table 1. Comparison of classification accuracy of the proposed feature combination and Mutual Information

Number of emotions recognized	Feature Type		
	HOC, 6 statistical, FD	HOC, 6 statistical, FD	Mutual Information
	4 channels	32 channels	32 channels
8	53.7	69.53	49.38
7	56.24	71.43	52.27
6	59.3	73.73	55.54
5	63.07	76.53	59.44
4	67.9	80	64.36
3	74.36	84.41	71.01
2	83.73	90.35	81

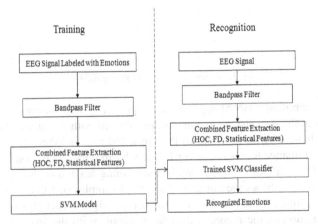

Fig. 1. Diagram of the emotion recognition algorithm with training session

features, a SVM classifier with polynomial kernel is trained and saved to be used in the real-time recognition. In the recognition phase, the EEG signals are passed to bandpass filter. Then, the FD, HOC and statistical features are extracted and fed into the SVM classifier obtained from the training session. Finally, the current emotional state of the subject is recognized.

3 Emotion Recognition Training System

The time it takes to extract one new sample of HOC, statistical and FD features is less than 0.1 second as shown in Table 2 and classifying this sample by SVM takes less than 0.05 seconds. As a result, the proposed algorithm can be used in real-time emotion recognition applications such as emotion-enabled adaptive games and adaptive advertisement. As the proposed algorithm is subject-dependent, a short system training session is needed for the user.

Table 2. Comparison of features computational time per channel

	HOC	Statistical	FD (Higuchi)
Approximate Time	0.07 seconds	0.001 seconds	0.004 second

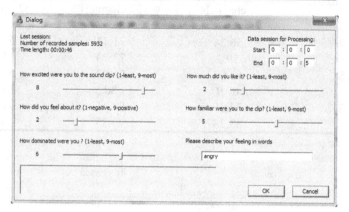

Fig. 2. Screenshot of the Training Session

EEG-based emotion-enabled applications require a system training session. In the training session, the user listens to sound clips labelled with emotions which are supposed to be elicited. After listening to the clips, the user is asked to assess arousal, valence and dominance levels of his/her feelings by moving the bar on a scale of 1 to 9. In Fig. 2, the screenshot of the menu of the training session is shown. The top left corner of the screen shows the number of recorded samples of EEG data and the recorded length of time for the training session. The top right corner allows the player to choose the duration of the recorded data for training. With the arousal, valence and dominance levels entered by the player to label the recorded EEG data, the SVM model is trained. The results are saved and later are used to classify new EEG data samples in the applications.

4   Adaptive Affective Applications

4.1   Data Acquisition

In the applications, we use Emotiv [23] device with 14 electrodes locating at AF3, F7, F3, FC5, T7, P7, O1, O2, P8, T8, FC6, F4, F8, AF4 standardized by the American Electroencephalographic Society [24] (plus CMS/DRL as references) to acquire EEG data. The technical parameters of the device are given as follows: bandwidth - 0.2-45Hz, digital notch filters at 50Hz and 60Hz; A/D converter with 16 bits resolution and sampling rate of 128Hz. The data are transferred via wireless receiver. Recently, the Emotiv device has become popular for research [25]. The reliability and validity of the EEG data collected by Emotiv device was done in [26] and [27].

4.2 Games

Two original EEG-based emotion-enabled games were designed and implemented based on the real-time emotion recognition algorithm: the adaptive "Bar" game and "Girl Twins" emotional companion application. Both of them were created with UDK and Maya. The player wears a wireless Emotiv device which is portable and easy to mount on the head. The diagram for the game application is shown in Fig. 3. Since our proposed algorithm uses the sliding window and shifts by 128 samples (1 second) each time, the player's emotion is recognized every 1 second and the emotional state at that time is used to update the emotion statistics. In the "Bar" game, emotion statistics are taken into account when making a decision for adjusting the difficulty level of the game. In the "Girl Twins", emotion statistics are used to update the twin girls' behaviors.

In the "Girl Twins" emotional companion game, changes of the user's recognized emotions are reflected on the girl twins. For each emotion, the girls' dress style, hair color, facial expression and movement change according to the user's recognized emotions (happy, surprised, satisfied, protected, angry, frightened, unconcerned, and sad). Based on the requirements, the girls' behaviors change according to or opposite to the player's emotions recognized from EEG. In Fig. 4, the screenshot of the game with girl twins with "happy" emotion is shown. Such an emotional companion could improve the player's engagement, for example, in the case of e-learning games.

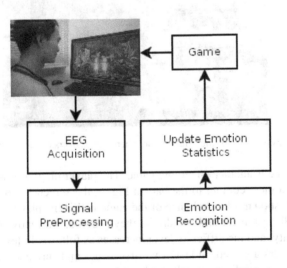

Fig. 3. Overall diagram of EEG-based emotion-enabled game

Fig. 4. Screenshot of the "Girl Twins" game representing "happy" player's emotion

Table 3. Decision for changing the Difficulty levels

Answers matching in the game	Dominant emotion while playing the current round	Difficulty of the next round
Correct	Negative	No change
Correct	Positive	More difficult
Incorrect	Negative	Less difficult
Incorrect	Positive	No change

Fig. 5. Screenshot of the "Bar" game where the customer orders the drink

The "Bar" game is another e-learning game. The player plays as a waiter who takes orders from customers coming to the bar. In Fig. 5, the screenshot of a customer ordering a drink is shown. The challenge of the game is that the player has to memorize the names of all customers and the drinks they ordered. Currently, the game has 3 levels of difficulty, and the difficulty level increases as follows. In level one, only first names of customers are used, in level two first names and surnames are used, and in level three names from different cultures have to be memorized. At each level, after the last order, a Customer-Drink table pops up for the player to match the names and the drinks. In this game, only negative and positive emotions defined on the valence dimension are used. The player's emotions are being assessed continuously through the game. The decisions for changing difficulty levels in the game are shown in Table 3. An emotion is considered dominant while playing the current level if it is recognized in more than 50% of the playing time.

4.3   Adaptive Advertising Movie

To optimize the viewer's experience towards the advertisement and to maximize the advertising effect such as memorization of the products, in [28], we proposed a real-time EEG-based emotion-enabled algorithm to personalize advertising movies.

As the EEG-based emotion recognition algorithm used in the emotion-adaptive advertisement movie can recognize up to 8 discrete emotions based on the VAD model, the recognized results need to be decoded into the valence, arousal, and dominance emotional dimensions. The mapping of discrete emotions in the 3D model is illustrated in Fig. 6. "Angry" corresponds to negative high arousal high dominance; "fear" corresponds to negative high arousal low dominance; "unconcerned" corresponds to negative low arousal high dominance; "sad" corresponds to negative low arousal low dominance; "happy" corresponds to positive high arousal high dominance, "surprise" corresponds to positive high arousal low dominance; "satisfied" corresponds to positive low arousal high dominance; "protected" corresponds to positive low arousal low dominance.

The flow chart of the proposed emotion-enabled advertisement algorithm is given in Fig. 7. First, the advertising movie is shown to the user. The user's EEG signals are acquired by the EEG device. Then, the emotion recognition algorithm including bandpass filter, feature extraction and classification is applied to the EEG signals. As a result, the user's current emotional state is identified. The recognized emotion label is decoded to the corresponding arousal, valence and dominance levels as shown in Fig. 6. Then, the identified arousal, valence and dominance levels are compared with

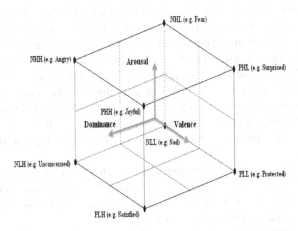

Fig. 6. 3D emotion classification model (Adopted from [9])

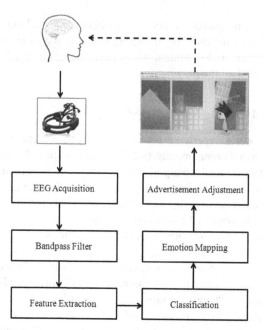

Fig. 7. Flow chart of the proposed emotion-enabled advertisement system

the targeted states respectively and the corresponding adjustment is made. If the recognized arousal, valence and dominance levels are compatible with the targeted levels, the default scenes of the advertising movie are shown. If at least one of them is incompatible, the movie is adjusted. For example, if the current state of the user is high arousal, but the desired state is low arousal which aims at making the audience remember the brand information, the scene colours in the advertisement are changed to cool colours to calm down the viewer.

We design and implement an emotion-adaptive advertisement for national library as an example of the real-time EEG-based emotion-enabled advertising system. In the designed movie, the national library is advertised as a place where a student can follow his/her creative imagination and discover the world via books. Five scenes are included as follows. In the 1st scene, a boy comes into the library. He is attracted by imaginary fireflies and chases them. In the 2nd, 3rd and 4th scene, the boy comes across several imaginary places such as a forest, a building and a path through the mountains. In the last scene, the boy catches up with the fireflies. The scene ends up by closing the book symbolizing the end of his discovery journey, and the logo of the library is shown.

A positive valence and high dominance are targeted throughout the advertisement. A high arousal is targeted at the beginning to make the subject more immersed and a low arousal is targeted when the information about the brand is shown to make the subject memorize the sign of national library.

If the viewer's recognized emotions are always compatible with the targeted emotions during the advertisement, there is no change, and the animation just follows the

Fig. 8. The scene of the basic animation when the recognized emotion is compatible with the targeted emotion

original basic design as shown in Fig. 8. If the current recognized arousal level is low but the targeted arousal level is high arousal level, the red colour is added to the scene to excite the viewer. If the recognized arousal level is high but the targeted arousal level of the advertisement is low arousal level, the blue colour is added to the scene to calm down the viewer. As the targeted valence level throughout the advertisement is always positive, if the recognized valence is positive, there is no change; if the recognized valence is negative, the head size of the character increases to induce positive emotion, and some curvy characters are added to make the viewer's feelings more positive.

5 Conclusion

In this paper, we propose and implement adaptive affective applications based on the real-time EEG-based subject-dependent emotion recognition algorithm. Two adaptive games and one advertising movie are designed and implemented. The "Bar" game uses 2 recognized emotions to adapt the difficulty level of the game. In the "Girl Twins" which is the emotional companion game, 8 emotions can be recognized in real time from the player's EEG signal and interpreted as the girl twins avatars' behaviors changes according to the user's emotions. The implemented EEG-based emotion-enabled applications need short system training for the player. Real-time EEG-based emotion recognition can help to improve the user's enjoyment and effectiveness of the game and advertisement since it allows personalizing the games and advertising movie in real time. It is possible to adjust the games and advertisement in real time according to the user's emotion to make the applications more effective. Assessment of the effectiveness of the game design and proposed advertisement will be the next step in our project.

Acknowledgment. The characters of "Bar", "Girl Twins" and "adaptive advertisement movie" are original and designed by NTU final year students Haoze Zhang, Mengying Ai, and Mohammad Rizqi Hafiyyandi respectively.

References

1. Mauss, I.B., Robinson, M.D.: Measures of emotion: A review. Cognition and Emotion 23(2), 209–237 (2009)
2. Tsai, T.W., Lo, H.Y., Chen, K.S.: An affective computing approach to develop the game-based adaptive learning material for the elementary students. In: Proceedings of the 2012 Joint International Conference on Human-Centered Computer Environments, pp. 8–13 (2012)
3. Tijs, T.J.W., Brokken, D., IJsselsteijn, W.A.: Dynamic game balancing by recognizing affect. In: Markopoulos, P., de Ruyter, B., IJsselsteijn, W.A., Rowland, D. (eds.) Fun and Games 2008. LNCS, vol. 5294, pp. 88–93. Springer, Heidelberg (2008)
4. Tijs, T.J.W., Brokken, D., IJsselsteijn, W.A.: Creating an emotionally adaptive game. In: Stevens, S.M., Saldamarco, S.J. (eds.) ICEC 2008. LNCS, vol. 5309, pp. 122–133. Springer, Heidelberg (2008)
5. Saari, T., Turpeinen, M., Kuikkaniemi, K., Kosunen, I., Ravaja, N.: Emotionally adapted games – An example of a first person shooter. In: Jacko, J.A. (ed.) HCI International 2009, Part IV. LNCS, vol. 5613, pp. 406–415. Springer, Heidelberg (2009)
6. Gilleade, K.M., Dix, A.: Using frustration in the design of adaptive videogames. In: Proceedings of the 2004 ACM SIGCHI International Conference on Advances in Computer Entertainment Technology, pp. 228–232 (2004)
7. Poels, K., Dewitte, S.: How to capture the heart? Reviewing 20 years of emotion measurement in advertising. Journal of Advertising Research 46(1), 18–37 (2006)
8. Liu, Y., Sourina, O.: EEG Databases for Emotion Recognition. In: Proc. 2013 Int. Conf. on Cyberworlds, pp. 302–309 (2013)
9. Mehrabian, A.: Framework for a comprehensive description and measurement of emotional states. Genetic, Social, and General Psychology Monographs 121(3), 339–361 (1995)
10. Mehrabian, A.: Pleasure-Arousal-Dominance: A general framework for describing and measuring individual differences in temperament. Current Psychology 14(4), 261–292 (1996)
11. Bolls, P.D., Lang, A., Potter, R.F.: The effects of message valence and listener arousal on attention, memory, and facial muscular responses to radio advertisements. Communication Research 28(5), 627–651 (2001)
12. Liu, Y., Sourina, O., Nguyen, M.K.: Real-time EEG-based Human Emotion Recognition and Visualization. In: Proceedings of the 2010 International Conference on Cyberworlds, pp. 262–269 (2010)
13. Liu, Y., Sourina, O., Nguyen, M.K.: Real-Time EEG-Based Emotion Recognition and Its Applications. In: Gavrilova, M.L., Tan, C.J.K., Sourin, A., Sourina, O. (eds.) Trans. on Comput. Sci. XII. LNCS, vol. 6670, pp. 256–277. Springer, Heidelberg (2011)
14. Koelstra, S., Muhl, C., Soleymani, M., Lee, J.-S., Yazdani, A., Ebrahimi, T., Pun, T., Nijholt, A., Patras, I.: DEAP: A Database for Emotion Analysis; Using Physiological Signals. IEEE Transactions on Affective Computing 3(1), 18–31 (2012)
15. Bechara, A., Damasio, H., Damasio, A.R.: Emotion, decision making and the orbitofrontal cortex. Cerebral Cortex 10(3), 295–307 (2000)
16. Kringelbach, M.L.: The human orbitofrontal cortex: Linking reward to hedonic experience. Nature Reviews Neuroscience 6(9), 691–702 (2005)
17. Dolcos, F., Labar, K.S., Cabeza, R.: Dissociable effects of arousal and valence on prefrontal activity indexing emotional evaluation and subsequent memory: An event-related fMRI study. NeuroImage 23(1), 64–74 (2004)

18. Demaree, H.A., Everhart, D.E., Youngstrom, E.A., Harrison, D.W.: Brain lateralization of emotional processing: Historical roots and a future incorporating "dominance". Behavioral and Cognitive Neuroscience Reviews 4(1), 3–20 (2005)
19. Petrides, M., Pandya, D.N.: Projections to the frontal cortex from the posterior parietal region in the rhesus monkey. Journal of Comparative Neurology 228(1), 105–116 (1984)
20. Banks, S.J., Eddy, K.T., Angstadt, M., Nathan, P.J., Phan, K.L.: Amygdala–frontal connectivity during emotion regulation. Social Cognitive and Affective Neuroscience 2(4), 303–312 (2007)
21. Chanel, G., Kierkels, J.J.M., Soleymani, M., Pun, T.: Short-term emotion assessment in a recall paradigm. International Journal of Human Computer Studies 67(8), 607–627 (2009)
22. Moddemeijer, R.: On estimation of entropy and mutual information of continuous distributions. Signal Processing 16(3), 233–248 (1989)
23. Emotiv, http://www.emotiv.com
24. American electroencephalographic society guidelines for standard electrode position nomenclature. Journal of Clinical Neurophysiology 8(2), 200–202 (1991)
25. Ranky, G.N., Adamovich, S.: Analysis of a commercial EEG device for the control of a robot arm. In: Proceedings of the 2010 IEEE 36th Annual Northeast Bioengineering Conference, pp. 1–2 (2010)
26. Stytsenko, K., Jablonskis, E., Prahm, C.: Evaluation of consumer EEG device Emotiv EPOC. Poster session presented at MEi:CogSci Conference 2011 (2011)
27. Duvinage, M., Castermans, T., Dutoit, T., Petieau, M., Hoellinger, T., Saedeleer, C.D., Seetharaman, K., Cheron, G.: A P300-based quantitative comparison between the emotiv epoc headset and a medical EEG device. In: Proceedings of the IASTED International Conference Biomedical Engineering, pp. 37–42 (2012)
28. Liu, Y., Sourina, O., Hafiyyandi, M.R.: EEG-Based Emotion-Adaptive Advertising. In: 2013 Humaine Association Conference on Affective Computing and Intelligent Interaction (ACII), pp. 843–848 (2013)

Author Index